D1479757

ROGER WILLIAMS UNIV. LIBRARY

WILLIAMS UNIV. LIBRARY

RWBB
LB1055 .S6   ROGER WILLIAMS COLLEGE LIBRARY
Sprinthall, Richard
Educational psychology: selected reading

3 1931 00100 1089

ROGER WILLIAMS COLLEGE LIBRARY

595

EDUCATIONAL PSYCHOLOGY

Selected Readings

Edited by

RICHARD C. SPRINTHALL AND NORMAN A. SPRINTHALL

Department of Psychology   Graduate School of Education
American International College   Harvard University

VAN NOSTRAND REINHOLD COMPANY

New York   Cincinnati   Toronto   London   Melbourne

LB1055 .S6
Sprinthall, Richard C.,
1930-
Educational psychology;
selected readings,

TO STUDENTS

"The future of any country which is dependent upon the will and wisdom of its citizens is damaged, and irreparably damaged, whenever any of its children are not educated to the full extent of their talents . . ."

John F. Kennedy
State of the Union Message to Congress
January 14, 1963

VAN NOSTRAND REINHOLD COMPANY REGIONAL OFFICES:

Cincinnati   New York   Chicago   Millbrae   Dallas

VAN NOSTRAND REINHOLD COMPANY FOREIGN OFFICES:

London   Toronto   Melbourne

Copyright © 1969 by LITTON EDUCATIONAL PUBLISHING, INC.

Library of Congress Catalog Card Number 69-15243

All rights reserved. No part of this work covered by the copyright hereon may be reproduced or used in any form or by any means—graphic, electronic, or mechanical, including photocopying, recording, taping, or information storage and retrieval systems—without written permission of the publisher.

Manufactured in the United States of America

Published by VAN NOSTRAND REINHOLD COMPANY
450 West 33rd Street, New York, N. Y. 10001

Published simultaneously in Canada by
D. VAN NOSTRAND COMPANY (Canada), LTD.

13 12 11 10 9 8 7 6 5 4 3

LB1055   SPRINTHALL
S6
    EDUCATIONAL
    PSYCHOLOGY

PREFACE

We have presented many developments and issues in introducing educational psychology in this volume. We have attempted to maintain a balanced treatment in content when selecting the readings and writing the commentary for each chapter. Introductions have been provided for each of the eight basic areas in this book, which not only are designed to put the readings in perspective in relation to the total field, but also to extract the major points being stressed in each article. These introductions were developed to supply continuity to the various articles, and show how each reading is integrated into the total field.

The readings represent a careful blend of the old and the new, the classics with the most recent and provocative statements in the field. The inclusion of the "classics" was not merely to take the student on a guided tour of an antique gallery but to provide him with a background whereby he can more fully understand the most modern approaches in educational psychology. The current readings will be all the more meaningful to the student, therefore, because he has also been allowed exposure to the classic statements.

The selection of readings was demanding. On the basis of our own experience in teaching at both the undergraduate and graduate level, we preferred articles designed to foster intellectual and personal growth. Above all, we wanted articles within the technical competence of the student new to the field.

We ultimately decided upon a division into eight major areas for the study of educational psychology: (1) Growth, Development, and Education; (2) Children and Adolescents; (3) Learning: Theory and Practice; (4) Learning and the Classroom; (5) Personality Factors and School Achievement; (6) Measurement and Intelligence; (7) The Psychology of Teaching; and (8) Cultural Deprivation. Within these eight areas representing the total framework of educational psychology, we have attempted to achieve a balance between the classic and contemporary articles. The classic articles include those by Anastasi, Bruner, Piaget, Benedict, Frank, Anna Freud, Cronbach, Skinner, Rogers, Allport, Erikson, Banning, James, Riesman, and Stoddard. The challenging, more recent articles are those of Bloom, Hunt, Scott, Krech, O. K. Moore, Neill, Torrance, Rosenthal and Jacobson, Malone, and Moynihan.

Rather than present an array of articles dealing with a potpourri of current issues confronting education and psychology we decided to focus the eighth area on one major current issue—cultural deprivation and education. Set against one of the basic themes of this volume, e.g., the crucial importance of initial learning experiences, we selected a particular set of perplexing problems of education for the culturally deprived. In our view these problems were too critical to avoid and therefore needed a special section for presentation. We hope that in this way we can bring particular attention to the most important challenges of this century in our educational systems.

We wish to thank our colleagues and friends who provided invaluable technical assistance—Dr. Arthur Bertrand, Dr. Robert MacLachlan, Dr. George Grosser, Professor Lee Sirois, and Professor Robert Bohlke in Springfield. From Cambridge, Dr. Ralph Mosher and Professors William Perry, David Tiedeman, and John Shlien have continued to be an important source of questions and comments for us. Special thanks are in order for Professor Lawrence Kohlberg who kindly revised his original selection and provided some new data that we were able to include with his work.

A particular note should be made with regard to Lawrence K. Frank who died just as we were completing the manuscript. If we were to single out a major thesis regarding education and children, it would be his view that the fundamental needs of children represent the needs of society. Our responses to those needs are, in his words, "probably the most sensitive indicators of the quality and integrity of our national life. . . ." We are sure that his ideas will continue to find relevance with those who are concerned about such issues.

We also wish to thank our wives Dianne and Barbara who provided moral encouragement and practical help. Thanks are also due to our typists Catherine Boudreau and Barbara Goff who converted our scribbling into a finished manuscript.

Most of all, we are deeply indebted to the authors who allowed us to use their works.

R. C. S.

N. A. S.

November 1968

CONTENTS

Chapter I

GROWTH, DEVELOPMENT, AND EDUCATION

Human growth and development is a continuous stream of dynamic change. From conception to maturity and old age, the organism is in a constant state of flux, rather like a mountain stream, and like the stream, development continues over the stormy and stressful rapids on to more placid pools of relative calm. Even the tempo is ever-changing. For each individual the change itself is different. There are no fixed growth tables, for each individual grows, matures, changes at a different rate. Whereas one boy at age fourteen is already shaving and speaking in a baritone voice, another may not reach this point until he's seventeen. We are thus faced with the problem of individual differences, the basic theme of human development.

Human behavior is now seen as the result of heredity interacting with environment. At that incredible moment of conception, at that precise point in time when the microscopic speck of watery material known as the zygote is formed, the genetic stage is set in motion, and the role of environment becomes crucial.

Environment even shapes our behavior throughout the prenatal stages, zygote to embryo to fetus. This can be done in such obvious ways as toxic agents attacking the fetus in its uterine environment, or perhaps even in more subtle ways as an experiment by D. K. Spelt (1948) has suggested. In this experiment a fetus was actually conditioned to respond while still in the uterus, implying that even learning may begin before birth. At birth, as William James so aptly describes it, the infant enters the "world of blooming, buzzing confusion," and the effects of environmental stimulation become ever more pronounced.

And yet we cannot lose sight of the fact that one's inherited traits, set in motion at conception, will constantly be guiding, overseeing the direction and scope of the environmental influence. Heredity sets the potential limits of how much environment can ultimately accomplish. This current view is a far cry from the arguments of years ago as to whether environment or heredity was more important in determining behavior. We now understand that it's not an "either-or" argument; that behavior is, after all, a function of both.

Perhaps this can be most dramatically illustrated by the work of the great German ethologist Konrad Lorenz. Lorenz (1935) found that when young ducklings, who usually obediently follow their mother, were exposed to other stimuli, such as Lorenz himself, they would just as obediently follow these other stimuli, again including Lorenz himself. He actually had dozens of incubator-hatched ducklings following him around, as though he were their mother. Lorenz called this phenomenon imprinting, and he found that it occurred only during the first day of the bird's life. During this critical period the duckling would form an attachment to almost any stimulus that moves. It is important, however, to note that imprinting *does require a stimulus* during the critical period; that is, that this phenomenon, unlike instinct, is a form of learning. Imprinting illustrates, par excellence, the behavioral effects of the precise blending of heredity and environment.

Hess, following the lead of Lorenz, carried out a series of rigorously controlled experiments on imprinting in ducklings (1959), and found that the critical period itself was of very brief duration. Hess found that imprinting was most effective between the thirteenth and sixteenth hour after hatching, and that beyond 30 hours it hardly ever occurred.

Although imprinting has not yet been demonstrated on humans, it has been shown to occur on some mammals, such as guinea pigs and sheep.

Sigmund Freud maintained that early childhood experiences could have a profound effect on later adult behavior, and most current theories of personality and psychological development are in agreement with this principle.

Freud theorized that the developing child passed through three early sensitive stages: oral, anal, and phallic. Because of environmental stimulation, mostly parental influence, the child could be "fixated" in any of these stages, and this would leave an indelible mark which would affect his adult behavior. For example, trauma experienced during the oral stage, first year of life, can result in a constellation of personality traits called the "oral character." This individual is basically overly dependent, and still receives great pleasure from oral activities. Fixation during the anal stage, or second year of life, results in the "anal character" syndrome. Individuals of this type are overly frugal, stubborn, and compulsively neat. They seemingly don't want to let go of a thing, including their bowel movements. During the fourth or fifth year the child enters the phallic period, a time of great sexual curiosity and universal masturbation. The central theme of this stage, however, is the "oedipal conflict," in which the child attaches basic sexual desires onto the opposite-sexed parent. This is usually resolved through the fear of punishment (castration anxiety) or loss of love of the like-sexed parent, and should result in the boy identifying with his father or the girl with her mother. Trauma during this period results in extreme selfishness, egocentricism, anxiety, or homosexuality.

The psychoanalytic hypothesis just outlined was, of course, the result of armchair speculation, and the clinical observation of individual cases. Freud was not an experimental psychologist, and yet his theory does, to some extent, foreshadow at the human level experimental animal studies.

Melzak and Scott (1957) obtained important experimental evidence on the issue of early experience. They raised ten puppies in complete isolation, the puppies being placed in separate cages where thy could neither see, hear, nor detect in any way the presence of the others. When later compared to litter-mates who had been raised normally, the isolated pups displayed a marked immaturity at all levels. Their problem solving ability was even impaired, and they were never able to make up for the deficiencies brought about by their early experience.

Harry Harlow's concept of "Learning Sets," describing the fact that one really has to learn how to learn, is further evidence of the importance of childhood experience. Without practice in learning, without a "learning set," a child may have great difficulty when faced with the formal learning situation of the schoolroom.

The physiological psychologist, D. O. Hebb, though working from a different theoretical framework, offers conclusions which are very similar to those of Harry Harlow. Noting that the brain is composed of both association and sensory areas, and that the human brain has a far higher proportion of association area to total area than do lower organisms, such as rats, Hebb argues that the human is not nearly as "sensory bound" as is the white rat. This point, of course, is an apt warning to psychologists not to be too quick in generalizing the results of rat studies to the human level. Further, Hebb feels that during infancy and early childhood, the human brain is relatively unorganized and capable of only primitive forms of learning. Through experience or repeated stimulation, however, the brain does become organized. A group of neurons begin working together; or, as Hebb phrases it, a cell assembly is formed. This process is slow but cumulative during infancy. But as more and more cell assemblies are slowly and perhaps painstakingly formed, these cell assemblies themselves become organized into phase sequences. With the accumulation of many sequences the brain becomes more totally organized and learning can then take place very rapidly. The difference between a child haltingly learning a task during the cell-assembly phase and the adult quickly perceiving a relationship which depended on phase sequences is, to use the Bugelski analogy, like the difference between a do-it-yourself handyman building a house piece by piece and a team of professional carpenters putting up a "pre-fab" home. The handyman might take years doing a job that the experienced "pre-fab" crew would do in days.

And yet without the early period of cell assembly and phase sequence formation as postulated by Hebb, or the formation of "learning sets" as hypothesized by Harlow, the human adult would be a slow learner indeed.

Early experience is the crucial ingredient in the ability to take full advantage of one's inherited intellectual potential. During early childhood the background of stimulation should be rich and varied. During infancy, during the critical periods for the formation of learning sets or cell assemblies, the child must be provided with a full range of sensory experience.

The evidence is thus compelling that education must become increasingly aware of the early development of the child, even before the child becomes of legal school age. This is especially true with regard to culturally disadvantaged groups. A child reared in a culturally impoverished family may be permanently damaged by this early experience even before he ever gets the opportunity to go to school. Perhaps several critical periods have already passed by the time the child gets to school, and this may prevent him from ever catching up with his age mates who have had more stimulating backgrounds. Projects such as "Head Start" are beginning to attack what may be one of education's and society's major problems today. In Chapter VIII of this volume we will present a specific focus on this aspect of cultural deprivation, especially in the article by Malone on the so-called "danger orientation." Malone presents a dramatic picture of the paralyzing effects on cognitive development caused by the slum environment. The need for early positive intervention is compelling.

AN OVERVIEW OF THE READINGS FOR THIS CHAPTER

In the first of the articles to follow (Selection 1), Anne Anastasi discusses the problem of heredity and environment. The age-old nature-nurture question takes on a new look in this intriguing article. The question of the relative contribution of heredity versus environment in determining individual differences is posed in a new way. The significant question now is just *how* do heredity and environment interact in producing variability in behavior. The contribution of heredity is not a constant factor, but is instead a contribution which itself varies under differing environmental conditions. So too does the contribution of environment differ under differing conditions of heredity. Viewing both heredity and environment as interaction mechanisms, Anastasi details the research on both animals and humans in this area, and shows that both factors vary along a "continuum of indirectness." Factors of heredity are especially indirect in causing behavioral differences, and the more indirect the cause the wider the range of possible behavioral variations.

The solution to the problem is to focus on the interaction process, the "how" of the relationship. Anastasi suggests seven basic techniques for studying the interaction process: (1) the study of the behavioral effects of selective breeding studies on animals; (2) the study of the influence of physiological factors on behavior; (3) the study of the influence of prenatal physiological factors on later behavior; (4) the study of early experience in influencing later behavior; (5) the study of cultural differences on behavior patterns; (6) the study of the influence of body-type and physical traits on behavior; and (7) the study of twins, both monozygotic and dizogotic, and especially a longitudinal study which could follow the twins from infancy to school age.

Hopefully, Anastasi has expunged forever the simplistic yet unanswerable question, "which is more important, heredity or environment?"

In the next article (Selection 2), J. P. Scott outlines the theory and research in the very important area of "critical periods." There are apparently certain things which are best learned, indeed only learned, at very specific points of time in an organism's development. If that point in time is allowed to pass unrecognized the organism may be permanently damaged, and may never be able to learn what would have been almost automatic during the critical period. Scott explains that this point in time for many critical periods is not on any rigid timetable, but is more a function of the developmental process. For example, though it had seemed that postnatal development, like embryonic development, would be basically the same for all vertebrates, a comparison of only two species, man and the dog, uncovers the fact that the periods can even occur in reverse order. The actual timing mechanisms, though basically maturational in nature, depend on the development of social behavior patterns, as well as sensory and motor development. Attempts, for example, to teach a child too early in a developmental period may be as harmful as waiting too late. Training too early may result in the learning of bad habits, or in learning "not to learn."

Scott emphasizes the importance of the concept of critical periods by predicting that as the process becomes more fully understood we may be able to control or even alter the critical periods themselves. Knowledge thus far suggests the possibility that the critical period for primary socialization might be extended.

In the next reading (Selection 3), Benjamin S. Bloom discusses the influence of early environment and experience. Bloom feels that it is folly to assume that changes in behavior and personality can take place at any age, and that these changes, regardless of age or stage of development, are of equal significance. Bloom maintains that there is a negatively accelerated curve of development, that is, that development is most rapid during the first few years of life and then begins to level off. The midpoint of this curve is reached before the age of five, and Bloom further feels that environment has its most significant effect during this period of most rapid development.

To substantiate this hypothesis, Bloom cites three major reasons. (1) Early environment is extremely important because it shapes characteristics during their most rapid period of formation. (2) Human development is sequential in nature, and each new characteristic is formed on a base of that same characteristic, or other characteristics which precede it. (3) Learning theory teaches us that it is far easier to learn something new if one is not bogged down with the problem of having to unlearn an older, less appropriate series of responses.

Bloom concludes by stating that today's *most vital* research problem in all the behavioral sciences is the one focusing on the effects of early learning and early environments on human development.

In the following paper (Selection 4), J. S. Bruner addresses himself to the problem of the cognitive consequences of early sensory deprivation. Bruner presents a brief history of the problems surrounding the evolution of the concept of perception, and points to some of the recent physiological findings which have furthered our understanding of perception. Bruner, citing the physiological work of Granit, Galambos, Pribram and Magoun, warns us that there is no simple one-to-one relationship between the physical world and our perception of it. The old Sherrington formula of stimuli impinging on receptors, which then trigger a flow of afferent or sensory neurons which then connect in the central nervous system and trigger a flow of efferent or motor neurons, is a formula that has constricted our thinking and prevented a real appreciation of the sensory process. The new evidence indicates that when the receptor is stimulated, not only is there an afferent neural flow to the central nervous system, but also an efferent neural flow *back to the receptor*. Because of this, the organism cannot possibly receive all the potential information in the environment, for there is some filtering taking place even at the receptor point. Bruner sees this as beneficial since the ability to minimize the environmental surprises helps the organism to survive.

New developments in psychology have also helped to free us from our complacent attitudes. No longer are we so smugly accepting a fixed relationship between the physical stimulus on one side and stable characteristics of the brain on the other, with variability accounted for only in what Bruner calls that favorite American vehicle, the response.

The new trend in psychology which has had the most profound effect in shedding further light in this area is the recent work in early experience. Perceptual and cognitive sophistication in the adult depend on early contact with a variety of stimuli and a shifting environment. Crucial is one's opportunity to experience stimulus heterogeneity at an early age. Thus, if the child is deprived of this varied sensory stimulation, then his entire cognitive growth will be arrested, for he will be unable to form the necessary rules, models and strategies for coping with his environment. Cognitive growth depends on this very process of model formation, and the failure to master techniques for utilizing information before a certain period of growth may lead to irreversible loss.

Piaget, in the next paper (Selection 5), discusses the ways in which children form concepts. For over forty years at the University of Geneva, Switzerland, Piaget has studied human development, and especially the development of the knowing process and concept formation. Calling himself a genetic epistemologist, he has, through carefully detailed, hour-by-hour observations of the developing child, formulated a theory of how children go about the business of learning to know. His theory encompasses both the child's attempts to develop a concept of himself as an entity separate from his environment, and also the child's strivings to form other concepts, such as time, cause and effect, and number. It is Piaget's belief that the child's intellectual growth consists of the learning of certain strategies which allow the child to utilize the information his environment provides. These strategies or concepts are sequential in nature, and that, for example, in mathematics, the child must understand the concept of conservation of quantity before he can develop the concept of numbers. If the child has not discovered logical relationships, that is, for example, that seven large blocks is equal numerically to seven small blocks, then his later understanding of geometrical concepts or even the concept of number itself will be impaired.

Piaget points out that the process of knowing involves two basic components, the formal and the dynamic. The formal aspect, that is one's basic perceptions, provides the raw material for the later development of the dynamic aspect, which is a higher level thought process. The example Piaget cites of the child witnessing liquid being poured from a large, low glass into a tall, narrow glass illustrates the point. At age four or five the child utilizes the formal viewpoint and believes that the amount of liquid has increased. By age seven or eight, however, the child utilizes the dynamic viewpoint, and, understanding the process of the transformation, knows that the amount of liquid has not increased, that the level of liquid has risen simply as a result of the loss of width. Piaget's genetic approach, therefore, is to explain how these dynamic structures grow and evolve from the formal. This development is based on three principal factors, maturation, physical experiences and social interaction. Finally, Piaget stresses another crucial principal, equilibrium, a process without which the previously mentioned factors remain as only partial explanations. The whole growth process, Piaget sees, depends on equilibration, or the child's response to his environment on the basis of two processes, accomodation and also assimilation. This equilibrium is between *accomodation,* the child's response to immediate and compelling environmental demands, and *assimilation,* the child's ability to internalize and conceptualize his environmental experience. This is ultimately the basis for the child's formation of strategies for coping with his environment. As the child's knowledge increases, so too do his strategies for dealing with his environment, which in turn further increases his knowledge. This is a never ending chain of concept formation.

For example, a child may have the response of reaching out and touching and this soon includes everything in his reachable environment, i.e. he can assimilate. If, however, the child happens to reach out and touch a hot stove he withdraws his hand and quickly accommodates to the idea that some things are painful to touch. This now makes it possible to avoid other hot and painful objects; that is, he can assimilate the notion that any hot object is potentially dangerous.

Piaget believes that this can be a spontaneous process on the part of the child, but implicit is the assumption that this spontaneity, this development of strategies, depends on a fairly varied and rich environment.

In the final selection (6), J. McV. Hunt revisits the hypotheses and techniques developed by Maria Montessori over fifty years ago. Montessori's approach was based on her work first with mentally retarded children and later with the culturally deprived children living in the slums of Rome. Her success in educating the slum children was truly extraordinary, teaching them to read, write, and count often before the age of five. As an interesting by-product, delinquency in the area was greatly reduced. Hunt briefly traces (in the Introduction to a recent edition of *The Montessori Method*) the ebbs and flows of Montessori's popularity through the years, and indicates the various reasons for these fluctuations in vogue. For many years Montessori's notions about child development were too divergent from the emerging theories of psychoanalysis, behaviorism, and intelligence testing to capture popular support. The fact that Montessori's concepts were dissonant with some of our cherished beliefs, especially our naive belief that intelligence was almost totally determined by heredity and our equally absurd conviction that early experience was really rather unimportant, led the majority of professional psychologists and educators to reject the Montessori position.

Current research, however, which emphasizes both the tremendous importance of early experience and the fallacy of our belief in fixed intelligence throws the spotlight once again on the Montessori method. The method, with its insistence on sensory training, especially at an early age, now fits more closely with today's facts and theories, and with today's problem of education for the culturally deprived.

Hunt also sees the Montessori techniques as being of benefit to what he has been referring to as "the problem of the match." It is Hunt's thesis that effective education must "match" the child's current capabilities with just enough complexity and novelty to keep the child's interest. Too much incongruity and the child rebels or withdraws, too little and the child becomes bored.

Perhaps the major past weakness of the Montessori method was its possibly inappropriate use with middle and upper-middle class children, children who were already receiving a rich variety of sensory training at home. Maria Montessori developed her system through her work with slum children and it may be precisely with this group, whose homes lack stimulus variety, where it can have its most dramatic impact today.

1. HEREDITY, ENVIRONMENT, AND THE QUESTION "HOW?" *

ANNE ANASTASI

Two or three decades ago, the so-called heredity-environment question was the center of lively controversy. Today, on the other hand, many psychologists look upon it as a dead issue. It is now generally conceded that both hereditary and environmental factors enter into all behavior. The reacting organism is a product of its genes and its past environment, while present environment provides the immediate stimulus for current behavior. To be sure, it can be argued that, although a given trait may result from the combined influence of hereditary and environmental factors, a specific difference in this trait between individuals or between groups may be traceable to either hereditary or environmental factors alone. The design of most traditional investigations undertaken to identify such factors, however, has been such as to yield inconclusive answers. The same set of data has frequently led to opposite conclusions in the hands of psychologists with different orientations.

Nor have efforts to determine the proportional contribution of hereditary and environmental factors to observed individual differences in given traits met with any greater success. Apart from difficulties in controlling conditions, such investigations have usually been based upon the implicit assumption that hereditary and environmental factors combine in an additive fashion. Both geneticists

and psychologists have repeatedly demonstrated, however, that a more tenable hypothesis is that of interaction (15, 22, 28, 40). In other words, the nature and extent of the influence of each type of factor depends upon the contribution of the other. Thus the proportional contribution of heredity to the variance of a given trait, rather than being a constant, will vary under different environmental conditions. Similarly, under different hereditary conditions, the relative contribution of environment will differ. Studies designed to estimate the proportional contribution of heredity and environment, however, have rarely included measures of such interaction. The only possible conclusion from such research would thus seem to be that both heredity and environment contribute to all behavior traits and that the extent of their respective contributions cannot be specified for any trait. Small wonder that some psychologists regard the heredity-environment question as unworthy of further consideration!

But is this really all we can find out about the operation of heredity and environment in the etiology of behavior? Perhaps we have simply been asking the wrong questions. The traditional questions about heredity and environment may be intrinsically unanswerable. Psychologists began by asking *which* type of factor, hereditary or environmental, is responsible for individual differences in a given trait. Later, they tried to discover *how much* of the variance was attributable to heredity and how much to environment. It is the primary contention of this paper that a more fruitful

* Anastasi, Anne, "Heredity, Environment and the Question How?," *Psychological Review*, 1958, 65, pp. 197-208. Copyright 1958 by the American Psychological Association, and reproduced by permission.

approach is to be found in the question "How?" There is still much to be learned about the specific *modus operandi* of hereditary and environmental factors in the development of behavioral differences. And there are several current lines of research which offer promising techniques for answering the question "How?"

VARIETY OF INTERACTION MECHANISMS

HEREDITARY FACTORS. If we examine some of the specific ways in which hereditary factors may influence behavior, we cannot fail but be impressed by their wide diversity. At one extreme, we find such conditions as phenylpyruvic amentia and amaurotic idiocy. In these cases, certain essential physical prerequisites for normal intellectual development are lacking as a result of hereditary metabolic disorders. . . .*

A somewhat different situation is illustrated by hereditary deafness, which may lead to intellectual retardation through interference with normal social interaction, language development, and schooling. In such a case, however, the hereditary handicap can be offset by appropriate adaptations of training procedures. It has been said, in fact, that the degree of intellectual backwardness of the deaf is an index of the state of development of special instructional facilities. As the latter improve, the intellectual retardation associated with deafness is correspondingly reduced.

A third example is provided by inherited susceptibility to certain physical diseases, with consequent protracted ill health. If environmental conditions are such that illness does in fact develop, a number of different behavioral effects may follow. Intellectually, the individual may be handicapped by his inability to attend school regularly. On the other hand, depending upon age of onset, home conditions, parental status, and similar factors, poor health may have the effect of concentrating the individual's energies upon intellectual pursuits.

*Since the publication of this article it has been found that phenylketonuria (PKU) can be diagnosed shortly after birth and treated with a special diet low in phenylalanine. See W. Centerwall, *et al.* Phenylketonuria: screening programs and testing methods. *American Journal Public Health*, 1960, *50*, 1667-1677.—ED.

The curtailment of participation in athletics and social functions may serve to strengthen interest in reading and other sedentary activities. Concomitant circumstances would also determine the influence of such illness upon personality development. And it is well known that the latter effects could run the gamut from a deepening of human sympathy to psychiatric breakdown.

Finally, heredity may influence behavior through the mechanism of social stereotypes. A wide variety of inherited physical characteristics have served as the visible cues for identifying such stereotypes. These cues thus lead to behavioral restrictions or opportunities and —at a more subtle level—to social attitudes and expectancies. The individual's own self concept tends gradually to reflect such expectancies. All of these influences eventually leave their mark upon his abilities and inabilities, his emotional reactions, goals, ambitions, and outlook on life.

The geneticist Dobzhansky illustrates this type of mechanism by means of a dramatic hypothetical situation. He points out that, if there were a culture in which the carriers of blood group AB were considered aristocrats and those of blood group O laborers, then the blood-group genes would become important hereditary determiners of behavior (*12*, p. 147). Obviously the association between blood group and behavior would be specific to that culture. But such specificity is an essential property of the causal mechanism under consideration.

More realistic examples are not hard to find. The most familiar instances occur in connection with constitutional types, sex, and race. Sex and skin pigmentation obviously depend upon heredity. General body build is strongly influenced by hereditary components, although also susceptible to environmental modification. That all these physical characteristics may exert a pronounced effect upon behavior within a given culture is well known. It is equally apparent, of course, that in different cultures the behavioral correlates of such hereditary physical traits may be quite unlike. A specific physical cue may be completely unrelated to individual differences in psychological traits in one culture, while closely correlated with them in another. Or it may be associated with totally dissimilar behavior characteristics in two different cultures.

It might be objected that some of the illustrations which have been cited do not properly exemplify the operation of hereditary mechanisms in behavior development, since hereditary factors enter only indirectly into the behavior in question. Closer examination, however, shows this distinction to be untenable. First it may be noted that the influence of heredity upon behavior is always indirect. No psychological trait is ever inherited as such. All we can ever say directly from behavioral observations is that a given trait shows evidence of being influenced by certain "inheritable unknowns." This merely defines a problem for genetic research; it does not provide a causal explanation. Unlike the blood groups, which are close to the level of primary gene products, psychological traits are related to genes by highly indirect and devious routes. Even the mental deficiency associated with phenylketonuria is several steps removed from the chemically defective genes that represent its hereditary basis. Moreover, hereditary influences cannot be dichotomized into the more direct and the less direct. Rather do they represent a whole "continuum of indirectness," along which are found all degrees of remoteness of causal links. The examples already cited illustrate a few of the points on this continuum.

It should be noted that as we proceed along the continuum of indirectness, the range of variation of possible outcomes of hereditary factors expands rapidly. At each step in the causal chain, there is fresh opportunity for interaction with other hereditary factors as well as with environmental factors. And since each interaction in turn determines the direction of subsequent interactions, there is an ever-widening network of possible outcomes. If we visualize a simple sequential grid with only two alternatives at each point, it is obvious that there are two possible outcomes in the one-stage situation, four outcomes at the second stage, eight at the third, and so on in geometric progression. The actual situation is undoubtedly much more complex, since there will usually be more than two alternatives at any one point.

In the case of the blood groups, the relation to specific genes is so close that no other concomitant hereditary or environment conditions can alter the outcome. If the organism survives at all, it will have the blood group determined by its genes. Among psychological traits, on the other hand, some variation in outcome is always possible as a result of concurrent circumstances. Even in cases of phenylketonuria, intellectual development will exhibit some relationship with the type of care and training available to the individual. That behavioral outcomes show progressive diversification as we proceed along the continuum of indirectness is brought out by the other examples which were cited. Chronic illness *can* lead to scholarly renown or to intellectual immaturity; a mesomorphic physique *can* be a contributing factor in juvenile delinquency or in the attainment of a college presidency! Published data on Sheldon somatotypes provide some support for both of the latter outcomes.

Parenthetically, it may be noted that geneticists have sometimes used the term "norm of reaction" to designate the range of variation of possible outcomes of gene properties (cf. *13*, p. 161). Thus heredity sets the "norm" or limits within which environmental differences determine the eventual outcome. In the case of some traits, such as blood groups or eye color, this norm is much narrower than in the case of other traits. Owing to the rather different psychological connotations of both the words "norm" and "reaction," however, it seems less confusing to speak of the "range of variation" in this context.

A large portion of the continuum of hereditary influences which we have described coincides with the domain of somatopsychological relations, as defined by Barker et al. (*6*). Under this heading, Barker includes "variations in physique that affect the psychological situation of a person by influencing the effectiveness of his body as a tool for actions or by serving as a stimulus to himself or others" (*6*, p. 1). Relatively direct neurological influences on behavior, which have been the traditional concern of physiological psychology, are excluded from this definition, Barker being primarily concerned with what he calls the "social psychology of physique." Of the examples cited in the present paper, deafness, severe illness, and the physical characteristics associated with social stereotypes would meet the specifications of somatopsychological factors.

The somatic factors to which Barker refers, however, are not limited to those of hereditary origin. Bodily conditions attributable to environmental causes operate in the same sorts of somatopsychological relations as those traceable to heredity. In fact, heredity-environment distinctions play a minor part in Barker's approach.

ENVIRONMENTAL FACTORS: ORGANIC. Turning now to an analysis of the role of environmental factors in behavior, we find the same etiological mechanisms which were observed in the case of hereditary factors. First, however, we must differentiate between two classes of environmental influences: (a) those producing organic effects which may in turn influence behavior and (b) those serving as direct stimuli for psychological reactions. The former may be illustrated by food intake or by exposure to bacterial infection; the latter, by tribal initiation ceremonies or by a course in algebra. There are no completely satisfactory names by which to designate these two classes of influences. In an earlier paper by Anastasi and Foley (4), the terms "structural" and "functional" were employed. However, "organic" and "behavioral" have the advantage of greater familiarity in this context and may be less open to misinterpretation. Accordingly, these terms will be used in the present paper.

Like hereditary factors, environmental influences of an organic nature can also be ordered along a continuum of indirectness with regard to their relation to behavior. This continuum closely parallels that of hereditary factors. One end is typified by such conditions as mental deficiency resulting from cerebral brain injury or from prenatal nutritional inadequacies. A more indirect etiological mechanism is illustrated by severe motor disorder—as in certain cases of cerebral palsy—without accompanying injury to higher neurological centers. In such instances, intellectual retardation may occur as an indirect result of the motor handicap, through the curtailment of educational and social activities. Obviously this causal mechanism corresponds closely to that of hereditary deafness cited earlier in the paper.

Finally, we may consider an environmental parallel to the previously discussed social stereotypes which were mediated by hereditary physical cues. Let us suppose that a young woman with mousy brown hair becomes transformed into a dazzling golden blonde through environmental techniques currently available in our culture. It is highly probable that this metamorphosis will alter, not only the reactions of her associates toward her, but also her own self concept and subsequent behavior. The effects could range from a rise in social poise to a drop in clerical accuracy!

Among the examples of environmentally determined organic influences which have been described, all but the first two fit Barker's definition of somatopsychological factors. With the exception of birth injuries and nutritional deficiencies, all fall within the social psychology of physique. Nevertheless, the individual factors exhibit wide diversity in their specific modus operandi—a diversity which has important practical as well as theoretical implications.

ENVIRONMENTAL FACTORS: BEHAVIORAL. The second major class of environmental factors— the behavioral as contrasted to the organic— are by definition direct influences. The immediate effect of such environmental factors is always a behavioral change. To be sure, some of the initial behavioral effects may themselves indirectly affect the individual's late behavior. But this relationship can perhaps be best conceptualized in terms of breadth and permanence of effects. Thus it could be said that we are now dealing, not with a continuum of indirectness, as in the case of hereditary and organic-environmental factors, but rather with a continuum of breadth.

Social class membership may serve as an illustration of a relatively broad, pervasive, and enduring environmental factor. Its influence upon behavior development may operate through many channels. Thus social level may determine the range and nature of intellectual stimulation provided by home and community through books, music, art, play activities, and the like. Even more far-reaching may be the effects upon interests and motivation, as illustrated by the desire to perform abstract intellectual tasks, to surpass others in competitive situations, to succeed in school, or to gain social approval. Emotional and social traits may likewise be influenced by the nature of interpersonal relations characterizing homes at different socio-economic levels. Somewhat more restricted in scope than social class, although still exerting a relatively broad influence, is amount of formal schooling which the individual is able to obtain.

A factor which may be wide or narrow in its effects, depending upon concomitant circumstances, is language handicap. Thus the bilingualism of an adult who moves to a foreign country with inadequate mastery of the new language represents a relatively limited handicap which can be readily overcome in most cases. At most, the difficulty is one of communication. On the other hand, some kinds of bilingualism in childhood may exert a retarding influence upon intellectual development and may under certain conditions affect personality development adversely (*2, 5, 10*). A common pattern in the homes of immigrants is that the child speaks one language at home and another in school, so that his knowledge of each language is limited to certain types of situations. Inadequate facility with the language of the school interferes with the acquisition of basic concepts, intellectual skills, and information. The frustration engendered by scholastic difficulties may in turn lead to discouragement and general dislike of school. Such reactions can be found, for example, among a number of Puerto Rican children in New York City schools (3). In the case of certain groups, moreover the child's foreign language background may be perceived by himself and his associates as a symbol of minority group status and may thereby augment any emotional maladjustment arising from such status (*34*).

A highly restricted environmental influence is to be found in the opportunity to acquire specific items of information occurring in a particular intelligence test. The fact that such opportunities may vary with culture, social class, or individual experiential background is at the basis of the test user's concern with the problem of coaching and with "culture-free" or "culture-fair" tests (cf. *1, 2*). If the advantage or disadvantage which such experiential differences confer upon certain individuals is strictly confined to performance on the given test, it will obviously reduce the validity of the test and should be eliminated.

In this connection, however, it is essential to know the breadth of the environmental influence in question. A fallacy inherent in many attempts to develop culture-fair tests is that the breadth of cultural differentials is not taken into account. Failure to consider breadth of effect likewise characterizes certain discussions of coaching. If, in coaching a student for a college admission test, we can improve his knowledge of verbal concepts and his reading comprehension, he will be better equipped to succeed in college courses. His performance level will thus be raised, not only on the test, but also on the criterion which the test is intended to predict. To try to devise a test which is not susceptible to such coaching would merely reduce the effectivenes of the test. Similarly, efforts to rule out cultural differentials from test items so as to make them equally "fair" to subjects in different social classes or in different cultures may merely limit the usefulness of the test, since the same cultural differentials may operate within the broader area of behavior which the test is designed to sample.

METHODOLOGICAL APPROACHES

The examples considered so far should suffice to highlight the wide variety of ways in which hereditary and environmental factors may interact in the course of behavior development. There is clearly a need for identifying explicitly the etiological mechanism whereby any given hereditary or environmental condition ultimately leads to a behavioral characteristic—in other words, the "how" of heredity and environment. Accordingly, we may now take a quick look at some promising methodological approaches to the question "how."

Within the past decade, an increasing number of studies have been designed to trace the connection between specific factors in the hereditary backgrounds or in the reactional biographies of individuals and their observed behavioral characteristics. There has been a definite shift away from the predominantly descriptive and correlational approach of the earlier decades toward more deliberate attempts to verify explanatory hypotheses. Similarly, the cataloguing of group differences in psychological traits has been giving way gradually to research on *changes* in group characteristics following altered conditions.

Among recent methodological developments, we have chosen seven as being particularly relevant to the analysis of etiological mechanisms. The first represents an extension of selective breeding investigations to permit the identification of specific hereditary conditions underlying the observed behavioral differences. When early selective breeding investigations such as those of Tryon (*36*) on rats indicated that "maze learning ability" was inherited, we were still a long way from knowing what was actually being transmitted by the genes. It was obviously not "maze learning ability" as such. Twenty—or even ten—years ago, some psychologists would have suggested that it was probably general intelligence. And a few might even have drawn a parallel with the inheritance of human intelligence.

But today investigators have been asking: Just what makes one group of rats learn mazes more quickly than the other? Is it differences in motivation, emotionality, speed of running, general activity level? If so, are these behavioral characteristics in turn dependent upon group differences in glandular development, body weight, brain size, biochemical factors, or some other organic conditions? A number of recent and ongoing investigations indicate that attempts are being made to trace, at least part of the way, the steps whereby certain chemical properties of the genes may ultimately lead to specified behavior characteristics.

An example of such a study is provided by Searle's (*31*) follow-up of Tryon's research. Working with the strains of maze-bright and maze-dull rats developed by Tryon, Searle demonstrated that the two strains differed in a number of emotional and motivational factors, rather than in ability. Thus the strain differences were traced one step further, although many links still remain to be found between maze learning and genes. A promising methodological development within the same general area is to be found in the recent research of Hirsch and Tryon (*18*). Utilizing a specially devised technique for measuring individual differences in behavior among lower organisms, these investigators launched a series of studies on selective breeding for behavioral characteristics in the fruit fly, *Drosophila*. Such research can capitalize on the mass of available genetic knowledge regarding the morphology of *Drosophila*, as well as on other advantages of using such an organism in genetic studies.

Further evidence of current interest in the specific hereditary factors which influence behavior is to be found in an extensive research program in progress at the Jackson Memorial Laboratory, under the direction of Scott and Fuller (*30*). In general, the project is concerned with the behavioral characteristics of various breeds and crossbreeds of dogs. Analyses of some of the data gathered to date again suggest that "differences in performance are produced by differences in emotional, motivational, and peripheral processes, and that genetically caused differences in central processes may be either slight or non-existent" (*29*, p. 225). In other parts of the same project, breed differences in physiological characteristics, which may in turn be related to behavioral differences, have been established.

A second line of attack is the exploration of possible relationships between behavioral characteristics and physiological variables which may in turn be traceable to hereditary factors. Research on EEG, autonomic balance, metabolic processes, and biochemical factors illustrates this approach. A lucid demonstration of the process of tracing a psychological condition to genetic factors is provided by the identification and subsequent investigation of phenylpyruvic amentia. In this case, the causal chain from defective gene, through metabolic disorder and consequent cerebral malfunctioning, to feeble-mindedness and other overt symptoms can be described step by step (cf. *32; 33*, pp. 389-391). Also relevant are the recent researches on neurological and biochemical correlates of schizophrenia (*9*). Owing to inadequate methodological controls, however, most of the findings of the latter studies must be regarded as tentative (*19*).

Prenatal environmental factors provide a third avenue of fruitful investigation. Especially noteworthy is the recent work of Pasamanick and his associates (*27*), which demonstrated a tie-up between socioeconomic level, complications of pregnancy and parturition, and psychological disorders of the offspring.

In a series of studies on large samples of whites and Negroes in Baltimore, these investigators showed that various prenatal and paranatal disorders are significantly related to the occurrence of mental defect and psychiatric disorders in the child. An important source of such irregularities in the process of childbearing and birth is to be found in deficiencies of maternal diet and in other conditions associated with low socioeconomic status. An analysis of the data did in fact reveal a much higher frequency of all such medical complications in lower than in higher socioeconomic levels, and a higher frequency among Negroes than among whites.

Direct evidence of the influence of prenatal nutritional factors upon subsequent intellectual development is to be found in a recent, well controlled experiment by Harell et al. (*16*). The subjects were pregnant women in low-income groups, whose normal diets were generally quite deficient. A dietary supplement was administered to some of these women during pregnancy and lactation, while an equated control received placebos. When tested at the ages of three and four years, the offspring of the experimental group obtained a significantly higher mean IQ than did the offspring of the controls.

Mention should also be made of animal experiments on the effects of such factors as prenatal radiation and neonatal asphyxia upon cerebral anomalies as well as upon subsequent behavior development. These experimental studies merge imperceptibly into the fourth approach to be considered, namely, the investigation of the influence of early experience upon the eventual behavioral characteristics of animals. Research in this area has been accumulating at a rapid rate. In 1954, Beach and Jaynes (*8*) surveyed this literature for the *Psychological Bulletin,* listing over 130 references. Several new studies have appeared since that date (eg., *14, 21, 24, 25, 35*). The variety of factors covered ranges from the type and quantity of available food to the extent of contact with human culture. A large number of experiments have been concerned with various forms of sensory deprivation and with diminished opportunities for motor exercise. Effects have been observed in many kinds of animals and in almost all aspects of behavior, including perceptual responses, motor activity, learning, emotionality, and social reactions.

In their review, Beach and Jaynes pointed out that research in this area has been stimulated by at least four distinct theoretical interests. Some studies were motivated by the traditional concern with the relative contribution of maturation and learning to behavior development. Others were designed in an effort to test certain psychoanalytic theories regarding infantile experiences, as illustrated by studies which limited the feeding responses of young animals. A third relevant influence is to be found in the work of the European biologist Lorenz (*23*) on early social stimulation of birds, and in particular on the special type of learning for which the term "imprinting" has been coined. A relatively large number of recent studies have centered around Hebb's (*17*) theory regarding the importance of early perceptual experiences upon subsequent performance in learning situations. All this research represents a rapidly growing and promising attack on the *modus operandi* of specific environmental factors.

The human counterpart of these animal studies may be found in the comparative investigation of child-rearing practices in different cultures and subcultures. This represents the fifth approach in our list. An outstanding example of such a study is that by Whiting and Child (*38*), published in 1953. Utilizing data on 75 primitive societies from the Cross-Cultural Files of the Yale Institute of Human Relations, these investigators set out to test a number of hypotheses regarding the relationships between child-rearing practices and personality development. This analysis was followed up by field observations in five cultures, the results of which have not yet been reported (cf. *37*).

Within our own culture, similar surveys have been concerned with the diverse psychological environments provided by different social classes (*11*). Of particular interest are the study by Williams and Scott (*39*) on the association between socioeconomic level, permissiveness, and motor development among Negro children, and the exploratory research by Milner (*26*) on the relationship between reading readiness in first-grade children and patterns of parent-child interaction. Milner found that upon school entrance the lower-class child seems to lack chiefly two advantages enjoyed by the middle-class child. The first is described as "a warm positive family atmosphere or adult-relationship pattern which is more and more being recognized as a motivational prerequisite of any kind of adult-controlled learning." The lower-class children in Milner's study perceived adults as predominantly hostile. The second advantage is an extensive opportunity to interact verbally with adults in the family. The latter point is illustrated by parental attitudes toward mealtime conversation, lower-class parents tending to inhibit and discourage such conversation, while middle-class parents encourage it.

Most traditional studies on child-rearing practices have been designed in terms of a psychoanalytic orientation. There is need for more data pertaining to other types of hypotheses. Findings such as those of Milner on opportunities for verbalization and the resulting effects upon reading readiness represent a step in this direction. Another possible source of future data is the application of the intensive observational techniques of psychological ecology developed by Barker and Wright (7) to widely diverse socioeconomic groups.

A sixth major approach involves research on the previously cited somatopsychological relationships (6). To date, little direct information is available on the precise operation of this class of factors in psychological development. The multiplicity of ways in which physical traits—whether hereditary or environmental in origin—may influence behavior thus offers a relatively unexplored field for future study.

The seventh and final approach to be considered represents an adaptation of traditional twin studies. From the standpoint of the question "How?" there is need for closer coordination between the usual data on twin resemblance and observations of the family interactions of twins. Available data already suggest, for example, that closeness of contact and extent of environmental similarity are greater in the case of monozygotic than in the case of dizygotic twins (cf. 2). Information on the social reactions of twins toward each other and the specialization of roles is likewise of interest (2). Especially useful would be longitudinal

studies of twins, beginning in early infancy and following the subjects through school age. The operation of differential environmental pressures, the development of specialized roles, and other environmental influences could thus be more clearly identified and correlated with intellectual and personality changes in the growing twins.

Parenthetically, I should like to add a remark about the traditional applications of the twin method, in which persons in different degrees of hereditary and environmental relationships to each other are simply compared for behavioral similarity. In these studies, attention has been focused principally upon the amount of resemblance of monozygotic as contrasted to dizygotic twins. Yet such a comparison is particularly difficult to interpret because of the many subtle differences in the environmental situations of the two types of twins. A more fruitful comparison would seem to be that between dizygotic twins and siblings, for whom the hereditary similarity is known to be the same. In Kallmann's monumental research on psychiatric disorders among twins (20), for example, one of the most convincing bits of evidence for the operation of hereditary factors in schizophrenia is the fact that the degrees of concordance for dizygotic twins and for siblings were practically identical. In contrast, it will be recalled that in intelligence test scores dizygotic twins resemble each other much more closely than do siblings—a finding which reveals the influence of environmental factors in intellectual development.

SUMMARY

The heredity-environment problem is still very much alive. Its viability is assured by the gradual replacement of the questions, "Which one?" and "How much?" by the more basic and appropriate question, "How?" Hereditary influences—as well as environmental factors of an organic nature—vary along a "continuum of indirectness." The more indirect their connection with behavior, the wider will be the range of variation of possible outcomes. One extreme of the continuum of indirectness may be illustrated by brain damage leading to mental deficiency; the other extreme, by physical characteristics associated with social stereotypes. Examples of factors falling at intermediate points include deafness, physical diseases, and motor disorders. Those environmental factors which act directly upon behavior can be ordered along a continuum of breadth or permanence of effect, as exemplified by social class membership, amount of formal schooling, language handicap, and familiarity with specific test items.

Several current lines of research offer promising techniques for exploring the *modus operandi* of hereditary and environmental factors. Outstanding among them are investigations of: (*a*) hereditary conditions which underlie behavioral differences between selectively bred groups of animals; (*b*) relations between physiological variables and individual differences in behavior, especially in the case of pathological deviations; (*c*) role of prenatal physiological factors in behavior development; (*d*) influence of early experience upon eventual behavioral characteristics; (*e*) cultural differences in child-rearing practices in relation to intellectual and emotional development; (*f*) mechanisms of somatopsychological relationships; and (*g*) psychological development of twins from infancy to maturity, together with observations of their social environment. Such approaches are extremely varied with regard to subjects employed, nature of psychological functions studied, and specific experimental procedures followed. But it is just such heterogeneity of methodology that is demanded by the wide diversity of ways in which hereditary and environmental factors interact in behavior development.

REFERENCES

1. ANASTASI, ANNE. *Psychological testing.* New York: Macmillan, (2nd ed., 1961).
2. ANASTASI, ANNE. *Differential psychology.* (3rd ed.) New York: Macmillan, 1958.
3. ANASTASI, ANNE, and CORDOVA, E. A. Some effects of bilingualism upon the intelligence test performance of Puerto Rican children in New York City. *J. educ. Psychol.*, 1953, *44*, 1-19.
4. ANASTASI, ANNE, and FOLEY, J. P., JR. A proposed reorientation in the heredity-environment controversy. *Psychol. Rev.*, 1948, *55*, 239-249.
5. ARSENIAN, S. Bilingualism in the post-war world. *Psychol. Bull.*, 1945, *42*, 65-86.
6. BARKER, R. G., WRIGHT, BEATRICE A., MYERSON, L., and GONICK, MOLLIE R. Adjustment to physical handicap and illness: A survey

of the social psychology of physique and disability. *Soc. Sci. Res. Coun. Bull.*, 1953, No. *55* (Rev.).
7. BARKER, R. G., and WRIGHT, H. F. *Midwest and its children: The psychological ecology of an American town.* Evanston, Ill.: Row, Peterson, 1955.
8. BEACH, F. A., and JAYNES, J. Effects of early experience upon the behavior of animals. *Psychol. Bull.*, 1954, *51*, 239-263.
9. BRACKBILL, G. A. Studies of brain dysfunction in schizophrenia. *Psychol. Bull.*, 1956, *53*, 210-226.
10. DARCY, NATALIE T. A review of the literature on the effects of bilingualism upon the measurement of intelligence. *J. genet. Psychol.*, 1953, *82*, 21-57.
11. DAVIS, A., and HAVIGHURST, R. J. Social class and color differences in child rearing. *Amer. sociol. Rev.* 1946, *11*, 698-710.
12. DOBZHANSKY, T. The genetic nature of differences among men. In S. Persons (Ed.), *Evolutionary thought in America.* New Haven: Yale Univer. Press, 1950. Pp. 86-155.
13. DOBZHANSKY, T. Heredity, environment, and evolution. *Science*, 1950, *111*, 161-166.
14. FORGUS, R. H. The effect of early perceptual learning on the behavioral organization of adult rats. *J. comp. physiol. Phychol.*, 1954, *47*, 331-336.
15. HALDANE, J. B. S. *Heredity and politics.* New York: Norton, 1938.
16. HARRELL, RUTH F., WOODYARD, ELLA, and GATES, A. I. *The effect of mothers diets on the intelligence of the offspring.* New York: Bur. Publ. Teach. Coll., Columbia Univer., 1955.
17. HEBB, D. O. *The organization of behavior.* New York: Wiley, 1949.
18. HIRSCH, L. and TRYON, R. C. Mass screening and reliable individual measurement in the experimental behavior genetics of lower organisms. *Psychol. Bull.*, 1956, *53*, 402-410.
19. HORWITT, M. K. Fact and artifact in the biology of Schizophrenia. *Science*, 1956, *124*, 429-430.
20. KALLMANN, F. J. *Heredity in health and mental disorder; Principles of psychiatric genetics in the light of comparative twin studies.* New York: Norton, 1953.
21. KING, J. A., and GURNEY, NANCY L. Effect of early social experience on adult aggressive behavior in C57BL10 mice. *J. comp. physiol. Psychol.*, 1954, *47*, 326-330.
22. LOEVINGER, JANE. On the proportional contributions of differences in nature and in nurture to differences in intelligence. *Psychol. Bull.*, 1943, *40*, 725-756.
23. LORENZ, K. Der Kumpan in der Umwelt des Vogels. Der Artgenosse als auslösendes Moment sozialer Verhaltungsweisen. *J. Orn., Lpz.*, 1935, *83*, 137-213; 289-413.
24. LUCHINS, A. S., and FORGUS, R. H. The

effect of differential postweaning environment on the rigidity of an animal's behavior. *J. genet. Psychol.*, 1955, *86*, 51-58.

25. MELZACK, R. The genesis of emotional behavior: An experimental study of the dog. *J. comp. physiol. Psychol.*, 1954, *47*, 166-168.

26. MILNER, ESTHER A. A study of the relationships between reading readiness in grade one school children and patterns of parent-child interaction. *Child Develpm.*, 1951, *22*, 95-112.

27. PASAMANICK, B., KNOBLOCH, HILDA, and LILIENFELD, A. M. Socioeconomic status and some precursors of neuropsychiatric disorder. *Amer. J. Orthopsychiat.*, 1956, *26*, 594-601.

28. SCHWESINGER, GLADYS C. *Heredity and environment.* New York: Macmillan, 1933.

29. SCOTT, J. P., and CHARLES, MARGARET S. Some problems of heredity and social behavior. *J. gen. Physchol.*, 1953, *48*, 209-230.

30. SCOTT, L. P., and FULLER, J. L. Research on genetics and social behavior at the Roscoe B. Jackson Laboratory, 1946-1951—A progress report. *J. Hered.*, 1951, *42*, 191-197.

31. SEARLE, L. V. The organization of hereditary maze-brightness and maze-dullness. *Genet. Psychol. Monogr.*, 1949, *39*, 279-325.

32. SNYDER, L. H. The genetic approach to human individuality. *Sci. Mon., N.Y.*, 1949, *68*, 165-171.

33. SNYDER, L. H., and DAVID, P. R. *The principles of heredity.* (5th ed.) Boston: Heath, 1957.

34. SPOERL, DOROTHY T. Bilinguality and emotional adjustment. *J. abnorm. som. Psychol.*, 1943, *38*, 37-57.

35. THOMPSON, W. R., and MELZACK, R. Early environment. *Sci. Amer.*, 1956, *194* (1), 38-42.

36. TRYON, R. C. Genetic differences in maze-learning ability in rats. *Yearb. nat. Soc. Stud. Educ.*, 1940, *39*, Part I, 111-119.

37. WHITING, J. W. M., *et al. Field guide for a study of socialization in five societies.* Cambridge, Mass.: Harvard Univer., 1954 (mimeo.).

38. WHITING, J. W. M., and CHILD, I. L. *Child training and personality. A cross-cultural study.* New Haven: Yale Univer. Press, 1953.

39. WILLIAMS, JUDITH R., and SCOTT, R. B. Growth and development of Negro infants: IV. Motor development and its relationship to child rearing practices in two groups of Negro infants. *Child Develpm.*, 1953, *24*, 103-121.

40. WOODWORTH, R. S. Heredity and environment: A critical survey of recently published material on twins and foster children. *Soc. Sci. Res. Coun. Bull.*, 1941, No. 47.

2. CRITICAL PERIODS IN BEHAVIORAL DEVELOPMENT *

JOHN P. SCOTT

A number of years ago I was given a female lamb taken from its mother at birth. My wife and I raised it on the bottle for the first 10 days of life and then placed it out in the pasture with a small flock of domestic sheep. As might have been expected from folklore, the lamb became attached to people and followed the persons who fed it. More surprisingly, the lamb remained independent of the rest of the flock when we restored it to the pasture. Three years later it was still follow-

ing an independent grazing pattern. In addition, when it was mated and had lambs of its own it became a very indifferent mother, allowing its offspring to nurse but showing no concern when the lamb moved away with the other members of the flock (*1*).

Since following the flock is such a universal characteristic of normal sheep, I was impressed by the extensive and permanent modification of this behavior that resulted from a brief early experience. The results suggested that Freud was right concerning the importance of early experience, and pointed toward the existence of critical periods in behavioral

* From: "Critical Periods in Behavioral Development," *Science*, Vol. 138, pp. 949-958, 30 November 1962, Copyright 1962 by the Association for the Advancement of Science.

development. As I soon discovered, there is considerable evidence that a critical period for determining early social relationships is a widespread phenomenon in vertebrates; such a critical period had long been known in ants (*2*).

The theory of critical periods is not a new one in either biology or psychology. It was strongly stated by Stockard in 1921, in connection with his experiments on the induction of monstrosities in fish embryos, although he gave credit to Dareste for originating the basic idea 30 years earlier (*3*). In experimenting with the effects of various inorganic chemicals upon the development of *Fundulus* eggs, Stockard at first thought one-eyed monsters were specifically caused by the magnesium ion. Further experiments showed him that almost any chemical would produce the same effect, provided it was applied at the proper time during development. These experiments and those of Child (*4*) and his students established the fact that the most rapidly growing tissues in an embryo are the most sensitive to any change in conditions, thus accounting for the specificity of effects at particular times.

Meanwhile Freud had attempted to explain the origin of neuroses in human patients as the result of early experience and had implied that certain periods in the life of an infant are times of particular sensitivity. In 1935, Lorenz (*5*) emphasized the importance of critical periods for the formation of primary social bonds (imprinting) in birds, remarking on their similarity to critical periods in the development of the embryo, and McGraw soon afterward (*6*) pointed out the existence of critical periods for optimal learning of motor skills in the human infant.

Since then, the phenomenon of critical periods has excited the imagination of a large group of experimenters interested in human and animal development. In describing this fast-moving scientific field, I shall point out some of the most significant current developments. More detailed information is available in some excellent recent reviews (*7, 8*).

To begin with, three major kinds of critical-period phenomena have been discovered. These involve optimal periods for learning, for infantile stimulation, and for the formation of basic social relationships. The last of these has been established as a widespread phenomenon in the animal kingdom and consequently receives major attention in this article.

PERIODS ARE BASED ON PROCESSES

In the dog, the development of behavior may be divided into several natural periods marked off by important changes in social relationships (Table 1). Only a few other species have been studied in sufficient detail for making adequate comparisons, but enough data have been accumulated to show that similar periods can be identified in other mammals and in birds (*9, 10*). I originally expected to find that the course of postnatal development, like that of embryonic development, would be essentially similar in all vertebrates, and that while the periods might be extended or shortened, the same pattern of development would be evident in all (*11*). However, comparison of only two species, man and the dog, shows that the periods can actually occur in reverse order, and that there is an astonishing degree of flexibility in behavioral development (*12*).

This leads to the conclusion that the important aspect of each developmental period is not time sequence but the fact that each represents a major developmental process. Thus, the neonatal period is chiefly characterized by the process of neonatal nutrition—nursing in mammals and parental feeding in many birds. The transition period is characterized by the process of transition to adult methods of nutrition and locomotion and the appearance of adult patterns of social behavior, at least in immature form. The period of socialization is the period in which primary social bonds are formed. If we consider processes alone, it is apparent that they are not completely dependent on each other and that they can therefore be arranged in different orders. It is also apparent that certain of these processes persist beyond the periods characterized by them. For example, a mammal usually retains throughout life the ability to suck which characterizes the neonatal period, although in most cases this ability is little used.

PROCESS OF PRIMARY SOCIALIZATION

Since one of the first acts of a young mammal is to nurse, and since food rewards are known to modify the behavior of adult animals, it once seemed logical to suppose that the process of forming a social attachment begins with food rewards and develops as an acquired drive. However, the experimental evidence does not support this extreme viewpoint. Brodbeck reared a group of puppies during the critical period of socialization, feeding half of them by hand and the other half by machine, but giving all of them the same degree of human contact (13). He found that the two sets of puppies became equally attached to people. The result was later confirmed by Stanley and his co-workers (14), who found that the only difference in response between the machine-fed and the hand-fed puppies was that the latter yelped more when they saw the experimenter. Elliot and King (15) fed all their puppies by hand but overfed one group and underfed another. The hungry puppies became more rapidly attached to the handlers. We can conclude that, in the dog, food rewards per se are not necessary for the process of socialization, but that hunger will speed it up.

Fisher (16) reared fox terrier puppies in isolation boxes through the entire socialization period. The puppies were fed mechanically (thus, food was entirely eliminated as a factor in the experiment), but they were removed from the boxes for regular contacts with the experimenter. One group of puppies was always rewarded by kind social treatment. A second group was sometimes rewarded and sometimes punished, but in a purely random way. Still a third group was always punished for any positive approach to the experimenter. The puppies that were both rewarded and punished showed most attraction and dependency behavior with respect to the experimenter, and the puppies that were always punished showed the least. After the treatment was discontinued, all the puppies began coming toward the experimenter, and the differences rapidly disappeared. This leads to the surprising conclusion that the process of socialization is not inhibited by punishment and may even be speeded up by it.

At approximately 3 weeks of age—that is, at the beginning of the period of socialization—young puppies begin to bark or whine when isolated or placed in strange places. Elliot and Scott (17) showed that the reaction to isolation in a strange place reaches a peak at 6 to 7 weeks of age, approximately the midpoint of the critical period, and begins to decline thereafter. Scott, Deshaies, and Morris (18) found that separating young puppies overnight from their mother and litter mates in a strange pen for 20 hours per day produced a strong emotional reaction and speeded up the process of socialization to human handlers. All this evidence indicates that any sort of strong emotion, whether hunger, fear, pain, or loneliness, will speed up the process of socialization. No experiments have been carried out to determine the effects of pleasant types of emotion, such as might be aroused by play and handling, but these were probably a factor in Brodbeck's experiment with machine-fed puppies.

The results of these experiments on dogs agree with evidence from other species. While they were going on, Harlow (19) was performing his famous experiments with rhesus monkeys isolated at birth and supplied with dummy "mothers." When given the choice between a comfortable cloth-covered mother without a nipple and an uncomfortable mother made of wire screening but equipped with a functional nursing bottle, the young rhesus monkeys definitely preferred the cloth-covered models from which they had received no food rewards. Harlow concluded that the acquired-drive theory of the origin of social attachment could be discarded.

Later, Igel and Calvin (20) performed a similar but more elaborate experiment with puppies. These animals had more opportunity to choose, being provided with four kinds of mother models: comfortable and uncomfortable, each type with and without nipples. Like rhesus monkeys, the puppies preferred the comfortable "mother" but usually chose one with a nipple. Thus it appears that food rewards do contribute something to the social relationship, although they do not form its prime basis.

Since then Harlow (21) has raised to maturity the monkeys raised on dummy mothers, has mated them, and has observed their behavior toward their own young. They become uniformly poor mothers, neglecting their offspring and often punishing them when they cry. In spite of such rejection, the young rhesus infants desperately crawl toward their mothers and give every evidence of becoming attached to them, although perhaps not as strongly as in the normal relationship. Here again punishment does not inhibit the formation of a social bond.

The hypothesis that the primary social bond originates through food rewards had already been shown to be invalid in the precocial birds, many of which form attachments prior to the time when they begin to feed. Lorenz (5) was the first to point out the significance of this phenomenon, which he called "imprinting." He also stated that it differed from conditioning, primarily in that it was very rapid and apparently irreversible. However, rapid formation and great persistence are also characteristic of many conditioned responses and other learned behavior. Fabricius (22) pointed out that no sharp line can be drawn between imprinting and conditioning, and Collias (23) concluded that imprinting is a form of learned behavior that is self-reinforcing.

The process of imprinting in young ducklings and chicks has since been experimentally analyzed in much detail, with results that invariably confirm the conclusion that it takes place without any obvious external rewards or reinforcement. Hess (24) found that if he caused young ducklings to follow a model over varying distances or over hurdles, the ducklings which had to make the greater effort became more strongly imprinted. He also found that the drug meprobamate and its congener carisoprodol, which are muscle relaxants as well as tranquilizers, greatly reduce imprinting if given during the critical period. James (25) found that chicks would become attached to an object illuminated by a flickering light, even though they were not allowed to follow, and Gray (26) later showed that they will become attached to a motionless object illuminated by a steady light and viewed from an isolation box. It is therefore apparent that chicks can become imprinted without following, although muscular tension may still be important.

Guiton (27) found that chicks allowed to follow a model in a group become less strongly imprinted than chicks exposed singly, and he attributed the results to the greater fear shown by the isolated chicks. Recently, Pitz and Ross (28) subjected young chicks following a model to a loud sound and found that this increased the speed with which they formed a social bond. Hess (29) has given a mild electric shock to chicks following a model and finds that this also increases the strength of imprinting. Instead of avoiding the model, the distressed chick runs after it more closely.

We may conclude that these young birds become attached to any object to which they are long exposed during the critical period, even when their contact is only visual. We may also conclude that the speed of formation of a social bond is dependent upon the degree of emotional arousal, irrespective of the nature of that arousal. Whether attachment is the result of the emotion itself or of the reduction of emotions as the chick or duckling approaches the model is still a matter of conjecture (30).

TIMING MECHANISMS

The basic timing mechanisms for developmental periods are obviously the biological processes of growth and differentiation, usually called maturation. For various reasons, these are not precisely correlated with age from birth or hatching. For example, birds often retain newly formed eggs in their bodies overnight, thus incubating them for several hours before laying. By chilling duck eggs just before placing them in an incubator (thus killing all embryos except those in the earliest stages of development) Gottlieb (31) was able to time the age of ducklings from the onset of incubation rather than from hatching and found that variation in the timing for the critical period was much reduced. No such exact timing studies have been made in mammals, but I have estimated that there is at least a week's variation in development among puppies at 3 weeks of age, and the variation among human infants must be considerably greater (32).

Another approach to the problem is to try to identify the actual mechanisms which open and close a period. Since an important part of forming a primary social relationship appears to be emotional arousal while the young

TABLE 1 Periods of development in the puppy and song sparrow. The six periods of development described by Nice (**10**) for the song sparrow correspond to the first four periods in the puppy, as indicated in the table. The young of the two species are born or hatched in an immature state, require intensive parental care and feeding, and go through much the same stages before becoming independent. Development is much more rapid in the bird than in the puppy, although small mammals such as mice mature at about the same rate as birds.

Puppy			Song sparrow		
Name of period	Length of period (weeks)	Initial event	Name of period	Length of period (days)	Initial event
I. Neonatal	0–2	Birth, nursing	Stage 1 (nestling)	0–4	Hatching, gaping
II. Transition	2–3	Eyes open	Stage 2	5–6	Eyes open
III. Socialization	3–10	Startle to sound	Stage 3	7–9	Cowering—first fear reactions
			Stage 4 (fledgling)	10–16	Leaving nest— first flight
			Stage 5	17–28	Full flight
IV. Juvenile	10–	Final weaning	Stage 6 (juvenile)	29–	Independent feeding

animal is in contact with another, it is obvious that the critical period for socialization could be timed by the appearance of behavioral mechanisms which maintain or prevent contact, and this indeed is the case. There are demonstrable positive mechanisms, varying from species to species, which bring young animals close to other members of their kind: the clinging response of young rhesus monkeys; the following response of chicks, ducklings, and lambs and other herd animals; the social investigation, tail wagging, and playful fighting of puppies; and the visual investigation and smiling of the human infant (*33*). These are, of course, accompanied by interacting responses from adult and immature members of the species: holding and clasping by primate mothers, brooding of mother hens and other birds, calling by mother sheep, investigation and play on the part of other young puppies, and the various supporting and nurturing activities of human mothers.

If contact and emotional arousal result in social attachment, there must be negative mechanisms which prevent such attachment once the critical period is past. Perhaps the most widespread of these is the development of a fear response which causes the young animal to immediately leave the vicinity of a stranger and hence avoid contact. This developing fear response is found in young chicks (*7*), ducklings (*22, 34*), dogs (*35*), rhesus monkeys (*36*) and in many other birds and mammals. Even in children there is a period between the ages of 5 and 12 months in which there is a mounting fear of strangers (*37*), sometimes called "8-months anxiety" (*38*). As already pointed out, there is a time in development when certain fear responses actually facilitate imprinting, but, as they grow stronger, the escape reaction follows so quickly that it prevents contact altogether.

Another sort of negative mechanism is the rejection of strange young by adult sheep, goats, and many other herd animals (*39*). In these species the mothers become strongly attached to the young within a few hours after birth and refuse to accept strangers thereafter. This indicates that the rapid formation of emotional bonds is not limited to young animals.

These timing mechanisms all depend primarily on the development of social behavior patterns, but both sensory and motor development can also influence timing. For example, a very immature animal cannot maintain contact by following, and in slowly developing altricial birds such as jackdaws and doves (5, 40), the period of imprinting comes much later than it does in the precocial species. In the human infant the process of socialization begins before the adult motor patterns develop, but contact is maintained by visual exploration and by the smiling response to human faces (33). Thus, understanding the process of socialization and its timing mechanisms in any particular species requires a systematic study of the development of the various capacities which affect the time of onset and the duration of the critical period. These include sensory, motor, and learning capacities as well as the ability to perform essential patterns of social behavior.

The fact that emotional arousal is so strongly connected with the process of primary socialization suggests that the capacity to produce emotional reactions may also govern the time of onset of a critical period. Figure

1 * summarizes the results of a study of emotional development in the dog during the critical period. If puppies are kept in large fields, totally isolated from people, fear and escape responses toward human beings very nearly reach a maximum by the time the puppies are 14 weeks old—a finding that fixes the upper limit of the period of socialization (35). On the other hand, the peak of the emotional response to isolation in a strange place occurs when puppies are approximately 6 to 7 weeks old, as does the peak of the heart-rate response to handling. At this age, such emotional arousal actually contributes to the strength of the social bond. Fuller (41) was unable to condition the heart-rate response consistently until puppies were 5 weeks old. This indicates that one of the factors that brings the critical period to a close may be the developing ability of the young puppy to associate fear responses with particular stimuli.

* Figure 4 in the original article.—EDS.

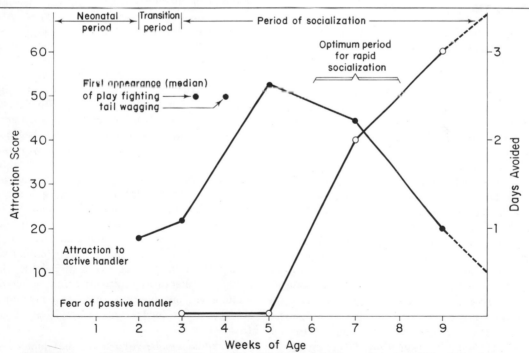

FIGURE 1 Timing mechanisms for the critical period in puppies (see **35**). The period is initiated by positive behavior mechanisms, such as playful fighting, which result in attraction to a strange individual, and it is brought to a close by the development of a fear response which causes the attraction to decline. The optimum period for rapid and permanent socialization comes shortly after the appearance of prolonged avoidance reactions.

All this suggests that if the development of the escape response to strangers could be held in check, the critical period might be extended indefinitely. Raising puppies in small isolation boxes during the critical period inhibits the development of the escape response, but they still show obvious signs of fear when they are first removed from their cages. Fuller (42) reports some success in socializing these older pups by overcoming their fear responses, either by careful handling or through the use of tranquilizing drugs.

Fear responses thus have the dual effect of facilitating the formation of the social bond during the critical period (along with other emotions) and of bringing the period to a close. This is understandable because the type of fear which terminates the critical period is a developing fear of strange animals. In the early part of the critical period the escape reaction is either lacking or is momentary and weak. At the close of the period it is strong enough to prevent contact altogether.

FORMATION OF AFFECTIONAL BONDS IN ADULT LIFE

Until recently, most investigators have concentrated their attention on the critical period for primary socialization or imprinting and few have gone on to study similar phenomena in later development. This field of investigation is just beginning to open up, though many related facts have long been known. For example, many birds form strong pair bonds which are maintained as long as both members survive. In studying the development of various types of social bonds in different species of ducks, Schutz (43) finds that, while attachments to particular individuals may be formed in the early critical period from 12 to 17 hours after hatching, the critical period for the attachment to the species may not come until sometime later, in some cases as late as 30 days after hatching, and the attachment to a particular member of the opposite sex, or the pair bond, does not come until the age of 5 months or so. Schutz also finds that female mallards cannot be sexually imprinted with respect to other species but always mate with other mallards no matter what their earliest experience has been. A similar phenomenon is reported by Warriner (44), who finds that male pigeons

prefer to mate with birds whose color is similar to that of the parents who reared them, whether of the same or another color from themselves, but females show no preference.

Certain species of mammals, such as foxes (45), form long-lasting mating bonds. It is possible that the violence of the sexual emotions contributes to the formation of the adult bond, just as other sorts of emotional arousal are important to the primary socialization of the infant. Klopfer (46) has suggested that the rapid formation of the social bond in a mother goat toward her kid is the result of the high degree of emotional arousal which accompanies the birth of the offspring.

In short, it seems likely that the formation of a social attachment through contact and emotional arousal is a process that may take place throughout life, and that although it may take place more slowly outside of certain critical periods, the capacity for such an attachment is never completely lost.

At this point it may be remarked that, in attempting to analyze the development of affection and social bonds objectively, scientists have often tried to simplify the problem by postulating various unitary, unromantic, and sometimes unesthetic explanations. One of these was the "acquired drive" hypothesis—that children love you because you feed them. Taking a more moderate view Harlow (19) has emphasized "contact comfort" as a major variable—that the young monkey begins to love its mother because she feels warm and comfortable—but that a number of other factors are involved. As this article indicates, evidence is accumulating that there is a much less specific, although equally unromantic, general mechanism involved—that given any kind of emotional arousal a young animal will become attached to any individual or object with which it is in contact for a sufficiently long time. The necessary arousal would, of course, include various specific kinds of emotions associated with food rewards and contact comfort.

It should not be surprising that many kinds of emotional reactions contribute to a social relationship. The surprising thing is that emotions which we normally consider aversive should produce the same effect as those which appear to be rewarding. This apparent paradox is partially resolved by evidence that the positive effect of unpleasant emotions is normally limited to early infancy by the development of escape reactions.

Nevertheless, this concept leads to the somewhat alarming conclusion that an animal (and perhaps a person) of any age, exposed to certain individuals or physical surroundings for any length of time, will inevitably become attached to them, the rapidity of the process being governed by the degree of emotional arousal associated with them. I need not dwell on the consequences for human behavior, if this conclusion should apply to our species as well as to other animals, except to point out that it provides an explanation of certain well-known clinical observations such as the development by neglected children of strong affection for cruel and abusive parents, and the various peculiar affectional relationships that develop between prisoners and jailors, slaves and masters, and so on. Perhaps the general adaptive nature of this mechanism is that since the survival of any member of a highly social species depends upon the rapid development of social relationships, a mechanism has evolved which makes it almost impossible to inhibit the formation of social bonds.

CRITICAL PERIODS OF LEARNING

Unlike the process of socialization, the phenomenon of critical periods of learning was first noticed in children rather than in lower animals. McGraw's (47) famous experiment with the twins Johnny and Jimmy was a deliberate attempt to modify behavioral development by giving one of a pair of identical twins special early training. The result varied according to the activity involved. The onset of walking, for example, was not affected by previous practice or help. Other activities, however, could be greatly speeded up—notably roller skating, in which the favored twin became adept almost as soon as he could walk. In other activities performance was actually made worse by early practice, simply because of the formation of unskillful habits. McGraw (6) concluded that there are critical periods for learning which vary from activity to activity; for each kind of coordinated muscular

activity there is an optimum period for rapid and skillful learning.

In an experiment with rats, Hebb (48) used the technique of providing young animals with many opportunities for spontaneous learning rather than formal training. Pet rats raised in the rich environment of a home performed much better on learning tasks than rats reared in barren laboratory cages. Since then, other experimenters (49) have standardized the "rich" environment as a large cage including many objects and playthings and have gotten similar effects.

Forgays (see 50) finds that the age at which the maximum effect is produced is limited to the period from approximately 20 to 30 days of age, immediately after weaning. A similar experience in adult life produces no effect. In rats, at any rate, the critical period of learning seems to coincide with the critical period of primary socialization, and it may be that the two are in some way related. Candland and Campbell (51) find that fearful behavior in response to a strange situation begins to increase in rats between 20 and 30 days after birth, and Bernstein (52) showed earlier that discrimination learning could be improved by gentle handling beginning at 20 days. It may well be that the development of fear limits the capacity for future learning as well as the formation of social relationships.

In addition to these studies on motor learning and problem solving, there are many experiments demonstrating the existence of critical periods for the learning of social behavior patterns. It has long been known that many kinds of birds do not develop the characteristic songs of their species if they are reared apart from their own kind (53). More recently, Thorpe (54) discovered a critical period for this effect in the chaffinch. If isolated at 3 or 4 days of age, a young male chaffinch produces an incomplete song, but if he hears adults singing, as a fledgling 2 or 3 weeks old or in early juvenile life before he sings himself, he will the next year produce the song characteristic of the species, even if he has been kept in isolation. In nature, the fine details of the song are added at the time of competition over territory, within a period of 2 or 3 weeks, when the bird is about a year old. At this time it learns the songs of two or three of its neighbors, and never learns any others in subsequent years. The critical period for song learning is thus a relatively long one, but it is definitely over by the time the bird is a year old. There is no obvious explanation for its ending at this particular time, but it is possible that learning a complete song pattern in some way interferes with further learning.

King and Gurney (55) found that adult mice reared in groups during youth fought more readily than animals isolated at 20 days of age. Later experiments showed that most of the effect was produced in a 10-day period just after weaning, and that similar experience as adults produced little or no effect (56). Thus, there appears to be a critical period for learning to fight through social experience, and this experience need be no more than contact through a wire. In this case the effect is probably produced by association with other mice before the fear response has been completely developed. Similarly, Fisher (16) and Fuller (57) inhibited the development of attacking behavior in fox terriers by raising them in isolation through the critical period for socialization. The animals would fight back somewhat ineffectually if attacked, but did not initiate conflicts. Tinbergen (58) found a critical period in dogs for learning territorial boundaries, coinciding with sexual maturity.

The results of corresponding experiments on sexual behavior vary from species to species. In mice, rearing in isolation produced no effects (59). Beach (60) found that male rats reared with either females or males were actually slower to respond to sexual behavior than isolated males, and he suggested that habits of playful fighting established by the group-reared animals interfered with sexual behavior later on. In guinea pigs, contact with other young animals improves sexual performance (61).

On the other hand, young chimpanzees (62) reared apart from their kind can only be mated with experienced animals. Harlow (21) discovered that his rhesus infants reared on dummy mothers did not develop normal patterns of sexual behavior, and he was able to obtain matings only by exposing females to experienced males. Normal behavior can be developed by allowing 20-minute daily play periods with other young monkeys, but if rhesus infants are reared apart from all other monkeys beyond the period when they spontaneously play with their fellows, patterns of both sexual and maternal behavior fail to develop normally. These results suggest that play has an important role in developing adult patterns of social behavior in these primates, and that the decline of play behavior sets the upper limit of the critical period during which normal adult behavior may be developed.

Such great changes in the social environment rarely occur in humans even by accident, but Money, Hampson, and Hampson (63) have studied the development of hermaphroditic children who have been reared as one sex and then changed to the other. They find that if this occurs before 2½ years of age, very little emotional disturbance results. Thus, there is a critical period for learning the sex role, this capacity persisting unchanged up to a point in development which roughly corresponds to the age when children begin to use and understand language. Perhaps more important, this is the age when children first begin to take an interest in, and play with, members of their own age group.

It is difficult to find a common factor in these critical periods for learning. In some species, such as rats, mice, dogs, and sheep, certain critical periods for learning coincide with the period for primary socialization and seem to be similarly brought to a close by the development of fear reactions. Other critical periods, in chaffinches and dogs, coincide with the formation of adult mating bonds. However, the critical period for sexual learning in the rhesus monkey comes later than that for primary socialization (64), as do critical periods for various kinds of learning in human beings.

Part of this apparent inconsistency arises from our ignorance regarding timing mechanisms. One such mechanism must be the development of learning capacities, and we have evidence in dogs (65), rhesus monkeys (66), and human infants (12) that learning capacities change during development, sometimes in a stepwise fashion. One element in these capacities is the ability to learn things which facilitate subsequent learning.

It is equally possible, however, to "learn not to learn," and such a negative learning set may act to bring the critical period to a close.

At this point, we can only state a provisional general hypothesis: that the critical period for any specific sort of learning is that time when maximum capacities—sensory, motor, and motivational, as well as psychological ones—are first present.

CRITICAL PERIODS FOR EARLY STIMULATION

Experiments to determine the effects of early stimulation have been mainly performed on infant mice and rats, which are usually weaned at about 21 days at the earliest, and have been concerned with the effect of stimulation during this pre-weaning period. All investigators beginning with Levine (67) and Schaefer (68), agree that rats handled during the first week or 10 days of life have a lessened tendency to urinate and defecate in a strange "open field" situation, learn avoidance behavior more readily, and survive longer when deprived of food and water. In short, early stimulation produces an animal that is less timorous, learns more quickly, and is more vigorous. Levine found that the effect could be obtained by a variety of stimuli, including electric shock and mechanical shaking as well as handling. This ruled out learned behavior as an explanation of the effect, and Levine, Alpert, and Lewis (69) discovered that animals handled in the early period showed a much earlier maturation of the adrenocortical response to stress. Levine interpreted these results as indicating that the laboratory environment did not provide sufficient stimulation for the proper development of the hormonal systems of the animals. This interpretation is in agreement with Richter's finding (70) that laboratory rats are quite deficient in adrenocortical response as compared with the wild variety. Schaefer, Weingarten, and Towne (71) have duplicated Levine's results by the use of cold alone, and have suggested temperature as a possible unitary mechanism. However, their findings are not necessarily in disagreement with those of Levine, as the hormonal stress response can be elicited by a variety of stimuli, and temperature may simply be another of the many kinds of stimuli which produce the effect.

According to Thompson and Schaefer (72) the earlier the stimulation the greater the effect. If the hormonal mechanism is the chief phenomenon involved, we can say that there is a critical period during the first week or 10 days of life, since the adrenal response in any case matures and becomes fixed by 16 days of age.

Denenberg (73) takes a somewhat different approach, pointing out that there should be optimal levels of stimulation, so that either very weak or very strong stimulation would produce poor results. He suggests that there are different critical periods for the effect of early stimulation, depending on the intensity of stimulation and the kind of later behavior measured. Working within the critical first 10 days, Denenberg found that the best avoidance learning was produced by stimulation in the second half of the period, whereas the best survival rates were produced by stimulation in the first half. Weight was approximately equally affected, except that there was little effect in the first 3 days (74).

Analyzing the effect on avoidance learning, Denenberg (75) and his associates found that both unhandled controls and rats handled for the first 20 days performed poorly, the former because they were too emotional and the latter because they were too calm to react quickly. An intermediate amount of emotional response produces the best learning, and this can be produced by handling only in the first 10 days of life; handling during the second 10 days has a lesser effect. No handling produces too much emotionality, and handling for 20 days results in too little. Irrespective of the effect on learning, the data lead to the important conclusion that emotional stimulation during a critical period early in life can lead to the reduction of emotional responses in later life.

More precisely, there appear to be two critical periods revealed by research on early stimulation of rats, one based on a physiological process (the development of the adrenal cortical stress mechanism) and extending to 16 days of age at the latest, the other based on a psychological process (the reduction of fear through familiarity) (51), beginning about 17 days when the eyes first open and extending to 30 days. The effects of handling during these two periods are additive, and many experiments based on arbitrary time rather than developmental periods undoubtedly include both.

The deleterious effects of excessive stimulation in the life of the infant may also be interpreted as a traumatic emotional experience. Bowlby (76), in studying a group of juvenile thieves, found that a large proportion of them had been separated from their mothers in early infancy, and he postulated that this traumatic emotional experience had affected their later behavior. Since this conclusion was based on retrospective information, he and his co-workers have since studied the primary symptoms of separation and have described in detail the emotional reactions of infants sent to hospitals, and thus separated from their mothers (77). Schaefer (78) found a difference in reaction to separation before 7 months and separation afterward. Both sets of infants were disturbed, but they were disturbed in different ways. Infants show increasingly severe emotional reactions to adoption from 3 through 12 months of age (33). It seems logical to place the beginning of the critical period for maximum emotional disturbance at approximately 7 months—at the end of the critical period for primary socialization, which Gray (79) places at approximately 6 weeks to 6 months. Infants whose social relationships have been thoroughly established and whose fear responses toward strangers have been fully developed are much more likely to be upset by changes than infants in which these relationships and responses have not yet been developed.

However, not all apparently "traumatic" early experiences have such a lasting effect. Experimental work shows that young animals have a considerable capacity to recover from unpleasant emotions experienced in a limited period in early life (80), and that what is traumatic in one species may not be in another. While young rats become calmer after infantile stimulation, young mice subjected to excessive auditory stimulation later become more emotional (81). At this point it is appropriate to point out that critical periods are not necessarily involved in every kind of early experience. Raising young chimpanzees in the dark produces degeneration of the retina, but this is a long and gradual process (82).

Another approach to the problem is to stimulate emotional responses in mothers and observe the effect on the offspring. Thompson (83) and other authors (84) have shown that the offspring of rats made fearful while pregnant are more likely to be overemotional in the open-field situation than the offspring of animals not so stimulated. Since any direct influence of maternal behavior was ruled out by cross-fostering experiments, it seems likely that the result is produced by modification of the adrenocortical stress mechanism—in this case, by secretion of maternal hormones acting on the embryo rather than by stimulation after birth of the young animal itself. No precise critical period for the effect has been established, but it is probably confined to the latter part of pregnancy. Similar effects have been obtained in mice (85), and if such effects can be demonstrated in other mammals, the implications for prenatal care in human beings are obvious.

It is interesting to note that, whereas shocking the mother both before and after parturition has the effect of increasing emotional responses in the young, the emotional responses of young rats are *decreased* when the treatment is applied directly to them. The explanation of this contradiction must await direct experiments on the endocrine system.

GENERAL THEORY OF CRITICAL PERIODS

There are at least two ways in which experience during critical periods may act on behavioral development. The critical period for primary socialization constitutes a turning point. Experience during a short period early in life determines which shall be the close relatives of the young animal, and this, in turn, leads the animal to develop in one of two directions—the normal one, in which it becomes attached to and mates with a member of its own species, or an abnormal one, in which it becomes attached to a different species, with consequent disrupting effects upon sexual and other social relationships with members of its own kind.

The concept of a turning point applies equally well to most examples of critical periods for learning. Up to a certain point in development a chaffinch can learn several varieties of song, but once it has learned one of them it no longer has a choice. Similarly, the human infant can learn either sex role up to a certain age, but once it has learned one or the other, changing over becomes increasingly difficult. What is learned at particular points limits and interferes with subsequent learning, and Schneirla and Rosenblatt (86) have suggested that there are critical stages of learning—that what has been learned at a particular time in development may be critical for whatever follows.

A second sort of action during a critical period consists of a nonspecific stimulus producing an irrevocable result, not modifiable in subsequent development. Thus, almost any sort of stimulus has the effect of modifying the development of the endocrine stress mechanism of young rats in early infancy.

Is there any underlying common principle? Each of these effects has its counterpart in embryonic development. Up to a certain point a cell taken from an amphibian embryo and transplanted to a new location will develop in accordance with its new environment. Beyond this turning point it develops in accordance with its previous location. Some cells retain a degree of lability, but none retain the breadth of choice they had before. Similarly, specific injuries produced by nonspecific causes are also found in embryonic development: damage to an embryonic optic vesicle results in a defective eye, no matter what sort of chemical produces the injury. It is obvious that the similarity between this case and the critical period for early stimulation can be accounted for by the single common process of growth, occuring relatively late in development in the case of the endocrine stress mechanism and much earlier in the development of the eye. The effects are nonspecific because of the fact that growth can be modified in only very limited ways, by being either slowed down or speeded up.

Both growth and behavioral differentiation are based on organizing processes. This suggests a general principle of organization: that once a system becomes organized, whether it is the cells of the embryo that are multiplying and differentiating or the behavior patterns of a young animal that are becoming organized through learning, it becomes progressively more difficult to reorganize the system. That is, organization inhibits reorganization. Further, organization can be strongly modified only when active processes of organization are going on, and this accounts for critical periods of development.

CONCLUSION

This concept of critical periods is a highly important one for human and animal welfare. Once the dangers and potential benefits for each period of life are known, it should be possible to avoid the former and take advantage of the latter.

The discovery of critical periods immediately focuses attention on the developmental processes which cause them. As these processes become understood, it is increasingly possible to deliberately modify critical periods and their results. For example, since the development of fear responses limits the period of primary socialization, we can deliberately extend the period by reducing fear reactions, either by psychological methods or by the use of tranquilizing drugs. Or, if it seems desirable, we can increase the degree of dependency of a child or pet animal by purposely increasing his emotional reactions during the critical period. Again, if infantile stimulation is desirable, parents can be taught to provide it in appropriate amounts at the proper time.

Some data suggest that for each behavioral and physiological phenomenon there is a different critical period in development. If this were literally true, the process of development, complicated by individual variability, would be so complex that the concept of critical periods would serve little useful purpose. Some sort of order can be obtained by dealing with different classes of behavioral phenomena. For example, it can be stated that the period in life in which each new social relationship is initiated is a critical one for the determination of that relationship. Furthermore, there is evidence that critical-period effects are more common early in life than they are later on, and that the critical period for primary socialization is also critical for other effects, such as the attachment to particular places (87), and may overlap with a critical period for the formation of basic food habits (88).

We may expect to find that the periods in which actual physiological damage through environmental stimulation is possible will turn out to be similarly specific and concentrated in early life.

A great deal of needed information regarding the optimum periods for acquiring motor and intellectual skills is still lacking. These skills are based not merely on age but on the relative rate of maturation of various organs. Any attempt to teach a child or animal at too early a period of development may result in his learning bad habits, or simply in his learning "not to learn," either of which results may greatly handicap him in later life. In the long run, this line of experimental work should lead to greater realization of the capacities possessed by human beings, both through avoidance of damaging experiences and through correction of damage from unavoidable accidents (89).

REFERENCES AND NOTES

1. J. P. Scott, *Comp. Psychol. Monogr. 18*, 1 (1945).
2. A. M. Field, *Biol. Bull. 7*, 227 (1904).
3. C. R. Stockard, *Am. J. Anat. 28*, 115 (1921).
4. C. M. Child, *Patterns and Problems of Development* (Univ. of Chicago Press, Chicago, 1941).
5. K. Lorenz, *J. Ornithol. 83*, 137, 289 (1935).
6. M. B. McGraw, in *Manual of Child Psychology*, L. C. Carmichael, Ed. (Wiley, New York, 1946), pp. 332-369.
7. E. H. Hess, in *Nebraska Symposium on Motivation* (Univ. of Nebraska Press, Lincoln, 1959), pp. 44-77.
8. H. Moltz, *Psychol. Bull. 57*, 291 (1960); J. L. Gewirtz, in *Determinants of Infant Behaviour*, B. M. Foss, Ed. (Methuen, London, 1961), pp. 213-299.
9. J. P. Scott, in *Social Behavior and Organization in Vertebrates*, W. Etkin, Ed. (Univ. of Chicago Press, Chicago, in press).
10. M. M. Nice, *Trans. Linnaean Soc. N.Y. 6*, 1 (1943).
11. J. P. Scott and M. V. Marston, *J. Genet. Psychol. 77*, 25 (1950).
12. J. P. Scott, *Child Develop. Monogr.*, in press.
13. A. J. Brodbeck, *Bull. Ecol. Soc. Am. 35*, 73 (1954).
14. W. C. Stanley, private communication (1962).
15. O. Elliot and J. A. King, *Psychol. Repts. 6*, 391 (1960).
16. A. E. Fisher, thesis, Pennsylvania State Univ. (1955).
17. O. Elliot and J. P. Scott, *J. Genet. Phychol. 99*, 3 (1961).
18. J. P. Scott, D. Deshaies, D. D. Morris, "Effect of emotional arousal on primary socialization in the dog," address to the New York State Branch of the American Psychiatric Association, 11 Nov. 1961.
19. H. Harlow, *Am. Psychologist 13*, 673 (1958).
20. G. J. Igel and A. D. Calvin, *J. Comp. Physiol. Psychol. 53*, 302 (1960).
21. H. F. Harlow and M. K. Harlow, personal communication (1962).
22. E. Fabricius, *Acta Zool. Fennica 68*, 1 (1951).
23. N. Collias, in *Roots of Behavior*, E. L. Bliss, Ed. (Harper, New York, 1962), pp. 264-273.
24. E. H. Hess, *Ann. N.Y. Acad. Sci. 67*, 724 (1957); in *Drugs and Behavior*, L. Uhr and J. G. Miller, Eds. (Wiley, New York, 1960), pp. 268-271.
25. H. James, *Can. J. Psychol. 13*, 59 (1959).
26. P. H. Gray, *Science 132*, 1834 (1960).
27. P. Guiton, *Animal Behavior 9*, 167 (1961).
28. G. F. Pitz and R. B. Ross, *J. Comp. Physiol. Psychol. 54*, 602 (1961).
29. E. H. Hess, "Influence of early experience on behavior," paper presented before the American Psychiatric Association, New York State Divisional Meeting, 1961.
30. H. Moltz, L. Rosenblum, N. Halikas, *J. Comp. Physiol. Psychol. 52*, 240 (1959).
31. G. Gottlieb, *ibid. 54*, 422 (1961).
32. J. P. Scott, *Psychosomat. Med. 20*, 42 (1958).
33. B. M. Caldwell, *Am. Psychol. 16*, 377 (1961).
34. R. A. Hinde, W. H. Thorpe, M. A. Vince, *Behaviour 9*, 214 (1956).
35. D. G. Freedman, J. A. King, O. Elliot, *Science 133*, 1016 (1961).
36. H. F. Harlow and R. R. Zimmermann, *ibid. 130*, 421 (1959).
37. D. G. Freedman, *J. Child Psychol. Psychiat. 1961*, 242 (1961).
38. R. A. Spitz, *Intern. J. Psychoanalysis 31*, 138 (1950).
39. N. E. Collias, *Ecology 37*, 228 (1956).
40. W. Craig, *J. Animal Behavior 4*, 121 (1914).
41. J. L. Fuller and A. Christake, *Federation Proc. 18*, 49 (1959).
42. J. L. Fuller, private communication.
43. F. Schutz, private communication.
44. C. C. Warriner, thesis, Univ. of Oklahoma (1960).
45. R. K. Enders, *Sociometry 8*, 53-55 (1945).
46. P. H. Klopfer, *Behavioral Aspects of Ecology* (Prentice-Hall, New York, in press).
47. M. B. McGraw, *Growth: a Study of Johnny and Jimmy* (Appleton-Century, New York, 1935).
48. D. O. Hebb, *Am. Pychologist 2*, 306 (1947).
49. D. G. Forgays and J. W. Forgays, *J. Comp. Physiol. Psychol. 45*, 322 (1952).
50. D. G. Forgays, "The importance of experience at specific times in the development of an organism," address before the Eastern Psychological Association (1962).
51. D. K. Candland and B. A. Campbell, private communication (1962).
52. L. Bernstein, *J. Comp. Physiol. Psychol. 50*, 162 (1957).

53. W. E. D. Scott, *Science 14*, 522 (1901).
54. W. H. Thorpe, in *Current Problems in Animal Behaviour*, W. H. Thorpe and O. L. Zangwill, Eds. (Cambridge Univ. Press, Cambridge, 1961).
55. J. A. King and N. L. Gurney, *J. Comp. Physiol. Psychol. 47*, 326 (1954).
56. J. A. King, *J. Genet. Psychol. 90*, 151 (1957).
57. J. L. Fuller, "Proceedings, International Psychiatric Congress, Montreal," in press.
58. N. Tinbergen, *The Study of Instinct* (Oxford Univ. Press, Oxford, 1951).
59. J. A. King, *J. Genet. Psychol. 88*, 223 (1956).
60. F. A. Beach, *ibid. 60*, 121 (1942).
61. E. S. Valenstein, W. Riss, W. C. Young, *J. Comp. Physiol. Psychol. 47*, 162 (1954).
62. H. Nissen, *Symposium on Sexual Behavior in Mammals, Amherst, Mass.* (1954), pp. 204-227.
63. J. Money, J. G. Hampson, J. L. Hampson, *Arch. Neurol. Psychiat. 77*, 333 (1957).
64. H. Harlow, in *Determinants of Infant Behaviour*, B. M. Foss, Ed. (Wiley, New York, 1961), pp. 75-97.
65. J. L. Fuller, C. A. Easler, E. M. Banks, *Am. J. Physiol. 160*, 462 (1950); A. C. Cornwell and J. L. Fuller, *J. Comp. Physiol. 54*, 13 (1961).
66. H. F. Harlow, M. K. Harlow, R. R. Rueping, W. A. Mason, *J. Comp. Physiol. Psychol. 53*, 113 (1960).
67. S. Levine, J. A. Chevalier, S. J. Korchin, *J. Personality 24*, 475 (1956).
68. T. Schaefer, thesis, Univ. of Chicago (1957).
69. S. Levine, M. Alpert, G. W. Lewis, *Science 126*, 1347 (1957).
70. C. P. Richter, *Am. J. Human Genet. 4* 273 (1952).
71. T. Schaefer, Jr., F. S. Weingarten, J. C. Towne, *Science 135*, 41 (1962).
72. W. R. Thompson and T. Schaefer, in *Functions of Varied Experience*, D. W. Fiske and S. R. Maddi, Eds. (Dorsey, Homewood, Ill., 1961), pp. 81-105.
73. V. H. Denenberg, in *The Behaviour of Domestic Animals*, E. S. E. Hafez, Ed. (Bailliere, Tindall and Cox, London), 109-138.
74. ———, *J. Comp. Physiol. Psychol.*, in press.
75. ——— and G. G. Karas, *Psychol., Repts. 7*, 313 (1960).
76. J. Bowlby, *Intern. J. Psychoanalysis 25*, 19, 107 (1944).
77. C. M. Heinicke, *Human Relations 9*, 105 (1956).
78. H. R. Schaffer, *Brit. J. Med. Psychol. 31*, 174 (1950).
79. P. H. Gray, *J. Psychol. 46*, 155 (1958).
80. M. W. Kahn, *J. Genet. Psychol. 79*, 117 (1951). A. Baron, K. H. Brookshire, R. A. Littman, *J. Comp. Physiol. Psychol. 50*, 530 (1957).
81. G. Lindzey, D. T. Lykken, H. D. Winston, *J. Abnormal Soc. Psychol. 61*, 7 (1960).
82. A. H. Riesen, in *Functions of Varied Experience*, D. W. Fiske and S. R. Maddi, Eds. (Dorsey, Homewood, Ill., 1961), pp. 57-80.
83. W. R. Thompson, *Science 125*, 698 (1957).
84. C. H. Hockman, *J. Comp. Physiol. Psychol. 54*, 679 (1961); R. Ader and M. L. Belfer, *Psychol. Repts. 10*, 711 (1962).
85. K. Keeley, *Science 135*, 44 (1962).
86. T. C. Schneirla and J. S. Rosenblatt, *Am. J. Orthopsychiat. 31*, 223 (1960).
87. W. H. Thorpe, *Learning and Instinct in Animals* (Methuen, London, 1956).
88. E. H. Hess, in *Roots of Behavior*, E. L. Bliss, Ed. (Harper, New York, 1962), pp. 251-263.
89. Part of the research described in this article was supported by a Public Health Service research grant (No. M-4481) from the National Institute of Mental Health.

3. IMPORTANCE AND INFLUENCE OF EARLY ENVIRONMENT AND EXPERIENCE *

BENJAMIN S. BLOOM

The prolongation of the period of dependency for youth in the Western cultures has

* Bloom, Benjamin S., "Importance and Influence of Early Environment and Experience" in *Stability and Change in Human Characteristics*, New York, John Wiley and Sons, 1964, pp. 214-216.

undoubtedly been a factor in desensitizing parents, school workers, and behavioral scientists to the full importance of the very early environmental and experiential influences. Youth are usually required to attend school until at least 16 years of age and the majority live at home and attend school until about age 18.

Another factor which has contributed to our lack of full awareness of the enormous influence of the early environment is the limited evidence on the effects of the early environment. And, even when such evidence is available from longitudinal studies of intelligence and personality, it has most frequently been interpreted as indicating little predictive significance for early measures of these characteristics. There appears to be an implicit assumption running through the culture that change in behavior and personality can take place at any age or stage in development and that the developments at one age or stage are no more significant than those which take place at another.

A central finding in this work is that for selected characteristics there is a negatively accelerated curve of development which reaches its midpoint before age 5. We have reasoned that the environment would have its greatest effect on a characteristic during the period of its most rapid development.

These findings and reasoning are supported by the results of selected studies: Lee (1951) and Kirk (1958) on intelligence, Dreizen et al. (1950) and Sanders (1934) on height, Sears et al. (1957) and Baldwin et al. (1949) on selected personality characteristics. Alexander (1961) and Bernstein (1960) further support the importance of the home environment on the language achievement of students in the early years of school. Additional support for the importance of the environment on early as well as later development may be found in the studies of siblings, fraternal, and identical twins reared together and reared apart (Newman, Freeman, and Holzinger, 1937; Burt, 1958). Finally, the animal research of Scott and Marston (1950) and Hebb (1949) gives support to the importance of the early environment in influencing the development of selected characteristics. The evidence referred to in the foregoing . . ., makes it very clear that the environment, and especially the early environment, has a significant effect on the development of selected characteristics.

We believe that the early environment is of crucial importance for three reasons. The first is based on the very rapid growth of selected characteristics in the early years and conceives of the variations in the early environment as so important because they shape these characteristics in their most rapid periods of formation. We have already referred in brief detail to the evidence for this.

However, another way of viewing the importance of the early environment has to do with the sequential nature of much of human development. Each characteristic is built on a base of that same characteristic at an earlier time or on the base of other characteristics which precede it in development. Hebb (1949) has pointed out the differences in activity and exploratory behavior of animals reared in very stimulating environments in contrast to those reared under very confining conditions. Such differences in initial behavior are of significance in determining the animal's activity and intelligence at later stages in its development. Erickson (1950) has described stages in the development of human beings and the ways in which the resolution of a developmental conflict at one stage will in turn affect the resolutions of subsequent developmental conflicts. The entire psychoanalytic theory and practice is based on a series of developmental stages (Freud, 1933; Freud, 1937; Horney, 1936; Sullivan, 1953) with the most crucial ones usually taking place before about age 6. The resolution of each stage has consequences for subsequent stages. Similarly, other more eclectic descriptions of development (Havighurst, 1953; Piaget, 1932; Murray, 1938; Gesell, 1945) emphasize the early years as the base for later development. All these theoretical as well as empirical descriptions of development point up the way in which the developments at one period are in part determined by the earlier developments and in turn influence and determine the nature of later developments. For each of these viewpoints, the developments that take place in the early years are crucial for all that follows.

A third reason for the crucial importance of the early environment and early experiences stems from learning theory. It is much easier to learn something new than it is to stamp out one set of learned behaviors and replace them by a new set. The effect of earlier learning on later learning is considered in most learning theories under such terms as habit, inhibition, and restructuring. Although each learning theory may explain the phenomena in different ways, most would agree that the first learning takes place more easily than a later one that is interfered with by an earlier learning. Observation of the difficulties one experiences in learning a new language after the adolescent period and the characteristic mispronunciations which tend to remain throughout life are illustrations of the same phenomena.

Several explanations for the difficulties in altering early learning and for the very powerful effects of the early learning have been advanced. Schachtel (1949) and McClelland (1951) believe that the learning which takes place before language development is so powerful because it is not accessible to conscious memory. Others, such as Dollard and Miller (1950), Mowrer (1950), and Guthrie (1935), would attribute the power of early learning to the repeated reinforcement and overlearning over time such that the early learning becomes highly stabilized. More recently, the experimental work on imprinting in animals by Hess (1959) demonstrates the tremendous power of a short learning episode at critical moments in the early history of the organism. Hess has demonstrated that ducklings at ages 9 to 20 hours may be imprinted to react to a wooden decoy duck as a mother duck in a ten minute learning experience and that the duckling will thereafter respond to the decoy duck in preference to real mother ducks.

Although it is possible that each type of explanation is sound, especially as it applies to different phenomena, all three tend to confirm the tremendous power of early learning and its resistance to later alteration or extinction.

The power of early learning must still, for humans, remain largely an inference drawn from theory, from descriptive developmental studies, and from quantitative longitudinal studies. In many respects, the attempts to describe the learning process as it takes place in the first few years of life are still far from satisfactory. We know more about the early learning of experimental animals than we do about human infants. In this writer's opinion, the most vital research problems in the behavioral sciences are those centered around the effects of early learning and early environments on humans.

REFERENCES

ALEXANDER, M., 1961. The relation of environment and achievement: a longitudinal study. Unpublished Master's Thesis, Univ. of Chicago.

BALDWIN, A. L., KALHORN, J., and BREESE, F. H., 1949. The appraisal of parent behavior. *Psychol. Monogr.*, *63*, No. 4, Whole No. 299.

BERNSTEIN, B., 1960. Aspects of language and learning in the genesis of the social process. *J. Child Psychol. and Psychiatry* (Great Britain), *1*, 313-324.

BURT, C., 1958. The inheritance of mental ability. *Amer. Psychologist*, *13*, 1-15.

DOLLARD, J., and MILLER, N. E., 1950. *Personality and psychotherapy*. New York: McGraw-Hill.

DREIZEN, S., CURRIE, C., GILLEY, E. J., and SPIES, T. D., 1950. The effect of milk supplements on the growth of children with nutritive failure: II. Height and weight changes. *Growth*, *14*, 189-211.

ERICKSON, E. H., 1950. *Childhood and society*. New York: Norton.

FREUD, A., 1937. *The ego and mechanisms of defense*. London: Hogarth Press.

FREUD, S., 1933. *New introductory lectures on psychoanalysis*. New York: Garden City.

GESELL, A., 1945. *The embryology of behavior*. New York: Harper.

GUTHRIE, E. R., 1935. *The psychology of learning*. New York: Harper.

HAVIGHURST, R. J., 1953. *Human development and education*. New York: Longmans, Green.

HEBB, D. O., 1949. *The organization of behavior*. New York: Wiley.

HESS, E., 1959. Imprinting. *Science*, *130*, 133-141.

HORNEY, K., 1936. *The neurotic personality of our time*. New York: Norton.

KIRK, S. A., 1958. *Early education of the mentally retarded*. Urbana: Univ. of Illinois.

LEE, E. S., 1951. Negro intelligence and selective migration: A Philadelphia test of the Klineberg hypothesis. *Am. Sociol. Rev.*, *16*, 227-233.

McCLELLAND, D. C. et al., 1951. *Personality*. New York: William Sloane Associates.

MOWRER, Q. H., 1950. *Learning theory and personality dynamics*. New York: Ronald Press.

MURRAY, H., 1938. *Explorations in personality*. New York: Oxford Univ. Press.

NEWMAN, H. H., FREEMAN, F. N., and HOLZINGER, K. J., 1937. *Twins: a study of heredity and environment*. Chicago: Univ. of Chicago Press.

PIAGET, J., 1932. *The moral judgment of the child*. New York: Harcourt, Brace.

SANDERS, B. K., 1934. *Environment and growth*. Baltimore: Warwick and York.

SCHACHTEL, E. G., 1949. "One memory and childhood amnesia," in Mullahy, P. (Ed.), *A study of interpersonal relations*. New York: Hermitage Press.

SCOTT, J. P., and MARSTON, M., 1950. Critical periods affecting the development of normal and maladjustive behavior of puppies. *J. Genet Psychol.*, 77, 26-60.

SEARS, R. R., MACCOBY, E. E., LEVIN, H., 1957. *Patterns of child rearing.* Evanston: Row, Peterson.

SULLIVAN, H. S., 1953. *The interpersonal theory of psychiatry.* New Haven: Norton.

4. COGNITIVE CONSEQUENCES OF EARLY SENSORY DEPRIVATION

JEROME S. BRUNER

Growth in any field of science is almost always uneven. The past decade, for example, has been a period of turbulent growth in the field of perception, a period in which parallel inquiries in neurophysiology, physics, and psychology have each in turn thrown light upon the nature of the perceptual process, light of such an order as to dazzle us all a bit with respect to the fundamental nature of perceiving. I should like briefly to review some of these developments before turning to the principal topic of this symposium: the problems of sensory deprivation.

Let me consider first the field of physics. The classical metrics of physics up to the end of the 19th century were the centimeters, grams, and seconds of classical mechanics. Until very recently in psychology, our description of ambient stimuli and of their effect at a sensory surface has been couched in terms of this system. The effort, moreover, to construct a set of experiential attributes for any modality has been guided by this classical system of physical mensuration, and it is not surprising that Titchener (*17*) and later Boring (*2*) ended with the ensemble of intensity, protensity, quality, and attensity (the last a never-ending source of embarrassment!). Today, physics has revolutionized its way of looking at the physical world of potential stimulation. In quantum theory, for example, one specifies the state of a system and the set of transitional probabilities leading to next states.

Emphasis upon probability of events and transitional probability have become central. These developments in physics have telegraphed themselves into psychology principally via the development of the mathematical theory of communication or information theory, an approach to the analysis of the reduction of uncertainty in physical systems that rests upon Boltzmann's insight that entropy in a system is best described as residual uncertainty. The result of all of this ferment in physics is that attention has been focussed on two related and hitherto neglected features of the physical stimulus: first, the set of *possible* stimulating states that might have occurred at any given moment, and, second, the bias in their likelihood of occurrence. The importance of this probabilistic metric for an understanding of the development of environmentally appropriate sets or attitudes will shortly become apparent.

Developments in neurophysiology have also provided a new challenge to the psychologist interested in perception. As in the case of our contact with physics, we as psychologists have been operating until very recently with a 19th or early 20th century conception of the nervous system, an image of a switching and transmission system made up of an afferent or sensory side, a central segment, and an efferent or motor outflow. The work of Granit (*7*), of Galambos (*5*) of Magoun and his associates, (e.g., *11*), and of Pribram (*14*) have seriously brought into question whether such a simple input-output model corresponds with the find-

* Bruner, Jerome S., "Cognitive Consequences of Early Sensory Deprivation," *Psychosomatic Medicine*, Vol. 21, No. 2, pp. 89-95 (1959).

ings of electrophysiology over the past decade and a half. Indeed, we know now that even in so simple a case as the flexion reflex of the spinal mammalian cat, close inspection indicates that a third of the fibres in the efferent nerve trunk going to a muscle has nothing whatever to do with motor activity but with the programming or gating of the sensory stretch receptors in the muscle, setting these receptors to feed back to the spinal cord on the afferent side either a lot or a little sensory information about the state of the muscle. And Granit (7) has shown that centrifugal control fibres operate from the center to the periphery in altering the sensitivity of retinal cells to stimulation. Indeed, Galambos has recently shown that fibres of central origin operate outward to the periphery of the auditory system, serving to "turn off" the sensitivity of hair cells in the organ of Corti when attention is turned elsewhere. Some of these fibres have already been traced back as far as the superior olive, and experiments have been done on the effects of severing them, the result of such section being to prevent centrifugal control from operating. Add to this work the continuing experimentation on the boosting operations of the reticular system in facilitating sensory input to the cortex, discharges which, as Lord Adrian puts it (1), clear the cortex of alpha activity in order to give sensory messages a clear field, and still another blow is struck in the interest of freeing psychologists from the rigid model of neural activity that is a heritage from the early Sherrington. What this work indicates, as Robert Oppenheimer put it in his first William James lecture of last year, is that the price of perceiving anything at all is that not everything is perceived that can potentially be perceived. And so, if you will, the problem for an organism which would hope to minimize the surprise of its environment to a level where he might survive, is to match his programming to the likelihood and significance of events in the environment.

Now consider some of the developments in psychology, for we on our part have not been quiet. I want to single out only two of these. The first is the shift in emphasis in the study of perception from a consideration of classical problems of space-time-quality organization as so well represented by the work of the Gestalt psychologists to what Prentice (13) has called a functional emphasis. I should take "functional emphasis" to mean that interest has shifted to the manner in which perceiving relates to and is instrumental in the various ongoing enterprises of an organism, whether these enterprises be simply getting around in a familiar environment or as seemingly complex as looking for food or for a mate or for the Holy Grail. What has been healthy about the new emphasis is that, first, it has confused us out of our smug assumption that perception was some sort of fixed relationship between an impinging pattern of physical energy, on the one side, and certain enduring and highly stable properties of the brain on the other, leaving the variability in perception to that favorite American vehicle of variance, the response. The second and more positive effect of the shift in emphasis is that we have been sent scurrying for independent variables that lie outside the comforting stimulus metric of centimeters, grams, and seconds.

A second development in psychology, new work on the effects of early experience, brings us to the heart of the problem to which we are addressing ourselves: the development of perception. It is a problem with a tortured background, tortured by the pains of yesterday's metaphysical deadlocks. One such deadlock is the so-called nativist-empiricist controversy which has about it some of the scent of a wrongly formulated dichotomy. I say this unkind thing about the so-called controversy simply because it has had no issue, and because it yields on the very margins where it should stay firm. Nobody in his right mind has ever urged that an organism begins with no built-in equipment for perceiving, nor has anybody been so brashly foolish as to claim that experience has no effect whatever on the nature of what we perceive. If the controversy had any real meaning in the study of space perception, where it originated, it certainly has none in the study of perception generally. Or rather, I should say, it has about the same meaning as a quarrel in physics between those who would proclaim that weight was more important than the force-fulcrum distance in Archimedean Type II levers. It is not a controversy but a question of plotting functions.

For bringing this matter into a proper empirical perspective, we must be grateful for the work of Hebb and his students in investigating the effects of early sensory deprivation in animals. I do not propose to review the work, for it is well known. In general, an impoverished environment, one with diminished heterogeneity and a reduced set of opportunities for manipulation and discrimination produces an adult organism with reduced abilities to discriminate, with stunted strategies for coping with roundabout solutions, with less taste for exploratory behavior, and with a notably reduced tendency to draw inferences that serve to cement the disparate events of its environment such as between the light of a candle flame and the likelihood of its burning when you put your nose into it. Add to these reduced capacities—which may indeed be irreversible, although there has not yet been a full scale attempt to provide adequate therapy toward overcoming these deficits—add to these the fact that there seem to be critical periods operative. Unless certain forms of stimulation-cum-learning take place before a certain point in a puppy's life or a rat's life, there appear to be certain very intractable changes.

Let me speculate a little about the meaning of these challenging findings. But before I do, let me remind you of the parallel findings on prolonged sensory deprivation in adult organisms that have the effect of disorganizing cognitive function, upsetting the constancies, even disrupting the perception of continuous contours that extend beyond the immediate focus of attention at the center of the visual field. I remind you of these matters in advance of setting forth some speculations to underline the likelihood that perception and cognitive activity generally depend upon a dynamically stable though ultimately disruptible equilibrium that depends, even in adult life, upon contact with stimulus heterogeneity and a shifting environment. Indeed, even more dramatic evidence is given by Ditchburn and his associates (4) indicating that if a visual pattern is stabilized on the retina such that it is not even displaced by the natural tremor of the eye, it will disappear from view within six or so seconds.

Let me see if I can pull the threads of the discussion together now. To operate effectively in an environment, an organism must develop a model of the environment, and this for at least two reasons. In the first place, it is a way of conserving information in the form of concepts or universals, the means whereby, to use the ancient Aristotelian language, we separate essences from accidents, or in modern terms signal from noise. If you will, the recurrent regularities and the higher probability relationships between and among events are conserved in this model. Given such models —call them trace systems or cell assemblies or templates or whatever term seems most appropriate to your imagery—it becomes possible, secondly, for an organism to extrapolate and interpolate on the basis of partial information, to perform the kind of inference that may be called "going beyond the information given." This is a task that is learned gradually at first and then, to use Lashley's (10) phrase, as the grammatical character of learning develops, proceeds at an accelerated pace as we convert masses of connected or associated events into more highly ordered systems, as when the children in the ingenious experiments of Inhelder and Piaget go from trial and error concreteness in bouncing a ball off a wall at a target to the reorganization of the situation as one in which the angle of incidence and the angle of reflexion are recognized as equal. This kind of learning is neither S-S nor S-R in the usual senses of those shopworn terms. It consists of a process of organizing "rules" or "transforms" that conserve and represent the redundant structure of the environment.

Without such prior learning, the centrifugal control functions of the nervous system are without a program—speaking now of a program as one does in computer language. A system without a program, without a basis for predicting that certain events are more likely than others or preclude others, has no basis for selectivity toward stimuli. I would make a small wager at this point. Consider the cats in the experiment of Hernandez-Péon et al. (8) Click stimulation produces large spike discharges in the cochlear nucleus. If now the click stimulation is continued but some white mice are introduced into the field under a bell jar, the electrical discharge produced by continuing click stimulation is markedly reduced. Attention is directed elsewhere with attendant gating of the auditory system. The wager is this: if cats are reared in a highly restricted sensory environment, one with a minimum of stimulus variation in either the visual or auditory fields, the selective gating found will be considerably less marked than in normally reared cats. The prediction is based upon several considerations about the nature of perceptual development as perceptual differentiation, a point of view most intimately associated with the Gibsons (6). Continued contact with a rich sensory environment, the view would hold, permits the development of differentiation of spheres of activity, of sensory modalities, of events within modalities. Sensory deprivation prevents such differentiation, prevents the development of selective gating.

This leads to another prediction: part of the process of perceptual development consists of the capacity to utilize cues, to extract information from cue-significate encounters. One of the more interesting forms of information utilization is to be found in the weighing of probable in contradistinction to certain cues, for the process requires a sorting out and evaluation of negative and positive instances. A given sign leads not always but sometimes and in excess of chance to a given significate. To master such cues requires either the gradual build-up of excitatory strength as required by such learning theories as Hull's (9) or Spence's (16), or it requires the use of a strategy like that proposed by such analysts of the decision process as Marschak (12) or Savage (15). In the first case, the process would be very slow and informationally very inefficient, particularly if one worked with a two-cue discrimination situation where, say, a white signal led to food 70% of the time and to non-food 30% and a black cue to food 30% and to non-food 70%. In the second, more informationally efficient strategy, as soon as the animal discriminated the difference in the probability of payoff, he would opt for the more probable cue and ride with it. Let us take groups of sensorially deprived and normal animals and set them two-choice discrimina-

tion tasks where the two cues lead 100:0/0:100 to their respective consequences, then 80:20/20:80, and finally 70:30/30:70 as in the well-known experiment of Brunswik (3). I would predict that the two groups would differ least on the certain cues, and as one moved in the direction of the equiprobable case, the groups would diverge more and more. The reason for the prediction is based on quite a simple premise. Not only does early deprivation rob the organism of the opportunity of constructing models of the environment, it also prevents the development of efficient strategies for evaluating information, for finding out what leads to what and with what likelihood. And robbed of development in this sphere, it becomes the more difficult to utilize probable than certain cues, the former requiring a more efficient strategy than the latter.

Let me conclude these notes by reference to the problem of transferability in learning. The McGill experiments and those inspired by the work at McGill have given us a striking example of what has been called non-specific transfer of training. Savings effected in learning something new by virtue of having learned something before cannot in such instances be credited to the transfer of specific responses or of priorly established associations. Yet it is precisely this type of so-called non-specific transfer that is perhaps the most typical and the most ubiquitous. It consists of the establishment of models or constructs or concepts that represent the environment in such a way that when one encounters a new task, it is possible to handle it as an exemplar of an old concept in connection with which appropriate responses have already been learned. Such transfer has the function, almost, of saving us from having to do much new learning and it is indeed the case that after a certain age in life, we do indeed get saved from such new learning.

But non-specific or generic transfer also involves the learning of general rules and strategies for coping with highly common features of the environment. And it is here that I think Piaget's vision is the clearest. He remarks upon the fact that cognitive growth consists of learning how to handle the great informational transformations like reversibility, class identity, and the like. In his most recent writing, he speaks of these as strategies for dealing with or, better, for creating usable information. I would propose that exposure to normally rich environments makes the development of such strategies possible by providing intervening opportunity for strategic trial and error. Whether failure to master the elements of such strategies for transforming information before a certain period of growth produces an irreversible loss, I cannot say, nor do I have a clue as to why critical periods are so critical. That there is impairment of strategy under a deprived regimen seems, however, to be fairly evident.

One word of conclusion about the effects of early deprivation. Little is served by fighting over the stale battlegrounds of yesterday's theorizing. I remarked in passing that there has been a strong arousal of interest in the manner in which cognitive functioning and perception are shaped by the instrumental role they play in the enterprises of an organism. In the past there have been pleas of protest that this instrumental bedding of perception played no role in shaping its character or laws, that only responses altered by virtue of instrumental requirements. Such a view comes from the ancient and honorable assumption that all there is to perceiving is the pattern of intensities, durations, and sensory qualities. It is obvious that inference is also a formidable factor in perceiving, else there would not be such a huge difference in recognizing the random word *yrulpzoc* and the fourth-order word *vernalit,* or frequent and infrequent words would be recognized with equal ease. Inference depends upon the establishment of rules and models, and it also depends upon the development of strategies for arriving at rules and models. I have proposed in this paper that early experience with a normally rich perceptual environment is needed for such learning, that deprivation prevents it.

Let me, finally, explore the implication of work on early deprivation for our understanding of the effects of sensory deprivation on the functioning adult organism. It would seem, first of all, that not only are there critical problems in the development of adequate models of the environment and adequate coping strategies, but that there are also maintenance problems of an order of delicacy that were not

even imagined before the pioneering experiments of Hebb and his associates at McGill. In listening to the papers of our symposium over the past several days, I have been struck by not only the need for variable sensory stimulation as a condition for maintaining a functioning organism, but also by the need for continuing social contact and stimulation. We have yet to study the relative effects of each of these sources of maintenance, but it would appear as if they may serve a vicarious function for each other: where social contact is maintained, as in the efforts at Mt. Sinai in New York to keep up the family contacts of children in respirators, the cognitively debilitating effects of reduced stimulation are notably reduced. It would not be unreasonable to guess that social contact provides a symbolic analogue or vicar for sensory intake.

What is this maintenance problem? I would like to suggest that it perhaps relates to a kind of continuing feedback-evaluation process by which organisms guide their correction strategies in perceiving, cognizing, and manipulating their environments. Let me suggest that the unhampered operation of this evaluation process is critical in the continuing adaptation of the organism, both in the development of adequate cognitive functioning, as I have suggested, and in moment-to-moment functioning. Consider the massive effects that occur when the evaluation process is interfered with by various means. Disrupt auditory feedback in speech by the conventional technique of delaying the return of the speech pattern to the speaker's ear by a fraction of a second, and the effect is highly disruptive. Stuttering occurs and the speaker reports a lively discomfort, sometimes bordering on panic. So, too, with the discomfort of a visual Ganzfeld, where virtually all orienting cues are removed and only a white unstructured space remains. Distorting spectacles often have the same effect of disrupting and preoccupying the organism, setting him off on a battle for adequate feedback that makes all else seem trivial. One may suggest that one of the prime sources of anxiety is a state in which one's conception or perception of the environment with which one must deal does not "fit" or predict that environment in a manner that makes action possible. If there is anything to this view of anxiety, then it follows that when one prevents an organism from monitoring the fittingness of his percepts and his cognitive structures, one is cutting him off from one of his principal sources of maintaining adjustment.

The work reported by Goldberger and Holt in this symposium on "individual differences in reaction to experimental interference with reality contact" and also by Bennett on the effect of sensory isolation in high altitude flying suggests that people respond differently to the initial stages of isolation, some finding it exciting and even intoxicating, others, terrifying and disrupting. I do not know what bearing this has on our present problem, save that when one is isolated from external stimulation one is thrown on internal resources, and people differ in the degree to which they live comfortably and confidently with their inner impulses and cognitive models. Over and beyond this important distinction, I would make one other in the form of a guess. It is this. To get any pleasure from being cut off temporarily from adequate evaluation of one's coping, whether by sensory deprivation or by "non-problem drinking" of five martinis, say, suggests that one is able to rely more on criteria of congruence and consistency in testing one's notions about the world, that one is less fearful of errors of overdaring and overgeneralization. The "strategies of evaluation" of such a person will tend to be more nominalistic and relativistic in the philosophical meaning of those terms. The person who is more easily thrown off by isolation and sensory deprivation and interference will be more the empiricist and realist, oriented outward for testing ideas. Each will show a different developmental pattern with respect to strategies for dealing with reality. We have seen such differences developing in eleven-year-old children whose cognitive patterns are now being studied intensively by the Cognition Project at Harvard, and as I listened to Drs. Goldberger and Holt reporting their findings, I was tempted to make the guess I am reporting here. Perhaps its only virtue, however, is that it is a testable guess that can be rejected easily!

In conclusion, then, I have suggested that early sensory deprivation prevents the formation of adequate models and strategies for dealing with the environment and that later sensory deprivation in normal adults disrupts the vital evaluation process by which one constantly monitors and corrects the models and strategies one has learned to employ in dealing with the environment.

REFERENCES

1. ADRIAN, E. D. The Physiological basis of perception. In E. D. ADRIAN et al. (Eds.), Brain mechanisms and consciousness. Oxford, Blackwell, 1954.
2. BORING, E. G. The physical dimensions of consciousness. New York, The Century Company, 1933.
3. BRUNSWIK, E. Organismic achievement and environmental probability. Psychol. Rev. 50, 255, 1943.
4. DITCHBURN, R. W. Report of the Experimental Psychology Group. Reading, England, January, 1957.
5. GALAMBOS, R. Suppression of auditory nerve activity by stimulation of efferent fibers to cochlea. J. Neurophysiol., 19, 424, 1956.
6. GIBSON, J. J., and GIBSON, E. J. Perceptual learning: Differentiation or enrichment? Psychol. Rev., 62, 32, 1955.
7. GRANIT, R. Receptors and sensory perception. New Haven, Yale Univer. Press, 1955.
8. HERNANDEZ-PÉON, R., SCHERRER, H., and JOUVER, M. Modification of electric activity in the cochlear nucleus during "attention" in unanesthetized cats. Science, 123, 331, 1956.
9. HULL, C. L. Principles of behavior. New York, D. Appleton-Century, 1943.
10. LASHLEY, K. S. Dynamic processes in perception. In E. D. ADRIAN et al. (Eds.), Brain mechanisms and consciousness. Oxford, Blackwell, 1954.
11. MAGOUN, H. W. The ascending reticular system and wakefulness. In E. D. ADRIAN et al. (Eds.), Brain mechanisms and consciousness. Oxford, Blackwell, 1954.
12. MARSCHAK, J. Rational behavior, uncertain prospects, and measurable utility. Econometrica, 18, 111, 1950.
13. PRENTICE, W. C. H. "Functionalism" in perception. Psychol. Rev., 63, 29, 1955.
14. PRIBRAM, K. The Brain and Thinking. Paper given at Cambridge Conference on Thinking, Cambridge, England, August, 1955.
15. SAVAGE, L. J. The foundations of statistics. New York, Wiley, 1954.
16. SPENCE, K. W. Behavior theory and conditioning. New Haven, Yale Univer. Press, 1956.
17. TITCHENER, E. B. Lectures on the elementary psychology of feeling and attention. New York, Macmillan Co., 1908.

5. THE GENETIC APPROACH TO THE PSYCHOLOGY OF THOUGHT * 1

JEAN PIAGET

From a developmental point of view, the essential in the act of thinking is not contemplation—that is to say, that which the Greeks called "theorema"—but the action of the dynamics.

Taking into consideration all that is known, one can distinguish two principal aspects:

1. The formal viewpoint which deals with the configuration of the state of things to know —for instance, most perceptions, mental images, imageries.

2. The *dynamic* aspect, which deals with transformations—for instance, to disconnect a motor in order to understand its functioning, to disassociate and vary the components of a physical phenomenon, to understand its causalities, to isolate the elements of a geometrical figure in order to investigate its properties, etc.

The study of the development of thought shows that the dynamic aspect is at the same time more difficult to attain and more important, because only transformations make us understand the state of things. For instance: when a child of 4 to 6 years transfers a liquid from a large and low glass into a narrow and higher glass, he believes in general that the quantity of the liquid has increased, because he is limited to comparing the initial state (low level) to the final state (high level) without

concerning himself with the transformation. Toward 7 or 8 years of age, on the other hand, a child discovers the preservation of the liquid, because he will think in terms of transformation. He will say that nothing has been taken away and nothing added, and, if the level of the liquid rises, this is due to a loss of width, etc.

The formal aspect of thought makes way, therefore, more and more in the course of the development to its dynamic aspects, until such time when only transformation gives an understanding of things. To think means, above all, to understand; and to understand means to arrive at the transformations, which furnish the reason for the state of things. All development of thought is resumed in the following manner: a construction of operations which stem from actions and a gradual subordination of formal aspects into dynamic aspects.

The operation, properly speaking, which constitutes the terminal point of this evolution is, therefore, to be conceived as an internalized action reversible (example: addition and subtraction, etc.) bound to other operations, which form with it a structured whole and which is characterized by well defined laws of totality (example: the groups, the lattice, etc.). Dynamic totalities are clearly different from the "gestalt" because those are characterized by their non-additive composition, consequently irreversible.

So defined, the dynamics intervene in the construction of all thought processes; in the structure of forms and classifications, of relations and serialization of correspondences, of numbers, of space and time, of the causality, etc. One could think at first glance that space

* Piaget, Jean, "The Genetic Approach to the Psychology of Thought," *Journal of Educational Psychology*, 1961, *52*, 275-281.

1 This paper, transmitted by Ernest Harms, is the text of an address made by Jean Piaget, from notes, at the New York Academy of Sciences' Conference on the Psychology of Thinking on April 28-29, 1960. The translation was made by Ruth Golbin, who has skillfully succeeded in retaining Piaget's individualistic style of expression.

and geometry add to the formal aspects of thought. In this way one conceived of the geometric science in the past, considering it impure mathematics, but applicable to perception and intuition. Modern geometry, since *Le Programme d'Erlangen* by F. Klein, has tended, like all other precise disciplines, to subordinate the formal to the dynamic. The geometries are, indeed, understood today as relying all on groups of transformation, so that one can go from one to the other by characterizing one less general "subgroup" as part of a more inclusive group. Thus geometry too rests on a system of dynamics.

Any action of thought consists of combining thought operations and integrating the objects to be understood into systems of dynamic transformation. The psychological criteria of this is the appearance of the notion of conservation or "invariants of groups." Before speech, at the purely sensory-motor stage of a child from 0 to 18 months, it is possible to observe actions which show evidence of such tendencies. For instance: From 4-5 to 18 months, the baby constructs his first invariant, which is the schema of the permanent object (to recover an object which escaped from the field of perception). He succeeds in this by coordinating the positions and the displacements according to a structure, which can be compared to what the geometricians call "group displacements."

When, with the beginning of the symbolic function (language, symbolic play, imagerie, etc.), representation through thought becomes possible, it is at first a question of reconstructing in thought what the action is already able to realize. The actions actually do not become transformed immediately into operations, and one has to wait until about 7 to 8 years for the child to reach a functioning level. During this preoperative period the child, therefore, only arrives at incomplete structures characterized by a lack in the notion of combinations and, consequently, by a lack of logic (in transitivity, etc.).

In the realm of causality one can especially observe these diverse forms of precausality, which we have previously described in detail. It is true that a certain number of authors— Anglo-Saxon above all—have severely criticized these conclusions, while others have recognized the same facts as we have (animism, etc.). Yet, in an important recent book two Canadian authors, M. Laurendeau and A. Pinard, have taken the whole problem up once again by means of thorough statistics. In the main points they have come to a remarkable verification of our views, explaining, moreover, the methodological reasons for the divergencies among the preceding authors.

At about 7 to 8 years the child arrives at his first complete dynamic structures (classes, relations, and numbers), which, however, still remain concrete—in other words, only at the time of a handling of objects (material manipulation or, when possible, directly imagined). It is not before the age of 11 to 12 years or more that operations can be applied to pure hypotheses. At this latter level, a logic of propositions helps complete the concrete structures. This enlarges the structures considerably until their disposition.

The fundamental genetic problem of the psychology of thought is hence to explain the formation of these dynamic structures.

Practically, one would have to rely on three principal factors in order to explain the facts of development: maturation, physical experience, and social interaction. But in this particular case none of these three suffice to furnish us with the desired explanations—not even the three together.

MATURATION

First of all, none of these dynamic structures are innate, but they form very gradually. (For example: The transitivity of equalities is acquired at approximately $6\frac{1}{2}$ to 7 years, and the ability of linear measure comes about only at 9 years, as does the full understanding of weights, etc.) But progressive construction does not seem to depend on maturation, because the achievements hardly correspond to a particular age. Only the order of succession is constant. However, one witnesses innumerable accelerations or retardations for reasons of education (cultural) or acquired experience. Certainly one cannot deny the inevitable role which maturation plays, but it is determined above all by existing possibility (or limitation). They still remain to be actualized, which brings about other factors. In addition, in the domain of thought, the factors of innateness seem above all limitative. We do not have, for example, an intuition of space in the fourth dimension; nevertheless we can deduce it.

PHYSICAL EXPERIENCE

Experiencing of objects plays, naturally, a very important role in the establishment of dynamic structures, because the operations originate from actions and the actions bear upon the object. This role manifests itself right from the beginning of sensory-motor explorations, preceding language, and it affirms itself continually in the course of manipulations and activities which are appropriate to the antecedent stages. Necessary as the role of experience may be, it does not sufficiently describe the construction of the dynamic structures—and this for the following three reasons.

First, there exist ideas which cannot possibly be derived from the child's experience—for instance, when one changes the shape of a small ball of clay. The child will declare, at 7 to 8 years, that the quantity of the matter is conserved. It does so before discovering the conservation of weight (9 to 10 years) and that of volume (10 to 11 years). What is the quantity of a matter independently of its weight and its volume? This is an abstract notion corresponding to the "substance" of the pre-Socratic physicists. This notion is neither possible to be perceived nor measurable. It is, therefore, the product of a dynamic deduction and not part of an experience. (The problem would not be solved either by presenting the quantity in the form of a bar of chocolate to be eaten.)

Secondly, the various investigations into the learning of logical structure, which we were able to make at our International Center of Genetic Epistemology, lead to a very unanimous result: one does not "learn" a logical structure as one learns to discover any physical law. For instance, it is easy to bring about the learning of the conservation of weight because of its physical character, but it is difficult to obtain the one of the transitivity of the relationship of the weight:

$$A = C \text{ if } A = B \text{ and } B = C$$

or the one of the relationship of inclusion, etc. The reason for this is that in order to arrive

at the learning of a logical structure, one has to build on another more elementary logical (or prelogical) structure. And such structures consequently never stem from experience alone, but suppose always a coordinating activity of the subject.

Thirdly, there exist two types of experiences:

1. The physical experiences show the objects as they are, and the knowledge of them leads to the abstraction directly from the object (example: to discover that a more voluminous matter is more or less heavy than a less voluminous matter).

2. The logicomathematical experience supposes to interrelate by action individual facts into the world of objects, but this refers to the result of these actions rather than to the objects themselves. These interrelations are arrived at by process of abstractions from the actions and their coordinates. For instance, to discover that 10 stones in a line always add up to 10, whether they are counted from left to right or from right to left. Because then the order and the total sum have been presented. The new knowledge consists simply in the discovery that the action of adding a sum is independent of the action of putting them in order. Thus the logicomathematical experience does not stem from the same type of learning as that of the physical experience, but rather from an equilibration of the scheme of actions, as we will see.

SOCIAL INTERACTION

The educative and social transmission (linguistic, etc.) plays, naturally, an evident role in the formation of dynamic structures, but this factor does not suffice either to entirely explain its development, and this for two reasons:

First, a certain number of structures do not lend themselves to teaching and are prior to all teaching. One can cite, as an example, most concepts of conservation, of which, in general, the pedagogs agree that they are not problematic to the child.

The second, more fundamental, reason is that in order to understand the adult and his language, the child needs means of assimilation which are formed through structures preliminary to the social transmission itself—

for instance, an ancient experience has shown us that French-speaking children understand very early the expression *"quelques unes de mes fleurs"* [some of my flowers] in contrast to *"toutes mes fleurs"* [all my flowers], and this occurs when they have not yet constructed the relation of inclusion:

Some A are part of all B; therefore $A < B$

In conclusion, it is not exaggerated to maintain that the basic factors invoked before in order to explain mental development do not suffice to explain the formation of the dynamic structures. Though all three of them certainly play a necessary role, they do not constitute in themselves sufficient reason and one has to add to them a fourth factor, which we shall try to describe now.

This fourth factor seems to us to consist of a general progression of equilibration. This factor intervenes, as is to be expected, in the interaction of the preceding factors. Indeed, if the development depends, on one hand, on internal factors (maturation), and on the other hand on external factors (physical or social), it is self-evident that these internal and external factors equilibrate each other. The question is then to know if we are dealing here only with momentary compromises (unstable equilibrium) or if, on the contrary, this equilibrium becomes more and more stable. This shows that all exchange (mental as well as biological) between the organisms and the milieu (physical and social) as composed of two poles: (*a*) of the *assimilation* of the given external to the previous internal structures, and (*b*) of the *accommodation* of these structures to the given ones. The equilibrium between the assimilation and the accommodation is proportionately more stable than the assimilative structures which are better differentiated and coordinated.

It is this equilibrium between the assimilation and accommodation that seems to explain to us the functioning of the reversible operations. This occurs, for instance, in the realm of notions of conservation where the invariants of groups do not account for the maturation and the physical experience, nor for the sociolingual transmission. In fact, dynamic reversibility is a compensatory system of which the idea of conservation constitutes precisely the

result. The equilibrium (between the assimilation and the accommodation) is to be defined as a compensation of exterior disturbances through activities of the subject orientated in the contrary direction of these disturbances. This leads us directly to the reversibility.

Notice that we do not conceive of the idea of equilibrium in the same manner as the "gestalt theory" does, which makes great use of this idea too, but in the sense of an automatical physical equilibrium. We believe, on the contrary, that the mental equilibrium and even the biological one presumes an activity of the subject, or of the organism. It consists in a sort of matching, orientated towards compensation—with even some over-compensation—resulting from strategies of precaution. One knows, for instance, that the homeostasis does not always lead to an exact balance. But it often leads to overcompensation, in response to exterior disturbances. Such is the case in nearly all occurrences except precisely in the case of occurrences of a superior order, which are the operations of reversible intelligence, the reversible logic of which is characterized by a complete and exact compensation (inverted operation).

The idea of equilibrium is so close to the one of reversibility that G. Brunner, in a friendly criticism of one of our latest books appearing in the *British Journal of Psychology,* proposes to renounce the idea of equilibrium because the notion of the reversibility seems sufficient to him. We hesitate to accept this suggestion for the following three reasons:

First, reversibility is a logical idea, while the equilibrium is a causal idea which permits the explanation of reforms by means of a probabilistic schema. For instance, in order to explain the formation of the idea of conservation, one can distinguish a certain number of successive stages, of which each is characterized by the "strategy" of a progress of compensation. Now it is possible to show that the first of these strategies (only bearing upon one dimension, to the neglect of others) is the most probable at the point of departure, and further, that the second of these strategies (with the emphasis on a second dimension) *becomes* the most likely—as a function of the result of the first. And, finally, that the third of these strategies (oscillation between the observed modifications upon the different dimensions and the discovery of their solidarity) *becomes* the most likely in the functioning of the results of the preceding, etc. From such a point of view the process of equilibration is, therefore, characterized by a sequential control with increasing probabilities. It furnishes a beginning for casual explanations of the reversibility and does not duplicate the former idea.

Secondly, the tendency of equilibrium is much broader for the operation than the reversibility as such, which leads us to explain the reversibility through the equilibrium and not the reverse. In effect, it is at this level of the obvious regulations and sensory-motor feedbacks that the process of equilibration starts. This in its higher form becomes intelligence. Logical reversibility is therefore conceivable as an end result and not as a beginning and the entire reversibility follows the laws of a semireversibility of various levels.

Thirdly, the tendency to equilibrate does not only explain this final reversibility, but also certain new synthesis between originally distinct operations. One can cite in this regard an example of great importance: the serial of whole numbers. Russell and Whitehead have tried to explain the basic set of numbers through the idea of equivalent classes, without recourse to the serial order. This means that two classes are believed to be equivalent, if one can put their respective elements into a reciprocal arrangement. Only when this relationship relies on the quality of the objects (an A put into relation with an A, a B with a B, etc.) one does not get the quantity. If this relationship is made exclusive of the qualities (an Individual A or B put into relationship with an Individual B or A) then there exists only one way to distinguish the elements from each other. In order not to forget one, or not to count the same twice, one must deal with them in succession and introduce the serial factor as well as the structure of classes. We

may then say, psychologically speaking, that the sequence of whole numbers is synthesis between two groupings qualitatively distinct, the fitting of the classes and serialization, and that this synthesis takes place as soon as one excludes the qualities of the elements in question. But how does this synthesis occur? Precisely by a gradual process of equilibration.

On the one hand the child who develops his ideas from numbers is in possession of structures enabling him to fit them into classes (classifications). But if he wants to be exclusive of qualities in order to answer to the question "how many," he becomes unable to distinguish the elements. The disequilibrium which appears, therefore, obliges the child to resort to the idea of order and take recourse to arranging these elements into a lineal row. On the other hand, if the child arranges the elements as 1, 1, 1, etc., how would he know, for instance, how to distinguish the second from the third? This new disequilibrium brings him back to the idea of classification: The "second" is the element which has but one predecessor, and the "third" is one that has two of them. In short, every new problem provokes a disequilibrium (recognizable through types of dominant errors) the solution of which consists in a re-equilibration, which brings about a new original synthesis of two systems, up to the point of independence.

During the discussion of my theories, Brunner has said that I have called disequilbrium what others describe as motivation. This is perfectly true, but the advantage of this language is to clarify that a cognitive or dynamic structure is never independent of motivational factors. The motivation in return is always solidary to structural (therefore cognitive) determined level. The language of the equilibrium presents that activity, that permits us to reunite into one and the same totality those two aspects of behavior which always have a functional solidarity because there exists no structure (cognition) without an energizer (motivation) and vice versa.

6. REVISITING MONTESSORI *

J. McV. HUNT

The enlightened self-interest that provided the first *Casa dei Bambini* in the slum tenements of Rome will find a responsive note today. Modern administrators and educators are faced with vandalism and aimless violence among economically and culturally deprived children who reject and are rejected by the traditional school system. In offering Dr. Montessori space for the new enterprise, the director of the Roman Association for Good Building and the owners of the buildings in the San Lorenzo district were motivated in large part by the hope that keeping the unruly young children, usually left alone during the day by their working parents, in something like a school would prevent vandalism and save damage to their property.

It is 70 years since Montessori became interested, while yet a medical student serving as an intern in the psychiatric clinic of Rome, in the "idiot children" then housed in the insane asylums. It is 66 years since she began the work with mentally deficient children that led her to examine Jean Itard's (1801) attempts at educating the "wild boy of Aveyron" and to utilize the materials and methods devised by Edouard Sèguin (1844, 1866) for educating the mentally deficient children. It is 57 years since she extended her modified Sèguin-approach in education of retarded children to the education of normal young children in the first *Casa dei Bambini,* or "Homes of Children" as Dorothy Canfield Fisher translated the term.

According to the reports (Fisher 1912, Stevens 1913), Montessori's success far surpassed her sponsors' fondest hopes, if not also hers. Not only was vandalism prevented, but these children, three to seven years old, became avid pupils. Not only did they learn "cleanliness," "manners," "some grace in action," and "something about proper diet," but they became acquainted with animals and plants and with the manual arts. They got both sensory and motor training with the didactic apparatus and even learned the basic symbolic skills of counting, reading, and writing, often before they were five years old. People were impressed. When, in 1909, Montessori published her *Scientific Pedagogy as Applied to Education in the Children's Houses,* people from all over the world beat Emersonian paths to her door and pressed her to communicate her methods to others.

Americans were among the first to become interested, and their interest rapidly exploded into a social movement. Perhaps the explosion of interest and its waning is best illustrated by rates of publication about Montessori's work. Jenny Merrill first described Montessori's work in the December, 1909, and March, 1910, issues of the *Kindergarten Primary Magazine.* The year 1911 brought six reports of Montessori's work. The number rose to 54 in 1912, and then jumped to a maximum of 76 in 1913. Then the explosion appears to have rapidly subsided: in 1914 the number of publications declined to 55; they dwindled to 15 in 1915, to eight in 1917, and amounted to less than five a year thereafter.

Why this sudden explosion of interest? Why the equally sudden fall? Why revisit today what may appear from such evidence to have been a mere fad in American education? What

* Reprinted by permission of Schocken Books Inc. from *The Montessori Method,* Copyright © 1964 by Schocken Books Inc.

concerns does such a revisit arouse? These are the issues I would like to discuss.

WHY THE EXPLOSION OF INTEREST?

A definitive accounting for this explosion of interest in Montessori's work is hardly possible, but certain factors help to explain it. Americans had been primed to hope for progress with all kinds of problems. Winning the West had encouraged such hope. The "muckrakers" had been uncovering, in article after article on "the shame of the cities" in *McClure's Magazine*, the seamy side of the human urban condition. American excitement about reform, recently fostered by the progressive Republicanism of Theodore Roosevelt, was still high. Many people, moreover, had become accustomed to see in children the chief hope of fundamental reform. This hope had been fostered by a half-century of activity of the Froebel Society, by nearly a quarter-century of G. Stanley Hall's child-study movement, and by John Dewey's (1900, 1902) attempts—inspired chiefly by the "reform Darwinism" of Lester F. Ward and Albion Small (Cremin, 1962)—to make that age-old institution, the school, an instrument of progress and social reform.

Reports of Montessori's success in the "Houses of Children" made her pedagogic methods look to many of the most progressive-minded like the way to a new day, or like the most rapid route yet uncovered to fundamental reform. Many of these progressive-minded people who visited Montessori or became interested in her work had, like Alexander Graham Bell, tremendous prestige; some of them, like McClure, controlled major sources of mass communication; others, like Dorothy Canfield Fisher (1912) and Ellen Yale Stevens (1913), had facile pens. They got the news out fast, and they spread it wide. These factors help explain the explosion of interest.

But why did the interest subside almost as rapidly as it exploded? Perhaps it failed, at least in part, because the Dottoressa rejected McClure's offer in 1913 to build her an institution in America. On the other hand, her rejection may merely have saved her a painful defeat.

Conceptions of nature and how to deal with any problem may fail either because they run

counter to the facts of empirical observation or because they run counter to other conceptions which are somehow better anchored in the beliefs of men at a given time, or because of some combination of these two. On the side of empirical observation, the impressions of Montessori's great educational success reported by American writers lent support to the validity of her conceptions. Some of these people should have been good observers; they included, for instance, such psychologists as Dorothy Canfield Fisher (who is better known for her novels), Arnold and Beatrice Gesell, Joseph Peterson, Howard C. Warren, and Lightner Witmer (see Donahue, 1962, for their publications). However, various conceptions of Montessori ran into almost head-on dissonance with conceptions which, from a variety of communicative influences, were becoming dominant in the minds of those Americans who became most influential. Most of Montessori's support had come from the elite of the political and educational progressives and through popular magazines; it had not come from those formulating the philosophy of education. Although Montessori got support from Howard C. Warren (1912), then president of the American Psychological Association, and from Lightner Witmer (1914), founder of the first Psychological Clinic at the University of Pennsylvania, she failed to get support from those psychologists of the functional school or of the emerging behavioristic school whose conceptions were shortly to become dominant. With such emerging theories, with the conceptions of the intelligence-testing movement, and with the psychoanalytic theory of psychosexual development, then just beginning to get a foothold in America following Freud's visit of 1909 at the invitation of G. Stanley Hall, Montessori's notions were too dissonant to hold their own.

WHY REVISIT MONTESSORI TODAY?

All this was a half-century ago, when the beliefs of Stimulus-response theory, the intelligence testers, and psychoanalysis were becoming dominant. They remained dominant for the period between the two World Wars and through World War II. Stimulus-response methodology was highly productive of observational evidence. Ironically, it is this evidence from S-R methodology which has been the undoing of the beliefs dominant in psychological theory, even some of those central to S-R theory. Moreover, it is this evidence from S-R methodologies which suggests that Montessori built pedagogically better than her critics knew, even though the language of her constructs may seem even more quaint today than Kilpatrick found it in 1912. Consider in turn the various beliefs synopsized.

BELIEF IN THE UNIMPORTANCE OF EARLY EXPERIENCE. It was Freud's (1905) observation that the free associations of his patients led back to infancy, and his imaginative interpretation in the theory of psychosexual development, that began to lend force to the notion that very early experience, even preverbal experience, might be important for the development of adult characteristics. Freud's theory, however, put the emphasis on the fate of instinctive modes of infantile pleasure-striving, i.e., sucking, elimination, and genitality. To a substantial degree, objective studies of the effects of these factors explicitly concerned in early psychosexual development have generally tended to depreciate their importance (see Child, 1954; Hunt, 1945; Orlansky, 1949; Sears, 1943).[1] On the other hand, studies of the effects of various kinds of early infantile experience in animal subjects have left very little room for doubt that early experience is a factor in behavioral development. Ready-made infantile responses, like the sucking of the calf—as any farmer knows—or of the human infant (Sears & Wise, 1950), the pecking response in chicks (Padilla, 1935), or the flying response of young birds (Spalding, 1873), will wane if these patterns go unused for too long a time. Similarly, such presumably instinctive patterns as mothering fail to develop in female rats that have been deprived of licking themselves by means of Elizabethan collars worn from weaning to adulthood (Birch, 1956). Even certain aspects of the anatomical maturation itself appear to depend upon experience. Chimpanzees (Riesen, 1958),

[1] I must except here a growing variety of factors in parent-child relationships which are being shown to be quite important (see Becker, 1962). These studies stem in large part from the psychoanalytic conception of the Oedipal relationship as that conception has been elaborated in the learning theory of Dollard & Miller (1950).

kittens (Weiskrantz, 1958), rabbits (Brattgård, 1952), and rats (Liberman, 1962) that are reared in darkness develop anomalous retinae which are deficient in Müller fibers and show deficient RNA production in the retinal ganglion cells (Brattgård, 1952; Liberman, 1962; Rasch, Swift, Riesen, & Chow, 1961). Moreover, rats deprived of vision for the 10 days immediately after the eyes open are not as quickly responsive to visual cues in adulthood as are litter-mates which were deprived of hearing for 10 days after their ears opened, and vice versa (Wolf, 1943; Gauron & Becker, 1959). (That is, the rats deprived of hearing are not as quickly responsive to aural cues as are rats deprived of vision.) Although there is still much confusion concerning this issue, rats petted, shook, or submitted to electric shock and to marked drops in temperature have shown repeatedly, as adults, a reduction in the tendency to defecate and urinate in a strange open field, increased readiness to enter strange places, and more rapid learning to avoid shock than controls left unmolested in the maternal nest (see Denenberg, 1962; Levine, 1961). These are but a sample of the various kinds of effects of infantile experience on the adult behavior of animal subjects (see also Beach & Jaynes, 1954). Still others will be noted in connection with other beliefs. Clearly, Montessori's concern with the experience of three- and four-year-olds need be no will-o'-the-wisp.

BELIEF IN FIXED INTELLIGENCE. The belief in fixed intelligence was based in considerable part upon the notion that the genes which carry the heredity of the individual fix his intellectual capacity. It is probably true that the genes determine an individual's potential to develop intellectual capacity, but they do not guarantee that the individual will achieve his potential capacity. Elsewhere (Hunt, 1961), I have summarized the evidence (a) that scores from tests administered in the preschool years predict very poorly scores for tests administered at adolescence, (b) that substantial differences in the I.Q. have been found for identical twins reared apart and that the degree of difference of I.Q. is related to the degree of difference between the sets of circumstances under which the twins have developed, and (c) that the commonly predicted drop in intelligence to be expected from the fact that the majority of each new generation comes from the lower half of the population intellectually has failed to occur and that, instead, rather substantial increases have been found.

It is especially interesting to note that Harold Skeels has recently followed up those individuals in the study by Skeels & Dye (1939). In this study, a group of 13 infants with a mean I.Q. of 64.3 and a range between 36 and 89 and with chronological ages ranging from seven to 30 months, was transferred from an orphanage to a school for the mentally retarded. There they were placed on a ward where the older and brighter girls became very much attached to them and would play with them during most of the infants' waking hours. After being on this ward for periods ranging between six months, for the seven-month-old youngster, and 52 months for the 30-month-old youngster, they were retested. Each of the 13 showed a gain in I.Q.: the minimum gain was seven points, the maximum was 58 points, and all but four showed gains of more than 20 points. In the same study, for purposes of contrast, were 12 other orphanage inmates, this group having a mean I.Q. of 87, an I.Q. range from 50 to 103, and an age range from 12 to 22 months. These infants were left in the orphanage. When they were retested after periods varying from 21 to 43 months, they all showed a decrease in I.Q. One decrease was only eight points, but for the remaining 11 children, the decreases varied between 18 and 45 points, with five exceeding 35 points. In the follow-up study, all of these cases were located after a lapse of 21 years. The findings are startling. Of the 13 in the group transferred from the orphanage to the school for the mentally retarded: all are self-supporting; none is a ward of any institution, public or private; 11 of the 13 are married, and nine of these have had children. On the other hand, of the 12 children, originally higher in I.Q., who were kept in the orphanage: one died in adolescence following continuous residence in a state institution for the mentally retarded; five are still wards of state institutions, one in a mental hospital and the other four in institutions for the mentally retarded; of the six no longer wards of state institutions, only two have been married and one of these is divorced. In education, the disparity between the two groups is similarly great. For the 13 transferred from the orphanage to the school for the mentally retarded, the median grade completed is the twelfth (*i.e.*, graduation from high school); four have gone on for one or more years of college work, with one of the boys having a bachelor's degree from a big state university. Occupationally, the range is from professional and semi-professional to semi-skilled laborers or domestics. For the 12 who remained in the orphanage, half failed to complete the third grade, and none got to high school. Only three of the six not now in state institutions are now employed (Skeels, personal communication, 1964). Clearly there is a difference here that counts. The superiority of the foster home, where the child receives a variety of experience and stimulation, over the old orphanage is relevant here (see Goldfarb, 1963).

Evidence that early experience influences adult problem-solving capacity comes also from studies with animal subjects. This work stems from the neuropsychological theorizing of Donald Hebb (1949). Hebb was concerned with the facts of attention and thought. For him, the switchboard conception of brain-function could not be true, for these facts imply that semi-autonomous processes must be operating within the brain. He also found evidence for these in neurophysiology, and he termed them *cell assemblies*, based upon early learning perceptual experiences, and *phase sequences*, based upon the sequential organizations of later learning. The electronic computer has replaced the telephone switchboard as the mechanical model of brain function. On the assumption that problem-solving would be a function of the richness of these semi-autonomous central processes, Hebb (1947) compared the problem-solving ability of rats reared in cages in the laboratory with that of rats reared as pets in his home. The problem-solving ability was measured by the Hebb-Williams (1946) test of animal intelligence. The pet-reared animals were superior to their cage-reared litter-mates. Thompson & Heron (1954), also at McGill, have done a similar experiment with dogs as subjects. Some were reared under isolation in laboratory cages from weaning to eight months of age. Their litter-mates were reared for this same period in homes as pets. The cage-reared and the pet-reared dogs were put together in a dog-pasture for 10 months; then, at 18 months of age, their problem-solving ability was assessed in the Hebb-Williams mazes. The pet-reared dogs were superior to their cage-reared litter-mates. In fact, the superiority of the pet-reared dogs over the cage-reared dogs appears to have been even more marked than the superiority of the pet-reared rats over the cage-reared rats. This suggests that the degree of effect of infantile experience on adult problem-solving capacity may well be a function of the proportion of the brain not directly connected with either receptor inputs or motor outputs. This proportion, termed the A/S ratio by Hebb (1949) increases up the phylogenetic scale.

There is a good possibility that the cultural deprivation involved in being reared under slum conditions may be somewhat analogous to cage-rearing while being reared in a family of the educated middle class most resembles pet-rearing. This possibility suggests that an enrichment of early experience during the preschool years might well serve as an antidote for this cultural deprivation, if it comes early enough (see Hunt, 1964). It might thereby give those children whose lot it has been to be born to parents living in slums a more nearly even opportunity to hold their own in the competitive culture of the public school once they get there. The "House of Children" established by Montessori in the San Lorenzo district of Rome and the methods of teaching that she developed there provide a splendid beginning precisely adapted for this purpose of counteracting cultural deprivation.

BELIEF IN PREDETERMINED DEVELOPMENT. The notions that psychological development is predetermined by the genes and that the response repertoire emerges automatically as a function of anatomic maturation are no longer tenable. The early evidence appearing to support such a conception of development was either based on investigations with such lowly organisms as Amblystoma and frogs (see Hunt, 1961), or it was based upon the effects of practicing a given kind of skill. Such lower organisms as these amphibia used as subjects by Carmichael (1926) and Coghill (1929) differ from mammals, and especially from human beings in two very fundamental ways. They have substantially greater regenerative ca-

pacity, and this fact suggests that biochemical determiners may well be considerably more prepotent in determining their development than such factors are in determining the development of mammals. They also have a much lower proportion of the brain not directly connected with receptor inputs or motor outputs (in Hebb's terms, a lower A/S ratio). This fact suggests that semi-autonomous central processes deriving from experience must have a much smaller role in determining their behavior than it has in mammals, and especially in man. Moreover, the evidence concerning the effects of very early experience both on the anatomical development of the retinae and on adult behavior in animal subjects is clearly dissonant with this notion of predetermined development.

Those studies showing that practice has but evanescent effects on such early abilities as tower-building, ladder-climbing, buttoning, and cutting with scissors (see Gesell & Thompson, 1929; Hilgard, 1932) missed the point that abilities appear to be hierarchically organized, that the experiences governing the age at which such abilities appear do not constitute exercise in those abilities themselves. Rather, they constitute encounters with quite different circumstances important in establishing abilities lower in the hierarchy. At the level of school subjects, this can be illustrated by noting how useless practice in long division is if the child has not learned to add and subtract. More to the point, however, is such evidence from animal studies as Birch's (1956) finding that female rats do not mother their young properly if they have been deprived of licking themselves by means of Elizabethan collars. Still more to the point, at the level of human beings, is that dramatic finding of Dennis (1960) that children being reared in a Teheran orphanage where visual and auditory inputs are relatively homogeneous are markedly delayed in their *locomotor* development. Of these children, 60% were still not sitting up alone at two years of age, and 85% were still not walking at four years of age. Variations of visual and auditory input would appear in terms of our conceptions of practice to have little to do with locomotor skills. Thus, while the genotype does set limits on an individual's potential, it does not guarantee that this potential in capacity will be reached. The achievement of genotypic potential appears to be a function of a continuous interaction between the organism and its environment. It has long been obvious that there must be a biochemical interaction manifested in the processes of food and water intake and elimination, but it now appears that psychological development is also highly dependent upon what one may characterize as the organism's informational interaction with the environment.

One more factor relevant to the role of early experience in psychological development. During the earliest phases, the longer a developing organism is deprived of a given sort of experience, or, to put it another way, the longer an organism is deprived of a given kind of informational interaction with the environment, the more likely is the effect of that deprivation to become permanent. For instance, in the work of Cruze (1935, 1938) chicks reared in darkness for only five days quickly developed their expected accuracy in pecking, but chicks allowed only some 15 minutes out of darkness for pecking each day for 20 days not only failed to improve but also appeared to be permanently deficient in pecking accuracy. Moreover, when Padilla (1935) kept newly-hatched chicks from pecking for eight consecutive days or longer, the chicks lost completely their inclination or capacity to peck. Such relationships are still inadequately understood, but they have a clear implication for childhood education. They imply that the longer cultural deprivation lasts, the greater and the more permanent will be its effects. Such considerations make it important to consider ways to enrich preschool experience as an antidote for such cultural deprivation, and the earlier the better (see Hunt, 1964). Moreover, from the observations of Americans who visited Montessori's Houses of Children, one gathers they were successful at precisely this business of counteracting the effects of cultural deprivation on these symbolic skills required for success in school and in an increasingly technological culture. Here, having based her pedagogy on earlier attempts to educate the mentally retarded was probably a highly pertinent advantage.

BELIEF THAT "ALL BEHAVIOR IS MOTIVATED." The proposition that all behavior is motivated by painful stimulation, homeostatic needs, or sex, or by acquired drives based upon these, has run into an accumulation of dissonant evidence. One of the most obvious implications of this commonly-believed proposition is that organisms will become quiescent in the absence of such motivation. They do not. For instance, play in animals is most likely to occur in the absence of such motivating conditions (Buhler, 1928; Beach, 1945). Similarly, manipulative behavior in chimpanzees (Harlow, Harlow & Meyer, 1950), spatial exploration in rats (Berlyne, 1960; Nissen, 1930), spontaneous alternation in rats (Montgomery, 1953, 1955), and visual and auditory exploration in monkeys (Butler, 1953, 1958) have all been found to occur repeatedly in the absence of such motivation (see Hunt, 1963a).

Such evidence has recently been given theoretical recognition in the postulation of a variety of new drives and needs. Such drives and needs however, are no more than descriptions of the behavior they propose to explain. Moreover, in motive-naming we are merely revisiting the instinct-naming popularized by McDougall (1908) early in this century and rejected immediately after World War I. We should know better. This evidence has also been unfortunately recognized in motives named in terms of their telic significance, such as the "urge of mastery" of Ives Hendrick (1943) and the "competence motivation" of White (1959), and in terms of spontaneous activity by such people as Hunt (1960). I say unfortunately recognized because such conceptual approaches provide no means of developing hypotheses about testable antecedent-consequent relationships.

Elsewhere I have proposed a mechanism for motivation inherent in information processing and action (Hunt, 1963a) or, if you will within the organism's informational interaction with the environment. The nature of this mechanism has been suggested by the recent radical change in our conception of the functional unit of the nervous system from that of reflex arc to that of feedback loop From the standpoint of the feedback loop activity is instigated, not merely by the onset of some kind of stimulation, but by the occurrence of a discrepancy between the input of the moment and some standard existing within the organism. This discrepancy I have termed following the lead of Miller, Galanter, & Pribram (1960), *incongruity*. As I see it, some standards, like those for homeostatic needs, are built into the organism, but some standards are established through experience as coded residues of encounters with the environment which are stored within the nervous system. In the language of common sense, they are expectations. Probably these residues are stored within those intrinsic portions of the brain not directly connected with receptor inputs and motor outlets. Incongruity is typically accompanied by emotional arousal, but emotional arousal does not appear to be, by itself, a sufficient determiner of whether the organism will approach or withdraw from a source of stimulation (see Haywood & Hunt, 1963). The determiners of approach and withdrawal, presumably associated with the hedonic value of the source of input, appear to inhere within the organism's informational interaction with circumstances. If there is too little incongruity, the organism approaches sources of incongruity, but if there is too much incongruity, the organism withdraws from sources of incongruous inputs (see Hebb, 1949). The former condition is illustrated in the study of Bexton, Heron, & Scott (1954). There, McGill students refused to remain within a situation where variation in receptor inputs was minimized even though they were paid $20 a day. On the other hand, withdrawal from too much incongruity is illustrated in Hebb's (1946) studies of fear. There, chimpanzees encountering various familiar situations in an unfamiliar guise retreated with distressed vocalizing and pupils wide open. Such withdrawal appeared in a young pet chimpanzee when the highly-familiar and much-loved experimenter appeared in a halloween mask or even merely in the coat of the animal keeper. These facts appear to mean that there is an optimum incongruity which is continually sought (Hunt, 1963a). It is a basis for continuous cognitive growth with joy. It also justifies the older notions that children have a spontaneous interest in learning. In basing her pedagogy on such motivation, I now believe Montessori was on solid ground.

The notion of an optimum of incongruity, coupled with the notion that the standard upon which incongruity is based derives from experience, gives rise to what I have termed "the problem of the match" (Hunt, 1961). This "problem of the match" implies that if the circumstances encountered are to be attractive and interesting and are yet to be challenging enough to call forth those accommodative changes, within the structure of central processes, that presumably constitute learning, they must be properly matched to those "standards" which the child has already developed in the course of his past experience. The status of our knowledge about these matters is entirely inadequate for us to arrange such matches entirely from the outside. It would appear that the child must have some opportunity to follow his own bent. Thus, we come to the importance of that liberty emphasized by the Rousseau-Pestalozzi-Froebel tradition and by Montessori.

It was this "problem of the match" that prompted my interest in Montessori's work. When I wrote *Intelligence and Experience*, this problem of the match loomed as a large obstacle in the way of maximizing intellectual potential. I deserve no credit for discovery, however, because as recently as two years ago, the name of Montessori would have meant to me only one of those educational "faddists" who came along shortly after the turn of the century. It was after a day-long discussion of such matters with Lee Cronbach and Jan Smedslund at Boulder in the summer of 1962, that Jan Smedslund asked me if I knew of Montessori and her work. When I claimed no such knowledge, he advised me to look her up, because, and I quote his words as I remember them, "she has a solution to your problem of the match—not a theoretical solution, but a practical one." I believe Smedslund is correct, for in arranging a variety of materials in graded fashion, in putting together children ranging in age from three to seven, and in breaking the lock-step in infant education, Montessori went a long way toward a practical solution. Grading the materials permits the child to grow as his interests lead him from one level of complexity to another. Having children aged from three to seven years together should permit the younger children a graded series of models for imitation and the older ones an opportunity to learn by teaching. Breaking the lock-step provides that opportunity for the child to make his own selection of materials and models. In the present state of our knowledge about the match, I believe only the child can make an appropriate selection. Thus, I believe there is an important psychological basis for Montessori's practice.

BELIEF IN THE RELATIVE IMPORTANCE OF MOTOR RESPONSE AND RECEPTOR INPUT. The belief that it is the motor response that is all-important in learning is less tenable than it was half a century ago. Although the issue is still far from settled, recent evidence appears to indicate that the role of the eyes and the ears, and perhaps the tactile organs, may be much more important in the organism's on-going informational interaction with the environment than are the motor outlets. In this connection, it is exceedingly interesting to recall that Hopi children reared on cradleboards walked as soon as did Hopi children reared with the free use of their arms and legs. Tying of the arms and legs to the cradleboard inhibits movement almost completely during the waking hours. Dennis & Dennis (1940) found that the distributions of ages of walking for the cradleboard-reared Hopi children and those allowed free movement could be super-imposed, one on the other. The average age for both conditions of rearing was about 15 months. Consider, in this same connection, the finding by Dennis (1960) that 60% of the Teheran-orphanage children are not yet sitting up alone at two years of age and that 85% are not walking at four years of age. The children in this orphanage have free use of their arms and legs, but the variety of visual and auditory inputs encountered is highly restricted. Note too that those Hopi children reared on cradle-boards were often carried about on their mothers' backs. Thus, while their arms and legs might be restricted, their eyes and ears could feast upon a rich variety of inputs. From such considerations and from the evidence assembled by Fiske & Maddi (1961), it would appear that variations in the circumstances with which an infant has informational interaction is an exceedingly important determiner of his rate of early development and of his achieving his genotypic potential in ability.

Still another line of suggestive evidence comes from the work of O. K. Moore. This concerns what he calls "responsive environ-ments." In teaching nursery-school children to read, he has them strike the keys of an electric typewriter so arranged that, as each key is struck, the child sees the letter struck and hears the name of the letter. Nursey-school children are introduced to the apparatus by a child who explains that "we take turns." Each day a child is asked if he wishes his turn. Given this opportunity, each child nearly always does. After a period of free exploration of the keyboard, the speaker in the apparatus can be used to tell the child what letter to strike. By keeping all keys but the named one fixed, the child can gradually be taught the keyboard. By means of further programmed changes in the experience, children can fairly rapidly be led to the point where they are typing from dictation. While this program concerns reading, it minimizes the motor side and is based on visual and auditory responses from the typing on the apparatus. When children with several months of such experience are provided with a blackboard, Moore reports that after noting that some of their marks resemble the letters they have learned on the typewriter, they quickly explore making all those letters with chalk. Moreover, the motor dexterity and the control of these four-and five-year-olds, as it appears in their writing, has been judged by experts to be like that typical of seven-and eight-year-olds (Moore, personal communication). Such observations suggest that motor control may be less a matter of educating the child's muscles than it is of his having clear images of what he is trying to make with his hands. On the basis of such evidence, perhaps Montessori's pedagogical emphasis on "sensory learning," based as it was on careful clinical observation of the learning of mentally retarded children was closer to reality than the theories of those who held such emphasis in contempt. Her theoretical attribution of the effects of "sensory learning" to increased power of a discriminative faculty may have been logically circular, but it was no more wrong than the emphasis on the response side.

In view of the various lines of recent evidence that I have been synopsizing, Montessori's pedagogy appears to fall into step with what may well be a new *Zeitgeist*. Moreover developments in technology are putting a new premium on the ability to solve problems in linguistic and mathematical terms. Those lacking these skills are finding less and less opportunity to participate in the culture, even to the degree that they can make a living. Futhermore, those children born to parents without these skills suffer that cultural deprivation associated with poverty and slums which makes them retarded in the underlying capacities required to succeed in the public schools. It would appear from the evidence cited that enrichment of preschool experience would be a promising antidote to such cultural deprivation. Montessori's Houses of Children in the San Lorenzo district of Rome supply an apt model with which to start. Thus, these changing beliefs about child development and the problem of coping with cultural deprivation in a culture where technology is playing an increasingly important role are reasons sufficient for revisiting Montessori's approach to child pedagogy.

WORDS OF CAUTION

On the other hand, there are dangers in revisiting Montessori's approach. While her practice is no longer out of step with the conceptions emerging from recent evidence, her theory was never the kind that supplies a good guide to the observation and investigation required to settle the various issues that are still highly problematical. Those who turn to Montessori's approach to pedagogy should simultaneously examine the changes in the conception of psychological development now being formulated. One hopes that these changes are more than another one of those swings in the pendulum of opinion that have so commonly characterized our notions of education and child-rearing. But, like the new conceptions of half a century ago, these of today may be wrong in substantial part, and it is highly important to confront them with evidence that will correct them.

In revisiting Montessori's pedagogical practice, there may be the danger of developing a cult which will restrict innovation and evaluation. Let me be concrete. Interesting and valuable as the didactic apparatus assembled and invented by Montessori is, there should be nothing sacrosanct about it. What has become the standard assembly of didactic materials may be too rich for a start with children who

are severely deprived culturally. This may be true even though the children in the original San Lorenzo houses were indeed culturally deprived. From conversations with teachers, I have gathered that some of these culturally deprived children become uncontrollably excited when confronted with this standard assembly. These children remind one of the cage-reared dogs of Thompson & Heron (1954) when they are first released from their cages into a laboratory room filled with objects. On the other hand, with children of upper-middle-class families, the standard assembly may already be "old stuff." Of the same order is the dissatisfaction with kindergarten commonly shown by children who have already been in nursery school for a year or two (see Simmons, 1960). This dissatisfaction can be attributed to boredom. It may be seen as a consequence of too little variation in the match between the circumstances available to such children and the information and skills they have already assimilated (see Hunt, 1961, 1963a). Children of the middle class who have encountered a rich variety of situations and things become "I-do-myself-ers" very early. They may become avidly interested, even at only three years of age, in learning to read, to write, to count, and to experience quantity in its various aspects. Unless someone is making approval and affection contingent upon a child's show of such interest, no one need fear for over-stimulation. Gratifying their interest in acquiring such skills can be a source of exhilaration. Gratifying their interest in reading may be facilitated by means of new kinds of didactic apparatus. Electronics make feasible what O. K. Moore calls "responsive environments." These were outside the ken of Montessori. Even now no one can anticipate their full pedagogical potential. The point is that the standard assembly should be viewed only as a starting point, and those revisiting Montessori should imitate her resourcefulness in inventing pedagogical apparatus and in adapting it to the use of individual children.

There may be another aspect to this danger of cultishness. This is the danger of standardizing the ways in which each child is supposed to utilize the various didactic materials. In response to my recommendation that Montessori's pedagogy be reexamined, various people have complained about Montessori teachers who insist that each child must pass through each of a set of prescribed steps of work with each kind of material. Such insistence obviously misses the meaning of what I call the "problem of the match" and ruins the practical solution of it that Jan Smedslund found in Montessori pedagogy. It loses the basic advantage of breaking the lock-step of having all children doing the same thing at the same time by demanding that all children do the same series of things with each kind of didactic material. Either way, the basic pedagogical implication of individual differences is missed, and children lose the growth-fostering pleasure of following their own predilections in their informational interaction with the environment.

In revisiting Montessori's pedagogy, there may also be dangers of underemphasis, first, on the role and importance of interpersonal relationships, and, second, on the importance of the affective and aesthetic aspects of life concerned with art and music. In recent years, emphasis on social and emotional adjustment has tended to over-stress social and affective matters at the expense of cognitive development, but this does not justify an over-correction and neglect of these matters. Even though the traditional three "R"'s are important channels for the enrichment of a child's future informational interaction with the environment, and even though learning them is fun under proper circumstances, they are not all of life. Montessori teacher-training might well borrow some of the social and disciplinary skills so much emphasized recently in the education of nursery-school teachers. Moreover, Montessori schools might well increase the variety of sensory materials; they might well supply opportunities for children to encounter more in the way of art and music, to make music, and to learn musical technique.

Perhaps one of the most important things to be gained by revisiting Montessori's pedagogy is her willingness and ability to observe children working with the didactic apparatus, and from observation to invent, on the spot, modifications of the situation that will foster a child's psychological development. She referred to this variously as "scientific peda-

gogy," as "pedagogical anthropology," and even as "experimental psychology." When she considered Itard's work with the "wild boy of Aveyron" as "practically the first of attempts at experimental psychology" (Montessori, 1909), however, she confused experimentation with clinical observation, as indicated by the fact that she notes further, that "Itard was perhaps the first educator to practice the observation of the pupil in the way in which the sick are observed in hospitals" (1909)). Careful clinical observation is needed in pedagogy, but it is not easy to teach this to teachers. Those who have attempted to do so have commonly fallen back upon metaphors and similes for their communication. I would now guess that the cutting edge of psychological development resides chiefly in the individual's attention and intention or plan. If a teacher can discern what a child is trying to do in his informational interaction with the environment, and if that teacher can have on hand materials relevant to that intention, if he can impose a relevant challenge with which the child can cope, supply a relevant model for imitation, or pose a relevant question that the child can answer, that teacher can call forth the kind of accommodative change that constitutes psychological development or growth. This sort of thing was apparently the genius of Maria Montessori.

Another of the most important things to be gained from revisiting Montessori's pedagogy is a scheme of preschool education nicely adapted by its origins to contribute toward the solution of one of the major educational challenges of our day. Children from the homes of many parents of the lower class come to the first grade, and even to kindergarten, unprepared to profit from regular school experience. In the light of the evidence which has become available largely since World War II, we can no longer rest upon the assumption that their lack of preparation is predetermined by the genes received from their parents of lower-class status. Regular schooling, moreover, may come too late. We must try to help these children overcome their handicap by enriching their experience during their preschool years. Montessori has provided a model. According to the impressionistic reports of observers, her "Houses of Children" worked quite well. We can well emulate Montessori's model, but we should not stop with it. Moreover, in the future those who become concerned with the question of the effectiveness of Montessori's model, and of revisions to come, should have more than the impressionistic reports of observers to go on. They should have demonstrations employing the experimental method and the best techniques available for educational and psychological assessment.

Chapter II

CHILDREN AND ADOLESCENTS

From earliest times of recorded history, all societies have confronted the problem of what to do with their young. From Herodotus, reportedly the first historian, down through the ages each society has had its share of prophets, soothsayers, advice givers, and pressure groups—all in on the art of child-rearing practices. Each new generation or each society has had its own analogue to the present day child psychologist. It is impossible to document the beginning. As Friendenberg wryly notes, "When Adam and Eve had Cain they did not have Gesell" (or Spock)! So society's development of ideas and concepts toward child-rearing, the nature of childhood, and (more recently) adolescence obviously started some time after that.

By the natural laws of physiological and biological development, the species homo sapiens has the longest period of dependence of all animals because the human neonate is so primitive instinctually. Although eventually he passes all other species in achieving a sophisticated developmental repertoire, he starts from a position of extreme and continuing dependency. This dependency exposes children to external control while it also creates the demand that society "invent" ways to respond to these dependent needs. The word "invent" is deliberate in view of the widely disparate methods that societies have used over the course of history, and it underscores the artificial nature of these "inventions." Also it is not an overstatement to say that most adults have relatively little understanding of the basic nature of children and adolescents. The result is that perhaps all too often child-rearing becomes in fact training with a capital "T." The training systems themselves may indeed come primarily from adult needs. For example, adults may like it better when children are "seen and not heard," for life may be more peaceful under such conditions of domestic tranquility with fewer interruptions and more time to read the paper after a tiring day at the office! Even the idea that the natural parents have prime responsibility for raising children is not stable across cultures. There is wide cultural variation in who actually raises children. The practice may be specific to the culture and thus "culture-bound." For example, in Russia children as early as age two may spend the entire day in school. In the Israeli kibbutzim, children are raised in communes, and in some few "traditional" English homes, the aristocratic children are still raised by a "nanny." We cite these few examples (there are many others) as reminders of variation but more importantly as indicators that child-rearing practices may be in fact based on adult wishes and desires, not on the real needs of the child. "After all," the adult can say, "he's too little to know what he wants."

Unfortunately, all too frequently, as we have suggested in the above, child-rearing practices, including the deliberate education of the child, is based solely or predominately on adult needs and adult values. We either can't or don't want to remember what children are really like. .

In part we all suffer from a selective memory, and it is impossible for adults to remember the "way it really was" to be a child. For one thing so much experience in childhood is emotional, or composed of affective feeling states, that we can't really recall how it felt then. Another reason comes from a basic human tendency to repress and forget the painful events of the past, or at worst to remember only bits and pieces. The more upsetting were these early experiences in childhood and adolescence the more we repress and "forget." Since we can't remember, we all too often fall into a trap of accepting ideas about children and adolescents that are fictions or myths, not based on the reality of how children perceive the world. An example of such myths would be the view that a child is simply a miniature version of an adult, an homonculus (a little man inside the body of a child). This view may lead us to severely reprimand the child whenever there is any indication of immaturity. Another common adult assumption is that children don't really want to "grow up," or, (in educational circles) that children don't really want to "learn." Such assumptions obviously carry with them a whole series of unfortunate and wrong-headed ideas that we must *force* children to learn, *make* them pay attention, *demand* that they listen, mark, and "inwardly digest" what we have to tell them. We would ask the reader to review in his own mind how many times he has heard teachers, parents, or educators (for that matter) talk about children as if they were, or should be, small-sized adults!

With the rise of industrialization, modern societies have created more problems than just those of children. As our society has lengthened the time between preparation for and implementation of a career, we have created a great "marginal state" called adolescence. There is probably no aspect of human development that generates as much controversy today as does adolescent development. While on the one hand it is perfectly obvious that many changes are taking place, it does not follow that we know the best way to respond to these changes. In fact one educator reportedly quipped, "Working with adolescents as a teacher or a counselor is like trying to give someone artificial respiration while he's still thrashing around in the lake." It seems difficult to discern appropriate programs for teaching and learning when adolescents seem to be floundering around so much just on their own while maintaining a strong affinity toward independence. The familiar cry, "Please let me do it myself," is typically the adolescents' plea.

If adults find it difficult to understand and remember what children are like, they find it impossible to comprehend adolescents. The adolescent turmoil, their fads in dress and appearance, their mercurial emotions, their inconsistencies, their "causes" and crusades—in short their ever changing extremisms—are so often just too much for adults to tolerate. If we remember, however, that adolescents exist by definition in a twilight zone or no man's land somewhere between the world of children and the world of adults we may begin to sense why adolescence as a stage is hardly a "golden age." Their physical changes are enormous—witness, for example, the differences between girls and boys in junior high school in terms of maturation. The boys in the seventh and eighth grade look as if they would be more comfortable in the elementary school. The girls look more like high school students. The gap couldn't be wider.

The rapid change in body size also carries with it implications for the adolescent's self concept, that is, how he views himself. An adolescent boy with pimples on his face, only a few hairs to shave and a voice that always "cracks" at the wrong time, has a difficult time maintaining a sense of self assurance and confidence. This all leaves the adolescent particularly sensitive to peer group pressures. To do what the group says, to dress the way the group does, to wear one's hair in accord with dictates of the group are all ironic indicators of the lack of individuality and absence of inner or self direction so common in adolescence. It is ironic because simultaneous with such "conformity," an adolescent may lecture an adult on the virtues and values of individual self expression! It may help if adults realize that the "groupiness" and the "cliques" really serve as a protective coating for the excessive self-consciousness of all adolescents—a self-concern that accompanies a period of change. The adolescents are in the process of reformulating an identity as to who they are as people—not children and obviously not adults.

The reformulation of a sense of personal identity during the course of adolescence thus is not a smooth path upon which to trod. We have suggested that much of the difficulty derives from the change in psychological and physiological status during this period. Also it should be noted that the adult ambivalence toward adolescents further heightens the problems of this period. Adult society is not at all clear in its response to the adolescence stage of development. For example, our laws are extremely inconsistent so that the legal status of young people remains ambiguous. A young man may be old enough to die for his country but not old enough to vote. In some states he can "drink" legally at one age but when he crosses the state line it becomes suddenly illegal. If we trained rats in a maze with such inconsistency they'd never learn even the T maze!

It is small wonder then that human beings in a period both of identity reformulation and inconsistent treatment occasionally respond with visible and stormy outbursts against society.

The stage also involves a new and different recognition of the opposite sex with all that follows in self concern and acceptability as a "date." But perhaps most apparent is the beginning of the changing relationship between a teenager and his parents. It's almost as if all at once the teenager suddenly finds out that adults are neither omnipotent nor perfect. Disillusionment follows quickly, for it's like finding out that a personal ideal or hero is only a statue with clay feet. Here are the seeds for the well known rebellion against adult authority. The teenager's father who was seen in the past as a successful businessman is now a "petty bourgeois." The reactions are extreme. Adolescents who find out there are *some* adults they can't trust, generalize to "You can't trust *anyone* over thirty." The helpful mother of the past may now be regarded by the teenage daughter as hopelessly old fashioned in everything—still living in the Stone Age— a faded relic of yesteryear!

These are a few of the elements that create within many adults the view that adolescents (as Churchill said of Russia) remain a mystery wrapped in an enigma. This view also carries with it adult feelings of anger, despair, and upset.

In this chapter we will present readings that point up the developmental stage nature of the pupils as children and adolescents. The problem for educational programs in general and for teachers in specific has been and will always be to view and understand the nature of children and adolescents on their own terms and not on our terms as adults. With this as a starting point, relevant school programs guided by genuinely understanding adults can reach out to both children and adolescents.

AN OVERVIEW OF THE READINGS FOR THIS CHAPTER

The first selection (7) is a classic article by Ruth Benedict on cultural conditioning. By comparing and contrasting our culture with more so-called primitive cultures, she illustrates a very important point—the extent to which primitive society allows growth and development of children to proceed smoothly in a step by step manner versus our culture which abruptly confronts children with change and discontinuity. The culture itself defines the means of transition.

Miss Benedict selects three aspects of human development to illustrate her thesis—a thesis in contrast—continuous development in primitive societies and discontinuous development in our own. The three dimensions she picks are (1) *Responsible vs Non-Responsible Role,* (2) *Dominance vs Submission* and (3) *Sex Role.* She shows how in the first dimension we carefully distinguish between a child's play and an adult's work while in primitive societies the child is carefully conditioned through a succession of tasks toward responsible social participation. Her other two examples help to make the point that much clearer. Her basic question to our society and culture, of course, is the extent to which we neither provide for continuous conditioning of cultural expectations nor provide ways to minimize the strain of discontinuous expectations. It is as if our society has chosen the worst of both worlds for its children and adolescents. She even suggests that much adult personality maladjustment results from our society's failure to develop institutions to adequately support individuals as they progress from stage to stage. Although she doesn't mention this directly it certainly might be most relevant to view the school, at least potentially, as such an institution of society.

In the second article (Selection 8), famed child psychologist L. K. Frank specifically instructs us to revise our traditional views about child-rearing. He seeks a complete reversal from a society that uses children for society's misconceived purposes to a position in which the child's own needs should be the primary determinants. The process of child growth is uneven, halting, elliptical, and filled with temporary regressions. He shows how adults may handle transitions and changes, almost as if he were answering the questions Benedict raised in the previous article. He notes changes as far ranging as from weaning and toilet training to learning to handle fear and grief. His main point is that the way the adult responds to these changes teaches the child not only at the moment but also in the long run. With support, encouragement, and unflagging effort, the adult *lends* the child enough strength so the child can move toward maturity, self control, and self direction. Also, as Frank makes clear, children have an inborn tendency to grow and become self sustaining adults. Whether or not they make it is directly dependent on how much support and encouragement adults have conveyed to the growing child.

The L. K. Frank position concerning the fundamental needs of children provides us with a picture of children and adolescents developing at individually determined rates. It is important to underscore the difference between this view and the rigid picture of child development portrayed in the 1930s and 40s by Gesell. In his Institute for the study of child development Gesell derived a series of year-specific definitions of what (for example) all five year olders are like. The specification of a relatively rigid set of age norms meant that the children in this country were constantly compared to the average on the Gesell growth charts by anxious parents. Both the uneven, halting process of growth and the wide range of individual differences were seriously compromised by such specific age-norms. Dr. Frank on the other hand presents a significantly different understanding of each child's fundamental needs as he emerges from dependence to independence.

The third article (Selection 9), Lawrence Kohlberg's *Sequence in the*

Development of Moral Thought, represents an important aspect of child and adolescent development long neglected. In the late 1920's Hartshorne and May demonstrated, to the shock and amazement of many, that moral conduct was relative. Cheating, for example, was normally distributed in children and adolescents—that is, most will cheat in certain circumstances. The early Hartshorne and May experiments were as simple as they were revealing. For example, pupils would be given a paper containing a series of blank circles. Then the children would be asked to close their eyes and write numbers within the circles. If the investigator then left the room, the children would apparently perform remarkable feats of accuracy. They concluded that moral conduct was highly specific to the situation (rather than to an internal set of reliable controls). Their results indicated that activities like cheating would depend on circumstances such as the risk of detection, the effort required to cheat, peer group approval, and examples set by others. Hartshorne and May, then, made us realize that simplistic notions about morality were irrelevant. Other more recent studies have shown for example that there is no relation between a trait such as honesty and Sunday School attendance, Boy Scout membership, special education classes designed to teach morality, or child rearing practices designed to build good "habits."

These findings began to question whether there was any such thing as moral judgment or moral conduct at all! Such questions created the stage for Kohlberg's work. His highly original approach indicates that all children pass through a specific set of stages of moral development—that moral development like cognitive development proceeds according to a sequence. Kohlberg presents six stages of moral development which describe the sequence. This means that moral judgment is determined developmentally and not by specific teaching or direct learning. Factors such as age, degree of social experience, and cognitive growth determine judgment, and thus it isn't until relatively late in adolescence that large groups of moral concepts and attitudes acquire meaning. This would indicate that it may be most important to teach adults what stage of moral development a child or an adolescent is presently occupying, rather than continue with empty prescriptions about what to do with today's youth! We have included as an addendum to the Kohlberg article, the moral judgment situations (the "Dilemmas") as well as the schema of developmental types.

The last three articles in this chapter all focus exclusively on the adolescent problem. Anna Freud's article (Selection 10), titled simply "Adolescence," describes this stage of development in terms of psychoanalytic psychology. She makes a series of important points; first, that adolescent upset is inevitable. In fact, the lack of upset indicates a delay in normal development. The reason for this in dynamic terms is that with puberty comes a surge of instinctual energy ("id" forces), which is too strong for the rational part of the personality (the "ego") to contain. Since upset then is both inevitable and indeed desirable, Anna Freud then describes the "defenses" that are most common to adolescence—displacement, reversal, withdrawal, regression. With this in mind much of adolescent behavior becomes understandable as a "symptom" of internal changes. As she notes at the end in a classic statement, it may be the parents who need help to bear through adolescence. "There are few situations in life which are more difficult to cope with than an adolescent son or daughter during the attempt to liberate themselves."

If adolescent upset is inevitable, Edgar Friendenberg's article (Selection 11) makes clear his view that we have responded to adolescents the wrong way. We have emphasized accomodation and adjustment as if adults want adolescents to be ingratiating, innocuous, and conforming. He particularly singles out schools for the part they play in emphasizing conformity and obedience. His central thesis is stark. Authentic self-definition (the process through which one becomes a person in his own right) occurs only through conflict and confrontation. Without this process of conflict an adolescent cannot become a genuine full-fledged adult, instead he becomes bland, conventional, a junior version of the men in grey' flannel suits.* Friendenberg challenges schools and school men to stop manipulating students for adult convenience since the present circumstance promotes unhealthy reactions—either an apathetic "fawning acceptance of authority" or the other extreme toward organized delinquency. Each he sees as understandable but dangerous expedients.

One note of caution to the reader concerning the above selection. It may seem at first glance that Friendenberg's views are diametrically opposed to those of Benedict. A careful reading is necessary to discern the common elements. Benedict is not suggesting that we eliminate conflict or discontinuities. She is proposing that if a society does contain such conflicts then it is necessary to take specific measures to promote successful resolution of the conflict. Similarly, Friendenberg notes that we do not genuinely support adolescents as they struggle towards manhood and womanhood. Instead, we, with the best of intentions, try to smooth and ease the transition. This way we may end up by eliminating both the support they need and the genuine success they also need.

The concluding article (Selection 12) in this chapter brings specific focus to adolescents in secondary school. James Coleman reports on his study of attitudes toward school, values of adolescents, and the influence of the peer group. His results give us major cause for concern because he infers from his data the existence of a monolithic and rather monstrous subculture. Adolescents, he avers, form themselves into a separate group, almost as if they form a separate society with their own norms and values that are imposed rather mercilessly on all members. He finds the dominance of

---

* This is a somewhat dated analogy, but in the 50s the prototype of the conforming, organizational yes-man was the man in the grey flannel suit!

the natural leaders—"school elites" who positively value athletics and externals such as good looks and clothes. At the same time these school pace-setters devalue learning and scholarship. Thus the adolescent society creates a school atmosphere or classroom climate opposed to learning. Coleman then suggests that the anti-intellectual school atmosphere can be revised if we examine carefully the difference between competition and cooperation. His ideas for a productive academic atmosphere in schools are well worthy of attention.

His major criticism is that academic competition sets students against one another. This means that pupils perceive grades as measures of invidious personal comparison. For one pupil to receive a good mark is seen as an achievement at the expense of others, and although Coleman doesn't mention it specifically, it is a well known phenomenon that some students who do well academically in high school keep very quiet about the grades they receive. What may appear as false modesty on the part of such students may indeed signify a deeper concern. The fact that Coleman found that social acceptance ranked as more important than "learning" in the wealthy suburban school in his sample was a case in point.

Especially for adolescents, then, we need to reconsider the role of the secondary school. Coleman's data indicates quite clearly that the energies of adolescents are not directed toward studies, toward ideas, nor toward learning. The school as an agent of significant effect is rather questionable. There are significant effects but such effects are not derived from the teachers or from the academic subjects studied. Instead the school climate seems governed by the teenage cliques, so that the secondary school has exchanged its learning climate for a social climate dominated by teenage values. The school as a potent institution then becomes compromised amid the flurry of pep rallies, football games, or dress styles. Such forces not only compete for attention, interest and energy, but do so with an unnerving success. Perhaps the most damaging assertion is that the adolescent society is basically a mirror image of the adult society. The adolescent subculture that values the superficial, that is so concerned over status and social acceptability, does not too greatly distort the image— these dimensions perhaps too often are just as important in the adult world as well. This would indicate that before we leap to any conclusion as to how "bad" teenagers are, we may be well served by examining perhaps more closely than before our own adult values. We transmit these values to teenagers not so much by what we say but rather by what we do.

7. CONTINUITIES AND DISCONTINUITIES IN CULTURAL CONDITIONING

RUTH BENEDICT

All cultures must deal in one way or another with the cycle of growth from infancy to adulthood.

Nature has posed the situation dramatically: on the one hand, the new born baby, physiologically vulnerable, unable to fend for itself, or to participate of its own initiative in the life of the group, and, on the other, the adult man or woman. Every man who rounds out his human potentialities must have been a son first and a father later and the two roles are physiologically in great contrast; he must first have been dependent upon others for his very existence and later he must provide such security for others. This discontinuity in the life cycle is a fact of nature and is inescapable. Facts of nature, however, in any discussion of human problems, are ordinarily read off not at their bare minimal but surrounded by all the local accretions of behavior to which the student of human affairs has become accustomed in his own culture. For that reason it is illuminating to examine comparative material from other societies in order to get a wider perspective on our own special accretions. The anthropologist's role is not to question the facts of nature, but to insist upon the interposition of a middle term between "nature" and "human behavior"; his role is to analyse that term, to document local man-made doctorings of nature and to insist that these doctorings should not be read off in any one culture as nature itself. Although it is a fact of nature that the child becomes a man, the way in which this transition is affected varies from one society to an-

other, and no one of these particular cultural bridges should be regarded as the "natural" path to maturity.

From a comparative point of view our culture goes to great extremes in emphasizing contrasts between the child and the adult. The child is sexless, the adult estimates his virility by his sexual activities; the child must be protected from the ugly facts of life, the adult must meet them without psychic catastrophe; the child must obey, the adult must command this obedience. These are all dogmas of our culture, dogmas which, in spite of the facts of nature; other cultures commonly do not share. In spite of the physiological contrasts between child and adult these are cultural accretions.

It will make the point clearer if we consider one habit in our own culture in regard to which there is not this discontinuity of conditioning. With the greatest clarity of purpose and economy of training, we achieve our goal of conditioning everyone to eat three meals a day. The baby's training in regular food periods begins at birth and no crying of the child and no inconvenience to the mother is allowed to interfere. We gauge the child's physiological make-up and at first allow it food oftener than adults, but, because our goal is firmly set and our training consistent, before the child is two years old it has achieved the adult schedule. From the point of view of other cultures this is as startling as the fact of three-year-old babies perfectly at home in deep water is to us. Modesty is another sphere in which our child training is consistent and economical; we waste no time in clothing the baby and, in contrast to many societies where the child runs naked till it is ceremonially

* Benedict, Ruth, "Continuities and Discontinuities in Cultural Conditioning," *Psychiatry*, 1938, *1*, 161-167. Reprinted by special permission of The William Alanson White Psychiatric Foundation, Inc.

given its skirt or its public sheath at adolescence, the child's training fits it precisely for adult conventions.

In neither of these aspects of behavior is there need for an individual in our culture to embark before puberty, at puberty or at some later date upon a course of action which all his previous training has tabued. He is spared the unsureness inevitable in such a transition.

The illustration I have chosen may appear trivial, but in larger and more important aspects of behavior, our methods are obviously different. Because of the great variety of child training in different families in our society, I might illustrate continuity of conditioning from individual life histories in our culture, but even these, from a comparative point of view, stop far short of consistency and I shall therefore confine myself to describing arrangements in other cultures in which training, which with us is idiosyncratic, is accepted and traditional and does not therefore involve the same possibility of conflict. I shall choose childhood rather than infant and nursing situations not because the latter do not vary strikingly in different cultures but because they are nevertheless more circumscribed by the baby's physiological needs than is its later training. Childhood situations provide an excellent field in which to illustrate the range of cultural adjustments which are possible within a universally given, but not so drastic, set of physiological facts.

The major discontinuity in the life cycle is of course that the child who is at one point a son must later be a father. These roles in our society are strongly differentiated; a good son is tractable, and does not assume adult responsibilities; a good father provides for his children and should not allow his authority to be flouted. In addition the child must be sexless so far as his family is concerned, whereas the father's sexual role is primary in the family. The individual in one role must revise his behavior from almost all points of view when he assumes the second role.

I shall select for discussion three such contrasts that occur in our culture between the individual's role as child and as father: 1. responsible—non-responsible status role, 2. dominance—submission, 3. contrasted sexual role. It is largely upon our cultural commitments to these three contrasts that the discontinuity in the life cycle of an individual in our culture depends.

1. RESPONSIBLE—NON-RESPONSIBLE STATUS ROLE

The techniques adopted by societies which achieve continuity during the life cycle in this sphere in no way differ from those we employ in our uniform conditioning to three meals a day. They are merely applied to other areas of life. We think of the child as wanting to play and the adult as having to work, but in many societies the mother takes the baby daily in her shawl or carrying net to the garden or to gather roots, and adult labor is seen even in infancy from the pleasant security of its position in close contact with its mother. When the child can run about it accompanies its parents still, doing tasks which are essential and yet suited to its powers, and this dichotomy between work and play is not different from that [which] its parents recognize, namely, the distinction between the busy day and the free evening. The tasks it is asked to perform are graded to its powers and its elders wait quietly by, not offering to do the task in the child's place. Everyone who is familiar with such societies has been struck by the contrast with our child training. Dr. Ruth Underhill tells me of sitting with a group of Papago elders in Arizona when the man of the house turned to his little three-year old granddaughter and asked her to close the door. The door was heavy and hard to shut. The child tried, but it did not move. Several times the grandfather repeated, "Yes, close the door." No one jumped to the child's assistance. No one took the responsibility away from her. On the other hand there was no impatience, for after all the child was small. They sat gravely waiting till the child succeeded and her grandfather gravely thanked her. It was assumed that the task would not be asked of her unless she could perform it, and having been asked the responsibility was hers alone just as if she were a grown woman.

The essential point of such child training is that the child is from infancy continuously conditioned to responsible social participation while at the same time the tasks that are expected of it are adapted to its capacity. The contrast with our society is very great. A child does not make any labor contribution to our industrial society except as it competes with an adult; its work is not measured against its own strength and skill but against high-geared industrial requirements. Even when we praise a child's achievement in the home we are outraged if such praise is interpreted as being of the same order as praise of adults. The child is praised because the parent feels well disposed, regardless of whether the task is well done by adult standards, and the child acquires no sensible standard by which to measure its achievement. The gravity of a Cheyenne Indian family ceremoniously making a feast out of the little boy's first snowbird is at the furthest remove from our behavior. At birth the little boy was presented with a toy bow, and from the time he could run about serviceable bows suited to his stature were specially made for him by the man of the family. Animals and birds were taught him in a graded series beginning with those most easily taken, and as he brought in his first of each species his family duly made a feast of it, accepting his contribution as gravely as the buffalo his father brought. When he finally killed a buffalo, it was only the final step of his childhood conditioning, not a new adult role with which his childhood experience had been at variance.

The Canadian Ojibwa show clearly what results can be achieved. This tribe gains its livelihood by winter trapping and the small family of father, mother and children live during the long winter alone on their great frozen hunting grounds. The boy accompanies his father and brings in his catch to his sister as his father does to his mother; the girl prepares the meat and skins for him just as his mother does for her husband. By the time the boy is 12, he may have set his own line of traps on a hunting territory of his own and return to his parent's house only one in several months—still bringing the meat and skins to his sister. The young child is taught consistently that it has only itself to rely upon in life, and this is as true in the dealings it will have with the supernatural as in the business of getting a livelihood. This attitude

he will accept as a successful adult just as he accepted it as a child.[1]

2. DOMINANCE—SUBMISSION

Dominance-submission is the most striking of those categories of behavior where like does not respond to like but where one type of behavior stimulates the opposite response. It is one of the most prominent ways in which behavior is patterned in our culture. When it obtains between classes, it may be nourished by continuous experience; the difficulty in its use between children and adults lies in that an individual conditioned to one set of behavior in childhood must adopt the opposite as an adult. Its opposite is a pattern of approximately identical reciprocal behavior, and societies which rely upon continuous conditioning characteristically invoke this pattern. In some primitive cultures the very terminology of address between father and son, and more commonly, between grandchild and grandson or uncle and nephew, reflects this attitude. In such kinship terminologies one reciprocal expresses each of these relationships so that son and father, for instance, exchange the same term with one another, just as we exchange the same term with a cousin. The child later will exchange it with his son. "Father—son," therefore, is a continuous relationship he enjoys throughout life. The same continuity, backed up by verbal reciprocity, occurs far oftener in the grandchild-grandson relationship or that of mother's brother-sister's son. When these are "joking" relationships, as they often are, travellers report wonderingly upon the liberties and pretensions of tiny toddlers in their dealings with these family elders. In place of our dogma of respect to elders such societies employ in these cases a reciprocity as nearly identical as may be. The teasing and practical joking the grandfather visits upon his grandchild, the grandchild returns in like coin; he would be led to believe that he failed in propriety if he did not give like for like. If the sister's son has right of access without leave to his mother's brother's possessions, the mother's brother has such rights also to the child's possessions

[1] Landes, Ruth, *The Ojibwa Woman*, Part 1 Youth—Columbia University Contributions to Anthropology, Volume XXXI.

They share reciprocal privileges and obligations which in our society can develop only between age mates.

From the point of view of our present discussion, such kinship conventions allow the child to put in practice from infancy the same forms of behavior which it will rely upon as an adult; behavior is not polarized into a general requirement of submission for the child and dominance for the adult.

It is clear from the techniques described above by which the child is conditioned to a responsible status role that these depend chiefly upon arousing in the child the desire to share responsibility in adult life. To achieve this little stress is laid upon obedience but much stress upon approval and praise. Punishment is very commonly regarded as quite outside the realm of possibility, and natives in many parts of the world have drawn the conclusion from our usual disciplinary methods that white parents do not love their children. If the child is not required to be submissive, however, many occasions for punishment melt away; a variety of situations which call for it do not occur. Many American Indian tribes are especially explicit in rejecting the ideal of a child's submissive or obedient behavior. Prince Maximilian von Wied who visited the Crow Indians over a hundred years ago describes a father's boasting about his young son's intractibility even when it was the father himself who was flouted; "He will be a man," his father said. He would have been baffled at the idea that his child should show behavior which would obviously make him appear a poor creature in the eyes of his fellows if he used it as an adult. Dr. George Devereaux tells me of a special case of such an attitude among the Mohave at the present time. The child's mother was white and protested to its father that he must take action when the child disobeyed and struck him. "But why?" the father said, "he is little. He cannot possibly injure me." He did not know of any dichotomy according to which an adult expects obedience and a child must accord it. If his child had been docile he would simply have judged that it would become a docile adult—an eventuality of which he would not have approved.

Child training which brings about the same result is common also in other areas of life than that of reciprocal kinship obligations between child and adult. There is a tendency in our culture to regard every situation as having in it the seeds of a dominance-submission relationship. Even where dominance-submission is patently irrelevant we read in the dichotomy, assuming that in every situation there must be one person dominating another. On the other hand some cultures, even when the situation calls for leadership, do not see it in terms of dominance-submission. To do justice to this attitude it would be necessary to describe their political and especially their economic arrangements, for such an attitude to persist must certainly be supported by economic mechanisms that are congruent with it. But it must also be supported by—or what comes to the same thing, express itself in—child training and familial situations.

Continuity of conditioning in training the child to assume responsibility and to behave no more submissively than adults is quite possible in terms of the child's physiological endowment if his participation is suited to his strength. Because of the late development of the child's reproductive organs continuity of conditioning in sex experience presents a difficult problem. So far as their belief that the child is anything but a sexless being is concerned, they are probably more nearly right than we are with an opposite dogma. But the great break is presented by the universally sterile unions before puberty and the presumably fertile ones after maturation. This physiological fact no amount of cultural manipulation can minimize or alter, and societies therefore which stress continuous conditioning most strongly sometimes do not expect children to be interested in sex experience until they have matured physically. This is striking among American Indian tribes like the Dakota; adults observe great privacy in sex acts and in no way stimulate children's sexual activity. There need be no discontinuity, in the sense in which I have used the term, in such a program if the child is taught nothing it does not have to unlearn later. In such cultures adults view children's experimentation as in no way wicked or dangerous but merely as innocuous play which can have no serious consequences. In some societies such play is minimal and the children manifest little interest in it. But the same attitude may be taken by adults in societies where such play is encouraged and forms a major activity among small children. This is true among most of the Melanesian cultures of Southeast New Guinea; adults go as far as to laugh off sexual affairs within the prohibited class if the children are not mature, saying that since they cannot marry there can be no harm done.

It is this physiological fact of the difference between children's sterile unions and adults' presumably fertile sex relations which must be kept in mind in order to understand the different mores which almost always govern sex expression in children and in adults in the same culture. A great many cultures with preadolescent sexual license require marital fidelity and a great many which value premarital virginity in either male or female arrange their marital life with great license. Continuity in sex experience is complicated by factors which it was unnecessary to consider in the problems previously discussed. The essential problem is not whether or not the child's sexuality is consistently exploited— for even where such exploitation is favored in the majority of cases the child must seriously modify his behavior at puberty or at marriage. Continuity in sex expression means rather that the child is taught nothing it must unlearn later. If the cultural emphasis is upon sexual pleasure the child who is continuously conditioned will be encouraged to experiment freely and pleasurably, as among the Marquesans; [2] if emphasis is upon reproduction, as among the Zuni of New Mexico, childish sex proclivities will not be exploited, for the only important use which sex is thought to serve in his culture is not yet possible to him. The important contrast with our child training is that although a Zuni child is impressed with the wickedness of premature sex experimentation he does not run the risk as in our culture of associating this wickedness with sex itself rather than with sex at his age. The adult in our culture has often failed to unlearn the wickedness of the dangerousness of sex, a lesson which was impressed upon him strongly in his most formative years.

DISCONTINUITY IN CONDITIONING

Even from this very summary statement of continuous conditioning the economy of such mores is evident. In spite of the obvious advantages, however, there are difficulties in its way. Many primitive societies expect as different behavior from an individual as child and as adult as we do, and such discontinuity involves a presumption of strain.

Many societies of this type however minimize strain by the techniques they employ, and some techniques are more successful than others in ensuring the individual's functioning without conflict. It is from this point of view that age-grade societies reveal their fundamental significance. Age-graded cultures characteristically demand different behavior of the individual at different times of his life and persons of a like age-grade are grouped into a society whose activities are all oriented toward the behavior desired at that age. Individuals "graduate" publicly and with honor from one of these groups to another. Where age society members are enjoined to loyalty and mutual support, and are drawn not only from the local group but from the whole tribe as among the Arapaho, or even from other tribes as among the Wagawaga of Southeast New Guinea, such an institution has many advantages in eliminating conflicts among local groups and fostering intra-tribal peace. This seems to be also a factor in the tribal military solidarity of the similarly organized Masai of East Africa. The point that is of chief interest for our present discussion, however, is that by this means an individual who at any time takes on a new set of duties and virtues is supported not only by a solid phalanx of age mates but by the traditional prestige of the organized "secret" society into which he has now graduated. Fortified in this way, individuals in such cultures often swing between remarkable extremes of opposite behavior without apparent psychic threat. For example, the great majority exhibit prideful and non-conflicted behavior at each stage in the life cycle even when a prime of life devoted to passionate and aggressive head hunting must be followed by a later life dedicated

[2] Ralph Linton, class notes on the Marquesans.

to ritual and to mild and peaceable civic virtues.[3]

Our chief interest here, however, is in discontinuity which primarily affects the child. In many primitive societies such discontinuity has been fostered not because of economic or political necessity or because such discontinuity provides for a socially valuable division of labor, but because of some conceptual dogma. The most striking of these are the Australian and Papuan cultures where the ceremony of the "Making of Man" flourishes. In such societies it is believed that men and women have opposite and conflicting powers, and male children, who are of undefined status, must be initiated into the male role. In Central Australia the boy child is of the woman's side and women are tabu in the final adult stages of tribal ritual. The elaborate and protracted initiation ceremonies of the Arunta therefore snatch the boy from the mother, dramatize his gradual repudiation of her. In a final ceremony he is reborn as a man out of the men's ceremonial "baby pouch." The men's ceremonies are ritual statements of a masculine solidarity, carried out by fondling one another's *churingas*, the material symbol of each man's life, and by letting out over one another blood drawn from their veins. After this warm bond among men has been established through the ceremonies, the boy joins the men in the men's house and participates in tribal rites.[4] The enjoined discontinuity has been tribally bridged.

West of the Fly River in southern New Guinea there is a striking development of this Making of Men cult which involves a childhood period of passive homosexuality. Among the Keraki [5] it is thought that no boy can grow to full stature without playing the role for some years. Men slightly older take the active role, and the older man is a jealous partner. The life cycle of the Keraki Indians includes, therefore, in succession, passive homosexuality, active homosexuality and heterosexuality. The Keraki believe that pregnancy will result from post-pubertal passive homosexuality and see evidences of such practices in any fat man whom, even as an old man, they may kill or drive out of the tribe because of their fear. The ceremony that is of interest in connection with the present discussion takes place at the end of the period of passive homosexuality. This ceremony consists in burning out the possibility of pregnancy from the boy by pouring lye down his throat, after which he has no further protection if he gives way to the practice. There is no technique for ending active homosexuality, but this is not explicitly tabu for older men; heterosexuality and children however are highly valued. Unlike the neighboring Marindanim who share their homosexual practices, Keraki husband and wife share the same house and work together in the gardens.

I have chosen illustrations of discontinuous conditioning where it is not too much to say that the cultural institutions furnish adequate support to the individual as he progresses from role to role or interdicts the previous behavior in a summary fashion. The contrast with arrangements in our culture is very striking, and against this background of social arrangements in other cultures the adolescent period of *Sturm und Drang* with which we are so familiar becomes intelligible in terms of our discontinuous cultural institutions and dogmas rather than in terms of physiological necessity. It is even more pertinent to consider these comparative facts in relation to maladjusted persons in our culture who are said to be fixated at one or another pre-adult level. It is clear that, if we were to look at our social arrangements as an outsider, we should infer directly from our family institutions and habits of child training that many individuals would not "put off childish things"; we should have to say that our adult activity demands traits that are interdicted in children, and that far from redoubling efforts to help children bridge this gap, adults in our culture put all the blame on the child when he fails to manifest spontaneously the new behavior or, overstepping the mark, manifests it with untoward belligerence. It is not surprising that in

[3] Henry Elkin, manuscript on the Arapaho.

[4] Spencer, B., and Gillen, F. J., *The Arunta;* N. Y., Macmillan, 1927 (2 vols.). Róheim, Géza, Psycho-Analysis of Primitive Cultural Types. *Internat. J. Psychoanal.* (1932) 13:1-224—in particular, Chapter III, on the Aranda, The Children of the Desert.

[5] Williams, Francis E., *Papuans of the Trans-Fly;* Oxford, 1936.

such a society many individuals fear to use behavior which has up to that time been under a ban and trust instead, though at great psychic cost, to attitudes that have been exercised with approval during their formative years. Insofar as we invoke a physiological scheme to account for these neurotic adjustments we are led to overlook the possibility of developing social institutions which would lessen the social cost we now pay; instead we elaborate a set of dogmas which prove inapplicable under other social conditions.

8. THE FUNDAMENTAL NEEDS OF THE CHILD *

L. K. FRANK

Every society and every generation uses children for its own purposes. It is significant that to-day we are beginning to speak of the needs of the child as entitled to consideration in his nurture and education or even as the controlling factor in child care. Contrast this emerging conception of the child's nature and needs with the practices all over the world, among so-called civilized people and so-called primitive people, in which the nurture and education of children are dictated by religious, ethical, and moral ideas, by political and economic requirements, by social class lines, indeed by an extraordinary variety of ideas and purposes all more or less remote from the child himself. The children in all these cultures are molded by the dominant ideas and beliefs and the group purposes into greater or less conformity in which they may sacrifice much or little.

Consider also the variety of practices in regard to the physical make-up or form of children. Among certain Indian tribes, the infant's head is flattened to a board. Among certain African tribes, the lips or ears may be stretched or the neck encased in coils of brass. Everyone is familiar with the ancient Chinese practice of binding the feet of female infants. As children grow older, many peoples have puberty rites involving tattooing, skin incisions, various forms of mutilation of the male

and female genitals, and the inculcation of rigidly prescribed motor patterns of action that may involve anatomical deformities. The catalogue of practices that deform, distort, or otherwise manipulate the physical structure is endless, but all are regarded by those who use them as essentially necessary to make over the child into the image prescribed by the culture as the only right form for a man or a woman. In their cultural context these practices and beliefs may be purposeful and valid.

Not only is the physical structure of the child made over into the patterns of the culture, but so are the physiological functions, as we see in the diverse standards imposed upon the young child by different societies. In the matter of nutrition, for example, every group teaches the child to like the food of its traditional choice, which means developing an appetite for an incredible array of foodstuffs, or supposed foodstuffs, and abhorring other foodstufls of equal or greater nutritive value. Many of these food choices represent a wise, economical use of available animal and vegetable resources, while others are obviously dictated by various beliefs in sympathetic magic, by rigid taboos, and by religious convictions that have little or no relation to the nutritional requirements of the growing child or even of the adult. Every society, again, imposes some kind of training upon children with respect to elimination. In some cultures the requirements are minimal, but in others they may be so severe and so

* Frank, L. K., "The Fundamental Needs of the Child," *Mental Hygiene*, 1938, *22*, pp. 353-379 (abridged).

rigorously imposed upon the very young child as to create lifelong impairment of physiological efficiency. Even breathing, in some cultures, is subject to special training, and sleeping patterns, peculiar to each group, are inculcated at an early age.

It is safe to say that most of these traditional patterns of child training and nurture derive from ideas and beliefs and strong convictions that have little or no relevance to the immediate needs of the child. Civilized man in many cases has survived *despite*, not because of, these methods of child care, as we are now beginning to realize in the light of recent investigation.

Curious as are these practices of physical and physiological training, the variety of practices in psychological training are even more astonishing, since here we find methods and procedures for bringing up children in the most fantastic, distorted patterns of conduct and feeling. The belief in using the child for social purposes is revealed here more convincingly than in the realm of physical care, where the organic limits of deformation impose some restraint; whereas in the area of conduct and belief there apparently are no limits to the grotesque, the cruel and brutal, the diabolical ingenuity of man in warping and twisting human nature to cultural patterns which originally may have been useful or even desirable, but which have become rigid and perverse.

When we reflect upon these various beliefs and practices that are imposed upon the child to make him conform to group-sanctioned patterns, we can begin to understand how extraordinarily significant it is to-day that we are discussing the needs of the child as a basis for his nurture and education. We can also see how questions of education and training become the focus of bitter conflicts, as contending factions in a society struggle to direct the nurture of children in order to control the group life. As we meet to-day to discuss programs of education for the young child in the home and in the nursery school, we are not concerned merely with questions of technique and procedures, with this or that pedagogical device; we are faced with the major issues of the future of our culture and the direction of our whole social, economic,

and political life, since an effective program of early-childhood education based upon the needs of the child will inevitably change our society far more effectively than any legislation or other social action.

We must, therefore, be humble and deliberate in our discussion, not only because of the gravity of the larger social issues involved, but also because we know so little about the needs of the child. It is safe to say that whenever you hear any person or group speaking with strong convictions about specific needs of the child and how to meet them, that person or group is probably sustained more by emotional fervor and loyalty to cultural traditions than by dependable knowledge of actual children.

Anyone who is prepared seriously and fairly to consider the question of the child's needs must begin by trying to be honest about his or her own personality bias and beliefs, emotional attitudes, religious loyalties, and social-economic and political leanings, because these often unconscious feelings and values play so large a rôle in our attitudes toward the child and in our willingness to recognize some of his needs or our strong denial of them. Probably the most general statement that we can make about the child's needs is that he should be protected from distortions, from unnecessary deprivations and exploitations by adults— parents, teachers and nurses, physicians, psychologists, and others engaged in dealing with children.

It is difficult to realize the extent of these often subtle coercions and pressures exerted upon the child. Before the infant is born, the parents may have built up a picture of the kind of child he or she is to be, with a pronounced bias toward the male or the female sex, or toward a certain kind of temperament, physique, and ability. The infant, having within him the genes of countless previous generations as well as the characteristics of his parents, enters into a family situation that even at birth may be threatening and out of harmony with his peculiar, idiosyncratic temperamental make-up and needs. Parents who are eager to minister to the infant's need for warmth, food, and safety may be doggedly determined to deny the child's sex and his many personal, temperamental characteristics, which gives rise to needs as important and urgent as the need for physical care.

It is not without reason, therefore, that we stress this primary and inalienable need of the child to be accepted as a unique individual, or, if the parents cannot or will not accord that acceptance, the need to be protected and reinforced against the destructive, warping influence of these parental biases. Every child suffers to a greater or less extent from this denial of his own personal, temperamental individuality, because even the most emancipated parents are not wholly free from the desire to see their children conform to the images they have constructed. Moreover, every teacher has these partialities, often unconscious, which incline her toward one child and away from another. Further, the child himself is subject to the strong desire to be like the parents, however out of harmony with his own make-up such an identification may be. It is interesting to see how the recognition of individual differences is resisted even by professionally trained persons, such as teachers, who will accept the fact of such differences with respect to mental capacity, as shown by standardized mental tests, but deny it with respect to personality, temperament, physical maturity, and other obvious characteristics.

The infant, as he grows into childhood and youth, faces a series of life tasks that cannot be evaded or denied. The way in which he meets those life tasks and his attempts to master them give rise to the various needs for which we to-day believe his nurture and education should provide. It is obvious that we have only a fragmentary knowledge of those needs, since we have studied so briefly the process of growth and development and the life tasks presented by our culture. But it is highly significant, as we suggested earlier, that we are genuinely concerned with understanding child growth and development and are trying to discover the child's needs, as a basis for his education and nurture.

The processes involved in living and growing create needs for warmth, nutrition, and bodily care concerning which we are gaining more knowledge and technical competence. Much of the research in the field of nutrition and its results are still in terms of uniform standardized rules based on pure-strain rat colonies, with no allowance made for individual differences in vitamin and mineral requirements, so that, in the name of scientific standards, we may create serious deficiencies in the individual child as contrasted with the standardized laboratory animal. Even rats in the same litter differ, as Streeter has recently shown, in their susceptibility to rickets. The nutritional and other physical needs of the individual child are to be viewed dynamically, not statically, in terms of continuing growth and development rather than fixed height-weight standards which are purely statistical averages. Moreover, these needs should be viewed in terms of physiological functioning, not merely of structural size and shape, since it is functional efficiency, not structure, that is important.

How many problem children, hypochondriacs, and psychoneurotics have been created by blind adherence to these standardized tables which physicians and nurses, health educators, and teachers have given to mothers as scientific laws and which mothers have then used on their children! Surely we should allow for individual differences in children and not increase parental anxiety in this area of physical needs by insisting upon these standardized height and weight tables for chronological-age groups. The child's need is for food, rest, sleep, and play, so that he will continue to grow and develop *at his own rate*. The emphasis should be upon growing, not upon fixed dimensions for chronological ages based upon the assumption that all children grow at the same rate.

*   *   *

It is also the confusion and anxiety and insecurity of capricious, vacillating teaching that damages the personality in search of something stable and constant to build upon. Children love order, regularity, repetition of the same pattern endlessly, and they need consistent adult guidance and help in learning these patterns of what is essential to their adult life and social living. But they do not need, nor can they safely endure, the fears, the anxieties, the feelings of inadequacy and of guilt that so many parents and teachers instill during this socialization process. Indeed fear seems to be the chief psychological instrument in early child-rearing—either the arousal of fears by cruel and coercive treatment or the inculcation of fears of experience, of people, of living, which cripple the child for life. Fear, and the resentment or hostility it often generates, are indeed the major emotional drives in our social life and give rise to much unsocial and antisocial behavior. What the child needs, but seldom receives, is a clear cut definition of the situation and of the conduct appropriate therein, so that he can and will learn what conduct is permitted and what is not permitted without the emotional disturbances he now experiences during these lessons. Practically, this means that the teaching by parents and teachers should stress the desirability or undesirability of the action without imputing blame to the child, so that instead of the usual admonishment, "You are a bad, naughty boy!" the statement should be, "That action is not desirable or not kind, not generous or not permissible, and I don't like it." The important difference is in the personal imputation of guilt and the emotional disturbance it creates in the child.

As many writers have pointed out, the child accepts socialization and the inevitable frustrations and repressions involved largely because he wants love and security from the parent and teacher. The long-popular method of asking the child to do this or that "if you love me," is especially damaging because it fails to create a recognition of impersonal authority in situations. The love for parents should never be exploited to control the child whose anxiety lest he lose that love is already great. The traditional manner of teaching, by calling the child bad or wicked when it is the behavior that should be defined as undesirable, makes the child fearful, guilty, and unhappy, and, if continued, may establish a persistent feeling of guilt and inadequacy and of being rejected. To assuage that feeling of guilt and to overcome the sense of inadequacy and rejection, the child may commit more antisocial or forbidden acts to get the punishment he needs for his guilty feelings or to prove that he is not worthless. As Dr. William Healy and Dr. Augusta Bronner have recently shown in their study, *New Light on Delinquency*, the delinquent generally has had an unhappy childhood, characterized by feelings of rejection, inadequacy, and guilt, and by lack of affection.

This point about the necessity of socialization for the child without undue emotional stress and strain during the process is being emphasized here because it has such great consequences for our social life. If we could persuade parents and teachers to avoid characterizing the child as bad or naughty, while defining the behavior, and then give the child ample reassurance when receiving such lessons, undoubtedly we could make an immense contribution to the reduction of delinquency, criminality, and other non-criminal, but socially destructive conduct on the part of those who spend their adult lives proving by the acquisition of property, prestige, and power that they are not as guilty or as worthless as they were repeatedly told in childhood.

This question of socialization of the child without distortion and emotional disturbances must be seen in the light of the great individual differences among children in intelligence, temperament, rate of maturation, and need of reassurance, so that each child may be treated individually. The professional urge to standardize, to routinize, to substitute academic training for sympathetic interest and insights into children and to look for uniformities and generalizations that will save thinking, all must be critically reexamined by nursery-school educators who are aware of these large social responsibilities. Especially is there is a need for questioning the well established principle that nursery-school teachers should be impersonal and should repress all affective responses to and from children. This principle came into vogue in the 1920's when behavioristic theories of child-rearing were dominant. The ideal of education was seen as that of almost complete emotional anesthesia and continually rational conduct, which is the ideal of the neurotic who is afraid of life and is seeking to suppress all feelings, of which he is fearful. As we realize how much the child is in need—as indeed all adults are also—of warm personal, human relations, of affectionate interest and real concern, and of opportunities to give and receive affection and to *feel*, we must challenge this old principle as directly contrary to the deepest need of the child and as destructive of human values, which can be preserved only by sensitivity and feeling tones toward people and situations.

Here it is necessary to ask why are we so afraid to recognize that the child needs mothering, not only at home, but in the nursery school, and that nursery-school teachers, by the very nature of their work, must be mother surrogates, ready and capable of giving affection and tenderness and warm emotional response to the children and of accepting them from the children. Is it because mothering does not seem scientific that we have tried to exclude it from the nursery schools or because —and I say this in no critical spirit, but as a statement based upon the actual situation—so many of those in nursery-school education are unmarried and childless and have unconsciously projected their own personal life adjustment into the training of nursery-school teachers? When we reflect upon the number of children in all classes of society who are raised by fear, terror, punishment, and other sadistic methods, with little or no experience of love and affection, we may well ask whether mothering (not smothering) may not be the most important service the nursery school can render to little children. Mothering does not mean babying or pampering, but rather giving a feeling of being liked and wanted, of belonging to someone who cares, and of being guided in the conduct of life with benevolent interest and confidence.

Dr. David Levy, a year or so ago, told this story at a meeting of the American Orthopsychiatric Association. He said that the social workers in the Bureau of Child Guidance were having unusually successful results with problem children, just because they were being maternal to these boys and girls so frequently denied real mothering. But they gave up this procedure because, said he, it did not seem scientific and was so hard to record! Perhaps if the nursery-school teacher were to consider her function as not only educational, but clinical, it might be easier to accept what the psychotherapeutic clinician accepts—namely, the rôle of parent surrogate, who gives the child individual personal interest and attention and tries to help that child work out a design for living by providing direction and deprivation, but always with interest and helpful concern.

Finally, we must look at the question of socialization in the light of the cultural changes through which we are now living, which are bringing about the destruction of so many of our traditional ideas, beliefs, and older certainties. The men and women of tomorrow will have to live in a shifting, uncertain world of rapidly changing ideas and conceptions; with few or no absolutes or certainties. What is to guide their lives, to help them find fulfillment and a design for living sanely, wholesomely, and coöperatively? Probably no previous generation has had to face such acute personal problems without help from religion, custom, and tradition. Either they will demand an authoritarian state because they cannot endure uncertainty or tolerate the destructive hostility and aggressions of unhappy individuals, or they will learn to seek in constructive work and recreative play, in the warm human relations of marriage, parenthood, and the family, a way of life that will permit realization of the enduring human values.

The nursery school, in close and coöperative relationship with the home and parents, is the primary agency for mental hygiene. The opportunity in preschool education to build wholesome, sane, coöperative, and mature personalities, and to determine the future of our culture, is unlimited. The discharge of that responsibility lies in helping the young child to meet the persistent life tasks and to fulfill his insistent needs. But the nursery school cannot do this alone. It must have collaboration from the kindergarten and the grade schools, and it must find some way of coöperating with the home and the family, despite the frequent blindness and resistance of the parents. If nursery-school teachers were to realize that they are like parents, with their personal peculiarities, their emotional resistance and susceptibilities, their ignorance and rigid convictions—which may be just as undesirable for the child as the home practices they deprecate—perhaps such a realization would make them more tolerant and more willing to seek a basis of collaboration in meeting the fundamental needs of the child. The family can and does provide the child with a place, a status, with "belongingness" and often much needed love and affection. Can the nursery school organize its procedures and prepare its teachers to meet these same needs and also those other educational needs which the family has difficulty in supplying?

The fundamental needs of the child are in truth the fundamental needs of society.

9. DEVELOPMENT OF CHILDREN'S ORIENTATIONS TOWARD A MORAL ORDER *

L. KOHLBERG

Since the concept of a moral attitude forms the basic building block of the social psychological theories of *Freud* (1922), *Durkheim* (1906), *Parsons* (1960) and others, there is reason to agree with *McDougall* (1908) that "the fundamental problem of social psychology is the moralization of the individual by the society."

Following the leads of *Freud* and *Durkheim*, most social scientists have viewed moralization as a process of *internalizing* culturally given external rules through rewards, punishments, or identification. Without questioning the view that the end point of the moralization process is one in which conduct is oriented to internal standards, one may well reject the assumption that such internal standards are formed simply through a process of "stamping in" the external prohibitions of the culture upon the child's mind. From the perspective of a developmental psychology such as that of *Piaget* (1932) or *J. M. Baldwin* (1906), internal moral standards are rather the outcome of a set of transformations of primitive attitudes and conceptions. These transformations accompany cognitive growth in the child's perceptions and orderings of a social world with which he is continuously interacting.

Directed by this developmental conception of the moralization process, our research has been oriented to the following tasks:

1. The empirical isolation of sequential stages in the development of moral thought.

2. The study of the relation of the development of moral thought to moral conduct and emotion.

3. The application of a stage analysis of moral judgment to subcultural differences as well as pathological deviance in moral orientations.

4. The isolation of the social forces and experiences required for the sequential development of moral orientations.

In the present paper, we shall summarize our findings as they relate to moralization as an age-developmental process, and we shall compare this characterization with that of *Piaget*.

THE ISOLATION OF SIX STAGES OF DEVELOPMENT IN MORAL THOUGHT

Our developmental analysis of moral judgment is based upon data obtained from a core group of 72 boys living in Chicago suburban areas. The boys were of three age groups: 10, 13, and 16. Half of each group was upper-middle class; half, lower to lower-middle class. For reasons to be discussed in the sequel to this paper, half of each group consisted of popular boys (according to class-room sociometric tests), while half consisted of socially isolated boys. All the groups were comparable in I.Q.

We have also used our procedures with a group of 24 delinquents aged 16, a group of 24 six-year-olds, and a group of 50 boys and girls aged 13 residing outside of Boston.

The basic data were two-hour tape-recorded interviews focussed upon hypothetical moral dilemmas. Both the content and method of the interviews were inspired by the work of *Piaget*

* Kohlberg, L., "Development of Children's Orientations Toward a Moral Order: I, Sequence in the Development of Moral Thought," *Vita Humana*, 1963, *6*, pp. 11-32 (abridged).

(1932). The ten situations used were ones in which acts of obedience to legal-social rules or to the commands of authority conflicted with the human needs or welfare of other individuals. The child was asked to choose whether one should perform the obedience-serving act or the need-serving act and was then asked a series of questions probing the thinking underlying his choice.

Our analysis of results commenced with a consideration of the action alternatives selected by the children. These analyses turned out to shed little light on moral development. Age trends toward choice in favor of human needs, such as might be expected from *Piaget's* (1932) theory, did not appear. The child's reason for his choice and his way of defining the conflict situations did turn out to be developmentally meaningful, however.

As an example, one choice dilemma was the following:

Joe's father promised he could go to camp if he earned the $50 for it, and then changed his mind and asked Joe to give him the money he had earned. Joe lied and said he had only earned $10 and went to camp using the other $40 he had made. Before he went, he told his younger brother Alex about the money and about lying to their father. Should Alex tell their father?

Danny, a working class 10-year-old of I.Q. 98 replied: "In one way it would be right to tell on his brother or his father might get mad at him and spank him. In another way it would be right to keep quiet or his brother might beat him up."

Obviously whether Danny chooses to fulfill his "obligation" to adult authority or to peer loyalty will depend on which action he perceives as leading to the greater punishment. What interests us most, however, is the fact that Danny does not appear to have a conception of moral obligation. His judgments are predictions; they are not expressions of moral praise, indignation, or obligation. From one to the next of the situations presented him, Danny was not consistently "authoritarian" or "humanistic" in his choices, but he was consistent in choosing in terms of the physical consequences involved.

A careful consideration of individual cases eventually led us to define six developmental types of value-orientation. A Weberian ideal-typological procedure was used to achieve a combination of empirical consistency and logical consistency in defining the types. The six developmental types were grouped into three moral levels and labelled as follows:

LEVEL I. PRE-MORAL LEVEL

Type 1. Punishment and obedience orientation.

Type 2. Naive instrumental hedonism.

LEVEL II. MORALITY OF CONVENTIONAL ROLE-CONFORMITY

Type 3. Good-boy morality of maintaining good relations, approval of others.

Type 4. Authority maintaining morality.

LEVEL III. MORALITY OF SELF-ACCEPTED MORAL PRINCIPLES

Type 5. Morality of contract and of democratically accepted law.

Type 6. Morality of individual principles of conscience.

These types will be described in more detail in subsequent sections of this paper. The typology rests upon 30 different general aspects of morality which the children brought into their thinking. One such aspect was the child's use of the concept of rights, another his orientation toward punitive justice, a third his consideration of intentions as opposed to consequences of action, etc. Each aspect was conceived as a dimension defined by a six-level scale, with each level of the scale corresponding to one of the six types of morality just listed.

A "motivational" aspect of morality was defined by the motive mentioned by the subject in justifying moral action. Six levels of motive were isolated, each congruent with one of the developmental types. They were as follows:

1. Punishment by another.
2. Manipulation of goods, rewards by another.
3. Disapproval by others.
4. Censure by legitimate authorities followed by guilt feelings.
5. Community respect and disrespect.
6. Self-condemnation.

These motives fall into three major levels. The first two represent on the verbal level what *McDougall* (1905) termed "the stage in which the operation of the instinctive impulses is modified by the influence of rewards and punishments." The second two correspond to *McDougall's* second stage "in which conduct is controlled in the main by anticipation of social praise and blame." The fifth, and especially the sixth, correspond to *McDougall's* third and "highest stage in which conduct is regulated by an ideal that enables a man to act in the way that seems to him right regardless of the praise or blame of his immediate social environment."

A more cognitive aspect of morality, conceptions of rights, was defined in terms of the following levels:

1. No real conception of a right. "Having a right" to do something equated with "being right," obeying authority.

2. Rights are factual ownership rights. Everyone has a right to do what they want with themselves and their possessions, even though this conflicts with rights of others.

3. Same as the second level concept but qualified by the belief that one has no right to do evil.

4. Recognition that a right is a claim, a legitimate exception, as to the actions of others. In general, it is an earned claim, e.g., for payment for work.

5. A conception of unearned, universal individual or human rights in addition to rights linked to a role or status.

6. In addition to level 5 conceptions, a notion of respecting the individual life and personality of the other.

Each of the 50 to 150 moral ideas or statements expressed by a child in the course of an interview could be assigned to one of 180 cells (30 dimensions $\times$ 6 levels per dimension) in the classification system. This classification yielded scores for each boy on each of the six types of thought based on the percentage of all his statements which were of the given type. Judges were able to assign responses to the moral levels with an adequate degree of agreement, expressed by product moment correlations between judges ranging from .68 to .84.

In spite of the variety of aspects of morality tapped by the 30 dimensions, there appeared to be considerable individual consistency in level of thought. Thus 15 boys in our original group of 72 were classified (in terms of their modal response) as falling in the first of our six types. On the average, 45% of the thinking of these 15 boys could be characterized as Type 1.

The differences between our age groups offer evidence concerning the developmental nature of the typology. The age trends for usage of the six types of thought are presented in figure 1.

It is evident that our first two types of thought decrease with age, our next two types increase until age 13 and then stabilize, and our last two types increase until age 16. Analyses of variance of the percentage usage of each type of thought by the 10-, 13-, and 16-year-old groups were carried out.[1] The differences between the three age groups in usage of all types of thought but one (Type 3) were found to be significant beyond the .01 level.

If our stages of moral thinking are to be taken as supporting the developmental view of moralization, evidence not only of age trends, but of sequentiality is required. While the age trends indicate that some modes of thought are generally more difficult or advanced than other modes of thought, they do not demonstrate that attainment of each mode of thought is prerequisite to the attainment of the next higher in a hypothetical sequence.

Because the higher types of moral thought replace, rather than add to, the lower modes of thought, the *Guttman* (1950) scaling technique used by other investigators to establish certain cognitive developmental sequences (*Schuessler and Strauss*, 1950; *Wohlwill*, 1960) is not appropriate for our material. A more appropriate statistical model is derived from *Guttman's* (1954) quasi-simplex correlation matrix. The "simplex" pattern of intercorrelations derives from the expectation that the more two types of thought are separated from one another in a developmental sequence, the lower should be the correlations between them. This expectation can be compared with the actual intercorrelations obtained among the six types of thought.

Each child had a profile showing the percent

[1] The means in figure 1 for age 7 are based on only 12 boys and a limited number of responses per child, compared to the older group.

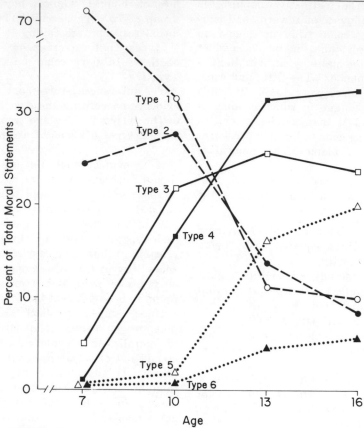

FIGURE 1   Use of six types of moral judgments at four ages.

of his responses that fell within each of the six types of thought. These profiles permitted us to correlate each of the six types of thought with each of the others across the sample of 72 boys, aged 10 to 16. The resulting product-moment correlation matrix is presented in Table I. Each correlation reflects the extent to which the individuals who use the type of thought identified by the numbers at the left margin of the matrix also use a second type of thought identified by the numbers above the matrix.

The expectation applied to the matrix is that the correlations between two types of thought should decrease as these two types are increasingly separated in the developmental hierarchy. The matrix presented in Table I indicates general agreement with the expectation. The correlations diminish as we move away

TABLE 1   Matrix of intercorrelations between six types of moral judgment.

Type	1	2	3	4	5	6
1	x					
2	55	x				
3	−41	−19	x			
4	−52	−41	18	x		
5	−52	−58	09	00	x	
6	−37	−43	−29	−07	23	x

from the main diagonal entries, whether we go across the columns or down the rows. (The correlations are markedly negative, partially because of the necessity for one percentage score to decrease as another increases.) Furthermore, correlations of types within the three main levels are higher than between levels, supporting our distinction of levels.[2]

THE FIRST TWO STAGES
(TYPE 1 AND 2)

Our Moral Type 1 shares such characteristics of Piaget's heteronomous as concern for consequences rather than intentions, lack of awareness of relativity of value, definition of right as obedience to authority. These and other Type 1 characteristics are illustrated by an excerpt from an interview with Tommy (age 10, working class, I.Q. 128). The excerpt also illustrates how the interview method traces back the child's immediate judgments to the unstated but basic assumptions or "principles" behind them.

This portion of the interview is in response to the third of the 10 moral dilemmas:

In Europe, a woman was near death from a special kind of cancer. There was one drug that the doctors thought might save her. It was a form of radium that a druggist in the same town had recently discovered. The drug was expensive to make, but the druggist was charging ten times what the drug cost him to make. He paid $200 for the radium and charged $2000 for a small dose of the drug. The sick woman's husband, Heinz, went to everyone he knew to borrow the money, but he could only get together about $1000 which is half of what it cost. He told the druggist that his wife was dying and asked him to sell it cheaper or let him pay later. But the druggist said: "No, I discovered the drug and I'm going to make money from it." So Heinz got desperate and broke into the man's store to steal the drug for his wife. Should the husband have done that?

The interview proceeded as follows:

"His wife was sick and if she didn't get the drug quickly, she might die. Maybe his wife is an important person and runs a store and the man buys stuff from her and can't get it any other place. The police would probably

<hr>

[2] These cross-sectional findings need to be supplemented by a longitudinal analysis if we are to accept the stages as a genuine developmental sequence. We are presently engaged in a semilongitudinal analysis, in which we have reinterviewed 54 of our original subjects after a three-year interval. The findings will be reported in a subsequent publication.

blame the owner that he didn't save the wife. That would be like killing with a gun or knife."

(Interviewer: Would it be all right to put the druggist in the electric chair for murder?)

"If she could be cured by the drug and they didn't give it to her, I think so, because she could be an important lady like Betsy Ross, she made the flag. And if it was President Eisenhower, he's important, and they'd probably put the man in the electric chair because that isn't fair."

(Should the punishment be more if she's an important person?)

"If someone important is in a plane and is allergic to heights and the stewardness won't give him medicine because she's only got enough for one and she's got a sick one, a friend, in back, they'd probably put the stewardess in a lady's jail because she didn't help the important one."

(Is it better to save the life of one important person or a lot of unimportant people?)

"All the people that aren't important because one man just has one house, maybe a lot of furniture, but a whole bunch of people have an awful lot of furniture and some of these poor people might have a lot of money and it doesn't look it."

On the one hand we notice Tommy's reasoning ability, his utilitarian calculation of the economics of the greater good. On the other hand we notice that the calculation of value is based on a "primitive" assumption as to the basis of moral values. A prosaic and commendable concern about the wife's life is eventually based on the notion that the value of a life is determined by its "importance" and that such importance is essentially a function of the amount of furniture owned.

Why are we justified in using the term "primitive" in describing the derivation of the value of life from the value of furniture? Awarding moral value to furniture involves a failure to differentiate the self's point of view from that of others, or to differentiate what the community holds as a shared or moral value (the value of life) and what the individual holds as a private value (the desire for furniture). Such a lack of a sense of subjectivity of value is also suggested by Tommy's definition of culpability in terms of consequences rather than intentions (the wickedness of the druggist depends on his causing the loss of an important life).

In a Type One response the value of what is right and what is wrong is based on external physical events and objects as good or bad. This is clear in the following response to punishment as defining what is good or bad. An example is provided by 10 year old Danny, who in Situation II, a situation of conflict between brother and father, defined the right choice in terms of a prediction as to which one would retaliate more heavily. Danny went on to say:

"My brother would say, 'If you tell on me, I'll whip you with my belt real hard'."

(What would you do then?)

"Well, if I was to tell my Dad if my brother Butchie was still hurting me, my brother would go find another house to live in."

The emergence of individualistic hedonism out of such growing cognitive differentiation is suggested by the responses which fall in our Type 2. Just as our first stage of morality coincides descriptively with *Piaget's* "heteronomous stage" but differs from it in interpretation, so our second stage coincides descriptively with *Piaget's* autonomous stage but differs from it in interpretation. Like *Piaget* and others, we found an increase in the use of reciprocity (exchange and retaliation) as a basis for choice and judgment in the years six to ten, though not thereafter. We also found age increases in notions of relativism of value, and in egalitarian denial of the moral superiority of authorities.

These reactions were common enough and well enough associated in our 10-year-olds to help define our Type 2. The tendency to define value relative to private needs is reflected in the response of Jimmy (a 10-year-old working-class boy, I.Q. 105) to our test situation about mercy-killing. The story continues the plight of the wife dying of cancer as follows:

The doctor finally got some of the radium drug for Heinz's wife. But it didn't work, and there was no other treatment known to medicine which could save her. She was in terrible pain, but she was so weak that a good dose of a pain-killer like ether or morphine would make her die sooner. She was delirious and almost crazy with pain, and in her calm periods, she would ask the doctor to give her enough ether to kill her. She said she couldn't stand the pain and she was going to die in a few months anyway.

Should the doctor do what she asks and make her die to put her out of her terrible pain?

Jimmy replied, "It's according to how you look at it. From the doctor's point of view, it could be a murder charge. From her point of view, it isn't paying her to live anymore if she's just going to be in pain."

(How about if there were a law against it?)

"It should be up to her; it's her life. It's the person's life, not the law's life."

In this situation Jimmy defines right action instrumentally, as means to individual values; he defines it relativistically, in relation to the conflicting values of various individuals; and he defines it hedonistically, in terms of "paying" in pleasure and pain. The woman has ownership rights over herself, she is her own property. In more mature types of thought rights are defined relative to duties, the law is seen as defending and defining rights, and the law's respect for the woman's rights represents a respect for her personality and life.

Jimmy also relied heavily on reciprocity in defining role relations as indicated by such remarks as the following:

(Why should someone be a good son?)

"Be good to your father and he'll be good to you."

The advance in cognitive differentiation of this type of response over that of Type 1 seems evident. It seems clear that such definition of value in terms of ego-need and reciprocity of needs is in a sense internal; i.e., it is not simply a reflection of direct teaching by others. It reflects rather Type 2's increasing awareness of its own ego-interests and of the exchange of ego-interests underlying much of social organization.

THE INTERMEDIATE STAGES OF MORAL DEVELOPMENT

It is clear that Type 1 and Type 2 children do not express attitudes toward "the good" and "the right" like those we take for granted in adults and which we often regard as moral cliches or stereotypes. These stereotypes first appear in our Type 3 and Type 4 preadolescents, whose verbal judgments and decisions are defined in terms of a concept of a morally good person (the implication of labelling Type 3 as a "good boy" morality).

A fairly typical Type 3 "good boy" response to the story about stealing the drug is the following response by Don (age 13, I.Q. 109, lower-middle class):

"It was really the druggist's fault, he was unfair, trying to over-charge and letting someone die. Heinz loved his wife and wanted to save her. I think anyone would. I don't think they would put him in jail. The judge would look at all sides, and see that the druggist was charging too much."

Don's response defines the issues in terms of attitudes toward the kinds of people involved; "the loving husband," "the unfair druggist," "the understanding judge," "what anyone would do," etc. He assumes that the attitude he expresses are shared or community attitudes.

In terms of motivation, this second level is one in which conduct is controlled in the main by anticipation of praise and blame. Praise and blame are, of course, effective reinforcers even in the child's earliest years. In these early years, however, disapproval is but one of the many unplesant external consequences of action that are to be avoided. In contrast, our Type 3 and Type 4 pre-adolescents attempt to make decisions and define what is good for themselves by *anticipating* possible disapproval in thought and imagination and by holding up approval as a final internal goal. Furthermore, the pre-adolescent is bothered only by disapproval if the disapproval is expressed by legitimate authorities. This attitude is naively expressed by Andy (age 16, working class, I.Q. 102) in his reply to the second story about telling one's father about one's brother's lie:

"If my father finds out later, he won't trust me. My brother wouldn't either, but I wouldn't have *a conscience* that he (my brother) didn't."

"I try to do things for my parents, they've always done things for you. I try to do everything my mother says, I try to please her. Like she wants me to be a doctor and I want to, too, and she's helping me to get up there."

Unlike the statements of compliance to the wishes of superiors (as in Level I), Andy's statements imply an identification of his own goals with his parent's wishes and a desire to anticipate them, somewhat independent of sanctions.

For children of Type 4, the moral order is seen as a matter of rules; and role-taking is based on "justice," on regard for the rights and expectations of both rule-enforcers and other rule-obeyers. The distinction between Type 3 and Type 4 styles of role-taking in moral judgment may be illustrated by two explanations as to the wrong of stealing from a store. Carol (13, I.Q. 108, lower-middle class, Type 3) says:

"The person who owns that store would think you didn't come from a good family, people would think you came from a family that didn't care about what you did."

James, 13, I.Q. 111, lower-middle class, Type 4) says:

"You'd be mad, too, if you worked for something and someone just came along and stole it."

Both Carol and James define the wrong of stealing by putting themselves in the role of the victim. James, however, expresses the "moral indignation" of the victim, his sense that the rights of a community member have been violated, rather than expressing merely the owner's disapproval of the thief as a bad and unloved person. In both, Type 3 and Type 4, regard for rules is based upon regard for an organized social order. For Type 3, this order is defined primarily by the relations of good or "natural" selves; for Type 4 it is rather defined by rights, assigned duties, and rules.

MORAL ORIENTATION AT THE THIRD DEVELOPMENTAL LEVEL

Children of Types 5 and 6 accept the possibility of conflict between norms, and they attempt something like a "rational" decision between conflicting norms. This is most clear in our Type 6 children who attempt to choose in terms of moral principles rather than moral rules. Conventional examples of moral principles are the Golden Rule, the utilitarian principle (the greatest good for the greatest number) and Kant's categorical imperative. A moral principle is an obligatory or ideal rule of choice between legitimate alternatives, rather than a concrete prescription of action (*Dewey and Tufts*, 1936; *Kohlberg*, 1958). Philosophically such principles are designed to abstract the basic element that exists in various concrete rules, and to form an axiomatic basis for justifying or formulating concrete rules.[3] Moral principles, of course, are not legally or socially prescribed or sanctioned, they are social ideals rather than social realities.

An example of the use of the utilitarian maxim as a moral principle is provided by Tony (age 16, I.Q. 115, upper-middle class). He is replying to a situation involving a choice of leaving or staying at a civilian air-defense post after a heavy bombing raid may have endangered one's family:

"If he leaves, he is putting the safety of the few over the safety of many. I don't think it matters that it's his loved ones, because people in the burning buildings are someone's loved ones too. Even though maybe he'd be miserable the rest of his life, he shouldn't put the few over the many."

Tony says that leaving the post is wrong, not because of the actual consequences, but because he evaluated the situation wrongly, and "put the few over the many." This is not merely a matter of utilitarian economics but of the requirement of justice that all lives be treated as of equal value.

Moral principles are principles of "conscience," and Type 6 children tend to define moral decisions in these terms. When Type 6 children are asked "What is conscience?", they tend to answer that conscience is a choosing and self-judging function, rather than a feeling of guilt or dread.

A more easily attained "rationality" in moral choice than that of Type 6 is embodied in the Type 5 orientation of social contract legalism. Type 5 defines right and wrong in terms of legal or institutional rules which are seen as having a rational basis, rather than as

[3] It is historically true that all philosophic formulations of moral principles, such as those just mentioned, are variations of a basic prescription to take the role of all other involved in the moral situations.

being morally sacred. Laws are seen as maximizing social utility or welfare, or as being necessary for institutional functioning. It is recognized that laws are in a sense arbitrary, that there are many possible laws and that the laws are sometimes unjust. Nevertheless, the law is in general the criterion of right because of the need for agreement.

While Type 5 relies heavily on the law for definitions of right and wrong, it recognizes the possibility of conflict between what is rationally "right" for the individual actor, and what is legally or rationally right for the society. George (16, upper-middle class, I.Q. 118) gives a fairly typical response to the questions as to whether the husband was wrong to steal the drug for his dying wife:

"I don't think so, since it says the druggist had a right to set the price since he discovered it. I can't say he'd actually be right; I suppose anyone would do it for his wife though. He'd prefer to go to jail than have his wife die. In my eyes he'd have just cause to do it, but in the law's eyes he'd be wrong. I can't say more than that as to whether it was right or not."

(Should the judge punish the husband if he stole the drug?)

"It's the judge's duty to the law to send him to jail, no matter what the circumstances. The laws are made by the people and the judge is elected on the basis that he's agreed to carry out the law."

George's belief is that the judge must punish even though the judge may not think the act is wrong. This is quite consistent with his belief that the act was individually "just," but legally wrong. It reflects a typical distinction made at this level between individual person and social role, a distinction which contrasts with the earlier fusion of person and role into moral stereotypes. The judge's role is seen as a defined position with a set of agreed-upon rules which the role-occupant contractually accepts on entering office. At the level of definition of role-obligation, then, contract replaces earlier notions of helping the role-partner, just as legality replaces respect for social authority in defining more general norms.

IMPLICATIONS OF THE STAGES FOR CONCEPTIONS OF THE MORALIZATION PROCESS

We may now briefly consider some of the implications of our stages for conceptions of the process and direction of moral development. Our age trends indicate that large groups of moral concepts and ways of thought only attain meaning at successively advanced ages and require the extensive background of social experience and cognitive growth represented by the age factor. How is this finding to be interpreted?

From the internalization view of the moralization process, these age changes in modes of moral thought would be interpreted as successive acquisitions or internalizations of cultural moral concepts. Our six types of thought would represent six patterns of verbal morality in the adult culture which are successively absorbed as the child grows more verbally sophisticated.

In contrast, we have advocated the developmental interpretation that these types of thought represent structures emerging from the interaction of the child with his social environment, rather than directly reflecting external structures given by the child's culture. Awareness of the basic prohibitions and commands of the culture, as well as some behavioral "internalization" of them, exists from the first of our stages and does not define their succession. Movement from stage to stage represents rather the way in which these prohibitions, as well as much wider aspects of the social structure, are taken up into the child's organization of a moral order. This order may be based upon power and external compulsion (Type 1), upon a system of exchanges and need satisfactions (Type 2), upon the maintenance of legitimate expectations (Type 3 and 4), or upon ideals or general logical principles of social organization (Types 5 and 6). While these successive bases of a moral order do spring from the child's awareness of the external social world, they also represent active processes of organizing or ordering this world.

We have cited two major results from our quantitative analyses which support this developmental interpretation. The first result was the approximation of the matrix of type inter-correlations to a quasi-simplex form. This suggested that individual development through the types of moral thought proceeded stepwise through an invariant sequence. If our moral types form an invariant sequence, acquisition of a higher type is not likely to be a direct learning of content taught by cultural agents, but is rather a restructuring of preceding types of thought. This interpretation is strengthened by the trend toward negative correlations between the higher and lower types of thought. Such negative relations suggest that higher modes of thought replace or inhibit lower modes of thought rather than being added to them. This in turn suggests that higher types of thought are reorganizations of preceding types of thought.

More strongly than the quantitative data, we believe that the qualitative data and interpretations contained in our stage descriptions makes the notion of developmental transformations in moral thought plausible and meaningful. We have described characteristics of the types which suggest that each type is qualitatively different than previous types. Such qualitative differences would not be expected were development simply a reflection of greater knowledge of, and conformity to, the culture. We have also attempted a logical analysis of the characteristics of the types which allows us to see each type as a conceptual bridge between earlier and later types.

The developmental conception of the moralization process suggested by our analysis of age changes has some definite further implications. Implications as to relations of the development of moral thought to social environmental factors on the one hand, and to the development of moral conduct on the other, will be considered in the sequel to this paper.

SUMMARY

The paper presents an overview of the author's findings with regard to a sequence of moral development. It is based on empirical data obtained mainly from boys aged 10, 13, and 16 in lengthy free interviews around hypothetical moral dilemmas. Ideal-typological procedures led to the construction of six types of moral thought, designed to form a developmental hierarchy. The first two types parallel *Piaget's* heteronomous and autonomous moral stages, but various findings fail to support *Piaget's* view that these stages are derived from heteronomous or mutual respect.

More mature modes of thought (Types 4-6) increased from age 10 through 16, less mature modes (Types 1-2) decreased with age. Data were analyzed with regard to the question of sequence, e.g., to the hypothesis that attainment of each type of thought is the prerequisite to attainment of the next higher type. A quasi-simplex pattern of intercorrelations supported this hypothesis.

Such evidence of developmental sequence in moral attitudes and concepts is believed to be of great importance for conceptions of the process of moralization. It indicates the inadequacy of conceptions of moralization as a process of simple internalization of external cultural rules, through verbal teaching, punishment, or identification. In contrast, the evidence suggests the existence of a series of internally patterned or organized transformations of social concepts and attitudes, transformations which constitute a developmental process.

ADDENDUM

Compiled by Norman Sprinthall

Since the publication of Professor Kohlberg's work, he has continued to investigate the growth of moral development in children. This most recent work includes a cross-cultural replication of his earlier work. With children at ages 10, 13 and 16 in Taiwan, he has administered the moral judgment situations and has scored their responses. In the accompanying figure (2) the results are presented and compared to similar ratings made on children in the same age ranges in the United States. The figures indicate that the same age trends hold for both groups of pupils. This means that children in Taiwan exhibit the same age specific systems for moral judgment as American students. For example, Type 1, moral judgment based on fearful avoidance of stealing and punishment is relatively common for both groups of children at age 10. Approximately 40% of the statements made by Taiwan pupils were classified as Type 1, and 30% for the American pupils. By age 16, the percentages were 8% in Taiwan and 10% for

American children. Thus both groups over the period of 6 years declined significantly in the use of that category. Similarly Type 4, a judgment based on "doing duty" and respect for authority increased for both groups of pupils, from 10% to almost 60% over the same time period in Taiwan and from 15% to 35% for the Americans. Although there are differences in degree, the age trend is similar. This indicates that the development of types of judgment are similar even though the cultural background of the pupils may be vastly different.

It is, of course, interesting to note that a greater proportion in Taiwan use Type 4 statements than in America. The American pupils at the same age (16) manifest a greater use of Type 5—20% versus 6% on Taiwan. This means that more American pupils reach this level than do the pupils from Taiwan. Type 5 is a judgment based upon duty as a legal contract that takes into consideration the rights of others and the sanctions of the majority. This difference may reflect the difference between a democratically oriented society versus one based upon obedience to authority to maintain a social order.

Professor Kohlberg has also replicated his stages of moral development in other countries besides Taiwan. Thus far the results from all these cross cultural samples indicate support for the general sequence of developmental stages in moral judgment.

MORAL JUDGMENT SITUATIONS
(Probing questions not included)

I. Joe is a 14-year-old boy who wanted to go to camp very much. His father promised him he could go if he saved up the money for it himself. So Joe worked hard at his paper route and saved up the $40 it cost to go to camp and a little more besides. But just before camp was going to start, his father changed his mind. Some of his friends decided to go on a special fishing trip, and Joe's father was short of the money it would cost. So he told Joe to give him the money he had saved from the paper route. Joe didn't want to give up going to camp, so he thought of refusing to give his father the money.

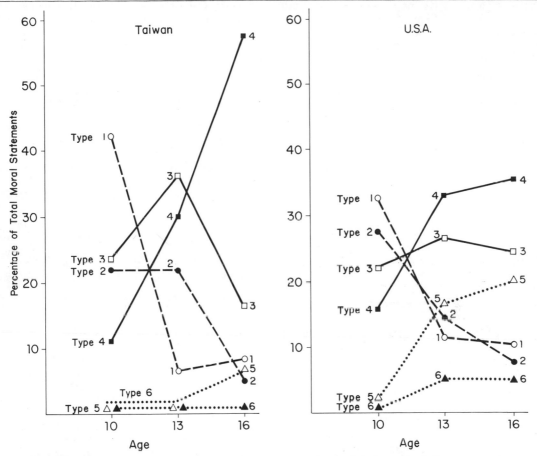

FIGURE 2   Mean per cent of use of six stages of moral judgment at three ages in Taiwan and the United States.

Should Joe refuse to give his father the money or should he give it to him? Why?

II. Joe lied and said he only made $10, and went to camp with the other $40 he made. Joe had an older brother Bob. Before Joe went to camp, he told Bob about the money and about lying to their father.

Should Bob tell their father? Why?

III. In Europe, a woman was near death from a special kind of cancer. There was one drug that the doctors thought might save her. It was a form of radium that a druggist in the same town had recently discovered. The drug was expensive to make, but the druggist was charging ten times what the drug cost him to make. He paid $200 for the radium and charged $2,000 for a small dose of the drug. The sick woman's husband, Heinz, went to everyone he knew

to borrow the money, but he could only get together about $1,000 which is half of what it cost. He told the druggist that his wife was dying and asked him to sell it cheaper or let him pay later. But the druggist said, "No, I discovered the drug and I'm going to make money from it." So Heinz got desperate and broke into the man's store to steal the drug for his wife.

Should the husband have done that? Why?

IV. The doctor finally got some of the radium drug for Heinz's wife. But it didn't work, and there was no other treatment known to medicine which could save her. So the doctor knew that she had only about six months to live. She was in terrible pain, but she was so weak that a good dose of a pain-killer like ether or morphine would make her die sooner. She was delirious and almost crazy with pain, and in her calm periods, she would ask the doctor to give her enough ether to kill her. She said she couldn't stand the pain and she was going to die in a few months anyway.

Should the doctor do what she asks and make her die to put her out of her terrible pain? Why?

V. In Korea, a company of Marines was way outnumbered and was retreating before the enemy. The company had crossed a bridge over a river, but the enemy were mostly still on the other side. If someone went back to the bridge and blew it up as the enemy were coming over it, it would weaken the enemy. With the head start the rest of the men in the company would have, they could probably then escape. But the man who stayed back to blow up the bridge would probably not be able to escape alive; there would be about a 4 to 1 chance he would be killed. The captain of the company has to decide who should go back and do the job. The captain himself is the man who knows best how to lead the retreat. He asks for volunteers, but no one will volunteer.

Should the captain order a man to stay behind, or stay behind himself, or leave nobody behind? Why would that be best?

VI. The captain finally decided to order one of the men to stay behind. One of the men he thought of was one who had a lot of strength and courage but he was a bad trouble maker. He was always stealing things from the other men, beating them up and wouldn't do his work. The second man he thought of had gotten a bad disease in Korea and was likely to die in a short time anyway, though he was strong enough to do the job.

If the captain was going to send one of the two men, should he send the trouble maker or the sick man? Why?

VII. Two young men were in trouble. They were secretly leaving town in a hurry and needed money. Al, the older one, broke into a store and stole $500. John, the younger one, went to a man who was known to help people in town. John told the man that he was very sick and he needed $500 to pay for the operation. Really he wasn't sick at all, and he had no intention of paying the man back. Although the man didn't know John

very well, he loaned him the money. So John and Al skipped town, each with $500.

Who did worse, Al who broke into the store or John who borrowed the money with no intention of paying it back? Why?

VIII. While all this was happening, Heinz was in jail for breaking in and trying to steal the medicine. He had been sentenced for ten years. But after a couple of years, he escaped from the prison and went to live in another part of the country under a new name. He saved money and slowly built up a big factory. He gave his workers the highest wages and used most of his profits to build a hospital for work in curing cancer. Twenty years had passed when a tailor recognized the factory owner as being Heinz, the escaped convict whom the police had been looking for back in his home town.

Should the tailor report Heinz to the police? Why should(n't) he?

IX. During the war in Europe, a city was often heavily bombed. All the men in the city were assigned to different fire-fighting and rescue stations all over the city. A man named Diesing was in charge of one fire engine station near where he worked. One day after an especially heavy bombing, Diesing left the shelter to go to his station. But on the way, he decided he had to see whether his family was safe. His home was quite far away, but he went there first.

Was it right or wrong for him to leave the station to protect his family?

SCHEMA OF DEVELOPMENTAL TYPES

LEVEL 1—Value resides in external quasi-physical happenings, in bad acts, or in quasi-physical needs rather than in persons and standards.

Type 1: Obedience and punishment orientation. Egocentric deference to superior power or prestige, or a trouble-avoiding set. Objective responsibility.

Type 2: Naively egoistic orientation. Right action is that instrumentally satisfying the self's needs and occasionally other's. Awareness of relativism of value to each actor's needs and perspective. Naive egalitarianism and orientation to exchange and reciprocity.

LEVEL II—Moral value resides in performing good or right roles, in maintaining the conventional order and the expectancies of others.

Type 3: Good boy orientation. Orientation to approval and to pleasing and helping others. Conformity to stereotypical images of majority or natural role behavior, and judgment by intentions.

Type 4: Authority and social order maintaining orientation. Orientation to "doing duty" and to showing respect for authority and maintaining the given social order for its own sake. Regard for earned expectations of others.

LEVEL III—Moral value resides in conformity by the self to shared or shareable standards, rights or duties.

Type 5: Contractual legalistic orientation. Recognition of an arbitrary element or starting point in rules or expectations for the sake of agreement. Duty defined in terms of contract, general avoidance of violation of the will or rights of others, and majority will and welfare.

Type 6: Conscience or principle orientation. Orientation not only to actually ordained social rules but to principles of choice involving appeal to logical universality and consistency. Orientation to conscience as a directing agent and to mutual respect and trust.

10. ADOLESCENCE *

ANNA FREUD

INTRODUCTION

I return to the subject of adolescence after an interval of twenty years. During this time much has happened in analytic work to throw added light on the problems concerned and to influence the conditions of life for young people, whether normal or abnormal. Nevertheless, in spite of partial advances, the position with regard to the analytic study of adolescence is not a happy one, and especially unsatisfactory when compared with that of early childhood. With the latter period, we feel sure of our ground, and in possession of a wealth of material and information which enables us to assume authority and apply analytic findings to the practical problems of upbringing. When it comes to adolescence, we feel hesitant and, accordingly, cannot satisfy the parents or educational workers who apply for help to our knowledge. One can hear it said frequently that adolescence is a neglected period, a stepchild where analytic thinking is concerned.

These complaints, which come from two sides, from the parents as well as from the analytic workers themselves, seem to me to warrant closer study and investigation than they have received so far.

*   *   *   *

What follows is an attempt to apply at least some of our hard-won insights to three of the most pressing problems concerning adolescence.

IS THE ADOLESCENT UPSET INEVITABLE?

There is, first, the ever recurrent question whether the adolescent upheaval is welcome and beneficial as such, whether it is necessary and, more than that, inevitable. On this point, psychoanalytic opinion is decisive and unanimous. The people in the child's family and school, who assess his state on the basis of

* Freud, Anna, "Adolescence," *Psychoanalytic Study of the Child*, 1958, *13*, pp. 255, 264-265 and 267-276. Reprinted by permission of International Universities Press.

behavior, may deplore the adolescent upset which, to them, spells the loss of valuable qualities, of character stability, and of social adaptation. As analysts, who assess personalities from the structural point of view, we think otherwise. We know that the character structure of a child at the end of the latency period represents the outcome of long drawn-out conflicts between id and ego forces. The inner balance achieved, although characteristic for each individual and precious to him, is preliminary only and precarious. It does not allow for the quantitative increase in drive activity, nor for the changes of drive quality which are both inseparable from puberty. Consequently, it has to be abandoned to allow adult sexuality to be integrated into the individual's personality. The so-called adolescent upheavals are no more than the external indications that such internal adjustments are in progress.

On the other hand, we all know individual children who as late as the ages of fourteen, fifteen or sixteen show no such outer evidence of inner unrest. They remain, as they have been during the latency period, "good" children, wrapped up in their family relationships, considerate sons of their mothers, submissive to their fathers, in accord with the atmosphere, ideas and ideals of their childhood background. Convenient as this may be, it signifies a delay of normal development and is, as such, a sign to be taken seriously. The first impression conveyed by these cases may be that of a quantitative deficiency of drive endowment, a suspicion which will usually prove unfounded. Analytic exploration reveals that this reluctance to "grow up" is derived not from the id but from the ego and superego aspects of the personality. These are children who have built up excessive defenses against their drive activities and are now crippled by the results, which act as barriers against the normal maturational processes of phase development. They are, perhaps more than any others, in need of therapeutic help to remove the inner restrictions and clear the path for normal development, however, "upsetting" the latter may prove to be.

PATHOLOGY IN ADOLESCENCE

This leaves us with a third problem which, to my mind, outweighs the preceding ones so far as clinical and theoretical significance are concerned. I refer to the difficulty in adolescent cases to draw the line between normality and pathology. As described above, adolescence constitutes by definition an interruption of peaceful growth which resembles in appearance a variety of other emotional upsets and structural upheavals.[1] The adolescent manifestations come close to symptom formation of the neurotic, psychotic or dissocial order and merge almost imperceptibly into borderline states, initial, frustrated or fully fledged forms of almost all the mental illnesses. Consequently, the differential diagnosis between the adolescent upsets and true pathology becomes a difficult task.

For the discussion of this diagnostic problem I leave most other authors in the field to speak for themselves and summarize my own impressions based on past and present clinical experience.

In 1936, when I approached the same subject from the aspect of the defenses, I was concerned with the similarity between the adolescent and other emotional disturbances rather than with the differences between them. I described that adolescent upsets take on the appearance of a neurosis if the initial, pathogenic danger situation is located in the superego with the resulting anxiety being felt as guilt; that they resemble psychotic disturbances if the danger lies in the increased power of the id itself, which threatens the ego in its existence or integrity. Whether such an adolescent individual impresses us, then, as obsessional, phobic, hysterical, ascetic, schizoid, paranoid, suicidal, etc., will depend on the one hand on the quality and quantity of the id contents which beset the ego, on the other hand on the selection of defense mechanisms which the latter employs. Since, in adolescence, impulses from all pregenital phases rise to the

[1] Adolescence, of course, is not the only time in life when alterations of a physiological nature cause disturbances of mental equilibrium. The same happens in later years in the climacterium; and recently, Grete L. Bibring has given a convincing description of similar damage to the equilibrium of mental forces during pregnancy

surface and defense mechanisms from all levels of crudity or complexity come into use, the pathological results—although identical in structure—are more varied and less stabilized than at other times of life.

Today it seems to me that this structural description needs to be amplified, not in the direction of the similarity of the adolescent to other disorders but in that of their specific nature. There is in their etiology at least one additional element which may be regarded as exclusive to this period and characteristic for it: namely that the danger is felt to be located not only in the id impulses and fantasies but in the very existence of the love objects of the individual's oedipal and preoedipal past. The libidinal cathexis to them has been carried forward from the infantile phases, merely toned down or inhibited in aim during latency. Therefore the reawakened pregenital urges, or —worse still—the newly acquired genital ones, are in danger of making contact with them, lending a new and threatening reality to fantasies which had seemed extinct but are, in fact, merely under repression.[2] The anxieties which arise on these grounds are directed toward eliminating the infantile objects, i.e., toward breaking the tie with them. Anny Katan (1937) has discussed this type of defense, which aims above all at changing the persons and the scene of conflict, under the term of "removal." Such an attempt may succeed or fail, partially or totally. In any case, I agree with Anny Katan that its outcome will be decisive for the success or failure of the other, more familiar line of defensive measures which are directed against the impulses themselves.

A number of illustrations will serve to clarify the meaning of this assumption.

[2] An important clinical instance of this can be found in adolescent girls with anorexia nervosa. Here the infantile fantasies of oral impregnation receive added impetus from the new real possibilities of motherhood opened up by genital development. Consequently, the phobic measures adopted against the intake of food on the one hand and identification with the mother on the other hand are overemphasized to a degree which may lead to starvation.

(I) DEFENSE AGAINST THE INFANTILE OBJECT TIES

Defense by Displacement of Libido.—There are many adolescents who deal with the anxiety aroused by the attachment to their infantile objects by the simple means of flight. Instead of permitting a process of gradual detachment from the parents to take place, they withdraw their libido from them suddenly and altogether. This leaves them with a passionate longing for partnership which they succeed in transferring to the environment outside the family. Here they adopt varying solutions. Libido may be transferred, more or less unchanged in form, to parent substitutes, provided that these new figures are diametrically opposed in every aspect (personal, social, cultural) to the original ones. Or the attachment may be made to so-called "leaders," usually persons in age between the adolescent's and the parents' generation, who represent ideals. Equally frequent are the passionate new ties to contemporaries, either of the same or of the opposite sex (i.e., homosexual or heterosexual friendships) and the attachments to adolescent groups (or "gangs"). Whichever of these typical solutions is chosen, the result makes the adolescent feel "free," and revel in a new precious sense of independence from the parents who are treated, then, with indifference bordering on callousness.

Although the direction taken by the libido in these instances is, in itself, on lines of normality, the suddenness of the change, the carefully observed contrast in object selection, and the overemphasis on the new allegiances mark it as defensive. It represents an all too hasty anticipation of normal growth rather than a normal developmental process.

It makes little further difference to the emotional situation whether the libidinal flight is followed by actual flight, i.e., whether the adolescent also "removes" himself bodily from his family. If not, he remains in the home in the attitude of a boarder, usually a very inconsiderate one so far as the older and younger family members are concerned.

On the other hand, the withdrawal of cathexis from the parents has most decisive consequences for the rest of the defensive processes. Once the infantile objects are stripped of their importance, the pregenital and genital impulses cease to be threatening to the same degree. Consequently, guilt and anxiety decrease and the ego becomes more tolerant. Formerly repressed sexual and aggressive wishes rise to the surface and are acted on, the actions being taken outside the family in the wider environment. Whether this acting out will be on harmless, or idealistic, or dissocial, or even criminal lines will depend essentially on the new objects to which the adolescent has attached himself. Usually the ideals of the leader, of the adolescent group, or of the gang, are taken over wholeheartedly and without criticism.

Adolescents of this type may be sent for treatment after their actions have brought them into conflict with their schools, their employers, or the law. As far as psychoanalytic therapy is concerned, they seem to offer little chance for the therapeutic alliance between analyst and patient without which the analytic technique cannot proceed. Any relationship to the analyst and, above all, the transference to him would revive the infantile attachments which have been discarded; therefore the adolescent remains unresponsive. Also, the escape from these attachments has suspended the feeling of internal conflict, at least temporarily; consequently, the adolescent does not feel in need of psychological help. A. Aichhorn had these points in mind when he maintained that adolescents of the dissocial and criminal type needed a long period of preparation and inner rearrangement before they could become amenable to analytic treatment. He maintained that the latter would be successful only if, during this preparation in a residential setting, the adolescent made a new transference of object love, reawakened his infantile attachments, internalized his conflicts once more, in short, became neurotic.

To try and analyze an adolescent in his phase of successful detachment from the past seems to be a venture doomed to failure.

Defense by Reversal of Affect.—A second typical reaction to the same danger situation is, although less conspicuous outwardly, more ominous in nature inwardly.

Instead of displacing libido from the parents —or, more likely, after failing to do so—the adolescent ego may defend itself by turning the emotions felt toward them into their opposites. This changes love into hate, dependence into revolt, respect and admiration into contempt and derision. On the basis of such reversal of affect the adolescent imagines himself to be "free" but, unluckily for his peace of mind and sense of conflict, this conviction does not reach further than the conscious surface layer of his mind. For all deeper intents and purposes he remains as securely tied to the parental figures as he has been before; acting out remains within the family; and any alterations achieved by the defense turn out to his disadvantage. There are no positive pleasures to be derived from the reversed relationships, only suffering, felt as well as inflicted. There is no room for independence of action, or of growth; compulsive opposition to the parents proves as crippling in this respect as compulsive obedience to them can prove to be.[3] Since anxiety and guilt remain undiminished, constant reinforcement of defense is necessary. This is provided in the first place by two methods: denial (of positive feeling) and reaction formations (churlish, unsympathetic, contemptuous attitudes). The behavioral picture that emerges at this stage is that of an uncooperative and hostile adolescent.

Further pathological developments of this state of affairs are worth watching. The hostility and aggressiveness, which serve as a defense against object love in the beginning, soon become intolerable to the ego, are felt as threats, and are warded off in their own right. This may happen by means of projection; in that case the aggression is ascribed to the parents who, consequently, become the adolescent's main oppressors and persecutors. In the clinical picture this appears first as the adolescent's suspiciousness and, when the projections increase, as paranoid behavior.

Conversely, the full hostility and aggression may be turned away from the objects and employed inwardly against the self. In these cases, the adolescents display intense depression, tendencies of self-abasement and self-injury, and develop, or even carry out, suicidal wishes.

During all stages of this process, personal suffering is great and the desire to be helped

---

[3] S. Ferenczi has pointed to this effect of "compulsive disobedience" many years ago.

intense. This, in itself, is no guarantee that the adolescent in question will submit to analytic therapy. He will certainly not do so if treatment is urged and initiated by the parents. Whenever this happens, he will consider analysis as their tool, extend his hostility or his suspicions to include the person of the analyst, and refuse cooperation. The chances are better if the adolescent himself decides to seek help and turns to analysis, as it were, in opposition to the parents' wishes. Even so, the alliance with the analyst may not be of long duration. As soon as a true transference develops and the positive infantile fantasies come into consciousness, the same reversal of affect tends to be repeated in the analytic setting. Rather than relive the whole turmoil of feelings with the analyst, many adolescent patients run away. They escape from their positive feelings, although it appears to the analyst that they break off treatment in an overwhelmingly strong negative transference.

Defense by Withdrawal of Libido to the Self.—To proceed in the direction of increasing pathology:

Withdrawal of libido from the parents, as it has been described above, does not, in itself, decide about its further use, or fate. If anxieties and inhibitions block the way toward new objects outside the family, the libido remains within the self. There, it may be employed to cathect the ego and superego, thereby inflating them. Clinically this means that ideas of grandeur will appear, fantasies of unlimited power over other human beings, or of major achievement and championship in one or more fields. Or, the suffering and persecuted ego of the adolescent may assume Christ-like proportions with corresponding fantasies of saving the world.

On the other hand, the cathexis may become attached to the adolescent's body only and give rise there to the hypochondriacal sensations and feelings of body changes that are well known clinically from initial stages of psychotic illness.

In either case analytic therapy is indicated as well as urgent. Treatment will dispel the appearance of severe abnormality if it reopens a path for the libido, either to flow backwards and recathect the original infantile objects, or to flow forward, in the direction described

above, to cathect less frightening substitutes in the environment.

What taxes the analyst's technical skill in these cases is the withdrawn state of the patient, i.e., the problem of establishing an initial relationship and transference. Once this is accomplished, the return from narcissistic withdrawal to object cathexis will relieve the patient, at least temporarily.

I believe, there are many cases where the analyst would be wise to be content with this partial success without urging further treatment. A further, and deeper, involvement in the transference may well arouse all the anxieties described above and, again, lead to abrupt termination of the analysis due to the adolescent's flight reaction.

Defense by Regression.—The greater the anxiety aroused by the object ties, the more elementary and primitive is the defense activity employed by the adolescent ego to escape them. Thus, at the extreme height of anxiety, the relations with the object world may be reduced to the emotional state known as "primary identification" with the objects. This solution with which we are familiar from psychotic illnesses implies regressive changes in all parts of the personality, i.e., in the ego organization as well as in the libido. The ego boundaries [3] are widened to embrace parts of the object together with the self. This creates in the adolescent surprising changes of qualities, attitudes and even outward appearance. His allegiance to persons outside himself betrays itself in these alterations of his own personality (i.e., his identifications) rather than in an outflow of libido. Projections, together with these identifications, dominate the scene and create a give-and-take between the self and object which has repercussions on important ego functions. For example, the distinction between the external and internal world (i.e., reality testing) becomes temporarily negligible, a lapse in ego functioning which manifests itself in the clinical picture as a state of confusion.

Regression of this kind may bring transitory relief to the ego by emptying the oedipal (and many of the preoedipal) fantasies of their libi-

[3] See P. Federn (1952) and, following him T. Freeman et al. (1958).

dinal cathexis.[4] But this lessening of anxiety will not be long-lived. Another and deeper anxiety will soon take its place which I have characterized on a former occasion (1951) as the fear of emotional surrender, with the accompanying fear of loss of identity.

(II) DEFENSE AGAINST IMPULSES

Where the defenses against the oedipal and preoedipal object ties fail to achieve their aim, clinical pictures emerge which come nearest to the borderline toward psychotic illness.

The "ascetic" adolescent.—One of these, the "ascetic" adolescent, I have described before as fighting all his impulses, preoedipal and oedipal, sexual and aggressive, extending the defense even to the fulfillment of the physiological needs for food, sleep, and body comfort. This, to me, seems the characteristic reaction of an ego, driven by the blind fear of overwhelming id quantities, an anxiety which leaves no room for the finer distinctions between vital or merely pleasant satisfactions, the healthy or the morbid, the morally permitted or forbidden pleasures. Total war is waged against the pursuit of pleasure as such. Accordingly, most of the normal processes of instinct and need satisfaction are interfered with and become paralyzed. According to clinical observation, adolescent asceticism is, with luck, a transitory phenomenon. For the analytic observer it provides precious proof of the power of defense, i.e., of the extent to which the normal, healthy drive derivatives are open to crippling interference by the ego.

On the whole, analytic treatment of the ascetic type does not present as many technical difficulties as one would expect. Perhaps, in these individuals, defense against the impulses is so massive, that they can permit themselves some object relationship to the analyst and, thus, enter into transference.

The "Uncompromising" Adolescent.—Another, equally abnormal adolescent, is described best as the "uncompromising" type. The term, in this instance, does refer to more than the well-known conscious, unrelenting position adopted by many young people who stand up for their ideas, refuse to make concessions to the more practical and reality-

adapted attitudes of their elders, and take pride in their moral or aesthetic principles. "Compromise," with these adolescents, includes processes which are as essential for life as, for example, the cooperation between impulses, the blending of opposite strivings, the mitagation of id strivings by interference from the side of the ego. One adolescent whom I observed in analysis did his utmost, in pursuit of this impossible aim, to prevent any interference of his mind with his body, of his activity with his passivity, his loves with his hates, his realities with his fantasies, the external demands with his internal ones, in short, of his ego with his id.

In treatment this defense was represented as a strong resistance against any "cure," the idea of which he despised in spite of intense suffering. He understood correctly that mental health is based in the last resort on harmony, i.e., on the very compromise formations which he was trying to avoid.

THE CONCEPT OF NORMALITY IN ADOLESCENCE

Where adolescence is concerned, it seems easier to describe its pathological manifestations than the normal processes. Nevertheless, there are in the above exposition at least two pronouncements which may prove useful for the concept: (1) that adolescence is by its nature an interruption of peaceful growth, and (2) that the upholding of a steady equilibrium during the adolescent process is in itself abnormal. Once we accept for adolescence disharmony within the psychic structure as our basic fact, understanding becomes easier. We begin to see the upsetting battles which are raging between id and ego as beneficient attempts to restore peace and harmony. The defensive methods which are employed either against the impulses, or against the object cathexis, begin to appear legitimate and normal. If they produce pathological results, this happens not because of any malignancy in their nature, but because they are overused, overstressed, or used in isolation. Actually each of the abnormal types of adolescent development, as it is described above, represents also a potentially useful way of regaining mental stability, normal if combined with other defenses, and if used in moderation.

[4] See in this connection M. Katan (1950).

To explain this last statement in greater detail: I take it that it is normal for an adolescent to behave for a considerable length of time in an inconsistent and unpredictable manner; to fight his impulses and to accept them; to ward them off successfully and to be overrun by them; to love his parents and to hate them; to revolt against them and to be dependent on them; to be deeply ashamed to acknowledge his mother before others and, unexpectedly, to desire heart-to-heart talks with her; to thrive on imitation of and identification with others while searching unceasingly for his own identity; to be more idealistic, artistic, generous, and unselfish than he will ever be again, but also the opposite: self-centered, egoistic, calculating. Such fluctuations between extreme opposites would be deemed highly abnormal at any other time of life. At this time they may signify no more than that an adult structure of personality takes a long time to emerge, that the ego of the individual in question does not cease to experiment and is in no hurry to close down on possibilities. If the temporary solutions seem abnormal to the onlooker, they are less so, nevertheless, than the hasty decisions made in other cases for one-sided suppression, or revolt, or flight, or withdrawal, or regression, or asceticism, which are responsible for the truly pathological developments described above.

While an adolescent remains inconsistent and unpredictable in his behavior, he may suffer, but he does not seem to me to be in need of treatment. I think that he should be given time and scope to work out his own solution. Rather, it may be his parents who need help and guidance so as to be able to bear with him. There are few situations in life which are more difficult to cope with than an adolescent son or daughter during the attempt to liberate themselves.

SUMMARY

In the foregoing paper the author has reviewed and summarized some of the basic literature on adolescence, as well as her own views on the subject. Her former description of the defensive processes in adolescence has been amplified to include specific defense activities directed against the oedipal and pre-oedipal object ties.

11. THE COMPETITION FOR ADOLESCENT ENERGIES *

JAMES S. COLEMAN

When a child is a small child, he must learn if he is to stay alive. His energies must be fiercely concentrated toward understanding the world in which he lives, toward becoming what he is not. When a man is a grown man, he may distribute his energies as he sees fit. His security and shelter are often assured, and when they are not, the activities which make them so have little to do with learning. I saw my young son recently, intensely concentrating on cutting a paper in the shape of a circle. He *must* do that, and he would do it, trying until he someday pulled himself to an "adult" level of competence. In the meantime his father, who could already cut a circle reasonably well, sat, newspaper in hand, mind wandering, eyes scanning, energies dissipated in a multitude of directions. The young son, having to fight his way out of the ignorance and incompetence of childhood, has his energies focused by that fight. The father, having won that battle, can relax his energies.

Somewhere in between is the adolescent—

* Coleman, James S., "The Competition for Adolescent Energies," *Phi Delta Kappan*, 1961, *42*, pp. 231-236.

old enough to make his way in the physical world, yet too young to manage the complexities of modern industrial society. He can handle himself in the society of his peers, and, to be sure, in the company of adults as well. A boy can hold a job if he likes, he can own and drive a car; a girl suddenly finds herself able to hold her own in the world of womanly competition—in the same league with adult women, if she so chooses. And adolescents today have more of the equipment of adult life than ever before. Cars are the most important, but there are other things. Adolescents have become an important market not only for popular music (where they have always constituted the major part of the audience), but also for movies, which have turned more and more to adolescents, since television diverted the mass adult audience. Similarly for many other commodities, particularly clothes and sporting goods, adolescents now constitute a very important market with their own considerable buying power. For several years they have even had their own special market researcher, discovering their tastes and locating their weaknesses for wide-awake entrepreneurs.

In short, the adolescent no longer faces the barriers of illiteracy, inarticulateness, and inability to comprehend which focused his energies and forced him to learn as a child. These fundamental hurdles overcome, his energies may spread themselves in the diverse directions toward which our affluent society pulls. For the first time, "learning" has serious competitors for his attention and energy. The primacy of the school can no longer be taken for granted, and formal education must take its place alongside the other activities which compete for an adolescent's energy. If formal education can successfully compete with these other matters, well and good, but compete it must, for learning no longer has the unquestioned primacy it once had when the child was unable to cut a paper into the shape of a circle.

Not so very long ago in our society, and even yet in most other societies, the natural hurdles offered by the child's environment were quickly followed by others just as natural. Children were thrust into a man's world when they had reached a man's size: they quickly went into

an occupation, whether on the farm, or in their father's shop, or as a houseservant, or into academic training for a specific occupation such as law, medicine, ministry, or teaching. In every case, the occupation offered its specific and very visible hurdles, whether physical or mental, hurdles which continued to focus energies until some security was gained.

THE LIMBO WE CALL ADOLESCENCE

These immediate hurdles leading to a specific occupation which once existed for a boy or girl of fourteen or fifteen are no longer in evidence. The requirements of industrial society have greatly extended the period of general education, and have created a state of limbo which we know as adolescence. The adolescent is no longer child, not yet adult; he is uncommitted to any specific occupation with its specific hurdles, yet he is "committed" to an institution which is devoted to educating him. That institution, of course, is the high school.

If that institution is to succeed, it must manage to capture the energies and attention of the inmates who are committed to it. It must compete "in the open market," so to speak, for the energies which are no longer focused on learning by the natural hurdles of the environment. It has some advantages over other competing activities, for it has physical control over adolescents for a large portion of each day, and it has a stamp of approval in the form of a diploma and records for college admission, which it can give or withhold.

These are important weapons in the competition for adolescent energy, and they are used implicitly or explicitly by every high school, and by every teacher. But these weapons are of a coercive sort, reminding one of the dictum, "You can lead a horse to water, but you can't make him drink." The horse is under the external control of the master, and the adolescent under the external control of the adult, but the horse and the adolescent will drink at their respective fountains only if they want to do so—disdaining the master's or adult's plea that it is in their own interest.

That such external control is not highly effective is obvious to any observer of our society. The casual observer of modern "youth culture" might easily wonder whether these weapons are at all effective in the competition for adolescent energy. Adolescents' lives are filled with many things, their energies flow in many directions, and much as adults might wish that the flow toward learning be great, the hard facts of the case suggest otherwise.

I have just finished a detailed study of ten high schools—city, suburban, and small town; upper class, middle class, and working class—and some of the results of the research are relevant here, to answer the question: "What, in fact, *are* adolescents interested in? What captures their collective and individual attention and directs their energy?"

The schools I have studied are extremely diverse. The smallest has an enrollment of 100, the largest 2,000. The poorest is a parochial school in big city slums, with a dark, dingy, and tiny building. The richest is in a very well-to-do suburb, with a new building in a country club atmosphere. In the former, only 1 per cent of the fathers have finished college; in the latter, 40 per cent have finished college. In two schools, farmers are the largest occupational group; one school in a new suburb contains almost nothing but blue-collar workers' children, and in the well-to-do suburban school, managers and owners of large businesses are the largest occupational group, closely followed by professionals.

IMPORTANCE OF ATHLETICS, "RIGHT" CROWD

These schools, in short, were selected for their very diversity. Yet most striking to the naive adult observer are the similarities from school to school in the directions teen-agers' energies flow. In the questionnaire, we asked several questions which show this well. Each boy was asked to rank several items according to their importance in making a boy "looked-up-to" or important in the eyes of other boys. In every school—small town, suburban, and big city; working class, middle class, and upper class—being an athlete ranked highest, when compared with numerous other things (getting good grades, being an activities leader, having a car, etc.). And in every school "being in the leading crowd" ranked second highest. Girls, asked a similar question, ranked being in the leading crowd *highest* by far in every school, surpassing activities

leadership, good clothes, good grades, and other goals.

Anyone who has had any contact with high schools is well aware of this powerful element in the social system of the school. Schools larger than the ones I have studied (that is, larger than about 2,000) may be able to support more than one leading crowd, just as large adult communities are able to support more than one social elite. However, in schools of the size I studied there is one leading crowd, and it exerts a powerful force in focusing the energies of adolescents. Its activities and interests constitute the norm of the adolescent society, toward which others strive. Though some students reject the leading crowd, most do not, but strive to be part of it. If they cannot, then the psychological consequences are far from trivial: they more often say they would like to trade and be someone different from themselves when they are asked such a question; their self-confidence is undercut in various other ways, and they spend considerably more time watching television and listening to records than do the others (a fact which strongly reinforces the oft-suggested theory that television is used as an escape from a disturbing situation).

ENERGY GOES IN JOCKEYING FOR STATUS

Thus a great amount of the energy of adolescents goes toward purely social matters, toward a continuous jockeying for status in the adolescent society or in some sub-section of it; or, in cases where this status is not forthcoming, to a more rewarding fantasy life such as television and popular music provide.

Now we as adults may bemoan this fact, this continual struggle for status and recognition, and the powerful hold of "the group" among adolescents. But in this, adolescent societies are not different from adult societies, where status is equally important, and the struggle for status, recognition, and respect is equally great.

This is not to say that high schools are invariant in the importance of "the crowd": some high schools constitute societies more nearly than do others. In city schools which are not built around distinct geographic communities, "the group" and the "leading crowd" are less powerful than in suburbs and in small towns. The leading crowd was of *most* importance, and social acceptance of highest importance, in the well-to-do suburban school. For example, all students in the ten schools studied were asked to rank several items according to importance "among the things you strive for during your high school days." One item was "learning as much as possible in school," another was "being accepted and liked by other students." The way these two items were ranked gives some indication of the relative importance "learning" and "social" matters have among these teen-agers. On the average, these two items were ranked about the same; but in the well-to-do suburban school which encompassed the greatest part of an adolescents' life (the school where 40 per cent of the fathers completed college, and where 75 per cent of the students were planning to go to college), social acceptance ranked considerably higher than did learning. In fact, social acceptance was accorded more importance relative to that of "learning as much as possible" in this school than in *any* of the other nine schools.

This was true despite the educated parents of these children, despite the excellent school facilities, despite the fact that their teachers were far better trained and could offer far more challenge than those in other schools, despite the fact that they were preparing for college, and despite the fact that their actual preparation was undoubtedly the best of all these schools. (This school is no peculiar deviant; it is on several current lists of "best" schools in the country, lists based not upon the interest in learning which these schools generate in their students but on physical facilities, curriculum, and teacher salaries.)

It is interesting to note that in this school, as in most of the others, the importance of social acceptance *rises* over the four years from freshman to senior, while the importance of learning *drops;* and in this school these shifts were more marked than in any other.

PARENTS MAKE SCHOOL
A SOCIAL COSMOS

There are several reasons for the great importance attached to social matters, but one is quite clear: in this school, as in many other well-to-do suburban schools, the parents have expanded the functions of the school to encompass the total social life of the students: dancing classes before and after school, parties, extracurricular activities, and various diversions to keep them busy, off the street, and out of their parents' lives. In other words, the parents have created of the school a true social system (so that two of the outstanding items in the school newspaper are the gossip column and the social events column, which reports on recent houseparties). This has the desired effect of pulling a greater and greater part of the adolescents' energies and interests into the school, but it does so in such a way that the "school" toward which the adolescents' energies are directed is hardly recognizable to the adult whose conception of school is a more traditional one.

This is not to say, of course, that classes do not go on as usual (and under far better instructional techniques and far better trained teachers than in schools of some years ago, or than in more traditional schools today); it is to say, rather, that the classroom activities are embedded within a powerful culture whose interests are diverse. The sweater a girl wears to class takes on great significance, overshadowing the significance of the algebra lesson to be learned; apparently casual conversations become loaded with the significance of getting into a certain clique; a boy's response to a teacher is fashioned with regard for the impression it makes upon other boys in his group; between-class conversation centers around recent social events.

The strategy, then, of this community and many other modern upper middle class suburbs in making "adolescent social centers" of their schools has somewhat unanticipated consequences: though it captures energies within the school, it does so by changing the school into a very different institution.

It is important not to misunderstand what I am saying. It has nothing to do with the "life-adjustment" vs. "academic emphasis" controversy. This often-forced dichotomy is a false one, for it forgets that most of the teen-ager's energy is not directed toward either of these goals. Instead, the relevant dichotomy is on the one hand an interest in cars and cashmere sweaters, backbiting and social exclusion, cliques and crowds, versus *learning* on the other hand, whether of the academic or life-adjustment variety.

But, one might argue, these highly social activities are themselves preparation for life, adjustment to life. I would certainly agree that boys and girls learn more about the hard realities of social life through their cliques and crowds than through their social studies courses. A girl comes to learn that discrimination is bad, not through the moral preachments of her social studies classes, but in "learning by living" when she is excluded from the group she aspires to. Another girl, on the other end of the excluding process, also learns by living; but she learns that discrimination does a pretty good job of enhancing the status of her clique.

That such training for life is effective no one will dispute. What is questionable, however, is whether it is adjustment to a civilized society or to a society of the jungle, where the war of all against all rages at its fiercest.

A SOLUTION THAT IS NO SOLUTION

I'm suggesting, then, that one solution, one way in which adolescent's energies are incorporated within the school, is not a solution at all. Every evidence from my research suggests, in fact, that it diverts energies even further away from learning than they usually are. How, then, is learning to capture the energies of teen-agers, to effectively compete against the other activities which struggle for an adolescent's attention? If it cannot do so by incorporating those outside activities, what is the alternative?

SOME ALTERNATIVE SOLUTIONS

One alternative is exemplified by the parochial boys' school in the city, a school which was stripped down and barren in both its physical aspect and its extracurricular and social activities. Many of the boys did not know each other outside school, for the school drew boys from many neighborhoods. In this school the social system of adolescents was hardly admitted into the school—partly by the absence of girls, partly by the absence of community or neighborhood, partly by the lack of extracurricular activities.

As a consequence, these boys were at the opposite extreme from the well-to-do suburban school in the relative importance they gave to "learning as much as possible in school" and "being accepted and liked by other students." The rank of social acceptance, relative to that of learning, was lowest of all in this school. There was, in short, far less infiltration of social relations into the classroom here. The jungle of dating activities and of social maneuver was excluded by the very barrenness of the school program. As a consequence, prestige among the boys in school depended almost solely upon two things: athletic achievement and scholastic achievement. The athletes and the scholars were admired and envied here, the athletes somewhat more than the scholars. It was evident in numerous ways that the energies of the parochial school boys were more nearly directed toward learning, less infused with extraneous matters.

Is this, then, the answer—that learning can best compete for an adolescent's energies by shedding itself of external allures (the opposite sex, extra-curricular activities, clubs, and the like)? It would seem so but for one slight omission in the above description of the parochial boys' school: The total energies which these boys brought to school were far less than in the other nine schools. Of those energies which the school captured, a great many were directed toward learning, but the sum total of these energies was not high. For many of these boys lived their real lives, and had their greatest interests, outside the school. After-school jobs—or more frequently, street corner gangs—constituted some considerable part of their interests.

These, then, appear to be the two horns of the dilemma: to incorporate adolescent social life into the school and see it pervade every corner of scholastic activity, or to keep it outside and see the adolescent energies stay outside as well. The first alternative is the modern one, taken on by more and more schools, as parents force the schools into taking their adolescents off their hands. The second is the more traditional one, the one which kept schools to a single pure function, that of teaching and learning.[1]

A FAMILIAR DILEMMA TO THE SOCIOLOGIST

To a sociologist, this dilemma is similar to problems faced by many other institutions. To cite just one example, the TVA found itself with these alternatives: to keep its goals intact but face possible destruction at the hands of vested local interests, or to gain the support of these powerful farmers and give up one of its goals, the goal of developing conservation areas surrounding its lakes. It chose the latter course.

But is this the best an institution can do— to choose one of the two evils facing it? I think not. There are a number of hints to the contrary. One such hint comes from some peculiar results in my research concerning the girls in the well-to-do suburban school. By all evidences, these girls (and the boys as well) are more socially mature than those in any of the other schools. Their parents have given them dancing lessons, have taught them manners, have often treated them as equals. In other ways they have been brought to a level of social assurance and independence greater than that of students in other schools. It is a surprise, then, to find that among these girls the brilliant student's popularity with boys, relative to that of the girl who is an activities leader, is *lowest* of all the schools. Consistent with this, girls in this school shy away from the label of "brilliant student" and are drawn to the label of activities leader more often than those in any other school. Why? The reason seems in part to be this: These

[1] Speaking conjecturally, I suppose that the traditional, single-sex, single-function barren schools are better for the bright, college-bound boy or girl whose energies are already directed toward learning; the modern, luxurious, multi-function school most typified by Scarsdale in New York or New Trier in Illinois is best for the boy or girl whose energies wander away from learning. That is, most of the students in the well-to-do suburban school I studied would have been better off in the boys' barren parochial school; more of their energies would have been captured by *learning* and by a desire to learn. In contrast, the boys of the slum, uninterested in school, would have had more of their energies captured for learning in the enticing suburban school.

adolescents are no longer children, and the girl who is admired and sought after by boys is the *active* girl, not the girl who is still conforming to adult standards by her concern with studies and good grades.

That is, "good grades" and concentration upon studies are seen by the adolescent community, and rightly so, as acquiescence and conformity to adult constraints. By contrast, social affairs, extracurricular activities, and athletics are activities of their "own," activities in which adolescents can carry out positive actions on their own, in contrast to school work, where they carry out "assignments" from teachers. Such assignments are galling to any community which feels itself at all autonomous. It is no wonder that the acquiescent girls, who are still conforming to parental and school "assignments," are not more popular with boys.

It needn't be this way, of course, for academic achievement is inherently no more passive than is any extracurricular activity. It is only that academic matters in school are still largely presented to adolescents as something to be received, as prescribed "exercises," as "assignments"; that is, they are matters which require more receptivity than positive action.

The first hint, then, is this: Adolescent energy is not going to be successfully won for learning by keeping the learner in a passive role, one in which "grades" dispensed by the teachers (like gold stars to kindergarteners) are the only mark of achievement. The energy needs somewhere to *go*, some goals to be won. Many extracurricular activities have such goals, goals which involve active effort, sometimes creative effort: dramatic presentations, music concerts, putting together a newspaper or a yearbook, and (as the best example) winning an athletic game.

Athletics provides, in fact, a second hint; for athletics has a peculiar role in most high schools. For boys it far outdistances any other school activities in the energy it captures. The time and effort expended by high-school athletes is phenomenal. It subjects boys to a rigid discipline, yet captures nearly all the energies not only of school-oriented boys but also of those for whom the pull of cars and gangs is strong. How and why does it do this? To even a casual observer the answer is straightforward, and research only reinforces it: People are willing to work very hard when they're sufficiently rewarded. An athlete who helps win a game is a star and a hero. He is rewarded by his fellows, and by the adult community as well. He receives the kind of personal rewards—the prestige, attention, and popularity—for which adults strive in their own ways. No other achievement in school gives a boy the same amount of immediate recognition and respect from others. If we wonder why boys work so hard at athletics, we should wonder why men work so hard at becoming successful businessmen, for the successful athlete gains as many of the rewards that accrue to adolescents as the successful businessman gains of the rewards that accrue to adults.

WHY DO WE REWARD THE ATHLETE?

But this does not explain why the adolescent community—and, to be sure, the adult community as well—gives such extra rewards to the star athlete, lifts him on their shoulders, symbolically or in fact, and makes of him a popular hero. Why is the student who achieves highly not acclaimed in the same way, rather than being seen as a grind or a bookworm? The answer is that once in awhile he *does* receive such acclaim, but only under special circumstances: When the star student achieves something for the *school*, as does the star athlete in winning his game, he too becomes a popular hero. A star debater who wins his contests, a National Merit Scholarship winner who brings attention to the school, such boys gain attention and prestige in their school as the ordinary scholar does not. The reason is simple: These boys' achievements are not solely for themselves; they are winning for the school as well, just as is the star athlete. In contrast, the boy or girl who simply gets high grades is achieving for himself alone— he's in competition only with his classmates. His efforts do nothing to give his classmates a sense of communal pride; they only force everyone else to work harder, to keep up. It's no wonder he's often seen by his fellows as a "grind" and a "curve-raiser," whose efforts must be stifled rather than encouraged.

Thus the peculiar fact emerges that the very structure of education acts to *hold down* the adolescent's expenditure of energy toward learning. To be sure, he receives encouragement from teachers and sometimes from parents, and his efforts are sharpened by the classroom competition—but that very competition sets in motion the forces which hold down efforts, forces which "restrict production," so that no one will have to work too hard. In contrast, these same institutions—that is, high schools—have found a marvelous device to capture energy, not for learning but for athletics. The device is interscholastic games, which give an athlete a chance to achieve not only for himself, but for his team and school and community—and receive his just rewards in return. The struggling student, who's often regarded as a little queer because his goals are purely selfish and individual, is deprived of such a chance—not by the nature of intellectual activity, but by the way this activity is structured in the schools.

There exist intellectual games of numerous sorts, and others could easily be invented. Games of strategy can have any content imposed upon them, from mathematics to football. An excellent example is provided by a recent development in executive training. It's called "management games," and involves several teams representing firms competing in a market. An electronic computer serves as the market and responds to the decisions made by each firm. Those firms whose economic knowledge is not sharp slowly lose their share of the market as their competitors' strategies and knowledge overcome them.

One result is already clear from these games: They create an intense involvement among usually staid businessmen, and keep them up till all hours, plotting charts and calculating the market. The game itself, plus the encouragement one receives from teammates, creates such involvement and captures the energies which ordinarily lie dormant as the executives yawn through training films and other audio-visual aids.

LET GOOD STUDENT ACHIEVE
FOR THE SCHOOL

The point, then, is this: Adolescent energies can be successfully captured for learning, intellectual activities can come to captivate their interest, if they are allowed to do so. If a good student is given a chance to achieve for his school and receive the rewards attendant upon doing so, more adolescents will be interested in becoming good students. If interscholastic games were not only athletic games but contained the contents of mathematics and English and sewing and bricklaying, the distribution of adolescent energies would be very different than it now is. If schools in a city or county competed in a "scholastic fair," with teams, exhibits, and tournaments, the impact on adolescents' distribution of energies would be impressive. The solution is not simple in its execution, for it consists of something more than a new course in the curriculum, or graded classes, or sifting out the "gifted children." Yet if it is carried out, and carried out well, it could pull adolescent energies into those directions of learning, of creativity, and of intellectual excitement for its own sake toward which a democratic society aims.

12. SELF DEFINITION AND CONFLICT *

E. Z. FRIEDENBERG

One of the most precise clues to what is actually going on psychologically in a culture is its use of language. People only bother to name those aspects of their experience that mean something to them. Those who share the language, therefore, share to some extent a common situation and a common concern.

If a people have no word for something, either it does not matter to them or it matters too much to talk about. If they *do* have a word for something, it is worth asking why they have included in their concept just what they have, and not other aspects which might, from a slightly different point of view, easily have been included. And if they cannot use the words they have without becoming arch, coy, or diffuse—if they cannot discuss a subject of apparent importance to them with vigor and precision—they are clearly in some kind of trouble about it. When experience is deformed by conflict or anxiety, language no longer quite fits. The personal needs of those who are trying to discuss a problem come between their experience and their common symbols, and they find it difficult to speak about it normally.

Adolescence is one of the topics which is subject to all these difficulties and which is correspondingly difficult to discuss intelligibly in English. Despite our exaggerated concern for and almost prurient interest in the "teen-ager," we have no neutral term for persons between the ages of, say, fourteen and twenty-one. "Adolescent" has overtones at once pedantic and erotic, suggestive of primitive fertility rites and of the orgies of classical antiquity. "Young person" meets the requirements of British jurisprudence in referring precisely to a portion of this age range, but is too poor in connotations to be a useful phrase in ordinary speech. "Teen-ager" remains the choice for popular usage. It is patronizing, and sounds rather uneasy and embarrassed; but these qualities may add to its appeal, for many of us do indeed respond to adolescence with forced joviality.

There is no English noun which simply identifies precisely persons between the ages of fourteen and twenty-one, leaving the reader free to feel what he pleases about them. This is odd. We have neutral nouns for persons and things that arouse feeling in nearly everyone: child, adult, hangman, cancer, mother, mistress, senator. These are exact; they mean what they mean. They can be dissociated from

* Reprinted by permission of the Beacon Press, copyright © 1959, 1964 by Edgar Z. Friedenberg.

their connotations if the context demands it. "Teen-ager" cannot be. What does one call an eighteen-year-old girl if one wishes to note that she has triumphed as Joan of Arc or Anne Frank, or written another successful novel? What does one call an eighteen-year-old boy in reporting that he has been killed in a training maneuver at boot camp? Such things do not happen to "teen-agers," absorbed as they are in delinquency and in endless telephone discussions of rock and roll.

Yet, if we have no convenient language for discussing adolescence we seem equally unable to dismiss it. And this too is rather odd. What is there about these eight or so years that lingers so in the psyche? Granted that puberty is a notable event, that the onset of sexual maturity and the bodily changes which ensue are dramatic, and that no language applies its word for "child" to persons beyond the early teens. Nothing so conspicuous demarcates the adolescent from the young adult; yet adults who are no longer young are likely to feel much more at ease with a young man of twenty-five than with a boy of eighteen. They place the two in different classes of humanity, while allotting thirty years, more or less, to middle age. These thirty years also bring changes in personality and body build, but we see them as gradual and have not divided them up with conceptual barriers.

This conception of an upper limit to adolescence is by no means universal. In most primitive cultures—variable as these are—young people are usually initiated into adult life shortly after puberty. They are conducted through *rites de passage* of varying degrees of harshness designed to "separate the men from the boys"; the separation is not a genuine period of adolescence but a brief *interregnum*. Essentially, in such societies, one is either a child or an adult, though adult society is marked by status differences quite as complex and elaborate as ours.

Adolescence is conceived as a distinct stage of life in societies so complicated and differentiated that each individual's social role and function takes years to define and learn. When years of special preparation for adult life are required, these years become a distinguishable period with its own rules, customs, and relationships. The ordeal of the classical British

preparatory and public school, for example, could not simply be sweated out in a burst of adolescent pluck; the initiation became a way of life. To instill into youth the complex code of the empire-builder and gentleman so thoroughly that this would be maintained in loneliness and isolation, and even under conditions in which it had become something of a nuisance to all concerned, took time and more than time. It took experience, under discipline, in relating to many different kinds of people whose status with respect to oneself varied sharply. In this way, the schoolboy learned to respond with spontaneous and often deep personal feeling to some of the people and events in his life, while limiting the *range* of his response to persons and situations he had learned to regard as worth noticing.

The British public school, at its most imposing, made adolescence much more than an interregnum. It made it an epoch. Its austerity could be relieved by a sensitive husbanding of sparse human resources; its heroes became myths, and in turn clichés, but the schoolboy had strong feelings about them. The prefect who caned you for specific offenses might, at other times, offer brusque understanding when you seriously needed it. He might also be a sadistic bully, or simply a rather stupid boy who was good at games. There were classmates with whom you could share brief, vivid perceptions and long, comfortable silences, though there were many more with whom you could share nothing. There were masters who had some respect for scholarship and for boys, and there were others who respected neither. All these defined themselves through the years as individuals as well as parts of a system. They could be fought, but there was no getting away from them or erasing your experiences with them. At best, they helped the adolescent make himself into a strongly characterized human being who was ready to go on to something more: at worst, their impact made adolescence interminable and their victims permanently fixated "old boys." In any case, they defined the content of adolescence; they gave the adolescent something to be adolescent about.

In a society that sets up special institutions for inducting the young into it, and takes several years doing it, the developmental process that we call adolescence can occur. This institutional provision need not, however, be formal or intentionally planned. A delinquent gang is such an institution. And even institutions as formal and coercive as the classical British public school or the old-fashioned military school influenced their students most strongly in ways that were not consciously planned, though they were certainly the consequence of powerful unconscious intentions.

The unconscious and conscious intentions that dominate a society are, of course, expressed through all its institutions, including those that deal with adolescents. The institutions which mold the adolescence of most young people in technically developed countries today are the instruments of a very different society from that which created the British public school or the military school. They are intended to yield young people predisposed to very different social behavior. They are seldom coercive or immediately painful, but rather informal, democratic, and apparently mild in operation. They make use of sanctions that hardly hurt at all when applied, but that often make their victims ill much later.

The kind of character these institutions—whether the school, the TV, or even the modern army and navy—tend to develop is in many ways the very opposite of that which the British public school, or the old-fashioned school of any kind, sought consciously and unconsciously to produce. All the contemporary institutions that bear on the young, diverse as they seem to be, are united in their insistence of cultivating sensitivity and pliability to the demands and expectations of other persons. Other-direction, adapability, adjustment, conformity—call it what you will, the idea is familiar enough—is a trait of great short-run social usefulness in today's relatively open and rootless society; and that society has done a formidable job of creating institutions which mold other-directed and adjustable character structure.

One might expect that the general increase in blandness and good humor which has resulted would also have sweetened the relationship between adults and adolescents; and in many ways it has. There are real friendships between adolescents and adults in contemporary society, especially in America; it is taken

for granted that there should be. This would not have been possible earlier, and it is still most unusual in many European or Latin-American countries. It is a basic development in human relations, scarcely less important than the simultaneous improvement in relations among different racial groups, which is resulting from quite similar social changes.

But the modern emphasis on cooperation and group adjustment has also injured the relationship between adolescents and adults in two very significant ways. These are not very widely recognized, but they lie, I believe, at the root of our difficulty in considering adolescence without self-consciousness or conflict. The first of these is rather superficial; the second is much more serious.

The tolerant, reasonable, democratic approach to "teen-agers"—like the comparable approach to formerly discriminated racial groups—is based on a premise of greater respect for them than the earlier attitude of coercive, if paternalistic, dominance. This much is valuable. But the same difficulty arises as in the improvement of interracial relations. In order for this to occur smoothly, the members of the dominant group must like and respect the subordinate group a good deal in the first place. If adults dislike or fear adolescents, the change will make those adults more frightened and more hostile, because it is a very real threat to their continued domination. In today's society they will probably have to be "nice to the kids" despite their fear and hostility; but they will most certainly try to maintain by seduction and manipulation the dominance they previously achieved by coercion and punishment.

This, it seems to me, is what usually does happen. Certainly, there are many exceptions, and the proportion seems to be growing nicely; but I think a detached observer of the behavior and attitudes of school personnel, juvenile court officials, and so forth would probably conclude that, on the whole, these individuals dislike and distrust youngsters more often than they like them. They are often disturbed at the prospect of being involved with young people in any situation that is not under their quite complete control; a dean who has grown accustomed to functioning as a rather fair-minded though rigid martinet is likely to become unscrupulous and conspiratorial if changes in his school force him to act as "adviser" to an ostensibly self-governing student disciplinary committee. Such officials are usually willing to abandon coercive techniques of control in favor of manipulative ones, since these help them preserve a more favorable image of themselves as guides who are liked and accepted by their charges; and, in any case, manipulative techniques work better than coercive ones with modern youngsters, who are usually quite skilled themselves at making tyrants feel guilty. But the teacher, dean, or probation officer who genuinely sees youngsters as persons of dignity equal to himself and who is satisfied to have purely rational authority over them is still rather the exception. The point can be overstressed, and I do not mean to suggest that the planet has become a sort of Madison Avenue streamlined version of Dotheboy's Hall. But the perception of the orientation of the world of adults toward adolescents so well and movingly expressed by Holden Caulfield in *The Catcher in the Rye* seems to me almost wholly valid.

Much of the ambivalence of adults toward "teen-agers" is, I should judge, simply a kind of repressed panic-response to the liquidation of authority over them. It must be understood, however, that the loss of authority is real; the adult empire is tottering. All empires are; this is the era of skepticism about the relationship between authority and status. It is an error, I believe, to interpret what is happening as a decline in respect for authority as such. American youngsters today are generous in according respect to parents, teachers, and other adults who earn it as individuals; and they are far more perceptive of individual quality in their elders than they could possibly have been when all adults were regarded as potentially or actually hostile and dangerous. But it is true that they are less likely to respect an adult today simply because he occupies a position of authority. It is also true that a boy who can be punished for insulting you is far less frightening—even if he is *very* insulting—than a boy who offers out of sheer kindness to share his analyst with you because he has noticed, correctly, that you need help worse than he does.

Adults who do not basically like and respect

adolescents—and this includes a large proportion of those who make a career of working with them—are badly frightened by the increasingly democratic relationships between adolescents and adults that are coming to prevail in our society. They have become more tense in their attitude toward youngsters, and contribute greatly to the difficulties of young people in our society. Their manipulative and covert hostility demoralizes adolescents and forms the basis of real personal and social problems. It is easier, and less damaging, for a youngster to face bad grades, disappointment at being passed over for a team or a club, or formal punishment, than it is for him to deal with gossip about his character or his manners, with teachers who pass the word along that he is a troublemaker or that he needs special patience and guidance because his father drinks.

Nevertheless, this is probably not too serious a matter, for it is pretty certain to work itself out in the course of time. Newer and better trained teachers and social workers tend to be of a somewhat different stamp. The youngsters themselves grow more accustomed to respectful handling and more confident of it; they become less rebellious but also easily diverted from their own moral judgments and decisions. When they *do* nevertheless have to deal with a hostile or tricky adult, they are more likely to know what they want and what they are doing, and can face him coolly. He, in turn, is *not* really confident of himself or his authority, and rapidly becomes more anxious. He may stubbornly refuse to listen; he may lose his temper and really try to hurt them, and this time he may succeed. But he also finds that his efforts to dominate the young cause him more anxiety than he can easily bear. Unless his superiors support him in a counterattack, he is likely to withdraw gradually behind a barrage of indignant complaint. Ultimately, he becomes picturesque; the young may grow quite fond of him.

What is far more serious is that the emphasis on cooperation and group adjustment characteristic of modern life interferes specifically with the central developmental task of adolescence itself. *This task is self-definition. Adolescence is the period during which a young person learns who he is, and what he really feels. It is the time during which he differentiates himself from his culture, though on the culture's terms. It is the age at which, by becoming a person in his own right, he becomes capable of deeply felt relationships to other individuals perceived clearly as such.* It is precisely this sense of individuality which fails to develop, or develops only feebly, in most primitive cultures or among lower-status social groups. A successful initiation leads to group solidarity and a warm sense of belonging; a successful adolescence adds to these a profound sense of self—of one's own personality.

Personalization is the métier of adolescence. Of all persons, adolescents are the most intensely personal; their intensity is often uncomfortable to adults. As cooperation and group adjustment become pervasive social norms; as tolerance supersedes passion as the basis for social action; as personalization becomes false-personalization, adolescence becomes more and more difficult. Conceivably, it might become again a rather rare event, having no function in the new world of glad-handing primitives happy among their electronic trinkets. But, for the present at least, the old norms of individual character, personal devotion, particular love and hate retain enough authority to make those who remain faithful to them, as adolescents tend to do, extremely troublesome to their contemporaries.

Adolescents often behave much like members of an old-fashioned aristocracy. They maintain private rituals, which they often do not really understand themselves. They are extremely conservative in their dress and tastes, but the conventions to which they adhere are purely those of their own social group; they try to ignore the norms of the larger society if these conflict with their own. They can be extravagantly generous and extravagantly cruel, but rarely petty or conniving. Their virtues are courage and loyalty; while the necessity for even a moderate degree of compromise humiliates them greatly. They tend to be pugnacious and quarrelsome about what they believe to be their rights, but naïve and reckless in defending them. They are shy, but not modest. If they become very anxious they are likely to behave eccentrically, to withdraw, or to attack with some brutality; they are less likely to blend themselves innocuously into the environment with an apologetic smile. They are honest on occasions when even a stupid adult would have better sense.

They are therefore at a considerable disadvantage in many relationships of modern life. Modern life is hostile to the aristocratic social principle. Aristocratic attitudes and modes of action snarl its very mainsprings. They interfere with the conduct of practical affairs and impede administrative action. In busy, anxious, and ambitious people, they arouse anger and resentment; but beneath the anger and resentment there is shame and guilt.

Adolescents insult us by quietly flaunting their authenticity. They behave as if they did not even know that passion and fidelity are expensive, but merely assumed that everyone possessed them. This, certainly, is inexcusably valorous; and it is not excused. But it makes us awkward in their presence, and embarrassed in our approach to them.

Not all adolescents, by any means, retain this quality. There are many who learn to soothe adults ruffled by encounters with their more ardent and challenging peers, and charm them on suitable occasions by an ingratiating youthfulness. When a boy or girl is needed for display, they are available; in the same clothes all the others wear, they look a little—not too much—neater. Having them in charge of the school paper and the student government saves a good deal of wear and tear all around; they are described in their school records as having qualities of leadership.

At certain times and places—perhaps here and now—such boys and girls predominate. Processes comparable to natural selection almost insure that they will. Schools nudge them into the pathways believed to lead to success in adult life and rehearse them for it in carefully designed facsimiles of adult institutions. Student life in the modern high school is now conducted through a veritable rat-maze of committees. The big man on campus is a perfectly executed scale model of a junior executive. It may therefore seem either inconsistent or willfully sentimental that I have described my heuristic model of an adolescent as a knight in shining chino pants.

But I think it is valid to maintain this, not just because I have encountered a goodly few such errant defenders of the faith in the course of half a lifetime, but because I am concerned here with a process of growth rather than with a statistical norm. There is certainly no doubt that modern society has power to corrupt, and that it starts early. But the function of adolescence is growth and individuation, and these can be fruitful only if a reasonable and increasing degree of integrity is maintained.

A youngster who has abandoned the task of defining himself in dialectical combat with society and becomes its captive and its emissary may be no rarity; but he is a casualty. There is not much more to be said about him: one can only write him off and trust that the world will at least feed him well if it cannot keep him warm. The promise of maturity must be fulfilled by those who are strong enough to grow into it at their own rate as full bargaining members.

Must there be conflict between the adolescent and society? The point is that adolescence *is* conflict—protracted conflict—between the individual and society. There are cultures in which this conflict seems hardly to occur; but where it does not, the characteristic development of personality which we associate with adolescence does not occur either.

There are cultures, as in Margaret Mead's classic description of coming of age in Samoa, where the young pass delicately as Ariel through puberty into adulthood. But their peoples do not seem to us like adults; they are charming people, but they are from our point of view insufficiently characterized. There is not much difference between them, and they do not seem to make much difference to one another.

In other simple cultures, in which the role of the adult is likewise thoroughly familiar to the child by the time he reaches puberty, the young are initiated into adult life much more harshly. Sometimes the process is more loving than it appears to be, though the very fact that adults find it necessary to inflict it is conclusive evidence of some hostility toward the young. In any case, it is comparatively brief. Some of these cultures are primitive; others are relatively stable subcultures of the Western world like that of British coal miners whose sons are hazed into adult status by their

elders when they first enter the mines themselves. But in these as well, the adults seem curiously indistinguishable by our criteria of personality. Differences of temperament and of attitude toward life may be very conspicuous indeed. But they stop short of what we regard as normal variation of human personality; the range is as wide, but not as deep.

And there are other cultures in which there is no conflict because conflict is thoroughly repressed. Not by externally applied brutality —this suppresses; it does not effectively repress. There are adolescents even in totalitarian countries, as the Polish and Hungarian authorities discovered in 1956. But where totalitarianism really sinks in, even the young will be so intensely anxious that no conflict will arise. Only those feelings and attitudes approved by society will then even occur to them as possibilities. There can be no adolescence in *1984*.

Conflict between the individual and society, as Lionel Trilling has so clearly stated in *Freud and the Crisis of Our Culture*,[1] is inherent in the development of personality by the standards of Western man. Freud is still the source of our most tough-minded psychodynamic system, and this point is basic to it. And it is in adolescence that this conflict is critical to individual development. Or to put it another way, and perhaps more truly, adolescence *is* this conflict, no matter how old the individual is when it occurs. Adolescent conflict is the instrument by which an individual learns the complex, subtle, and precious difference between himself and his environment. In a society in which there is no difference, or in which no difference is permitted, the word "adolescence" has no meaning.

But conflict is not war; it need not even involve hostile action. It must, to be sure, produce some hostile feelings, among others. But there need be no intent to wound, castrate, or destroy on either side. Conflict between the adolescent and his world is dialectical, and leads, as a higher synthesis, to the youth's own adulthood and to critical participation in society as an adult. Some of the experiences of adolescence which turn out to be most beneficial to growth are, it is true, painful at the

[1] Boston: The Beacon Press, 1955.

time. Looking for your first job, among strangers; learning that your first love is the girl she is but not the girl you need; getting soundly beaten in your first state-wide track meet when you are used to being the fastest runner in town—none of this is fun. But such experiences are not sickening, heartbreaking, or terrifying because, even at the time, they can be felt as bringing you in closer touch with reality. The pain they produce is somehow accepted as benign, like soreness following unaccustomed physical exercise or the pain or normal childbirth. Growth is more satisfying and far more reassuring, than comfort; though normal growth is comfortable most of the time.

One cannot, therefore, use the inevitability of conflict in adolescence as a justification for actions which hurt adolescents on the pretext of "toughening them up." If "growing pains" are never sickening, heartbreaking, or terrifying, it is equally true that heartbreak, terror, and a sense of insult and violation contribute nothing to growth. They stunt it or twist it, and the grower is more or less deformed. Perhaps the commonest deformation which these cause in persons too young to know how to handle themselves in pain is apathy.

In their encounters with society, youngsters are frequently badly hurt, and there is no mistaking this kind of agony for growing pains. They are sickened and terrified; they feel their pride break, cringe from the exposure of their privacy to manipulation and attack, and are convulsed with humiliation as they realize that they cannot help cringing and that, in fact, their responses are now pretty much beyond their control. Control once regained is consolidated at a less humane level; there will be no more love lost or chances taken on the adversary.

A number of psychological and social dynamisms can take over at this juncture; none of them is a part of the process of healthy growth, though some at least give time for scars to form so that growth may be resumed later. But most of these defense mechanisms are dangerous in their total context, although they make perfectly good sense in the light of the victim's immediate emotional condition. This is the fundamental dilemma of organism. A severe heart attack is not such a bad idea from the immediate viewpoint of the exhausted heart, if only the rest of the body and the heart itself, as a muscle, were not so thirsty for blood. Somehow, however it has been insulted, the heart must be kept in action, for its own sake as well as for that of the body as a whole; though a wise physician knows when to keep demands on it to a minimum, and also knows that the minimum may still be more than can be borne.

Growth, too, must continue. Apathy, a fawning acceptance of authority, or a hard-eyed campaign of organized delinquency with enough real violence to show you mean business, may all be understood as functional for adolescents bearing certain kinds of wounds. But understandable or not, functional or not, these are dangerous expedients for the young. They may provide cover for the processes of healing, and facilitate the formation of strong emotional scar tissue. But they not only lead to more trouble with society; they lead away from the kinds of relationships by which growth continues, and from the kind of self-perception of which growth consists.

Delinquency, apathy, and seductive fawning are not aspects of the essential conflict between youth and society which constitutes adolescence. They are the consequences of the conflict having gone terribly wrong, and a corresponding wisdom and patience—more than is usually available under actual working conditions—are needed to restore it as a fruitful process. For most young people, of course, things do not go terribly wrong. They go moderately wrong, but we nevertheless grow up, more or less, and conduct ourselves toward the next generation in its need with such humanity as we can muster. For the result, no blame attaches. Adam and Eve, at the time that Cain was born, had no opportunity to read the works of Gesell.

I know of no reason to suppose that, at the present time, there is a crisis in our relationship to youth; and, in any case, this is certainly not a book of instructions to be supplied with adolescents. But if the function of adolescence is self-definition, one would expect it to be very difficult in a society which suffers from a dearth of individuality and in which alienation is a crucial problem. And if the instrument of self-definition is the conflict between the adolescent and a basically humane society—which nevertheless has purposes of its own, and more to do than take care of kids—one would expect the self-defining process to break down as that society became less humane and more manipulative. A society which has *no purposes* of its own, other than to insure domestic tranquillity by suitable medication, will have no use for adolescents, and will fear them; for they will be among the first to complain, as they crunch away at their benzedrine, that tranquilizers make you a square. It will set up sedative programs of guidance, which are likely to be described as therapeutic, but whose apparent function will be to keep young minds and hearts in custody till they are without passion.

We have by no means gone so far as yet; but the sort of process of which I speak is already discernible. In this extended essay, I hope to analyze the social processes bearing on adolescence as these show themselves in the social institution officially responsible for their nurture—the school. It will also be necessary to examine the processes of personal and emotional growth fundamental to adolescence, so that we may come to an understanding of what it means to a young person, called a "teen-ager," to try to grow into individual adulthood under the conditions of contemporary life.

Chapter III

LEARNING: THEORY AND PRACTICE

The merging of the disciplines, Psychology and Education, can be seen most clearly in the area of learning. Psychology's contribution, mainly in the form of experimental data on animals, and Education's contribution, chiefly in the form of observations of the child in the learning situation, have blended to further our understanding of the learning process.

Because of its extreme importance to both Psychology and Education, perhaps no other topic has generated the heated controversy that has marked the history of attempts to understand the concept of learning. But controversy is still the "name of the game" in educational psychology, and out of the study of learning has come a large number of actual facts for the social scientist's book of knowledge.

Learning can be defined as a relatively permanent change in behavior produced by environmental stimulation, as opposed to changes due to maturation, and this change in behavior is thought to be accompanied by a change within the organism, most probably in the nervous system. Learning is man's crowning glory, for it allows behavior to be constantly modified. Unlike insects, which are virtually slaves to their never-changing instincts, man and the higher organisms can profit by experience by modifying their behavior to account for changing conditions.

Since their earliest days Psychology and Education have focused attention on learning. Early in the nineteenth century J. F. Herbart outlined the now famous five formal steps of instruction, a kind of teaching formula for ensuring that learning would take place most efficiently. Later in the nineteenth century William James discussed learning and consciousness as a continuous dynamic stream.

About 1885 Hermann Ebbinghaus provided the first actual experimental evidence regarding one kind of learning. He spent long hours memorizing lists of nonsense syllables, and then later checked himself to see how much he had retained. This type of learning is called rote memorization, and research in this area is still being carried out today.

In 1899 a book was published entitled "Animal Intelligence," and its author, Edward L. Thorndike, established himself as the biggest single name in Educational Psychology, a title he was to hold for the next forty years. Thorndike's first experiments involved the study of how cats learned to solve the problem of escaping from a "problem box." It was once said that if one of these cats acted at all unpredictably it would change educational curricula throughout the nation. Although this is an obvious overstatement, it does convey an idea of the tremendous impact Thorndike had on the field of education.

Perhaps Thorndike's most famous contribution to learning theory was his Law of Effect, which stated that a response would tend to be repeated if its consequences led to a satisfying state of affairs, while it would be discontinued if its consequences led to annoyance. Thorndike saw learning as basically trial and error, with the organism slowly eliminating responses that did not lead to success.

Other studies of learning began appearing just after the turn of the century. From Russia came the work of Ivan P. Pavlov who introduced the concept of the conditioned reflex. Pavlov, utilizing the salivary reflex, trained dogs to salivate to previously neutral stimuli, such as the sound of a tone. This procedure is now called Classical Conditioning, and it involves the presentation of a conditioned stimulus (such as a tone), followed immediately by the unconditioned stimulus (meat powder placed in the dog's mouth). After a number of these paired associations, the conditioned stimulus itself will come to elicit the salivation, now called a conditioned response. It was Pavlov's point that the previously neutral stimulus (conditioned stimulus) will take on the power to elicit the response through its having been constantly associated with the unconditioned stimulus. The conditioned stimulus, after training, comes to act as a signal that the meat powder is to follow. There is renewed interest in Classical Conditioning today because of the dramatic success of Wolpe and other conditioning therapists in using this technique to cure neurotics, especially phobics. Almost all the learning theorists up to the present time have borrowed from or used as a point of reference the pioneering work of Pavlov. This can be most obviously seen in the works of the behaviorists, Watson and Guthrie, but Pavlov's work also modified the later thinking of Thorndike.

Another important learning tradition stemmed from a series of experiments originating (1912) in the laboratory of Max Wertheimer. This approach, called *Gestalt Psychology,* emphasized that real understanding was more than just the learning of specific bits of information or specific responses. The term "Gestalt" means the totality, or configuration or "whole," and Wertheimer maintained that the whole was more than just the sum of its specific parts. Thus, the Gestaltists were concerned with the whole learning act, from start to finish, and not with the tiny muscular responses of which it might be composed.

Kohler during the 1920s, and other Gestalt psychologists, also took violent issue with Thorndike, maintaining that insight could occur, that individuals could suddenly see novel relationships, that learning was not simply a function of blind trial and error. Since Harlow's work on "learning sets," described in Chapter I, the concept of "insight" is no longer widely held in modern psychology.

The Gestaltists, especially in the work of Kurt Lewin in the 1930s, saw learning as the forming of concepts, the grasping of facts and ideas as opposed to the learning of muscular responses. E. C. Tolman, following in the Wertheimer-Lewin tradition, has stated (1948) that both rats and men learn by forming hypotheses and seeing relationships. Tolman feels that "cognitive maps" of one's environment are formed, and on the basis of these maps the organism is able to select the appropriate response. Tolman uses his concept of the "cognitive map" to explain how the organisms, rats or men, use their environments to get from place to place. Unlike the S-R psychologists, who see learning as a result of an association formed between the stimulus and response, Tolman hypothesizes that learning is instead a result of an association formed among the stimuli themselves. That is, the organism associates some new stimulus, or *sign*, with a previously encountered and therefore meaningful stimulus, or *significate*. This led Tolman to be labeled as an S-S (sign-significate) psychologist, as opposed to S-R (stimulus-response) theorists such as Guthrie and Watson.

Another historic date in the field of learning is 1938, which saw the publication of B. F. Skinner's *The Behavior of Organisms*. Skinner made the important distinction between two kinds of responses: (1) respondents, which can be automatically elicited by an unconditioned stimulus, such as salivating to food in the mouth; and (2) operants, which may occur on their own, with no specific stimulus having been identified. Skinner saw these two kinds of responses as following distinctly different learning principles. Skinner, however, emphasized operant, as opposed to respondent, conditioning, and with the use of his technique he even envisaged the conditioning of a society. (See Walden II, 1948.)

In the Skinnerian distinction, a respondent is essentially a reflex, and its conditioning conforms to the laws of Classical Conditioning. An operant, however, whose stimulus need not be identified must be conditioned in a different way, since, by definition, an operant cannot be triggered by an unconditioned stimulus.

If an operant is allowed to occur, is "emitted," and is then followed by a positive reinforcement, the rate of response for that operant will increase. Typically, Skinner places a rat in a box which contains a small lever and a food tray. When the rat finally happens to press the lever, reinforcement (a pellet of food) immediately drops into the tray. After a few trials the rate of response jumps dramatically. A rat that might normally emit three or four bar presses per hour before conditioning, might emit presses at a rate of as high as five or six hundred an hour after conditioning has taken place. Even higher rates have been recorded when an animal is on one of the intermittent reinforcement schedules, that is, when the reinforcement does not follow every bar press.

Since the teacher cannot be delivering pellets of food or candy bars every time a student emits an appropriate response, the concept of secondary or conditioned reinforcement is of great importance in educational psychology. With a rat in a Skinner box, conditioned reinforcement can be demonstrated by allowing the response to occur, following it with some previously neutral stimulus (such as a light), and then presenting the pellet of food. Through repeated association with the food, the light eventually takes on reinforcing properties of its own. In a sense, the rat will begin pressing the lever "just to see the light go on." This is secondary or conditioned reinforcement, and examples from life outside the Skinner box are extremely numerous. Perhaps money is the prime example. Notice that the sequence of events is exactly the same as for the rat in the box. One works (emits operants), is paid the money (a neutral stimulus in and of itself), and then is able to buy food or other primary reinforcements. Another obvious example of conditioned reinforcement is the grade assigned after an exam or term paper, or the scholarship awarded to the "Dean's List" student. Implicit also in the operation of the teaching machine is the concept of conditioned reinforcement, usually in the form of allowing the student to progress to the next frame when the correct response has been emitted. Unlike the scholarships or even assigned grade, the teaching machine can provide less distant conditioned reinforcers, in that the delay between response and reinforcement is only a fraction of a second. Skinner's research leads to the conclusion that this is far more efficacious than a delay of a few seconds, never mind a few weeks or months.

Educational psychology today views learning from many points of view, and as the dust settles on the historic theoretical duels of the past a new appreciation of the nature and complexity of learning has emerged. Certainly classical conditioning is a fact. A dog can be trained to salivate to the sound of a tone, but all learning is not of this type. Nor is Thorndike's trial and error learning, nor Kohler's "insight," nor Skinner's operant, nor Tolman's sign-significate, the prototype of all learning. Bruner's idea of concept learning, and Harlow's notion of "learning sets," both of which were mentioned in the first chapter, are also contributing to our knowledge of the total learning process. And finally, as will be seen in the article by Krech, has come startling new evidence regarding the chemistry of learning.

The great theoretical arguments of the past were due in large measure to the adoption of narrow views and to the rigid adherence to one point of view. The debates were often of an "either-or" nature, that, for example, if Tolman were right then surely Skinner must be wrong.

It is becoming increasingly apparent that there is not just one way to learn or one kind of learning, that many of the seemingly diverse positions in learning offer genuine contributions both to our understanding of behavior and to our ability to provide meaningful learning experiences in the classroom.

AN OVERVIEW OF THE READINGS FOR THIS CHAPTER

In the first selection (13) to follow, R. M. Gagné traces the rather stormy history of learning theory in American psychology. Gagné cites five fundamental positions as being at the core of most of the disputes, and the ensuing proliferation of learning theories in psychology he sees as variations on these five basic themes. He lists the following: (1) Associationism —based on the British empirical tradition of explaining how complex ideas are constructed out of simple sense impressions; (2) Animal Trial and Error—based on the use of animals in learning studies, and thought by Gagné to be consistent only with the acquisition of simple motor skills at the human level; (3) The Conditioned Response—founded on Pavlov's classical conditioning paradigm, and again a very restricted formula for explaining human learning; (4) The Learning of Verbal Associates—based on the famous Ebbinghaus study on the memory of nonsense syllables, and again a limited prototype of learning; and (5) Insight—based on the Gestalt premise that learning takes place suddenly as experience is reorganized, a premise that is seriously challenged by the recent work of Harlow on learning sets.

Gagné feels that these quarrels have actually hampered our understanding of learning. Since the various theories were always placed in opposition to each other, they have, in a very real sense, prevented our understanding of "learning as an event."

In the next article (Selection 14), Robert C. Craig focuses on the dilemma of the teacher who is faced with these varieties of learning theories. In attempting to relate theory and the practice of actually teaching, Craig chooses three positions and indicates how each could be applied in the classroom. By contiguity, Craig means those theories, such as Guthrie's or Watson's, which maintain that learning is the result of sensory impressions being immediately followed by impulses to action. The second position, reinforcement, refers to those theories, such as Thorndike's or Skinner's, which see learning as depending on the fact that appropriate responses be consistently followed by positive stimulation. Thirdly, the cognitive approach assumes that learning is the organization of principles or relationships. Without being doctrinaire, Craig offers many useful teaching techniques which logically derive from these three theoretical positions.

Probably no concept in learning has been of more interest to educators than the concept of transfer. In the next article (Selection 15) by Andrews and Cronback, the experimental evidence for transfer, and the resulting educational implications, are carefully detailed. The goal, after all, of education is to provide learning that will transfer to other situations, both in and outside of the classroom. Without transfer the school would have to at least attempt to train the individual for every possible activity he might ever be called upon to face, clearly an impossibility. Fundamental to the construction of any curriculum is the question of what disciplines and areas and even techniques provide for the most transfer.

Many years ago, the teaching of Latin, Greek, and Logic was grounded in the belief that these subjects would discipline the mind, or provide the individual with the mental training which would allow him to cope with the life situation. This notion was merely the product of blind faith, not experimental evidence, but the notion was strengthened when the German faculty psychologists began talking about "thinking" as a separate, *trainable,* faculty of the mind. This view, now discredited, of "mental discipline," though not grounded on the empirical data of transfer, did provide the ground work which allowed the transfer concept eventually to have such a forceful impact in the field of education.

Transfer itself is the experimental fact that the learning and performance in Situation A can affect the learning and performance in Situation B. When the effect is facilitating we speak of positive transfer, and when the effect is inhibitory we call it negative transfer.

After reviewing the actual research on transfer, Andrews and Cronback present five major principles to aid the teacher in taking advantage of transfer in the educational process. This article is extremely important in that it neatly bridges the gap between theory and teaching techniques.

In the next paper (Selection 16), Herbert Thelen, clearly espousing a cognitive view of learning, discusses the question of programmed instruction. Thelen dismisses the use of the teaching machine in conditioning as simply the learning of isolated facts and bits of information. Conditioning, Thelen argues, is the only method for the teaching of nonsense. If, however, concept learning is the goal, as Thelen believes it should be, then insight learning, not conditioning, should be utilized. Is this possible with the teaching machine? Thelen feels it is, and presents a series of eight helpful deductions to prove his case.

Next (in Selection 17), B. F. Skinner presents his case for the teaching machine. Unlike Thelen, Skinner sees the use of the teaching machine as a conditioning device as extremely beneficial in the educational process. Through the proper use of the teaching machine the human organism is more likely to reach full development.

Skinner sees some of the advantages of the machine as allowing the student to proceed at his own pace; the fact that students prefer to study by machine and are, thus, more motivated; the fact that the student gets immediate feed-back; and the fact that aversive control is not necessary. Unlike Thelen in the previous article, Skinner argues that the use of the teaching machine through conditioned reinforcement is not a mere conveyor of trivia and bits of information. Instead, it allows for the teaching of the behavior directly, the very behavior from which we infer that concept formation, for example, has taken place. That is, instead of "transmitting information to the student," the behavior can be set up which is *"taken as a sign that he possesses information."* Rather than teaching the concepts of mathematics, we teach directly the behavior from which the knowledge of these concepts is inferred.

Skinner also feels that for a teaching machine to be truly effective, the student must be made to respond, to take some kind of action. The student must be an active participant, not a passive recipient, in the educational process. Various operants must be emitted in order to be conditioned, and then from this conditioned behavior, we can infer that learning has ocurred. After all, the fact that any learning has ocurred must be inferred from behavior, since we have no way yet of measuring the process itself. We say no way yet, since the evidence to be presented in the next paper suggests that this may be a possibility in the future.

In the final article (Selection 18) for this section, David Krech surveys the extremely exciting and promising research in the chemistry of learning. Krech, pointing to the two-stage memory storage process theory, indicates that the processes involved in short-term memory are somewhat different from those involved in long-term memory. Short-term memory is basically electrochemical, but long-term memory is more biochemical, apparently actually producing new proteins and higher levels of enzyme activity in the brain cells. Thus, while short-term memory does not cause the formation of new proteins, long-term memory does. Krech also cites evidence showing that there is now a rather extensive array of drugs which can increase learning and memory, at least in animals. Does this mean, as Krech whimsically asks, that the teacher should turn in his "schoolmaster's gown for a pharmacists jacket?" The answer, Krech reassures us, is "no," and backs this up with a description of his own extremely exciting research.

Krech reasoned that since numerous experiments had shown that chemical injections can affect memory storage, then perhaps it might work both ways, that is, that environmental stimulation of responses might affect the chemistry of the brain. This rather astonishing hypothesis turned out to be the case. Krech found that when rats were raised in an educationally enriched environment, that is, in well-lighted cages with creative "rat toys" and learning tasks, the actual chemistry of their brains changed. Further, the brains of these environmentally stimulated rats showed *structural changes.* Their brains were more developed, larger and heavier, than the brains of a control group of rats which had been raised in impoverished environments. This, of course, is consistent with Hebb's theory of cell assemblies and phase sequences as outlined in Chapter One of this volume.

Thus, Krech shows that the chemistry and structure of the brain are dependent on the rat's early psychological and educational environment. The weight and density of the cortex was increased by this early rat-type "Head Start Program." Krech's conclusion is: "The biochemist's work can be only half effective without the educator's help."

13.   LEARNING IN AMERICAN PSYCHOLOGY *

ROBERT M. GAGNÉ

How people learn, and the conditions under which they learn, are questions that have been investigated by several generations of American psychologists, as well as by those in other parts of the world. But learning has always been a favorite problem for American writers and researchers, partly no doubt because of a philosophical tradition that tended to place great emphasis on experience as a determiner of knowledge. It is of some value, therefore, to spend a little time in describing what these historically important ideas about the nature of learning have been, since they will point the way to the influences that have shaped current learning theory, and that will undoubtedly affect future developments as well.

Research on learning has generated several typical "models," or *prototypes*, which are frequently referred to by writers on the subject. There are the conditioned response, trial-and-error learning, insight, and others, which are often used to communicate basic similarities and contrasts among situations in which learning occurs. It is important for an understanding of the varieties of learning, to become acquainted with these prototypes of learning and the situations in which they have typically been observed.

THE ASSOCIATIONIST TRADITION

One of the oldest lines of thinking about learning in American psychology derives from

* From *The Conditions of Learning* by Robert M. Gagné. Copyright © 1965 by Holt, Rinehart and Winston, Inc. Reprinted by permission of Holt, Rinehart and Winston, Inc.

the British associationist psychologists, who formulated a number of theories about how ideas are associated. These theorists were primarily concerned with the question of how complex ideas like "flower" or "number" are constructed in the human mind from elementary sense impressions. In other words, they were interested in the question of how such "complex ideas" were learned in the first place. On this latter point, they were generally agreed that acquiring a new idea necessitated (1) *contiguity* of the sense impressions or simple ideas that were to be combined to form the new idea, and (2) *repetition* of these contiguous events. Some of these psychologists also discussed "mental concentration" (which is now usually called attention) as an important condition for the learning of new ideas by association (Mill, 1869).

American psychologists like William James and John Dewey added some distinctly new interpretations to this associationist tradition. The ideas of Darwin concerning the functions of living phenomena in adaptation exerted a considerable influence on these American scholars. Accordingly, they sought to discover the *functions* of behavioral events like learning and thinking, rather than simply the composition of these events. A most important characteristic of learning was considered to be its function in the life of the organism. This view led them to place the *nervous system*, rather than "the mind" in a position of central importance to an understanding of how sense impressions get connected with behavior. And perhaps most significant of all, they assigned a critical role to *action* as a factor in learning. Action did not simply follow ideas, as the British associationists had proposed, but became an essential feature of the process of behavioral organization called learning.

ANIMAL TRIAL AND ERROR

Another direction taken by American psychology in its treatment of learning established perhaps the most important trend of all. This was the use of animals for the performance of experiments on learning. Edward L. Thorndike (1898) was a pioneer in these efforts to understand the learning of animals by performing experiments rather than by collecting anecdotes about animal behavior. From his controlled observations of cats, dogs, and chickens escaping from problem boxes, he concluded that many previous accounts of animal thought were erroneous in that they attributed greater power to animal intelligence than actually existed. His investigations suggested the possibility that all that was necessary to explain animal learning were specific bonds between "sense impressions" and "impulses to action." These associations he considered to be stamped in by the consequences resulting from the completed act (such as escape from the problem box). Thorndike believed that associations of this sort also made up a large part, although not all, of what human beings learned and remembered.

A hungry animal, such as a cat, is placed in a box with slatted sides and a door that can be opened by pressing a wooden lever to release a latch, allowing the animal to reach food placed within his view outside the box. At first, the cat is observed to engage in a variety of acts, including scratching at the sides and door of the box. Sooner or later, these various activities lead by chance to the depression of the latch that opens the door. The animal then immediately leaves the box and eats the bit of food. When placed in the box again, the animal's behavior is obviously changed. He spends less time scratching at the sides of the box, and more time making movements in the region of the latch. On this second trial, it takes him much less time to release the latch and get to the food. Subsequent trials reduce the time still more, until he is releasing the latch only a few seconds after he is placed in the box.

The view of learning that is represented by this prototype situation may be described briefly as follows. When confronted with a novel situation, the motivated learner engages in various "tries" to attain satisfaction. Sooner or later, largely by chance, he makes a set of responses that lead to motive satisfaction. The particular responses that are immediately followed by motive satisfaction (eating the food, in this case) become "stronger" in relation to others. Thus, when the animal is placed in the box a second time, the latch-pressing responses occur sooner, whereas the other responses (like scratching the floor of the box) tend to be shorter in duration or entirely absent. On subsequent trials in the box these "errors" progressively weaken and disappear. The correct responses, in contrast, are progressively strengthened by being followed immediately by motive satisfaction. This generalization was called the "law of effect" by Thorndike. The learning situation does not differ in basic characteristics from that of the rat pressing a lever, employed later by Skinner (1938). "Reinforcement" is the term Skinner uses to identify the events that Thorndike called the law of effect.

Is the animal trial-and-error prototype representative of human learning? The answer is clearly in the negative. It is, in fact, rather difficult to relate it to the learning that might occur in a human being. If a person is put in a problem box, we know that he is likely to adopt a strategy of searching for a way out. He recognizes latches, knobs, or other devices as having certain functions. He "thinks out" the consequences of his actions before he takes them, and chooses the most likely alternative. Once he finds his way out, he will under most circumstances remember it, and there will be no gradual error reduction on subsequent trials. How can such behavior be in any sense comparable to "trial-and-error"? The strategies, the recalling, the recognizing, the thinking, the choosing are all there in his behavior; they can readily be observed if the proper experimental conditions are provided.

By searching hard, one can probably find some degree of comparability between the trial-and-error prototype and the acquisition of a motor skill by young children, such as balancing blocks, making a simple knot, or learning language sounds. Insofar as the prototype helps us to understand such learning, it is useful. But this is, of course, an extremely circumscribed usefulness for the field of learning in general.

A number of more modern learning theorists have made the individual association, as seen in animal behavior, the basis of their ideas on learning. Among these are Edwin R. Guthrie (1935), Clark L. Hull (1943), and B. F. Skinner (1938), each of whom has proposed somewhat different interpretations of the basic idea that the *association*, as observed in animal learning of simple acts, is the typical form of learning. Other investigators of animal learning opposed this tradition, however. Chief among these was Edward C. Tolman (1932), whose experiments convinced him that Thorndike and those who followed him were wrong in asserting that nothing but an "association" existed between a situation and the response that followed it. Tolman's theory maintains that association is an internal matter, between a representation (within the animal's nervous system) of the stimulus situation, and a representation of the alternatives of action to be taken. He thus attempted to restore to animal behavior the "ideas" (although this was not his term) that had been considered unnecessary by Thorndike.

THE CONDITIONED RESPONSE

I. P. Pavlov found that when a signal such as a buzzer was sounded at the time food was given to a hungry dog, and this set of events was repeated several times, the dog came to salivate at the sound of the buzzer alone. Whereas the salivation to the taste of food could be considered a natural (or unconditioned) response, salivation to a buzzer had to be acquired as a conditioned response. This learning occurred when the new signal (the buzzer) was presented together with the food in a number of trials. A new signal-response connection was thereby established.

John B. Watson (1919) championed the view of learning suggested by the work of Pavlov in his studies of conditioning in dogs. In Watson's writings, learning was viewed as a matter of establishing individual associations (conditioned responses) firmly based in the nervous system. More complex human acts were considered to be chains of conditioned responses.

Most investigators of Pavlovian conditioning now believe it to be a very special kind of learning, representative of the establishment of *involuntary*, "anticipatory" responses such as the startled eyeblinking that may follow a threatening gesture (Kimble, 1961). It is likely, of course, that human beings acquire many conditioned responses of this sort in the course of their lives. One may find oneself, for example, waking with a start at the slight click the alarm clock makes before it actually rings. Hearing an automobile horn from an unexpected direction may evoke a tensing of muscles in the hands on the wheel and in the foot on the brake. In the schoolroom, the teacher's pointing to an object to be described may become a conditioned signal for students to be alert for other stimuli to come from that direction. It is even possible that learned anticipatory responses may be largely what is meant by "paying attention" to something. Conditioned emotional reactions of an involuntary sort may be involved in reactions to snakes, spiders, or other events that are accompanied by unexpected signals. Perhaps they also play a part in the determination of attitudes.

Despite the widespread occurrence of conditioned responses in our lives, they remain unrepresentative of most of the events we mean by the word "learning." Voluntary acts can be conditioned only with difficulty, if at all. If a child wants to learn to ride a bicycle, he will get no help in this activity by arranging the pairing of a conditioned and unconditioned stimulus, because voluntary control of his actions is not acquired in this way. The same is true, needless to say, for most other kinds of things he must learn, beginning with reading, writing, and arithmetic. There can be little doubt that Watson's idea that most forms of human learning could be accounted for as chains of conditioned responses is wildly incorrect; and this has been pretty generally conceded for many years.

THE LEARNING OF VERBAL ASSOCIATES

Hermann Ebbinghaus carried out an ingenious set of experimental studies of learning and memorization. He used himself as an experimental subject, and as materials, series of nonsense syllables of the sort NOF-VIB-JEX, and so on. These constructed syllables were employed in the attempt to gain control over the unwanted variable of previous practice, since it was immediately apparent to Ebbinghaus that an association like BOY-MAN was already more or less well learned. In committing to memory these series of nonsense syllables, he was able to study the effects of such variables as length of series, order of presentation, and many others. Later investigators saw in the nonsense syllable a versatile tool for the study of *verbal association*.

An important and productive line of investigation of the learning of nonsense syllables and other verbal units was carried on by Robinson (1932), McGeoch (1942), and down into the present day by Melton (1940, 1964), Underwood (1964), Postman (1964), and many others. Generally speaking, investigators in this tradition have championed empirical research rather than the development of comprehensive theory.

For a period of some years, investigators of verbal associate learning apparently believed that their findings could account for the learning of *single* associations. But even Ebbinghaus's results showed that committing one syllable to memory was strongly influenced by the presence of other syllables. During the many years of research following Ebbinghaus, the number of factors that have been found to affect the learning of nonsense lists has constantly increased, and the difficulty of experimental control has similarly become greater. The learning of any single association in a sequence has been shown to be markedly affected by the *interference* of other associations both within the list and outside it. A great many of the characteristics previously thought to describe the learning of single associates are now attributed to the effects of interference.

The verbal associate prototype must also be considered to represent a very limited range of actual learning situations. The differences in learning and retaining logically connected prose and poetry, as opposed to nonsense lists, have been apparent for many years, and it is doubtful whether the interference that occurs within these two types of material follows the same laws. There may be a limited number of instances in which human beings engage in the learning of material whose members are arbitrarily related, as in learning the alphabet, or π to ten places. But the vast majority of verbal learning that occurs must be affected strongly by its meaningfulness, as experiments on verbal associates have themselves demonstrated.

INSIGHT

Opposed to these associationist trends in studies of learning has been the *Gestalt* tradition, reflected in the writings of Max Wertheimer, Wolfgang Köhler, and Kurt Koffka. As conceived by these writers, learning typically takes the form of an *insight,* which is a suddenly occurring reorganization of the field of experience, as when one "has a new idea" or "discovers a solution to a problem."

Köhler used a variety of problem situations to study insightful learning in chimpanzees (1927). For example, a banana was suspended from the top of the animal's cage, out of his reach. Several wooden boxes were available within the cage, but the animal could not reach the banana by standing on any one of them. A great variety of restlessness and trial and error was exhibited. On occasion, however, an animal was observed to act suddenly, as though he were carrying out a plan, by placing one box on top of another, then immediately climbing on this structure to reach the banana. As another example, one chimpanzee was observed, again after much trial and error, to put together two joined sticks, which he then used as a single long stick to reach a banana placed outside his cage. Köhler called such learning *insight,* and emphasized the discontinuity it had with the previous trial-and-error behavior. The total successful act was put together and exhibited suddenly, without error and as if by plan. Köhler's interpretation was that insight involved a "seeing" of relationships, a putting together of events that were internally represented.

This form of learning by human beings has also been described by other Gestalt writers like Wertheimer and Katona. For example, Wertheimer describes solutions to a geometric problem by children, insightful and otherwise. Children who knew the "formula" for the area of a rectangle as $h \times b$ were asked to derive a means of finding the area of a parallelogram. Some proceeded in a "rote" fashion to multiply the length of the base times the length of the side, which, of course, is incorrect. Others were able to see the correct solution by cutting a right triangle from one side of the parallelogram, and attaching it to the other side, thus constructing a known figure, the rectangle. Still others were able to see the problem as one of dividing up the entire parallelogram into little squares (a very sophisticated solution). Although a child may have tried several wrong approaches, a "good" solution was arrived at, according to Wertheimer, when the child could see the essential structure of the problem situation.

The most frequent criticism of the "insight" explanation of these learning events is, however, a very serious one. This is to the effect that animals and children solve these problems by *transfer from previous learning*. The chimpanzee is able to pile boxes one upon another because he has previously learned to do this, although not necessarily in this particular situation. The child is able to identify the triangles as similar because he has previously done this with other right triangles. It cannot be said that such an explanation is not true, because in fact in these Gestalt examples the factor of prior learning has not been controlled. Despite the neatness of a theory that accounts for insight on the basis of the structure of the observed situation, the phenomena of insight have in one instance after another been shown to be affected by previous learning.

One of the most impressive modern evidences of the effects of prior learning on insightful behavior occurs in Harlow's studies of *learning set* (1949). Harlow trained monkeys to solve problems in which the correct choice among three objects was the "odd" one, the object dissimilar to the others. By trial-and-error learning, monkeys learned to choose the odd one of three objects when they were consistently rewarded for doing so. In the next problem, three new objects were presented, including an odd one, and the monkeys again learned to choose the odd one, somewhat faster

this time. A third problem, again with a new set of objects, was solved faster than the second. After solving a few more oddity problems of this sort, the animal was able to solve oddity problems (involving objects he had not previously encountered) at once, without any hesitation. He had acquired, Harlow said, a learning set that enabled him to solve oddity problems correctly without trial and error.

This evidence implies that previous learning, acquired through a number of encounters with similar problems, can establish a kind of internal capability that makes the animal quite different from naïve monkeys of the same age and strain. He becomes an "oddity-problem solver" monkey, who displays insight when given an oddity problem to solve. Obviously, this capability for insight did not arise because of a "structuring of the situation." It came, rather, from accumulated experience based on many individual trials of previous learning.

What can be said about the representativeness of insight as a prototype of learning? On the one hand, it does appear to represent some common learning occurrences that are rather easy to identify. When children are led to "see" relationships, such as those between addition and multiplication or between weight and the "pull" of gravity, they often display insight. On the other hand, it is difficult to find insight in the learning of a great variety of other things. A child cannot learn the names of plants or stars in an insightful manner. He cannot learn to read by insight, nor to speak a foreign language. A student of biology does not learn the structures and functions of animals by insight. In short, insight cannot be a prototype for a vast amount of learning that human beings ordinarily undertake. Perhaps it occurs when we learn by "solving problems," but we also learn many, many things that are not problems at all. They may simply be facts, or propositions, or principles.

THE SIGNIFICANCE OF LEARNING PROTOTYPES

Thus we see that learning in American psychology has usually been considered a problem of understanding the *association*. To the British associationists, the association of interest was between sense impressions and ideas, or between simple and complex ideas. Following James and Dewey, Watson, Thorndike and others set out to study the association between sense impressions and impulses to action, or, in more modern terms, between stimulus and response (S and R). Tolman believed that the essential kind of association in learning was an internal event connecting "significates" and "expectations." And then there have been those who, all along, have denied that association is a central event in learning at all.

Throughout the period of scientific investigation of learning, there has been frequent recourse to certain typical experimental situations to serve as *prototypes* for learning. Most prominently, these have been derived from animal learning studies, the conditioned response, the learning of verbal associates, or insight studies. Actually, the choice of these prototypes has had considerable influence on the course of learning research. When contrasting predictions are made by theories, it is these prototypes that are appealed to as concrete ways of settling the issue. And it is from these prototypes that experiments are designed to test theoretical predictions. They have become, in other words, the concrete models that investigators of learning think about when they set out to study learning experimentally.

As examples, the prototypes themselves represent a variety of kinds of learning. It has not been found possible to "reduce" one variety to another, although many attempts have been made. In addition, there are many instances of learning that these prototypes apparently do *not* represent. There seem, in fact, to be a number of varieties of learning that are not considered at all by these standard examples; their representativeness of all the varieties of actual learning phenomena is not all comprehensive.

These learning prototypes all have a similar history in this respect: each of them started to be a representative of a particular variety of learning situation. Thorndike wanted to study animal association. Pavlov was studying reflexes. Ebbinghaus studied the memorization of verbal lists. Köhler was studying the solving of problems by animals. By some peculiar semantic process, these examples became prototypes of learning, and thus were considered to represent the domain of learning as a whole, or at least in large part. Somehow, they came to be placed in opposition to each other: either all learning was insight or all learning was conditioned response. Such controversies have continued for years, and have been relatively unproductive in advancing our understanding of learning as an event.

14. RELATING THEORY AND PRACTICE *

ROBERT C. CRAIG

THE TEACHER'S PRESENTATION

We can envision many variations in teacher presentations, some using a variety of aids, but the teacher nearly always "shows" or

* Reprinted with permission of The Macmillan Company from *The Psychology of Learning in the Classroom* by Robert C. Craig. Copyright © by the Macmillan Company 1966.

"tells." The term "lecture" is sometimes a appropriate one; but classroom presentation are not very formal, and the teacher usuall welcomes occasional questions by students o punctuates his presentation with questions t them. Brief teacher presentations are ofte linked with other techniques in a larger uni of instruction.

Although teacher presentations can provid

motivation, guidance, or evaluation for other learning activities, the criticisms of teachers' presentations usually are directed at their use for transmitting or clarifying information, as though the teacher were an animated text. How may this familiar form of teacher presentation be made more compatible with the emphases of each theory?

FOR CONTIGUITY. The weakness of teacher presentation for this approach is that the student may not do what he is to learn. To put it another way, to improve contiguity learning a teacher must find ways to insure that students respond correctly to important cues when they are presented.

One common practice, which might be used even more widely, is that of interrupting a talk with requests for student responses. A teacher may write a word on the board and tell one student or all to say it aloud. If only one student responds aloud, it is assumed that the others will respond silently. Another teacher points to a map, names a city, and asks students to say the name or write it in their notebooks. In still another class a book is held aloft and the Spanish name is said, first by the teacher or an able student, then by others. Later students are expected to respond correctly to the sight of the word, the place on the map, or the book without an assist from the teacher. Longer responses, such as statements of principles, summaries of data, or the steps of solving mathematical problems, may be prompted in the same manner.

The teacher who attempts to schedule his informal prompting of students more systematically finds that his lectures begin to resemble an orally administered teaching program such as that suggested by Carpenter and Haddan.[1] In essence their plan is to have the speaker present information in a series of brief segments, each only a few minutes long. After each segment, students are to be asked to complete sentences or answer related questions. From the contiguity point of view students could be given the answers verbatim, at least when new material is being introduced. Another possibility would be to give each student a duplicated list of questions that he is to answer during the lecture. Under such a plan a lecturer would merely pause every few minutes to see if his pace is appropriate and to check the need for a review of previous points.

The teacher is obviously at some disadvantage with respect to the machine in administering a program. Try as he may, the teacher's materials will seldom be prepared with the rigorous attention to detail and sequence that characterizes the commercial program. The pacing certainly cannot be highly individualized. The teacher does have the great advantage, however, of being able to work toward objectives of his own choosing. The standardized program suffers from the same limitation as the standardized test—that is, it seldom quite suits the local course of study.

If we wish to be somewhat more speculative, contiguity theory suggests a further role for the teacher, one that future investigators may find crucial. The teacher may be an agent for increasing students' pleasure in course-related concepts and activities. While presenting his material he may use his personal charm and wit, praise, and assurances to reduce students' anxiety and arouse their positive feelings. According to the classical conditioning formula the material itself will then become a source of pleasure.

Having a happy class is not enough, of course. Regaling them with stories or giving all "A's" is not enough. Students must be stimulated by significant aspects of the subject-matter (conditioned stimuli) at the same time the teacher's devices (unconditioned stimuli) make them "feel good" (emotional responses). Furthermore, the teacher's approach to his subject is still systematic and analytical. His aim is to attach positive emotional reactions to as many specific elements of the course as possible in the time allotted to him. He judges his success by students' continued interest and activity. Do they take notes and review them? Do they wish further discussion of important ideas? Do they seek related readings? Later, do they take other courses or "major" in the same area?

In each additional experience the students should find pleasure in the facts, opinions, and conclusions, perhaps the actual words, of

[1] *Systematic Application of Psychology to Education* (New York: Macmillan, 1964), pp. 145-52.

the course. Whenever they express an idea, use a concept, or take a stand on an issue, agreeing with the course should tend to make them "feel better."

The language of reinforcement rather than that of conditioning might well be used to present these interesting possibilities for emotional training. The concepts of secondary drive and reinforcers suggest a way words and other course elements can come to motivate students later. Contiguity would still be an essential factor, however, in explaining how course elements acquire their influence initially.

FOR REINFORCEMENT. The suggestions for a contiguity approach can be endorsed here, *if*, and this is important, student responses are consistently followed by reinforcement. The more traditional descriptions of reinforcement learning suggest that right responses are selected and confirmed. We think, for example, of a teacher pointing to a city on the map of South America and inviting students to name it before he says, "That's right, it's Rio de Janeiro." In the contiguity approach, you will recall, the teacher would give the city's name, then have students repeat it. Even if errors are few, the confirmation of hearing the answer again from the teacher is said to result in greater learning. The teacher should give a full statement of the desired answer and supplement this with other reinforcements, perhaps praise or smiles, when he knows these work well with particular students.

The typical teachers' presentation assumes a great deal about both the responses of his students and their reaction to reinforcement. Ideally, he gets students to imitate his thought processes and paces his presentation so that they push ahead of him to answers or tentative conclusions. Questions aimed at one of the class or to the class at large may help. Then, he steps out in front again, as it were, with information that reinforces the responses he hopes they have made. This procedure can work well, but we cannot even be sure any substantial number of the class respond, unless we provide for them to do so overtly.

Short presentation segments may be used in a "programmed lecture," such as that described for a contiguity approach. The rein-

forcement practice might be to have all students answer oral questions or written ones duplicated in advance. The teacher talks or shows, then the students answer, then the teacher gives the intended answers as reinforcement.

In this or other types of presentation the teacher will wish to keep a close check on the difficulty of his material. Whenever too many errors are observed in students' comments or their responses to his probes, or if doubt is suggested by their perplexed expressions, he should slow up and give more details. Conversely, when no errors are evident and students begin to appear bored and disinterested, he might speed up and give fewer explanations and illustrations.

The reinforcement-minded teacher who uses presentation methods will be intrigued with the opportunity to experiment with sequences designed to develop learning sets. Repeated direct or vicarious reinforcements for responses to a series of problems involving the same principle may be a promising method of developing students' ability to cope with other problems involving this principle.

FOR COGNITIVE LEARNING. The teacher who is guided by cognitive theories uses presentation methods to display the natural structure of materials or activities. The teacher's own ability to find order and lawfulness in what he teaches is the first requirement. Then, he must seek words and examples that will make the relations he has found important to the student and crystal clear. There are only few guidelines to follow in doing this. Generally speaking, cognitive psychology offers the teacher a challenge rather than prescriptive statements. Those who accept the invitation need a high degree of both scholarship and professional judgment.

The contrast between cognitive and association emphases is often sharpest when association principles seem an obvious choice. Teaching the multiplication combinations involving nines is one example of this type. An association-minded teacher might see this as a matter of forming and strengthening a separate connection for each combination of the nines table. Let's suppose instead that the teacher asks himself if there is any opportunity here to develop a greater understanding of relations among numbers that may make this and future tasks easier and more interesting. As it happens, there is.

The teacher decides to use a brief lecture-demonstration. He begins by writing the list of combinations from 9×1 to 9×10 and from 10×1 to 10×10 on the chalkboard. He asks one or two students for the answers to previously learned combinations and accepts contributions from several volunteers. He also asks for the product of several combinations not yet studied in order to stimulate greater interest in the "easy way" he is about to show them.

A comparison of the nines table with the tens tables and the use of a row of numbers from 1 to 100 enable him to bring out the following—not in these words, of course: (1) The left digits of the products of both the nines and tens tables go up by one each time the multiplier increases by one, that is, 9×1=09, 9×2=18, 9×3=27, and so on; and 10×1=10, 10×2=20, 10×3=30, and so on. (2) The left digit of a tens product is always equal to the multiplier, that is, 10×1=10, 10×2=20, 10×3=30, and so on; but the left digit of the nines "lags behind" and is always one less, that is 9×1=09, 9×2=18, 9×3=27, etc. (3) Each time the *left* digit of the nines products goes *up* by one, the *right* digit does *down* by one, so that their *sum remains at nine*—09, 18, 27, 36, 45, 54, 63, 72, 81, 90.

All of the above points are especially clear to students when they are shown on an abacus, for each time a nine is to be added a ten marker is moved over and a one marker is brought back. Few students, even those who cannot put it into words, will fail to see that all they have to do to multiply nine by any number is to put down one less than the number and follow this with nine minus the first number (or ten minus the multiplier). For example, 9×8 is 7 (one less than the multiplier) followed by 2 (9−7) or 72. For homework, students might be given the task of extending the procedure to combinations above 9×10.

In many schools children would know one as the complement of nine and may easily be led to relate finding nines products, computing on an abacus and computing with complements. The use of complements is not limited to addi-

tion or the nines but has many applications in mathematics. A number of "high-speed" methods using complements would interest some students.

Our analogy with programmed learning is still useful, and we may think of this teacher's presentation as the information segment of a program with large task units. The oral or written questions that usually follow are an informal "adjunct program" to confirm understanding and to show where "branching" for review or further explanation is needed.

STUDENT ACTIVITIES

When the teacher of a class is not presenting material, he is, more often than not, trying to elicit or guide student activity. An observer may recognize the familiar "oral quiz" or recitation over an assignment, the relatively free verbal interchange of the discussion, or something neither one nor the other but a little of both. He may find different individuals or small groups proceeding rather independently with only an occasional assist from the teacher and be told that they are working on projects or "a problem." He probably knows the project as a task that students complete somewhat independently and may think of a problem as either the same thing or as something entirely new.

Actually, learning experiences that extend beyond a single class period are often planned within the general framework of a problem. This approach is not so much a new method as a different emphasis in the use of familiar methods. In this approach, which resembles scientific research in some ways, the teacher assumes the role of a guide or co-investigator in (1) selecting and defining interesting and worthwhile problems, (2) formulating and evaluating proposed solutions or hypotheses, (3) planning and completing study or experimentation pertaining to proposed solutions, and (4) applying and using the conclusions.

As our observer noted, the possible combinations of activities in a problem-solving approach are many. A discussion is well adapted to selecting and defining problems and the planning stages of other steps, as well as for reaching conclusions when the data have been collected. The teacher may present some of the data needed by students or explain some of their difficulties. More data are gathered in assignments or projects. The application of conclusions may lead to still further projects.

Some of the steps of problem solving parallel the elements of learning as we have presented them. This is one of the reasons why a problem-solving organization is often advised in methods courses for teachers. When the learner accepts a class problem as one that is important to him, the correspondence is particularly close. It is well to remember, however, that learning does not require this classroom emphasis. A motivated student may find a goal and attain it in a lecture or in reading a text. He learns from question to question in programmed texts, as well as by completing the several steps in the development and solution of a formal problem.

FOR CONTIGUITY. An active response by the learner is the first requirement for learning by association. Increased student participation during teacher presentations was suggested; but student participation can be more continuous when the teacher only reviews, in a sense, material previously covered in less controlled situations, such as outside reading. Associations formed under conditions where the teacher cannot control both stimuli and response would be considered somewhat haphazard without such a review.

The stage is set for student participation in controlled contiguity learning when the students have prepared and the teacher has a series of questions with the expected answers before him:

T: "What are the three purposes for which nonfiction is written?"
S1: "To entertain. To inform other people."

The teacher writes these ideas on the board, and there is silence in the room.

T: "You have two of the purposes of nonfiction. What is the third? Janice? Bill?"
S1: "The book said to give ideas."

Teacher writes "ideas" on the board.

T: "What do we mean 'to give ideas'?"
S2: "Well, to tell other people what you think."
T: "Is that all?"
S3: (Glancing at his open book) "To convince others that what you think is right."

T: "Now you have it. The next question is . . ."

At some point in this fairly typical recitation the teacher may have a student state the question again and read the answers aloud from the board, while other students repeat them silently. Later, he may ask the students to copy the list in their notebook, thus providing still another repetition.

The spirit of contiguity learning carries over into the assignment of a teacher. Assignments are often considered preparation for conditioning in class, but the right kind of an assignment provides additional opportunity to form associations. Consider the homework instructions of a German teacher, for example: "Copy each of the next 50 vocabulary words beginning with 'klein' on the left of a small card. To study, look first at 'klein' while covering 'little,' then look at 'little.' Do the same with each word. After a number of repetitions of this kind you will have learned them all." He might have said that when they can say "little" to the stimulus "klein" without looking they will be conditioned. Other lists, formulas, speeches, or poems may be learned in the same way. It is laborious to learn an entire poem a word or phrase at a time with each word or phrase serving as a stimulus for the next, but that is the way of learning by association.

Lessons may be built of such deliberately planned associations. The combined associations of lessons are the outcomes of units, and they in turn form blocks of instruction or courses. There is provision, of course, for a variety of responses. Statements of specific fact, illustrations, comparisons, conventions, trends, cause-and-effect relations, and evaluations are a few of the verbal associations that may be systematically conditioned.

Contiguity partisans are not indifferent to the possibilities for more complex learning during student participation. They say that students may be conditioned to enjoy and seek course-related activities of all kinds. Our speculations on the conditioning of emotional responses to the teacher's presentation have suggested some of the possibilities. In general, students are believed to learn whatever they are led to do. If they are led to trace and develop a thought, question it, and relate it to other thoughts, this is what they learn. The example of the teacher or other students may be the way to get them to do and learn such things. However, how will they tell the good examples from the poor? Obviously by the effect on the teacher and other students. The teacher will not wish to leave this effect to chance, of course, so he will try to act in such a way as to rather consistently differentiate the better from the poorer actions of students. At this point we are so close to the reinforcement explanation that we may simply refer to it. In doing so, we do not say the contiguity explanation is wrong, merely that the reinforcement position is much the same, yet still more helpful.

FOR REINFORCEMENT. A commitment to reinforcement obligates the teacher to arrange satisfying consequences. Other than this his tactics with respect to teaching specific associations are similar to those of teachers who follow contiguity theory. In these associations both the stimuli and the response are well defined and fairly easily shown to the learner.

The most unique contribution of reinforcement is in the encouragement of student responses that the teacher cannot control fully or call forth at will. Our objectives for students with respect to problem-solving skills provide some familiar examples. Consider the process of clarifying a problem. To be more specific, this can be subdivided into (1) effective use of related information, (2) willingness to suspend judgment, (3) thoroughness in exploring the possibilities, (4) identifying the criteria of a good solution, and so on. If such attitudes and skills were to be encouraged during a class discussion of a plan for the study of an assigned topic, what might a teacher do?

We will assume that such a teacher has illustrated the techniques of problem solving and that his students have worked several other problems together. The teacher reviews his knowledge of students' prior experience and present competencies as individuals and as a group. He recalls that they are prone to jump to conclusions and decides that today he will give particular attention to their willingness to suspend judgment. At the same time he will use such opportunities as he has to reinforce other skills and attitudes important in this part of the problem-solving process. He will try also to encourage progress toward several other objectives related to participation in group decisions and to oral communication.

The teacher plans a free discussion, for he does not know exactly what more he can do or say in this particular situation to help students learn to hold back and be less precipitous in their decisions. Although he knows student suggestions and actions relative to the objectives he has chosen will vary in quality, he cannot specify in advance the particular response that should be reinforced. If he stopped to reflect on the matter, he might be encouraged or amused by the fact that psychologists who shape the behavior of rats might also have difficulty in describing exactly what movement their "pupil" should make at any given point in training. This teacher is confident, however, of his ability to recognize the right kind of response, and he will be ready to reinforce it when it occurs. He knows the reactions of students as individuals and will try to choose words and actions that will work best for each. He expects that several students will help him by recognizing and approving several types of appropriate behavior.

Shaping is an apt term for what this teacher plans. We have described this process before. He will try to reinforce any improvement— that is, any act or suggestion that is better than that typical for individuals of this group up to this time. Of course, today's improvement may be ignored or noted as a step backward next week. His judgment is sometimes faulty also, so that under his tutelage there is some retracing of steps, some learning that must be forgotten later. Even an especially skillful administration of reinforcement does not produce dramatic changes in a single discussion; but to be optimistic he hopes that after today there will be an increase in probability, if not a detectable difference, in some student's willingness to look for more facts, to consider different alternatives, and so on, before urging that they "get started on something."

Any teacher would be more optimistic of his chances for success in shaping problem-solving ability, laboratory skills, effective styles of communication, artistic expression, or other complex behavior if he could work with students individually. The teacher would like to think of his role as that of continuously monitoring the progress of an individual to help and reinforce him. Some of this takes place in school situations but not in the typical class. In group situations we again depend on the somewhat unpredictable results of vicarious learning. When we give a verbal "pat on the back" to the student whose contribution turns the attention of the class to exploring other aspects of the problem more thoroughly, do we increase the probability of similar response in other students? Can we arrange a response to the suggestion of a slower student that will reinforce him at his level without misleading others who are more advanced? These and other problems contribute to the inefficiency of group procedures for the attainment of a number of important objectives.

The importance of the concept of shaping warrants the inclusion of a further brief example from the classroom. We have chosen one from beginning work on the writing of poetry. This class is making a start with respect to one of the most essential elements of poetic composition and will work on other elements and the consideration of poetical devices and structures later.

The teacher begins dramatically by having students close their eyes and imagine they will never see again. "Think about what single thing you would most like to have in your memory . . ." They spend a few minutes thinking and reporting, and then the teacher reads a short passage in which Helen Keller has expressed the joy and beauty she finds in nature. Miss Keller urges that others use their eyes as if tomorrow they would become blind.

> T: "She sort of implies that we are all a little blind, doesn't she? Now take a look at your hand and tell me what you see."
> S: "Shape of an M." "Wrinkles." "Knuckles." "Fingernails."
> T: "Well, I hope you have one nail to each finger."
> S: (Laughing appreciatively) "On someone who uses his hands in his work, you'd see calluses."
> T: "That's good observing, but let's restrict this to our own hands."
> S: "A tree."

> T: "He's speaking poetically, which is good. Someone else?"

The teacher shifts the attention of the class to a green vase and then to "something that will make me see winter changing into spring." The process is slow; but as the teacher continues to comment favorably on responses he likes and to ignore the others, the contributions become more and more specific, detailed, and original.

FOR COGNITIVE LEARNING. Student participation in learning has been given a prominent place in the cognitive teaching strategy also, but not for reasons of association. For S-R purposes responding *is* learning, while from the cognitive view it merely *aids* learning, that is, understanding. A student's action aids understanding when its consequences confirm tentative hypotheses or lead to their revision.

One view of learning is that the learner's activities are always appropriate to the situation as he understands it. Consequently his actions give the teacher evidence of the adequacy of his interpretation. They tell the teacher when further explanation or experience is needed and perhaps what kind as well. Because his objective is increased understanding rather than fixing a response, the teacher is not satisfied with merely indicating adequate and inadequate responses; he will do his best to make it clear *why* a student's action is more or less adequate.

An attempt to implement this view in the contexts of the examples of the preceding section—that is, to clarify a problem or encourage keener observation and poetic expression—would be marked by greater efforts to teach a pattern of generalizations and supporting ideas so that it would be clear where various student suggestions might lead and why some contributions might be considered better or more useful than others. If you reread the examples of shaping in the preceding section carefully, you may now find the process somewhat mechanical and contrived, perhaps even slightly unethical. If this process were much more reliable than it is, we might raise a question about the desirability of molding students to our ends, perhaps without their knowledge or consent (Skinner, 1948).

The value of student responses for diagnosing learning and providing feedback would lead many teachers to plan the learning of the nines table, as described under "The Teacher's Presentation," as a group experience in discovery. Students' attention would be directed to a comparison of the nines and tens tables and to the progression of products in the two tables, but they would be encouraged to supply reasons and rules in their own words. "The 9×1 is one less than the 10×1 so the nines never can catch up," suggests either incomplete insight or inexact expression. One teacher who did not settle for this response was pleased with, "The left one goes up one each time and the right one goes down one. One more cancels one less so the sum remains the same!"

Understanding is one of two traditional cognitive emphases that has encouraged teachers to organize the curriculum around problems of some duration or substantial units of content. A broader context obviously increases the opportunities for the patterning of ideas. It is equally essential if students are to relate these ideas to goals that appear realistic and worthwhile.

An increased emphasis on students' own goals and larger, more inclusive units of work leads to frequent group discussions in the planning and carrying out of activities, often in the problem-solving pattern. Such discussions differ from those of classes managed by reinforcement principles in that the problems to be clarified are more often ones that students have chosen to implement their own interests in an area of study. Small group or individual work within the broader problem context is encouraged to provide for some diversity of interests and to adapt materials and methods to be intellectual operations (levels) of the students.

CONCLUDING STATEMENT

Without minimizing the importance of verified facts and principles, we have assumed that the teacher's "personal theory" and his efforts to "be consistent" have an even greater effect on his classroom practices. To a degree, theory and fact are complementary; when knowledge is meager, theory assumes a proportionately larger role. This is believed to be the case in much of teaching.

We have urged more attention to psychological explanations in efforts to be consistent educationally. Despite the limitations of these theories, they are the results of systematic explorations of evidence and ideas about learning. Their differing emphases reduce in summary to several general questions that a teacher might ask first in any situation:

Contiguity: What models or prompts will direct learners' attention and elicit appropriate responses simultaneously?

Reinforcement: What reinforcers are effective and how can they be administered (scheduled) optimally?

Cognitive: What organization of materials or activities will lead to an understanding of general ideas and supporting details in relation to important personal goals?

What should the teacher do about diverse theoretical emphases? He would not want to ignore the proven contributions of any theory, obviously, but he may give priority to one view regularly or as difficulties arise in his present practices. Another alternative, of course, is a synthesis of the several explanations, not haphazardly or uncritically, but by assigning a definite educational role to each. The contiguity principle, for example, is definite about arrangements for teaching somewhat arbitrary associations and emotional responses; the cognitive approach is concerned with intellectual tasks that involve complex symbolic behavior in relation to content that may be structured to facilitate understanding and use; and reinforcement concepts may have unique advantages for forming a variety of attitudes and skills with few or inconspicuous cognitive elements.

Finally, there is admittedly insufficient evidence of how well the concepts derived in psychological theory or the laboratory apply in the classroom. The risks of overgeneralization are great; but they may be reduced somewhat if extensions of psychological concepts to teaching are proposed, not as fact, but as hypotheses that merit further tryout in classrooms. This is what we have advised. With this proviso, we suggest that any remaining risk in the use of learning theories is preferable to the alternative hazards of dependence on hunches, uncritical imitation, or habit.

15. TRANSFER OF TRAINING *

T. G. ANDREWS AND L. J. CRONBACH

All educational efforts aim at learning which can be transferred to new situations. Some of these new situations are to be met within the school curriculum; others are life situations outside the classroom. Ultimately it is to the latter type of situation that educational interest in transfer of training is pointed. When one practices a response to a specific stimulus situation, *learning* (*q.v.*) takes place. When a particular learning experience also influences an individual's ability to respond effectively to stimuli different in some ways from those he reacted to during learning, transfer of training is said to have taken place.

If transfer were not possible, it would be necessary to train the individual in every specific situation he will ever face. The mechanic who has learned to repair one tractor would have to begin learning anew on each new model, and the rifleman who is an expert with one weapon would begin as a novice when he changes to another.

There are several important psychological questions concerning transfer of training. For educational purposes two of these questions are most important: To how wide a range of different situations will a particular learning transfer? What instructional methods promote the greatest degree of transfer? Transfer is apparent in impressive proportions in everyday life, but it cannot be taken for granted in all educational situations. The transfer problem is a question of degree and

of the relative efficiency of educational or training procedures.

Individuals do not always transfer to the same extent from one learning experience to another. Research is required to establish how and when training will transfer. Will practice firing at towed targets improve the combat firing of an aerial gunner? Will study of logical propositions in mathematics improve reasoning about life problems? Will lectures on mental hygiene improve adjustment to frustrating situations? Will the study of Latin aid in mastering law? Such questions underlie all curriculum construction.

EMERGENCE OF THE TRANSFER PROBLEM

So long as the curriculum was supposed primarily to transmit knowledge of Western culture, the problem of transfer was not important. A man learned Latin, geometry, and natural history because these knowledges were the mark of an educated man. With the emergence of a less aristocratic notion of education in America during the 1800's there developed gradual acceptance of the axiom that the function of any teaching is to change behavior. The place of skill subjects such as reading and arithmetic was secure under this philosophy. Classical knowledge had less obvious value for everyday behavior and the classical subjects were defended on the ground that they strengthened certain mental faculties—reasoning, judgment, memory, will, etc. According to this *faculty psychology*, exercising a faculty by appropriate training developed the mind, and so improved behavior. Conventional school subjects were said to provide "mental discipline."

* "Transfer of Training" by W. S. Monroe. Reprinted with permission of the Macmillan Company from *Encyclopedia of Educational Research*, pp. 1483-1489. © American Educational Research Association 1950.

Experimental psychology began to challenge this theory of transfer when James, about 1890, attempted to measure the effect of training on memory. He and his students timed their speed of memorizing passages from Victor Hugo's *Satyr*. Daily for a month or longer they memorized selections from another author, and then retested themselves on new passages from Hugo. According to the faculty theory, memorization of the classics develops the memory. James and his group found some improvement, but results were so slight as to throw into question the entire value of mental discipline. Further tests were made of transfer effects in memory, perception, reasoning, and other alleged faculties. These studies showed rather small transfer and were considered adequate to disprove the claims of formal discipline.

Transfer through specific habits was emphasized in the theory of Thorndike and Woodworth (1901), which replaced the faculty aproach. Under this theory, curriculum makers sought to provide learning experiences which would give training in the particular skills, habits, and responses likely to be used in later life. Thus in citizenship training, study of political thought was superseded by training in how to mark a ballot, how to read editorials, and how to acquire facts specifically needed about current problems and in forming judgments about them.

More recent emphasis in education points to broader posibilities of transfer. In addition to habits and facts, school experiences engender attitudes and broad understandings which have great significance. Feelings of inadequacy fostered in school may transfer to an adult's performance on his job and to his methods of dealing with his children. A concept of fair dealing, learned in childhood, may reflect itself in an adult's marital relations, treatment of his employees, and attitudes on international affairs. Judd (1908) contributed to this viewpoint by showing experimentally that teaching meaningful general principles permits more effective transfer than a curriculum which is merely a collection of useful habits. Current methods of teaching for transfer are discussed at the end of this article.

METHODOLOGY

Studies of transfer have been pursued both in the laboratory and in classroom situations. The essential features of transfer as a psychological process are best studied in the experimental approach. By designing experiments in which the crucial variables are controlled, we can assess with considerable assurance the importance of each factor for transfer. In actual school situations, learning and transfer cannot be explained by such a simple formula as "so much presentation plus so much motivation plus so much generalization result in so much transfer." Changes in pupils come from a complex interaction of factors. To understand this interaction (e.g. why does presentation Z improve the work of some pupils but not others?) careful studies in the classroom are needed to supplement laboratory findings.

A crucial difficulty in studies of transfer has been the problem of assessing all outcomes of a learning experience. Results of instruction are usually thought of in terms of gains in knowledge or skill, and these are readily measured. Each instructional process, however, affects in many ways the personality, and attitudes of the pupil. If it is established that two procedures (e.g. study of civics vs. student self-government) produce equal gains in ability to reach logical decisions about new political questions, we still do not know their relative effect on such behavior as concern about political problems, tendency to vote on election day, and tendency to seek information on civic problems as they arise. We do not know whether the adult, capable as he is in reasoning as a result of the teaching, will have the confidence to follow his own thinking or will be swayed by partisan appeals. Few studies have attempted to evaluate the transfer effects of learning procedures in terms of these crucial but subtle concomitants.

Transfer may be positive (facilitating subsequent performance), negative (inhibitory), or mixed. Study of past political debates may produce some positively transferring effects, such as ability to interpret a new question in terms of its historical antecedents. It may produce such negative effects as an attitude that politics and civics are boring and to be thought about only under a teacher's compulsion. Study of the Latin verb *cedere* may lead to positive transfer in spelling the English *precede* but to negative transfer in spelling *supersede*. The usual experiment, in which "total" learning is measured by some test, can rarely disentangle such positive and negative outcomes. It is impossible to prove or demonstrate zero transfer, because an experimentally measured zero gain may represent cancelling positive and negative effects. Attempts to express amount of transfer on a scale from 0 to 100 per cent have been confusing, in the absence of an accepted operational definition of 100 per cent transfer (Woodworth, 1938, pp. 176-207).

The methodology of transfer investigations involves several important problems of control. The simplest and most fundamental experimental design involves the following steps: (a) Subjects are tested to determine their initial proficiency on the final task. (b) Two groups are equated, either as matched pairs or as total groups with equal means and equal variances. One of these groups is arbitrarily identified as the experimental group and the other as the control group. (c) The educational experience from which we expect transfer is now given to the experimental group. During this period of practice, the control group receives no training. (d) At the end of the period of practice, or some time later, both groups are retested on the final task, in which we expect the experimental group to have improved as a result of the intervening experience.

Such an experimental design may be represented by the following schema:

Experimental Group:
　　Test R_2; Training on R_1; Test on R_2
Control Group:
　　Test on R_2; . . . . ; Test on R_2

We would expect the control group, and also the experimental group, to better their performance on R_2 merely by virtue of their previous experience on R_2. Over a long period of time, maturational effects would also produce better scores in both groups. It is important to note that we may claim transfer effect only to the extent that the two groups are accurately matched or equated in terms of their initial ability on the final task and on such additional relevant factors as intelligence, previous training, and motivation for taking the pretest. The methodology of transfer studies is like that for learning experiments in every respect save one, that gains are measured not on the practiced task but on a different performance. James's learning of poetry was shown by his better knowledge of the poetry he studied; the transfer to memory in general was tested by his ability to master new poetry.

Various modifications of the above procedure are used when we intend to compare different types of intermediate training. When no pretest on the final task is possible because neither group has skill in it at the outset (as in testing whether experience with one gun transfers to ability to assemble a different piece), we must equate groups on supplementary variables such as intelligence or mechanical aptitude. Attention should be drawn to two rather precise statistical controls which obviate the usual loss of individual subjects in forming groups. We may "match through regression" (Peters and Van Voorhis, 1940, pp. 463-468) or apply the Neyman-Johnson method (Butch, 1944). Both these methods, although complicated, are powerful tools. The Neyman-Johnson method has the added advantage of identifying differences in amount of transfer for different types of subjects. We should expect this method to be used more frequently in future studies.

STUDIES OF TRANSFER

The research on transfer may be summarized in terms of three significant questions:

1. What types of responses can be improved through transfer?
2. Do some school subjects possess greater "transfer value" than others, in terms of their effect on the pupil's general mental functioning?
3. What eduational procedures produce the greatest amount of transfer?

1. CHARACTERISTIC TRANSFER EFFECTS. The first point of attack for research on transfer was to determine whether such broad mental powers as memory, observation, judgment, reasoning, and volition could be improved by training. Following the pioneer study of

James (1890, pp. 666-668), Thorndike and Woodworth (1901) performed an important series of investigations. Their first experiments were designed to determine the transfer effects of training in observation and perceptual discrimination. Subjects practiced estimating areas of certain geometric figures. The investigators then determined the effects of this practice on the accuracy of estimation of figures not previously presented. The transfer effects were found to vary between 30 and 50 per cent of the gains on the practiced figures. Training in estimating lengths of lines, however, produced little or no improvement in estimating lines not previously presented. Improvement in the accuracy of estimating weights from an initial test to a final test, with an intervening practice period on a different set of weights, was found to be about 40 per cent of the efficiency gained with the material practiced. Such studies indicated that transfer was evident but by no means considerable.

In other experiments Thorndike and Woodworth found that practicing the cancellation of certain letters of the alphabet from material on a printed page increased the efficiency of cancelling other letters only by 25 per cent of the gain observed during the practice period itself. The same general result was found for the relative improvement in finding and cancelling parts of speech in prose material.

These experiments represented a critical attack on the claims of formal discipline and gave little encouragement to the concept of a general observational ability which could be improved significantly through training. Much of the transfer effect found by Thorndike and Woodworth was interpreted by them as due to the carrying over of specific methods and rules of procedure or to the similarity in the practiced and the tested material.

Following these studies on observational ability there was an emphasis on research directed at rather specific aspects of transfer, such as problems of bilateral transfer (cross education) and memory for specific elements, such as nonsense syllables. Swift (1903) found that there was approximately 66 per cent transfer of ball-tossing skill from the right hand to the left hand. Ebert and Meumann (1904) found that subjects made considerable transfer from learning nonsense syllables, mainly by becoming adapted to the experimenter, the task, and the laboratory conditions. Seemingly as a result of practicing the learning of nonsense syllables, the subjects investigated by Ebert and Meumann were improved in the learning of letters, numbers, prose, and poetry, as well as meaningless visually perceived forms. But when the experiment of Ebert and Meumann was repeated by Reed (1917) with the use of a control group, it was found that any spread of ability from specialized memory practice is relatively small and undependable.

There were a large number of such investigations on specific learning functions early in the century and further analysis of the problems produced important interpretations. Thus, Swift noted in his experiment on balltossing that the method of handling the balls was carried over from one hand to the other. Dearborn (1909) showed that the "transfer" of Ebert and Meumann was largely due to gains made within the test series and the remainder was due to general improvement in orientation, attention, and technique of learning. Bray (1928), in a study of target-aiming transfer from hand to foot, found that methods, tricks, and modes of adjustment seem to be the primary media of transfer from one member to another.

An experiment by Sleight (1911) is somewhat representative of early attempts to identify the particular learnings transferred. He equated four groups of young girls on the basis of performance on several memory tasks. Each of three groups was given training in one task of memorizing either poetry, the substance of prose passages, or tables of measures and other quantitative data. Before, during, and after the practice period of 12 days, the subjects of the three experimental groups and one control group were measured on several kinds of learning, such as orally given names and dates, nonsense syllables, and a series of letters. There were some gains and some losses, and in general Sleight's experiment showed no general improvement in memory attributable to practice.

It became evident that transfer produced little generalized improvement. In a study by Woodrow (1927), however, the interest was shifted to determine whether it was possible to train subjects so that the *techniques* of memorizing acquired during the training period will be used to advantage on later occasions. Two experimental groups and one control group were studied. All groups were tested to determine their initial memorizing ability. One experimental group had a total of about 3 hours of practice at memorizing with no special instruction or training. The other experimental group was given the same amount of time in training on several simple rules and how or when to use them. The practice time of this latter experimental group was spent in consciously applying these techniques. All three groups then took final tests which were like the initial tests and included poetry, prose, miscellaneous factual items, Turkish-English vocabulary, and little-known historical dates. The two experimental groups dealt only with nonsense syllables and with poetry during their practice and training periods. The results indicated that simple practice, with no special aid or set, produces little transfer, whereas the learning of memory techniques with intent to use them definitely transfers to the final memory test.

In the psychological domain of reasoning Barlow (1937) found that instruction in analysis, abstraction, and generalization produces appreciable transfer to problems requiring understanding and reasoning—e.g. getting the point of Aesop's fables.

In addition to investigations of transfer of particular capacities, there is a large amount of evidence that attitudes, emotional reactions, and habits of character can and do transfer. (See Attitudes; Character Education, in Monroe, 1950, pp. 77-84, 126-134.) Watson and Rayner (1920) called attention to the transfer of an emotional response in one of his experiments on conditioning. In a young child who had learned to fear a furry animal, the fear response readily transferred to other furry animals, cotton, wool, and Santa Claus whiskers.

A pioneering experiment on the transfer of moral or character habits was performed by Voelker (1921), who gave six groups of boys a series of initial tests of honesty or trustworthiness, such as not returning over-change, not returning borrowed property, cheating in scoring one's own examination paper, peeping

in blindfold tests, and the like. Two of the groups were then given intensive Boy Scout work on trustworthiness, including discussions, learning of codes, and exhortations. In two other groups the regular Scout training was given, but there was far less emphasis on honesty. The remaining two groups served as controls and received no Boy Scout training and no training in trustworthiness. All of the six groups were retested with measures similar to those constituting the initial tests. Most progress had been made by the two Boy Scout groups which received the intensive training, and the least progress was made by the two control groups.

Such studies as that of Barlow and of Voelker have largely reversed the earlier conclusions that broad mental processes are relatively immune to transfer. The development of attitudes is demonstrated by an important experiment performed by Bond (1940) in a course in genetics which emphasized generalizations about racial characteristics. The training produced measurable changes not only in knowledge of facts but also in reduction of superstition and in improved ability to solve new problems in human genetics, and it significantly changed attitudes regarding imperialism, Jews, Italians, Latin Americans, and Orientals. Bond's method of teaching for transfer had greater effect for students in some ranges of intelligence and initial knowledge than for others. The study illustrates the significant advantages of the Neyman-Johnson technique for this type of research.

Transfer is also in question in the several investigations on the effect of nurture on general intellectual development. See Nature and Nurture, in Monroe (1950, pp. 772-777).

2. TRANSFER VALUE OF SCHOOL SUBJECTS. Proponents of various subjects, particularly the traditional ones, have been anxious to claim general mental improvement as an outcome of their subjects. The most important research on this problem is found in studies by Thorndike (1924), Broyler, Thorndike, and Woodyard (1927), and Wesman (1945). Thorndike devised a plan for comparing the tested intelligence of pupils exposed to different school subjects. By working with thousands of cases, he was able to establish subgroups taking exactly the same subjects except

that one group took mathematics whereas the other took stenography or cooking. Similar groups permitted comparing the transfer values of each important pair of subjects. The final conclusions, which have been supported by later studies with similar technique, are that gains in intelligence as a result of following particular subjects are negligible and that the differences in effect on intelligence of particular subjects are far too small to be given weight in planning curriculums. This finding was startling to those who had confidence in the importance of classical subjects in producing superior intellects. Thorndike considered this widespread belief to be the result of uncontrolled observation, pointing out that if all the best pupils took classical subjects, those subjects would seem to be producing better graduates than other curriculums.

3. METHODS OF INCREASING TRANSFER. Much attention has been given to methods of promoting transfer. Judd (1908) trained two groups to throw darts at a target 12 inches under water. One group used a trial-and-error method, while the other was taught the principles of refraction. When the target was moved to a depth of 4 inches, the former group was unable to adapt its previously acquired skill, but the group taught by generalizations adapted to the new conditions rapidly. Hamblen (1925) reached similar conclusions in studying the value of Latin for increasing ability to understand English derivatives. In classes where no special teaching for transfer was attempted, automatic transfer was negligible. Where teachers introduced many derivations, transfer was greater, but substantial improvement in dealing with unfamiliar derivations was obtained only where illustrative derivatives were related to rules and principles of derivation. Many other studies have confirmed the importance of conscious generalizing in other fields (Katona, 1940, Chaps. III and IV).

Other studies have brought out the importance of recognition in transfer. If the learner does not identify a problem as an opportunity to apply his knowledge, it will not transfer. Smith (1940) found that many pupils who, for example, were able to erect a perpendicular to a horizontal line could not construct a perpendicular to an oblique side of a triangle. He

therefore proposed a teaching method in which responses were taught both in simple and complex settings, with specific teaching in methods of analyzing the complex problems. Significant gains in solving new complex problems were found. Fawcett (1938) developed a course in mathematics stressing "the nature of proof" rather than particular theorems. He helped pupils see the need for definitions, assumptions, and proofs in connection with problems from their everyday lives and made them aware of methods of proof. Tests showed that the group made normal progress on geometry itself and made impressive gains in ability to analyze nonmathematical reasoning about unfamiliar problems. The control groups, learning traditional geometry, did not show transfer to nonmathematical materials.

The reader is referred to more complete bibliographies and summaries for detailed listings of the thousand or so studies bearing on transfer (Coover, 1916; McGeoch, 1942, pp. 394-452; Norem, 1933, pp. 3-35; Sandiford, 1928, pp. 275-300; Stroud, 1946, pp. 555-597; Swenson, 1941). Attention may be drawn to the steady improvement in research technique shown in these studies. Earlier work was open to criticism for failure to use an adequate control group, small numbers of cases, emphasis on meaningless learning unrelated to problems of school or life, training of such short duration that little transfer could be expected, failure to study long-term transfer effects, and failure to measure all types of outcomes. The reader must bear these criteria in mind in considering particular studies of transfer.

THEORIES OF TRANSFER

From time to time, as findings on transfer have accumulated, theories to account for the results have been advanced. With the exception of the initial theory of formal discipline, that practice develops mental strength, the subsequent theories may be considered successive refinements of a basic idea, rather than competing and incompatible notions. The most widely discussed theory is Thorndike's (1906, p. 243 f.) *theory of identical components.* When first proposed, under the name "identical elements," the theory sought to account for the fact that transfer was negligible unless the practiced task and the final task had a great deal in common. In keeping with his theory that each specific act of learning made use of a specific neural bond. Thorndike assumed that transfer was greatest when the practiced learning and the new learning had the largest number of bonds in common.

Association theory has been modified with the passage of time, as research has shown that the neural-chain theory is inadequate to account for learning. In its modern form, the theory of identical components states that the extent to which a response transfers to a new situation depends on the degree to which the new situation resembles the practiced one (Gibson, 1941). Situations may resemble each other in the specific configuration of the stimulus (*péche* and *péché* are very similar, although one means *peach* and one means *sin*) or in the general character of the situation even though all details are different (as when a child transfers to an employer attitudes and anxieties learned in relation to his father).

If responses to new situations depend entirely on familiarity with the various components to be encountered, it is necessary for education to equip the pupil with responses to all the many components of the situations he will meet in life. This led to the "social utility" curriculum, which stressed the particular facts adults encountered after leaving school. This was a major advance, for it removed from arithmetic deliberately difficult fractions (e.g. 121/318, 23/79) which were supposed to provide mental development under the discipline theory, and replaced them with the limited number of fractions actually found in business, carpentry, and so on (3/8, 5/32, etc.). In social studies, topics and concepts which represented only general culture were eliminated in favor of the concepts represented in current live issues.

Unfortunately, the highly specific theory of identical components made the curricular task overwhelming, because of the large number of specific learnings needed to solve all future problems. Judd added greatly to the design of sound curriculums with his stress on a *theory of generalization* (Judd, 1908). This theory pointed out that a response could be generalized so that the learner would apply it to every new situation of a given type. One then need not practice with every important fraction, but merely learn the general principles of fractions. Mastery of general social and historical principles would equip the subject to attack new situations subsumed under those principles. One may readily combine the Judd and Thorndike theories by considering that one way in which two situations may have an "identical component" is by falling under the same generalization. For a curriculum based on generalization, it is necessary that the pupil learn generalizations explicitly and that he know where they can be applied.

Gestalt psychologists have made much of the fact that learning often is not applied to a new situation, no matter how nearly identical to an old one, because the subject does not recognize the familiar in the new situation. Such criticisms force one to rephrase the theory of transfer as follows. *Transfer of a previously acquired behavior-pattern to a new situation will occur whenever an individual recognizes the new situation as similar to the situation for which the behavior was learned.* We have therefore swung through a cycle, from blind assumption that transfer is widespread, through a period of skepticism when transfer was expected only in the narrowest specific knowledge and habits, to a theory which looks on transfer as common and to be expected, provided certain conditions are met.

IMPLICATIONS FOR EDUCATION

The educator may draw implications for curriculum and classroom practice from many of the studies in this area. One of the major contributions of the research has been to demonstrate that no particular school subject has, in itself, any magical transfer value. To argue for teaching geometry, Latin, or philosophy because it "develops the mind," "increases understanding of the common problems of modern and ancient civilization," or "strengthens the control of reason over emotion," is to ignore an indisputable body of evidence. To examine the likelihood of transfer, one must question not what school subject is offered but what responses the pupil learns. From a study of Latin, one can probably improve his English, or become aware of the problems of man and the state, or establish a lifelong enjoyment of Roman poetry, or become antagonistic to Latin, the teacher, the school, and "culture" in general. There is no superior subject matter for transfer, there are only superior learning experiences. No doubt, under skilled teaching, educational psychology, art, or cooking can be made the vehicle for developing reasoning, a sense of values, or superior study habits.

The teacher in any subject may choose between teaching for mastery of his narrow strip of subject matter and teaching for transfer to life beyond the algebra or the economics book. Transfer will not be automatic. The A student in algebra or economics will often fail to use his skills in problems outside the classroom unless the subjects have been taught for transfer. There are five major steps in teaching for transfer:

1. POINT OUT THE POSSIBILITY OF TRANSFER. If pupils expect that what they learn will help in later situations, they are most likely to use it when opportunity arises. The teacher can introduce specific materials illustrating life situations where the principles of the school subject are applicable: shortcut calculations based on algebra, hidden assumptions in the reasoning of advertisements for comparison with geometric postulates, and habits of dental care as an application of knowledge about bacteria. Instances of confusingly similar situations may be specifically pointed out to reduce negative transfer.

2. USE VARIED TEACHING MATERIALS, LIKE THOSE TO WHICH THE LEARNING IS EXPECTED TO TRANSFER. Beyond merely pointing out situations to which learning may transfer, the teacher should base the classroom work on life-like materials whenever possible. The more a pupil experiences the real situation, the more likely he is to recognize his next opportunity to respond to it. This principle is illustrated in the gradual reduction of verbalism in the schools, exercises with words being replaced by exercises with objects, charts, and motion pictures. The experience of conducting a student-body election has more in common with the experience of a citizen than does memorizing the life history of a bill introduced in Congress. The class which experiments on white rats learns more about the effect of nutrition on growth than the class which merely learns the verbal principles. If the algebra class works with the equations in

s, a, and g, habits will not become stereotyped around the familiar x. The school can never provide experience with all important life situations and one must still teach for transfer beyond the materials studied.

3. DEVELOP MEANINGFUL GENERALIZATIONS. Each classroom topic can be thought of as something to be learned in itself or as an illustration of a broad principle. One may memorize Caesar's biography, or one may observe in it the consequences of concentrated power. One may learn how the gasoline engine operates, or one may derive from it principles applicable to all thermodynamic systems. One may do an arithmetic problem, or one may learn from it a general plan for all problem solving. It is these broader principles which make a particular learning most widely transferable. It is not enough, however, to present generalizations. They must be understood by the learner, not merely parroted.

4. PROVIDE PRACTICE IN APPLYING THE GENERALIZATION. An essential stage in transfer is recognizing a new situation as a special case of an old type. One cannot practice such recognition by drilling on a page of exercises, all of one labelled type. Practice is obtained by encountering a new situation in a setting which does not carry a sign identifying the generalization to be used. Some of the best experiences for transfer come through encountering algebra in the science text or science in the home-economics project. Any teacher can set up transfer experiences by introducing problems calling for application of generalizations in a context which forces the student to decide for himself what procedures or principles apply.

5. EVALUATE THE LEARNING EXPERIENCE BY DETERMINING HOW THE PUPIL'S BEHAVIOR IN NEW SITUATIONS IS CHANGED. Such evaluation stresses for the pupil that learning goes beyond memorizing and points out for the teacher his achievements and failures. Test materials requiring transfer of principles to new problems in most school subjects are illustrated in *The Measurement of Understanding* (National Society for the Study of Education, 1946).

In the long run transfer has reduced to a special case of the problem of learning. One learns the response one practices, if that response has satisfying consequences.

BIBLIOGRAPHY

SUMMARIES AND BIBLIOGRAPHIES

1. COOVER, J. E. Formal Discipline from the Standpoint of Experimental Psychology. *Psychological Monograph, No. 87*, 1916, 255 pp.
2. MCGEOCH, J. A. *The Psychology of Human Learning*. Longmans, Green, 1942, pp. 394-452.
3. NOREM, C. M. Transfer of Training Experiments Revalued. *University of Iowa Studies in Education*, Vol. 8, No. 6, 1933, pp. 3-35.
4. SANDIFORD, P. *Educational Psychology*. Longmans, Green, 1928, pp. 275-300.
5. STROUD, J. B. *Psychology in Education*. Longmans, Green, 1946, pp. 555-597.
6. SVENSON, E. J. *Retroactive Inhibition; A Review of the Literature*. University of Minnesota Press, 1941. 59 pp.

INVESTIGATIONS

7. BARLOW, M. D. Transfer of Training in Reasoning. *J. Educ. Psychol., 28*, 122-128, 1937.
8. BOND, A. D. *An Experiment in the Teaching of Genetics*, Teachers College, 1940, 99 pp.
9. BRAY, C. W. Transfer of Learning. *J. Exper. Psychol., 11*, 443-467, 1928.
10. BROLYER, C. R., E. L. THORNDIKE, and E. WOODYARD. A Second Study of Mental Discipline in High School Studies. *J. Educ. Psychol., 18*, 377-404, 1927.
11. BUTSCH, R. L. C. A Work Sheet for the Johnson-Neyman Technique. *J. Exper. Educ., 12*, 226-241, 1944.
12. DEARBORN, W. F. The General Effects of Special Practice in Memory. *Psychological Bulletin*, Vol. 6, No. 1, 1909, 44 pp.
13. EBERT, E., and MEUMANN, E. Über einige Grundfragen der Psychologie der Übungsphänomene in Berichte des Gedächtnisses. *Archive für des gesamte Psychologie, 4*, 1-232, 1905.
14. FAWCETT, H. P. The Nature of Proof. *National Council of Teachers of Mathematics, Thirteenth Yearbook*. Teachers College, Columbia University, 1938.
15. GIBSON, E. J. Retroactive Inhibition as a Function of Degree of Generalization Between Tasks. *J. Exper. Psychol., 28*, 93-115, 1941.
16. HAMBLEN, A. A. *The Extent to Which the Effect of the Study of Latin upon a Knowledge of English Derivations Can Be Increased*. University of Pennsylvania, 1925, 81 pp.
17. HENRY, N. B. (Ed.). The Measurement of Understanding. *Firty-fifth Yearbook Nat'l Soc. Study of Educ., Part I*, University of Chicago Press, 1946, 338 pp.
18. JAMES, W. *Principles of Psychology*, Vol. I, Holt, 1890, pp. 666-668.
19. JUDD, C. H. The Relation of Special Training to General Intelligence. *Educ. Rev., 36*, 28-42, 1908.
20. KATONA, G. *Organizing and Memorizing*. Columbia University Press, 1940, Chaps. III and IV.
21. PETERS, C. C., and W. R. VAN VOORHIS. *Statistical Procedures and Their Mathematical Bases*, McGraw-Hill, 1940, pp. 463-468.
22. REED, H. B. A Repetition of Ebert and Meumann's Practice Experiment on Memory. *J. Exper. Psychol., 2*, 315-346, 1917.
23. SLEIGHT, W. G. Memory and Formal Training. *Brit. J. Psychol., 4*, 386-457, 1911.
24. SMITH, R. R. Three Major Difficulties in the Learning of Demonstrative Geometry. *Mathematics Teacher, 33*, 99-134, 1940.
25. SWIFT, E. J. Studies in the Psychology and Physiology of Learning. *Amer. J. Psychol., 14*, 201-251, 1903.
26. THORNDIKE, E. L. *The Principles of Teaching*, A. G. Seiler, 1906, p. 243f.
27. THORNDIKE, E. L. Mental Discipline in High School Studies. *J. Educ. Psychol., 15*, 1-22, 83-98, 1924.
28. THORNDIKE, E. L., and R. S. WOODWORTH. The Influence of Improvement in One Mental Function upon the Efficiency of Other Functions. *Psychol. Rev., 8*, 247-261, 384-395, 553-564, 1901.
29. VOELKER, P. F. *The Functions of Ideals and Attitudes in Social Education: An Experimental Study*, Teachers College, 1921, 126 pp.
30. WATSON, J. B., and R. RAYNER. Conditioned Emotional Reactions. *J. Exper. Psychol., 3*, 1-14, 1920.
31. WESMAN, A. G. A Study of Transfer of Training from High School Subjects to Intelligence. *Teachers College Contributions to Education, No. 909*. Teachers College, Columbia University, 1945, 82 pp.
32. WOODROW, HERBERT. The Effect of Type of Training upon Transference. *J. Educ. Psychol., 18*, 159-172, 1927.
33. WOODWORTH, R. S. *Experimental Psychology*, Holt, 1938, pp. 176-207.

16. PROGRAMMED INSTRUCTION: INSIGHT VS. CONDITIONING *

HERBERT A. THELEN

Suppose I want you to learn that the chemical symbol for Sodium is Na, for Potassium, K, for Calcium, Ca, and so on down through a list of 25 elements. By "learn" I mean becoming able, without hesitation, to respond with "Na" when I say "Sodium," with "K" when I say "Potassium."

Probably the simplest way to teach you is through drill. You would read the list of elements and symbols and would try to memorize the connections. Then I would give you a list of elements and you would try to write the correct symbols. I would correct your mistakes and you would try again. We could also drill orally, with me naming the elements, you responding, me correcting. Or we could conduct the drill on a machine which would give you immediate "feedback" of "right" or "wrong."

CONDITIONING

This sort of learning occurs through "repetition and "reinforcement"—some sort of feedback or response which tends to "fix" the connection between element and symbol in your mind. The objective is to develop the specific habit of associating names and symbols. This process is called "conditioning."

Conditioning is the only process through which nonsense (or near-nonsense) can be learned. It can also be used to teach pigeons to tread on the right lever in order to get grain. It is an efficient way to learn *isolated* bits of information, such as the year in which Columbus discovered America, the months of the year, and the density of lead.

* Reprint from the March, 1963, issue of *Education*. Copyright, 1963, by the Bobbs-Merrill Company, Inc., Indianapolis, Indiana.

It is hoped that being told your response is correct will make you want to make further effort; but, if you don't really care about it, then we will fall back on the notion that generally speaking, if a person makes a response (never mind for what reason) he is more likely to make the same response the next time the stimulus is presented. Programmers say that such learning tactics "increase the verbal repertoire."

AN EXPERIMENT

Let us consider another type of task. Suppose I want you to learn the quantitative law "governing" the period of back-and-forth oscillation of a pendulum. I can give you a ball of twine, an assortment of weights (different sizes, shapes, weights, and colors), and a support from which you can hang the weights by means of the twine. I would probably also give you a yardstick and a stop-watch, although I might prefer to wait until you asked for them.

My instructions would be to play with the things I had just given you and see if you could discover what it is that determines how rapidly the pendulum will swing back and forth; and also just what the relationship is between this factor and the rate of swing.

You would probably begin by using a piece of string to hang one of the weights from the support, and you would set it in motion and notice its regular rate of swing. Your next move would probably be either to lengthen or to shorten the string and see what happened. You would soon get the notion that changing the weights (color, weight, shape) made no difference, but lengthening or shortening the string resulted in the pendulum swinging slower or faster.

You would then use the yardstick to measure the length of the string, and the watch to time the swings. You would make several measurements and you would find that the shorter the string the faster the pendulum, but not in direct proportion.

I might have to give you a hint about trying the square root of the length. But we would keep at it until you found the relationship that worked—which would also mean you would have to realize that you had to measure from the "middle" (center of gravity) of the weight rather than from the hook on its top.

We would discuss what you had done, and I would be interested both in your findings and your strategy. I would probably want to see next if you could make use of the law you had discovered to work some problems, and if you could use the strategy of controlled experimentation more efficiently in another discovery situation.

"INSIGHT" LEARNING

The kind of learning process I have been describing is "insight" learning. You explore various hunches and at some point you are aware of the principle. Then you move systematically to demonstrate the principle. You cannot make "mistakes" because each "mistake" furthers your inquiry by eliminating an unfruitful possibility.

This sort of insight learning is most effective for the learning of principles (the law of the pendulum) as distinguished from discrete bits of information (how many seconds a 12-inch pendulum requires to swing back and forth once). Principles learned through this sort of discovery tend to be "internalized"; they can be used in many unfamiliar or different situations later.

If I had merely told you the principle, you would memorize my words, but all you would have learned is the answer to the specific question: What is the law of the pendulum?

If I had told you the principle and then given you some problems to work, you would learn to use the formula for making calculations, but it would not necessarily be useful to you for any other purpose.

If I had tried to develop the principle through question and answer discussion with you, you might develop the insight required to use it as part of verbal expositions, but you would not be very likely to "see" its operation in a wide range of situations in nature later (when I was not there).

Eighty per cent of present programs (those using Skinner-linear and Crowder-branching rules) teach by the first method, conditioning. The remaining twenty per cent teach by a miscellaneous variety of rules, but tend more toward their authors' conceptions of insight learning. There is considerable controversy about the worth and usefulness of the eighty per cent. (The twenty per cent have mostly not been available to the public. Their turn will come later.)

THE MAJOR ISSUE

It seems clear to me that the major issue concerning programmed learning is primarily the large educational issue of conditioning versus insight. This issue, unresolved for two thousand years, is still unresolved. Teaching programs, educational television, the place and nature of achievement tests, the differences between education for the masses and for the elite—answers to these questions hinge on one's position about conditioning versus insight learning as the means of education.

To say this does not mean that there isn't plenty to criticize about present learning programs even for conditioning, but I do not think that is the main issue. The issue is whether "increasing the verbal repertoire" is a legitimate educational objective; whether conditioned learning of a very large number of fragments of information can in any way contribute to the development of character, ability to think critically, ability to apply principles, development of interests, and so on.

This is yet to be demonstrated; and it will be hard to demonstrate because we do not have the sort of evaluation devices and techniques we need to assess most of these major educational objectives.

THREE COURSES OF ACTION

Not having the necessary assessment instruments to measure the significant objectives what shall we do? Three courses of action are possible.

One is to develop the instruments, but the present pattern of "achievement tests" is so well entrenched at present that I don't have much immediate hope.

The second course of action is to give up our educational mission and settle for a lesser one. For the most part this is what the programmers are trying to persuade us to do: a good program, they would have us believe, is one that does as good a job as an average teacher in teaching the things that are typically measured on achievement tests. This seems to me to be a cynical view, the counsel of despair.

The third alternative is the oldest and best; it is actually the basis of most teaching. This is to study the experiences of the children *during* the learning activity. Thus one may assume that if students work absorbedly, come up with ideas that are new to them, try to build on each other's ideas, think up alternative ways to do things, offer and evaluate conclusions drawn from experiences they can describe—in such a case we would probably say they were having "worthwhile educative experiences" even though we have *not* yet given them a "test."

What we are working from is a model in our minds of what productive study looks and feels like. As long as a classroom full of students fits the teacher's model (even though he doesn't know he has one) the teacher simply tries to maintain interaction as it is; but the moment the experiences begin to lose their thrust or go sour, the teacher acts to change the situation and get back on the track.

The best model for classrooms is that of educated people utilizing knowledge effectively to conduct inquiries into problems, questions and issues that they feel are important. This model assumes that one becomes educated by acting more and more like an educated person.

The teacher is satisfied if he believes the children are doing this as well as they can, given their immature status, lack of experience, and present skills. If the teacher has no sound internalized image of such an operation, then he will act in accordance with some non-educative substitute, such as simply being comfortable and polite, becoming an audience for his play-acting of the expert or executive, becoming a congregation for his moralizing, becoming glibly informed with a lot of talk about (rather than understanding of) phenomena, becoming "independent" (which usually boils down to getting over being immobilized in an anarchic situation).

As I say, the big question is what we really *mean* by education—as shown by our actions as teachers. What is the nature of an educative situation?

THE BEST POLICY

There is little doubt that most competent opinion by people who have no vested interest in particular materials or in the sacred traditions of public schools is that we should maximize insight learning and minimize conditioned learning as much as possible.

There are both theoretical and practical objections to conditioned learning as the way to useful and utilizable knowledge (even though most attitudes and many skills are learned through conditioning in the family). There are only practical objections (too much work) to insight learning.

SOME HELPFUL DEDUCTIONS

As applied to programming of materials, the following deductions may serve as a starting set:

1. The student would be able to define his purpose in using the materials in terms of a question to be answered, a relationship to be sought, a skill to be learned, and he would have solid reasons which, for him, justify his learning of these things.

2. The materials would present reasonably large or molar "situations" containing many elements, and the student would devise his own path through these elements, taking them in any order he chooses, going back and forth among them, having free choice.

3. Each of these molar situations would involve at least two phases: discovery of the pattern followed by immediate application, summarizing, prediction, or raising of further questions that occurred to the student as he was working.

4. During the "search" phase, the student

would get immediate feedback when he had classified each element appropriately.

5. During the application or assimilation phase, feedback could not be built into the program because any of a large number of speculations or answers might be right—at least from the point of view of the student. The feedback for this phase would have to be reserved for a non-material third phase: class discussion which begins with the testimony of several students.

6. The programmed materials thus would lead into class discussion: the reported specu-

lations and difficulties of the students during the second phase would be testimony from which the agenda for discussion is generated.

7. The discussion would be concerned both with the students' speculations and conclusions and with the way in which the students arrived at these answers.

8. Diagnosis of the discussion would lead into the formulation of what the students need to study next, and a variety of activities as appropriate, including further work with programmed materials, would then be initiated.

17. WHY WE NEED TEACHING MACHINES *

B. F. SKINNER

Current suggestions for improving education are familiar to everyone. We need more and better schools and colleges. We must pay salaries which will attract and hold good teachers. We should group students according to ability. We must bring textbooks and other materials up-to-date, particularly in science and mathematics. And so on. It is significant that all this can be done without knowing much about teaching or learning. Those who are most actively concerned with improving education seldom discuss what is happening when a student reads a book, writes a paper, listens to a lecture, or solves a problem, and their proposals are only indirectly designed to make these activities more productive. In short, there is a general neglect of education method. (Television is no exception, for it is only a way of amplifying and extending *old* methods, together with their shortcomings.)

It is true that the psychology of learning has so far not been very helpful in education. Its learning curves and its theories of learning

* From *Cumulative Record*, Enlarged Edition, by B. F. Skinner. Copyright © 1961 by Appleton-Century-Crofts, Inc. Reprinted by permission of Appleton-Century-Crofts, Division of Meredith Corporation.

have not yielded greatly improved classroom practices. But it is too early to conclude that nothing useful is to be learned about the behavior of teacher and student. No enterprise can improve itself very effectively without examining its basic processes. Fortunately, recent advances in the experimental analysis of behavior suggest that a true technology of education is feasible. Improved techniques are available to carry out the two basic assignments of education: constructing extensive repertoires of verbal and nonverbal behavior and generating that high probability of action which is said to show interest, enthusiasm, or a strong "desire to learn."

The processes clarified by an experimental analysis of behavior have, of course, always played a part in education, but they have been used with little understanding of their effects, wanted or unwanted. Whether by intention or necessity, teachers have been less given to teaching than to holding students responsible for learning. Methods are still basically aversive. The student looks, listens, and answers questions (and, incidentally, sometimes learns) as a gesture of avoidance or escape. A good teacher can cite exceptions, but it is a mistake to call them typical. The birch rod and cane are gone, but their place has been taken by equally effective punishments (criticism, possibly ridicule, failure) used in the same way: the student must learn, or else!

By-products of aversive control in education range from truancy, early drop-outs, and school-vandalism to inattention, "mental fatigue," forgetting, and apathy. It does not take a scientific analysis to trace these to their sources in educational practice. But more acceptable techniques have been hard to find. Erasmus tells of an English gentleman who tried to teach his son Greek and Latin without punishment. He taught the boy to use a bow and arrow and set up targets in the shape of Greek and Latin letters, rewarding each hit with a cherry. Erasmus suggested cutting letters (from "delicious biscuits.") As a result, we may assume that the boy salivated slightly upon seeing a Greek or Latin text and that he was probably a better archer; but any effect on his knowledge of Greek and Latin is doubtful.

Current efforts to use rewards in education show the same indirection. Texts garnished with pictures in four colors, exciting episodes in a scientific film, interesting classroom activities—these will make a school interesting and even attractive (just as the boy probably liked his study of Greek and Latin), but to generate specific forms of behavior these things must be related to the student's behavior in special ways. Only then will they be truly rewarding or, technically speaking, "reinforcing."

We make a reinforcing event contingent on behavior when, for example, we design a piece of equipment in which a hungry rat or monkey or chimpanzee may press a lever and immediately obtain a bit of food. Such a piece of equipment gives us a powerful control over behavior. By scheduling reinforcements, we may maintain the behavior of pressing the lever in any given strength for long periods of time. By reinforcing special kinds of responses to the lever—for example, very light or heavy presses or those made with one hand or the other—we "shape" different forms or topographies of behavior. By reinforcing only when particular stimuli or classes of stimuli are present, we bring the behavior

under the control of the environment. All these processes have been thoroughly investigated, and they have already yielded standard laboratory practices in manipulating complex forms of behavior for experimental purposes. They are obviously appropriate to educational design.

In approaching the problem of the educator we may begin by surveying available reinforcers. What positive reasons can we give the student for studying? We can point to the ultimate advantages of an education—to the ways of life which are open only to educated men—and the student himself may cite these to explain why he wants an education, but ultimate advantages are not contingent on behavior in ways which generate action. Many a student can testify to the result. No matter how much he may *want* to become a doctor or an engineer, say, he cannot force himself to read and remember the page of text in front of him at the moment. All notions of ultimate utility (as, for example, in economics) suffer from the same shortcoming: they do not specify effective contingencies of reinforcement.

The gap between behavior and a distant consequence is sometimes bridged by a series of "conditioned reinforcers." In the laboratory experiment just described a delay of even a fraction of a second between the response to the lever and the appearance of food may reduce the effectiveness of the food by a measurable amount. It is standard practice to let the movement of a lever produce some visual stimulus, such as a change in the illumination in the apparatus, which is then followed by food. In this way the change in illumination becomes a conditioned reinforcer which can be made immediately contingent on the response. The marks, grades, and diplomas of education are conditioned reinforcers designed to bring ultimate consequences closer to the behavior reinforced. Like prizes and medals, they represent the approval of teachers, parents, and others, and they show competitive superiority, but they are mainly effective because they signalize progress through the system—toward some ultimate advantage of, or at least freedom from, education. To this extent they bridge the gap between behavior and its remote consequences; but they are still not contingent on behavior in a very effective way.

Progressive education tried to replace the birch rod, and at the same time avoid the artificiality of grades and prizes, by bringing the reinforcers of everyday life into the schools. Such natural contingencies have a kind of guaranteed effectiveness. But a school is only a small part of the student's world, and no matter how real it may seem, it cannot provide natural reinforcing consequences for all the kinds of behavior which education is to set up. The goals of progressive education were shifted to conform to this limitation, and many worthwhile assignments were simply abandoned.

Fortunately, we can solve the problem of education without discovering or inventing additional reinforcers. We merely need to make better use of those we have. Human behavior is distinguished by the fact that it is affected by small consequences. Describing something with the right word is often reinforcing. So is the clarification of a temporary puzzlement, or the solution of a complex problem, or simply the opportunity to move forward after completing one stage of an activity. We need not stop to explain *why* these things are reinforcing. It is enough that, when properly contingent upon behavior, they provide the control we need for successful educational design. Proper contingencies of reinforcement, however, are not always easily arranged. A modern laboratory for the study of behavior contains elaborate equipment designed to control the environment of individual organisms during many hours or days of continuous study. The required conditions and changes in conditions cannot be arranged by hand, not only because the experimenter does not have the time and energy, but because many contingencies are too subtle and precise to be arranged without instrumental help. The same problem arises in education.

Consider, for example, the temporal patterning of behavior called "rhythm." Behavior is often effective only if properly timed. Individual differences in timing, ranging from the most awkward to the most skillful performances, affect choice of career and of artistic interests and participation in sports and crafts. Presumably a "sense of rhythm"

is worth teaching, yet practically nothing is now done to arrange the necessary contingencies of reinforcement. The skilled typist, tennis player, lathe operator, or musician is, of course, under the influence of reinforcing mechanisms which generate subtle timing, but many people never reach the point at which these natural contingencies can take over.

The relatively simple device supplies the necessary contingencies. The student taps a rhythmic pattern in unison with the device. "Unison" is specified very loosely at first (the student can be a little early or late at each tap) but the specifications are slowly sharpened. The process is repeated for various speeds and patterns. In another arrangement, the student echoes rhythmic patterns sounded by the machine, though not in unison, and again the specifications for an accurate reproduction are progressively sharpened. Rhythmic patterns can also be brought under the control of a printed score.

Another kind of teaching machine generates sensitivity to properties of the environment. We call an effective person "discriminating." He can tell the difference between the colors, shapes, and sizes of objects, he can identify three-dimensional forms seen from different aspects, he can find patterns concealed in other patterns, he can identify pitches, intervals, and musical themes and distinguish between different tempos and rhythms—and all of this in an almost infinite variety. Subtle discriminations of this sort are as important in science and industry and in everyday life as in identifying the school of a painter or the period of a composer.

The ability to make a given kind of discrimination can be taught. A pigeon, for example, can be *made* sensitive to the color, shape, and size of objects, to pitches, and rhythms, and so on—simply by reinforcing it when it responds in some arbitrary way to one set of stimuli and extinguishing responses to all others. The same kinds of contingencies of reinforcement are responsible for human discriminative behavior. *The remarkable fact is that they are quite rare in the environment of the average child.* True, children are encouraged to play with objects of different sizes, shapes, and colors, and are given a passing acquaintance with musical patterns; but they are seldom exposed to the precise contingencies needed to build subtle discriminations. It is not surprising that most of them move into adulthood with largely undeveloped "abilities."

The number of reinforcements required to build discriminative behavior in the population as a whole is far beyond the capacity of teachers. Too many teachers would be needed, and many contingencies are too subtle to be mediated by even the most skillful. *Yet relatively simple machines will suffice.* The apparatus is adapted from research on lower organisms. It teaches an organism to discriminate selected properties of stimuli while "matching to sample." Pictures or words are projected on translucent windows which respond to a touch by closing circuits. A child can be made to "look at the sample" by reinforcing him for pressing the top window. An adequate reinforcement for this response is simply the appearance of material in the lower windows, from which a choice is to be made.

The child identifies the material which corresponds to the sample in some prescribed way by pressing one of the lower windows, and he is then reinforced again—possibly simply because a new set of materials now appears on the windows. If he presses the wrong window, all three choices disappear until the top window has been pressed again—which means until he has again looked at the sample. Many other arrangements of responses and reinforcements are, of course, possible. In an auditory version, the child listens to a sample pattern of tones and then explores other samples to find a match.

If devices similar to these were generally available in our nursery schools and kindergartens, our children would be far more skillful in dealing with their environments. They would be more productive in their work, more sensitive to art and music, better at sports, and so on. They would lead more effective lives. We cannot assert all this with complete confidence on the present evidence, but there is no doubt whatsoever *that the conditions needed to produce such a state of affairs are now lacking.* In the light of what we know about differential contingencies of reinforcement, the world of the young child is shamefully impoverished. And only machines will remedy this, for the required frequency and

subtlety of reinforcement cannot otherwise be arranged.

The teacher is, of course, at a disadvantage in teaching skilled and discriminative behavior because such instruction is largely nonverbal. It may be that the methods of the classroom, in which the teacher is said to "communicate" with the student, to "impart information," and to build "verbal abilities," are better adapted to standard subject matters, the learning of which is usually regarded as more than the acquisition of forms of behavior or of environmental control. Yet a second look may be worthwhile. Traditional characterizations of verbal behavior raise almost insuperable problems for the teacher, and a more rigorous analysis suggests another possibility. We can define terms like "information," "knowledge," and "verbal ability" by reference to the behavior from which we infer their presence. *We may then teach the behavior directly.* Instead of "transmitting information to the student," we may simply set up the behavior which is taken as a sign that he possesses information. Instead of teaching a "knowledge of French" we may teach the behavior from which we infer such knowledge. Instead of teaching "an ability to read" we may set up the behavioral repertoire which distinguishes the child who knows how to read from one who does not.

To take the last example, a child reads or "shows that he knows how to read" by exhibiting a behavioral repertoire of great complexity. He finds a letter or word in a list on demand; he reads aloud; he finds or identifies objects described in a text; he rephrases sentences; he obeys written instructions; he behaves appropriately to described situations; he reacts emotionally to described events; and so on, in a long list. He does none of this before learning to read and all of it afterwards. To bring about such a change is an extensive assignment, and it is tempting to try to circumvent it by teaching something called "an ability to read" from which all these specific behaviors will flow. But this has never actually been done. "Teaching reading" is always directed toward setting up specific items in such a repertoire.

It is true that parts of the repertoire are not independent. A student may acquire some kinds of response more readily for having acquired others, and he may for a time use some in place of others (for example, he may follow written directions not by responding directly to a text but by following his own spoken instructions as he reads the text aloud). In the long run all parts of the repertoire tend to be filled in, not because the student is rounding out an ability to read, but simply because all parts are in their several ways useful. They all continue to be reinforced by the world at large after the explicit teaching of reading has ceased.

Viewed in this way, reading can also be more effectively taught with instrumental help. A pupil can learn to distinguish among letters and groups of letters in an alphabet simply as visual patterns in using the device and procedures just described. He can be taught to identify arbitrary correspondences (for example, between capitals and lower-case letters, or between handwritten and printed letters) in a more complex type of stimulus control which is within reach of the same device. With a phonographic attachment, correspondences between printed letters and sounds, between sounds and letters, between words and sounds, between sounds and printed words, and so on, can be set up. (The student could be taught all of this without pronouncing a word, and it is possible that he would learn good pronunciation more quickly if he had first done so.)

The same device can teach correspondences between words and the properties of objects. The pupil selects a printed or spoken word which corresponds in the language to, say, a pictured object or another printed or spoken word. These semantic correspondences differ in important respects from formal matches, but the same processes of programming and reinforcement can—indeed, must—be used. Traditional ways of teaching reading establish all these repertoires, but they do so indirectly and, alas, inefficiently. In "building a child's need to read," in motivating "his mental readiness," in "sharing information," and so on, the teacher arranges, sometimes almost surreptitiously, many of the contingencies just listed, and these are responsible for whatever is learned. An explicit treatment clarifies the program, suggests effective procedures, and

guarantees a coverage which is often lacking with traditional methods. Much of what is called reading has not been covered, of course, but it may not need to be taught, for once these basic repertoires have been established, the child begins to receive automatic reinforcement in responding to textual material.

The same need for a behavioral definition arises in teaching other verbal skills (for example, a second language) as well as the traditional subjects of education. In advancing to that level, however, we must transcend a limitation of the device. The student can *select* a response without being able to speak or write, but we want him to learn to *emit* the response, since this is the kind of behavior which he will later find most useful. The emission of verbal behavior is taught by another kind of machine. A frame of textual material appearing in the square opening is incomplete: in place of certain letters or figures there are holes. Letters or figures can be made to appear in these holes by moving sliders (a keyboard would be an obvious improvement). When the material has been completed, the student checks his response by turning a crank. The machine senses the settings of the sliders and, if they are correct, moves a new frame of material into place, the sliders returning to their home position. If the response is wrong, the sliders return home, and a second setting must be made.

The machine can tell the student he is wrong without telling him what is right. This is an advantage, but it is relatively costly. Moreover, correct behavior is rather rigidly specified. Such a machine is probably suitable only for the lower grades. A simpler and cheaper procedure, with greater flexibility, is to allow the student to compare his written response with a revealed text. The device uses this principle. It is suitable for verbal instruction beyond the lower primary grades—that is, through junior high school, high school, and college, and in industrial and professional education. Programmed material is stored on fan-folded paper tapes. One frame of material, the size of which may be varied with the nature of the material, is exposed at a time. The student writes on a separate paper strip. He cannot look at unauthorized parts of the material without recording the fact that he has done so, because when the machine has been loaded and closed, it can be opened only by punching the strip of paper.

The student sees printed material in the large window at left. This may be a sentence to be completed, a question to be answered, or a problem to be solved. He writes his response in an uncovered portion of a paper strip at the right. He then moves a slider which covers the response he has written with a transparent mask and uncovers additional material in the larger opening. This may tell him that his response is wrong without telling him what is right. For example, it may list a few of the commonest errors. If the response he wrote is among them, he can try again on a newly uncovered portion of the paper strip. A further operation of the machine covers his second attempt and uncovers the correct response. The student records a wrong response by punching a hold alongside it, leaving a record for the instructor who may wish to review a student's performance, and operating a counter which becomes visible at the end of the set. Then the student records the number of mistakes he has made and may compare it with a par score for the set.

Exploratory research in schools and colleges indicates that what is now taught by teacher, textbook, lecture, or film can be taught in half the time with half the effort by a machine of this general type. One has only to see students at work to understand why this is a conservative estimate. The student remains active. If he stops, the program stops (in marked contrast with classroom practice and educational television); but there is no compulsion for he is not inclined to stop. Immediate and frequent reinforcement sustains a lively interest. (The interest, incidentally, outlasts any effect of novelty. Novelty may be relevant to interest, but the material in the machine is always novel.) Where current instructional procedures are highly efficient, the gain may not be so great. In one experiment involving industrial education there was approximately a 25% saving in the time required for instruction, something of the order of a 10% increase in retention, and about 90% of the students preferred to study by machine. In general, the student generally likes what he is doing; he makes no effort to escape—for example,

by letting his attention wander. He need not force himself to work and is usually free of the feeling of effort generated by aversive control. He has no reason to be anxious about impending examinations, for none are required. Both he and his instructor know where he stands at all times.

No less important in explaining the success of teaching machines is the fact that each student is free to proceed at his own rate. Holding students together for instructional purposes in a class is probably the greatest source of inefficiency in education. Some efforts to mechanize instruction have missed this point. A language laboratory controlled from a central console presupposes a group of students advancing at about the same rate, even though some choice of material is permitted. Television in education has made the same mistake on a colossal scale. A class of twenty or thirty students moving at the same pace is inefficient enough, but what must we say of all the students in half a dozen states marching in a similar lock step?

In trying to teach more than one student at once we harm both fast and slow learners. The plight of the good student has been recognized, but the slow learner suffers more disastrous consequences. The effect of pressure to move beyond one's natural speed is cumulative. The student who has not fully mastered a first lesson is less able to master a second. His ultimate failure may greatly exaggerate his shortcoming; a small difference in speed has grown to an immense difference in comprehension. Some of those most active in improving education have been tempted to dismiss slow students impatiently as a waste of time, but it is quite possible that many of them are capable of substantial, even extraordinary, achievements if permitted to move at their own pace. Many distinguished scientists, for example, have appeared to think slowly.

One advantage of individual instruction is that the student is able to follow a program without breaks or omissions. A member of a class moving at approximately the same rate cannot always make up for absences, and limitations of contact time between student and teacher make it necessary to abbreviate material to the point at which substantial gaps are inevitable. Working on a machine, the student can always take up where he left off or, if he wishes, review earlier work after a longer absence. The coherence of the program helps to maximize the student's success, for by thoroughly mastering one step he is optimally prepared for the next. Many years ago, in their *Elementary Principles of Education*, Thorndike and Gates considered the possibility of a book "so arranged that only to him who had done what was directed on page one would page two become visible, and so on." With such a book, they felt, "much that now requires personal instruction could be managed by print." The teaching machine is, of course, such a book.

In summary, then, machine teaching is unusually efficient because (1) the student is frequently and immediately reinforced, (2) he is free to move at his natural rate, and (3) he follows a coherent sequence. These are the more obvious advantages, and they may well explain current successes. But there are more promising possibilities: the conditions arranged by a good teaching machine make it possible to apply to education what we have learned from laboratory research and to extend our knowledge through rigorous experiments in schools and colleges.

The conceptions of the learning process which underlie classroom practices have long been out of date. For example, teachers and textbooks are said to "impart information." They expose the student to verbal and non-verbal material and call attention to particular features of it, and in so doing they are said to "tell the student something." In spite of discouraging evidence to the contrary, it is still supposed that if you tell a student something, he then knows it. In this scheme, teaching is the transmission of information, a notion which, through a false analogy, has acquired undue prestige from communication engineering. Something is undoubtedly transmitted by teacher to student, for if communication is interrupted, instruction ceases; but the teacher is not merely a source from which knowledge flows into the student. We cannot necessarily improve instruction by altering the conditions of transmission—as, for example, by changing to a different sensory modality. This is a mistake made by some so-called teaching machines which, accepting our failure to teach reading, have tried to restore communication by using recorded speech. The student no longer pores over a book, as in the traditional portrait; he stares into space with earphones on his head. For the same reasons improvements in the coding of information may not be immediately relevant.

The student is more than a receiver of information. He must take some kind of action. The traditional view is that he must "associate." The stream of information flowing from teacher to student contains pairs of items which, being close together or otherwise related, become connected in the student's mind. This is the old doctrine of the association of ideas, now strengthened by a scientific, if uncritical, appeal to conditioned reflexes: two things occurring together in experience somehow become connected so that one of them later reminds the student of the other. The teacher has little control over the process except to make sure that things occur together often and that the student pays attention to them—for example, by making the experiences vivid or, as we say, memorable. Some devices called teaching machines are simply ways of presenting things together in ways which attract attention. The student listens to recorded speech, for example, while looking at pictures. The theory is that he will associate these auditory and visual presentations.

But the action demanded of the student is not some sort of mental association of contiguous experiences. It is more objective and, fortunately, more controllable than that. To acquire behavior, *the student must engage in behavior*. This has long been known. The principle is implied in any philosophy of "learning by doing." But it is not enough simply to acknowledge its validity. Teaching machines provide the conditions needed to apply the principle effectively.

Only in the early stages of education are we mainly interested in establishing *forms* of behavior. In the verbal field, for example, we teach a child to speak, eventually with acceptable accent and pronunciation, and later to write and spell. After that, topography of behavior is assumed; the student can speak and write and must now learn to do so appropriately—that is, he must speak or write in given ways under given circumstances. How he comes to do so is widely misunderstood. Education usually begins by establishing so-called formal repertoires. The young child is taught to "echo" verbal behavior in the sense of repeating verbal stimuli with reasonable accuracy. A little later he is taught to read—to emit verbal behavior under the control of textual stimuli. These and other formal repertoires are used in later stages of instruction to evoke new responses without "shaping" them.

In an important case of what we call instruction, control is simply transferred from so-called formal to thematic stimuli. When a student learns to memorize a poem, for example, it is clearly inadequate to say that by reading the poem he presents to himself its various parts contiguously and then associates them. He does not simply read the poem again and again until he knows it. (It is possible that he could never learn the poem in that way.) Something else must be done, as anyone knows who has memorized a poem from the text. The student must make tentative responses while looking away from the text. He must glance at the text from time to time to provide fragmentary help in emitting a partially learned response. If a recalled passage makes sense, it may provide its own automatic confirmation, but if the passage is fragmentary or obscure, the student must confirm the correctness of an emitted response by referring to the text after he has emitted it.

A teaching machine facilitates this process. It presents the poem line by line and asks the student to read it. The text is then "vanished" —that is, it becomes less and less clear or less and less complete in subsequent presentations. Other stimuli (arising from the student's own behavior in this case) take over. In one procedure a few unimportant letters are omitted in the first presentation. The student reads the line without their help and indicates his success by writing down the omitted letters, which are confirmed by the machine. More of the line is missing when it again appears, but because he has recently responded to a fuller text, the student can nevertheless read it correctly. Eventually, no textual stimulus remains, and he can "recite" the poem.

(If the reader wishes to try this method on a friend or member of his family without a machine, he may do so by writing the poem on a chalk board in a clear hand, omitting a few unimportant letters. He should ask his subject to read the poem aloud but to make no effort to memorize it. He should then erase another selection of letters. He will have to guess at how far he can go without interfering with his subject's success on the next reading, but under controlled conditions this could be determined for the average student quite accurately. Again the subject reads the poem aloud, making no effort to memorize, though he may have to make some effort to recall. Other letters are then erased and the process repeated. For a dozen lines of average material, four or five readings should suffice to eliminate the text altogether. The poem can still be "read.")

Memorized verbal behavior is a valuable form of knowledge which has played an important role in classical education. There are other, and generally more useful, forms in which the same processes are involved. Consider, for example, a labeled picture. To say that such an instructional device "tells the student the name of the pictured object" is highly elliptical—and dangerous if we are trying to understand the processes involved. Simply showing a student a labeled picture is no more effective than letting him read a poem. He must take some sort of action. As a formal stimulus, the label evokes a verbal response, not in this case in the presence of other verbal behavior on the part of the student, but in the presence of the picture. The control of the response is to pass from the label to the picture; the student is to give the name of the pictured object without reading it.

The steps taken in teaching with labeled pictures can also be arranged particularly well with a machine. Suppose we are teaching medical-school anatomy at the textbook level. Certain labeled charts represent what is to be learned in the sense that the student will eventually (I) give the names of indicated parts and describe relations among them and (2) be able to point to, draw, or construct models of parts, or relations among them, given their names. To teach the first of these, we induce the student to describe relations among the parts shown on a fully labeled chart. One effect of this is that he executes the verbal behavior at issue—he writes the names of the parts. More important, he does this while, or just after, looking at corresponding pictured details. He will be able to write the names again while looking at a chart which shows only incomplete names, possibly only initial letters. Finally, he will be able to supply the complete names of parts identified only by number on still another chart. His verbal responses have passed from the control of textual stimuli to that of pictured anatomical details. Eventually, as he studies a cadaver, the control will pass to the actual anatomy of the human body. In this sense he then "knows the names of the parts of the body and can describe relations among them." . . .

Learning a poem or the names of pictured objects is a relatively straightforward task. More complex forms of knowledge require other procedures. At an early point, the main problem becomes that of analyzing knowledge. Traditionally, for example, something called a "knowledge of French" is said to permit the student who possesses it to do many things. One who possesses it can (1) repeat a French phrase with a good accent, (2) read a French text in all the senses of reading listed above, (3) take dictation in French, (4) find a word spoken in French on a printed list, (5) obey instructions spoken in French, (6) comment in French upon objects or events, (7) give orders in French, and so on. If he also "knows English," he can give the English equivalents of French words or phrases or the French equivalents of English words or phrases.

The concept of "a knowledge of French" offers very little help to the would-be teacher. As in the case of reading, we must turn to the behavioral repertoires themselves, for these are all that have ever been taught when education has been effective. The definition of a subject matter in such terms may be extraordinarily difficult. Students who are "competent in first-year college physics," for example, obviously differ from those who are not—but in what way? Even a tentative answer to that question should clarify the problem of teaching physics. It may well do more. In the not-too-distant future much more general issues in epistemology may be approached from the same direction. It is possible that we shall fully understand the nature of knowledge only

after having solved the practical problems of imparting it.

Until we can define subject matters more accurately and until we have improved our techniques of building verbal repertoires, writing programs for teaching machines will remain something of an art. This is not wholly satisfactory, but there is some consolation in the fact than an impeccable authority on the excellence of a program is available. The student himself can tell the programmer where he has failed. By analyzing the errors made by even a small number of students in a pilot study, it is usually possible to work a great improvement in an early version of a program. . . .

The teaching machine . . . falls far short of the "electronic classrooms" often visualized for the schools and colleges of the future. Many of these, often incorporating small computers, are based on misunderstandings of the learning process. They are designed to duplicate current classroom conditions. When instruction is badly programmed, a student often goes astray, and a teacher must come to his rescue. His mistakes must be analyzed and corrected. This may give the impression that instruction is largely a matter of correcting errors. If this were the case, an effective machine would, indeed, have to follow the student into many unprofitable paths and take remedial action. But under proper programming nothing of this sort is required. It is true that a relatively important function of the teacher will be to follow the progress of each student and to suggest collateral material which may be of interest, as well as to outline further studies, to recommend changes to programs of different levels of difficulty, and so on, and to this extent a student's course of study will show "branching." But changes in level of difficulty or in the character of the subject need not be frequent and can be made as the student moves from one set of material to another.

Teaching machines based on the principle of "multiple choice" also often show a misunderstanding of the learning process. When multiple-choice apparatuses were first used, the organism was left to proceed by "trial and error." The term does not refer to a behavioral process but simply to the fact that contingencies of reinforcement were left to chance: some responses happened to be successful and others not. Learning was not facilitated or accelerated by procedures which increased the probability of successful responses. The results, like those of much classroom instruction, suggested that errors were essential to the learning process. But when material is carefully programmed, both subhuman and human subjects can learn while making few errors or even none at all. Recent research by Herbert S. Terrace, for example, has shown that a pigeon can learn to discriminate colors practically without making mistakes. The control exerted by color may be passed, *via* a vanishing technique, to more difficult properties of stimuli—again without error. Of course we learn something from our mistakes—for one thing, we learn not to make them again—but we *acquire* behavior in other ways.

The teaching machines of S. J. Pressey, the first psychologist to see the "coming industrial revolution in education," were mechanical versions of self-scoring test forms, which Pressey and his students also pioneered. They were not designed for programmed instruction in the present sense. The student was presumed to have studied a subject before coming to the machine. By testing himself, he consolidated what he had already partially learned. For this purpose a device which evaluated the student's selection from an array of multiple-choice items was appropriate. For the same purpose multiple-choice material can, of course, be used in all the machines described above. But several advantages of programmed instruction are lost when such material is used in straightforward instruction.

In the first place, the student should *construct* rather than *select* a response, since this is the behavior he will later find useful. Secondly, he should advance to the level of being able to emit a response rather than merely recognize a given response as correct. This represents a much more considerable achievement, as the difference between the sizes of reading and writing vocabularies in a foreign language demonstrates. Thirdly, and more important, multiple-choice material violates a basic principle of good programming by inducing the student to engage in erroneous behavior. Those who have written multiple-choice tests know how much time, energy, and ingenuity are needed to construct plausible wrong answers. (They must be plausible or the test will be of little value.) In a multiple-choice *test*, they may do no harm, since a student who has already learned the right answer may reject wrong answers with ease and possibly with no undesirable side-effects. The student who is *learning*, however, can scarcely avoid trouble. Traces of erroneous responses survive in spite of the correction of errors or the confirmation of a right answer. In multiple-choice material designed to teach "literary appreciation," for example, the student is asked to consider three or four plausible paraphrases of a passage in a poem and to identify the most acceptable. But as the student reads and considers unacceptable paraphrases, the very processes which the poet himself used in making his poem effective are at work to destroy it. Neither the vigorous correction of wrong choices nor the confirmation of a right choice will free the student of the verbal and nonverbal associations thus generated.

Scientific subjects offer more specific examples. Consider an item such as the following, which might be part of a course in high school physics:

As the pressure of a gas increases, volume decreases. This is because:

  (a) *the space between the molecules grows smaller*
  (b) *the molecules are flattened*
  (c) etc. . . .

Unless the student is as industrious and as ingenious as the multiple-choice programmer, it will probably not have occurred to him that molecules may be flattened as a gas is compressed (within the limits under consideration). If he chooses item (b) and is corrected by the machine, we may say that he "has learned that it is wrong," but this does not mean that the sentence will never occur to him again. And if he is unlucky enough to select the right answer first, his reading of the plausible but erroneous answer will be corrected only "by implication"—an equally vague and presumably less effective process. In either case, he may later find himself recalling that "somewhere he has read that mole-

cules are flattened when a gas is compressed."
And, of course, somewhere he has.

Multiple-choice techniques are appropriate
when the student is to learn to compare and
choose. In forming a discrimination, . . . an
organism must be exposed to at least two stimuli, one of which may be said to be wrong.
Similarly, in learning to "troubleshoot" equipment there may be several almost equally
plausible ways of correcting a malfunction.
Games offer other examples. A given hand at
bridge may justify several bids or plays, no
one of which is wholly right and all the others
wrong. In such cases, the student is to learn
the most expedient course to be taken among
a natural array of possibilities. This is not
true in the simple acquisition of knowledge—
particularly verbal knowledge—where the task
is only rarely to discriminate among responses
in an array. In solving an equation, reporting
a fact of history, restating the meaning of a
sentence, or engaging in almost any of the
other behavior which is the main concern of
education, the student is to *generate* responses.
He may generate and reject, but only rarely
will he generate a set of responses from which
he must then make a choice.

It may be argued that machines which provide for branching and decision-making are
designed to teach more than verbal repertoires
—in particular, that they will teach thinking.
There are strategies in choosing from an
array, for example, which require kinds of behavior beyond the mere emission of correct
responses. We may agree to this without questioning the value of knowledge in the sense of
a verbal repertoire. (The distinction is not
between rote and insightful learning, for programmed instruction is especially free of rote
memorizing in the etymological sense of wear-
ing down a path through repetition.) If an
"idea" or "proposition" is defined as something
which can be expressed in many ways, then it
may be taught by teaching many of these
"ways." What is learned is more likely to
generalize to comparable situations than a
single syntactical form, and generalization is
what distinguishes so-called deeper understanding.

But not all thinking is verbal. There are,
first of all, alternative, parallel nonverbal repertoires. The mathematician begins with a
verbal problem and ends with a verbal solution, but much of his intervening behavior may
be of a different nature. The student who
learns to follow or construct a proof entirely
by manipulating symbols may not engage in
this kind of thinking. Similarly, a merely verbal knowledge of physics, as often seen in the
student who has "memorized the text," is of
little interest to the serious educator. Laboratories and demonstrations sometimes supply
contingencies which build some nonverbal
knowledge of physics. Special kinds of teaching machines could help, for machines are not
only not confined to verbal instruction, they
may well make it possible to reduce the emphasis on verbal communication between
teacher and student.

A more clear-cut example of the distinction
between verbal and nonverbal thinking is musical composition. The composer who "thinks
musically" does more than perform on an instrument or enjoy music. He also does more
than use musical notation. In some sense he
"thinks" pitches, intervals, melodies, harmonic
progressions, and so on. It should not surprise
us that individuals differ greatly in their
"abilities" to do this, since the necessary contingencies are in very short supply. One might
attack the problem by setting up an explicit
kinesthetic repertoire in which "thinking a
pitch" takes the form of identifying a position
on a keyboard. A device which arranges the
necessary contingencies is under development.
With its help we may discover the extent to
which students can in general learn (and at
what ages they can learn most effectively) to
strike a key which produces a tone which has
just been heard. Similar devices might generate important forms of nonverbal mathematical behavior or the behavior exhibited say, by
an inventor conceiving of a device in three
dimensions, as well as creative repertoires in
other forms of art. Here is an extraordinary
challenge to the technology of instrumentation.

There is another sense in which the student
must learn to think. Verbal and nonverbal
repertoires may prepare him to behave in effective ways, but he will inevitably face novel
situations in which he cannot at first respond
appropriately. He may solve such problems,
not by exercising some mental ability, but by
altering either the external situation or the

relative probabilities of parts of his own repertoire. In this way he may increase the probability of an adequate response.

In this sense, thinking consists of a special repertoire which we may call self-management. For example, the student may alter the extent to which the environment affects him by "attending" to it in different ways. As one step in teaching thinking we must teach effective attending. The phrase "Pay attention!" is as common on the lips of teachers as "Open, please" on those of dentists—and for much the same reason: both phrases set up working conditions. The student may pay attention to avoid punishment and in doing so may learn to pay attention, but where aversive sanctions have been given up, teachers have resorted to attracting and holding attention. The techniques of the publication and entertainment industries are extensively invoked. Primers are usually decorated with colored pictures, and high school textbooks are sometimes designed to resemble picture magazines. Films dramatize subject matters in competition with noneducational films and television.

Attention which is captured by attractive stimuli must be distinguished from attention which is "paid." Only the latter must be learned. Looking and listening are forms of behavior, and they are strengthened by reinforcement. A pigeon can learn to match colors, for example, only if it "pays attention to them." The experimenter makes sure that it does so, not by attracting its attention, but by reinforcing it for looking. Similarly, a well-taught student pays attention to sentences, diagrams, samples of recorded speech and music, and so on, not because they are attractive but because something interesting occasionally happens *after* he has paid attention.

Most audio-visual devices fail to teach attention because they stimulate the student *before* he looks or listens closely. No matter how well a four-colored text or a dramatically filmed experiment in physics attracts attention, it prepares the student only for comics, advertising, picture magazines, television programs, and other material which is *interesting on its face*. What is wanted is an adult who, upon seeing a page of black-and-white text, will read it because it may *prove* interesting. Unfortunately, the techniques associated with

captured and paid attention are incompatible. Whenever a teacher attracts the attention of a student, he deprives him of an opportunity to learn to pay attention. Teaching machines, with their control over the consequences of action, can make sure that paying attention will be effectively reinforced.

Another activity associated with thinking is studying—not merely looking at a text and reading it but looking and reading *for the sake of future action*. Suppose we show a child a picture and later, in the absence of the picture, reinforce him generously for correct answers to questions about it. If he has done nothing like this before, he will probably not be very successful. If we then show him another picture, he may begin to behave in a different way: he may engage in behavior which will increase the probability that he will later answer questions correctly. It will be to his advantage (and to ours as educators) if this kind of behavior is taught rather than left to chance. We teach a student "how to study" when we teach him to take notes, to rehearse his own behavior, to test himself, to organize, outline, and analyze, to look for or construct mnemonic patterns, and so on. Some of these behaviors are obvious, but others are of more subtle dimensions and admittedly hard to teach. Machines have an advantage in maintaining the contingencies required for indirect or mediated reinforcement.

Other aspects of thinking, including the solution of personal problems, can also be analyzed and directly programmed. This is not current practice, however. Students are most often "taught to think" simply by thrusting them into situations in which already established repertoires are inadequate. Some of them modify their behavior or the situation effectively and come up with solutions. They may have learned, but they have not necessarily been taught, how to think.

Logicians, mathematicians, and scientists have often tried to record and understand their own thinking processes, but we are still far from a satisfactory formulation of all relevant behaviors. Much remains to be learned about how a skillful thinker examines a situation, alters it, samples his own responses with respect to it, carries out specific verbal manipulations appropriate to it, and so on. It is quite possible that we cannot teach thinking adequately until all this has been analyzed. Once we have specified the behavior, however, we have no reason to suppose that it will then be any less adaptable to programmed instruction than simple verbal repertoires.

Teaching machines and the associated practices of programmed instruction will have proved too successful if their practical consequences are allowed to overshadow their promise for the future. We need teaching machines to help solve a very pressing problem, but we also need them to utilize our basic knowledge of human behavior in the design of entirely new educational practices.

Teaching machines are an example of the technological application of basic science. It is true that current machines might have been designed in the light of classroom experience and common sense, and that explanations of why they are effective can be paraphrased in traditional terms. The fact remains that more than half a century of the self-conscious examination of instructional processes had worked only moderate changes in educational practices. The laboratory study of learning provided the confidence, if not all the knowledge, needed for a successful instrumental attack on the *status quo*. Traditional views may not have been actually wrong, but they were vague and were not entertained with sufficient commitment to work substantial technological changes.

As a technology, however, education is still immature, as we may see from the fact that it defines its goals in terms of traditional achievements. Teachers are usually concerned with reproducing the characteristics and achievements of already educated men. When the nature of the human organism is better understood, we may begin to consider not only what man has already shown himself to be but what he may become under carefully designed conditions. The goal of education should be nothing short of the fullest possible development of the human organism. An experimental analysis of behavior, carried out under the advantageous conditions of the laboratory, will contribute to progress toward that goal. So will practical experiments conducted in schools and colleges with the help of adequate instrumentation.

18. THE CHEMISTRY OF LEARNING *

DAVID KRECH

American educators now talk a great deal about the innovative hardware of education, about computer-assisted instruction, 8 mm cartridge-loading projectors, microtransparencies, and other devices. In the not too distant future they may well be talking about enzyme-assisted instruction, protein memory consolidators, antibiotic memory repellers, and the chemistry of the brain. Although the psychologists' learning theories derived from the study of maze-running rats or target-pecking pigeons have failed to provide insights into the education of children, it is unlikely that what is now being discovered by the psychologist, chemist, and neurophysiologist about rat-brain chemistry can deviate widely from what we will eventually discover about the chemistry of the human brain.

Most adults who are not senile can repeat a series of seven numbers—8, 4, 8, 8, 3, 9, 9—immediately after the series is read. If, however, they are asked to repeat these numbers thirty minutes later, most will fail. In the first instance, we are dealing with the immediate memory span; in the second, with long-term

* David, Krech, "The Chemistry of Learning," *Saturday Review*, January 20, 1968, 48-50.

memory. These basic behavioral observations lie behind what is called the two-stage memory storage process theory.

According to a common variant of these notions, immediately after every learning trial—indeed, after every experience—a short-lived electrochemical process is established in the brain. This process, so goes the assumption, is the physiological mechanism which carries the short-term memory. Within a few seconds or minutes, however, this process decays and disappears; but before doing so, if all systems are go, the short-term electrochemical process triggers a second series of events in the brain. This second process is chemical in nature and involves, primarily, the production of new proteins and the induction of higher enzymatic activity levels in the brain cells. This process is more enduring and serves as the physiological substrate of our long-term memory.

It would follow that one approach to testing our theory would be to provide a subject with some experience or other, then interrupt the short-term electro-chemical process immediately—before it has had an opportunity to establish the long-term process. If this were done, our subject should never develop a long-term memory for that experience.

At the Albert Einstein Medical School in New York, Dr. Murray Jarvik has devised a "step-down" procedure based on the fact that when a rat is placed on a small platform a few inches above the floor, the rat will step down onto the floor within a few seconds. The rat will do this consistently, day after day. Suppose that on one day the floor is electrified, and stepping onto it produces a painful shock. When the rat is afterward put back on the platform—even twenty-four hours later—it will not budge from the platform but will remain there until the experimenter gets tired and calls the experiment quits. The rat has thus demonstrated that he has a long-term memory for that painful experience.

If we now take another rat, but this time interfere with his short-term memory process immediately after he has stepped onto the electrified floor, the rat should show no evidence of having experienced a shock when tested the next day, since we have not given his short-term electrochemical memory process an opportunity to initiate the long-term pro-

tein-enzymatic process. To interrupt the short-term process, Jarvik passes a mild electric current across the brain of the animal. The current is not strong enough to cause irreparable harm to the brain cells, but it does result in a very high level of activation of the neurons in the brain, thus disrupting the short-term electrochemical memory process. If this treatment follows closely enough after the animal's first experience with the foot shock, and we test the rat a day later, the rat acts as if there were no memory for yesterday's event; the rat jauntily and promptly steps down from the platform with no apparent expectation of shock.

When a long time-interval is interposed between the first foot shock and the electric-current (through the brain) treatment, the rat *does* remember the foot shock, and it remains on the platform when tested the next day. This, again, is what we should have expected from our theory. The short-term electro-chemical process has now had time to set up the long-term chemical memory process before it was disrupted.

Some well known effects of accidental human head injury seem to parallel these findings. Injuries which produce a temporary loss of consciousness (but no permanent damage to brain tissue) can cause the patient to experience a "gap" in his memory for the events just preceding the accident. This retrograde amnesia can be understood on the assumption that the events immediately prior to the accident were still being carried by the short-term memory processes at the time of the injury, and their disruption by the injury was sufficient to prevent the induction of the long-term processes. The patient asks "Where am I?" not only because he does not recognize the hospital, but also because he cannot remember how he became injured.

Work conducted by Dr. Bernard Agranoff at the University of Michigan Medical School supports the hypothesis that the synthesis of new brain proteins is crucial for the establishment of the long-term memory process. He argues that if we could prevent the formation of new proteins in the brain, then—although the short-term electrochemical memory process is not interfered with—the long-term memory process could never become established.

Much of Agranoff's work has been done with goldfish. The fish is placed in one end of a small rectangular tank, which is divided into two halves by a barrier which extends from the bottom to just below the surface of the water. When a light is turned on, the fish must swim across the barrier into the other side of the tank within twenty seconds—otherwise he receives an electric shock. This training is continued for several trials until the animal learns to swim quickly to the other side when the light is turned on. Most goldfish learn this shock-avoidance task quite easily and remember it for many days. Immediately before—and in some experiments, immediately after—training, Agranoff injects the antibiotic puromycin into the goldfish's brain. (Puromycin is a protein inhibitor and prevents the formation of new proteins in the brain's neurons.) After injection, Agranoff finds that the goldfish are not impaired in their acquisition of the shock-avoidance task, but, when tested a day or so later, they show almost no retention for the task.

These results mean that the short-term memory process (which helps the animal remember from one trial to the next and thus permits him to learn in the first place) is not dependent upon the formation of new proteins, but that the long-term process (which helps the animal remember from one day to the next and thus permits him to retain what he had learned) is dependent upon the production of new proteins. Again, as in the instance of Jarvik's rats, if the puromycin injection comes more than an hour after learning, it has no effect on later memory—the long-term memory process presumably has already been established and the inhibition of protein synthesis can now no longer affect memory. In this antibiotic, therefore, we have our first chemical memory erasure—or, more accurately, a chemical long-term memory preventative. (Almost identical findings have been reported by other workers in other laboratories working with such animals as mice and rats, which are far removed from the goldfish.)

Thus far I have been talking about disrupting or preventing the formation of memory. Now we will accentuate the positive. Dr. James L. McGaugh of the University of California at Riverside has argued that injections of central nervous system stimulants such as strychnine, picrotoxin, or metrazol should enhance, fortify, or extend the activity of the short-term electrochemical memory processes and thus increase the probability that they will be successful in initiating long-term memory processes. From this it follows that the injection of CNS stimulants immediately before or after training should improve learning performance. That is precisely what McGaugh found—together with several additional results which have important implications for our concerns today.

In one of McGaugh's most revealing experiments, eight groups of mice from two different hereditary backgrounds were given the problem of learning a simple maze. Immediately after completing their learning trials, four groups from each strain were injected with a different dosage of metrazol—from none to five, 10, and 20 milligrams per kilogram of body weight. First, it was apparent that there are hereditary differences in learning ability—a relatively bright strain and a relatively dull one. Secondly, by properly dosing the animals with metrazol, the learning performance increased appreciably. Under the optimal dosage, the metrazol animals showed about a 40 per cent improvement in learning ability over their untreated brothers. The improvement under metrazol was so great, in fact, that the dull animals, when treated with 10 milligrams, did slightly better than their untreated but hereditarily superior colleagues.

In metrazol we not only have a chemical facilitator of learning, but one which acts as the "Great Equalizer" among hereditarily different groups. As the dosage was increased for the dull mice from none to five to 10 milligrams their performance improved. Beyond the 10-milligram point for the dull mice, however, and beyond the five-milligram point for the bright mice, increased strength of the metrazol solution resulted in a deterioration in learning. We can draw two morals from this last finding. First, the optimal dosage of chemical learning facilitators will vary greatly with the individual taking the drug (There is, in other words, an interaction between heredity and drugs); second, there is a limit to the intellectual power of even a hopped-up Southern California Super Mouse!

We already have available a fairly extensive class of drugs which can facilitate learning and memory in animals. A closer examination of McGaugh's results and the work of others, however, also suggests that these drugs do not work in a monolithic manner on something called "learning" or "memory." In some instances, the drugs seem to act on "attentiveness"; in some, on the ability to vary one's attacks on a problem; in some, on persistence; in some, on immediate memory; in some, on long-term memory. Different drugs work differentially for different strains, different individuals, different intellectual tasks, and different learning components.

Do all of these results mean that we will soon be able to substitute a pharmacopoeia of drugs for our various school-enrichment and innovative educational programs, and that most educators will soon be technologically unemployed—or will have to retool and turn in their schoolmaster's gown for a pharmacist's jacket? The answer is no—as our Berkeley experiments on the influence of education and training on brain anatomy and chemistry suggest. This research is the work of four—Dr. E. L. Bennett, biochemist; Dr. Marian Diamond, anatomist; Dr. M. R. Rosenzweig, psychologist; and myself—together, of course, with the help of graduate students, technicians, and, above all, government money.

Our work, started some fifteen years ago, was guided by the same general theory which has guided more recent work, but our research strategy and tactics were quite different. Instead of interfering physiologically or chemically with the animal to determine the effects of such intervention upon memory storage (as did Jarvik, Agranoff, and McGaugh), we had taken the obverse question and, working with only normal animals, sought to determine the *effects* of memory storage on the chemistry and anatomy of the brain.

Our argument was this: If the establishment of long-term memory processes involves increased activity of brain enzymes, then animals which have been required to do a great deal of learning and remembering should end up with brains enzymatically different from those of animals which have not been so challenged by environment. This should be specially true for the enzymes involved in trans-synaptic neural activity. Further, since such neural activity would make demands on brain-cell action and metabolism, one might also expect to find various morphological differences between the brains of rats brought up in psychologically stimulating and psychologically pallid environments.

I describe briefly one of our standard experiments. At weaning age, one rat from each of a dozen pairs of male twins is chosen by lot to be placed in an educationally active and innovative environment, while its twin brother is placed in as unstimulating an environment as we can contrive. All twelve educationally enriched rats live together in one large, wire-mesh cage in a well lighted, noisy, and busy laboratory. The cage is equipped with ladders, running wheels, and other "creative" rat toys. For thirty minutes each day, the rats are taken out of their cages and allowed to explore new territory. As the rats grow older they are given various learning tasks to master, for which they are rewarded with bits of sugar. This stimulating educational and training program is continued for eighty days.

While these animals are enjoying their rich intellectual environment, each impoverished animal lives out his life in solitary confinement, in a small cage situated in a dimly lit and quiet room. He is rarely handled by his keeper and never invited to explore new environments, to solve problems, or join in games with other rats. Both groups of rats, however, have unlimited access to the same standard food throughout the experiment. At the age of 105 days, the rats are sacrificed, their brains dissected out and analyzed morphologically and chemically.

This standard experiment, repeated dozens of times, indicates that as the fortunate rat lives out his life in the educationally enriched condition, the bulk of his cortex expands and grows deeper and heavier than that of his culturally deprived brother. Part of this increase in cortical mass is accounted for by an increase in the number of glia cells (specialized brain cells which play vital functions in the nutrition of the neurons and, perhaps, also in laying down permanent memory traces); part of it by an increase in the size of the neuronal cell bodies and their nuclei; and part by an increase in the diameters of the blood vessels supplying the cortex. Our postulated chemical changes also occur. The enriched brain shows more acetylocholinesterase (the enzyme involved in the trans-synaptic conduction of neural impulses) and cholinesterase (the enzyme found primarily in the glia cells).

Finally, in another series of experiments we have demonstrated that these structural and chemical changes are the signs of a "good" brain. That is, we have shown that either through early rat-type Head Start programs or through selective breeding programs, we can increase the weight and density of the rat's cortex and its acetylocholinesterase and cholinesterase activity levels. And when we do—by either method—we have created superior problem-solving animals.

What does all of this mean? It means that the effects of the psychological and educational environment are not restricted to something called the "mental" realm. Permitting the young rat to grow up in an educationally and experientially inadequate and unstimulating environment creates an animal with a relatively deteriorated brain—a brain with a thin and light cortex, lowered blood supply, diminished enzymatic activities, smaller neuronal cell bodies, and fewer glia cells. A lack of adequate educational fare for the young animal—no matter how large the food supply or how good the family—and a lack of adequate psychological enrichment results in palpable, measurable, deteriorative changes in the brain's chemistry and anatomy.

Returning to McGaugh's results, we find that whether, and to what extent, this or that drug will improve the animal's learning ability will depend, of course, on what the drug does to the rat's brain chemistry. And what it does to the rat's brain chemistry will depend upon the status of the chemistry in the brain to begin with. And what the status of the brain's chemistry is to begin with reflects the rat's early psychological and educational environment. Whether, and to what extent, this or that drug will improve the animal's attention, or memory, or learning ability, therefore, will depend upon the animal's past experiences. I am not talking about interaction between "mental" factors on the one hand and "chemical" compounds on the other. I am talking, rather, about interactions between chemical factors introduced into the brain by the biochemist's injection or pills and chemical factors induced in the brain by the educator's stimulating or impoverishing environment. The biochemist's work can be only half effective without the educator's help.

What kind of educational environment can best develop the brain chemically and morphologically? What kind of stimulation makes for an enriched environment? What educational experiences can potentiate the effects of the biochemist's drugs? We don't know. The biochemist doesn't know. It is at this point that I see a whole new area of collaboration in basic research between the educator, the psychologist, and the neurobiochemist—essentially, a research program which combines the Agranoff and McGaugh techniques with our Berkeley approach. Given the start that has already been made in the animal laboratory, an intensive program of research—with animals and with children—which seeks to spell out the interrelations between chemical and educational influences on brain and memory, can pay off handsomely. This need not wait for the future. We know enough now to get started.

Both the biochemist and the teacher of the future will combine their skills and insight for the educational and intellectual development of the child. Tommy needs a bit more of an immediate memory stimulator; Jack could do with a chemical attention-span stretcher; Rachel needs an anticholinesterase to slow down her mental processes; Joan, some puromycin—she remembers too many details and gets lost.

To be sure, all our data thus far come from the brains of goldfish and rodents. But is any one so certain that the chemistry of the brain of a rat (which, after all, is a fairly complex mammal) is so different from that of the brain of a human being that he dare neglect this challenge—or even gamble—when the stakes are so high?

Chapter IV

LEARNING AND THE CLASSROOM

Throughout the entire history of educational psychology there has been controversy over the question of how humans learn. If this controversy has been at times heated, virulent, and indeed vituperative, then we would quite naturally expect similar discordance when we turn to the question of learning in the classroom. In its most simple form the question would appear stark. What material do we want our pupils to know e.g. what are the goals or "objectives" of a curriculum? Having this in mind, it would seem that straightforward, uncomplicated answers could be derived through a series of rather simple experiments. If, for example, we want our pupils to learn history, it should be possible to develop a reasonably comprehensive curriculum with lectures, readings, and discussions, without untoward problems. Using this curriculum or "unit," it should be possible to present it to the pupils through different teaching procedures and then examine which procedures were most effective.

In a schematic sense, thus the curriculum would equal the "what" and the teaching process the "how to." By holding the curriculum content reasonably constant, we ought to be able to find out the "best way" to reach the goals of education in the classroom. This in essence is the scientific method applied to the problems of classroom learning. Hopefully such an approach would discover which method of teaching works best. The experimental model in every day terms is analogous to the television commercial about the effectiveness of a particular kind of toothpaste with ingredient "X." The way the claim is tested out is illustrative of the method. Have two groups similar in all ways except that one group has toothpaste with "X" and the other group has toothpaste without "X," then after a specified period of time see if one group has fewer cavities.

Although the example may seem mundane, it does fit the experimental method of hypothesis testing. The independent variable, the toothpaste, is actively manipulated. Some of the toothpaste contains "X" and some doesn't and, most importantly, the experimenter decides which subjects get which toothpaste. The dependent variable is the outcome or effect variable, that is, the number of cavities. Then, at a later point, or even concurrently with other groups of pupils, we could repeat the study to see if the original results hold up a second time. This would be a replication of the study to confirm the original results.

Unfortunately, it should come as no surprise to discover that the apparent simplicity of the classroom learning problem stated above came unglued before the type had time to dry in the first research reports. Measuring the effect of the teaching-learning process proved to be much more difficult than measuring the effect of toothpaste on cavities. The problem in a scientific study of classroom learning-teaching is the genuine difficulty in developing an adequate measure of outcome, e.g. learning as a dependent variable as well as the difficulty in systematically varying or manipulating the independent variable, teaching.

There were glimmers from some investigations that it might be possible to find the answers. An oft-quoted study by Lippitt and White purported to show that pupils learned "best" with democratic teaching procedures as compared to authoritarian or laissez-faire techniques. While such findings were pleasing because of the philosophical overtones and fit nicely into the American ethic, a closer examination of the research evidence indicated that no such interpretation was justified. In that study the various styles of teaching, democratic, laissez-faire, and authoritarian also included other differences beyond the styles that were of major importance. For example, the authoritarian teacher was not only "bossy" and enforced rigorous discipline, but he also kept the directions and plans for the task (making masks) exclusively to himself.*

In reviewing studies of classroom learning, each new study invariably raised more questions than it answered. Educational psychology seemed mired in a swamp without the slightest notion or direction as to how to extricate itself. Cynics could say educational psychology had met the classroom learning problem and had been defeated!

Of course the question can be immediately raised, "Why should it be so difficult to scientifically demonstrate the best way to teach children?" Perhaps the problem becomes more understandable if we remember that humans learn in many different ways and at different times. When we understand that children learn in school and outside of school, from teachers and from friends, with other people and independently by themselves, then the complications for our scientific method become even greater. If we add that the learning process itself has different dimensions we soon realize why the final answers are not yet in! On this latter question we can point up the variety of learning styles with a few examples. If we watch a Little League game we can see dramatically the amount of learning that

---

* Many such studies have been reviewed by Anderson. His carefully documented conclusions were that none of these studies provide sufficient evidence that authoritarian, laissez-faire, or democratic atmospheres necessarily have any effect upon pupil learning (see Anderson, R. C. "A Resume of the Authoritarian-Democratic Studies." *Harvard Educ. Review*, 1959, *29*, 201-215).

has taken place through imitation (or as it's sometimes called, identification). We can spot which major leaguer each particular little leaguer has patterned himself after. Obviously a great deal of teaching has taken place.

In addition to imitation, another learning style might be exemplified by the person who hears a joke and then suddenly the next day starts laughing. This delayed reaction, as it were, indicates that the person heard the joke all right but didn't get the point until sometime later, when for whatever reason, the joke took on a new meaning. It has often been reported that people who work on a problem without success for a long time, may then in an off-moment or even in the middle of the night wake up and "see" the answer. Many such examples can be found in the biographies of famous inventors. These serve as reminders that either in or outside of a classroom not everyone learns in a steady step by step sequence even if it could be assumed that *all* the pupils heard *all* the content that the teacher transmitted, all the same way—itself a highly dubious assumption. In fact these assumptions that all pupils pay equal attention, hear, see, and understand precisely the same way are not only dubious, but absurd. For example, when a math teacher turns to page 38 in the math book it would require a superman to keep the class moving at the same rate through the material on that page. If we had a way of accurately tuning into the thoughts and feelings of the pupils in that class at that moment, we would realize how different individuals in fact really are. We would "hear" some pupils thinking about the lesson at hand, some about the work in the prior period or yesterday, others about the other questions, some mundane (e.g. "I wonder what's coming up for lunch?"), some not so mundane (e.g. "If we used numbers to a different base than the base 10, the problem that the teacher is doing on the board would look this way . . ."). All such activities obviously work against what for the most part has been the model for traditional teaching in a classroom.

At the present time, then, we have to be content with the ambiguous problems inherent to the teaching-learning process. We have no answers but plenty of questions. For example in a regular classroom we would have to ask not only what effect the teacher might have on the children but also the obverse. Children do have an effect upon how the adult in the room actually teaches. It has been a tradition among college students in psychology on finding a teacher who has at some point avidly denounced for example B. F. Skinner's theory of conditioning, to then develop a scheme so that their friends on one side of the room make obvious signs of paying attention in the denouncer's class. They nod, smile, write their class notes quite obviously, and ask questions. The other side of the room is collectively mute, disinterested, and totally "tuned out." In a remarkably short time the teacher will start to focus almost all of his lecture to the side of the class where the action is and ignore the disinterested side. It should also be noted that young, "bright" school teachers often interact only with the young bright pupils in their classrooms and seldom even call on the other pupils. Thus the interaction "effect" really means that teaching and learning is a two-way street.

It is necessary to underscore how little is really known about classroom learning in order to understand the somewhat polemic nature of the readings in this section. Also, and this is particularly relevant to those entering teaching as a career, it is important to remember that we have no scientifically validated plan, or prescribed set of techniques, or single model for how to teach children. Pupil "gain," or how much a student learns in a formal class, remains an attractive though relatively difficult goal as the ultimate measure of the teaching-learning process. The "hard" evidence is not available, and perhaps because of the complexities involved in accurately assessing any interaction process, we may never really achieve final answers.

AN OVERVIEW OF THE READINGS FOR THIS CHAPTER

In the first article (Selection 19), B. F. Skinner, a behavioral psychologist, presents his views on "Why Teachers Fail." Skinner criticizes the teaching methods (e.g. pedagogy) that are usually employed as a kind of mixed bag of myths about instruction, romantic conceptions about pupils, and a generally inconsistent set of behaviors by teachers themselves. His position is that all behavior is determined by schedules of reinforcement and that all human beings are, in fact, conditioned among other stimuli by the responses of other people. Since this is taking place anyway, Skinner would suggest, we should make systematic use of reinforcement to gain specific ends. He presents some examples of how teachers may tend, unwittingly, to reinforce behaviors in class they don't really want. This is central to his position. He carefully distinguishes between the effective use of positive reinforcement by a teacher and the use of aversive controls. Without positive reinforcement Skinner would maintain the pupil receives little positive feedback for his efforts. It's like attempting to learn the piano without hearing the sound the notes make when struck. The latter brings with it a coercive atmosphere. A pupil may be compelled to pay attention for fear of teacher sanctions—ridicule, sarcasm, incarceration, extra homework, etc., but this only induces a counterattack by the pupils. The pupil will quickly develop other more subtle means of escaping punitive control. Dropouts and truants are examples of physical withdrawal, but there are other psychologically sophisticated means of withdrawing while remaining physically present. Although one may question the universality of his suggestions for corrective action solely through positive reinforcement, one can hardly question Skinner's analysis of the many aspects of teaching failures. The all too human tendency to punish children, even though it may take different forms than the "old fashioned" method of corporal punishment still effectively inhibits learning.

The second article (Selection 20) by Carl Rogers, "The Facilitation of Significant Learning," presents a somewhat different perspective on the problem. Rogers makes his position abundantly clear at the outset. He views teaching as an overrated function. He values as a goal of education not the transmittal of knowledge but the facilitation of learning. This is a critical point in his argument. Our usual conception of knowledge is that it is a body of codified information '(for example a lesson plan on the causes of World War I) that the teacher desires to transmit to the pupils. The teacher is the "expert" if you will, and *presents* the information to the children. Rogers finds such a view of learning as anathema. Self-directed learning, he avers, is the genuine goal and will occur only if the pupils feel "prized" as individuals by the teacher. Through non-possessive caring, the pupil is liberated and can learn in his own way and at his own pace.

Thus Rogers strongly emphasizes the importance of interpersonal attitudes as either facilitating or inhibiting significant learning. Attitudes that reflect genuineness as a person, non-judgmental acceptance of others, and empathy (note the difference here between sympathy and empathy), will facilitate learning. It is, of course, obvious what attitudes inhibit significant learning according to Rogers. The author concludes his presentation with some practical suggestions to encourage experiential learning. Since experiential learning is personal, self-initiated and judged, pervasive and meaningful, his suggestions should be examined quite carefully. The problem confronting the teacher is a difficult one indeed, e.g. to encourage learning without taking over *for* the pupil.

A third, rather different view is contained in the next article (Selection 21) by Jerome Bruner, "Learning and Thinking." While Skinner proposed the use of the positive reinforcement of behavior and Rogers suggested the importance of the interpersonal relationship, Bruner takes yet another view. He notes the need to distinguish between thinking and learning. Thinking, he equates with passive knowledge reception (in this way he agrees with Rogers), while learning is seen as an active process of discovery and insight. Discovery is intrinsically rewarding. In other words the teacher's primary responsibility is to create a curriculum that will maximize self-discovery and excitement. As a case in point he presents the example of fifth grade pupils engaged in "discovering" Chicago. Bruner suggests then that the problems of teaching and learning are in fact the problems of curriculum. The sets of ideas, e.g. the content of the curriculum has been too long neglected. Blandness and superficiality are too often the hallmark of the academic subjects we ask children to study. In such a context we may promote thinking but hardly any learning.

If the first three articles represent major theoretical positions on teaching and learning, the next three articles in the chapter present specific examples. O. K. Moore in his article (Selection 22), "Autotelic Responsive Environments and Exceptional Children," demonstrates how children can learn specifically under principles of reinforcement. Professor Moore's work started with the development of a "Responsive Environment Laboratory." In this laboratory, children are placed for short times deliberately beyond the reach of significant adults, and through the procedures he describes are "taught" to read, speak, write, and listen. The laboratory contains a "talking typewriter." The child's fingernails are painted with colors which match the colors on the keyboard, and when he strikes a key, the letter is printed and actually pronounced by the machine. This process is highly analogous to the concept and practice of teaching machines discussed in the preceeding chapter. Thus the child's activity, e.g. pressing the key, is immediately reinforced both visually and auditorially. From this beginning the process moves through phases until the child becomes capable of writing stories on his own. Moore finds that kindergarten and first grade children can produce stories for a class newspaper under such conditions. His main point in all of this is that children interact directly with the machine and learn without benefit of adults.

A. S. Neill in the next article (Selection 23), "The Idea of Summerhill," sketches a totally different learning environment than that portrayed by Moore. One can detect the influence of that most famous of all American educational philosophers, John Dewey, in "The Idea of Summerhill." Dewey stressed the importance of personal experience, participation and personal attitudes in what has been called the "whole-child" approach. Education is not just focused on the growing intellectual capacities or subject matter mastery, but on the growing personality. The life of the child is central. In Dewey's words: "Learning? Certainly, but living primarily, and learning through and in relation to this living." *

In Summerhill, then, the central idea is simple—make the school fit the child. Neill then goes on to present in somewhat vivid terms his assumptions about learning and children. He developed the school on just this premise, that children are innately wise and the environment should help each child unfold or develop in his own way. This is an idiographic approach to education since it rests on the singluar uniqueness of each child taken one at a time. The interests and wants of children determine what they learn. In this sense Summerhill could be viewed as an interest-centered curriculum. Also it is well to note how the management of the school is organized with general school meetings where all (teachers, children, and the director) have but one vote each. The atmosphere of equality pervades the school. An intriguing question might be to what degree this model of teaching and learning could be generalized—or to what extent does Summerhill's success derive from its very uniqueness. Being totally different and a separate residential community may mean it could only

---

* Dewey, John. *The School and Society*. Chicago: Phoenix, 1963 p. 36.

operate as an exception to regular schooling. This is not to suggest that it necessarily follows, but the question should be examined. This is certainly what Skinner suggests in the previous article. Skinner held that Summerhill was therapeutic not educational. To a very great extent, in any case, the atmosphere seems very close to what Carl Rogers mentioned on the necessity of the interpersonal relationship as one basis for learning.

The article by John Holt (Selection 24), an excerpt from his book *How Children Fail,* continues to develop the theme of this chapter on the elements and controversies that surround the question of teaching and learning. Holt is quite outspoken and perhaps somewhat less subtle than the other authors in this section. Adults (parents and teachers alike) destroy the intellectual and creative capacities in children through the misnamed process of education. Rather than nurturing inquiry, we develop fear and anxiety in pupils. We make them afraid of failing, being wrong, and making mistakes. How can we learn anything if we are afraid? Holt then goes on to describe the causes of the problem as well as the effects. Note carefully his comments on the stance usually assumed by teachers, a stance that soon squelches the excitement of discovery learning. He concludes on a deliberately provocative note. We had all better stop pushing children around in the name of teaching if we want to allow them to learn.

The final article (Selection 25) by Jules Henry is titled, "American School Rooms: Learning the Nightmare." In this essay Henry launches a broadside at the entire establishment of education. While the school's avowed purpose is to teach, its real function is to induct children into a predetermined culture. Thus while Henry skillfully takes apart schooling and lays bare its inequities, at the same time he is actually criticizing the culture of which the school is simply a reflection. Having observed teachers and pupils over a six year period, Henry quite obviously took umbrage at what he saw. The manipulation of pupils, the "agitated forest of hands," the inculcation of personal competition—these are aspects of the nightmare. He claims that the school ultimately transforms the child from his original "self" to a "self" that the school can manage. At least there is no ambiguity in the concluding article of the selection. Henry makes it frightfully clear what dangers he sees in such a system of education. A competitive culture, he notes, endures by tearing people down. "Why blame the children for doing it?"

It is probably necessary at this point to restate some of our own positions in order to provide a framework for understanding the variety of viewpoints represented in the readings. In the first place, it is obvious that honest people disagree on important issues, and psychologists and educators are no exception when the issues are teaching and learning. Of greater significance, however, may be the trend toward exclusiveness by all the authors. To some degree they all pose singular solutions. Skinner would emphasize positive reinforcement, Rogers the interpersonal dimension, Bruner discovery. Similarly, Moore, Neill, and Holt propose solutions almost as singular even though based in practice. Henry, in what really amounts to a *tour de force*, simply demolishes the entire concept of education. If we recall, however, that the teaching-learning process represents an interaction and that children learn in multiple ways, we may begin to see the enormous scope of the problem. Children do learn by discovery. Children do learn when they are positively "reinforced." Children do learn under conditions of a non-possessive "prizing" interpersonal relationship. In fact it is almost impossible to prevent a child from learning something, whether the "something" will help him grow toward intellectual and personal maturity or toward a hatred for learning with concomitant anxiety and despair. This is the real question that is constantly posed to all teachers all the time.

19. WHY TEACHERS FAIL * [1]

B. F. SKINNER

The most widely publicized efforts to improve education show an extraordinary neglect of method. Learning and teaching are not analyzed, and almost no effort is made to improve teaching as such. The aid which education is to receive usually means money, and the proposals for spending it follow a few familiar lines. We should build more and better schools. We should recruit more and better teachers. We should search for better students and make sure that all competent students can go to school or college. We should multiply teacher-student contacts with films and television. We should design new curricula. All this can be done without looking at teaching itself. We need not ask how those better teachers are to teach those better students in those better schools, what kinds of contact are to be multiplied through mass media, or how new curricula are to be made effective.

Perhaps we should not expect questions of this sort to be asked in what is essentially a consumer's revolt. Earlier educational reforms were proposed by teachers—a Comenius, a Rousseau, a John Dewey—who were familiar with teaching methods, knew their shortcomings, and thought they saw a chance to improve them. Today the disaffected are the parents, employers, and others who are unhappy about the products of education. When teachers complain, it is as consumers of education at lower levels: graduate school authorities want better college teaching, college teachers work to improve high school curricula, and so on. It is perhaps natural that consumers should turn to the conspicuous shortcomings of plant, personnel, and equipment rather than to method.

It is also true that educational method has not been brought to their attention in a

* Skinner, B. F., Why Teachers Fail, Lecture to Philosophy of Education Society, New York, 1965 (also appeared in *Saturday Review* October 16, 1965).

[1] Preparation of this manuscript has been supported by Grant K6-MH-21, 775 of the National Institute of Mental Health of the U. S. Public Health Service, and by the Human Ecology Fund.

favorable light. Pedagogy is not a prestigious word. Its low estate may be traced in part to the fact that under the blandishments of statistical methods, which promised a new kind of rigor, educational psychologists spent half a century measuring the results of teaching while neglecting teaching itself. They compared different methods of teaching in matched groups and could often say that one method was clearly better than another, but the methods they compared were usually not drawn from their own research or even their own theories, and their results seldom generated new methods. Psychological studies of learning were equally sterile—concentrating on relatively unimportant details of a few typical learning situations such as the memory drum, the maze, the discrimination box, and verbal "problems." The learning and forgetting curves which emerged from these studies were never useful in the classroom and came to occupy a less and less important place in textbooks on educational psychology. Even today many distinguished learning theorists insist that their work has no practical relevance.

For these and doubtless other reasons, what has been taught as pedagogy had not been a true technology of teaching. College teaching, indeed, has not been taught at all. The beginning teacher receives no professional preparation. He usually begins to teach simply as he himself has been taught, and if he improves it is only in the light of his own unaided experience. High school and grade school teaching is taught primarily through apprenticeships, in which students receive the advice and counsel of experienced teachers. Certain trade skills and rules of thumb are passed along, but the young teacher's own experience is to be the major source of improvement. Even this modest venture in teacher training is under attack. It is argued that a good teacher is simply one who knows his subject matter and is interested in it. Any special knowledge of pedagogy as a basic science of teaching is felt to be unnecessary.

The attitude is regrettable. No enterprise can improve itself to the fullest extent without examining its basic processes. A really effective educational system cannot be set up until we understand the processes of learning and teaching. Human behavior is far too complex to be left to casual experience, or even to organized experience in the restricted environment of the classroom. Teachers need help. In particular they need the kind of help offered by a scientific analysis of behavior.

Fortunately such an analysis is now available. Principles derived from it have already contributed to the design of schools, equipment, texts, and classroom practices. Some acquaintance with its basic formulation is beginning to be regarded as important in the training of teachers and administrators. This paper is not concerned with these positive contributions, however, but rather with the light which the analysis throws on current practices. There is something wrong with teaching. From the point of view of an experimental analysis of behavior, what is it?

AVERSIVE CONTROL

Corporal punishment has always played an important role in education. As Marrou (1956) has said

> Education and corporal punishment appeared as inseparable to a Hellenistic Greek as they had to a Jewish or Egyptian scribe in the time of the Pharoahs. . . . Montaigne's well-known description of "punished children yelling and masters mad with rage" is as true of Latin as it is of Greek schools. When the men of antiquity thought back to their school days they immediately remembered the beatings. "To hold out the hand for the cane"—*manun ferulae subducere*—was an elegant Latin way of saying "to study."

The cane is still with us, and efforts to abolish it are vigorously opposed. In Great Britain a split leather strap for whipping students called a taws can be obtained from suppliers who advertise in educational journals, one of whom is said to sell three thousand annually. (The taws has the advantage, shared by the rubber truncheon, of leaving no incriminating marks.)

The brutality of corporal punishment and the viciousness it breeds in both teacher and student have, of course, led to reform. Usually this has meant little more than shifting to noncorporal measures, of which education can boast an astonishing list. Ridicule (now largely verbalized, but once symbolized by the dunce cap or by forcing the student to sit facing a wall), scolding, sarcasm, criticism, incarceration (being "kept after school"), extra school or homework, the withdrawal of privileges, forced labor, ostracism, being put on silence, and fines—these are some of the devices which have permitted the teacher to spare the rod without spoiling the child. In some respects they are less objectionable than corporal punishment, but the pattern remains: the student spends a great part of his day doing things he does not want to do. A teacher's methods are basically aversive: (1) if students stop work immediately when a class is dismissed—dismissal being obviously a release from a threat, (2) if they welcome rather than regret vacations and unscheduled days of no school, (3) if they can be rewarded for good behavior by being excused from other assignments and punished by being given additional assignments, (4) if the teacher frequently resorts to injunctions like "Pay attention" or "Now remember" and other forms of "gentle admonition," and, of course, (5) if the teacher finds it necessary from time to time to "get tough" and warn his students of aversive measures. The teacher can use aversive control because he is either bigger and stronger than his students or able to invoke the authority of parents or police who are. He can coerce students into reading texts, listening to lectures, taking part in discussions, recalling as much as possible of what they have read or heard, writing papers, and so on. This is perhaps an achievement, but it is offset by an extraordinary list of unwanted by-products traceable to the basic practice.

The student who works mainly to escape aversive stimulation discovers other ways of escaping. He is tardy—"creeping like snail unwillingly to school." He stays away from school altogether. Education has its own word for this—"truancy"—from an old word meaning wretched. A special policeman, the truant officer, deals with offenders by threatening still more aversive consequences. The drop-out is a legal truant. Children who commit suicide are often found to have had serious trouble in school.

There are subtler forms of escape. Though physically present and looking at teacher or text, the student does not pay attention. He is hysterically deaf. His mind wanders. He daydreams. "Mental fatigue" is usually not a state of exhaustion but an uncontrollable disposition to escape, and schools deal with it by permitting escape to other activities which it is hoped, will also be profitable. The periods into which the school day is broken measure the limits of successful aversive control rather than the capacity for sustained attention. A child will spend hours absorbed in play or in watching movies or television who cannot sit still in school for more than a few minutes before escape becomes too strong to be denied. One of the easiest forms of escape is simply to forget all one has learned, and no one has discovered a still more aversive form of control to prevent this ultimate break for freedom.

An equally serious reaction to aversive treatment clarified by an experimental analysis of behavior is to attack the source. If the teacher is weak, the student may attack openly. Physical attacks on teachers are now common. Verbal attacks in the teacher's absence are legendary. When the teacher is present, attacks may take the form of annoyance, and students escape punishment by annoying surreptitiously—by groaning, shuffling the feet, or snapping the fingers. A "tormenter" was a surreptitious noise maker especially designed for classroom use.

Counterattack escalates. Slightly aversive action by the teacher evokes reactions which demand severer measures, to which in turn the student reacts still more violently. Escalation may continue until one party withdraws (the student leaves school or the teacher resigns) or dominates completely (the students establish anarchy or the teacher imposes a despotic discipline).

Vandalism is another form of counterattack which is growing steadily more serious. Many cities maintain special police forces to guard school buildings on weekends. Schools are now being designed so that windows cannot be easily broken from the street. A more sweeping counterattack comes later when, as tax payers or alumni, former students refuse to support educational institutions. Anti-intellectualism often represents a general attack on all that education represents.

A much less obvious but equally serious

effect of aversive control is plain inaction. The student is sullen and unresponsive. He "blocks." Inaction is sometimes a form of escape, in which, rather than carry out an assignment, the student simply takes punishment as the lesser evil, or of attack if he thus enrages his teacher; but it is also in its own right a predictable effect of aversive control.

All these reactions have emotional accompaniments. Fear and anxiety are characteristic of escape and avoidance, anger of counterattack, and resentment of sullen inaction. These are the classical features of juvenile delinquency, of psychosomatic illness, and of other maladjustments familiar to the administrations and health services of educational institutions.

In college and graduate schools the aversive pattern survives in the now almost universal system of "assign and test." The teacher does not teach, he simply holds the student responsible for learning. The student must read books, study texts, perform experiments, and attend lectures, and he is responsible for doing so in the sense that, if he does not correctly report what he has seen, heard, or read, he will suffer aversive consequences. Questions and answers are so staple a feature of education that their connection with teaching almost never occasions surprise. As a demand for a response which will meet certain specifications, a question is almost always slightly aversive. An examination is a collection of questions which characteristically generates the anxiety and panic appropriate to avoidance and escape. Reading a student's paper is still likely to be called "correcting" it. Examinations are designed to show principally what the student does *not* know. A test which proves to be too easy is made harder before being given again, ostensibly because an easy test does not discriminate, but more probably because the teacher is afraid of weakening the threat under which his students are working. A teacher is judged by his employers and colleagues by the severity of the threat he imposes: he is a good teacher if he makes his students work hard, regardless of how he does so or of how much he teaches them by doing so. He eventually evaluates himself in the same way; if he tries to shift to nonaversive methods, he may

discover that he resists making things easy as if this necessarily meant teaching less.

Proposals to add requirements and raise standards are usually part of an aversive pattern. A well known educator has written: "We must stiffen the work of our schools . . . we have every reason to concentrate on [certain subjects] and be unflagging in our insistence that they be really learned. . . . Senior year [in high school] ought to be the hardest. . . . [We should give] students work that is both difficult and important, and [insist] that it be well done. . . . We should demand more of our students." These expressions are probably intended to be synonymous with "students should learn more" or possibly "teachers should teach more." There may be good reasons why students should take more mathematics or learn a modern language more thoroughly or be better prepared for college or graduate school, but they are not reasons for intensifying aversive pressures. A standard is a level of achievement; only under a particular philosophy of education is it a criterion upon which some form of punishment is made contingent.

Most teachers are humane and well disposed. They do not want to threaten their students, yet they find themselves doing so. They want to help, but their offers to help are often declined. Most students are well disposed. They want an education, yet they cannot force themselves to study. They know they are wasting time. For reasons which they have probably not correctly identified, many are in revolt. Why should education continue to use the aversive techniques to which all this is so obviously due? Evidently because effective alternatives have not been found. It is not enough simply to abandon aversive measures. A Summerhill is therapeutic, not educational. By withholding characteristic punishment teachers may help students who have been badly treated elsewhere and prepare them to be taught, but something else is needed if they are to teach. What is that something else, and why has it not yet solved the problem?

TELLING AND SHOWING

A child sees things and talks about them accurately afterward. He listens to news and gossip and passes it along. He recounts in great detail the plot of a movie he has seen or a book he has read. He seems to have a "natural curiosity," a "love of knowledge," an "inherent wish to learn." Why not take advantage of these natural endowments and teach simply by bringing the student into contact with the world he is to learn about? There are practical problems, of course. Only a small part of the real world can be brought into the classroom even with the aid of films, tape recorders, and television, and only a small part of what remains can be visited outside. Words are easily imported, but the verbal excesses of classical education have shown how easily this fact may lead to a dangerous overemphasis. Within reasonable limits, however, is it not possible to teach simply by giving the student an opportunity to learn in a natural way?

Unfortunately, a student does not learn simply when he is shown or told. Something essential to his natural curiosity or wish to learn is missing from the classroom. That something is positive reinforcement. In daily life he looks, listens, and remembers because certain consequences are contingent upon his doing so. He responds to the things he sees and hears, and when his responses are reinforced, he acts in the same way again. He also learns to look and listen in special ways which encourage remembering because he is reinforced for recalling what he has seen and heard, just as a newspaper reporter knows and remembers things he sees because he is paid for reporting them. Consequences of this sort are lacking when a teacher simply shows a student something or tells him something. Aversive consequences contingent on not-looking, not-listening, and not-remembering are an effective replacement but raise other problems, as we have seen. Positive reinforcers occur in nature, but they are not well used in simple showing and telling.

Rousseau was the great advocate of natural learning. Émile was to be taught by the world of things. His teacher was to draw his attention to that world. Beyond that his education was to be negative. The teacher was not to arrange consequences, aversive or otherwise. But Émile was an imaginary student with imaginary learning processes, and when Rousseau's disciple, Pestalozzi, tried the methods on his own flesh-and-blood son, he ran into

trouble. His diary (1890) is one of the most pathetic documents in the history of education. As he walked with his young son beside a stream, Pestalozzi would repeat several times, "Water flows downhill." He would show the boy that "wood swims in water and . . . stones sink." Whether the child was learning anything or not he was not unhappy, and Pestalozzi could believe that at least he was using the right method. But when the world of things had to be left behind, failure could no longer be concealed. "I could only get him to read with difficulty; he has a thousand ways of getting out of it, and never loses an opportunity of doing something else." He could make the boy sit still at his lessons by first making him "run and play out of doors in the cold," but Pestalozzi himself was then exhausted. Inevitably, of course, he returned to aversive measures: "He was soon tired of learning to read, but as I had decided that he should work at it regularly every day, whether he liked it or not, I determined to make him feel the necessity of doing so, from the very first, by showing him there was no choice between this work and my displeasure, which I made him feel by keeping him in."

GETTING ATTENTION

The failure of showing and telling is sometimes attributed to lack of attention. We are often aware that we ourselves are not listening or looking carefully when we are not studying effectively. How can we keep our mind on a text? How can we concentrate? If we are not to punish the student for not-looking and not-listening, what alternatives are available? One possibility is to make sure that there is nothing else in the immediate environment to be seen or heard. The schoolroom is isolated and freed of distractions. Silence is often the rule. Physical constraints are helpful. Earphones reassure the teacher that only what is to be heard is going into the student's ears. The TV screen is praised for its isolation and hypnotic effect. A piece of equipment has been proposed which achieves concentration in the following desperate way: the student faces a brightly lighted text framed by walls which operate on the principle of the blinders once worn by carriage horses. His ears are between earphones. He reads part of the text aloud and then listens to his recorded voice as he reads it again. If he does not learn what he reads, it is certainly not because he has not seen it!

A less coercive practice is to make what is to be seen or heard attractive and attention-compelling. The advertiser faces the same problem as the teacher, and his techniques have been widely copied in the design of textbooks, films, and classroom practices. Bright colors, variety, sudden change, big type, animated sequences—all these have at least a temporary effect in inducing the student to look and listen. They do not, however, teach the student to look and listen, because they occur at the wrong time. A similar weakness is seen in making school itself pleasant. Attractive architecture, colorful interiors, comfortable furniture, congenial social arrangements, naturally interesting subjects—these are all reinforcing, but they reinforce only the behaviors they are contingent upon. An attractive school building reinforces the behavior of coming in sight of it. A colorful and comfortable classroom reinforces the behavior of entering it. Roughly speaking, these things could be said to strengthen a positive attitude toward school. But they provide merely the setting for instruction. They do not teach what students are in school to learn.

In the same way audiovisual aids usually come at the wrong time to strengthen the forms of behavior which are the principal concern of the teacher. An interesting page printed in four colors reinforces the student simply for opening the book and looking at it. It does not reinforce reading the page or even examining it closely; certainly it does not reinforce those activities which result in effective recall of what is seen. An interesting lecturer holds his listeners in the sense that they look at and listen to him, just as an interesting demonstration film reinforces the behavior of watching it, but neither the lecture nor the film necessarily reinforces listening or listening in those special ways which further recall. In good instruction interesting things should happen *after* the student has read a page or listened or looked with care. The four-color picture should *become* interesting when the text which accompanies it has been read. One stage in a lecture or film should be interesting only if earlier stages have been carefully ex-

amined and remembered. In general, naturally attractive and interesting things further the primary goals of education only when they enter into much more subtle contingencies of reinforcement than are usually represented by audiovisual aids.

MAKING MEMORABLE

It is possible that students may be induced to learn by making material not only attractive but memorable. An obvious example is making material easy. The child first learns to write in manuscript because it resembles the text he is learning to read; he may learn to read material printed in a phonetic alphabet; he may learn to spell only words he will actually use; and so on. This sort of simplification shows a lack of confidence in methods of teaching and often merely postpones the teacher's task, but it is sometimes a useful strategy. Material which is well organized is also, of course, easier to learn.

Some current psychological theories suggest that material may be made memorable in another way. Various laws of perception imply that an observer "cannot help" seeing things in certain ways. The stimulus seems to force itself upon the organism. Optical illusions are often cited as examples. These laws suggest the possibility that material may be presented in the form in which it is irresistibly learned. Material is to be so "structured" that is readily—and almost necessarily—"grasped." Instructional examples are, however, far less persuasive than the demonstration offered in support of them. In trying to assign an important function to the material to be learned, it is particularly easy to overlook other parts of the contingencies of reinforcement under which learning actually occurs.

THE TEACHER AS A MIDWIFE

No matter how attractive, interesting, and well structured material may be, the discouraging fact is that it is often not learned. Rather than continue to ask why, many educational theorists have concluded that the teacher cannot really teach at all but can only help the student learn. The dominant metaphor goes back to Plato. "Socrates . . . possessed no other art but maieutics, his mother Phaenarete's art of delivering; he drew out from souls what they have in them . . ." (Bréhier, 1963). The student already knows the truth; the teacher simply shows him that he knows. The archetype is the famous episode in the *Meno* in which Socrates takes an uneducated slave boy through Pythagoras' theorem for doubling the square.[2] In spite of the fact that this scene is still widely regarded as an educational triumph, there is no evidence that the child learned anything. He timidly agrees with Socrates' suggestions and answers leading questions, but it is inconceivable that he could have reconstructed the theorem by himself when Socrates had finished. Socrates says as much later in the dialogue: "If someone will keep asking him these same questions often and in various forms, you can be sure that in the end he will know about them as accurately as anybody." (Socrates was a frequency theorist!)

It must be admitted that the assignment was difficult. The boy was starting from scratch. In his little book, *How to solve it*, Polya (1957) uses the same technique in presiding at the birth of the formula for the diagonal of a parallelepiped. His students make a more positive contribution because they have already had some geometry. But any success due to previous teaching weakens the claim for maieutics. And Polya's prompting and questionings give more help than he wants to admit.

It is only because mathematical proofs seem to arise from the nature of things that they can be said in some sense to be "known by everyone" and simply waiting to be drawn out. Even Socrates could not argue that the soul knows the facts of history, say, or a second language. Impregnation must precede parturition. But is it not possible that a presentation which has not seemed to be learned is the seed from which knowledge grows to be delivered by the teacher? Perhaps the intellectual mid-

wife is to show the student that he remembers what he has already been shown or told. In *The Idea of a University* Cardinal Newman gave an example of the maieutic method applied to acquired knowledge. It will stir painful memories in many teachers. A Tutor is talking with a Candidate about a bit of history—a bit of history, in fact, in which Plato's Menon lost his life.

Tutor. What is the meaning of the word Anabasis? *Candidate is silent.*

T. You know very well; take your time, and don't be alarmed. Anabasis means . . . *C.* An ascent.

T. Who ascended. *C.* The Greeks, Xenophon.

T. Very well: Xenophon and the Greeks; the Greeks ascended. To what did they ascend? *C.* Against the Persian king: they ascended to fight the Persian king.

T. That is right . . . an ascent; but I thought we called it a *descent* when a foreign army carried war into a country? *C. Is silent.*

T. Don't we talk of a descent of barbarians? *C.* Yes.

T. Why then are the Greeks said to go *up?* *C.* They went up to fight the Persian king.

T. Yes; but why *up* . . . why not *down?* *C.* They came down afterwards, when they retreated back to Greece.

T. Perfectly right; they did . . . but could you give no reason why they are said to go *up* to Persia, not *down? C.* They went *up* to Persia.

T. Why do you not say they went *down? C. pauses, then,* . . . They went *down* to Persia.

T. You have misunderstood me . . .

Newman warned his reader that the Candidate is "deficient to a great extent . . . not such as it is likely that a respectable school would turn out." He recognized a poor student, but not a poor method. Thousands of teachers have wasted years of their lives in exchanges which have been no more profitable —and all to the greater glory of maieutics and out of a conviction that telling and showing are not only inadequate but wrong.

Although the soul has perhaps not always

[2] Karl Popper (1962) has argued that the significance of this episode extends far beyond education. "For Meno's slave is helped by Socrates' judicious questions to remember or recapture the forgotten knowledge which his soul possessed in its ante-natal state of omniscience. It is, I believe, this famous Socratic method, called in the *Theaetetus* the art of midwifery or *maieutic*, to which Aristotle alluded when he said that Socrates was the inventor of the method of induction."

known the truth nor ever been confronted with it in a half forgotten experience, it may still seek it. If the student can be taught to learn from the world of things, nothing else will ever have to be taught. This is the method of discovery. It is designed to absolve the teacher from a sense of failure by making instruction unnecessary. The teacher arranges the environment in which discovery is to take place, he suggests lines of inquiry, he keeps the student within bounds, and so on. The important thing is that he tell him nothing.

The human organism does, of course, learn without being taught. It is a good thing that this is so, and it would no doubt be a good thing if more could be learned in that way. Students are naturally interested in what they learn by themselves because they would not learn if they were not, and for the same reason they are more likely to remember what they learn in that way. There are reinforcing elements of surprise and accomplishment in personal discovery which are welcome alternatives to traditional aversive consequences. But discovery is no solution to the problems of education. The individual cannot be expected to rediscover more than a very small part of the facts and principles which have already been discovered by others. To stop teaching in order that the student may learn for himself is to abandon education as a medium for the transmission of the accumulated knowledge and wisdom of a culture.

There are other difficulties. The position of the teacher who encourages discovery is ambiguous. Is he to pretend that he himself does not know? (Socrates answered Yes. The point in Socratic irony is that those who do know enjoy a laugh at the expense of those who do not.) Or, for the sake of encouraging a joint venture in discovery, is the teacher to choose to teach only those things which he himself has not yet learned? Or is he frankly to say, "I know, but you must find out" and to accept the consequences for his relations with his students?

Still another difficulty arises when it is necessary to teach a whole class. How are a few good students to be prevented from making all the discoveries? When that happens other members of the class not only miss the excitement of discovery, they are left to

learn material which is presented in a slow and particularly confusing way.

Students should, of course, be encouraged to explore, to ask questions, to study by themselves, to be "creative." When properly analyzed the kinds of behavior referred to in such expressions can be taught. It does not follow, however, that they must be taught by the method of discovery. The difficulty is that effective instructional practices threaten the conception of teaching as a form of maieutics. If the student is to "exercise his rational powers," to "develop his mind," or to learn through "intuition or insight," and so on, then it may indeed be true that the teacher cannot teach but can only help the student learn. When these goals are restated in terms of explicit changes in behavior, however, effective methods of instruction can be designed.

THE IDOLS OF THE SCHOOL

In his famous four Idols Francis Bacon formulated some of the reasons why men arrive at false ideas. He might have added two special Idols of the School which affect those who want to improve teaching. *The Idol of the Good Teacher* is the belief that *what a good teacher can do, any teacher can do.* Some teachers are, of course, unusually effective. They are naturally interesting people, who make things interesting to their students. They are skillful in handling students, as they are skillful in handling people in general. They can formulate facts and principles and communicate them to others in effective ways. Possibly their skills and talents will someday be better understood and successfully imparted to new teachers. At the moment, however, good teachers are true exceptions. The fact that a method proves successful in their hands does not mean that it will solve important problems in education. *The Idol of the Good Student* is the belief that *what a good student can learn, any student can learn.* Because they have superior ability or have been exposed to fortunate early environments, some students learn without being taught. It is quite possible that they learn more effectively what they are not taught. Possibly we shall someday produce more of them. At the moment, however, the fact that a method works with good students does not mean that it will work with all. It is possible that we shall progress more rapidly toward effective education by leaving the good teacher and the good student out of account altogether. They will not suffer, because they do not need our help. We may then devote ourselves to the discovery of practices which are appropriate to the remaining— what?—ninety-five per cent of teachers and students.

The Idols of the School explain some of the breathless excitement with which educational theorists return again and again to a few standard solutions to their problems. The Idol of the Good Teacher suggests that students need more personal attention (but students learn—often quite effectively—without it). The Idol of the Good Student suggests that they need more freedom (but in abandoning aversive forms of control we need not weaken the power of an educational environment). Ingenious film demonstrations may make high school physics more meaningful and fascinating than textbook accounts (but purely verbal material may also be exciting, as any physicist knows).

All such proposals for improvement rest upon a generalized Idol of the School—that personal experience in the classroom is the primary source of pedagogical wisdom. It is actually very difficult for teachers to profit from experience. They almost never learn about their long-term successes or failures, and their short-term effects are not easily traced to the practices from which they pre-

sumably arose. Few teachers have time to reflect on such matters, and traditional educational research has given them little help. There may be practical reasons for asking whether one method of teaching is better than another, but the important thing is to say why one is better.

A much more effective kind of educational research is possible. Teaching may be defined as the arrangement of contingencies of reinforcement under which behavior changes. Such contingencies can be most successfully analyzed in studying the behavior of one student at a time under carefully controlled conditions. Few educators are aware of the extent to which human behavior is being examined in arrangements of this sort. A true technology of teaching is, however, imminent. It is beginning to suggest effective alternatives to the aversive practices which have caused so much trouble.

REFERENCES

BRÉHIER, EMILE. *The Hellenic Age.* Translated by Joseph Thomas. Chicago, 1963, p. 86.

GUIMPS, ROGER DE. *Pestalozzi: His Life and Work.* Translated by J. Russell. New York, 1890.

MARROU, H. I. *A History of Education in Antiquity.* Translated by George Lamb. London, 1956.

PESTALOZZI, see Guimps, Roger de.

POLYA, G. *How to solve it.* New York: Doubleday and Company, 1957.

POPPER, KARL. On the sources of knowledge and ignorance. *Encounter*, September, 1962.

20. THE FACILITATION OF SIGNIFICANT LEARNING

CARL R. ROGERS * [1]

In this chapter, I would like to describe two types of learning, two possible aims for edu-

* From *Instruction: Some Contemporary Viewpoints* by Lawrence Siegel, published by Chandler Publishing Company, San Francisco. Copyright © 1967 by Chandler Publishing Company. Reprinted by permission.

cation, and two sets of assumptions upon which the educational process can be based. It will be clear that for me the second member of each

[1] I am indebted to Miss Ann Dreyfuss for her assistance in various aspects of this chapter [CRR].

of these pairs seems more suitable for today's world. I shall then try to indicate some of the ways in which this second view might be implemented.

TWO TYPES OF LEARNING

COGNITIVE LEARNING. Some learning appears to be primarily cognitive, primarily the fixing of certain associations. A child can learn his letters and numbers in this fashion; at a later date he may learn to "rattle off" the multiplication table; at a still later date he may learn the rules for solving a binomial equation or the irregular verbs in French. Only very imperceptibly do any of these learning changes *him*. They are like the nonsense syllables which the psychologist asks him to learn as a participant in an experiment. They are learned as part of a task set before him, part of a "body of knowledge" which he is to acquire. Such learning is often painfully difficult and also often quickly forgotten.

EXPERIENTIAL LEARNING. The other type of learning is primarily experiential, or significant or meaningful. The student says, "I am discovering—drawing in from the outside and making that which is drawn in a real part of *me*." The adolescent who devours everything he can read or hear about gasoline engines in order to make his hot rod faster and more efficient exemplifies this type of learning. The child who is trying to draw a realistic house reads or hears a few simple rules of perspective. He reaches out to grasp this material, make it his, use it. This is another instance of meaningful learning. Still another is the child who goes to books and the library to satisfy his curiosity about earthworms or the hydrogen bomb or sex. The feeling in regard to any experiential learning is, "Now I'm grasping what I *need* and *want*."

I shall define a bit more precisely the elements which are involved in such significant or experiential learning.

1. *It has a quality of personal involvement.* The whole person in both his feeling and cognitive aspects is involved in the learning event.

2. *It is self-initiated.* Even when the impetus or stimulus comes from outside, the sense of discovery, of reaching out, of grasping and comprehending, comes from within.

3. *It is pervasive.* It makes a difference in the behavior, the attitudes, perhaps even the personality of the learner.

4. *It is evaluated by the learner.* "This is not quite what I want—doesn't go far enough—ah, this is better, this *is* what I want to know." The locus of evaluation may be said to reside definitely in the learner.

5. *Its essence is meaning.* When such learning takes place, the element of meaning to the learner is built into the whole experience.

TWO POSSIBLE AIMS FOR EDUCATION

To TRANSMIT STORED KNOWLEDGE. For the most part, the current educational system is geared to the aim of inculcating in the young the stored knowledge already accumulated, together with the values which have guided men in the past. Its natural product is the informed, essentially passive conformist.

Historically, there has been much to be said for this point of view. Because of a recent visit in Australia, I have been reading and hearing about the Australian aborigine. For twenty thousand years he and his kind have survived in a most inhospitable environment in which modern man would die. He has survived by passing on every bit of knowledge and skill he has acquired about a relatively unchanging world and frowning upon or tabooing any new ways of meeting the relatively unchanging problems. This has been the description of American educational goals as well.

To NURTURE THE PROCESS OF DISCOVERY. But modern man is face to face with a situation which has never before existed in history. The world—of science, of communication, of social relationships—is changing at such a pace that knowledge stored up in the past is not enough. The physicist cannot live by the stored knowledge of his science. His confidence, his basic trust, is in the *process* by which new knowledge is acquired. In like fashion, if society is to be able to meet the challenges of a more and more rapidly changing world—if civilization is to survive—people must be able increasingly to live in a process manner. The public, like the physicist, will have to put their trust in the *process* by which new problems are met, not in the *answers* to problems of the past.

This need implies a new goal for education.

Learning how to learn, involvement in a process of change—these become the primary aims of an education fit for the present world. There must evolve individuals who are capable of intelligent, informed, discriminating, adaptive, effective involvement in a process of change. Such involvement develops only in the individual who has discovered that significant learning is, though threatening, even more deeply rewarding; who has recognized that it is satisfying to take the risk of being open to his experience, both of his feelings and reactions within and of the evidence his senses bring him about the world without. Such an individual is in process of change, is continually learning, is constructively meeting the perplexities of a world in which problems are always spawning much faster than their answers. He has learned that the process of change is something in which he can live more comfortably than in rigidity, that the ability to face the new appropriately is more important than being able to repeat the old. This is a new type of aim for education.

TWO SETS OF ASSUMPTIONS IN EDUCATION

ASSUMPTIONS IMPLICIT IN CURRENT EDUCATION. From an observation of educational institutions at all levels (first grade through graduate study), I have attempted to abstract from the behavior of the educators those assumptions or principles upon which they act. It should be clear that these six assumptions are implicit, rather than explicit—that they are drawn from what teachers *do,* rather than from what they *say.*

1. *The student cannot be trusted to pursue his own learning.* The attitude of most teachers and faculty members tends to be one of mistrustful guidance. They look suspiciously on the student's aims and desires and devote their energies to guiding him along the pathway he "should" follow. I believe it is extremely rare that students have the feeling that they are being set free to learn, on their own.

2. *Presentation equals learning.* This assumption is evident in every curriculum, every lesson plan. It is especially clear if one observes a faculty committee trying to decide what topics a course shall "cover." It is clear that what is presented or covered is what is learned. Anyone who has used any method which taps the actual experience of students in a class knows that this assumption could not be further from the truth; yet it persists.

3. *The aim of education is to accumulate brick upon brick of factual knowledge.* There must be a "foundation of knowledge." These clearly defined building blocks must be assimilated before the student can proceed to learn on his own. Though this assumption flies in the face of everything known about the curve of forgetting, it remains an unquestioned assumption.

4. *The truth is known.* In almost every textbook, knowledge is presented as a closed book. "These are the facts"—about chemistry or history or literature. The student has almost no opportunity to realize that in every field it is the *search* for knowledge which is important and that the "knowledge" already gained is only the best working hypothesis that can be formulated at the moment. Only in recent years, in such developments as the teaching of the "new mathematics" has there been the slightest dent in this assumption.

5. *Constructive and creative citizens develop from passive learners.* There seems to be great unanimity in the verbalized aim of producing good citizens, able to act constructively, with an independence and originality adequate to the complex problems of today. Yet it is equally evident that the main virtue encouraged in classrooms at all levels is that of passively learning material which is presented by the instructor, which in turn has been selected by some educational group as being important for the student to learn. This is clearly the way in which it is assumed that an independent citizenry is developed.

6. *Evaluation is education, and education is evaluation.* Taking examinations and preparing for the next set of exams is a way of life for students. There is little or no thought of intrinsic goals, since the extrinsic have become all-important. Rarely does the student ask himself, "What aspect of this subject or this book interests me?" or "How could I find out about this particular aspect of life?" The sole question is, "What will be asked on the examination?" It has gradually come to be assumed by teachers, students, and parents that report

cards and grades *constitute* education. When a faculty member asked a student what he got out of a certain course, the student's response was what one would expect in this system: "I got a B."

ASSUMPTIONS RELEVANT TO SIGNIFICANT EXPERIENTIAL LEARNING. It is my belief that in the next few decades there is likely to be a revolution in education which will deeply challenge the foregoing assumptions. My reason for believing that such a revolution will occur is that I question whether our culture can afford to permit its citizens to develop under such an educational system. It cannot afford to develop citizens who are passive, whose knowledge is settled and closed, whose ways of thinking are rigid, who have no feeling for the *process* of discovering new knowledge and new answers.

The question for this newer approach to education will be, "How can the incorporation of the *process* of learning and changing be made the deepest purpose of the educational experience? In endeavoring to answer this, I list below a new set of assumptions which, I believe, will replace the present principles.

1. *Human beings have a natural potentiality for learning.* They are curious about their world, they are eager to develop and learn, and they have the capacity for making constructive discriminations between learning opportunities. This potentiality for learning, for discovery, can be released under suitable conditions (which I discuss below). In short, the student's desire to learn can be trusted.

2. *Significant learning takes place when the subject matter is perceived by the student as having relevance for his own purposes.* When an individual has a goal he wishes to achieve and when he sees the material available to him as relevant to achieving that goal, learning takes place with great rapidity. How long does it take an adolescent to learn to drive a car? A very reasonable hypothesis is that the time for learning various subjects would be cut to a small fraction of the time currently allotted if the material were perceived by the learner as related to his own purposes. The evidence from various sources indicates that in many instances one-third to one-fifth of the present time allotment would be sufficient.

3. *Much significant learning is acquired through doing.* When a student is attempting to cope with a problem which is directly confronting him, effective learning is likely to occur. The brief, intensive courses for teachers, doctors, farmers—individuals facing immediate problems—provide ample evidence of learning through doing. The class group which becomes involved in a dramatic production—selecting the play and the cast, designing and making the scenery and costumes, coaching the actors, selling tickets—provides similar evidence.

4. *Learning is facilitated when the student participates responsibly in the learning process.* This assumption is closely related to the preceding. When he chooses his own directions, helps to discover his own learning resources, formulates his own problems, decides his own course of action, and lives with the consequences of each of these choices, then significant learning is maximized. There is evidence from industry as well as from the field of education that participative learning is much more effective than is passive learning.

5. *Self-initiated learning, involving the whole person of the learner—feelings as well as intellect—is the most pervasive and lasting.* This hypothesis has been discovered in psychotherapy, where it is the totally involved learning of oneself by oneself which is most effective. This is not learning which takes place "only from the neck up." It is a "gut-level" type of learning—profound and pervasive. It can also occur in the tentative discovery of a new self-generated idea, in the learning of a difficult skill, or in the act of artistic creation—painting, poetry, sculpture. One of the most important aspects is that in these situations the learner knows it is his own learning, and thus can hold to it or relinquish it in the face of a more profound learning, without having to turn to some authority for corroboration of his judgment.

6. *Creativity in learning is best facilitated when self-criticism and self-evaluation are primary, and evaluation by others is of secondary importance.* Creativity blossoms in an atmosphere of freedom. The best research organizations, in industry as well as in the academic world, have learned that external evaluation is largely fruitless if the goal is creative work.

The individual must be permitted to make his own evaluation of his own efforts.

7. *The most socially useful learning in the modern world is the learning of the process of learning, a continuing openness to experience, an incorporation into oneself of the process of change.* I have already discussed this assumption in speaking of the second aim in education.

CONDITIONS FACILITATING EXPERIENTIAL LEARNING

If significant experiential learning is the preferred type, if the goal for education is to facilitate an openness to the process of change, if the educational approach is to be based on the assumptions or hypotheses stated in the preceding section, how may these purposes be implemented? Fortunately, much has been discovered (particularly in the field of psychotherapy) about the conditions which make for significant or experiential learning by the whole person. I would like to summarize these conditions as I understand them, as they apply not only to the climate created by the teacher in his classroom, but to the faculty of the teacher-training institution and to administrators of schools at all levels.

CONFRONTING A PROBLEM. There is no doubt that experiential learning takes place most effectively when the individual is face to face with a problem which is meaningful to him, a problem to which he desires a solution. It is perhaps not impossible to promote significant learning in the absence of such a confrontation with a problem but it is much more difficult. The current tendency to insulate the elementary- and high-school pupil from any of the real problems of life constitutes a difficulty for the teacher at these levels.

Teacher education is more fortunate in this respect. The prospective teacher can readily be given some experience in the classroom—observing, helping, being responsible for portions of the teaching—so that he becomes sharply and vividly aware of the difficult problems he will soon be facing on his own responsibility; hence, he is well motivated toward significant learning.

It is not quite so clear whether the teacher-training institution is aware of the problems it confronts. To the extent, however, that the faculty and administration of such an institution are aware of the intense critical public interest in education, to the extent that they are aware of the acute problems posed by a sharp increase in student population, to the extent that they realize the ineffectiveness of most professional education as carried on today—to this degree they will recognize the profound problems with which they are confronted and will also be in a mood for self-initiated learning.

DEVELOPING CERTAIN ATTITUDES. Once the individual or the institution is clearly aware of a problem, there seems to be evidence that certain attitudinal sets in the facilitator of learning increase the likelihood that experiential learning will take place. I will endeavor to describe three of these attitudes in somewhat general terms so that the principles apply to the facilitation of learning, whether in administrators and faculty members of the teacher-training institution, in the prospective teacher, in a classroom teacher taking further training on the job, or in the pupil in the classroom.

Realness. Perhaps the most basic of these essential attitudes is realness or genuineness. When the facilitator is a real person, being what he really is and entering into a relationship with the learner without presenting a front or a façade, he is likely to be effective. To be real in this sense means that the feelings which he is experiencing are available to him, available to his awareness, that he is able to live these feelings and able to communicate them if appropriate. It means that he comes into a direct personal encounter with the learner, meeting him on a person-to-person basis. It means that he is being himself, not denying himself.

With this attitude, the teacher can be a real person in his relationship with his students. He can be enthusiastic, he can be bored, he can be interested in students, he can be angry, he can be sensitive and sympathetic. Because he accepts these feelings as his own, he has no need to impose them on his students. He can dislike a student product without implying that it is objectively bad or that the student is bad. He is simply expressing a feeling of dislike for the product, a feeling which exists within himself. Thus, he is a *person* to his students, not a faceless embodiment of a curricular requirement or a sterile tube through which knowledge is passed from one generation to the next.

It is obvious that this attitudinal set, found to be effective in psychotherapy, is in sharp contrast with the tendency of most teachers to show themselves to their pupils simply in their teaching "role." It is quite customary for teachers rather consciously to put on the mask, the role, the façade, of being a teacher and to wear this façade all day, removing it only when they have left the school.

Acceptance. Another attitude which stands out in the work of those who have been successful in promoting experiential learning is acceptance, a prizing of the student, a prizing of his feelings and his opinions. When the facilitator values the individual learner as having worth and when this prizing extends to every facet of this individual, then the likelihood that experiential learning will take place is greatly increased. A teacher who has such an attitude can be fully acceptant of the fear and hesitation of the student as he approaches a new problem as well as of the satisfaction he feels in achievement. Such a teacher can accept the student's occasional apathy, his desire to explore byroads of knowledge, as well as his disciplined efforts to achieve major goals. If he can accept personal feelings which both disturb and promote learning—rivalry with a sibling, hatred of authority, concern about personal adequacy—then he is certainly such a teacher. What I am describing is a prizing of the learner as an imperfect human being with many feelings, many potentialities. It means that the facilitator cares for the learner in a nonpossessive way; he is willing for the learner to be a separate person. His prizing or acceptance of the learner is an operational expression of his essential confidence in the capacity of the human organism.

Empathic Understanding. A further element which establishes a climate for experiential learning is empathic understanding. When the teacher has the ability to understand the student's reactions from the inside, has a sensitive awareness of how the process of education and learning appears to the student, then again the likelihood of personally meaningful learning is increased.

This kind of understanding is sharply different from the usual evaluative understanding which follows the pattern of, "I understand what is wrong with you." When there is a sensitive empathy, however, the reaction in the learner follows something of this pattern: "At last someone understands how it feels and seems to be me without wanting to analyze me or judge me. Now I can blossom and grow and learn."

Summary. There is an increasing number of studies which lend confirmation to the view that when these three attitudes exist in the therapeutic relationship, they bring about constructive learning and change in the individual (Barret-Lennard, 1962; Rogers, 1957, 1967). There is at least one pilot study indicating that teachers who are regarded by their superiors as outstanding show these attitudinal qualities in much higher degree than teachers who are rated as less effective (Barrett-Lennard, 1960). Since the aim of education, like the aim of therapy, is to produce creative and adaptive individuals, well informed about themselves and their world, it does not seem too great a leap to suggest that these attitudes are as basic to the facilitation of learning in education as they are to the facilitation of learning in psychotherapy.

PROVIDING RESOURCES. In addition to the learner's face-to-face confrontation with a problem and the facilitator's evincing the attitudes described above, there must be resources for learning. It is usually the responsibility of the facilitator to see that all types of resources are made available. These may be material resources, tools, laboratory equipment, supplies, and the like. They may be opportunities for observation—visiting a classroom, listening to tape recordings, going to a children's hospital. They may be written resources presenting the stored experiences of others—books, articles, reprints, student papers and reports. They may be personal resources—contact with individuals whose work or experience can contribute to the learning. Certainly, much of the effectiveness of the facilitator depends upon his imaginative organization of resources and his ability to make these resources easily and psychologically available to the learner.

SOME PRACTICAL WAYS OF ENCOURAGING EXPERIENTIAL LEARNING

Keeping in mind the conditions which have been described, I turn now to some of the newer developments in education, practical approaches which may be used to facilitate a more experiential type of learning and which may be used to implement the hypotheses basic to the second educational goal. I have selected three examples which apply specifically to classroom instruction, and one which applies both to the classroom and to the training and supervision of the instructor himself.

THE CONDUCT OF INQUIRY. A specialized type of participative and experiential learning which has been receiving increasing emphasis in the last few years has been developing in science. Various individuals and national groups have been working toward a goal of helping students to become inquirers, working in a fluid way toward discovery in the scientific realm.

The impetus for this movement has grown out of an urgent need to have science experienced as a changing field, as it is in the modern world, rather than as a closed book of already discovered facts. The possession of a body of knowledge about science is not an adequate qualification for the teacher today. Hence the aim is to get the teacher away from the misleading image of science as absolute, complete, and permanent (Schwab, 1960). Suchman (1961, 1962) is one of those who have given rather specific details regarding the implementation of this aim. In trying to strengthen the autonomous process within the learner, Suchman advocates a new approach in which special training is necessary for teachers of science. The teacher sets the stage of inquiry by posing the problems, creating an environment responsive to the learner, and giving assistance to the student in his investigative operations. This climate makes it possible for pupils to achieve autonomous discoveries and to engage in self-directed learning. They become scientists *themselves,* on a simple level, seeking answers to real questions, discovering for themselves the pitfalls and the joys of the scientists's search. They may not learn as many scientific "facts," but they develop a real appreciation of science as a never-ending search, a recognition that there is no closure in science.

It is obvious that if prospective teachers are to stimulate the spirit of inquiry among their pupils, they must have experienced it themselves. Therefore, courses in the teacher-training institution must be taught in the same fashion as Suchman describes if teachers themselves are to experience the satisfaction of self-initiated discovery in the scientific realm. This new development in the area of science constitutes a deep challenge to present concepts of teaching. According to the evidence, current educational practice tends to make children less autonomous and less empirical in their search for knowledge and understanding as they move through the elementary grades. This tendency is strictly at variance with the aim of those who focus on inquiry. When children are permitted to think their way through to new understandings, the concepts they derive in the process have greater depth, meaning, and durability. The children have become more autonomous and more solidly based in an empirical approach.

SIMULATION. The trend toward a more experiential type of learning shows up in the increasing use of simulation in the classroom. The essence of this procedure is that a complex situation is simulated—the relationships among several nations (Solomon, 1963; Guetzkow, 1963), a historical situation, a social conflict, a problem in interpersonal relationships—and the students take the parts of those participating in the event. Though there is no conclusive research as yet indicating the outcome of this type of learning as compared with more conventional procedures, it is already being successfully used in half a dozen universities and a number of high schools. Since it is a relatively new type of approach, I shall outline a hypothetical example.

A social studies or civics course might well simulate a problem in community policy regarding education. Different pupils might be assigned respectively to be the mayor, the head of the board of education, the members of the board of education, the superintendent of schools, the president of the PTA, the head of the taxpayers' league. Now the problem is posed to them—from their own community or from any other community where the facts are available to them—that members of the board of education want a new bond issue to expand the building plant and hire new teachers. They prepare to take their parts in the simulated situation.

What are the types of learning that would follow upon this simulation? First, each student would turn to the factual resources in order to develop his own stance on the issue and to justify his point of view. There would be a degree of self-discipline involved in searching for this factual material. The student would find it necessary to make a personal decision based on his own informed stand. He would be involved in the handling of interpersonal relationships with those who hold different points of view. He would find himself bearing the responsibility for the consequences of his own decisions and actions. Throughout the experience, there would be necessary a disciplined commitment to learning, decision, action. Such an experience would appear to develop a positive type of learning rather than a negative, critical type of thinking. Current education often develops individuals who can readily criticize any proposal or idea but cannot make a positive plan or decision regarding constructive action.

Another interesting example of the use of a type of simulation is described by Ronald Lippitt (1962). A fifth-grade class was concerned about youngsters who were know-it-alls. The whole class participated either as actors or observers in dealing with the problem. As they did so, the pupils developed a real understanding of why know-it-alls behave as they do; the class came to recognize the insecurity which so often underlies such behavior. Gradually, an attitude evolved of working *with* the problem rather than *at* it. In the process, individual students showed significant personal development, and the class as a group showed increased freedom of communication, which encouraged and supported greater individuality of participation. It was a living experience in behavioral science.

PROGRAMMED INSTRUCTION. As educators well know, there has been a vast and explosive development in programmed instruction (Skinner, 1961; Fry, 1963; Gage, 1963; Pressey, 1963). This is not the place to review these developments or the theory of operant conditioning upon which this work is based. It is appropriate, however, to point out that programmed instruction may be used in a variety of ways. Programming can be seen as potentially providing for all learning, or it may be seen as one new and very useful tool in the facilitation of learning. As Skinner has pointed out, "To acquire behavior the student must engage in behavior" (1961, p. 389).

It is of particular interest to note that in the development of programmed instruction there is a tendency toward shorter, "plug-in" programs, rather than toward the development of whole courses covering a total field of knowledge. To me, the development of these shorter programs suggests the more fruitful way in which the student may be involved in the use of so-called teaching machines. When learning is facilitated in line with the second set of assumptions presented, the student frequently comes upon gaps in his knowledge, tools which he lacks, information which he needs to solve the problem he is confronting. Here the flexibility of programmed instruction is invaluable. A pupil who needs to know how to use a microscope can find a program covering this knowledge. The student who is planning to spend three months in France can utilize programmed instruction in conversational French. The pupil who needs algebra, whether for the solution of problems of interest to him or simply to get into college, can work on a program of instruction in algebra.

Used in these ways, a competently developed program undoubtedly gives the student immediate experiences of satisfaction, enables him to learn a body of knowledge when he needs it, gives him the feeling that any content is learnable, and fosters a recognition that the process of education is an intelligible and comprehensible one. He can work at his own rate and finds that the carefully designed program presents him with coherent, interrelated steps. Its stress on immediate reinforcement and reward rather than on punitive or evaluative measures is another factor in its favor. If programmed learning is used flexibly, it can constitute a large forward step in meeting the massive needs for functional learning of subject matter as the number of pupils grows sharply.

Programmed learning is developing in new and unexpected fields. Berlin and Wyckoff (1963) are developing programs for the improvement of interpersonal relationships in which two people work together at mutual tasks assigned by the programmed text, not only learning some of the cognitive concepts in regard to interpersonal relationships but also gradually experiencing deeper and deeper communication with each other. Both industry and educational institutions have begun to make use of this developing series of programs, impressed by the fact that the learnings involve both feelings and intellect and that they have significant personal meaning for the learner.

It should be obvious that programmed learning has great potential risks if it is unwisely used. If it becomes a substitute for thinking in larger patterns and gestalts, if it becomes a way of stressing factual knowledge more than creativity, then real damage may be done. But if it is perceived as an instrument which can be used by educators to achieve flexibility in education, then it is one of the most powerful tools which psychology has as yet contributed to the field.

"SENSITIVITY TRAINING." The final example of a new development which fosters a climate for experiential or significant learning is so-called sensitivity training. This is an approach which is of help in educating administrators and teachers for the newer goals in education. It also has relevance to the classroom situation.

Though not widely used as yet in educational institutions, there has been a burgeoning use of the intensive group experience in the development of business executives and government administrators. Under a variety of labels—the T-Group, the Laboratory Group, the Sensitivity Training Course, the intensive Workshop in Human Relations, the Basic Encounter Group—this approach has become an important part of the training function.

It is difficult to describe briefly the nature of such a group experience, especially since it varies greatly from group to group and from leader to leader. (See Wechsler and Reisel, 1959, for one description.) Essentially, the group begins with little imposed structure, so that the situation and the purposes are am-

biguous and up to the group members to decide. The leader's function is to facilitate expression and to clarify or point up the dynamic pattern of the group's struggle to work toward a meaningful experience. In such a group, after an initial "milling around," personal expressiveness tends to increase and involves an increasingly free, direct, and spontaneous communication among members of the group. Façades become less necessary, defenses are lowered, basic encounters occur as individuals reveal hitherto hidden feelings and aspects of themselves and receive spontaneous feedback—both negative and positive—from group members. Some or many individuals become much more facilitative in relationships to others, making possible greater freedom of expression.

In general, when the experience is a fruitful one, it is deeply personal, resulting in more direct person-to-person communication, sharply increased self-understanding, more realness and independence in the individual, and an increased understanding and acceptance of others. While much still remains to be learned about the intensive group experience in all its forms, it is already clear that it helps to create in most members of the group attitudes which, among other things, are highly conducive to experiential learning.

Perhaps a few examples will convey a more meaningful picture of what is already being done. The National Training Laboratory has begun to conduct "college labs" at Bethel, Maine (Bradford, Gibb, and Benne, 1964, p 109). Each of the T-Groups in these laboratories contains several students and several faculty members from the same college. As they share in the exploration of their interpersonal attitudes and relationships and of their work goals, their learnings have often been highly significant. There are reports that at least one department of English has been revolutionized by its experience in this college lab.

Various leaders in the group-dynamics field (Gibb, Herold, Zander, and Coffey) have transformed courses for teachers into T-Groups. So meaningful have been the learnings that in some of these institutions the demand for such groups, involving learning based on direct personal encounter, has grown beyond all expectations.

One elementary-school system in a Western city has made it possible for most of its principals and teachers to have experience in a sensitivity-training group. Likewise, when there is a difficult classroom situation, a member of the guidance department serves as leader of a "problem-solving group" in the classroom, the group including the teacher(s) as well as the pupils involved. Out of these experiences have come much more responsible behavior on the part of pupils, much improved communication in the classroom, and an administrative structure in which faculty-administrator interaction is much more free and real than is ordinarily achieved. In other words, there has been movement toward the establishment of a psychological climate in which pupils, teachers, and administrators can learn, in a self-initiated fashion, in regard to both the interpersonal problems which they face and the factual problems which they face in the world outside.

It appears highly likely that this particular development will become much more widespread in the educational world.

CONCLUSION

In this chapter, I have tried to present something of what would be involved if a new aim for education were adopted, that of achieving openness to change, and if focus were on that type of learning in which the whole person is involved, a meaningful experience of emotional as well as cognitive learning.

It is clear, I believe, that if this aim were selected, the basic reliance of the teacher would be upon the tendency toward fulfillment, toward actualization, in his students. The teacher would be basing his work on the hypothesis that students who are in real contact with life problems wish to learn, want to grow, seek to discover, endeavor to master, desire to create. The teacher would attempt to develop a quality of climate in the classroom and a quality of personal relationship with his students which would permit these natural tendencies to come to fruition.

The teacher or facilitator of learning who is desirous of creating the conditions for this self-fulfilling type of learning finds that there are a number of new methods already at hand which are congenial to this approach. The conduct-of-inquiry approach in science develops self-initiated learners in that field. The use of simulation techniques makes for responsible learning and decision making. The teaching machine, especially in the form of brief, specific programs, can provide the flexibility which enables the student to learn material when he most needs it. The utilization of sensitivity training for both facilitators and learners not only increases the freedom and depth of communication but also helps the individual to become more independent in his stance toward learning and toward life. These specific approaches suggest, but do not exhaust, the many ways in which the goals of the new education may be implemented.

As for the learner, the result of such self-initiated learning, such development in meeting and mastering new problems, is a more complete openness to all aspects of his experience, both the outer stimuli and his own internal reactions. He would thus be more fully and adaptively present in confronting a new problem. Martin Buber (1955 edition, p. 14) described this situation well: ". . . In spite of all similarities, every living situation has, like a newborn child, a new face that has never been before and will never come again. It demands of you a reaction which cannot be prepared beforehand. It demands nothing of what is past. It demands presence, responsibility; it demands you."

It is in this spirit that the learner would be able to deal creatively with an ever changing world.

REFERENCES

BARRETT-LENNARD, G. Dimensions of therapist response as causal factors in therapeutic change. *Psychol. Monogr.*, 1962, 76, No. 43 (Whole No. 562).

———. Personal communication, 1960.

BERLIN, J. I., and L. B. WYCKOFF. *Relationship improvement programs*. Atlanta, Ga.: Human Developm. Inst., 1963.

BRADFORD, L., J. GIBB, and K. BENNE, eds. *T-Group theory and laboratory method*. New York: Wiley, 1964.

BUBER, M. *Between man and man*. New York: Beacon Press, 1955. Works included were first published 1926-1939.

FRY, E. *Teaching machines and programmed instruction*. New York: McGrawHill, 1963.

GAGE, N. L. The educational psychology of American teachers. Paper presented to the advisory council of the Assn. of Organizations for Tchr. Educ., Washington, D.C., Oct. 1963.

GUETZKOW, H., *et al. Simulation in international relations: Developments for research and teaching*. Englewood Cliffs, N.J.: Prentice-Hall, 1963.

LIPPITT, R. *Teaching behavioral science in the elementary school*. Mimeo report. Ann Arbor: University of Michigan, 1962.

PRESSEY, S. Teaching machine (and learning theory) crisis. *J. Appl. Psychol.*, 1963, *47*, 1-6.

ROGERS, C. R. The necessary and sufficient conditions of therapeutic personality change. *J. Consult. Psychol.*, 1957, *21*, 95-103.

———, ed. *The therapeutic relationship and its impact: A study of psychotherapy with schizophrenics*. Madison: University of Wisconsin Press, 1967.

SCHWAB, J. J. Inquiry, the science teacher and the educator. *Sch. Rev.*, 1960, *68*, 176-195.

SKINNER, B. F. Why we need teaching machines. *Harv. Educ. Rev.*, 1961, *31*, 377-398.

SOLOMON, L. N. Reducing tensions in a test-tube world. *War/Peace Rep.*, July 1963, *3*, No. 7, 10-12.

SUCHMAN, J. R. *The elementary school training program in scientific inquiry*. Urbana: University of Illinois, 1962.

———. Inquiry training: Building skills for autonomous discovery. *Merrill-Palmer Quart. Behav. Developm.*, 1961, *7*, 147-169.

WECHSLER, I. R., and J. REISEL. *Inside a sensitivity training group*. Los Angeles: Inst. of Industr. Relat., UCLA, 1959.

21. LEARNING AND THINKING *

JEROME S. BRUNER

I

I have been engaged, these last few years, in research on what makes its possible for organisms—human and subhuman alike—to take advantage of past learning in attempting to deal with and master new problems before them now. It is a problem with a deceptively simple ring to it. In pursuit of it, my colleagues and I have found ourselves observing children in schoolrooms, watching them learning. It has been a revealing experience.

We have come to recognize in this work that one of the principal objectives of learning is to save us from subsequent learning. This seems a paradox, but it is not. Another way of putting the matter is to say that when we learn something, the objective is to learn it in such a way that we get a maximum of travel out of what we have learned. A homely example is provided by the relationship in arithmetic between addition and multiplication. If the principle of addition has been grasped in its deeper sense, in its generic sense, then it is unnecessary to learn multiplication. For, in principle, multiplication is only repeated addition. It is not, as we would say in our curricula, another "unit."

Learning something in a generic way is like leaping over a barrier. On the other side of the barrier is thinking. When the generic has been grasped, it is then that we are able to recognize the new problems we encounter as exemplars of old principles we have mastered. Once over the barrier, we are able to benefit from what William James long ago called "the electric sense of analogy."

There are two interesting features in generic learning—in the kind of learning that permits us to cross the barrier into thinking. One of them is *organization;* the other is *manipulation.* If we are to use our past learning, we must organize it in such a way that it is no longer bound to the specific situation in which the learning occurred. Let me give

* From Jerome S. Bruner, "Learning and Thinking," *Harvard Educational Review*, *29*: 3, Summer 1959, 184-192. Copyright © 1959 by President and Fellows of Harvard College.

an example from the history of science. It would have been possible for Galileo to have published a handbook of the distances traversed per unit time by falling bodies. School boys for centuries thereafter could easily have been tortured by the task of having to remember the Galilean tables. Such tables, cumbersome though they might have been, would have contained all the necessary information for dealing with free-falling bodies. Instead, Galileo had the inspiration to reorganize this welter of information into a highly simplified form. You recall the compact expression $S = \frac{1}{2} gt^2$: it not only summarizes all possible handbooks but organizes their knowledge in a way that makes manipulation possible. Not only do we know the distances fallen, but we can use the knowledge for bodies that fall anywhere, in any gravitational field—not just our own.

One of the most notable things about the human mind is its limited capacity for dealing at any one moment with diverse arrays of information. It has been known for a long time that we can deal only with about seven independent items of information at once; beyond that point we exceed our "channel capacity," to use our current jargon. We simply cannot manipulate large masses of information. Because of these limits, we must condense and recode. The seven things we deal with must be worth their weight. A simple formula that can regenerate the distance fallen by any free body, past or future, is under these conditions highly nutritious for its weight. Good organization achieves the kind of economical representation of facts that makes it possible to use the facts in the future. Sheer brute learning, noble though it may be, is not enough. Facts simply learned without a generic organization are the naked and useless untruth. The proper reward of learning is not that it pleases the teacher or the parents, nor is it that we become "quiz kids." The proper reward is that we can now use what we have learned, can cross the barrier from learning into thinking. Are we mindful of these matters in our conduct of teaching?

What has been said thus far must seem singularly lacking in relevance to magic, to art, and to poetry. It appears to relate principally to the learning the mathematics, science, and the social studies. But there is an analogous point to be made about the learning of the arts and literature. If one has read literature and beheld works of art in such a way as to be able to think with their aid, then one has also grasped a deeper, simplifying principle. The underlying principle that gives one the power to use literature and the arts in one's thinking is not of the order of a generic condensation of knowledge. Rather it is metaphoric in nature, and perhaps the best way of describing this class of principles is to call them guiding myths.

Let me take an example from mythology. Recall when you read for the first time the story of Perseus slaying the hateful Medusa. You recall that to look directly upon the Medusa was to be turned to stone. The secret of Perseus was to direct the killing thrust of his sword by the reflection of Medusa on his polished shield. It is an exciting story, full of the ingenuity that Hercules had taught us to expect. Beneath the story, beneath all great stories, there is a deeper metaphoric meaning. I did not understand this meaning for many years, indeed, not until my son asked me what the myth of Perseus "meant." It occurred to me that the polished shield might symbolize all of the devices by which we are able to take action against evil without becoming contaminated by it. The law suggested itself as one such device, enabling us to act against those who trespassed against morality without ourselves having to trespass in our action. I do not wish to hold a brief for my interpretation of the Perseus myth. But I would like to make one point about it.

Man must cope with a relatively limited number of plights—birth, growth, loneliness, the passions, death, and not very many more. They are plights that are neither solved nor by-passed by being "adjusted." An adjusted man must face his passions just as surely as he faces death. I would urge that a grasp of the basic plights through the basic myths of art and literature provides the organizing principle by which knowledge of the human condition is rendered into a form that makes thinking possible, by which we go beyond learning to the use of knowledge. I am not suggesting that the Greek myths are better than other forms of literature. I urge simply that there be exposure to, and interpretation of, literature that deals deeply with the human condition. I have learned as much from Charley Brown of *Peanuts* as I have learned from Perseus. The pablum school readers, stripped of rich imagery in the interest of "readability," stripped of passion in the erroneous belief that the deep human condition will not interest the child—these are no more the vehicles for getting over the barrier to thinking than are the methods of teaching mathematics by a rote parrotting at the blackboard.

II

I should like to consider now some conditions in our schools today that promote and inhibit progress across the barrier from learning to thinking. I should point out in advance that I am not very cheerful on this subject.

THE PASSIVITY OF KNOWLEDGE-GETTING. I have been struck during the past year or so, sitting in classrooms as an observer, by the passivity of the process we call education. The emphasis is upon gaining and storing information, gaining it and storing it in the form in which it is presented. We carry the remainder in long division so, peaches are grown in Georgia, transportation is vital to cities, New York is our largest port, and so on. Can the facts or the methods presented be mimicked? Is so, the unit is at an end. There is little effort indeed which goes into the process of putting the information together, finding out what is generic about it. Long division is a skill, like threading a needle. The excitement of it as a method of partitioning things that relates it to such matters as subtraction is rarely stressed. One of the great inventions of man—elementary number theory —is presented as a cookbook. I have yet to see a teacher present one way of doing division and then put it squarely to the class to suggest six other ways of doing it—for there are at least six other ways of doing it than any one that might be taught in a school. So too with algebra. Algebra is not a set of rules for manipulating numbers and letters except in a trivial sense. It is a way of thinking, a way of coping with the drama of the unknown. Lincoln Steffens, in his *Autobiography,* com-

plains upon his graduation from the University of California that his teachers had taught him only of the known, how to commit to mind, and had done little to instruct him in the art of approaching the unknown, the art of posing questions. How does one ask questions about the unknown? Well, algebra is one technique, the technique for arranging the known in such a way that one is enabled to discern the value of an unknown quantity. It is an enriching strategy, algebra, but only if it is grasped as an extended instance of common sense.

Once I did see a teacher specifically encourage a class to organize and use minimal information to draw a maximum number of inferences. The teacher modeled his technique, I suppose, on the tried method of the storyteller. He presented the beginnings of the Whiskey Rebellion and said to his pupils, much in the manner of Ellery Queen speaking to his readers, "You now have enough to reconstruct the rest of the story. Let's see if we can do it." He was urging them to cross the barrier from learning into thinking. It is unhappily true that this is a rare exception in our schools.

So knowledge-getting becomes passive. Thinking is the reward for learning, and we may be systematically depriving our students of this reward as far as school learning is concerned.

One experiment which I can report provides encouragement. It was devised and carried out by the research group with which I am associated at Harvard in collaboration with teachers in the fifth grade of a good public school. It is on the unpromising topic of the geography of the North Central States and is currently in progress so that I cannot give all of the results. We hit upon the happy idea of presenting this chunk of geography not as a set of knowns, but as a set of unknowns. One class was presented blank maps, containing only tracings of the rivers and lakes of the area as well as the natural resources. They were asked as a first exercise to indicate where the principal cities would be located, where the railroads, and where the main highways. Books and maps were not permitted and "looking up the facts" was cast in a sinful light. Upon completing this exercise, a class discussion was begun in which the children attempted to justify why the major city would be here, a large city there, a railroad on this line, etc.

This discussion was a hot one. After an hour, and much pleading, permission was given to consult the rolled up wall map. I will never forget one young student, as he pointed his finger at the foot of Lake Michigan, shouting, "Yipee, *Chicago* is at the end of the pointing-down lake." And another replying, "Well, OK: but Chicago's no good for the rivers and it should be here where there is a big city (St. Louis)." These children were thinking, and learning was an instrument for checking and improving the process. To at least a half dozen children in the class it is not a matter of indifference that no big city is to be found at the junction of Lake Huron, Lake Michigan, and Lake Ontario. They were slightly shaken up transportation theorists when the facts were in.

The children in another class taught conventionally, got their facts all right, sitting down, benchbound. And that was that. We will see in six months which group remembers more. But whichever does, one thing I will predict. One group learned geography as a set of rational acts of induction—that cities spring up where there is water, where there are natural resources, where there are things to be processed and shipped. The other group learned passively that there were arbitrary cities at arbitrary places by arbitrary bodies of water and arbitrary sources of supply. One learned geography as a form of activity. The other stored some names and positions as a passive form of registration.

THE EPISODIC CURRICULUM. In a social studies class of an elementary school in a well-to-do suburb of one of our great eastern cities, I saw groups of twelve-year-old children doing a "project" on the southeastern states. Each team was gathering facts that might eventually end up on a map or a chart or some other graphic device. The fact-gathering was atomized and episodic. Here were the industrial products of North Carolina. There was the list of the five principal cities of Georgia. I asked the children of one team what life would be like and what people would worry about in a place where the principal products

were peanuts, cotton, and peaches. The question was greeted as "unfair." They were gathering facts.

It is not just the schools. The informational environment of America seems increasingly to be going through such an atomization. Entertainment is in fifteen minute episodes on TV, to be taken while sitting down. The school curriculum is built of episodic units, each a task to itself: "We have now finished addition. Let us now move to multiplication." Even in our humor the "gag" threatens to replace the shrewd observer of the human comedy. I have seen an elementary school play fashioned entirely on a parody of radio commercials. It was a brave effort to tie the 10-second atoms together.

I do not wish to make it seem as if our present state of education is a decline from some previous Golden Age. For I do not think there has ever been a Golden Age in American public education. The difference now is that we can afford dross less well than ever before. The volume of positive knowledge increases at a rapid rate. Atomizing it into facts-to-be-filed is not likely to produce the kind of broad grasp that will be needed in the world of the next quarter century. And it is certainly no training for the higher education that more and more of our children will be getting.

I have not meant the above as a plea for the "central subject" or the "project" method of teaching. It is, rather, a plea for the recognition of the continuity of knowledge. One hears professional educators speak of "coverage," that certain topics must be covered. There are indeed many things that must be covered, but they are not unconnected things. The object of learning is to gain facts in a context of connectivity that permits the facts to be used generatively. The larger the number of isolated facts, the more staggering the number of connections between them—unles one can reduce them to some deeper order. Not all of them can. Yet it is an ideal worth striving for, be it in the fifth grade or in graduate school. As Robert Oppenheimer put it in a recent address before the American Academy, "Everything cannot be connected with everything in the world we live in. Everything can be connected with anything."

THE EMBARRASSMENT OF PASSION. I should like to consider now the guiding myth. Let me begin with a summary of the young Christopher Columbus as he is presented in a popular social studies textbook. Young Chris is walking along the water front in his home town and gets to wondering where all those ships go. Eventually he comes back to his brother's cobbler shop and exclaims, "Gee, Bart, I wonder where all those ships go, whether maybe if they just kept going they wouldn't come back because the world is round." Bart replies with pleasant brotherly encouragement. Chris is a well-adjusted kid. Bart is a nice big brother. And where is the passion that drove this obsessed man across uncharted oceans? What impelled this Columbus with such force that he finally enlisted the aid of Ferdinand and Isabella over the protest of their advisors? Everything is there in the story except the essential truth—the fanatical urge to explore in an age of exploration, the sense of an expanding world. Columbus did not have a schoolboy's whim, nor was he the well-adjusted grownup of this account. He was a man driven to explore, to control. The justification for the pablum that makes up such textbooks is that such accounts as these touch more directly on the life of the child.

What is this "life of the child" as seen by text writers and publishers? It is an image created out of an ideal of adjustment. The ideal of adjustment has little place for the driven man, the mythic hero, the idiosyncratic style. Its ideal is mediocentrism, reasonableness above all, being nice. Such an ideal does not touch closely the deeper life of the child. It does not appeal to the dark but energizing forces that lie close beneath the surface. The Old Testament, the Greek Myths, the Norse legends—these are the embarrassing chronicles of men of passion. They were devised to catch and preserve the power and tragedy of the human condition—and its ambiguity, too. In their place, we have substituted the noncontroversial and the banal.

Here a special word is needed about the concept of "expressing yourself," which is our conception of how one may engage the deeper impulses of the child. I have seen a book review class in a public school in which the children had the choice of reporting on any book they wished to choose, in or out of the school library, and where the discussion by the other children had to do entirely with the manner in which the reciting child presented his material. Nothing was said about the book in the discussion. The emphasis was on nice presentation, and whether the book sounded interesting. I have no quarrel with rewarding self-expression. I wonder simply whether it is not perhaps desirable, too, to make known the canons of excellence. The children in this class were learning to be seductive in their recounting; they were not concerned with an honest accounting of the human condition. The books they had read were cute; there was no excitment in them, none to be extracted. Increasingly the children in American elementary schools grow out of touch with the guiding myths. Self-expression is not a substitute. Adjustment is a worthy ideal, if not an ennobling one. But when we strive to attain it by shutting our eyes to the turmoils of human life, we will not get adjustment, but a niggling fear of the unusual and the excellent.

THE QUALITY OF TEACHERS. I do not wish to mince words. The educational and cultural level of the majority of American teachers is not impressive. On the whole they do not have a good grasp of the subject matter that they are teaching; courses on method will not replace the absent subject matter. In time and with teaching experience this deficiency is often remedied. But in so many cases there is no time: the turnover in the teaching profession as we all know is enormous; the median number of years of teaching before departure for marriage or motherhood is around three.

This leaves us with a small core of experienced teachers. Do we use them to teach the new teachers on the job? No. The organization of the school with respect to utilization of talent is something short of imaginative. It consists of a principal on top and a group of discrete teachers beneath her, and that is all. In large metropolitan high schools this is sometimes supplemented by having departments at the head of which is an experienced teacher. The communication that goes on between teachers is usually at a highly informal level and can scarcely be called comrehensive. It is usually about problem-children, not about social studies or mathematics or how to bring literature alive.

I would urge, and I believe that educators have taken steps in this direction, that we use our more experienced teachers for on-the-job training of less experienced, new teachers. I would also urge that there be established some means whereby the substantive topics taught in our elementary and high schools be included in some kind of special extension program provided by our eighteen hundred colleges and universities in the United States for the benefit of teachers. I am not speaking only of teachers colleges, but rather of all institutions of higher learning. Institutions of higher learning have a responsibility to the lower schools, and it can be exercised by arranging for continuous contact between those, for example, who teach history at the college level and those who are teaching history or social studies at the lower levels. And so, too, with literature or mathematics, or languages. To assume that somehow a teacher can be "prepared" simply by going through teacher training and then by taking courses in methods in summer school is, I think, fallacious. Often it is the case that the teacher, like her students, has not learned the material well enough to cross the barrier from learning to thinking.

III

It is quite plain, I think, that the task of improving the American Schools is not simply one of technique—however comforting it would be to some professional educators to think so. What is at issue, rather, is a deeper problem, one that is more philosophical than psychological or technogical in scope. Let me put it in all innocence. What do we conceive to be the end product of our educational effort? I cannot help but feel that this rather oversimplified question has become obscured a cant. There is such an official din in support of the view that we are "training well-rounded human beings to be responsible citizens" that one hestitates to raise the question whether such an objective is a meaningful guide to what one does in classroom teaching. Surely the objective is worthy, and it has influenced the techniques of education in America, not always happily. For much of what we have called the embarrassment of passion can, I think, be traced to this objective, and so too the blandness of the social studies curriculum. The ideal, sadly, has also led to the standardization of mediocrity by a failure of the schools to challenge the full capacity of the talented student.

Since the war, there has been a perceptible shift in the problems being faced by schools and parents alike. It is the New Competition. Will Johnny and Sally be able to get into the college of their first choice, or, indeed, into any college at all? The origins of the concern are obvious enough—the "baby bulge" has made itself felt. The results are not all bad, I would urge, or need not be. There are, to be sure, severe problems of overcrowding that exacerbate the difficulties already inherent in public education. And it is true that parental pressures for grades and production are increasing the proportion of children with "learning blocks" being referred to child guidance clinics.

But the pressures and the competition are also rekindling our awareness of excellence and how it may be nurtured. The shake-up of our smugness by the evident technical thrust of the Soviet Union has added to this awareness. Let me urge that it is this new awareness that requires shaping of expression in the form of a new set of ideals. Grades, admission to college, followed by admission to graduate school—these are surely not the ideals but, rather, the external signs.

Perhaps the fitting ideal is precisely as we have described it earlier in these pages, the active pragmatic ideal of leaping the barrier from learning into thinking. It matters not *what* we have learned. What we can *do* with what we have learned: this is the issue. The pragmatic argument has long been elaborated on extrinsic grounds, that the higher one has gone in the educational system the greater the economic gain. Indeed, at least one eminent economist has proposed that parents finance college education for their children by long-term loans to be repaid by the children on the almost certain knowledge that higher earning results from such education. All of this is the case, and it is indeed admirable that educational progress and economic success are so intimately linked in our society. I would only suggest that the pragmatic ideal be applied also the intrinsic aspects of education. Let us not judge our students simply on *what* they know. That is the philosophy of the quiz program. Rather, let them be judged on what they can generate from what they know—how well they can leap the barrier from learning to thinking.

22. AUTOTELIC-RESPONSIVE ENVIRONMENTS AND EXCEPTIONAL CHILDREN *

O. K. MOORE

In every society there are those who fail to learn the things which are held to be essential for carrying out the role of a competent adult, or who learn so slowly that they are generally out of phase with the age-graded societal demands imposed upon them. Slow learners are apt to be problems to themselves and to their friends. It is recognized, in scientific circles at least, that there are many and diverse causes for failure to learn at the socially prescribed rate: brain damage, emotional disturbance, social-cultural deprivation, and the like.[1]

What is not perhaps so generally recognized is that prodigies are sometimes out of phase with societal demands also; they tend to make people as uncomfortable as retarded children do. Both retarded children and prodigies unwittingly violate social expectations—they need help if they are to reach their full potential. Both the ultrarapid and the ultraslow are *exceptional* children. The main topic of this paper is to describe some methods whereby the acquisition of complex skills can be accelerated, for both ultraslow and ultrarapid learners.

For a number of years my staff and I have been conducting studies of early learning in prenursery, nursery, kindergarten and first grades, where children are in the process of acquiring complex symbolic skills. In the course of this work I formulated the notion of a responsive environment and decided to act on the assumption that an *autotelic responsive environment* is optimal for acquiring such skills (Moore, 1961). I will now try to make clear just what this assumption means.

I have defined a *responsive environment* as one which satisfies the following conditions:

1. It permits the learner to explore freely.
2. It informs the learner immediately about the consequences of his actions.
3. It is self-pacing, i.e., events happen within the environment at a rate determined by the learner.
4. It permits the learner to make full use of his capacity for discovering relations of various kinds.
5. Its structure is such that the learner is likely to make a series of interconnected discoveries about the physical, cultural or social world.

My colleague, Alan Ross Anderson, and I have defined an activity as *autotelic* if engaging in it is done for its own sake rather than for obtaining rewards or avoiding punishment that have no inherent connection with the

---

* From Moore, O. K., Autotelic-Responsive Environments and Exceptional Children, *Experience, Structure and Adaptability*, O. J. Harvey (ed.), New York: Springer, 1966, pp. 169-177.
[1] At present there is no way to measure the basic capacities of human beings independently of their experiences. Also, there undoubtedly are interactional effects between *capacities* and *experiences*. It is not assumed here that the retarded child is necessarily wanting in "basic capacity." The use here of such terms as "gifted" and "retarded" is simply intended to be consonant with standard usage in the field.

activity itself (Anderson and Moore, 1959). The distinction between the autotelic and non-autotelic activities is somewhat vague, but it can be applied in some cases without difficulty. Consider tennis playing as an example: we cannot play tennis without getting exercise, playing at all is a sufficient condition for exercising—so if we play for this reason, among others, this is an intrinsic reward. However, if we play for money, then the activity is not autotelic, since tennis and money need not go together—witness, amateur players.

In general, setting up a system of extrinsic rewards and punishments for engaging in an activity makes the learning environment more complex. As an illustration, consider a child who is learning to read aloud a list of words such as "fat" and "fate," "mat" and "mate," "rat" and "rate," etc.; pretend also that an experimenter rewards or punishes the learner depending upon success or failure. Imagine that the reward is candy and that the punishment is mild electric shock.

Under these circumstances, the child not only has the task of learning to read and pronounce these words, but also that of figuring out the relation between candy and electric shock, on the one hand, and his own efforts, on the other. There is no intrinsic relation between the words to be learned or between the letters of the words and the pronunciation, or between candy and the sensation of being shocked. It should be easy to see that learning to read and to pronounce words *and also* to anticipate the candy or the shock introduces irrelevancies which may distract or confuse the learner. It is not irrelevant, however, that after the child masters the words "fat" and "fate," he may be able to generalize to the words "mat" and "mate," or that he may be able to decipher new words not on the list such as "tin" and "tine." Children are pleased, and some become ecstatic, when they make discoveries of this kind. Pleasure thus derived, unlike the pleasure of eating candy, is inherently related to the internal structure of the task (and more broadly to the structure of the spoken and written language)—it is *not* pleasure arbitrarily associated with the task by the experimenter acting in accord with his own *ad hoc* rule. Of course, sophisticated adults manage to disentangle nonautotelic

irrelevancies from the essential features of many tasks; but we hold that this is not an optimal situation for learning difficult things.

The distinction between autotelic and non-autotelic activities is sometimes confounded with the issue as to whether rewards and punishments are either necessary or sufficient for learning to occur at all. Our objection to the use of extrinsic rewards and punishments is that they make learning situations unnecessarily complex. In effect, they add relations to be learned. However, to grant that, generally, there are intrinsic rewards and punishments associated with learning is not to prejudge the questions as to whether learning could take place without them.

As a theoretical matter it is very difficult to see how a learning experiment could be designed, which would be in any way meaningful to the learner, and in point of fact, we assume (for the sake of conceptual clarity *vis-à-vis* the making of a distinction between learning and performance, i.e., practicing what has been learned) that rewards and punishments, whether intrinsic or extrinsic, are neither necessary nor sufficient for the occurrence of learning. But of course no one would want to deny that they are highly relevant to the willingness of the learner to continue to learn more and to his desire to practice what he has learned

From what has been said above it is undoubtedly clear that not all responsive environments are autotelic, nor are all autotelic activities carried out within the context of responsive environments. It is the purpose of this chapter to describe an environment which is *both* autotelic and responsive. I feel that I have been able to contrive an environment of this kind, which takes the form of a research laboratory, for young children. Some aspects of the autotelic "responsive environments laboratory" to be described here are novel; for example, the children play with a "talking typewriter." But in order to interpret the behavior of children within this environment, it is well to keep the system as a whole steadily in view—to see it as a social as well as a mechanical system. For this reason, a physical description of the laboratory is followed by a description of the norms under which the laboratory is operated. A cultural characterization of what is to be learned is counterbalanced by a description of equipment and procedures which facilitate the learning. No one aspect of the environment should be thought of as constituting its essence; the laboratory was designed to fulfill all the conditions of an autotelic responsive environment. The techniques of operation are intricate and presuppose careful planning. And since the description of an environment without some reference to the behavior of its denizens is incomplete, at the end of this chapter information is given about the background and laboratory behavior of five children: two "educable retardates," one child on the borderline between the "educable retardate" and the "dull normal," one who is on the borderline between the "very bright" and the "gifted," and one "gifted" child (to use standard terminology).*

The emphasis in this paper on exceptional children should not be construed as a lack of interest in those who are within the normal range. As a matter of fact, most of my work has been with normal children. However, extreme cases are sometimes illuminating. I hope that this is true here.

To return to the problems of those who do not meet the age-graded demands imposed upon them, the relevance of the research reported here on retarded youngsters is patent: anything which may help them become more competent is of educational interest. On the other hand, it is not at all obvious that accelerating prodigies is a socially useful thing to do; society seems to be organized so as to slow them down, if anything. However, a case can be made for the acceleration of prodigies. Indications will be given as to how prodigies can develop some of their own potentialities while helping other children in the development of theirs.

LABORATORY—PHYSICAL DESCRIPTION [2]

The Responsive Environments Laboratory is located at Hamden Hall Country Day School, Hamden, Connecticut, a few yards from the

Hamden Hall preschool classrooms. It consists of two adjoining prefabricated metal sheds each 20′×40′, set on concrete foundations. One shed is windowless and the other has window only in a small office area; they are centrally heated and air conditioned. The sheds are as simple as modern construction permits; they are made up of one-foot modular sections, have exposed ceiling and wall beams, and so on. In Shed 1 are five portable soundproofed booths 7′×7′×7′, lined along two 40′ walls, leaving a middle aisle as well as small aisles between booths for observation through windows with one-way glass. Through a face and by-pass system the booths are separately air conditioned. One booth has camera ports and built in lighting equipment so that sound motion pictures can be made on a semi-automatic basis. Shed 1 also contains a desk, a conference table and a secretary's desk.

A central two-way communication system permits the staff to speak or listen either at the main console or at the booths themselves.

The interior of Shed 1 gives an impression of psychological warmth despite its spartan construction. Perhaps this is because the booths, which are its most prominent feature have a natural wood finish. (Booth interior are finished with off-white, sound-absorbent tiles.)

Shed 2 is divided into three areas separated by natural wood partitions: a small classroom an office-conference room which also contains a booth for testing and a bathroom. From the standpoint of construction the 16′×20′ classroom is an over-sized booth. Like the booth it is soundproofed, air conditioned, equipped with one-way glass, finished in natural wood (exterior) and natural wood and sound absorbent tile (interior). Again there is provision for the making of motion pictures on semi-automatic basis. Shed 2, like Shed 1, is warm and pleasant in emotional tone; together they form one functional unit.

This laboratory was designed in accord with one overriding objective, that of making it

under my personal direction—the others work cooperatively with me.

In order to avoid confusion, everything that said here pertains to the Hamden Hall laboratory although the children discussed in the section (below) "Children in a Responsive Environment" did not necessarily come to this laboratory.

---

* This extensive description of the children can be found in the original source—ED.

[2] The Responsive Environments Laboratory described here served as the model for four other laboratories. Two of the laboratories operate

conducive to carrying out autotelic activities by young children: it is simple, distinct, and separate. a) Simple in the sense that a game board or a playing field is devoid of irrelevancies, b) distinct in the sense that a playing field has clear-cut boundary lines, and c) separate in the sense that a grandstand sets barriers between participants and spectators.

The parts of the laboratory used by children are windowless; windows are an open invitation to digress. The absence of windows also increases the children's sense of privacy. . . . The booth interiors are free of the attention-grabbing patterns and whirligigs so typical of nursery and elementary classrooms. The soundproofing muffles irrelevant noises and further enhances a sense of privacy. The buildings are air conditioned in order to produce a constant comfortable environment; it makes no difference whether it is raining or snowing, sunny or cloudy, the general laboratory atmosphere is invariant. One-way windows, camera ports, semi-automatic motion-picture controls, and the like, make it possible to observe and document children's behavior without intruding upon them.

It is important to note that children spend only a small fraction of their day in this laboratory. It is not suggested here that gay designs and intriguing novelties are not appropriate in many other contexts.

LABORATORY—AUTOTELIC OPERATIONAL NORMS

Behavioral scientists take it for granted that human organizations function within the context of sets of interlocking social norms; this is certainly true of the Responsive Environments Laboratory as a social organization. By *operational norms* I mean the social rules which govern the relations between laboratory activities, on the one hand, and the school, the parents, and children, on the other. One problem with which I have been concerned in constructing a new environment is that of being explicit about its normative aspects. A fundamental part of the task of creating a special environment for carrying on activities autotelically is to differentiate these activities from other important aspects of children's lives.

It is worth noting that, in addition to the educational problems mentioned at the outset, all, or nearly all, human societies make provision for engaging in autotelic activities. This is not only a matter of specifying times and places for these activities—the basketball court at game time, the theater at 8:40—but it is also a matter of creating and observing norms which safeguard these activities as autotelic. For example, one is not supposed to bribe a basketball player to shave points. The general public reacts with moral indignation whenever it is discovered that a norm of this kind has been violated. A distinction should be drawn between the norms which surround or protect an activity in its autotelic status and the rules of the activity itself. For example in bridge, onlookers are forbidden to *kibitz*, but this injunction is not a rule of the *game* of bridge. More generally, it is always possible to relax the norms which make an activity autotelic while leaving the rules of the "game" intact. Conversely, autotelic conventions can remain invariant while the rules of the game are changed.

With respect to the Responsive Environments Laboratory, every effort is made to maintain a setting in which "kibitzing" by parents and friends of the children is virtually impossible [there is a rule against their visiting [3] and the physical arrangement ensures privacy *vis-à-vis* the "significant persons" in the child's life—more technically, the "significant others," in the sense of Mead (1934), are excluded].

The staff seeks to make the laboratory a child-centered milieu. Even the introduction of a child to the laboratory is done by another child rather than an adult. A child guide takes the newcomer through the laboratory (equipment is turned off; the introduction to its operation is made later). Sometimes three introductory visits are needed before a newcomer seems to be at ease, although one visit is sufficient for most children. The guide also explains some of the relevant rules: 1) that

[3] As a matter of practice, parents are allowed one visit per school year. The visit is arranged so that they do not see their own child in a booth and the child does not see his parents in the laboratory. However, the laboratory has many visitors—roughly 600 in the past three years. Most visitors are either behavioral scientists or professional educators.

he need not come to the laboratory unless he wants to, 2) that he can leave whenever he wishes, 3) that he must leave when his time is up (30 minutes maximum stay), 4) that he need not explain his coming or going, 5) that he go to the booth to which he is assigned for the day, 6) that if he says he wants to leave, or starts to leave, he *can* come back again the next day (but not the same day). Newcomers have the opportunity to explore every nook and corner of the laboratory. The guide watches this activity but does not interfere. After a while newcomers seem to feel satisfied that they have seen everything and are ready to leave.

It should be obvious that the role of the guide requires the ability to communicate clearly and to exercise self-restraint. The task of being a guide is assigned to gifted children; this is but one of many special tasks which they are given.

The laboratory staff is carefully instructed about treating the children. The import of the rules is that we want children to initiate activities. The staff is to respond to them rather than to teach them. Those who are in daily interaction with the children are not permitted to see the background information gathered by the project's professional staff: for example, the operating personnel do not know I.Q. test scores. Operating personnel are randomly assigned to booths every day. (There are two kinds of booths, automated and nonautomated. In nonautomated booths an adult is with the child. Since adults do not teach, we prefer to call them "booth assistants." [4] The members of the staff who are professional teachers [5] serve as supervisors of

the laboratory as a whole, as well as booths.) No booth assistant should be uniquely associated with any given booth and its equipment or with any particular child. (Children, as well as booth assistants, are randomly assigned to booths each day.[6]) The conduct of the operating staff is monitored by a supervisor who can talk directly to the booth assistant without interrupting a child. This is especially important in training new booth assistants. (The foregoing remarks are applicable to nonautomated booths. At present there is one fully automated booth, which requires no adult in the booth with the child; further details about automation appear below.)

The Hamden Hall children leave their classrooms (nursery, kindergarten and first grade) to come to the laboratory every school day. When it is a child's turn to come, his classroom teacher [7] lets him know. He then either accepts or rejects his turn for the day. If he decides to come he takes his "pass" and goes by himself the few yards to the laboratory where he is checked in and goes to the booth

[4] Booth assistants generally have been the wives of graduate students. (This means we have to train new assistants quite frequently because their husbands graduate.) One of the qualifications for the job of booth assistant is a strong aesthetic sense. Teacher training is not necessary. The importance assigned to aesthetics is perhaps a prejudice on my part. I assume that those who are artistically inclined are likely to find the subtle workings of children's minds to be of continuing interest, and that they are not apt to impose their views on children. This assumption may be unwarranted but it has resulted in the selection of remarkably empathic, nondirective and patient booth assistants.

[5] It has been my experience that professional teachers who work out well as laboratory super-

visors have both the ability to to empathize with children and to organize efficiently. The role of laboratory supervisor is a critical one for the successful employment of the methods we are considering. It is in this role that the teacher, as a professional, can use her training and experience to good advantage. The seasoned professional teacher can draw on her years of experience to do such things as spot the child who is ill and should be home, or to analyze the hitches which arise in the process of performing a task which requires nicely coordinated effort on the part of the staff.

[6] Of the 102 children, that I have studied there have been a few who, at times, have responded so much better to a particular booth assistant or to the nonautomated equipment, or to the automated instrumentation than they did to the other conditions, that the laboratory departed from the usual procedure of random assignment until these children were able to play with pleasure wherever they found themselves. It will be made clear in the section "Children in a Responsive Environment" that it is important to take individual variability into account.

[7] The regular classroom teacher, like the laboratory supervisor, is important to the successful employment of these methods in the context of a school. She must be flexible enough to organize her own classroom activities so that the short individual trips to the laboratory do not unsettle the general routine. Her attitudes toward early learning are also important.

assistant to whom he has been assigned. One of the most remarkable things about this environment is that, day in and day out, children elect to come to it. Sometimes several months go by without one child of the current group (which numbers 60) refusing his turn. However, it frequently happens that a child does not want to leave when his time is up, in which case he is gently picked up and told that another child is waiting.

From what has been said it should be clear that the adults the child encounters in the laboratory are *not* the significant adults in his life—they are *not* his mother, father, grandmother, etc. Those significant adults who ordinarily are in the best position to reward or punish him have no way of knowing how he spends his time in the laboratory on a day-to-day basis. It is therefore unlike Little League Baseball, with relatives and friends observing from the sidelines; the laboratory time represents 30 minutes *away from* the significant persons in his life.

To "cut off" 30 minutes from the rest of the day in this fashion does not necessarily mean that the experience is without consequences for the remainder of the child's day. Just as most autotelic activities make use of cultural objects (Anderson and Moore, 1957; Moore, 1958; Moore and Anderson, 1963; Moore and Lewis, 1963), which are formally isomorphic with significant features of many serious activities [as Anderson and I have argued before (Moore and Anderson, 1962): a) puzzles, b) games of chance, c) games of strategy, and d) aesthetic objects are formally similar to a) puzzling situations, b) the aleatory features of experience, c) cooperative and competitive undertakings, and d) the affective side of living] so, too, it is possible to design autotelic responsive environments in which a child can play with cultural objects, which though not ordinarily treated autotelically, are still structurally isomorphic with selected aspects of the world outside the laboratory.

REFERENCES

ANDERSON, A. & MOORE, O. K. Autotelic folkmodels. Technical Report No. 8, Office of Naval Research, Group Psychology Branch, Contract SAR/Nonr. 609(16), New Haven, 1959. Reprinted in *Sociological Quarterly*, *1*:204-216.

ANDERSON, A. R. & MOORE, O. K. The formal analysis of normative concepts. *Amer. Soc. Rev.*, 1957, *22*, 9-17.

MEAD, G. H. *Mind, Self and Society*. Chicago: Univer. of Chicago Press, 1934.

MOORE, O. K. *Dictation*. (Motion picture). Will be available through the Responsive Environments Foundation, Inc., 20 Augur Street, Hamden, Connecticut.

MOORE, O. K. Problem solving and the perception of persons. *In* R. Tagiuri & L. Petrullo (eds.), *Person Perception and Interpersonal Behavior*. Palo Alto: Stanford Univer. Press, 1958, pp. 131-150.

MOORE, O. K. Orthographic symbols and the preschool child—a new approach. Proceedings of the third Minnesota conference on gifted children, Minneapolis: University of Minnesota Press, 1960, pp. 91-101.

MOORE, O. K. *Automated Responsive Environments: Part 1*. (Motion picture). The Responsive Environments Foundation, Inc., Hamden, Connecticut.

MOORE, O. K. *Automated Responsive Environments: Part 2*. (Motion picture). The Responsive Environments Foundation, Inc., Hamden, Connecticut.

MOORE, O. K. & ANDERSON, A. R. *Early Reading and Writing, Part 1: Skills*. (Motion picture). Basic Education, Inc., Hamden, Connecticut.

MOORE, O. K. & ANDERSON, A. R. *Early Reading and Writing, Part 2: Teaching Methods*. (Motion picture). Basic Education, Inc., Hamden, Connecticut.

MOORE, O. K. & ANDERSON, A. R. *Early Reading and Writing, Part 3: Development*. (Motion picture). Basic Education, Inc., Hamden, Connecticut.

MOORE, O. K. & ANDERSON, A. R. Some puzzling aspects of social interaction. In J. H. Criswell, H. Solomon & P. Suppes (eds.), *Mathematical Methods in Small Group Processes*. Stanford Univer. Press, 1962, pp. 232-249. Also, *Rev. of Metaphys.*, 1062, *15*, 409-433.

MOORE, O. K. & ANDERSON, A. R. The structure of personality. Read at the ONR symposium on the "Social Self," University of Colorado, October 7-9, 1961. Also, *Rev. of Metaphys.*, *16*, 212-236. Also, O. J. Harvey (ed.), *Cognitive Determinants of Motivation and Social Interaction*. University of Colorado: Ronald Press, 1963.

MOORE, O. K. & LEWIS, D. J. Learning theory and culture. *Psych. Rev.*, *59*, 1962, 380-388. Also, E. P. Hollander & R. G. Hunt (eds.), *Current Perspectives in Social Psychology*. New York: Oxford University Press, 1963.

PIERCE, J. R. *Symbols, Signals and Noise: The Nature and Process of Communication*. New York: Harper & Brothers, 1961.

TERMAN, L. M. *Genetic Studies of Genius*, Vols. 1-5. Palo Alto: Stanford University Press, 1925-1959.

23. THE IDEA OF SUMMERHILL *

A. S. NEILL

This is a story of a modern school—Summerhill.

Summerhill was founded in the year 1921. The school is situated within the village of Leiston, in Suffolk, England, and is about one hundred miles from London.

Just a word about Summerhill pupils. Some children come to Summerhill at the age of five years, and others as late as fifteen. The children generally remain at the school until they are sixteen years old. We generally have about twenty-five boys and twenty girls.

The children are divided into three groups: The youngest range from five to seven, the intermediates from eight to ten, and the oldest from eleven to fifteen.

Generally we have a fairly large sprinkling of children from foreign countries. At the present time (1960) we have five Scandinavians, one Hollander, one German and one American.

The children are housed by age groups with a house mother for each group. The intermediates sleep in a stone building, the seniors sleep in huts. Only one or two older pupils have rooms for themselves. The boys live two or three or four to a room, and so do the girls. The pupils do not have to stand room inspection and no one picks up after them. They are left free. No one tells them what to wear: they put on any kind of costume they want to at any time.

Newspapers call it a *Go-as-you-please School* and imply that it is a gathering of wild primitives who know no law and have no manners.

* "The Idea of Summerhill," pp. 3-12, from *Summerhill: A Radical Approach to Child Rearing* by A. S. Neill, Copyright 1960, Hart Publishing Company, New York.

It seems necessary, therefore, for me to write the story of Summerhill as honestly as I can. That I write with a bias is natural yet I shall try to show the demerits of Summerhill as well as its merits. Its merits will be the merits of healthy, free children whose lives are unspoiled by fear and hate.

Obviously, a school that makes active children sit at desks studying mostly useless subjects is a bad school. It is a good school only for those who believe in *such* a school, for those uncreative citizens who want docile, uncreative children who will fit into a civilization whose standard of success is money.

Summerhill began as an experimental school. It is no longer such; it is now a demonstration school, for it demonstrates that freedom works.

When my first wife and I began the school we had one main idea: *to make the school fit the child*—instead of making the child fit the school.

I had taught in ordinary schools for many years. I knew the other way well. I knew it was all wrong. It was wrong because it was based on an adult conception of what a child should be and of how a child should learn. The other way dated from the days when psychology was still an unknown science.

Well, we set out to make a school in which we should allow children freedom to be themselves. In order to do this, we had to renounce all discipline, all direction, all suggestion, all moral training, all religious instruction. We have been called brave, but it did not require courage. All it required was what we had—complete belief in the child as a good, not an evil, being. For almost forty years, this belief in the goodness of the child has never wavered; it rather has become a final faith.

My view is that a child is innately wise and realistic. If left to himself without adult suggestion of any kind, he will develop as far as he is capable of developing. Logically, Summerhill is a place in which people who have the innate ability and wish to be scholars will be scholars; while those who are only fit to sweep the streets will sweep the streets. But we have not produced a street cleaner so far. Nor do I write this snobbishly, for I would rather see a school produce a happy street cleaner than a neurotic scholar.

What is Summerhill like? Well, for one thing, lessons are optional. Children can go to them or stay away from them—for years if they want to. There *is* a timetable—but only for the teachers.

The children have classes usually according to their age, but sometimes according to their interests. We have no new methods of teaching, because we do not consider that teaching in itself matters very much. Whether a school has or has not a special method for teaching long division is of no significance, for long division is of no importance except to those who *want* to learn it. And the child who *wants* to learn long division *will* learn it no matter how it is taught.

Children who come to Summerhill as kindergarteners attend lessons from the beginning of their stay; but pupils from other schools vow that they will never attend any beastly lessons again at any time. They play and cycle and get in people's way, but they fight shy of lessons. This sometimes goes on for months. The recovery time is proportionate to the hatred their last school gave them. Our record case was a girl from a convent. She loafed for three years. The average period of recovery from lesson aversion is three months.

Strangers to this idea of freedom will be wondering what sort of madhouse it is where children play all day if they want to. Many an adult says, "If I had been sent to a school like that, I'd never have done a thing." Others say, "Such children will feel themselves heavily handicapped when they have to compete against children who have been made to learn."

I think of Jack who left us at the age of seventeen to go into an engineering factory. One day, the managing director sent for him.

"You are the lad from Summerhill," he said. "I'm curious to know how such an education appears to you now that you are mixing with lads from the old schools. Suppose you had to choose again, would you go to Eton or Summerhill?"

"Oh, Summerhill, of course," replied Jack.

"But what does it offer that the other schools don't offer?"

Jack scratched his head. "I dunno," he said slowly; "I think it gives you a feeling of complete self-confidence."

"Yes," said the manager dryly, "I noticed it when you came into the room."

"Lord," laughed Jack, "I'm sorry if I gave you that impression."

"I liked it," said the director. "Most men when I call them into the office fidget about and look uncomfortable. You came in as my equal. By the way, what department did you say you would like to transfer to?"

This story shows that learning in itself is not as important as personality and character. Jack failed in his university exams because he hated book learning. But his lack of knowledge about *Lamb's Essays* or the French language did not handicap him in life. He is now a successful engineer.

All the same, there is a lot of learning in Summerhill. Perhaps a group of our twelve-year-olds could not compete with a class of equal age in handwriting or spelling or fractions. But in an examination requiring originality, our lot would beat the others hollow.

We have no class examinations in the school, but sometimes I set an exam for fun. The following questions appeared in one such paper:

Where are the following:—Madrid, Thursday Island, yesterday, love, democracy, hate, my pocket screwdriver (alas, there was no helpful answer to that one).

Give meanings for the following: (the number shows how many are expected for each)—Hand (3) . . . only two got the third right—the standard of measure for a horse. Brass (4) . . . metal, cheek, top army officers, department of an orchestra. Translate Hamlet's To-be-or-not-to-be speech into Summerhillese.

These questions are obviously not intended to be serious, and the children enjoy them thoroughly. Newcomers, on the whole, do not rise to the answering standard of pupils who have become acclimatized to the school. Not that they have less brain power, but rather because they have become so accustomed to work in a serious groove that any light touch puzzles them.

This is the play side of our teaching. In all classes much work is done. If, for some reason, a teacher cannot take his class on the appointed day, there is usually much disappointment for the pupils.

David, aged nine, had to be isolated for whooping cough. He cried bitterly. "I'll miss Roger's lesson in geography," he protested. David had been in the school practically from birth, and he had definite and final ideas about the necessity of having his lessons given to him. David is now a lecturer in mathematics at London University.

A few years ago someone at a General School Meeting (at which all school rules are voted by the entire school, each pupil and each staff member having one vote) proposed that a certain culprit should be punished by being banished from lessons for a week. The other children protested on the ground that the punishment was too severe.

My staff and I have a hearty hatred of all examinations. To us, the university exams are anathema. But we cannot refuse to teach children the required subjects. Obviously, as long as the exams are in existence, they are our master. Hence, the Summerhill staff is always qualified to teach to the set standard.

Not that many children want to take these exams; only those going to the university do so. And such children do not seem to find it especially hard to tackle these exams. They generally begin to work for them seriously at the age of fourteen, and they do the work in about three years. Of course they don't always pass at the first try. The more important fact is that they try again.

Summerhill is possibly the happiest school in the world. We have no truants and seldom a case of homesickness. We very rarely have fights—quarrels, of course, but seldom have I seen a stand-up fight like the ones we used to have as boys. I seldom hear a child cry, because children when free have much less hate to express than children who are downtrodden.

Hate breeds hate, and love breeds love. Love means approving of children, and that is essential in any school. You can't be on the side of children if you punish them and storm at them. Summerhill is a school in which the child knows that he is approved of.

Mind you, we are not above and beyond human foibles. I spent weeks planting potatoes one spring, and when I found eight plants pulled up in June, I made a big fuss. Yet there was a difference between my fuss and that of an authoritarian. My fuss was about potatoes, but the fuss an authoritarian would have made would have dragged in the question of morality—right and wrong. I did not say that it was wrong to steal my spuds; I did not make it a matter of good and evil—I made it a matter of *my* spuds. They were *my* spuds and they should have been left alone. I hope I am making the distinction clear.

Let me put it another way. To the children, I am no authority to be feared. I am their equal, and the row I kick up about my spuds has no more significance to them than the row a boy may kick up about his punctured bicycle tire. It is quite safe to have a row with a child when you are equals.

Now some will say: "That's all bunk. There can't be equality. Neill is the boss; he is bigger and wiser." That is indeed true. I am the boss, and if the house caught fire the children would run to me. They know that I am bigger and more knowledgeable, but that does not matter when I meet them on their own ground, the potato patch, so to speak.

When Billy, aged five, told me to get out of his birthday party because I hadn't been invited, I went at once without hesitation—just as Billy gets out of my room when I don't want his company. It is not easy to describe this relationship between teacher and child, but every visitor to Summerhill knows what I mean when I say that the relationship is ideal. One sees it in the attitude to the staff in general. Rudd, the chemistry man, is Derek. Other members of the staff are known as Harry, and Ulla, and Pam. I am Neill, and the cook is Esther.

In Summerhill, everyone has equal rights. No one is allowed to walk on my grand piano, and I am not allowed to borrow a boy's cycle without his permission. At a General School

Meeting, the vote of a child of six counts for as much as my vote does.

But, says the knowing one, in practice of course the voices of the grownups count. Doesn't the child of six wait to see how you vote before he raises his hand? I wish he sometimes would, for too many of my proposals are beaten. Free children are not easily influenced; the absence of fear accounts for this phenomenon. Indeed, the absence of fear is the finest thing that can happen to a child.

Our children do not fear our staff. One of the school rules is that after ten o'clock at night there shall be quietness on the upper corridor. One night, about eleven, a pillow fight was going on, and I left my desk, where I was writing, to protest against the row. As I got upstairs, there was a scurrying of feet and the corridor was empty and quiet. Suddenly I heard a disappointed voice say, "Humph, it's only Neill," and the fun began again at once. When I explained that I was trying to write a book downstairs, they showed concern and at once agreed to chuck the noise. Their scurrying came from the suspicion that their bedtime officer (one of their own age) was on their track.

I emphasize the importance of this absence of fear of adults. A child of nine will come and tell me he has broken a window with a ball. He tells me, because he isn't afraid of arousing wrath or moral indignation. He may have to pay for the window, but he doesn't have to fear being lectured or being punished.

There was a time some years back when the School Government resigned, and no one would stand for election. I seized the opportunity of putting up a notice: "In the absence of a government, I herewith declare myself Dictator. Heil Neill!" Soon there were mutterings. In the afternoon Vivien, aged six, came to me and said, "Neill, I've broken a window in the gym."

I waved him away. "Don't bother me with little things like that," I said, and he went.

A little later he came back and said he had broken two windows. By this time I was curious, and asked him what the idea was.

"I don't like dictators," he said, "and I don't like going without my grub." (I discovered later that the opposition to dictatorship had tried to take itself out on the cook, who promptly shut up the kitchen and went home.)

"Well," I asked, "what are you going to do about it?"

"Break more windows," he said doggedly.

"Carry on," I said, and he carried on.

When he returned, he announced that he had broken seventeen windows. "But mind," he said earnestly, "I'm going to pay for them."

"How?"

"Out of my pocket money. How long will it take me?"

I did a rapid calculation. "About ten years," I said.

He looked glum for a minute; then I saw his face light up. "Gee," he cried, "I don't have to pay for them at all."

"But what about the private property rule?" I asked. "The windows are my private property."

"I know that but there isn't any private property rule now. There isn't any government, and the government makes the rules."

It may have been my expression that made him add, "But all the same I'll pay for them."

But he didn't have to pay for them. Lecturing in London shortly afterward, I told the story; and at the end of my talk, a young man came up and handed me a pound note "to pay for the young devil's windows." Two years later, Vivien was still telling people of his windows and of the man who paid for them. "He must have been a terrible fool, because he never even saw me."

Children make contact with strangers more easily when fear is unknown to them. English reserve is, at bottom, really fear; and that is why the most reserved are those who have the most wealth. The fact that Summerhill children are so exceptionally friendly to visitors and strangers is a source of pride to me and my staff.

We must confess, however, that many of our visitors are people of interest to the children. The kind of visitor most unwelcome to them is the teacher, especially the earnest teacher, who wants to see their drawing and written work. The most welcome visitor is the one who has good tales to tell—of adventure and travel or, best of all, of aviation. A boxer or a good tennis player is surrounded at once, but visitors who spout theory are left severely alone.

The most frequent remark that visitors make is that they cannot tell who is staff and who is pupil. It is true: the feeling of unity is that strong when children are approved of. There is no deference to a teacher as a teacher. Staff and pupils have the same food and have to obey the same community laws. The children would resent any special privileges given to the staff.

When I used to give the staff a talk on psychology every week, there was a muttering that it wasn't fair. I changed the plan and made the talks open to everyone over twelve. Every Tuesday night, my room is filled with eager youngsters who not only listen but give their opinions freely. Among the subjects the children have asked me to talk about have been these: The Inferiority Complex, The Psychology of Stealing, The Psychology of the Gangster, The Psychology of Humor, Why Did Man Become a Moralist? Masturbation, Crowd Psychology. It is obvious that such children will go out into life with a broad clear knowledge of themselves and others.

The most frequent question asked by Summerhill visitors is, "Won't the child turn round and blame the school for not making him learn arithmetic or music?" The answer is that young Freddy Beethoven and young Tommy Einstein will refuse to be kept away from their respective spheres.

The function of the child is to live his own life—not the life that his anxious parents think he should live, nor a life according to the purpose of the educator who thinks he knows what is best. All this interference and guidance on the part of adults only produces a generation of robots.

You cannot *make* children learn music or anything else without to some degree converting them into will-less adults. You fashion them into accepters of the *status quo*—a good thing for a society that needs obedient sitters at dreary desks, standers in shops, mechanical catchers of the 8:30 suburban train—a society, in short, that is carried on the shabby shoulders of the scared little man—the scared-to-death conformist.

24. HOW CHILDREN FAIL *

J. S. HOLT

Nobody starts off stupid. You have only to watch babies and infants, and think seriously about what all of them learn and do, to see that, except for the most grossly retarded, they show a style of life, and a desire and ability to learn that in an older person we might well call genius. Hardly an adult in a thousand, or ten thousand, could in any three years of his life learn as much, grow as much in his understanding of the world around him, as every infant learns and grows in his first three years.

But what happens, as we get older, to this extraordinary capacity for learning and intellectual growth?

What happens is that it is destroyed, and more than by any other one thing, by the process that we misname education—a process that goes on in most homes and schools. We adults destroy most of the intellectual and creative capacity of children by the things we do to them or make them do. We destroy this capacity above all by making them afraid, afraid of not doing what other people want, of not pleasing, of making mistakes, of failing, of being *wrong*. Thus we make them afraid

* From Holt, J. S., "To Summarize" from *How Children Fail*, New York: Pitman, 1964, pp. 167-174, 179-181.

to gamble, afraid to experiment, afraid to try the difficult and the unknown. Even when we do not create children's fears, when they come to us with fears ready-made and built-in, we use these fears as handles to manipulate them and get them to do what we want. Instead of trying to whittle down their fears, we build them up, often to monstrous size. For we like children who are a little afraid of us, docile, deferential children, though not, of course, if they are so obviously afraid that they threaten our image of ourselves as kind, lovable people whom there is no reason to fear. We find ideal the kind of "good" children who are just enough afraid of us to do everything we want, without making us feel that fear of us is what is making them do it.

We destroy the disinterested (I do *not* mean *un*interested) love of learning in children, which is so strong when they are small, by encouraging and compelling them to work for petty and contemptible rewards—gold stars, or papers marked 100 and tacked to the wall, or *A*'s on report cards, or honor rolls, or dean's lists, or Phi Beta Kappa keys—in short, for the ignoble satisfaction of feeling that they are better than someone else. We encourage them to feel that the end and aim of all they do in school is nothing more than to get a good mark on a test, or to impress someone with what they seem to know. We kill, not only their curiosity, but their feeling that it is a good and admirable thing to be curious, so that by the age of ten most of them will not ask questions, and will show a good deal of scorn for the few who do.

In many ways, we break down children's convictions that things make sense, or their hope that things may prove to make sense. We do it, first of all, by breaking up life into arbitrary and disconnected hunks of subject matter, which we then try to "integrate" by such artificial and irrelevant devices as having children sing Swiss folk songs while they are studying the geography of Switzerland, or do arithmetic problems about rail-splitting while they are studying the boyhood of Lincoln. Furthermore, we continually confront them with what is senseless, ambiguous, and contradictory; worse, we do it without knowing that we are doing it, so that, hearing nonsense shoved at them as if it were sense, they come to feel that the source of their confusion lies not in the material but in their own stupidity. Still further, we cut children off from their own common sense and the world of reality by requiring them to play with and shove around words and symbols that have little or no meaning to them. Thus we turn the vast majority of our students into the kind of people for whom all symbols are meaningless; who cannot use symbols as a way of learning about and dealing with reality; who cannot understand written instructions; who, even if they read books, come out knowing no more than when they went in; who may have a few new words rattling around in their heads, but whose material models of the world remain unchanged and, indeed, impervious to change. The minority, the able and successful students, we are very likely to turn into something different but just as dangerous: the kind of people who can manipulate words and symbols fluently while keeping themselves largely divorced from the reality for which they stand; the kind of people who like to speak in large generalities but grow silent or indignant if someone asks for an example of what they are talking about; the kind of people who, in their discussions of world affairs, coin and use such words as megadeaths and megacorpses, with scarcely a thought to the blood and suffering these words imply.

We encourage children to act stupidly, not only by scaring and confusing them, but by boring them, by filling up their days with dull, repetitive tasks that make little or no claim on their attention or demands on their intelligence. Our hearts leap for joy at the sight of a roomful of children all slogging away at some imposed task, and we are all the more pleased and satisfied if someone tells us that the children don't really like what they are doing. We tell ourselves that this drudgery, this endless busywork, is good preparation for life, and we fear that without it children would be hard to "control." But why must this busywork be so dull? Why not give tasks that are interesting and demanding? Because, in schools where every task must be completed and every answer must be right, if we give children more demanding tasks they will be fearful and will instantly insist that we show them how to do the job. When you have acres of paper to fill up with pencil marks, you have no time to waste on the luxury of thinking. By such means children are firmly established in the habit of using only a small part of their thinking capacity. They feel that school is a place where they must spend most of their time doing dull tasks in a dull way. Before long they are deeply settled in a rut of unintelligent behavior from which most of them could not escape even if they wanted to.

School tends to be a dishonest as well as a nervous place. We adults are not often honest with children, least of all in school. We tell them, not what we think, but what we feel they ought to think; or what other people feel or tell us they ought to think. Pressure groups find it easy to weed out of our classrooms, texts, and libraries whatever facts truths, and ideas they happen to find unpleasant or inconvenient. And we are not even as truthful with children as we could safely be, as the parents, politicians, and pressure groups would let us be. Even in the most non-controversial areas our teaching, the books, and the textbooks we give children present a dishonest and distorted picture of the world.

The fact is that we do not feel an obligation to be truthful to children. We are like the managers and manipulators of news in Washington, Moscow, London, Peking, and Paris, and all the other capitals of the world. We think it our right and our duty, not to tell the truth, but to say whatever will best serve our cause—in this case, the cause of making children grow up into the kind of people we want them to be, thinking whatever we want them to think. We have only to convince ourselves (and we are very easily convinced) that a lie will be "better" for the children than the truth, and we will lie. We don't always need even that excuse; we often lie only for our own convenience.

Worse yet, we are not honest about ourselves, our own fears, limitations, weaknesses, prejudices, motives. We present ourselves to children as if we were gods, all-knowing, all-powerful, always rational, always just, always right. This is worse than any lie we could tell about ourselves. I have more than once shocked teachers by telling them that when kids ask me a question to which I don't know the answer, I say, "I haven't the faintest idea"; or

that when I make a mistake, as I often do, I say, "I goofed again"; or that when I am trying to do something I am no good at, like paint in water colors or play a clarinet or bugle, I do it in front of them so they can see me struggling with it, and can realize that not all adults are good at everything. If a child asks me to do something that I don't want to do, I tell him that I won't do it because I don't want to do it, instead of giving him a list of "good" reasons sounding as if they had come down from the Supreme Court. Interestingly enough, this rather open way of dealing with children works quite well. If you tell a child that you won't do something because you don't want to, he is very likely to accept that as a fact which he cannot change; if you ask him to stop doing something because it drives you crazy, there is a very good chance that, without further talk, he will stop, because he knows what that is like.

We are, above all, dishonest about our feelings, and it is this sense of dishonesty of feeling that makes the atmosphere of so many schools so unpleasant. The people who write books that teachers have to read say over and over again that a teacher must love all the children in a class, all of them equally. If by this they mean that a teacher must do the best he can for every child in a class, that he has an equal responsibility for every child's welfare, an equal concern for his problems, they are right. But when they talk of love they don't mean this; they mean feelings, affection, the kind of pleasure and joy that one person can get from the existence and company of another. And this is not something that can be measured out in little spoonfuls, everyone getting the same amount.

In a discussion of this in a class of teachers, I once said that I like some of the kids in my class much more than others and that, without saying which ones I liked best, I had told them so. After all, this is something that children know, whatever we tell them; it is futile to lie about it. Naturally, these teachers were horrified. "What a terrible thing to say!" one said. "I love all the children in my class exactly the same." Nonsense; a teacher who says this is lying, to herself or to others, and probably doesn't like any of the children very much. Not that there is anything wrong with that; plenty of adults don't like children, and there is no reason why they should. But the trouble is they feel they should, which makes them feel guilty, which makes them feel resentful, which in turn makes them try to work off their guilt with indulgence and their resentment with subtle cruelties—cruelties of a kind that can be seen in many classrooms. Above all, it makes them put on the phony, syrupy, sickening voice and manner, and the fake smiles and forced, bright laughter that children see so much of in school, and rightly resent and hate.

As we are not honest with them, so we won't let children be honest with us. To begin with, we require them to take part in the fiction that school is a wonderful place and that they love every minute of it. They learn early that not to like school or the teacher is *verboten,* not to be said, not even to be thought. I have known a child, otherwise healthy, happy, and wholly delightful, who at the age of five was being made sick with worry by the fact that she did not like her kindergarten teacher. Robert Heinemann worked for a number of years with remedial students whom ordinary schools were hopelessly unable to deal with. He found that what choked up and froze the minds of these children was above all else the fact that they could not express, they could hardly even acknowledge the fear, shame, rage, and hatred that school and their teachers had aroused in them. In a situation in which they were and felt free to express these feelings to themselves and others, they were able once again to begin learning. Why can't we say to children what I used to say to fifth graders who got sore at me, "The law says you have to go to school; it doesn't say you have to like it, and it doesn't say you have to like me either." This might make school more bearable for many children.

Children hear all the time, "Nice people don't say such things." They learn early in life that for unknown reasons they must not talk about a large part of what they think and feel, are most interested in, and worried about. It is a rare child who, anywhere in his growing up, meets even one older person with whom he can talk openly about what most interests him, concerns him, worries him. This is what rich people are buying

for their troubled kids when for $25 per hour they send them to psychiatrists. Here is someone to whom you can speak honestly about whatever is on your mind, without having to worry about his getting mad at you. But do we have to wait until a child is snowed under by his fears and troubles to give him this chance? And do we have to take the time of a highly trained professional to hear what, earlier in his life, that child might have told anybody who was willing to listen sympathetically and honestly? The workers in a project called Streetcorner Research, in Cambridge, Mass., have found that nothing more than the opportunity to talk openly and freely about themselves and their lives, to people who would listen without judging, and who were interested in them as human beings rather than as problems to be solved or disposed of, has totally remade the lives and personalties of a number of confirmed and seemingly hopeless juvenile delinquents. Can't we learn something from this? Can't we clear a space for honesty and openness and self-awareness in the lives of growing children? Do we have to make them wait until they are in a jam before giving them a chance to say what they think?

We cannot have real learning in school if we think it is our duty and our right to tell children what they must learn. We cannot know, at any moment, what particular bit of knowledge or understanding a child needs most, will most strengthen and best fit his model of reality. Only he can do this. He may not do it very well, but he can do it a hundred times better than we can. The most we can do is try to help, by letting him know roughly what is available and where he can look for it. Choosing what he wants to learn and what he does not is something he must do for himself.

There is one more reason, and the most important one, why we must reject the idea of school and classroom as places where, most of the time, children are doing what some adult tells them to do. The reason is that there is no way to coerce children without making them afraid, or more afraid. We must not try to fool ourselves into thinking that is not so. The would-be progressives, who until recently had great influence over most American public school education, did not recognize this

—and still do not. They thought, or at least talked and wrote as if they thought, that there were good ways and bad ways to coerce children (the bad ones mean, harsh, cruel, the good ones gentle persuasive, subtle, kindly), and that if they avoided the bad and stuck to the good they would do no harm. This was one of their greatest mistakes, and the main reason why the revolution they hoped to accomplish never took hold.

The idea of painless, non-threatening coercion is an illusion. Fear is the inseparable companion of coercion, and its inescapable consequence. If you think it your duty to make children do what you want, whether they will or not, then it follows inexorably that you must make them afraid of what will happen to them if they don't do what you want. You can do this in the old-fashioned way, openly and avowedly, with the threat of harsh words, infringement of liberty, or physical punishment. Or you can do it in the modern way, subtly, smoothly, quietly, by withholding the acceptance and approval which you and others have trained the children to depend on; or by making them feel that some retribution awaits them in the future, too vague to imagine but too implacable to escape. You can, as many skilled teachers do, learn to tap with a word, a gesture, a look, even a smile, the great reservoir of fear, shame, and guilt that today's children carry around inside them. Or you can simply let your own fears, about what will happen to you if the children don't do

what you want, reach out and infect them. Thus the children will feel more and more that life is full of dangers from which only the goodwill of adults like you can protect them, and that this goodwill is perishable and must be earned anew each day.

The alternative—I can see no other—is to have schools and classrooms in which each child in his own way can satisfy his curiosity, develop his abilities and talents, pursue his interests, and from the adults and older children around him get a glimpse of the great variety and richness of life. In short, the school should be a great smörgåsbord of intellectual, artistic, creative, and athletic activities, from which each child could take whatever he wanted, and as much as he wanted, or as little. When Anna was in the sixth grade, the year after she was in my class, I mentioned this idea to her. After describing very sketchily how such a school might be run, and what the children might do, I said, "Tell me, what do you think of it? Do you think it would work? Do you think the kids would learn anything?" She said, with utmost conviction, "Oh, yes, it would be wonderful!" She was silent for a minute or two, perhaps remembering her own generally unhappy schooling. Then she said thoughtfully, "You know, kids really like to learn; we just don't like being pushed around."

No, they don't; and we should be grateful for that. So let's stop pushing them around, and give them a chance.

25. AMERICAN SCHOOLROOMS: LEARNING THE NIGHTMARE

JULES HENRY

School is an institution for drilling children in cultural orientations. Educators have attempted to free the school from drill, but have

* From Henry, J., "American Schoolrooms: Learning the Nightmare," *Columbia University Forum*, Spring 1963, pp. 24-30.

failed because they have always chosen the most obvious "enemy" to attack. Furthermore, with every enemy destroyed, new ones are installed among the old fortifications that are the enduring contradictory maze of the culture. Educators think that when they have made arithmetic or spelling into a game; made it unnecessary for children to "sit up straight"; defined the relation between teacher and children as democratic; and introduced plants, fish, and hamsters into schoolrooms, they have settled the problem of drill. They are mistaken.

The paradox of the human condition is expressed more in education than elsewhere in human culture, because learning to learn has been and continues to be *Homo sapiens'* most formidable evolutionary task. Although it is true that mammals, as compared to birds and fishes, have to learn so much that it is difficult to say by the time we get to the chimpanzees which behavior is inborn and which is learned, the learning task has become so enormous for man that today, education, along with survival, constitutes a major preoccupation. In all the fighting over education we are simply saying that after a million years of struggling to become human, we are not yet satisfied that we have mastered the fundamental human task, learning.

Another learning problem inherent in the human condition is this: We must conserve culture while changing it, we must always be *more* sure of surviving than of adapting. Whenever a new idea appears, our first concern as *animals* must be that it does not kill us; then, and only then, can we look at it from other points of view. In general, primitive people solved this problem simply by walling their children off from new possibilities by educational methods that, largely through fear, so narrowed the perceptual sphere that nontraditional ways of viewing the world became unthinkable.

The function of education has never been to free the mind and the spirit of man, but to bind them. To the end that the mind and spirit of his children should never escape, *Homo sapiens* has wanted acquiescence, not originality, from his offspring. It is natural that this should be so, for where every man is unique there is no society, and where there is no society there can be no man. Contemporary American educators think they want creative children, yet it is an open question as to what they expect these children to create. If all through school the young were provoked to question the Ten Commandments, the

sanctity of revealed religion, the foundations of patriotism, the profit motive, the two-party system, monogamy, the laws of incest, and so on, we would have more creativity than we could handle. In teaching our children to accept fundamentals of social relationships and religious beliefs without question we follow the ancient highways of the human race.

American classrooms, like educational institutions anywhere, express the values, preoccupations, and fears found in the culture as a whole. School has no choice; it must train the children to fit the culture as it is. School can give training in skills; it cannot teach creativity. Since the creativity that *is* encouraged—as in science and mathematics, for example—will always be that which satisfies the cultural drives at the time, all the American school can do is nurture that creativity when it appears.

Creative intellect is mysterious, devious, and irritating. An intellectually creative child may fail in social studies, for example, simply because he cannot understand the stupidities he is taught to believe as "fact." He may even end up agreeing with his teachers that he is "stupid" in social studies. He will not be encouraged to play among new social systems, values, and relationships, if for no other reason than that the social studies teachers will perceive such a child as a poor student. Furthermore, such a child will simply be unable to fathom the absurdities that seem transparent *truth* to the teacher. What idiot believes in the "law of supply and demand," for example? But the children who do, tend to *become* idiots; and learning to be an idiot is part of growing up! Or, as Camus put it, learning to be *absurd*. Thus the intellectually creative child who finds it impossible to learn to think the absurd the truth, who finds it difficult to accept absurdity as a way of life, usually comes to think himself stupid.

Schools have therefore never been places for the stimulation of young minds; they are the central conserving force of the culture, and if we observe them closely they will tell us much about the cultural pattern that binds us.

Much of what I am now going to say pivots on the inordinate capacity of a human being to learn more than one thing at a time. A child writing the word "August" on the board, for example, is not only learning the word "August," but also how to hold the chalk without making it squeak, how to write clearly, how to keep going even though the class is tittering at his slowness, how to appraise the glances of the children in order to know whether he is doing it right or wrong. If a classroom can be compared to a communications system—a flow of messages between teacher (transmitter) and pupils (receivers) —it is instructive to recall another characteristic of communications systems applicable to classrooms: their inherent tendency to generate *noise*. *Noise,* in communications theory, applies to all those random fluctuations of the system that cannot be controlled, the sounds that are not part of the message. The striking thing about the child is that along with his "messages about spelling" he learns all the noise in the system also. But—and mark this well—it is *not* primarily the message (the spelling) that constitutes the most important subject matter to be learned, but the noise! The most significant cultural learnings—primarily the cultural drives—are communicated as *noise*. Let us see the system operate in some of the contemporary suburban classrooms my students and I studied over a period of six years.

It is March 17 and the children are singing songs from Ireland and her neighbors. The teacher plays on the piano, while the children sing. While some children sing, a number of them hunt in the index, find a song belonging to one of Ireland's neighbors, and raise their hands in order that they may be called on to name the next song. The singing is of that pitchless quality always heard in elementary school classrooms. The teacher sometimes sings through a song first, in her off-key, weakishly husky voice.

The usual reason for this kind of song period is that the children are "broadened" while they learn something about music and singing. But what the children in fact learn about singing is to sing like everybody else. (This phenomenon—the standard, elementary school pitchlessness of the English-speaking world—was impressive enough for D. H. Lawrence to mention it in *Lady Chatterley's Lover.* The difficulty in achieving true pitch

is so pervasive among us that missionaries carry it with them to distant jungles, teaching the natives to sing hymns off key. Hence on Sundays we would hear our Pilagá Indian friends, all of them excellent musicians in the Pilagá scale, carefully copy the missionaries by singing Anglican hymns, translated into Pilagá off key exactly as sharp or as flat as the missionaries sang.) Thus one of the first things a child with a good ear learns in elementary school is to be musically stupid; he learns to doubt or to scorn his innate musical capacities.

But possibly more important than this is the use to which teacher and pupils put the lesson in ways not related at all to singing or to Ireland and her neighbors. To the teacher this was an opportunity to let the children somehow share the social aspects of the lesson with her. The consequence was distraction from singing as the children hunted in the index, and the net result was to activate the children's drives toward competition, achievement, and dominance. In this way the song period was scarcely a lesson in singing, but rather one in extorting the maximal benefit for the Self from *any* situation.

The first lesson a child has to learn when he comes to school is that lessons are not what they seem. He must then forget this and act as if they were. This is the first step toward "school mental health"; it is also the first step in becoming absurd. The second lesson is to put the teachers' and students' criteria in place of his own. The child must learn that the proper way to sing is tunelessly and not the way he hears the music; that the proper way to paint is the way the teacher says, not the way he sees it; that the proper attitude is not pleasure, but competitive horror at the success of his classmates, and so on. And these lessons must be so internalized that he will fight his parents if they object. The early schooling process is not successful unless it has produced in the child an acquiescence in its criteria, unless the child *wants* to think the way school has taught him to think. What we see in kindergarten and the early years of school is the pathetic surrender of babies. How could it be otherwise?

Now nothing so saps self-confidence as alienation from the Self. It would follow that school, the chief agent in the process, must try to provide the children with "ego support," for culture tries to remedy the ills it creates. Hence the effort to give children recognition in our schools. Hence the conversion of the songfest into an exercise in Self-realization. That anything essential was nurtured in this way is an open question, for the kind of individuality that was recognized as the children picked titles out of the index was mechanical, without a creative dimension, and under the strict control of the teacher. In short, the school metamorphoses the child, giving it the kind of Self the school can manage, and then proceeds to minister to the Self it has made.

We can see this at work in another example:

The observer is just entering her fifth-grade classroom for the observation period. The teacher says, "Which one of you nice, polite boys would like to take [the observer's] coat and hang it up?" From the waving hands, it would seem that all would like to claim the honor. The teacher chooses one child, who takes the observer's coat. . . . The teacher conducted the arithmetic lessons mostly by asking, "Who would like to tell the answer to the next problem?" This question was followed by the usual large and agitated forest of hands, with apparently much competition to answer.

What strike us here are the precision with which the teacher was able to mobilize the potentialities in the boys for the proper social behavior, and the speed with which they responded. The large number of waving hands proves that most of the boys have already become absurd; but they have no choice. Suppose they sat there frozen?

A skilled teacher sets up many situations in such a way that *a negative attitude can be construed only as treason*. The function of questions like, "Which one of you nice, polite boys would like to take [the observer's] coat and hang it up?" is to bind the children into absurdity—to compel them to acknowledge that absurdity is existence, to acknowledge that it is better to exist absurd than not to exist at all. The reader will have observed that the question is not put, "Who *has* the answer to the next problem?" but, "Who *would like to tell*" it? What at one time in our culture was phrased as a challenge to skill

in arithmetic, becomes here an invitation to group participation. The essential issue is that *nothing is but what it is made to be by the alchemy of the system*.

In a society where competition for the basic cultural goods is a pivot of action, people cannot be taught to love one another. It thus becomes necessary for the school to teach children how to hate, and without appearing to do so, for our culture cannot tolerate the idea that babes should hate each other. How does the school accomplish this ambiguity? Obviously through fostering competition itself, as we can see in an incident from a fifth-grade arithmetic lesson.

Boris has trouble reducing 12/16 to the lowest terms, and could only get as far as 6/8. The teacher asked him quietly if that was as far as he could reduce it. She suggested he "think." Much heaving up and down and waving of hands by the other children, all frantic to correct him. Boris pretty unhappy, probably mentally paralyzed. The teacher, quiet, patient, ignores the others and concentrates with look and voice on Boris. After a minute or two, she turns to the class and says, "Well, who can tell Boris what the number is?" A forest of hands appears, and the teacher calls Peggy. Peggy says that four may be divided into the numerator and the denominator.

Boris's failure has made it possible for Peggy to succeed; his misery is the occasion for her rejoicing. This is the standard condition of the contemporary American elementary school. To a Zuñi, Hopi, or Dakota Indian, Peggy's performance would seem cruel beyond belief, for competition the wringing of success from somebody's failure, is a form of torture foreign to those noncompetitive cultures. Yet Peggy's action seems natural to us; and so it is. How else would you run our world?

Looked at from Boris's point of view, the nightmare at the blackboard was, perhaps, a lesson in controlling himself so that he would not fly shrieking from the room under enormous public pressure. Such experiences force every man reared in our culture, over and over again, night in, night out, even at the pinnacle of success, to dream not of success, but of failure. In school the external nightmare is internalized for life. Boris was not learning arithmetic only; he was learning the *essential nightmare* also. *To be successful in our culture one must learn to dream of failure.*

When we say that "culture teaches drives and values" we do not state the case quite precisely. We should say, rather, that culture (and especially the school) provides the occasions in which drives and values are *experienced in events* that strike us with *overwhelming and constant force.* To say that culture "teaches" puts the matter too mildly. Actually culture invades and infests the mind as an obsession. If it does not, it will be powerless to withstand the impact of critical differences, to fly in the face of contradiction, to so engulf the mind that the world is seen only as the culture decrees it shall be seen, to compel a person to be absurd. The central emotion in obsession is fear, and the central obsession in education is fear of failure. In school, one becomes absurd through being afraid; but paradoxically, *only by remaining absurd can one feel free from fear.*

Let us see how absurdity is reinforced: consider this spelling lesson in a fourth-grade class.

The children are to play "spelling baseball," and they have lined up to be chosen for the two teams. There is much noise, but the teacher quiets it. She has selected a boy and a girl and sent them to the front of the room as team captains to choose their teams. As the boy and girl pick the children to form their teams, each child takes a seat in orderly succession around the room. Apparently they know the game well. Now Tom, who has not yet been chosen, tries to call attention to himself in order to be chosen. Dick shifts his position to be more in the direct line of vision of the choosers, so that he may not be overlooked. He seems quite anxious. Jane, Tom, Dick, and one girl whose name the observer does not know are the last to be chosen. The teacher even has to remind the choosers that Dick and Jane have not been chosen. . . .

The teacher now gives out words for the children to spell, and they write them on the board. [Each word is a pitched ball, and each correctly spelled word is a base hit. The children move around the room from base to base as their teammates spell the words correctly.] The outs seem to increase in frequency as each side gets near the children chosen last. The children have great difficulty spelling "August." As they make mistakes, those in the seats say, "No!" The teacher says, "Man on third." As a child at the board stops and thinks, the teacher says, "There's a time limit; you can't take too long, honey." At last, after many children fail on "August" one child gets it right and returns, grinning with pleasure, to her seat. . . . The motivation level in this game seems terrific. All the children seem to watch the board, to know what's right and wrong, and seem quite keyed up. There is no lagging in moving from base to base. The child who is now writing "Thursday" stops to think after the first letter, and the children snicker. He stops after another letter. More snickers. He gets the word wrong. There are frequent signs of joy from the children when their side is right.

"Spelling baseball" is an effort to take the "weariness, the fever, and the fret" out of spelling by absurdly transforming it into a competitive game. Children are usually good competitors, though they may never become good spellers; and although they may never learn to *spell* success, they know what it *is*, how to go after it, and how it feels not have it. A competitive game is indicated when children are failing, because the drive to succeed in the *game* may carry them to victory over the subject matter. But once a spelling lesson is cast in the form of a game of baseball a great variety of *noise* enters the system; because the sounds of *baseball* (the baseball "messages") cannot but be *noise* in a system intended to communicate *spelling.* If we reflect that one could not settle a baseball game by converting it into a spelling lesson, we see that baseball is bizarrely irrelevant to spelling. If we reflect further that a child who is a poor speller might yet be a magnificent ballplayer, we are even further impressed that learning spelling through baseball is learning by absurd association.

In making spelling into a baseball game one drags into the classroom whatever associations a child may have to the impersonal sorting process of kid baseball, but there are differences between the baseball world and the "spelling baseball" world also. One's failure is paraded before the class minute upon minute, until, when the worst spellers are the only ones left, the conspicuousness of the failures has been enormously increased. Thus the *noise* from baseball is amplified by a *noise* factor specific to the classroom.

It should not be imagined that I "object" to all of this, for in the first place I am aware of the indispensable social functions of the spelling game, and in the second place, I can see that the rendering of failure conspicuous cannot but intensify the quality of the essential nightmare, and thus render an important service to the culture. Without nightmares human culture has never been possible. Without hatred competition cannot take place except in games.

The unremitting effort by the system to bring the cultural drives to a fierce pitch must ultimately turn the children against one another; and though they cannot punch one another in the nose or pull one another's hair in class, they can vent some of their hostility in carping criticism of one another's work. Carping criticism, painfully evident in almost any American classroom, is viciously destructive of the early tillage of those creative impulses we say we cherish.

Listen to a fifth-grade class: The children are taking turns reading stories they have made up. Charlie's is called *The Unknown Guest*.

"One dark, dreary night, on a hill a house stood. This house was forbidden territory for Bill and Joe, but they were going in anyway. The door creaked, squealed, slammed. A voice warned them to go home. They went upstairs. A stair cracked. They entered a room. A voice said they might as well stay and find out now; and their father came out. He laughed and they laughed, but they never forgot their adventure together."

Teacher: Are there any words that give you the mood of the story?

Lucy: He could have made the sentences a little better. . . .

Teacher: Let's come back to Lucy's comment. What about his sentences?

Gert: They were too short. [Charlie and Jeanne have a discussion about the position of the word "stood" in the first sentence.]

Teacher: Wait a minute; some people are forgetting their manners. . . .

Jeff: About the room: the boys went up the stairs and one "cracked," then they were in the room. Did they fall through the stairs, or what?

The teacher suggests Charlie make that a little clearer. . . .

Teacher: We still haven't decided about the short sentences. Perhaps they make the story more spooky and mysterious.

Gwynne: I wish he had read with more expression instead of all at one time.

Rachel: Not enough expression.

Teacher: Charlie, they want a little more expression from you. I guess we've given you enough suggestions for one time. [Charlie does not raise his head, which is bent over his desk as if studying a paper.] Charlie! I guess we've given you enough suggestions for one time, Charlie, haven't we?

If American children fail while one of their number succeeds, they carp. And why not? We must not let our own "inner Borises" befog our thinking. A competitive culture endures by tearing people down. Why blame the children for doing it?

The contemporary school is not all horrors; it has its gentler aspects as well. Nearing a conclusion, let us examine impulse release and affection as they appear in many suburban classrooms.

Impulse is the root of life, and its release in the right amount, time, and place is a primary concern of culture. Nowadays the problem of impulse release takes on a special character because of the epoch's commitment to "letting down the bars." This being the case, teachers have a task unique in the history of education: the fostering of impulse release rather than the installation of controls. Everywhere controls are breaking down, and firmness with impulse is no part of contemporary pedagogy of "the normal child." Rather, impulse release, phrased as "spontaneity," "life adjustment," "democracy," "permissiveness," and "mothering," has become a central doctrine of education. It persists despite toughminded critics from the Eastern Seaboard who concentrate on curriculum. The teachers know better; the real, the persisting, subject matter is *noise*.

How can the teacher release children's emotions without unchaining chaos? How can she permit so much *noise* and not lose the message? Were they alive, the teachers I had in P.S. 10 and P.S. 186 in New York City, who insisted on absolute silence, would say that chaos does prevail in many modern classrooms and that the message *is* lost. But lest old-fashioned readers argue that the social structure has fallen apart, I will point out what does *not* happen: The children do not fight or wrestle, run around the room, throw things, sing loudly, or whistle. The boys do not attack the girls or vice versa. Children do not run in and out of the room. They do not make the teacher's life miserable. All this occurs when the social structure *is* torn down, but in the average suburban classrooms we studied, it never quite happens. Why not? Here are some excerpts from an interview with a second-grade teacher I'll call Mrs. Olan.

> In the one-room schoolhouse in which I first taught, the children came from calm homes. There was no worry about war, and there was no TV or radio. Children of today know more about what is going on; they are better informed. So you can't hold a strict rein on them.
> Children need to enjoy school and like it. They also need their work to be done; it's not all play. You must get them to accept responsibility and to do work on their own.

To the question, "What would you say is your own particular way of keeping order in the classroom?" Mrs. Olan says:

> Well, I would say I try to get that at the beginning of the year by getting this bond of affection and a relationship between the children and me. And we do that with stories; and I play games *with* them—don't just teach them how to play. It's what you get from living together comfortably. We have "share" times. . . . These are the things that contribute toward discipline. Another thing is discipline—it took me a long time to learn it, too: I thought I was the boss, but I learned that even with a child, if you speak to him as you would to a neighbor or a friend you get a better response than if you say, "Johnny, do this or that."

Mrs. Olan has a creed: Love is the path to discipline through permissiveness; and school is a continuation of family life, in which the values of sharing and democracy lead to comfortable living and ultimately to discipline. She continues:

> With primary children the teacher is a mother during the day; they have to be able to bring their problems to you. They get love and affection at home, and I see no reason not to give it in school.

To Mrs. Olan, mother of a 21-year-old son, second-grade children are pussy-cats. When asked, "Do you think the children tend to be quieter if the teacher is affectionate?" she says:

> If a teacher has a well-modulated voice and a pleasing disposition, her children are more relaxed and quiet. Children are like kittens: If kittens have a full stomach and lie in the sun they purr. If the atmosphere is such that the children are more comfortable, they are quiet. It is comfortable living that makes the quiet child. When you are shouting at them and they're shouting back at you, it isn't comfortable living.

It is clear to the observer that Mrs. Olan is no "boss," but lodges responsibility in the children. She clarifies the matter further:

> It means a great deal to them to give them their own direction. When problems do come up in the room we talk them over and discuss what is the right thing to do when this or that happens. Usually you get pretty good answers. They are a lot harder on themselves than I would be; so if any punishment comes along like not going to an assembly you have group pressure.

As the interviewer was leaving, Mrs. Olan remarked, "My children don't rate as high [on achievement tests] as other children. I don't push, and that's because I believe in comfortable living." *Noise* has indeed become subject matter.

In such classrooms the contemporary training for impulse release and fun is clear. There the children are not in uniform, but in the jerkins and gossamer of *The Midsummer Night's Dream;* it is a sweet drilling without pain. Since impulse and release and fun are a major requirement of the classroom, and since they must be contained within the four walls, the instrument of containment can only be affection. The teacher must therefore become a parent, for it is a parent above all who deals with the impulses of the child.

It is hard for us to see, since we consider most people inherently replaceable, that there is anything remarkable in a parent-figure like a teacher showering the symbols of affection on a child for a year and then letting him walk out of her life. However, this is almost unheard of outside the stream of Western civilization; and even in the West it is not common. As a matter of fact, the existence of *children* willing to accept such demonstrations is in itself an interesting phenomenon, based probably on the obsolescence of the two-parent family. (Today our children *do not have enough parents,* because parents are unable to do all that has to be done *by* parents nowadays.) The fact that a teacher can be demonstrative without inflicting deep wounds on *herself* implies a character structure having strong brakes on involvement. Her expressions of tenderness, then, must imply "so far and no farther"; and over the years, children must come to recognize this. If this were not so, children would have to be dragged shrieking from grade to grade and teachers would flee teaching, for the mutual attachment would be so deep that its annual severing would be too much for either to bear. And so this noise, too, teaches two lessons important to today's culture. From regular replacement-in-affection children learn that the affection-giving figure, the teacher, is replaceable also, and so they are drilled in uninvolvement. Meanwhile, they learn that the symbols of affectivity can be used ambiguously, and that they are not binding—that they can be scattered upon the world without commitment.

Again, the reader should not imagine that I am "against" affectionate classrooms. They are a necessary adjunct to contemporary childhood and to the socialization of parenthood (the "three-parent family") at this stage of our culture. Meanwhile, the dialectic of culture suggests that there is some probability that when love like this enters by the door, learning leaves by the transom.

What, then, is the central issue? The central issue is *love of knowledge* for its own sake, not as the creature of drive, exploited largely for survival and for prestige. Creative cultures have loved the "beautiful person"— meditative, intellectual, and exalted. As for the individual, the history of great civilizations reveals little except that creativity has had an obstinate way of emerging only in a few, and that it has never appeared in the mass of the people. Loving the beautiful person more, we may alter this.

The contemporary school is a place where children are drilled in very general cultural orientations, and where subject matter becomes to a very considerable extent the instrument for instilling them. Because school deals with masses of children, it can manage only by reducing children all to a common definition. Naturally that definition is determined by the cultural pre-occupations and so school creates the *essential nightmare* that drives people away from something (in our case, failure) and toward something (success). Today our children, instead of loving knowledge, become embroiled in the nightmare.

Chapter V

PERSONALITY FACTORS AND SCHOOL ACHIEVEMENT

In order to attain a full, three-dimensional psychological picture of the student, we are ultimately confronted with the rather thorny concept of personality. Though almost everyone feels a kind of instinctive understanding of personality, most people seem hard-pressed when attempting to describe it. To the layman personality is a simple, common-sense term which is usually used to describe social desirability and personal appeal. The difference between an individual who "has" personality and one who is not so endowed, is almost always a difference in personal magnetism or even extraversion.

Technically, however, things are not that simple, nor should they be. People do not have more or less personality than others, but they do have different personalities. Psychologists have many differing views as to what the precise nature of personality is, but they all reject the simplistic "personal-appeal" definition. Among psychologists the number of different viewpoints regarding personality may even exceed the many positions regarding the nature of learning itself, and yet, to his eternal glory, some attempt at consensus has been formulated by Gordon W. Allport. Using a kind of factor-analytic approach, Allport has sorted, sifted, and finally gleaned from a whole host of differing conceptual frameworks, a working definition that is satisfactory to most psychologists. Though leaning toward the humanistic tradition, Allport extracts the "meat" from most of the diverse positions when he says, "Personality is the dynamic organization within the individual of those psychophysical systems that determine his characteristic behavior and thought." Here we see a description of personality in the context of patterned individuality, a concept which sees personality as dynamic yet stable, capable of change and growth, yet internally coherent. One's personality can change, and yet the basic organization is consistent enough for one's behavior to be recognized and to some extent predicted by a close friend, loved one, or teacher.

Although the above-cited Allport definition of personality gives us a working conceptual model, it must be remembered that this definition was the result of a painstaking analysis of many diverse views. Other than the straight physical-type personality theories, such as those of Sheldon and Kretschmer which stress the strong association between one's physique and one's temperament, most personality theorists owe some debt to Sigmund Freud and his psychoanalytic theory. With some exposure to the Freudian position as a background, the student will find the readings in this area more meaningful, if only from the point of view of the basic terminology.

Freud analyzed personality at two levels, the structural and the dynamic. At the structural level, Freud examined the basic building blocks of personality, much as a space scientist might examine the component parts of an Atlas missile, with its electrical connections and intricate series of valves, etc. At this level, Freud saw human personality as composed of three basic elements, the id, the ego, and the superego.

The Id. This is the part of the personality, inborn and largely unconscious, which is composed of man's most primitive and animal-like instincts. The basic physiological drives reside in the id, and at that level are not constrained by reality or morality. The newborn baby is all id, and is therefore a rather savage bundle of uncontrolled impulses.

The Ego. The second part of the personality, the ego, develops, at least in embryonic form, during the child's first year of life. The ego is that part of personality which is in contact with reality, which allows the child to separate self from non-self. As the child matures the ego becomes stronger and allows the child to tolerate some frustration, delay certain immediate pleasures, and avoid painful situations. An adult whose "ego is strong" is more reality oriented and more self-disciplined than one whose ego is weak.

The Superego. The third and the last of the personality structures, developed mostly during toilet training, is called the superego and is analogous to the "still, small voice of conscience." The superego is the child's internalization of inhibitory commands, such as "naughty," "mustn't," "don't," and "dirty." The superego is the child's introjection of cultural norms as mediated by the parents, and a later failure to heed the constraining voice of the superego may result in severe feelings of guilt and depression.

These, then, are the three components which form the structural aspect of personality. Freud also viewed personality from the dynamic standpoint. The previously mentioned space scientist looks not just at the missile's wiring and valves, but also at its driving force or thrust. Freud labeled the driving force, or dynamic aspect of personality, the libido. The libido is the total amount of personality energy that impels the individual to act, especially to act in the direction of pleasure. The libido is often focused on certain people or things, or it can, as seen in Chapter I, be blocked or "fixated" in various erogenous zones of the body.

Looking now at personality development, both structural and dynamic, the fundamental Freudian premise is that the mature personality evolves out of conflict. Virtually no personality theorist would disagree with this premise, and coupled with the emphasis on motivation, conscious and especially unconscious, we find the impact of the Freudian position as truly enormous.

Considering the significance of personality variables on human behavior, it is little wonder that students of educational psychology could never fully appreciate the concepts of learning or academic achievement without regard to personality. Teachers have long recognized that these personality or non-intellectual factors are critical in determining the achievement of their students. Even if we were to develop an absolutely reliable and valid measure of intelligence, no accurate prediction of achievement could be made without consideration of the non-intellectual variables. Implicit in the entire literature on under- and over-achievement is the assumption that personality and emotional variables play a crucial if not the crucial role in academic success. We have probably all known the individual who seems able to learn with little or no effort and yet, who, pathetically, flunks more courses than he passes. It is more than just a glib cliche that some students seem to be desperately, though probably unwittingly, trying not to achieve academically. The student's veiled little smile when his parents are presented with a report card filled with low grades is obvious evidence of a tragically self-defeating yet concerted effort at "striking back." "Show this around the country club," is the eloquent message to many a coercive parent.

Although we have stressed in chapter I the extreme importance of early experience on the developing child, the growth process of course does not cease abruptly at age five or six. From the very first day the child, especially the middle-class child, enters the school situation society exerts enormous pressures on him to succeed academically. The child often sees the entire adult world as though joined in an enormous conspiracy to urge, cajole, threaten him into believing that scholastic success is the single most important thing in the world. First grade teachers, and certainly parents of first graders, have been known to admonish a youngster who might be having some difficulty following the plot of a "See Puff jump" epic with the awesome threat, "You'll never get into college!" And the pressures increase geometrically as the child progresses on into high school. Many high school guidance counselors seem to believe their very existence depends on what percentage of their senior class is accepted for college.

One counselor proudly boasted that all but three of his graduating seniors had been placed in college, and two of those three would have gone to college but because of emotional problems they had been institutionalized. "But as soon as they get out, I'll get them into college," he proclaimed!

The pressures on the child's developing personality also come from many areas other than the scholastic. Every child is faced with the conflict of dependence versus independence, a conflict which seems to reach its crisis stage during adolescence. This conflict is due to the child's own desire to remain dependent, to have someone make decisions for him, to have a shoulder to cry on, and his equally strong desire to be a free, independent, self-reliant individual. From birth on the child is engaged in the long and painful process of slowly giving up dependence in order to attain independence, and, even as an adult, there must be some compromise and balance between these two needs.

Another source of frustration is in the area of sex. As the child advances through puberty he is confronted with the dilemma of becoming aware of his own strong sexual needs and also society's demand that these needs not be satisfied. Our society does not really accept any form of pre-marital sexual release. The dilemma is even more apparent in today's society, for with the advancing technology and need for more and more education to compete successfully, marriage, and thus guilt-free sexual expression, is further delayed.

Aggression is still another source of pressure and anxiety. We all have hostile tendencies, urges to fight back when our goals are blocked or our self esteem is threatened, and yet again society allows for overt aggression only in very prescribed situations. Although it's acceptable in football, boxing, and warfare, physical aggression can result in very serious legal consequences when practiced in day to day interaction.

Finally, the child faces the cultural paradox of achievement versus the Judeo-Christian ethic of "Love thy neighbor." Our children are urged to compete, to win, to succeed, and yet they are told that this should not be a "dog eat dog" world, that they should also be "good Samaritans."

Under these and many more assorted pressures individuals react differently. Some children, and adults too, seem to thrive in time of crisis, while others seem simply to fold up and develop a whole series of psychological symptoms. As Gordon Allport has said, "The same fire that melts the butter hardens the egg."

Teachers must be made aware that the manifestation of emotional symptoms may not always be obvious. The teacher usually devotes much time and attention to the rebellious, aggressive child. Thus by "acting out" his problems a child with this type of personality often gets the recognition he seems to need. However, a more serious symptom, withdrawal, often escapes the attention of the teacher and parent too. The child who withdraws, perhaps into a make-believe world of fantasy, does not upset the school routine, and, therefore, does not seem to present a problem. Some teachers actually wish they had more withdrawn children, more "little angels," in their classes. This syndrome, however, can be serious indeed, and the withdrawn child, by not getting the attention and recognition he needs, enters a vicious circle in which further withdrawal and perhaps a complete loss of contact with reality is the result.

The study of personality, especially as it relates to academic achievement, is indeed fascinating. As man better comes to understand himself, master himself, free himself, all of mankind will be the benefactor. To paraphrase L. K. Frank, the fundamental needs of the individual personality are precisely the fundamental needs of society. Ideally the school and the learning tasks in school should be organized in such a way as to promote the growth of personal competence and self mastery. An important goal then of the school should be to foster, nurture, and facilitate personality growth in a learning context, to counteract debilitating effects and to enhance the realization of human potential.

AN OVERVIEW OF THE READINGS FOR THIS CHAPTER

Gordon Allport leads off with a scholarly, yet highly readable, account (Selection 26) of the concept of personality, its historical roots, and its present status. Two divergent views on personality, essentialistic and positivistic, are outlined. The essentialist position, taken by Allport himself, sees personality as basically an internal structure. Several representative examples of essentialist definitions are discussed, and it should be noted that Allport's own definition will be comprised of what he considers to be the "meat" of these positions. Allport's task is to sift the theoretical wheat from the chaff.

Opposed to this, the positivists take the view that the only real scientific data in psychology comes from the direct observation of behavior, with no inferences allowed. If it can't be pointed at, it doesn't exist, and thus, as Allport says, personality "evaporates in a mist of method."

Allport then presents his own definition, with each of the separate terms defined with precision. Implied throughout the discussion is the fact that personality has independence, is something "out there" which exists as a separate entity independent of the methods used to measure it.

Erik H. Erikson next (in Selection 27) presents his life-cycle theory of personality development. The emphasis here is on the normal and healthy personality, and Erikson provides the guide-lines which designate the approximate period of life at which each of the characteristics should ideally occur. The mature personality, above all, should have a sense of identity, and although the climax of this search occurs during adolescence, the truly healthy personality almost instinctively knows the answer to the question, "Who am I?" He need not brag about the fact, nor must he consciously even have to pose the question. Perhaps it's one of those undefinable bits of self knowledge, and if you really have to ask, you'll never get to know.

Erikson sees life as a developmental process progressing through eight stages, each stage typifying a particular crisis. Through the resolution of these conflicts, the healthy personality emerges. Yet the conflicts are never permanently resolved, for the healthy personality must constantly overcome them, in the same way that the body's metabolism continuously must "resist decay." Even during adulthood, the individual may have to reconquer an old fear based on a mistrust developed during early infancy.

Erikson's point, however, is that these stages are sequential, and when a healthy adjustment to a particular crisis does not occur, it is even more difficult to resolve a similar crisis during a later stage.

After reading the first two selections, the student of educational psychology, and/or the prospective teacher, may feel that although the material is interesting, "what has this got to do with me? I'm not going to be a psychiatrist." The question is legitimate, yet as a teacher, as a member of one of the "helping professions," the teacher's ability to recognize, often in an early stage, the possible beginnings of neurotic or psychotic behavior disorders is critical. In "The Lonely Road of Unreality" (Selection 28), Evelyn Banning in one of the really classic statements in the literature points out the *specific ways* by which the teacher can aid in the task of diagnosing the pre-psychotic child.

The teacher, of course, is in an especially advantageous position in this regard, for outside of the parents, perhaps nobody else has the unique opportunity of being able to observe the child for so many hours and in such a variety of situations. The teacher can observe how the child relates to adults, to the peer group, to frustration, and can detect when these reactions seem at all deviant. Banning is especially insistent that the teacher should be aware that the real danger sign, the most significant warning, is not the overtly aggressive response, but the quiet withdrawal. Seclusiveness, daydreaming, and indifference are the first signs of a possible break with reality, and it does *not* take a trained psychiatrist to detect these signs. This is not to suggest that teachers become professional psychologists, but, like it or not, we do "psychologize" whenever we make inferences about how or why people behave as they do.

In another classic statement (Selection 29), Glen Heathers pursues the question, important in any discussion of personality, of dependence and independence as critical variables in the adjustment process. Before reading this selection, the student should become familiar with Gordon Allport's theory of motivation. The theory is called *functional autonomy*, and briefly stated, Allport indicated that a means to an end can become an end in itself. That is, that certain motives, such as needs for money, which were originally instrumental in achieving the goals of food, clothing, shelter, etc., can begin to function autonomously or independently of their original goals. A man who was once saving money in order to buy food or clothing, can have the means become an end in itself, and begin to save money for the sheer joy of saving the money. This theory implies that adult motivation can be, in a sense, a-historical (or no longer historically connected with the motivated origins formed during childhood).

Heathers makes the point that independence and dependence are learned, and that this learning process results in two forms, instrumental dependence-independence and emotional dependence-independence. For example, instrumental dependence is learned when a child seeks the help of another and depends on this other for help in reaching certain outside goals. Emotional dependence, however, is the result of having the other *individual's response,* such as reassurance, as the goal itself, without regard to any other outside goals. Thus, instrumental dependence precedes the development of emotional dependence, though once formed the emotional dependence can function independently or autonomously.

Since every motive must have both needs and goals, Heathers also examines the needs which are basic to the learning of emotional dependence. These needs are for reassurance, affection, and approval, and, thus, emotional dependence is more likely to occur when a child is in high-anxiety-provoking situations or situations of constant conflict.

The overly dependent child, however, can be taught to be more self-reliant. Since dependence, both instrumental and emotional, is learned, so too is independence; and Heathers offers some very helpful suggestions for both parents and teachers in helping a child to overcome a condition of extreme dependency.

The next article (Selection 30), by Hummel and Sprinthall, presents actual research evidence regarding one of education's most perplexing problems, underachievement. The problem of the underachieving child is one of the more tragic dilemmas in education, for when a student has the potential to learn and profit from the educational experience, it is indeed frustrating to witness, as every teacher has, the wasted talent of the underachiever. It is analogous to a "G.T." racing car with a high horsepower engine not being able to go more than 20 miles per hour because of some mechanical failure that prevents the driver from being able to depress the accelerator.

The problem of the underachiever illustrates par excellence the importance of the personality, or non-intellectual variables, as factors in academic success. It was Hummel and Sprinthall's problem to identify some of the personality variables which are associated with underachieving. The student should keep in mind that interests, attitudes, and values are three of the key factors in the overall concept of personality.

The authors hypothesize that academic achievement, holding intelligence constant, is a function of the student's ego strength, that is the student's reality orientation. The underachiever, therefore, probably possesses a weak ego, and would be unwilling to postpone pleasure, would be easily distracted, and be generally less able to set about his tasks with an organized approach. The underachiever, in short, would be less able to control his own basic impulses.

This is not to suggest, however, that high academic performance is the sole criterion of ego strength. The content of the ego-strength variables (a planning orientation, an ability to delay immediate gratification, an ability to examine alternatives) all point to a general competence orientation. Ego-strong individuals may indeed possess a generalized effectiveness in many areas.

In the final article (Selection 31), Paul Torrance discusses the extremely important topic, creativity. Although society depends for its survival on the amount and quality of its creative imagination, the academic establishment too often stifles and even totally prevents the flowering of the creative mind. One of the problems rests in the fact that our most creative students are not usually considered our "best" students in the traditional sense. The highly creative student is seen as less desirable by most teachers, and in some classrooms the interaction between teacher and creative student is little less than open warfare. Compounding the difficulty is that the creative student is also somewhat estranged from his peer group. He is less able to form friendships, is more apt to be self-absorbed, and is often seen as having silly and wild ideas.

Torrance has developed an intriguing array of creativity tests and has been quite successful in obtaining quantifiable measures. One of the most significant findings from these tests is that there is no one-to-one correspondence between intelligence and creativity. Following the lead of Getzels and Jackson (1958), Torrance noted the correlations between creativity and intelligence for students from the first to the sixth grade. Torrance confirms the Getzels and Jackson finding that although there is an association between creativity and intelligence at the lower and middle IQ range, above an IQ score of roughly 120 this correlation evaporates to near zero. Apparently it does take a certain intellectual level before high creativity can be displayed independently of IQ.

In the total context of personality development, Torrance sees creativity as extremely important. The forced suppression of the creative drive can cause emotional problems and may even, as Erich Fromm has also suggested, lead to a personality breakdown. Rather than pointing to the suppression of animal-like instincts as the root of personality problems, as Freud did, Torrance is isolating a very human characteristic, creative expression, as equally important to personal adjustment.

26. PERSONALITY, CHARACTER, AND TEMPERAMENT *

GORDON W. ALLPORT

ORIGINS OF THE TERM "PERSONALITY"

The word *personality* and its root *person* have long held fascination for students of language. Max Müller, for example, becomes enthusiastic over their abstractness and wide serviceability:

Let us take such a word as *person*. Nothing could be more abstract. It is neither male nor female, neither young nor old. As a noun it is hardly more than what *to be* is as a verb. In French it may even come to mean nobody. For if we ask our concièrge at Paris whether anybody has called us during our absence, he will reply, "Personne, monsieur," which means, "Not a soul, sir."

But this word *persona* has rolled along with wonderful bounds, striking right and left, suggesting new thoughts, stirring up clouds of controversy, and occupying to the present day a prominent place in all discussions on theology and philosophy, though a few only of those who use it know how it came to be there.[1]

The terms *personality* in English, *personnalité* in French, and *Persönlichkeit* in German closely resemble the *personalitas* of medieval Latin. In classical Latin *persona* alone was used. All scholars agree that this word originally meant *mask*. (This fact can give some comfort to those who prefer to define personality in terms of external effect. Appearance, not inner organization, receives

the emphasis.) But *persona*, even in ancient times, came to mean other things, including the player behind the mask, i.e., his true assemblage of inner and personal qualities. It also came to mean an important person (whence *personage, parson*). The term was also used to designate the three persons of the Trinity. And whether these *personae* were three masks of one God or three co-equal persons became a theological dispute of long duration. Perhaps the most famous definition of *persona* was given by Boethius in the sixth century: *Persona est substantia individua rationalis naturae*—a person is an individual substance of a rational nature.

And so we see that the term bounded along even in classical Latin with various meanings. Some of them anticipated the "external effect" definitions of the present day, some of them the "internal structure" definitions.

INTERNAL STRUCTURE

Most philosophers and psychologists (except for the modern positivists whom we shall soon consider) prefer to define personality as an objective entity, as something that is "really there." They grant that the person is open to the world around him, is affected by it and affects it at every step. Yet a personality has its own life-history and its own existence; it is not to be confused with society nor with the perceptions that other people have of it. Thus William Stern, who was both a philosopher and a psychologist speaks of personality as a "multiform dynamic unity." He adds that no one ever fully achieves a perfect unity but always has this as his aim.[2]

* From Chapter Two from *Pattern and Growth in Personality* by Gordon W. Allport. Copyright 1937, © 1961 by Holt, Rinehart and Winston, Inc. Copyright © 1965 by Gordon W. Allport. Reprinted by permission of Holt, Rinehart and Winston, Inc.

[1] F. M. Müller, *Biographies of words* (New York: Longmans, Green, 1888), p. 32.

[2] W. Stern, *Die menschliche Persönlichkeit* (Leipzig: Barth, 1923), pp. 4, 20.

Some writers add a note of "value" to this type of definition. Personality is something to be prized. Thus Goethe speaks of personality as the one thing in the world that has "supreme value." And Kant's moral philosophy is based on the same conviction. Everything in life can be used by men as a means to some end—save only personality. No one may exploit another. The integrity of personality must be forever respected. Judeo-Christian ethics initiated this line of thought.

Although Western psychologists likewise customarily place high value on the integrity of personality (because it is, after all, the creed of democracy), their definitions are less exalted. They drop out any attempt at evaluation, and give a simple descriptive statement. A typical example is the following. Personality is

> the sum-total of all the biological innate dispositions, impulses, tendencies, appetites, and instincts of the individual, and the acquired dispositions and tendencies—acquired by experience.[3]

Although this definition regards personality as an accessible datum for study, it fails to stress the integration of structure of the many listed component parts. It is representative of what we may call omnibus or "ragbag" definitions of personality. More "structural" is the following definition:

> Personality is the entire mental organization of a human being at any stage of his development. It embraces every phase of human character: intellect, temperament, skill, morality, and every attitude that has been built up in the course of one's life.[4]

Also the following:

> Personality is the organized aggregate of psychological processes and states pertaining to the individual.[5]

Some definitions stress the subjective cognitive factor that makes for internal organization, saying that personality is

a unified scheme of experience, an organization of values that are consistent with one another.[6]

My own definition will likewise be in terms of internal structure. (Some writers would call definitions of this type "essentialist.") But first we must examine a contrasting approach.

THE POSITIVIST VIEW

Some contemporary psychologists object strenuously to essentialist definitions. They argue that "internal structure" is inaccessible to science. We cannot know the "multiform dynamic unity" that is "really there." Inner structure, if it exists at all simply cannot be studied directly.

What we know about personality is merely our "operations." If we administer a personality test and obtain such and such a score—these are our operations, i.e., our method. From the positivist point of view, therefore, inner personality is a myth "a mere construct tied together by a proper name." The best we can do is to make guesses about it—"conceptualize" it. The conceptualization must not go beyond the scientific methods we use.

An example of such an operational definition is the following. Personality is

> the most adequate conceptualization of a person's behavior in all its detail that the scientist can give at a moment of time.[7]

Here we note a resemblance to "external effect" definitions. Personality is not what one has, but is someone else's perception, in this case, the scientist's. In other words, personality is a "construct," something thought about but not actually existing "out there."

To press the point still further there are psychologists who say we should never employ the concept of personality at all. If we knew enough about the "stimulus" and the "response" (so-called S-R psychology) we would not have to bother our heads with any "inter-

[3] M. Prince, *the unconscious* (2d ed., rev.; New York: Macmillan, 1924), p. 532.
[4] H. C. Warren and L. Carmichael, *Elements of human psychology* (Rev. ed.; Boston: Houghton Mifflin, 1930), p. 333.
[5] R. Linton, *The cultural background of personality* (New York: Appleton-Century-Crofts, 1945), p. 84.

[6] P. Lecky, *Self-consistency: a theory of personality* (New York: Island, 1945), p. 90.
[7] D. McClelland, *Personality* (New York: Sloane, 1951), p. 69. The problem under discussion is considered by C. S. Hall and G. Lindzey, *Theories of personality* (New York: Wiley, 1954), p. 9.

vening variable" like personality. This is the view of extreme positivistic behaviorism. Only outer, visible manipulable operations are tolerated. Personality as such evaporates in a mist of method.

Although such is the goal of some psychologists, it is questionable whether they are following the lead of the elder sciences. Does an astronomer who studies Arcturus think of the star as a construct tied together by a name? Hardly; to him it is a celestial body, truly existing, and possessing a composition and structure that he will try scientifically to comprehend. When a biologist dissects a plant he does not believe that the plant's structure and physiology reside only in his manipulations.

Personality is even more difficult to study than stars or plants, but the situation is the same. No psychologist and no layman ever fully understands any single personality, not even his own, but this fact does not negate the existence of the personality. Like the astronomer or the biologist we *try* to comprehend an existent fact of nature. We should adapt our methods so far as we can to the object, and not define the object in terms of our faulty methods.

A DEFINITION FOR THIS BOOK

There is, of course, no such thing as a correct or incorrect definition. Terms can only be defined in ways that are useful for a given purpose. For the purposes of the present volume we require a definition of personality that is "essentialist." We shall treat personality as a unit "out there," possessing internal structure in its own right. All phrasings are full of pitfalls, but for better or for worse our definition follows:

PERSONALITY IS THE DYNAMIC ORGANIZATION WITHIN THE INDIVIDUAL OF THOSE PSYCHOPHYSICAL SYSTEMS THAT DETERMINE HIS CHARACTERISTIC BEHAVIOR AND THOUGHT

We may now examine briefly the key concepts in this definition:

DYNAMIC ORGANIZATION. We have seen that omnibus or ragbag definitions are not adequate. The central problem of psychology is mental organization (the forming of patterns or hierarchies of ideas and habits that dynamically direct activity). Integration and other organizational processes are necessary to account for the development and structure of personality. Hence "organization" must appear in the definition. The term implies also the reciprocal process of *disorganization,* especially in those abnormal personalities that are marked by progressive disintegration.

PSYCHOPHYSICAL. This term reminds us that personality is neither exclusively mental nor exclusively neural (physical). Its organization entails the functioning of both "mind" and "body" in some inextricable unity.

SYSTEMS. A system (any system) is a complex of elements in mutual interaction. A habit is a system, so too a sentiment, a trait, a concept, a style of behaving. These systems are latent in the organism even when not active. Systems are our "potential for activity." [8]

DETERMINE. Personality *is* something and *does* something. The latent psychophysical systems, when called into action, either motivate or direct specific activity and thought. All the systems that comprise personality are to be regarded as *determining tendencies.* They exert a directive influence upon all the adjustive and expressive acts by which the personality comes to be known.

CHARACTERISTIC. All behavior and thought are characteristic of the person, and . . . they are unique to him. Even the acts and concepts that we apparently "share" with others are at bottom individual and idiomatic. It is true that some acts and concepts are more idiosyncratic than others, but none can be found that lacks the personal flavor. In a sense, therefore, it is redundant to employ the term *characteristic* in our definition. Yet redundancy is not necessarily a bad thing; it helps to drive a point home.

BEHAVIOR AND THOUGHT. These two terms are a blanket to designate anything what-

[8] R. R. Sears defines personality as "the potential for activity" in A theoretical framework for personality and social behavior, *Amer. Psychologist,* 1951, 6, 476–483. The aphorism has much to commend it. But its weakness lies in its failure to admit the necessary criterion of organization. A neurone has a potential for activity, but we cannot consider such a structure in isolation as having personality.

soever an individual may do. Chiefly what he does is to adjust to his environment. But it would be unwise to define personality only in terms of adjustment. We not only adjust to our environment but we reflect on it. Also, we strive to master it, and sometimes succeed. Behavior and thought, therefore, make both for survival and for growth. They are modes of adjustment and outreach elicited by the environmental situation we are in, always selected and directed by the psychophysical systems that comprise our personality.

The question may be asked whether, by this definition, animals have personality. The answer is a guarded "Yes." Animals no doubt have rudimentary forms of inherited and learned psychophysical systems that lead to characteristic (unique) activity. (We know nothing about their thought.) But this concession does not carry us very far. The psychophysical individuality of lower animals is exceedingly primitive and cannot serve as a helpful prototype of human personality. We venture to assert that the difference between any two species of subhuman vertebrates is not as great as the difference between any one human being and another. The enormous complexity of the human brain, in contrast to the simpler brains of other vertebrates, would seem to warrant this assertion.

A PHILOSOPHICAL OBJECTION

One term in our definition has as yet received no comment—the term *individual*. Some philosophers would say that we commit the unpardonable sin of begging the whole question. Who is this "individual" in whom personality resides? Are we not secretly admitting an organizer—a "self?" Do we not have on our hands an unexplained entity that somehow creates a unity of personality?

This objection comes especially from personalistic philosophers who feel that some continuing, unified agent is implied (or needed) by all definitions of personality. One such philosopher, Bertocci, would modify our definition as follows:

A self's personality is that self's dynamic organization of its own unique psycho-

physical wants and abilities which renders adjustments to its environment unique.[9]

That there is a pressing problem of relating *self* to *personality* we hasten to admit. . . . But for the moment it is enough to say that the objection misrepresents our use of the term *individual*. When we say that the dynamic organization lies within the individual we mean merely that it lies within the organism, i.e., "within the skin." It is our way of denying that personality is merely a matter of "external effect."

As for the concept of *self*, we see no need to include it in our definition. One's self is surely an important (no doubt the most important) psychophysical system within personality, as we shall later show. For the time being, however, the problem need not detain us.

CHARACTER

No less fascinating than the term *personality* is the term *character*. The two are often used interchangeably, although the first is of Latin derivation, the second of Greek χαραχτήρ means engraving. It is the mark of a man— his pattern of traits or his life-style. The most famous user of the term in ancient Greece was Theophrastus, a pupil of Aristotle. He wrote many perceptive character sketches, of which thirty survive. . . .

Today, as we have said, the two terms are often used synonymously. European psychologists, however, seem to have a preference for *character*, while American psychologists favor *personality*. There is an interesting reason for the difference. *Persona* originally meant mask; χαραχτήρ, engraving. The former term suggests appearance, visible behavior, surface quality; the latter suggests deep (perhaps inborn), fixed, and basic structure. Now American psychology has a preference for environmentalism; its behavioristic leaning leads it to stress outer movement, visible action. European psychology, on the other hand, tends to stress what is inborn in the nature of man, what is deeply etched and relatively unchanging. Freud, for example, speaks often of

[9] P. A. Bertocci, Personality. In P. L. Harriman (Ed.), *Encyclopedia of psychology* (New York: Philosophical Library, 1946), p. 458.

character-structure but seldom of personality. In Europe the term *characterology* is commonly used, but seldom in America. American psychologists have produced a great many books entitled *Personality* but few entitled *Character*. Thus the ancient difference in flavor of the two terms seems to account for present-day regional preferences.[10]

The term *character* has acquired a special connotation beyond its original meaning of engraving. When we say a man is of "good character" we are referring to his moral excellence. (If we say he has a "good personality" we mean merely that he is socially effective—the popular usage we discussed early in this chapter.) Thus whenever we speak of character we are likely to imply a moral standard and make a judgment of value. This complication worries those psychologists who wish to keep the actual structure and functioning of personality free from judgments of moral acceptability. It is largely for this reason that the present book favors the term *personality*. (The astute reader may say, "Your emphasis on internal structure corresponds well to what the ancient Greeks meant by character." And so it does, but it is the later accretions of value-judgment that make us hesitate to use it.)

Now one may, of course, make a judgment of value concerning a personality as a whole, or concerning any part of a personality: "He is a noble fellow." "She has many endearing qualities." In both cases we are saying that the person in question has traits which, when viewed by some outside social or moral standards, are desirable. The raw psychological fact is that the person's qualities are simply what they are. Some observers (and some cultures) may find them noble and endearing; others may not. For this reason—and to be consistent with our own definition—we prefer to define *character* as *personality evaluated;* and *personality,* if you will, as *character devaluated.*

The term *characteristic* is a bird of another feather. We have employed it in our defini-

tion of personality, for fortunately it has escaped the value-aura of the parent word. It has no reference to moral judgment. Since it stands close to the original meaning of character we shall find it useful. It will serve to cover habits, traits, attitudes, and interests—any graven mark of individuality. It is a curious fact that "characteristic" should have kept its primitive meaning, whereas its root-form gathered much ethical moss.

Before we leave the matter we should refer to one additional usage of the term *character.* *Some* psychologists regard it as a special part of personality. Thus one defines it as "the degree of ethically effective organization of all the forces of the individual." Another as "an enduring psychophysical disposition to inhibit impulses in accordance with a regulative principle." A certain amount of research has been published under the title *Studies in Character* or *Dimensions of Character.*[11] Such reports deal with investigations of children's honesty, self-control, thoughtfulness of others, religious loyalty.

Now the fact that a child or an adult has moral ideals, conscience, and religious beliefs is very important for a study of his personality, since they are features of his internal structure. It is also important to know whether a person has a "disposition to inhibit impulses in accordance with a regulative principle." But all these trends are within the *personality*. The fact that they are perceived and judged favorably does not alter the case. And so we prefer not to consider character as some special region of the personality. We can stand on our simple definition of character as *personality evaluated*. Ethical theory is an important branch of philosophy, but it should not be confused with the psychology of personality.

---

[10] For a fuller discussion of the differences, see G. W. Allport, European and American theories of personality. In H. P. David and H. von Bracken (Eds.), *Perspectives in personality theory* (New York: Basic Books, 1957), Chap. I.

[11] The first definition cited from W. S. Taylor, Character and abnormal psychology, *J. abnorm. soc. Psychol.*, 1926, 21, 86. The second is from A. A. Roback, *The psychology of character* (New York: Harcourt, Brace, 1927), p. 450. The series of *Studies in Character* are summarized in H. Hartshorne, M. A. May, and F. K. Shuttleworth, *Studies in the organization of character* (New York: Macmillan, 1930). See also E. M. Ligon, *Dimensions of character* (New York: Macmillan, 1956).

TEMPERAMENT

From ancient times down to the present comes the doctrine that a person's temperament is determined largely by the "humors" (glandular secretions) of the body. The term *temperament* came into English in the Middle Ages along with the doctrine of the four humors. It meant then, and still means, a "constitution or habit of mind, especially depending upon or connected with physical constitutional psychology."

Temperament, like *intelligence* and *physique*, might be said to designate a class of "raw material" from which personality is fashioned. All three factors lean heavily upon gene-determination, and are therefore the aspects of personality that are most dependent on heredity. Temperament refers to the chemical climate or "internal weather" in which personality evolves. The more anchored a disposition is in native constitutional soil the more likely it is to be spoken of as temperament. "Her native temperament is gay." "He has a slow and sluggish temperament."

A few authors, particularly in Great Britain, sometimes use the term as equivalent to personality—as when they say "temperament tests" rather than "tests of personality." But this usage is exceptional and decreasing. And some authors who are writing on the limited topic of temperament mistakenly use broader terms, as in the following book titles: *Glands regulating personality*, *Physique and character*, *Biological foundations of personality*. In all these cases "temperament" would fit the subject matter of the book more precisely.

In order to make needed advances in the study of temperament we require much more research in human genetics, biochemistry, neurology, endocrinology, and physical anthropology. We know that personality is largely conditioned by temperament, but we do not know the precise sources of temperament itself.

What does temperament include? No clear answer is possible. When we say that a person is easily startled, has powerful or weak sex urges, has a "frightful temper"; when we say that someone is by nature slow-moving and lethargic, that another is excitable, energetic, or has a "sour disposition," we are describing temperament. There have been various attempts to analyze out basic dimensions of temperament with the aid of psychological tests, but as yet no final agreement is reached.

It does seem probable that a primary factor relates to *drive and vigor* or its opposite, *apathy*. Constitutions high in drive and vigor may have high metabolic rates and strong thyroid functioning.[12] But our knowledge of the physical basis is not yet secure, nor do we know how many additional dimensions we need for the purpose of classifying major forms of temperament.[13]

Lacking more precise knowledge of the subject we offer the following definition as fairly representing current psychological usage, and as serving adequately the purposes of this book.

Temperament refers to the characteristic phenomena of an individual's emotional nature, including his susceptibility to emotional stimulation, his customary strength and speed of response, the quality of his prevailing mood, and all peculiarities of fluctuation and intensity in mood, these phenomena being regarded as dependent upon constitutional make-up, and therefore largely hereditary in origin.

This definition is not meant to imply that temperament is unchanged from birth to death. Like physique and intelligence, temperament may be altered (within limits) by medical, surgical, and nutritional influences as well as in the course of learning and life-experience. Temperament may alter as per-

---

[12] See C. J. Adcock, The differentiation of temperament from personality, *J. gen. Psychol.*, 1957, 57, 103–112.

[13] A useful survey of the present stage of knowledge is contained in S. Diamond, *Personality and temperament* (New York: Harper, 1957), Chaps. 7 and 8. Diamond is of the opinion that animal research and factorial analyses of human temperament "contain repeated assurances of the importance of dispositions to *affiliative*, *aggressive*, *fearful*, and *controlled* (or impulsive) behavior" (p. 171). The numerous authors he cites use, of course, varying terms, but Diamond believes that their labels point to the same basic dimensions of temperament. My criticism would be that his labels suggest traits of personality rather than constitutional dispositions (true temperament), but there may be underlying physiological dispositions to support this, or some similar, classification of trends in temperament. Continued research is needed.

sonality evolves. Yet the fact remains that in our endowment from birth onward there are constitutional, chemical, metabolic, neural levels that establish for us a characteristic stock in trade. Alteration is possible but not unlimited.

SUMMARY

Voltaire once wrote, "If you would converse with me, you must first define your terms." Especially do highly abstract words such as *personality, character,* and *temperament* call for definition in order to make conversation profitable.

My own definition of personality is "essentialist." Personality is what a person "really is," regardless of the way other people perceive his qualities or the methods by which we study them. Our perceptions and our methods may be in error, just as an astronomer may fall short in studying the constitution of a star. But the star is still there, a challenging object for study. My definition does not, of course, deny that a person is variable over time or that his behavior may change from situation to situation. It says simply that the person has an internal structure and range of characteristics (variable, to be sure, but ascertainable), and it is this structure that we hope to study.

Character is a term we can largely dispense with since it refers (by our definition) to the evaluation of personality. *Characteristic,* on the other hand, keeps its original meaning of engraving (a uniquely etched feature), and is therefore useful for our purposes.

Temperament, like intelligence and physique, refers to "raw materials" out of which personality is fashioned. One's temperamental endowment is not unchangeable though it sets limits upon the development of personality.

27. YOUTH AND THE LIFE CYCLE *

E. H. ERIKSON

THE EIGHT STAGES IN THE LIFE CYCLE OF MAN

"Personality," Erickson has written, "can be said to develop according to steps predetermined in the human organism's readiness to be driven toward, to be aware of, and to interact with a widening social radius, beginning with a dim image of a mother and ending with an image of mankind. . . ." Following are the steps he has identified in man's psychosocial development, and the special crises they bring. In presenting them, he has emphasized that while the struggle between the negatives and positives in each crisis must be fought through successfully if the next developmental stage is to be reached, no victory is completely or forever won.

I. INFANCY: TRUST VS. MISTRUST. The first "task" of the infant is to develop "the cornerstone of a healthy personality," a basic sense of trust—in himself and in his environment. This comes from a feeling of inner goodness derived from "the mutual regulation of his receptive capacities with the maternal techniques of provision" [1]—a quality of care that transmits a sense of trustworthiness and meaning. The danger, most acute in the second half of the first year, is that discontinuities in care may increase a natural sense of loss, as the child gradually recognizes his separate-

* Erikson, E. H., "Youth and the Life Cycle," from *Children,* Vol. 7, No. 2, March 1960, 43-49.

[1] Erik H. Erikson, "Growth and Crises of the 'Healthy Personality,' " *Symposium on the Healthy Personality* (New York: Josiah Macy, Jr. Foundation, 1950).

ness from his mother, to a basic sense of mistrust that may last through life.

II. EARLY CHILDHOOD: AUTONOMY VS. SHAME AND DOUBT. With muscular maturation the child experiments with holding on and letting go and begins to attach enormous value to his autonomous will. The danger here is the development of a deep sense of shame and doubt if he is deprived of the opportunity to learn to develop his will as he learns his "duty," and therefore learns to expect defeat in any battle of wills with those who are bigger and stronger.

III. PLAY AGE: INITIATIVE VS. GUILT. In this stage the child's imagination is greatly expanded because of his increased ability to move around freely and to communicate. It is an age of instrusive activity, avid curiosity, and consuming fantasies which lead to feelings of guilt and anxiety. It is also the stage of the establishment of conscience. If this tendency to feel guilty is "over-burdened by all-too-eager adults" the child may develop a deep-seated conviction that he is essentially bad, with a resulting stifling of initiative or a conversion of his moralism to vindictiveness.

IV. SCHOOL AGE: INDUSTRY VS. INFERIORITY. The long period of sexual latency before puberty is the age when the child wants to learn how to do and make things with others. In learning to accept instruction and to win recognition by producing "things" he opens the way for the capacity of work enjoyment. The danger in this period is the development of a sense of inadequacy and inferiority in a child who does not receive recognition for his efforts.

V. ADOLESCENCE: IDENTITY VS. IDENTITY DIFFUSION. The physiological revolution that comes with puberty—rapid body growth and sexual maturity—forces the young person to question "all sameness and continuities relied on earlier" and to "refight many of the earlier battles." The developmental task is to integrate childhood identifications "with the basic biological drives, native endowment, and the opportunities offered in social roles." The danger is that identity diffusion, temporarily unavoidable in this period of physical and psychological upheaval, may result in a permanent inability to "take hold" or, because of youth's tendency to total commitment, in the

fixation in the young person of a negative identity, a devoted attempt to become what parents, class, or community do not want him to be.

VI. YOUNG ADULTHOOD: INTIMACY VS. ISOLATION. Only as a young person begins to feel more secure in his identity is he able to establish intimacy with himself (with his inner life) and with others, both in friendships and eventually in a love-based mutually satisfying sexual relationship with a member of the opposite sex. A person who cannot enter wholly into an intimate relationship because of the fear of losing his identity may develop a deep sense of isolation.

VII. ADULTHOOD: GENERATIVITY VS. SELF-ABSORPTION. Out of the intimacies of adulthood grows generativity—the mature person's interest in establishing and guiding the next generation. The lack of this results in self-absorption and frequently in a "pervading sense of stagnation and interpersonal impoverishment."

VIII. SENESCENCE: INTEGRITY VS. DISGUST. The person who has achieved a satisfying intimacy with other human beings and who has adapted to the triumphs and disappointments of his generative activities as parent and coworker reaches the end of life with a certain ego integrity—an acceptance of his own responsibility for what his life is and was and of its place in the flow of history.

Question: *Are there any points about your concepts of psychosocial development which you would now like to stress in the light of what you have heard about how they have been interpreted during the past decade in the training of professional persons and through them of parents and future parents?*

Yes, I am grateful for the opportunity of making a few observations on the reception of these concepts. You emphasize their influence on teaching in various fields; let me pick out a few misunderstandings.

I should confess to you here how it all started. It was on a drive in the countryside with Mrs. Erikson that I became a bit expansive, telling her about a kind of ground plan in the human life cycle, which I seemed to discern in life histories. After a while she began to write, urging me just to go on; she had found my "plan" immediately convincing.

Afterwards, a number of audiences of different professional backgrounds had that same sense of conviction—so much so that I (and others) became somewhat uneasy: after all, these psychosocial signposts are hardly *concepts* yet, even if the whole plan represents a valid *conception,* one which suggests a great deal of work.

What Mrs. Erikson and I subsequently offered to the White House Conference of 1950 was a kind of worksheet, which has, indeed, been used by others as well as myself in scientific investigation, and well integrated in a few textbooks. But its "convincingness" has also led to oversimplifications. Let me tell you about a few.

There has been a tendency here and there to turn the eight stages into a sort of rosary of achievement, a device for counting the fruits of each stage—trust, autonomy, initiative, and so forth—as though each were achieved as a permanent trait. People of this bent are apt to leave out the negative counterparts of each stage, as if the healthy personality had permanently conquered these hazards. The fact is that the healthy personality must reconquer them continuously in the same way that the body's metabolism resists decay. All that we learn are certain fundamental means and mechanisms for retaining and regaining mastery. Life is a sequence not only of developmental but also of accidental crises. It is hardest to take when both types of crisis coincide.

In each crisis, under favorable conditions, the positive is likely to outbalance the negative, and each reintegration builds strength for the next crisis. But the negative is always with us to some degree in the form of a measure of infantile anxiety, fear of abandonment—a residue of immaturity carried throughout life, which is perhaps the price man has to pay for a childhood long enough to permit him to be the learning and the teaching animal, and thus to achieve his particular mastery of reality.

You may be interested to know that further clinical research has indicated that our dream life often depicts a recovery of mastery along the lines of these stages. Moreover, nurses have observed that any adult who undergoes serious surgery has to repeat the battle with these nemeses in the process of recovery. A person moves up and down the scale of maturity, but if his ego has gained a positive balance during his developmental crises the downward movements will be less devastating than if the balance, at one stage or another, was in the negative.

Of all the positive aspects mentioned, trust seems to have been the most convincing—so convincing, in fact, that some discussions never reach a consideration of the other stages. I don't mean to detract from the obvious importance of trust as the foundation of the development of a healthy personality. A basic sense of trust in living as such, developed in infancy through the reciprocal relationship of child and mother, is essential to winning the positive fruits of all the succeeding crises in the life cycle: maybe this is what Christmas, with its Madonna images, conveys to us. Yet, it is the nature of human life that each succeeding crisis takes place within a widened social radius where an ever-larger number of significant persons have a bearing on the outcome. There is in childhood, first, the maternal person, then the parental combination, then the basic family and other instructing adults. Youth demands "confirmation" from strangers who hold to a design of life; and later, the adult needs challenges from mates and partners, and even from his growing children and expanding works, in order to continue to grow himself. And all of these relationships must be imbedded in an "ethos," a cultural order, to guide the individual's course.

In our one-family culture (supported by pediatricians and psychiatrists who exclusively emphasize the mother-child relationship) we tend to lose sight of the fact that other people besides parents are important to youth. Too often we ask only where a given youth came from and what he once was, and not also where he was going, and who was ready to receive him and his intentions and his specific gifts. Thus we have movements to punish parents for the transgressions of their children, ignoring all other persons and environmental factors that entered into the production of a young person's unacceptable behavior and failed to offer support to his positive search.

Another way in which the life cycle theory has been oversimplified is in the omission of stages which do not fit into the preconceived ideas of the person who is adopting or adapting the theory. Thus a large organization devoted to parenthood distributed a list of the stages but omitted *integrity vs. despair*—the problem of senescence. This is too easy a way to dispose of grandparents, it robs life of an inescapable final step; and, of course, it defeats this whole conception of an intrinsic order in the life cycle.

This kind of omission ignores the "cog-wheeling" of infantile and adult stages—the fact that each further stage of growth in a given individual is not only dependent upon the relatively successful completion of his own previous stages, but also on the completion of the subsequent stages in those other individuals with whom he interacts and whom he accepts as models.

Finally, I should point to the fact that what my psychoanalytic colleagues warned me of most energetically has, on occasion, come to pass: even sincere workers have chosen to ignore my emphasis on the intrinsic relation of the psychosocial to the psychosexual stages which form the basis of much of Freud's work.

All of these misuses, however, may be to a large extent the fault of my choice of words. The use of simple, familiar words like "trust" and "mistrust" apparently leads people to assume that they know "by feel" what the theory is all about. Perhaps this semantic problem would have been avoided if I had used Latin terms, which call for definitions.

I may point out, however, that I originally suggested my terms as a basis for discussions —discussions led by people who have an idea of the interrelatedness of all aspects of human development. For the eight stages of psychosocial development are, in fact, inextricably entwined in and derived from the various stages of psychosexual development that were described by Freud, as well as from the child's stages of physical, motor, and cognitive development. Each type of development affects the other and is affected by it. Thus, I feel that discussants would do well to study each key word in its origins, in its usage in various periods and regions, and in other languages. Simple words that touch upon universal human values have their counterpart in every living language, and can become vehicles of understanding at international conferences.

Incidentally, I made up one new word because I thought it was needed. To me, "generativity" described the chief characteristic of the mature adult. It was turned into a comfortable, if inaccurate, homespun word before it ever left the Fact-Finding Committee of 1950. I had deliberately chosen "generativity" rather than "parenthood," or "creativity," because these narrowed the matter down to a biological and an artistic issue instead of describing the deep absorption in guiding the young or in helping to create a new world for the young, which is a mark of maturity in parents and nonparents, working people and "creative" people alike.

Enough of this fault-finding! But it *is* interesting to see what can happen to new ideas; and you *did* ask me.

Question: *During the past 10 years you have been treating and studying mentally ill young people at a public clinic in a low-income area in Pittsburgh and at a private, comparatively expensive, mental hospital in the Berkshires. Have you found any common denominator in the disturbances of these patients—from such opposite walks of life—that would seem to point to any special difficulty harassing the young people of our land today?*

Since 1950, I have concentrated on the life histories of sick young people in late adolescence and early adulthood primarily in order to study one of the crises magnified, as it were, with the clinical microscope. I think that our initial formulations of the identity crisis have been clinically validated and much refined.

Many of these sick young people in their late teens and early twenties had failed during their adolescence to win out in the struggle against identity confusion. They were suffering so seriously from a feeling of being (or, indeed, wanting to be) "nobody" that they were withdrawing from reality, and in some cases even attempting to withdraw from life itself: in other words, they were regressing to a position where trust had to be reinstated. Their malaise proved to be related to the same sense of diffuseness which drives other young adults to incessant and sometimes delinquent activity—an effort to show the world, including themselves, that they are "somebody" even if deep down they do not believe it.

In the meantime, of course, the identity issue has been taken up by many writers and by some magazines, almost in the form of a slogan. We are prone to think that we have cornered an issue when we have found a name for it, and to have resolved it when we have found something to blame. So now we blame "the changing world."

Actually, there is no reason why youth should not participate with enthusiasm in radical change; young people are freer for change than we are. The bewildering thing for them must be that we now complain about change, having eagerly caused it ourselves with inventions and discoveries; that we seem to have played at change rather than to have planned it. If we had the courage of our inventions, if we would grow into the world we have helped to create, and would give youth co-responsibility in it, I think that all the potential power of the identity crisis would serve a better world than we can now envisage.

Let me say a word about identity, or rather about what it is not. The young person seeking an identity does not go around saying, even to himself, "Who am I?" as an editorial in a national magazine suggested last year's college graduates were doing on their way home. Nor does the person with a secure sense of identity usually stop to think or to brag about the fact that he has this priceless possession, and of what it consists. He simply feels and acts predominantly in tune with himself, his capacities, and his opportunities; and he has the inner means and finds the outer ways to recover from experiences which impair this feeling. He knows where he fits (or knowingly prefers not to fit) into present conditions. . . .

This sense of a coincidence between inner resources, traditional values, and opportunities of action is derived from a fusion of slowly grown, unconscious personality processes—and contemporary social forces. It has its earliest beginnings in the infant's first feelings of affirmation by maternal recognition and is nurtured on the quality and consistency of the parental style of upbringing. Thus identity is in a sense an outgrowth of all the earlier stages; but the crucial period for its development to maturity comes with the adolescent crisis.

Every adolescent is apt to go through some serious struggle at one time or another. The crises of earlier stages may return in some form as he seeks to free himself from the alignments of childhood because of both his own eagerness for adulthood and the pressures of society. For a while he may distrust what he once trusted implicitly; may be ashamed of his body, and doubtful of his future. He experiments, looking for affirmation and recognition from his friends and from the adults who mean most to him. Unconsciously, he revamps his repertory of childhood identifications, reviving some and repudiating others. He goes in for extremes—total commitments and total repudiations. His struggle is to make sense out of what has gone before in relation to what he now perceives the world to be, in an effort to find a persistent sameness in himself and a persistent sharing of some kind of essential character with others.

Far from considering this process to be a kind of maturational malaise, a morbid egocentricity of which adolescents must be "cured," we must recognize in it the search for new values, the willingness to serve loyalties which prove to be "true" (in any number of spiritual, scientific, technical, political, philosophical, and personal meanings of "truth") and thus a prime force in cultural rejuvenation.

The strengths a young person finds in adults at this time—their willingness to let him experiment, their eagerness to confirm him at his best, their consistency in correcting his excesses, and the guidance they give him—will codetermine whether or not he eventually makes order out of necessary inner confusion and applies himself to the correction of disordered conditions. He needs freedom to choose, but not so much freedom that he cannot, in fact, make a choice.

In some adolescents, in some cultures, in some historical epochs this crisis is minimal;

in others it holds real perils for both the individual and society. Some individuals, particularly those with a weak preparation in their preceding developmental crises, succumb to it with the formation of neuroses and psychoses. Others try to resolve it through adherence—often temporary—to radical kinds of religious, political, artistic, or criminal ideologies.

A few fight the battle alone and, after a prolonged period of agony characterized by erratic dangerous behavior, become the spokesmen of new directions. Their sense of impending danger forces them to mobilize their capacities to new ways of thinking and doing which have meaning, at the same time, for themselves and their times. In my book "Young Man Luther" I have tried to show how identity is related to ideology and how the identity struggle of one intense young genius produced a new person, a new faith, a new kind of man, and a new era.

I think I chose to write about Luther and his time because there are many analogies between our time and his, although today the problems which beset all historical crises are global and, as it were, semifinal in character. Today, throughout the world, the increasing pace of technological change has encroached upon traditional group solidarities and on their ability to transmit a sense of cosmic wholeness and technological planfulness to the young.

To me one of the most disturbing aspects of our technological culture is the imbalance between passive stimulation and active outlet in the pleasures that are sanctioned for young people. With the passing of the western frontier and the accelerated appearance of automatic gadgets, young people have become increasingly occupied with passive pursuits which require little participation of mind or body—being conveyed rapidly through space by machines and watching violent fantasies at the movies or on television—without the possibility of matching the passive experience with active pursuits. When an adolescent substitutes passivity for the adventure and activity which his muscular development and sexual drives require, there is always the danger of explosion—and I think that this accounts for much of the explosive, unexpected, and delin-

quent acts on the part of even our "nice" young people.

This is probably why "Westerns," always on the borderline of the criminal and the lawful, capture the passive imagination of a youth which has traditionally substituted identification with the rugged individualist—the pioneer who ventures into the unknown—for commitment to a political ideology; and which now finds itself confronted with increasing demands for standardization, uniformity, and conformity to the rituals of a status-convention. While the national prototype has historically been based on readiness for change, the range of possibilities of what one might choose to be and of opportunities to make a change [has] narrowed. To this has been added most recently the rude shaking of the once "eternal" image of our Nation's superiority in productivity and technical ingenuity through the appearance of Sputnik and its successors.

Thus one might say the complexity of the adolescent state and the confusion of the times meet head on.

However, I believe that the "confusion" derives from a hypocritical denial of our true position, both in regard to obvious dangers and true resources. When youth is permitted to see its place in a crisis, it will, out of its very inner dangers, gain the strength to meet the demands of the time.

Clinical experience with young people has, it is true, verified that combination of inner and outer dangers which explains aggravated identity crises. On the other hand, it has convinced me and my colleagues, even in hospital work, of the surprising resources which young people can muster if their social responsibilities are called upon in a total environment of psychological understanding.

Question: *Does this kind of confusion have anything to do with juvenile delinquency?*

I would not want to add here to the many claims concerning distinct and isolated causes of juvenile delinquency. But I would like to stress one contributing factor: the confused attitudes of adults—both laymen and professionals—toward the young people whom we, with a mixture of condescension and fear, call teenagers.

Except perhaps in some rare instances of congenital defects resulting in a low capacity to comprehend values, juvenile delinquents are made, not born; and we adults make them. Here, I am not referring to their parents exclusively. True, many parents, because of their own personalities and backgrounds, are not able to give their children a chance for a favorable resolution of the identity crisis. Nor am I referring to the failure of society at large to correct those blights on the social scene—such as overcrowded slums and inequality of opportunities for minority groups —which make it impossible for tens of thousands of young people to envisage an identity in line with the prevailing success-and-status ideology.

Rather I am referring to the attitudes of adults—in the press, in court, and in some professional and social institutions—which push the delinquent young person into a "negative identity," a prideful and stubborn acceptance of himself as a juvenile delinquent—and this at a time when his experimentation with available roles will make him exquisitely vulnerable (although he may not admit or even know it) to the opinions of the representatives of society. When a young person is adjudicated as a potential criminal because he has taken a girl for a ride in somebody else's car (which he intended to abandon, not to appropriate), he may well decide, half consciously, of course, but none the less with finality, that to have any real identity at all he must be what he obviously *can* be—a delinquent. The scolding of young people in public for the indiscretions they have committed, with the expectation that they show remorse, often ignores all the factors in their histories that force them into a delinquent kind of experimentation. It is certainly no help toward a positive identity formation.

In his insistence on holding on to an active identity, even if it is temporarily a "negative" one from the point of view of society, the delinquent is sometimes potentially healthier than the young person who withdraws into a neurotic or a psychotic state. Some delinquents, perhaps, in their determination to be themselves at all costs and under terrible conditions have more strength and a greater potential for contributing to the richness of the national life than do many excessively con-

forming or neurotically defeatist members of their generation, who have given up youth's prerogatives to dream and to dare. We must study this problem until we can overcome the kind of outraged bewilderment which makes the adult world seem untrustworthy to youth and hence may seem to justify the choice of a delinquent identity.

Actually, transitory delinquency, as well as other forms of antisocial or asocial behavior, often may be what I have called a *psychosocial moratorium*—a period of delay in the assumption of adult commitment. Some youths need a period of relaxed expectations, of guidance to the various possibilities for positive identification through opportunities to participate in adult work, or even of introspection and experimentation—none of which can be replaced by either moralistic punishment or condescending forgiveness.

Question: *The theme of the 1960 White House Conference on Children and Youth charges the Conference with studying and understanding "the values and ideals of our society" in its efforts "to promote opportunities for children and youth to realize their full potential for a creative life in freedom and dignity." On the basis of the scheme which you presented to us in 1950, could you add a word about how these values, once identified, can be transmitted in a way that will insure their incorporation into the value systems of the young?*

Like every other aspect of maturity the virtues which we expect in a civilized human being grow in stages as the child develops from an infant to an adult. What is expected of a child at any time must be related to his total maturation and level of ego strength, which are related to his motor, cognitive, psychosexual, and psychosocial stages. You can't expect total obedience from a 2-year-old who must test a growing sense of autonomy, nor total truth from a 4-year-old involved in the creative but often guilt-ridden fantasies of the oedipal stage.

It would be in line with the course of other historical crises if in our Nation today a certain sense of moral weakness were producing a kind of frantic wish to enforce moral strength in our youth with punitive or purely exhortative measures.

Today, a sense of crisis has been aggravated by the long cold war and the sudden revelation of the technical strength of a supposedly "backward" rival. We are wondering whether we have made our children strong enough for living in such an unpredictably dangerous world. Some people, who suddenly realize that they have not been responsible guardians of all the Nation's young, now wonder whether they should have beaten moral strength into them or preached certain absolute values more adamantly.

No period, however, can afford to go back on its advances in values and in knowledge, and I trust that the 1960 White House Conference will find a way to integrate our knowledge of personality development with our national values, necessities, and resources. What we need is not a plan whereby relatively irresponsible adults can enforce morality in their children, but rather national insistence on a more *responsible* morality on the part of adults, paired with an *informed* attitude toward the *development* of moral values in children. Values can only be fostered gradually by adults who have a clear conception of what to expect and what not to expect of the child as, at each stage, he comes to understand new segments of reality and of himself, and who are firm about what they are sure they *may* expect.

It must be admitted that psychiatry has added relatively little to the understanding of morality, except perhaps by delineating the great dangers of moralistic attitudes and measures which convince the child only of the adult's greater executive power, not of his actual moral power or true superiority. To this whole question, I can, on the basis of my own work, only indicate that the psychosocial stages discussed in 1950 seem to open up the possibility of studying the way in which in each stage of growth the healthy child's developmental drives dispose him toward a certain set of qualities which are the necessary fundaments of a responsible character: in *infancy*, hope and drive; in *early childhood*, will and control; in the *play age*, purpose and direction; in the *school age*, skill and method; and in *adolescence*, devotion and fidelity. The development of these basic qualities in children, however, depends on the corresponding development in adults of qualities related to: in *young adulthood*, love, work, and affiliation; in *adulthood*, care, parenthood, and production; and in *old age*, "wisdom" and responsible renunciation.

Now I have given you another set of nice words, throwing to the winds my own warning regarding the way they can be misunderstood and misused. Let me point out, therefore, that I consider these basic virtues in line with our advancing psychoanalytic ego-psychology, on the one hand, and without advancing knowledge of psychosocial evolution, on the other, and that the conception behind this list can only be studied in the context of advancing science. I will discuss this further in a forthcoming publication, but I mention it now because I thought I owed you a reference to the way in which my contribution of 1950 has gradually led me in the direction of the great problem of the anchoring of virtue in human nature as it has evolved in our universe.

We ought to regard the breaking of a child's spirit—by cruel punishment, by senseless spoiling, by persistent hypocrisy—as a sin against humanity. Yet today we have back-to-the-woodshed movements. Last year in the legislature of one of our greatest States a bill was introduced to allow corporal punishment in the public schools and was lauded by part of the press. This gave the Soviets a chance to declare publicly against corporal punishment, implying that they are not sufficiently scared by their own youth to go back on certain considered principles in the rearing of the young. Actually, I think that we stand with the rest of the civilized world on the principle that if adult man reconsiders his moral position in the light of historical fact, and in the light of his most advanced knowledge of human nature, he can afford, in relation to his children, to rely on a forbearance which step by step will bring the best *out* of them . . .

28. THE LONELY ROAD OF UNREALITY *

EVELYN L. BANNING

Of the varied processes of adjustment in response to the child's inner needs, the natural events of his life, and the presence and activities of those about him, adjustment by withdrawal presents the greatest challenge to the teacher, not only because withdrawal responses often escape notice, but mainly because such avoidant modes, more insidious than others, may become habitual and pathological before recognition. According to Louttit, the boundaries between psychoneuroses and psychoses are no clearer than those between personality difficulties and psychoneuroses. In other words, between the child's seclusiveness and timidity, resulting from the withdrawing mode of behavior, and the borderlands of the functional psychosis of schizophrenia, there are no clearcut demarcations, no signposts that unquestionably indicate to the teacher that ahead lies the Lonely Road of Unreality. Nevertheless, the withdrawing, recessive personality, subjected to unbearable stresses and strains of his personal and social environment, may become the severely distorted and shattered personality of the psychotic.

Ten years ago Teresa, a slight, silent, and inactive child of seven completed grade one with a satisfactory record. The teacher's only comment at the time was, "Teresa is unsocial and shows no interest in playing with the other children." Today Teresa is institutionalized in a mental hospital, classified: schizophrenia, hebephrenic. And yet Teresa's behavior all through her eight years of public school received scarcely more than passing attention; indeed, no teacher considered her

withdrawn manner or her extreme seclusiveness a matter of concern since she caused no disturbance in the classroom and showed great solicitation for teacher approval in the early grades.

Two questions immediately present themselves for our consideration of the teacher's role in recognizing and in treating behavior anomalies.

1. What are the symptoms of prepsychotic behavior observable in school children?

2. What help can the teacher actually give the child after recognizing these early symptoms?

The predisposing causative factors of schizophrenia are not definitely known: on the other hand, the precipitating factors, whether organic illness, physical discomfort, emotional trauma, psychic conflicts, or the developmental crisis of childhood or adolescence, merely evoke and exaggerate the schizophrenic response when the pattern has already been established. Bleuler states "There is nothing to be gained by listing the factors that have been implicated in the precipitation of the functional psychosis; obviously any incident toward which an individual may have become sensitized can tip the balance." For the teacher, therefore, the important consideration lies not in the etiology of the psychosis, either generally or in any specific case such as that of Teresa, nor in the therapy possible after the onset of mental deterioration, but rather in the recognition of the early symptoms of behavior disorders for the purpose of planning the best methods of improving the child's adjustment to reality. Likewise the full social significance of the value of early recognition is clear in view of the fact that schizophrenia is usually

* From Banning, Evelyn L., "The Lonely Road of Unreality," *School and Society*, *72*, August, 1950, pp. 132–133.

found among adolescents and young adults and that it accounts for approximately one fourth of all mental disorders.

Although sufficient data regarding prepsychotic behavior of more serious disorders are unfortunately lacking, the preschizophrenic symptoms, in a broad sense, do resemble the introverted type of personality described by Jung and others. The most distinctive feature, according to Young, is the gradual and insidious development of inattention and emotional indifference to the world outside of the individual. Extreme seclusiveness, excessive daydreaming, regression of personal interests, and odd behavior are primary symptoms. The teacher needs to observe carefully the behavior of the shy, timid, and quiet pupil who may be overlooked, since he does not disturb class routine. Inasmuch as it is not always easy to determine whether the child's behavior is a normal striving for a satisfactory adjustment or an abnormal inability to meet regular daily experiences, the teacher should have a sound understanding of the psychology of adjustment and of human behavior.

The secondary symptoms are many and varied, depending upon the developmental stage, all symptoms that give evidence of a disordered contact with the environment. Out of the specific experiences, the individual comes to develop certain standard or habitual forms of reaction, substitute responses that in psychotics tend to involve the entire organization. Secondary symptoms include temper displays, a diminished breadth of general interest, emotional expressions, negativisms, psychomotor agitation, a variety of speech disorders, and overt sex practices. In these more severe cases, the teacher should not consider herself qualified for therapy, but should instead refer the child to a clinical specialist or psychiatrist. Such use of available resources for the treatment of severe behavior disorders is distinctly a credit to the professional alertness of the teacher.

The school and the teacher, however, do play a significant part in treating behavior problems before the developing personality of the child begins to deviate conspicuously from a normal path. Both through modifying the environmental factors of the school and through working directly with the child, the individual may be taught to meet social and cultural frustrations successfully and may be shielded from unattainable ideals of success. Work that is within the capacity of the child, that is meaningful, and that provides him with some sense of accomplishment is essential. Mental balance can also be aided by additional ambivalent activities that are approved outlets for deep and unsatisfied wishes: art, avocations, and hobbies. Most important of all, however, is the therapeutic attitude of the teacher, that teacher who, by her real understanding and knowledge of behavior anomalies, her resourcefulness, and encouragement, offers affectional security to the quiet, insecure child in a social setting not unduly exciting. Thus the teacher may be of help to the preschizophrenic child who is giving evidence of difficulty in making a reasonably adequate adjustment to the world of reality.

29. ACQUIRING DEPENDENCE AND INDEPENDENCE: A THEORETICAL ORIENTATION *

GLEN HEATHERS

A. PROBLEM

Everyone's personality develops in a social world and every aspect of personality reflects one's relationships and experiences with others. A central aspect of the process of becoming "socialized" is developing needs, perceptions, and response patterns having to do with dependence on others, or with independence. Currently, a major research program on the development of dependence-independence in preschool children is underway at the Fels Research Institute. This paper presents the general theoretical orientation basic to the research program. Its purposes are to define certain forms of dependence-independence and to indicate how they may be learned.

B. FORMS OF DEPENDENCE AND INDEPENDENCE

A person is dependent on others to the extent that he has needs [1] which require that others respond in particular ways if these needs are to be satisfied. A person is independent of others to the extent that he can satisfy his needs without requiring that others respond to him in particular ways.

One way of depending on others is *instrumental dependence* which is present when a

person seeks help in reaching goals. Thus, an infant depends on others for help in satisfying hunger and other bodily needs. When a child seeks help, as in getting food, help is the subgoal in relation to the end-goal of food.

With emotional dependence, the responses of others are the end-goals rather than means of reaching them. Thus, the need for affection is an emotional-dependence need which is satisfied by others' affectionate responses. Three forms of emotional dependence may be distinguished—needs for reassurance, for affection, and for approval. The need for *reassurance* occurs in situations when a person anticipates undesired or feared outcomes—failure, rejection, injury, etc. Seeking reassurance is a matter of placing oneself in the care of another person as a way of avoiding such outcomes. Thus, a child who fears the dark desires someone he trusts to share the darkness with him, and a child who is anxious about failing a task wants to be told that he will make out all right. A person's need for *affection* is the need for others to respond with physical signs of affection such as caresses and kisses or with words and deeds which show that they care for him. A person's need for *approval* is the need for others to make positive responses toward him either on the basis of his performance or on the basis of status-giving characteristics such as his appearance, his possessions, or his social rôles.

Instrumental independence means conducting activities and coping with problems without seeking help. It is the obverse of instrumental dependence.

Emotional independence means, first, the absence of needs for reassurance, affection, or

* From Heathers, Glen, "Acquiring Dependence and Independence: A Theoretical Orientation," *Journal of Genetic Psychology*, 1955, *87*, pp. 277–291.
[1] The term "need" is a theoretical construct which refers to perceptions and response patterns related to achieving and utilizing any goals in a particular class of goals (e.g., affection). Needs may be measured at the perceptual level by obtaining verbal reports (as in projective tests) or at the overt behavioral level by observing responses toward goals.

approval in particular situations. This aspect may be called "emotional self-reliance" and is the obverse of emotional dependence. In addition, emotional independence is defined to include "self-assertion" in the form of needs to master tasks, and to dominate others. It should be noted that emotional self-reliance does not assume any specific independence needs while self-assertion does. The need to master a task is assumed to be more than the need to complete it: it is the need for self-approval on the basis of one's performance. Similarly, the need to dominate is assumed to be a need for self-approval on the basis of one's assertive behavior. These definitions of self-reliance and self-assertion assume that the behavior expressing them is not used as a means of gaining approval. When approval is the goal, as when a person dominates in order to attract attention or praise, emotional dependence rather than independence is shown.

C. ASSUMPTIONS ABOUT THE LEARNING PROCESS

In offering an account of how dependence and independence are learned, it is assumed that learning takes place in relation to needs which a person tends to satisfy through making appropriate goal-directed responses. A person learns certain "meanings" of aspects of situations in relation to his needs and he learns "predispositions" to make or not to make certain goal directed responses when a given need is active in a situation. His overt responses depend on which of his needs are active as he enters the situation, on what *need-relevancies* he perceives in the situation, and on his *expectancies* of satisfying or not satisfying his needs by responses directed toward goals in the situation.

The need-relevancies of a situation may be divided into three categories: (*a*) need-arousal —a situation may evoke needs as when a person perceives the threat of injury; (*b*) goals— a situation may provide opportunities for satisfying needs; and (*c*) goal-pathways—a situation may provide opportunities to make responses which lead to goals.

A person learns the need-relevancies of a situation through the simultaneous association of his perceptions [2] of the situation, and of his responses in the situation, with positive or negative *reinforcement*. When perceptions of the situation and of his responses to it are associated with *positive* reinforcement (achieving goals) he learns to expect a positive outcome and acquires predispositions to make the goal-directed responses which led to positive reinforcement. Conversely, when perceptions of the situation and of his responses are associated with *negative* reinforcement (failure to achieve goals, punishment, injury) he learns to expect this sort of outcome and acquires predispositions not to make the responses which led to negative reinforcement.

A point which requires special emphasis is that the reinforcement value of a goal is not determined by the goal as such but by its relation to one's expectations. Thus a child who is seeking affection from his mother may perceive her hug as rejection because she doesn't take him on her lap and caress him as she usually has done. Another child may perceive a similar hug as rewarding because it equals or exceeds what he has learned to expect.

An important aspect of learning need-relevancies is that stimuli from a situation which are associated with reinforcement acquire reinforcement value. When this has occurred, these accompaniments or "signs" of reinforcement may function as goals in the absence of the previous reinforcement. Thus, if a child's mother smiles whenever she gratifies any of his needs, her smile will come to be a goal in its own right.

When substitute goals are learned, new needs are also acquired in the sense that a person tends to seek these substitute goals in the absence of the needs which were previously active. In this article, needs for reassurance, affection, approval, mastery, and domination are considered to be acquired needs. It is assumed that the reason one comes to need affection, approval, etc., is because of a gen-

[2] The use of the term "perception" in this paper may cause confusion because it is conventional to restrict this term to conscious process. The term is used in this paper to refer to all "psychological processes" which are active when a person reacts to a situation, regardless of the degree of conscious awareness or control of these processes.

eral tendency to seek positive reinforcement. So, when a person perceives the opportunity for achieving a goal (such as affection or approval) he not only has the expectancy of achieving it but also the predisposition to achieve it.

D. INSTRUMENTAL DEPENDENCE

At birth, and during his first months, the infant is relatively helpless and is *passively* dependent on others to satisfy almost all his needs. He can breathe, and, if his supply of air is interrupted, his struggling may restore it. He can suck in and swallow liquid brought to his mouth and he can digest and eliminate. He reacts to annoying stimuli by general bodily activity which may remove the annoyance. However, beyond such reflexes and such general bodily responses, the very young infant can do nothing to satisfy his needs.

Despite his helplessness, it is wrong to say that the neonate is *actively* dependent on others, since he must first learn to associate others with the satisfaction of his needs. Neither instrumental nor emotional dependence are present until the child has learned to perceive others as related to achieving goals, and until he has learned to use certain responses as means of inducing others to attend to his needs. For example, the basis for learning to use crying as an expression of instrumental dependence is the fact that a child's mother responds to his crying by trying to discover and satisfy his needs. Learning principles predict that through this sort of experience the child comes to associate crying with his mother's responding to him, and with relieving his distress. When this learning has taken place, crying may be used as a device to express instrumental dependence.

In developing instrumental dependence on others, the child learns various devices for stimulating others to help him reach his goals. Crying is generally effective in alerting others to the fact that he wants something, and also is apt to disturb others enough to make them try to find out what he wants and "pacify" him. But crying isn't a good way of indicating *what* he wants. A child learns to indicate what he wants by looking toward it, pointing at it, naming it, etc. In this process of learning instrumental-dependence devices, each child is taught by his mother and others to use certain ways of asking for help which are acceptable to them, and to which they will respond by helping him. He is also taught not to use certain devices because these are ineffective in getting help. Thus a child may be taught to stop crying, to smile, or to say "please" as conditions for getting others to help him.

One form of instrumental dependence is imitation in which one depends on another for his cues as to where to go or what to do in order to reach his goals. Imitation has been analyzed in detail by Miller and Dollard (2) who showed that one child will learn to imitate another child if following the other leads to reward while not following him leads to non-reward. They showed also that imitation "generalizes" from one situation to another. That is, imitation becomes a general instrumental-dependence device which may be used in any appropriate situation as a means of reaching a goal.

It is essential that the person from whom instrumental aid is sought be motivated to give help. Very often this means that a child must "earn" the help he seeks by offering his prospective helper some inducement. Thus a mother who desires that her child show signs of "growing up" may require that he try first before she will help him. This give-and-take is obviously important in developing the socialized individual. Instead of passive, one-sided relationships it requires active, mutual relations with other people. Sears (3) offers a beginning toward the systematic analysis of this interaction process in his consideration of the "dyadic group."

E. EMOTIONAL DEPENDENCE

1. ACQUIRING EMOTIONAL DEPENDENCE NEEDS. In explaining how emotional dependence develops, the first question is how others' responses become the end-goals which are sought rather than means toward end-goals as with instrumental dependence. In the analysis which follows, this will be discussed in relation to acquiring needs for reassurance, affection, and approval.

a. Needs for Reassurance. Reassurance satisfies needs for emotional support in "anxiety" situations when a person anticipates injury, failure, or rejection. In order to anticipate unpleasant experiences in a situation, one must previously have had such experiences in situations having something in common with the present one. The need for reassurance in situations perceived as threatening develops if other people, by their presence or their responses, have given instrumental aid which prevented the threatening outcomes. In this way, other people become associated with avoiding or relieving anxiety in threatening situations. More generally, the presence and responses of others, including their verbal assurance, come to be associated with anxiety reduction in any situation. Thus a person comes to "trust" others and to count on them to prevent undesired outcomes. The need for reassurance, and responses of seeking it, thus develop as means of preventing or relieving anxiety.

Obviously a person does not learn to trust everybody since in his experiences some people have failed to protect him from harm and some have punished him through frustrating, rejecting, or injuring him. On the basis of these differential experiences, each person learns to direct his needs for reassurance toward certain people or categories of people and not toward others.

b. Needs for Affection. To explain how a child's needs for affection develop, it is necessary to show how affectionate responses by others become associated with the satisfaction of certain of the child's "basic" needs. The infant's earliest experiences of receiving affection have to do with being made comfortable and relaxed, and with being given pleasant sensual stimulation. One of the primary expressions of affection is when a mother holds her infant as she feeds him. Another is holding him in her arms and caressing him while rocking him to sleep. Each of these classical expressions of affection involves a comfortable posture, warmth, and mild stimulation tending to relax the child. Also each involves direct sensual stimulation to which the child responds with signs of pleasure. After a few weeks, the child experiences affection from his mother and others through being played with—being tumbled about, being surprised in games like peek-a-boo, being given toys to play with, being teased with funny faces or funny sounds,

etc. On the basis of such experiences, the child comes to perceive its mother and others as sources of comfort and pleasure. Also it develops impulses toward being responded to in ways associated with such comfort and pleasure—it develops needs for affection.

While satisfying her child's needs in direct physical ways the mother also smiles at her child, talks gently to him, calls him pet names, and uses other verbal expressions of her affection. Since these responses are associated with the direct physical gratification of his needs, they come to have reward value in their own right so that needs which were satisfied originally by physical affection may now be satisfied (at least in part) by these symbolic expressions of affection.

c. Needs for Approval. When the child first learns to depend on others for instrumental aid, for reassurance, or for affection, nothing much is required of him beyond letting others know what his needs are. In other words, if his mother understands his capacities, she won't demand that he behave in any particular way as a condition for giving him help or reassurance or affection. However, after a time, she begins to require that he act in certain ways if he is to get her to coöperate in meeting his needs. The child's choice of response in a situation thus becomes a condition of his being rewarded, ignored, or punished by others.

When the child learns that his choice of response determines whether others will satisfy his needs, he develops the need to respond in ways which others approve. When they tell him "that's fine," "you're a big boy," "you did it by yourself," etc., at the same time they reward him in other ways, their verbal expressions of approval acquire reward value. Thereafter, when the need for approval is present, these signs of approval may satisfy the need.

On the other hand, signs of disapproval (frowning, yelling at the child, saying "don't" or "that's naughty") are associated with rejection or punishment and acquire negative reinforcement value. Disapproval thus becomes a basis for learning not to do certain things even when those acts are not discouraged in any other way. Also, since disapproval is often accompanied by punishment, it will tend to arouse anxiety about being punished. This anxiety will be relieved by getting others to respond positively.[3]

2. DEVELOPING RESPONSE PATTERNS FOR EXPRESSING DEPENDENCE NEEDS. In analyzing any need, three aspects may be distinguished: (*a*) a state of *tension* or expectancy which may be experienced as dissatisfaction, anxiety, or pleasant anticipation; (*b*) *goals* (objects, circumstances, others' responses) which are ways of satisfying the need; and (*c*) *response patterns* which are means of achieving these goals. The analysis to this point has dealt mainly with the tensional and goal aspects of emotional dependence. This section considers how a person develops or selects particular response patterns (devices) for stimulating others to satisfy his dependence needs.

In seeking a dependence relationship with another person, one's overtures should do three things—attract the other person's attention, indicate what is wanted, and motivate the other person to respond in the desired way. During the child's first year or so, crying is one of the most frequently used dependence devices. Crying usually induces the child's mother to approach, pick him up, and comfort him, thus satisfying needs for reassurance or for affection. One of the child's earliest learned dependence devices is turning or leaning toward his mother and reaching out his arms. This is a postural adjustment associated with being picked up; when it occurs in anticipation of being picked up it serves as a stimulus to the mother and is a dependence device. When the child is able to crawl or walk, he tends to approach his mother when seeking to satisfy dependent needs.

Language adds greatly to the child's ability to indicate what he wants and also give him

further weapons for motivating others to comply with his wishes. When he learns to say "mama" and "dada" he can indicate which one he wishes to serve him. As his vocabulary grows, he can say specifically what his wishes are, or what he wants others to do: "I'm scared," "I'm tired," "come here," "carry me," "watch me," "look what I made." Each of these verbal expressions is taught the child in association with the situations or acts to which it applied, and in association with the satisfaction of the needs which were present at the same time.

Each child learns his own unique set of dependence devices according to which of his response patterns his parents and others rewarded. Thus it is not possible to present a list of dependence response patterns which applies to all children. However, there are common elements in every child's set of dependence devices which reflect the fact that each child's needs for reassurance, affection, and approval call for certain kinds of responses from others. Also, each child in a cultural group tends to be taught a set of dependence devices which reflect the values and norms of the group.

F. REACTIONS WHEN DEPENDENCE OVERTURES ARE REJECTED

Sontag (*4*) proposes that the frustration of dependent needs leads to "defenses" against further frustration of one's dependence-seeking overtures. Obviously the most radical defense against rejection is to stop trying to induce others to satisfy one's dependence needs. However, before a child adopts this sort of reaction to felt rejection, he may respond to rejection by changes in his dependence-seeking devices, or by shifting his overtures away from one person toward another. Thus, if a child's mother rejects his requests to sit on her lap but offers affection in other ways, the child will tend to modify his affection-seeking overtures correspondingly. If the child's mother almost always refuses to pick him up and play with him while his father usually does so, he will tend to turn to his father rather than to his mother for this sort of expression of affection.

Sontag (*4*) has indicated how over-conformity may be adopted as a general device

---

[3] The present account of the development of instrumental and emotional dependence implies two basic steps in the socialization process. When the child has learned to depend on others for help, protection, reassurance, and affection the first step—acquiring "infantile dependence"—has been made. When he learns to seek approval by conforming to others' requirements, he takes the second step which leads him out of infantile dependence toward what may be called "social maturity." Social maturity is primarily the readiness for mutual relations with others where one tries to satisfy others' needs as a condition for their satisfying his own.

for avoiding rejection of dependence over-tures. As he points out, through being "good" a child lessens his chances of being disapproved or punished as well as increasing his chances of winning affection and approval from his parents or others. Being good, of course, means paying the price of catering to adults' standards of conduct as a way of inducing them to gratify his dependence needs.

In the cases described above, a child reacts to rejection by modifying his dependence-seeking overtures or by changing the person toward whom he directs such overtures. These types of adjustive reactions to rejection occur as the child perceives an alternative way of satisfying his dependence needs. However, if such alternative channels are not available to him, if he consistently meets rejection when he makes dependence-seeking overtures to the people around him, he may come to expect rejection generally. In such a case, expressing his emotional dependence needs becomes associated with punishing consequences (frustration) and the child tends to quit trying to induce others to satisfy these needs. Thus, constant rejection may produce a general withdrawal from seeking dependence relationships, although dependent needs may still be active. Experimental evidence in support of this point is offered by Carl (1) who showed that the frequency of dependence responses declines when the adult toward whom these responses are directed consistently fails to respond to them.

Where consistent rejection has produced strong withdrawal tendencies, one may find the child showing evidence of a conflict between the tendency to make dependence overtures and the tendency to hold back in anticipation of being rejected. Hesitant, timorous overtures may result from these opposed impulses. The child who wants affection may start toward his mother, then stop half way and stand there. Or he may go over and stand at her side, touch her dress, then wait for an encouraging sign from her before making more definite indications of his wishes.

G. INSTRUMENTAL INDEPENDENCE

When a child initiates his own activities and copes with difficulties he encounters without asking for help, he shows instrumental inde-pendence. Suppose a child starts working out a cut-out puzzle with the goal of completing it. If the puzzle is hard for him he will take quite a while and make many mistakes before he reaches his goal. The extent to which he persists in the task without asking for help may be taken as a measure of his instrumental independence.

Whether a child shows instrumental independence in a situation depends on a number of factors. The hypotheses which follow specify five of these factors and predict their effects on a child's tendencies to seek help.

(a). *The more frustration a child encounters while performing an activity, the more will he tend to seek help.* This hypothesis simply assumes that children learn to seek help as one way of overcoming obstacles in their goal-directed behavior.

(b). *The more a child expects that help is available, the more will he tend to seek it.* If a child has learned through repeated experiences that others will help him under certain conditions, he will tend to resort to help when those conditions exist. If he usually has been refused help at such times, he will tend not to expect or seek it.

(c). *The more a child expects he can reach his goal unaided, the less will he tend to seek help.* If the child has previously completed the activity or similar activities without help, he has a basis for expecting to succeed on his own and for going ahead without asking for help.

(d). *The more reassurance a child receives while performing an activity, the less is he apt to seek help.* This factor of reassurance is illustrated when someone says, "You're doing fine," or "You can finish it." The hypothesis assumes that reassurance fosters instrumental independence by lessening anxiety in instances when the child is anticipating failure.

(e). *The more a child expects approval for reaching a goal unaided, the less will he tend to seek help.* This assumes the child has the need for approval and that this need provides a positive incentive for finishing an activity without help if he expects approval upon completing it.

The development of "frustration tolerance" is an aspect of acquiring instrumental independence. The critical factor in learning to cope with frustrations is whether the child actually persists until he reaches his goal. When a parent helps a child "over the rough spots" so that he continues at the task rather than giving up, he is helping his child learn to tolerate frustration. Also, if he makes the task easy at the outset and gradually steps up its difficulty as the child's expectation of success increases along with increasing frustration, the chances are good that more and more frustration will be tolerated. Finally, if the desirability of the goal is increased, the child is more apt to persist until reaching it and so to develop the expectation of overcoming obstacles on future occasions.

In analyzing how instrumental independence develops, the rôle of emotional dependence deserves special consideration. If a situation is one in which the child anticipates injury or rejection, he may require reassurance (emotional dependence) in order to face the situation and so be enabled to develop instrumental independence. Also, as discussed by Stendler (5), the child's need for approval may play a key rôle in motivating him to exhibit instrumental independence rather than quitting or asking for help when he encounters difficulties.

H. EMOTIONAL INDEPENDENCE

Emotional dependence and independence are relative terms. No one at any age is emotionally dependent in every situation. However, comparing children or adults of the same age, there are great differences in the types of situation, and in the proportion of all situations, where emotional dependence and independence are shown. As an individual grows older, the situations in which he shows emotional dependence and independence change. It is these differences which require explanation.

1. DEVELOPING EMOTIONAL SELF-RELIANCE. A child may be called emotionally self-reliant (or self-confident) when he faces threats of injury or rejection without requiring emotional support. A lack of emotional self-reliance is shown by avoiding threat situations or by seeking emotional "props" which make one feel safer while coping with threats. These props may be means of reducing the actual threat in the situation, or "security symbols" such as the doll a child takes to bed with him, or reassurance from a trusted person.

In analyzing how emotional self-reliance is acquired, threats of injury and of rejection will be discussed separately.

a. *Acquiring self-confidence in physical threat situations.* Initially, each child is fearless in many situations where his parents know he may injure himself. When a 12-month-old crawls off the porch and tumbles to the ground he need not be showing self-confidence. He may simply not know any better. Eventually, a child will fall enough times in one situation or another to learn the painful consequences and to anticipate them whenever he is at the point of falling again. When he has learned to associate a situation with the threat of hurting himself, the issue of emotional dependence or independence in that situation is relevant. In responding to the threats he perceives in a situation where he may hurt himself, a child shows emotional independence if he copes with the situation without requiring any protective devices or without leaning on another person for reassurance.

The question of how self-confidence is learned applies in particular to situations where a child has been frightened or hurt and reacts by showing fear or avoidance, or by requiring emotional support in order to face the situation. Methods of learning self-confidence may be illustrated by ways in which children overcome the fear of deep water. Assume a child who swims a little, but is afraid to be in water over his head. Six methods of overcoming his fear are described below.

(1). *Sink-or-swim method.* In this case, the child is forced to cope with the situation by being tossed into the water and left to fend for himself. If he gets to land under his own power a few times, he may perceive himself as capable of coping with the situation and lose his fear. This is a hazardous method of teaching self-confidence, since the child may panic and have to be rescued. Or the experience may intensify his fear of the water even though he makes it to land.

(2) *Distraction method.* This method includes any means by which the child temporarily forgets or pushes aside his fear so that he jumps into the water and tries to swim. For example, if others say, "I dare you," or "coward," the child may be distracted from his fear long enough to plunge in. Swimming

uccessfully under these conditions is a way
or the child to replace his expectation of fail-
re and injury with the expectation of success.

(3). *Threshold method.* This is the method
f starting out a stroke or two from land and
oing a bit farther out each time as confidence
rows in one's ability to swim back. The
uccess of this method depends on the threat
n the situation increasing slowly enough that
he child's anxiety or fear does not exceed the
evel which he will tolerate.

(4). *Over-learning method.* This method
alls for practicing swimming under safe con-
itions to the point where one becomes so
killful and experienced that he becomes con-
dent he can take care of himself in the deep
ater.

(5). *Crutch method.* In this case the child
ses water wings or a life belt which he relies
n to keep him from sinking. With the protec-
ion this device gives him, he practices swim-
ing until he has sufficient confidence in his
bility that he will venture into water without
crutch.

(6). *Reassurance method.* In this method
he child depends on some person whom he
rusts to protect him. The reassurance given
im enables him to practice swimming and to
iscover that he can take care of himself.

Each of the six methods described applies
o acquiring self-confidence in the great
ariety of physical threat situations—over-
oming the fear of being alone in a room, the
ear of animals, the fear of high places, the
ear of fighting, etc. Acquiring self-confidence
y any of these methods depends on coping
ith the feared situation successfully and on
eveloping the expectation of being successful
n one's own.

b. Acquiring "rejection-tolerance." One form
f emotional self-reliance is the capacity to
olerate rejection by others. Two bases for
xhibiting rejection-tolerance are proposed.
irst, a person may be emotionally self-reliant
ollowing instances of being rejected if he has
lternative ways of satisfying his needs for
ffection and approval when they arise. If
e has usually been successful in satisfying
hese dependent needs he may expect to be
ble to satisfy them again and so will be secure
gainst specific instances of being rejected.
econd, a person while developing channels for

expressing his emotional dependence needs,
learns to discriminate the people who are important sources of gratification of these needs
from others who are not. When this learning
has occurred, he will be able to take rejection
from people who "don't matter" as long as
those whom he counts on are not rejecting.

2. DEVELOPING SELF-ASSERTION. Self-assertion expresses needs to master tasks or to
dominate other people. In satisfying these
needs the relevant goals are feelings of adequacy or superiority: "I did it," "I'm smarter
than you are," "I beat him," etc. In short, it
is assumed that self-assertion needs are satisfied by self-approval.

a. Acquiring mastery needs and behavior. A
basis for explaining how mastery develops is
the child's desire to win others' approval. On
this basis, three aspects of the process of
developing this form of self-assertion may be
distinguished, as follows: (a) acquiring needs
for approval, (b) learning to perform tasks
with persistence, speed, or skill in order to
win approval, and (c) "internalizing," i.e.,
adopting others' standards as to the sort of
performance required to gain approval, and
feeling self-approval when these standards are
satisfied. The first two aspects fall under emotional dependence and have been discussed
earlier in this paper. It is with the third aspect
that emotional independence enters the picture
since the child who has internalized his ap-
proval-seeking doesn't require approval from
others to motivate his performance.

Internalization of approval may be explained
as follows. After learning to do things which
win others' approval, a child anticipates approval whenever he performs the acts which
have been approved. It is assumed that anticipated approval is rewarding by itself, giving
a feeling of security or pleasure. Since it is
rewarding, it may function as a goal to reinforce the performance of the customarily
approved behavior.

The degree to which a child develops mastery needs, and the activities and standards
of performance he uses to express those needs,
are determined by his individual learning experiences. A child will tend to express mastery
needs in those activities in which he has been
successful in getting approval. Getting approval, of course, depends on doing things

which his parents and others value—going to the toilet, keeping clean, solving puzzles, catching a ball, reciting a rhyme, etc. Also a child learns to strive for the levels of accomplishment which others have set up as a basis for giving approval—speed, accuracy, grace, persistence, originality, etc.

b. Acquiring dominance needs and behavior. Learning dominance needs and behavior may be accounted for on the basis of winning others' approval in the same way that learning mastery was explained above. Once others' approval has been internalized, self-approval (from anticipated approval) serves as reinforcement for dominant behavior. The great differences in dominative behavior among children of the same age may be explained as due in part to differences in the amount of approval or disapproval others have given them for being dominant in particular ways in various situations.

A child does not have to win in order to satisfy dominance needs if approval has been given him for daring, for doing his best, or for making a good showing. However, other things being equal, the more often a child is defeated in tests for dominance, the less apt he will be to express dominative behavior. Since dominating others often has instrumental value in obtaining goals other than approval (as when two children want the same toy), being successful in competing for such goals reinforces one's tendencies toward expressing domination, while being unsuccessful sets up expectations of failure and tends to weaken those tendencies.

I. SUMMARY

This paper defines certain dependence-independence aspects of personality and outlines how they may be learned. In this analysis, the distinction is made between instrumental dependence (needs for help) and emotional dependence (needs for reassurance, affection or approval). Similarly, instrumental inde-

pendence is distinguished from emotional independence. Emotional independence is defined to include self-assertive needs to master tasks and to dominate other people.

An important link between dependence and independence is offered by the need for approval, which is not only a dependence need but also a basis for learning both instrumental and emotional independence.

Dependence and independence needs are discussed as acquired or "secondary" needs. Also this article discusses the acquisition of expectancies of satisfying or not satisfying these needs by making goal-directed responses in particular situations. It is assumed that such expectancies are associated with predispositions to make, or not to make, particular goal-directed responses, dependent on the outcomes which are anticipated.

In the analysis of instrumental and emotional dependence, this article stresses the fact that dependence needs require interaction with others since these needs can be satisfied only when others respond in certain ways. Since others must be motivated to satisfy one's dependence needs, and since others set up certain requirements the dependent person must meet before they will gratify his needs, it is evident that dependence needs play a central rôle in shaping one's personality to meet social expectations.

REFERENCES

1. CARL, L. J. An experimental study of the effect of nurturance on preschool children. Unpub. Ph.D. Dissertation, State Univ. Iowa, 1949.
2. MILLER, N. E. & DOLLARD, J. Social Learning and Imitation. New Haven: Yale Univ. Press, 1941.
3. SEARS, R. R. A theoretical framework for personality and social behavior. *Am. Psychol.*, 1951, *6*, 476-483.
4. SONTAG, L. W. Dynamics of personality formation. *Personality*, 1951, *6*, 119-130.
5. STENDLER, C. B. Critical periods in socialization and over-dependency. *Child Devel.* 1952, *23*, 3-12.

30. UNDERACHIEVEMENT RELATED TO INTERESTS, ATTITUDES, AND VALUES *

RAYMOND HUMMEL AND NORMAN SPRINTHALL

THE PROBLEM

Educators have long been perplexed by inferior academic performance on the part of students who otherwise evidence superior intellectual capacity. Research on academic underachievement, however, typically has been insignificant in its findings and inconsistent in its explanations (Hackett & DuBois, 1961; Peterson, 1963; Tiedeman & McArthur, 1956; Thorndike, 1963). Underachievement has been attributed variously to parental disinterest, cultural impoverishment, personality maladjustment, teacher inadequacy, and just plain laziness. Some social scientists have made it fashionable to justify underachievement as a symptom of adolescent alienation from absurd conditions in school and society (Friedenberg, 1959; Goodman, 1956). Whatever one's interpretation of its sources, underachievement is generally recognized to be a serious drain on society's reservoir of talent (McClelland et al., 1958; Miller, 1961) and on an individual's chances to realize a sense of worth and fulfillment in an increasingly technological society.

THEORETICAL CONSIDERATIONS

The present study, part of a larger research in counseling and underachievement,[1] examines

* Hummel, Raymond and Sprinthall, Norman, "Underachievement Related to Interests, Attitudes, and Values." *The Personnel and Guidance Journal*, December 1965, *44*, pp. 388-395.

[1] The larger project, entitled "Evaluation of a Model for Guidance Counseling," has been supported by the U. S. Department of Health, Education, and Welfare, SAE #8968, Project 1951. The authors are also grateful for support from the Graduate School of Education, Harvard University, and from the Computation Center, Massachusetts Institute of Technology.

academic underachievement as a problem in adaptive ego functioning. As an individual confronts the flow of demands and opportunities in daily living—for example, the tasks imposed by the school—he perceives and acts under the guidance of a system of psychic dispositions. This "guidance system," which comprises the mainly conscious, the rational and reality-oriented aspects of personality, is called the ego. The concept of ego as a dynamic organization of perceptual and value dispositions through which an individual guides and governs his efforts to adapt to his environment has been given its most important recent treatment in Rapaport (1951), Hartman (1959), and Gill (1959). Some of the elements of theory more specific to the present study appear in Hummel (1962).

The ego structure, the network of personal dispositions within the ego, changes and develops as an individual matures and learns from experience. At any given moment, however, it influences significantly the manner in which a person governs his needs and impulses and guides his instrumental behavior in response to the tasks and opportunities in his external world. It is in this sense that the ego can be construed as an agency, an "establishment" through which an individual adapts to his environment. Some of the indicators of an adaptive ego include: a rational orientation to problem situations; a readiness to deal with a set of prescribed tasks with minimal delay, distraction, or supervision; a planful orientation toward the future; and a willingness to postpone enjoyable activities in pursuit of a distant goal. The effectiveness of a student's academic performance is construed, in this context, to be an indicator of the adaptive strength of his ego.

EGO AND ACADEMIC PERFORMANCE. The relationship between academic achievement and ego adaptiveness is quite short of perfect. Many conditions other than ego capacity obviously determine an individual's level of academic achievement. Some courses in some high schools neither encourage nor merit maximal effort from bright students. Nor are teachers' grades arrived at with pure objectivity. Some bright adolescents, moreover, may give priority to enterprises outside the high school. If these nonacademic enterprises are socially constructive and personally satisfying, why downgrade the ego adaptiveness of adolescents so engaged? Nor is it necessarily maladaptive for some bright students to take a "moratorium" from intensive academic study, especially if they use such a period to examine critically the often contradictory values and performance standards being promoted by the adult world.

Despite such exceptions, we are still persuaded to the postulate that underachievement, in the general case of the bright student, is a valid indicator of an immature ego. The essential rationale for construing academic achievement to be an indicator of ego functioning lies in the consequences academic achievement has on an individual's freedom to choose and to exercise some control (in the future as well as in the present) over his life circumstances. The theory focuses on the "life in progress" (White, 1952) of each adolescent in a society that is becoming increasingly technological, corporate, and bureaucratic in its structure. With such social changes, access to socially valued and personally satisfying statuses (in terms of occupational level, marital eligibility, and civic influence) has come to pivot more and more around educational qualifications.

Whether one views these social trends to be desirable or not is—from the research perspective for this paper—immaterial; the trends exist, and they can be projected as facts for the future (Kimball & McClellan, 1962). Routes of access to valued statuses and to a fulfilling life, other than channels of formal education and training, have become increasingly scarce. Of course, an adequate theory of

underachievement as maladaptation ought still to provide for the adolescent who—out of protest or sheer individualism—would knowingly and responsibly choose to establish his identity outside the corporate mainstream. Such a person might have a strong, well-adapted ego. But considering the risks, he would have to be of heroic—and therefore rare—stature. Currently, the more likely conditions associated with adolescent alienation—at least in the suburban high school—are anomy and apathy.

INTERESTS, ATTITUDES AND VALUES. Efforts in the social sciences to employ interest, attitude, and value as discrete concepts have had a doubtful payoff. Super and Crites (1962) note that there is substantial overlap among these concepts and in the content of the instruments that purport to measure them. At the inception of the present study it was intended to construe these terms to represent different levels of psychological (ego) functioning. We were unable, however, despite having Kluckhohn's (1952) admirable analysis of the value concept as an example, to establish consistent logical distinctions among the concepts of interest, attitude, and value; nor were these terms separately useful in efforts to group and to examine our data. It was thus decided to consider them in this study to be interchangeable. Each scale within an instrument, regardless of the title of the instrument, was judged as to whether it might be an appropriate measure of certain ego qualities. On the Guilford-Zimmerman Temperament Survey, for example, only the Restraint and Thoughtfulness scales were judged to be directly relevant indicators of how the individual's ego might function. The scores on the other scales—Friendliness, Personal Relations, Masculinity, etc.—were judged to be too remote in their implications.

PLAN FOR THE STUDY

A postulate underlying the plan for the research is that an individual's level of academic achievement relative to intellectual capacity is a function of the strength of certain of his psychological (ego) dispositions. In the strategy for this study, selected measures of interest, attitude, and value were employed as indicators of relevant ego dispositions. The general hypothesis then follows: If measures of mental ability and relevant social variables are held constant, a significant relation will be found between level of school achievement and certain measures of interests, attitudes, and values.

INSTRUMENTS

The measuring instruments selected were: The Strong Vocational Interest Blank, the Strodtbeck V-Scale (modified by expanding the original 15 items to a 20- item scale), the Allport-Vernon-Lindzey Study of Values (Levy modification), and the Guilford-Zimmerman Temperament Survey.

The research population consisted of all the boys from the two high schools in a middle-class, suburban, residential community. This community provides strong support for public education; the schools are ably staffed and enjoy a national reputation for excellence. The high school curriculum has five tracks—three for college preparation, one for vocational training, and one for business training. Over 70 per cent of the students who graduate from high school attend four-year colleges.

SELECTION OF SAMPLE. A sample of boys in the sophomore, junior, and senior classes was drawn from both high schools of the community in the fall of 1960. Using the entire school population of about 1,500 high school boys, a regression equation was computed for each high school class. The combined Verbal and Quantitative scores of the School and College Abilities Test (SCAT) were used as a measure of academic ability and compared statistically with six differently computed measures of grade-point average (GPA). The measure of GPA finally selected was that which provided the highest correlations between ability and grades; this measure took into account for each course its level of difficulty, its number of credit points, and the teacher's grade. The regression equations were then used to compute a predicted GPA for each student. The difference between the actual weighted GPA and the predicted average was derived as a discrepancy score. Discrepancy scores were computed for the entire population of high school boys and then distributed on a continuum with the average score at zero.

The research sample drawn from this population included only boys who scored above the 70th percentile (national norms) on the SCAT test and who were currently enrolled in one of the college preparatory curricula. The final sample was divided into groups at three achievement levels: underachievers, par achievers, and superior achievers.

The Underachievers. The underachievers were defined as boys with grade-point discrepancy scores (GPA) that fell one or more standard deviations in the negative direction from the average discrepancy score of the population. The initial selection procedure provided a group of 137 possible underachievers picked from the population roster. This exhausted the population of bright underachievers (as defined by the criteria already mentioned in the two high schools.)

As a check on the SCAT, the subjects tentatively selected were administered the Wechsler Adult Intelligence Scale (WAIS). (A conversion scale was developed for subjects below age 16.) Students were included in the sample if SCAT and WAIS scores indicated high average ability. Twenty-seven underachievers were dropped when an inspection of both ability measures suggested that their intellectual ability was marginal for the research sample. Further screening by interview and by check of school records eliminated 15 students for whom it was felt that low achievement was an aspect of more pervasive emotional disturbance. The elimination of 42 cases thus reduced the number of underachievers to 95.

The Par Achievers. The par achievers were chosen through a similar screening procedure. The final group was composed of 24 students whose actual and predicted grades were equal; that is, their discrepancy score was close to zero.

The Superior Achievers. The superior achievers were selected by the same basic procedure. The final group was composed of 28 students whose discrepancy scores were one or more standard deviations in the positive direction from the average discrepancy score. The superior achievers were thus separated from the underachievers by at least two standard deviations on the continuum of discrepancy scores; the par achievers were located between these groups.

In summary, the procedures employed to refine the same were: (1) selection of the most efficient out of six tested formulas for defining academic grade-point average; (2) the combined use, for screening, of both group and individual tests of mental ability; (3) the elimination of subjects who manifested potentially severe emotional problems; (4) the selection of students from only the college preparatory curricula whose academic potential was estimated to be sufficiently high to justify planing for college, and (5) the separation of the three achievement groups from each other by at least one standard deviation in discrepancy score units, thus minimizing overlap and the effect of errors of measurement.

CHARACTERISTICS OF THE RESEARCH SAMPLE. The final sample consisted of 147 normal suburban high school boys who measured high in academic ability, divided into three groups: 95 underarachievers, 24 par achievers, and 28 superior achievers.

There were no significant differences in measured mental ability among the three achievement groups. On the SCAT, the average total converted score was 304 (approximately at the 93rd percentile on national norms); on the WAIS, the average total IQ was 118 (approximately at the 88th percentile on Wechsler's national norms). If the actual GPA's were plotted on a conventional scale, the underachievers would average approximately C− grades; par achievers, B−; and superior achievers, A grades.

The three groups were found to be similar with respect to a number of additional variables; namely, socio-economic status (Hamburger, 1957), age, level of educational aspiration, the extent of family dislocations (i.e., death or divorce of a parent), and place of family origin. Religious-cultural background was also coded into Jewish versus non-Jewish categories. It had been assumed on the basis of previous research (McClelland, 1958; Strodtbeck, 1958) that religious background would be relevant to academic achievement. In this sample, however, no such relationships were observed. Of the 48 boys who could be classified as Jewish, 32 (66 per cent) were un-

derachievers. Of the boys who could be classified as non-Jewish, 43 out of 64 (67 per cent) were underachievers. Of the boys who could not be classified in terms of religion, an equivalent of 57 per cent were underachievers. Similar percentages were found for the par and superior achiever groups, i.e., 21 per cent of the Jews and 15 per cent of the non-Jews were superior achievers—an insignificant difference in this population.

The homogeneity among the groups in this research on the variables noted above thus encourages the assumption that, in this sample, levels of academic achievement can be examined in relatively pure relationship to variables we have defined as ego dispositions.

RESULTS

STRONG VOCATIONAL INTEREST BLANK. On the SVIB, the superior achievers scored significantly higher on the Social Service, Occupational Level, and Interest Maturity scales while the underachievers scored higher on the Business Contact scale. To conserve space Table I lists only the Strong Scales for which significant differences were found.

The higher Social Welfare scale score suggests the closer similarity of the superior achievers to those of men whose occupations reflect a heightened social concern. The higher Interest Maturity score indicates that the interests of superior achievers more closely resemble the interests of 25-year-old men than do the other groups. The higher Occupational Level scores indicate that superior achievers have interests closer than the other groups to the interests of men in high-level professional and business careers.

The underachievers, by their higher scores on the Business Contact scale, display interests similar to those of men in real estate, life insurance and sales management—occupations which may reflect, more than those of the other scales, a practical, utilitarian orientation to living.

STRODTBECK V-SCALE. On the V-Scale, three factors emerged: (1) adherence to authority; (2) positive orientation to planning, education, mastery over the environment; and (3) positive orientation to work-success. Table 2 illustrates the factor clusters and the relative loadings.

TABLE 1 Strong Vocational Interest Blank: Means, standard deviations and analysis of variance ratios for three achievement groups.

Strong Groups	Achievement Groups			
	UA (N=95)	PA (N=24)	SA (N=28)	F Ratio (2+144ndf)
V. Social Service	175.70	191.71	224.75	3.20*
	95.16	72.82	84.21	
VII. C.P.A.	26.36	30.12	31.67	3.89*
	9.85	8.81	9.82	
IX. Business Contact	106.81	99.37	90.64	4.88‡
	23.01	28.49	25.33	
XII. Interest Maturity	45.40	47.54	50.07	3.18*
	9.80	5.85	6.83	
XIII. Occupational Level	52.00	54.08	55.57	3.43*
	6.48	6.09	7.60	

* Indicates F significance of $<.05$.
‡ Indicates F significance of $<.01$.
Note: UA=Underachievers; PA=Par Achievers; SA= Superior Achievers.

Only Factor II significantly differentiated among the three groups (using a one-way analysis of variance for Factor II scores, the F ratio was 7.63, p. $<.01$, ndf$=2+144$).

It is noteworthy that the first factor, Adherence to Authority, did not significantly distinguish underachievers from superior achievers. This finding is directly at odds with Strodtbeck's results (1958) and inconsistent with Perry's research (1959). In the present study, underachievers all consistently disavowed the concept of arbitrary loyalty to family authority. The great majority of subjects in each of the three groups rejected the view that parental ties—permanently and without exception—are binding.

The second factor revealed a more consistent pattern than the first. Superior achievers are morely likely to reject "fate" as a determining force in their lives. Not one superior achiever agreed with either of the first two items in Table 2. The same general attitude was apparent in their response to the other items. Superior achievers hold a more hopeful attitude than the other groups toward planning, toward the possibility of mastering their environment, and toward the importance of education and learning.

On the third factor there was no significant separation. The traditional values for hard work and success, the so-called Protestant ethic, as measured here do not seem to distinguish students in accord with level of school achievement. This is a quite tentative conclusion, since the factor basically was derived from only two highly similar items.

ALLPORT-VERNON-LINDZEY STUDY OF VALUES. On the Study of Values, only the Economic Scale differentiated significantly the three groups; the superior achievers obtained significantly lower scores on this scale than the par and underachievers. This finding may be influenced by the particular conditions in this research design. The students in this sample are all enrolled in a college preparatory curriculum with a strong emphasis on science and liberal arts; such courses may not be readily translatable into immediate practical outcomes. But strong economic values may be related to a desire for practical results, for early payoff to effort—an outcome which the liberal arts courses cannot guarantee. The low Economic scores of the superior achievers may signify their greater readiness to attack academic tasks with less concern for an immediate, practical payoff. The differences on the Economic scale also parallel to some extent the findings on the SVIB, especially the differences among the achievement groups on the Business Contact scale.

GUILFORD-ZIMMERMAN TEMPERAMENT SURVEY. On the G-Z, it was hypothesized that the

TABLE 2   Strodtbeck V-Scale: Factors, items and loadings.

	Factor Loadings		
	I	II	III
Items: Factor I			
3. Even if a teenager gets married, his main loyalty should still belong to his mother and father	—.32	.05	.21
4. The best kind of job to have is one where you are part of an organization, all working together even if you don't get individual credit	—.36	.07	—.13
5. When the time comes for a boy to take a job, he should stay near his parents, even if it means giving up a good job	—.52	—.09	—.09
7. Nothing in life is worth the sacrifice of moving away from your parents	—.62	—.06	.18
15. A good teacher's job is to keep his students from wandering from the right track	—.35	—.25	.07
16. The worst thing about a lazy student is that he is letting his parents down	—.43	—.08	.05
19. It helps the child in the long run if he is made to accept his parents' ideas	—.33	—.06	.14
Items: Factor II			
1. Planning only makes a person unhappy since your plans hardly ever work out	.01	—.37	.13
2. When a man is born, the success he's going to have is already in the cards, so he might as well accept it and not fight against it	—.10	—.28	.07
8. Nowadays, with the world the way it is, the smart person lives for today and lets tomorrow take care of itself	—.15	—.50	.01
9. Education and learning are more important in determining a person's happiness than money and what it will buy	—.24	.42	.06
10. Parents expect too much of their children	—.05	—.42	—.06
13. All I want out of life is a steady job that pays me enough to buy a nice car and comfortable home	—.12	—.45	—.04
Items: Factor III			
11. There's nothing a person can't be or do if he really wants to and works hard to do it	—.17	.22	.73
14. To benefit from his courses, a student should have a clear idea of what he intends to do when he gets out of high school	—.10	—.20	.26
18. Students sometimes get rebellious ideas, but as they grow up they ought to get over them	.01	—.10	.26
20. A person can attain anything in life if he wants it hard enough	—.19	.07	.73

Note: In general, factor loadings above plus or minus .25 can be considered significant.

superior achievers would be the highest on the Restraint and Thoughtfulness scales. The other eight scales were thought to be unrelated, in terms of ego theory, to academic achievement. Scales such as Friendliness, Sociability, Personal Relations, Emotional Stability, Masculinity, etc., were not thought to reveal dispositions that determine how an adolescent adapts to school tasks. The differentiation between groups was indeed significant, and *only* on the Restraint and Thoughtfulness scales. The superior achievers scored extremely high on these scales, underachievers scored quite low, and pa chievers averaged between these extremes. The Restraint and Thoughtfulness scales themselves possibly measure similar dispositions (the intercorrelation is moderately high, +.42; and at least 10 of the 29 items are similar). Both these scales include items dealing with the importance of planning, of thinking through complicated problems, of seriousmindedness, and of understanding reasons behind actions. The dimensions of planfulness and thoughtfulness seem to be of major significance in differentiating among the groups. The F ratios for these two scales (23.46 for Restraint, and 9.74 for Thoughtfulness) were the largest found on any relevant dimensions.

A discriminant analysis was performed on the data for the SVIB, the Study of Values, and the G-Z. This was done to check against the occurrence of chance differences, a likely accompaniment when univariate and bivariate statistical tests are used with multi-dimensional batteries. The Wilks-Lambda criterion, the most general test of overall discriminating power, was derived for each instrument. The Lambda was significant beyond the .001 level for all three instruments. Thus, on an overall basis, each test was found to provide significant separation across the three achievement groups.

DISCUSSION

The data suggest that the (prototypical) superior achiever—in comparison with the underachiever—is more mature, more thoughtful and planful in his orientation to tasks and problems, and more willing to postpone immediate gratifications to achieve distant goals. His interests more closely resemble those of older men. He is positively oriented to master his circumstances; he disavows more strongly than the underachiever the role of fate as a determinant in his life. The superior achiever does not appear to be any less well adjusted, at least in terms of such scales on the Guilford-Zimmerman Temperament Survey as Emotional Stability and Masculinity; nor does he perceive it to be any more difficult to relate to other persons, as might be indicated on such scales as those of Sociability and Friendliness. The general image of the superior achiever in these data is that he is an independent, purposive, and efficiently organized individual who is likely to deal with academic tasks—whether interesting or dull—as a necessary condition of getting on with his life. There is no evidence to support the stereotype of the superior achiever as a harried, neurotic conformer.

The underachiever, obversely, is less planful and thoughtful in his orientation to life; he is inclined to be fatalistic in his expectations concerning outcomes of personal effort. He is likely to put a premium on the immediate and practical effects to be gained from work, here academic work. He is less likely to relate his conduct to long-range consequences.

Such qualities as self-control, personal responsibility, and a thoughtful, planful orientation to the tasks of living are among those commonly ascribed to a mature ego. It is on such variables that the superior academic achievers in this sample differ most strikingly from the underachievers. The data thus support the postulate that academic performance is a kind of problem-solving behavior whose level of efficiency is, in each individual, a function of the structure and strength of his ego.

To interpret academic performance as a problem in adaptation, one need not ignore the often alienating conditions that adolescents face in school; academic underachievement is in itself not a sufficient indicator of maladaptation. In this study, however, underachievement was found to be accompanied by a number of signs of immature ego structure. Academic tasks, even in the most enlightened schools, cannot always be immediately meaningful in themselves. To meet them adaptively, an individual needs to be capable of investing in a plan, and of risking himself to pursue it. He must be able not only to control his performance of assigned learning tasks with appropriate efficiency; he must also trust in some degree the promise of the school that a current investment of time and energy in such assignments will, in the long run, help him to make a better life.

REFERENCES

DARLEY, J. G. & HAGENAH, THEDA. *Vocational interest measurement.* Minneapolis: Univ. Minnesota Press, 1955.

FRIEDENBERG, E. Z. *The vanishing adolescent.* Boston: Beacon, 1959.

GILL, M. M. The present state of psychoanalytic theory. *J. abnorm. soc. psychol.*, 1959, *58*, 1-8.

GOODMAN, P. *Growing up absurd.* New York: Random House, 1956.

HACKETT, E. V., & DuBOIS, P. H. The measurement and evaluation of over- and underachievement. Draft report of conference on research methodology in training. Washington Univ., St. Louis, 1961.

HAMBURGER, M. A revised occupational scale for rating socio-economic status. Career Pattern Study, Teachers College, Columbia Univ., 1957. (Mimeo).

HARTMAN, H. *Ego psychology and the problem of adaptation.* New York: International Press, 1959.

HUMMEL, R. Ego counseling in guidance concept and method. *Harvard Educ. Rev.*, 1962, *32*, 463-482.

KIMBALL, S. T., & McCLELLAN, J. E., JR. *Education and the new America.* New York: Random House, 1962.

KLUCKHOHN, C. Values and value-orientation in the theory of action: an exploration in definition and classification. In T. Parsons and E. A. Shils (Eds.), *Toward a general theory of action.* Cambridge, Mass.: Harvard Univ. Press, 1952, 388-433.

McCLELLAND, D. C., et al. *Talent and society.* Princeton: Van Nostrand, 1958.

MILLER, L. M. (Ed.). *Guidance for the underachiever with superior ability.* Washington, D. C.: U.S. Dept. of HEW, 1961.

MORGAN, H. H. A psychosomatic comparison of achieving and nonachieving college students of high ability. *J. consult. psychol.*, 1952, *16*, 292-298.

PERRY, W. Check list of educational values. Unpublished draft of explanatory material for a volume, Cambridge, Mass., 1959.

PETERSON, J. The researcher and the underachiever: never the twain shall meet. *Ph Delta Kappan*, 1963, *44*, 379-381.

RAPAPORT, D. *The organization and pathology of thought.* New York: Columbia Univ. Press 1951.

STERN, G. G., STEIN, M. I., & BLOOM, B. S *Methods in personality assessment.* Glencoe Ill.: Free Press, 1956.

STRODTBECK, F. Family interaction, values and achievement. In D. McClelland et al., *Talent and society.* Princeton: Van Nostrand, 1958 135-194.

SUPER, D. E., & CRITES, J. O. *Appraising vocational fitness.* New York: Harper, 1962.

THORNDIKE, R. L. *The concepts of over- and underachievement.* New York: Bureau of Publications, Teachers College, Columbia Univ. 1963.

TIEDEMAN, D. V., & McARTHUR, C. C. Over- and underachievement: if any! Paper read at National Council on Measurements used in Education, Atlantic City, N. J., Feb. 1956.

WHITE, R. W. *Lives in progress.* New York Dryden, 1952.

WILSON, W. C. Value differences between public and private school graduates. *J. educ. psychol.* 1959, *50*, 213-218.

31. EXPLORATIONS IN CREATIVE THINKING *

E. PAUL TORRANCE

There are many reasons for school guidance workers to consider the identification and development of creative thinking important.

First, creativity is important from the standpoint of personality development and mental health. There is little question but that prolonged, enforced repression of the creative desire may lead to breakdown of the personality.

* Reprinted from the December, 1960, issue of *Education.* Copyright, 1960, by the Bobbs-Merrill Company, Inc., Indianapolis, Indiana.

On tests of creative thinking, developed by the author and his associates, schizophrenic manifested amazingly impoverished imaginations, inflexibility and inadequacy of response and similar characteristics. Their production gave no evidence of the rich fantasy lives an wild imaginations popularly attributed t schizophrenics—only a tremendously impoverished and stifled creativity.

Second, creative thinking contributes importantly to the acquisition of information Indeed, it ultimately may be demonstrated that creative thinking is as important in this respect as are memory and other intellectual functions.

Third, creative thinking is essential in the application of knowledge and in the achievement of vocational success. In almost every field of human achievement, creativity is usually the distinguishing characteristic of the truly eminent. The possession of high intelligence, special talent, and high technical skill is not enough to produce outstanding achievement.

Fourth, it is tremendously important to society for our creative talent to be identified, developed, and utilized. The future of our civilization depends upon the quality of the creative imagination of our next generation.

The author and his associates are engaged in a program of studies concerned with the identification and development of creative thinking from kindergarten through graduate school and into professional life. Thus far, most of our attention has been focused on explorations in the early school years.

The purpose of this paper is to describe a few of the results from these studies, with their implications for school guidance. Problems of identifying creative talent and helping the highly creative individual adjust to his peer group without sacrificing his creativity will receive primary consideration.

IDENTIFYING CREATIVE TALENT

One of the first problems of interest to the guidance worker is that of identifying creative talent. Pioneering work in this field was done by Guilford (4), beginning in the late forties. He and his associates (5) identified the following kinds of thinking abilities involved in creative scientific thinking: sensitivity to problems, fluency of ideas, flexibility, originality, redefinition, ability to rearrange, abstracting ability, synthesis and closure, and coherence of organization.

Lowenfeld (6) identified essentially the same abilities in art. Other approaches have been reported by Barron (1), Getzels and Jackson (3), and others. The attempt to study the development of creative thinking from kindergarten through graduate school, however, has led the author and his colleagues in a number of new directions.

First, we introduced materials calculated to challenge the inventiveness of children (12). These materials consisted primarily of toys (nurse kit, fire truck, and dog), which the children were permitted to manipulate. Subjects were asked to think of ideas for improving each toy so that it would be "more fun to play with."

Responses provided quantifiable data for assessing several kinds of thinking ability which we believed were important in the creative individual. For example, flexibility of thinking was assessed reliably by analyzing the responses in terms of the number of different approaches used in modifying the toy. These approaches included the following well-known principles (8): addition, subtraction, multiplication, division, substitution, combination, magnification, minification, rearrangement, reversal, and sensory appeal (motion, sound, light, odor).

An inventive level score (13) was developed by adapting for our use some of the criteria used by the U. S. Patent Office (7) in making decisions about patent applications. A constructiveness score was devised by taking a cue from a finding by Rossman (9) that noninventors tend only to "cuss" the defects of their environment while inventors tend to say, "This is the way to do it."

A second direction in our innovations in the identification of creativity was stimulated by our definition of creativity as "the formation and testing of ideas and hypotheses" and by our desire to capitalize upon the child's curiosity. Our definition and desire gave birth to our "Ask-and-Guess Test" (14).

In this test, the subject was first shown a picture and asked to think of all the questions he would like to ask in order to understand what is happening in the picture. We asked subjects to pose only questions which could not be answered merely by looking at the picture. Next, we asked him to make as many guesses (formulate hypotheses) as he could about what caused the depicted event. Finally, we asked him to make guesses about all of the possible consequences of the action depicted.

Subjects of all ages found these materials interesting, and we established relatively simple principles for evaluating the quality of the responses. Scores also produced an extremely interesting set of growth curves. For example, we found that ability to formulate hypotheses concerning causation appears to develop slowly and gradually from first grade through the college years. In addition, we found that ability to formulate hypotheses concerning consequences develops much more rapidly in the early school years and is subject to a considerable amount of waxing and waning throughout this range.

The limits of this article do not permit a description and discussion of the other types of material developed to elicit creative ideation.

INTELLIGENCE AND CREATIVITY

Although the developmental patterns concerning the differentiation of intelligence and creativity are not yet clear, several consistent trends have emerged. The relationships between measures of intelligence and measures of creativity differ slightly from grade to grade and between the sexes. Most of the coefficients of correlation are relatively low (around .30), but are higher among girls than among boys. Within the ranges of IQ (132 to 186, as measured by Stanford-Binet) in a class of gifted youngsters, we found a coefficient of correlation of .03 between intelligence and a measure of creativity.

Following the pattern reported by Getzels and Jackson (3), in their study of high-school students, highly creative and highly intelligent groups were identified at each grade level from first through sixth grades. Members of the highly creative group ranked in the upper 20 per cent in their classes on measures of creativity, but not on traditional measures of intelligence. Members of the highly intelligent group ranked in the upper 20 per cent on measures of intelligence, but not on measures of creativity. Those in a third group ranked high on both measures.

Regardless of the measure of intelligence used (Stanford-Binet, Wechsler Intelligence Scale for Children, California Test of Mental Maturity, or Otis Quick-Scoring), about 70 per cent of the top 20 per cent on measures of creativity would have been excluded from gifted groups which were selected on the basis of intelligence only.

One of the most consistent findings, when the highly creative were compared with the highly intelligent, was that the latter were better known by their teachers and were considered as more desirable pupils than were the former. Even those pupils who were highly creative and highly intelligent were considered less desirable than the highly intelligent pupils who had lesser creative abilities. Students who were both highly creative and highly intelligent, in general, were considered by their teachers as more unruly, more dominant, more independent, more studious, and harder working than the students in other groups.

On the basis of peer nominations, those children who ranked highly on both measures were the "stars." They received the most nominations on talkativeness, good ideas, ideas for being naughty, and silly or wild ideas. Those who ranked high on intelligence, but lower on creativity, tended to have the most friends, while those who ranked high on creativity, but not on intelligence, tended to have the fewest friends.

On a measure of psychological accessibility derived from the House-Tree-Person Test (2) those who rated high on creativity, but lower on intelligence, tended to be least accessible psychologically. This tendency should be of special importance to guidance workers, inasmuch as these youngsters have apparently estranged their teachers, as indicated by the author's studies and those of Getzels and Jackson (3).

PEER SANCTIONS AND CREATIVITY

It will be no news to guidance workers that peer groups exercise rather severe sanctions against their most creative members. In no group thus far studied has the author failed to find relatively clear evidence of the operation of these pressures. Both sociometric studies and small-group experiments have been used thus far. Both types of study have yielded many clues for helping youngsters avoid some of the severity of peer sanctions without sacrificing their creativity. Inasmuch as the results of the experimental study were simpler and more straightforward than the others, only this one study will be described here.

In this study (11), we formed groups of five children. In each, we placed one of the most creative children in the class, as identified by tests administered earlier. We then placed each group in a situation requiring creative thinking and involving competition among groups.

This situation permitted the group to experiment for twenty-five minutes, trying to discover all of the things which could be done with a box of science toys and to discover the principles whereby they worked. After a period of five minutes, used for planning, demonstrations, and explanations, each group was given twenty-five minutes in which to present their demonstrations. The focus of observation was upon the techniques used by the groups to control the most creative member and the strategies of the most creative member in coping with these pressures. Much of the behavior observed suggested that the highly creative individual was, in many cases, responsible for his own woes.

At the second-grade level, the most highly creative individuals were generally unpleasant, showing little consideration for the group; little or no goal orientation; little or no identification with the group; and little or no heed to the leadership attempts of their less creative peers.

In the third grade, the most creative subjects tended to work independently—and were ignored for the most part. This tendency persisted into the fourth grade, where the most creative members assumed little responsibility for leadership. Moreover, in the final ratings, these individuals were given little credit for important contributions which they actually made to the success of the group.

The highly creative subjects in the fifth grade manifested more leadership and were more dominant than those in the fourth grade, but they left themselves open to criticism and attack for "being too scientific" and for "being too greedy." These tendencies became more pronounced in the sixth-grade groups.

An examination of almost any of the many lists of personality characteristics of highly creative individuals suggests a number of valid answers to the question, "Why do highly creative individuals alienate their peers and elders?" Many of the highly creative individuals are disturbing elements in classroom groups in elementary schools. The problem of teachers and guidance workers resolves itself into one of helping highly creative individuals maintain those characteristics which seem essential to the development of creative talent and, at the same time, helping them acquire skills for avoiding, or reducing to a tolerable level, the peer sanctions.

Stein (10) has offered a set of interesting suggestions concerning the social role of the creative industrial researcher. If we apply Stein's principles to teachers and guidance workers, the objective in helping creative youngsters would run something like this: Help the highly creative child to maintain his assertiveness without being hostile and aggressive.

SUMMARY

The identification and development of creative thinking should be of concern to guidance workers. It is important from the standpoint of personality development and mental health, acquisition of information, vocational success, and social welfare.

A variety of materials have been devised and tested for identifying creative thinking at all educational levels. New developments have been in the direction of manipulative materials which yield measures of inventiveness, materials which permit exploration through questioning and formulating hypotheses concerning the causes and consequences of behavior.

Both measures of intelligence and creativity appear to be essential in identifying giftedness. Children who rate highly on measures of creativity appear to become alienated from their peers and teachers and tend to manifest behaviors which call forth sanctions by their peers. One of the problems of the guidance worker is to help the highly creative child cultivate those personality characteristics which apparently are essential to his creativity and to help him avoid or reduce the sanctions of his peers without sacrificing his creativity.

REFERENCES

1. Barron, E. The Psychology of Imagination. *Scientific American*, Vol. 199 (September, 1958), pp. 150-166.
2. Buck, J. N. The H-T-P Technique, Monograph Supplement to *Journal of Clinical Psychology*, Vol. 5 (1948), pp. 1-120.
3. Getzels, J. W., and Jackson, P. W. The

Meaning of "Giftedness"—An Examination of an Expanding Concept. *Phi Delta Kappan*, Vol. 40 (1958), pp. 75-77.

4. GUILFORD, J. P. Creativity: *American Psychologist*, Vol. 9 (1950), pp. 444-454.

5. GUILFORD, J. P., and Others. *A Factor-Analytic Study of Creative Thinking*, Part I. *Hypotheses and Description of Tests* (Los Angeles: University of Southern California, 1951).

6. LOWENFELD, V. Current Research on Creativity, *NEA Journal*, Vol. 47 (1958), pp. 538-540.

7. MCPHERSON, J. H. A Proposal for Establishing Ultimate Criteria for Measuring Creative Output, in *The 1955 University of Utah Research Conference on the Identification of Creative and Scientific Talent*, ed. C. W. Taylor (Salt Lake City: University of Utah Press, 1956).

8. OSBORN, A. F. *Applied Imagination* (rev. ed.: New York: Charles Scribner's Sons, 1957).

9. ROSSMAN, J. *The Psychology of the Inventor* (Washington, D. C.: Inventors Publishing Co., 1931).

10. STEIN, M. I. A Transactional Approach to Creativity, in *The 1955 University of Utah Research Conference on the Identification of Creative and Scientific Talent*, ed. C. W. Taylor (Salt Lake City: University of Utah Press, 1956).

11. TORRANCE, E. P. *Explorations in Creative Thinking in the Early School Years*, Part V. *An Experimental Study of Peer Sanctions Against Highly Creative Children* (Minneapolis: Bureau of Educational Research University of Minnesota, 1959).

12. TORRANCE, E. P., and MICHIE, H. W. *Explorations in Creative Thinking in the Early School Years*, Part I, *Scoring Manual for "How Good Is Your Imagination" (Form C)* (Minneapolis: Bureau of Educational Research University of Minnesota, 1959).

13. TORRANCE, E. P., and PALM, H. *The Measurement of Inventivelevel and Constructiveness As Aspects of Creative Thinking* (Minneapolis: Bureau of Educational Research University of Minnesota, 1959).

14. TORRANCE, E. P., and RADIG, H. J. *The Ask-and-Guess Test: Rationale and Scoring Manual* (Minneapolis: Bureau of Educational Research, University of Minnesota, 1959).

Chapter VI

MEASUREMENT AND INTELLIGENCE

Students of educational psychology, indeed students in any of the social sciences, are often dismayed when first encountering the literature in the field of measurement. The rigors of complex statistical procedure, the vast and mysterious body of measurement jargon are both awe inspiring and intimidating to the uninitiated. Social scientists seem to make a fetish over the concept of measurement. Perhaps in no other area has the flow of words regarding measurement theory been so enormous. Educational psychologists, whose discipline is certainly at this point in time one of the more inexact sciences, spend countless hours debating and fretting over details of measurement which often seem trivial to the casual observer. "Never mind about the standard error of estimate or the amount of variance accounted for, tell me my son's IQ score," is the oft-heard anguished plea of many a harried parent. But is all this concern simply a case of sound and fury? The answer is, of course, "no." The seemingly endless statistical lexicon, the forbidding jargon of the trade, is due to an attempt to be precise in the communication of meaning. This is especially important in the social sciences where the concepts being measured are not always as precise or exact as they are in physics or chemistry.

Basically, measurement is the assigning of numbers to concepts. Taking an IQ test, stepping on a scale, placing a tape measure around one's waist, all are examples of measurement. So too are counting the number of times a student is absent, or noting the order of finish of the horses at the Kentucky Derby. In each case a number has been assigned to a "thing" or concept, such as intelligence, weight, clothing-size, or the speed of a horse. People are even measured in such complex areas as "scientific aptitude" or "need for affiliation", and yet the basic measurement theory is the same as it is for something as materialistic as being fitted for a new pair of golf shoes. In education, of course, the purpose of measurement is to provide the teacher with information about the abilities and characteristics of the students.

The way in which the numbers are assigned to concepts or events determines the scale of measurement being used. In measurement theory there are four basic scales, nominal, ordinal, interval and ratio. Any scale other than these four are variations on these basic themes.

Nominal Scales. Nominal scaling, or simply using numbers to label categories, is the lowest order of measurement. It is the assigning of events into various categories and then counting the frequency of occurrence within those categories. For example, we may simply categorize a group of students on the basis of whether or not they exhibit overt aggressive responses during recess and then note the frequencies or numbers of students falling in each of these categories. The farmer sorting strawberries is creating a nominal scale, as is the market researcher finding out which wash-day product is the most popular among housewives in Chester, New Jersey. In nominal scaling, therefore, we discover how many events have X or Y or Z in common.

Ordinal Scales. Often it is not enough to know simply that X or Y is present, but as inquiring scientists we wish to find out how much X or how much Y. The next scale of measurement, the ordinal scale, attempts this by going within a certain category and rank ordering the events. For example, if it were discovered that wash-day product X is the most popular among those housewives of Chester, New Jersey, we could then examine that category alone, and rank the women according to how much "brand X" they used. In the classroom, we might rank order the students according to scores on an achievement test, or height, or number of sociometric votes they received. The important point to remember about ordinal data is that although it does provide information regarding greater or less than, *it does not* specify how much greater or how much less. That is, if on some variable you find student A ranked number one and student B ranked number two, you do not know whether student A is just barely better than B, or whether he is far out in front.

Interval Scales. A still further refinement occurs when our data is in the form of an interval scale. Here we begin to get information on not just greater or less, but how much greater or less. Theoretically, the distances between the points on an interval scale are equal. A rigorously standardized IQ test yields interval data, so that we know that someone with a score of 130 is the same amount higher than a score of 125, as a score of 95 would be over a score of 90. The distance between interval scores has meaning, and because of this, inferences made from interval data can be broader and more meaningful than inferences made from ordinal or nominal data. The more information contained in the score, the more meaningful any conclusions might be that are based on the score.

Ratio Scales. Although this type of data is not yet available in the social sciences, it will be mentioned in order to complete the scaling discussion. Ratio scales, the most refined of the scales of measurement, not only have equal intervals between the points of the scales, but also have an absolute zero. Since we do not know what absolutely zero IQ is, we cannot imply that an IQ of 100 is twice that of an IQ of 50. True ratio scales allow for direct comparisons of that nature, but it is important to realize that none of our measurements in education or psychology pack that much precision. It is therefore incorrect for a teacher, using one of his own tests or even using a well-known, standardized achievement test, to say that Student A did twice as well as Student B.

Regardless of the scale employed, any measurement, to be useful, must satisfy two basic criteria: reliability and validity. Since entire books could be written about these two concepts, we will restrict ourselves only to a brief summary of each.

1. *Reliability.* Whenever we measure anything, whether that be as physical as laying a tape measure next to a piece of wood or as possibly vague as taking a certain aptitude test, there is always the possibility of chance errors occurring. With the tape measure, perhaps you do not lay it perfectly straight; or the pencil used to mark the wood has a point which is too thick, or any of a number of reasons prevents you from getting an error-free measurement. Of course when dealing with psychological or educational measurements, the possibility of random or chance errors increases tremendously. The less error contained in a measurement the more reliable it will be, and this very lack of error will result in a high degree of consistency. Reliability, then, results in consistency over repeated measurements. A reliable IQ test, for example, will yield roughly the same score if taken today and then say a month later, assuming of course that nothing dramatic has occurred which might change the thing being measured.

In constructing one's own test, the prospective teacher should keep in mind that, other things being fairly equal, the more items included in the test the higher the reliability of the test will be. Error is reduced by simply selecting a larger sample of items from the general population of items being covered.

2. *Validity.* Validity indicates the degree to which the test measures what it purports to measure. If a score is supposed to represent scholastic aptitude, for example, then that is what it should be measuring, not height or weight. The Scholastic Aptitude Test is supposed to measure just that, one's aptitude for college work, not, as is thought by some school administrators, the quality of the secondary school's educational curriculum or the effectiveness of the teachers. If that were what the Scholastic Aptitude Test constructors had in mind, they would have designed a different test.

The importance of validity cannot be stressed too much. It is absolutely crucial. A teacher should rightfully expect that a test of musical aptitude is in fact measuring musical aptitude and not IQ or knowledge of the historical facts of Beethoven's life. The teacher should also remember this when constructing his or her own classroom examinations. This is especially important in essay examinations, for if the teacher is truly interested in assessing the student's ability in History or Social Studies then the student should not be penalized for a lack of neatness or poor penmanship.

Statistically, the techniques used for computing coefficients of reliability or validity involve the use of correlation. Typically the Chi Square test, or some variation of it, is used with nominal data, the Spearman Rank Order correlation with ordinal data, and the Pearson Product-Moment correlation with interval data. The reasons for and precise nature of these statistical tests and techniques of data gathering are beyond the scope of this book. A basic understanding of this area, however, can usually be gained by taking a one-semester course in elementary statistics; or the reader may prefer the do-it-yourself method made possible by the use of a programmed text—for example, *Understanding Statistical Concepts* by Bradley and McClelland.

In educational psychology, measurement techniques have been most carefully and probably most successfully pursued in the area of intelligence testing. Since the pioneering work of Sir Francis Galton, the father of mental testing (late 19th century), literally thousands of intelligence tests have been constructed and used both in and outside the classroom. And since its inception the whole area has been embroiled in the controversy over whether intelligence is mostly a product of inheritance or environment, the so-called nature-nurture argument. It was even because of his interest in this age-old philosophical debate that led Galton to develop a kind of primitive IQ test. Although Galton's studies led him to believe that intelligence was basically an inherited trait, he did take note of the wide array of differences in intelligence. He produced a series of simple sensory-motor tests, such as reaction time and auditory range, and he believed that through these measurements of an individual's perceptual equipment some indication of one's genetically endowed intellect could be determined.

The next landmark in the history of mental testing was 1905 when Alfred Binet and Henry Simon introduced the first real intelligence test of the sort we know today. Binet and Simon introduced the concept of mental age which allowed for measurements of intelligence to be presented in the form of interval data. The current Stanford-Binet intelligence test, last revised in 1960, traces its origin back to this early Binet-Simon test.

Current also are the Wechsler intelligence tests, the Wechsler Adult Intelligence Scale (WAIS), and the Wechsler Intelligence Scale for Children (WISC). These tests actually allow for more than just an IQ score to be computed, for the skilled psychologist can tap many personality variables with the Wechsler tests.

Both the Stanford-Binet and the Wechsler are individual intelligence tests. That is, they are administered by a psychological specialist to just one person at a time. This makes testing large groups extremely time consuming, and therefore expensive.

During the first World War it became important to test large groups of men quickly, and a new approach to testing was devised. The so-called paper and pencil tests were introduced, beginning with the Army Alpha test of 1917. Tests of this nature, which virtually every American has taken at one time or another, can be administered to large groups of subjects at one sitting, the subject reading the multiple-choice item and then checking what he considers to be the correct alternative. Today there are hundreds of IQ tests of this type, such as the California Mental Maturity, the Iowa, or the Lorge-Thorndike.

But what about the concept purportedly being measured by all these tests? What, in fact, is "intelligence?" The definitions vary widely—from Wechsler's "global capacity of the individual to act purposefully, to think rationally, and to deal effectively with his environment" to E. G. Boring's positivistic statement that intelligence is simply that which an intelligence test measures. Perhaps most theorists would agree, however, that intelligence is the capacity or ability to learn quickly and generally retain what has been learned. This definition has the advantage of conforming to the intelligence tests themselves, because all tests measure, to a large extent, speed of acquisition, and to an even larger extent the ability to remember what has been acquired.

The question of heredity versus environment as the key factor in determining intelligence has finally, it seems, been put to rest. After years of futile argument over the relative percentage of nature or nurture in the intelligence equation, psychologists are today in basic agreement that intelligence is a function of both heredity and environment as an interaction. The question now is just how do heredity and environment interact, blend, merge to form the individual's intelligence. Heredity certainly sets the outer limits as to what environment can accomplish, but the key question now is concerned with the interaction process itself.

The renewed interest in the importance of early experience is aiding in the answer to this question. The concepts of imprinting and critical periods, and the work of Hebb, Bloom, Scott, Harlow, J. McV. Hunt, and others, all lead us to conclude that environmental stimulation during the child's first four or five years of life is absolutely crucial in determining adult mental ability. It is also becoming increasingly apparent that failure to provide stimulation during those early critical years leads to permanent intellectual impairment. The adult simply cannot make up for lost time during childhood. Bloom, for example, has pointed out that by age six, when a child usually starts school, roughly 67 percent of his intelligence has already been formed. This emphasizes once again the importance of experience prior to the age of formal schooling, and also that the school itself can still have an impact during the "finishing stages" of intelligence formation.

AN OVERVIEW OF THE READINGS FOR THIS CHAPTER

Angoff and Anderson, in the first article (Selection 32), present the case for the standardization of tests. Only tests that have been carefully standardized, they feel, allow for the objective, unbiased evaluation of the large masses of individuals who are competing for educational awards and/or better self-understanding.

In the past, standardized tests have been criticized on the basis that they are so universal they don't fit the needs of the local curriculum. The questions asked on the standardized test may not be the kinds of questions pursued in the local English class. But, perhaps we can make a fetish out of such an idiosyncratic and provincial approach. Perhaps it is important for us to be able to compare our students with those in other parts of the country, and further, as Angoff and Anderson point out, local norms can and should be assembled for the standardized test.

Angoff and Anderson see the standardized test as being consistent with the notion of individual differences, and it is precisely these differences that the tests are designed to better understand. With standardized tests, our understanding will be grounded in the objectivity of scientific inquiry, not the vagaries of wishful thinking.

How are tests standardized? The article outlines the procedures, and although these techniques are presented with regard to the national tests of major publishers, the reader will find many of the points relevant to the construction of the teacher-made test as well; after all, objectivity and uniformity are noble goals for any test.

In the second article (Selection 33), George D. Stoddard presents an extremely lucid account of that murky concept, intelligence. Basically, Stoddard argues that "intelligence is as intelligence does," that the meaning of intelligence is a function of the observed behavior. To satisfy Stoddard's definition, perhaps we should stop using intelligence as a noun, and instead use it as an adverb. An individual is intelligent when he acts *intelligently*.

Stoddard concedes that intelligence is indeed based on the brain, but as we have seen in Chapter III, even the brain itself can be influenced, both as to chemistry and structure, by environmental stimulation. Further, since men think in man-made symbols, intelligence must still be measured through man's ability to deal effectively with symbols, despite our recent knowledge regarding actual changes in the nervous system.

Like Anastasi, Bloom, and J. McV. Hunt, Stoddard views intelligence as a function of heredity interacting with environment, with the emphasis on the interaction process. Man *learns* to be intelligent, and the key to this kind of learning is early experience. We must maximize a beneficient early environment, for "with or without formal schooling, the first six years are the most important—logically because all of life follows, and psychologically because this is a period of rapid mental growth."

The next selection (34), by Benjamin S. Bloom, surveys some of the major studies in the area of intelligence and brings order to many of the seemingly conflicting results. Citing the studies of Newman, Freeman and Holzinger (1937), Burt (1958), and Husen (1959), Bloom finds that all tell about the same story—the more environments differ, the more differences there are in intelligence. For example, identical twins raised together have more similarity in intelligence than when they are raised apart, and this finding is also true for non-identical twins and siblings. Favorable, or what Bloom calls abundant, environments allow for significantly higher intelligence scores than do impoverished environments. This is true despite what proportion of the variance one assigns to the role of heredity.

Bloom argues that intelligence is a developmental characteristic, and is basically sequential in nature. Lack of environmental stimulation can hinder the development of intelligence at a given age, and this loss of precious time can be extremely harmful. A failure to learn during a given time period cannot be fully compensated for by even unusually excellent learning conditions in a later period. The reader will find this reminiscent of J. P. Scott's position on critical periods presented in Chapter I. It' may well be that there are critical periods in the development of intelligence, and Bloom would contend that these critical periods occur early in life.

Hypothesizing a negatively accelerated growth curve for intelligence (that is, that the opportunity for IQ gain becomes less and less the older the child becomes), Bloom points to the great importance of the abundant environment at an early age. This was especially borne out in a study by Lee (1951). Tracing the effect of environmental change on negro children who moved from the South up to Philadelphia, Lee found that IQ increases were more pronounced the younger the child was at the time of the move. With increasing age, there was a decreasing effect of an improved environment on intellectual development.

Using this hypothesis as a premise, Bloom *actually predicts* the amount of IQ change to be expected by a shift to a more stimulating environment. Whereas an improved environment during the first four years of life can add an average of 2.50 IQ points per year, improving the environment between the ages of 8 and 17 may add an average of only .40 IQ points per year. Although the empirical evidence doesn't substantiate Bloom's predictions to the very last decimal point, the correlation between the observed change and Bloom's predictions of change is a resounding +.95. If Bloom has erred, it's on the side of conservatism, since in many studies the actual results show Bloom's predictions to *underestimate* the amount of change.

Of all the misconceptions abounding in the field of psychology and education, perhaps few are as flagrant or as widespread as those in the area of intelligence testing. In the next paper (Selection 35), Warren R. Good explores these fallacies and finds that many of the myths are unfortunately supported and even promulgated, not only by the lay public, but by the professional teachers who are using the tests.

Good criticizes the traditional practice, based on the 1937 Stanford-Binet norms, of interpreting IQs as though they were fixed values. For example, the notion that an IQ of 70 places a child in the lowest one percent of the population, or that an IQ of 130 places him in the top one percent, is a fallacy. Since every IQ test (whether it be the Stanford-Binet, the Wechsler, or any of the various group tests) is independently standardized, they all have rather different standard deviations. This means that an IQ score of 120, for example, does not always mean the same thing—for whereas an IQ of 120 on one test may place the individual at the 85th percentile, the same IQ on another test may place an individual at the 70th percentile. As Good points out, a child "might have an IQ of 80 on one test and be judged a bit subnormal, and have an IQ of 48 on another and be classified as an Imbecile."

The author's solution is to do away with the term IQ completely, and convert all intelligence scores into Z scores. This would force intelligence scores to be computed on the basis of the mean and the standard deviation for each separate test, and end the statistical confusion surrounding the IQ score.

Good is also extremely critical of the "nonverbal" IQ test, maintaining that if an individual has not been alert enough to have developed some basic language skills he probably is not equipped with much intellectual ability. Unless the individual is physically handicapped, the nonverbal IQ test is of little use, according to the author.

Basically the same argument is used against the so-called culture-free tests, for again Good contends that despite environmentally differing backgrounds, there is a core of culture which is common to virtually every American child. To simply exclude the common culture in order to achieve pseudo fairness, Good feels, "is to throw out our most useful indicators of mental ability."

Finally, the author points out that many of our children are over-tested. Not only is the IQ score misinterpreted, but the felony is compounded by giving the tests far too often.

The reader should note that in this discussion Good defines intelligence as a capacity, whereas in the Stoddard article intelligence was defined as a contemporary ability. This is one of the issues that still divides theorists in this area, but whether seen as a capacity or an ability all agree that intelligence is inferred from behavior.

One problem faced sooner or later by every teacher is whether or not to tell the parents the results of their children's IQ tests. James H. Ricks, Jr., in the concluding paper (Selection 36) offers some very practical suggestions to the teacher faced with this dilemma. Ricks states that not only do the parents have the right to know whatever the school knows about their children, but the *school has the obligation* to communicate understandable and usable knowledge to the parent. The communication of the IQ score itself may not really be conveying useful information; it may, in fact, really be transmitting false impressions. Parents are often too quick to seize upon an IQ score as being some kind of fixed, immutable characteristic. The communication of the actual IQ score all too often leads to final conclusions, and Ricks therefore contends that it should *not be* reported. Though grade-placement scores, achievement scores, and even precise percentiles lead to less confusion of interpretation than does the IQ score, perhaps the safest course is not to use any numbers at all. Ricks then presents his formula for reporting test results: "You score like people who . . ." To complete this sentence the author provides a series of examples, all designed to convey real information and not just the illusion of information.

When we think of all the exacting technicalities regarding test scores and measurement theory, when we consider the problems of reliability, validity, error of measurement, etc., it is no wonder that Ricks warns that the communication to the parents of the exact scores is often like attempting to reach "TV watchers with an AM radio broadcast."

32. THE STANDARDIZATION OF EDUCATIONAL AND PSYCHOLOGICAL TESTS *

WILLIAM H. ANGOFF AND SCARVIA V. ANDERSON

The development and application of standardized tests probably represent one of the major contributions to educational progress of the last fifty years. But its success has not come without criticism; indeed, some of the success would not have been possible without the constructive criticism which has spurred test makers into improving their procedures and seeking new methods of assessing human mental processes. Some of the least constructive of the criticisms have stemmed from a fundamental view that testing is motivated by a mechanistic philosophy by which all men are cast into one mold, without regard for

* From Angoff, William R., and Anderson, Scarvia B., "The Standardization of Educational and Psychological Tests," *Illinois Journal of Education*, February 1963, pp. 19-23.

their essential individuality. The test makers, on the other hand, take the view that not only do they *not* disregard the essential differences among individuals, but also that these differences are precisely what they seek to understand. They also maintain that the pursuit of this understanding is best accomplished by adopting the methods of scientific inquiry by which they imply that all aspects of measurement be held constant and uniform, except for the individual's own performance. Only then can the variability in performance from one person to another be taken as evidence of the *abilities* of the individuals and of nothing else.

The test makers will also take the position that because it provides *uniform methods* and *uniform standards* for everyone standardized testing necessarily yields fair and equitable assesments of performance for everyone. Thus the process of standardization permeates all aspects of a test; the construction, administration, scoring, reporting, and evaluation of test results.

TEST CONSTRUCTION

Ordinarily a standardized test poses the same questions for all students. The test maker attempts to write questions that will be regarded in the same way by all students who take the test. He pretests his questions in an effort to weed out ambiguities that result in different meanings to different people. (Pretests are conducted for other reasons as well: to insure the proper degree of difficulty for the test and the highest degree of reliability.) In most cases he writes a variety of test questions in order to sample as widely as possible the distribution of knowledge covered in a particular test. In this way he avoids giving special advantage to a student for whom the test is heavily weighted with questions in which he happens to have special competence or for which he did special intensive preparation in an attempt to "beat the test." In order to achieve a test which gives uniform opportunity to all students, a test maker asks not one or three or five questions but fifty or a hundred, because only with large numbers of questions can he be confident of achieving an adequate sampling of knowledge. He also writes questions which will test specifically what he intends to test, say knowledge and understanding of the events leading up to World War II—not "test wiseness," not general intelligence, not handwriting ability, nor neatness, nor English composition. This is not to say, of course, that some of these other characteristics are unimportant; but fair assessment demands that they must be measured separately.

ADMINISTRATION AND SCORING

The test maker also prescribes that the test be administered under uniform conditions— the same directions for all, the same presentation of questions, the same time limits, and insofar as possible the same favorable environmental conditions: proper light, ventilation, and temperature; convenient working space; general quiet, with freedom from extraneous disturbances.

Uniformity is also achieved in the scoring process. By restricting the nature of the student's responses and by removing from the task any opportunity the student may seize upon to bias the grading of his paper, the test maker insures virtually perfect scoring reliability. On a subjectively scored test the teacher's ratings can be influenced by such diverse factors as neatness and legibility, good or poor prose, his own fatigue or boredom with the scoring task, his general feeling of well-being, and, not of least importance, *his prior biases toward the student*. The standardized test, on the other hand, is scored only for the student's performance on the questions that are asked him. Again this is not to say that such factors as prose style or legibility of handwriting should not be tested. But if they are considered important enough to be tested, they should be tested independently. They should not appear as unreliable riders to another purpose to be considered as part of the score or not, depending on the particular mood and predilections of the person who happens to be scoring the paper at the time. As in the administration of the tests, what is sought here is a fair and equitable score, uncontaminated by factors that can only be considered as irrelevant or biasing in terms of the stated purpose of the test.

Of course all standardized tests are not "multiple-choice" tests. There are numerous instances in which a student is asked an "open-ended" question, as in the Stanford-Binet, the Wechsler-Bellevue, and the Interlinear Section of the College Board English Composition Test. In such cases the rules for scoring are agreed upon in advance by a group of experts and set down to be followed rigidly in the scoring process. Thus, even with tests that call for some subjectivity in scoring, attempts are made in the standardized test to reduce to a minimum the influence of extraneous factors and to set uniform standards to be applied to all examinees without bias.

SCALING

Standardization is also achieved in the development of an appropriate score scale system. Very frequently tests are constructed in more than one form—to discourage students from memorizing the questions either for their own benefit on retest or to help other students achieve higher scores, to avoid the effects of practice in studies of educational change, and to allow a second measurement when the validity of the first is open to question. Even when the various forms are constructed according to common specifications and precautions are taken to adopt an item-sampling scheme that will yield a similar "mix" of items in all forms, there are almost certain to be small differences between forms. Occasionally the differences are large, not only with respect to the range of talent for which they are appropriate. In such cases it would be grossly unfair to compare the raw score earned by one student who is given an easier form with the raw score earned by another student who is given a more difficult form. Therefore, in order to correct the differences between forms and to provide scores that are independent of the particular form that happened to be administered in any instance, scores on the various forms of a test are equated—or "calibrated"—and converted to a common reporting scale. (In order to avoid confusion this scale is made independent and different from the raw-score system for any single form.) Then, within the limitations imposed by the reliability of the equating method one can be confident that a student's score was unaffected by the difficulty of the particular form he took. Teachers, admissions officers, and counselors are relieved of the obligation of taking into consideration the difficulty characteristic of each test form.

There are other advantages to equating. If the reporting scale is maintained intact and without change over a period of time during which new forms are introduced, it is possible to trace the quality of successive groups of examinees, to make studies of trends, and to compare individuals and groups tested at different times, in different places, and for different purposes.

The methods by which a scale is established and the methods by which it is maintained in the face of multiple forms constitute a sizable field of study by themselves. Frequently a representative group of individuals ("representative" in terms of the population for which the test is designed) is tested to become the "standard group" on whom the scale is based. In later uses of the test the "standard group," whose average performance provides the focal point of the scale, is used as the basic reference or normative group for the purposes of evaluating individual scores. This procedure expresses the view that the "standard group" gives normative meaning to the scale. Multiple forms of the test that are introduced at later times are equated, by procedures to be described below, to the scale defined by the original group, a process which allows scores on all of the forms to be reported in terms of this single standard scale.

There are other approaches to the problem of scale definition. One of these is based on the philosophy that because of changes in the population it is not always possible to give the scale lasting normative meaning. Moreover, even in those instances when the characteristics of the group may be expected to remain fairly constant, there is some question whether the scale should have any normative meaning or whether it should be a purely arbitrary scale of measurement, like the commonly used scales of inches, pounds, and Fahrenheit. The proponents of this view maintain that a measurement should be just a measurement and no more; that the evaluation of that measurement, as of the measurement of physical objects, should come from other sources: from continued experiences and increased familiarity with the scale and from comparison with the performance of groups of individuals who are either known to the test user or easily characterized for him.

The methods of equating two forms of a test all pre-suppose that the conversion of scores from one form to another involves simply an adjustment of units to account for differences in difficulty of the forms. Ideally this adjustment would be determined by administering both forms to all members of a group and observing the differences in performance on the forms—after first removing the effect of practice or fatigue on the form administered second. Variations on the approach, necessitated by practical considerations, include a) dividing a large group of individuals into two random halves, administering one form to each half and observing the difficulties in the statistics on the test form that each group took; and b) administering the same "equating" test to two groups, each of which has been tested with one of the major test forms. Here, too, the differences in performance on the two test forms are observed, but with adjustments made for any differences in the two groups by use of the equating test.

NORMING

An essential characteristic of the test standardization process is the presentation of reference data for appropriate norms groups. In some cases, as was just noted, the characteristics of the norms sample are built directly into the test scale itself. Tests which yield I.Q. scores fall into this category. In other cases an arbitrary scale is maintained, and the test is accompanied by norms appropriate for the principal uses for which the test is intended.

Tests designed for general surveys of ability, aptitude, and achievement are frequently related meaningfully to "national" norms collected by grade or age. But for these tests and for other tests in specific areas other types of norms may be desirable—norms differentiated by sex, geography, type of curriculum, rural-urban-suburban, public-private-parochial, etc. It is then the task of the test user to choose the appropriate norms from those that are available and to apply them in evaluating the performance of the individuals he has tested.

The norms that are developed for a test may be as elaborate as the test demands or the test maker can afford. The process of norms development, however, is fundamentally the same, regardless of the number and type of norms that are constructed. The test maker defines the characteristics of the population from which he decides to sample, and proceeds to select a sample from this population which will be as nearly representative of the population as possible. Ideally this would mean selecting all individuals at random from the population; however, for practical reasons other procedures are ordinarily employed. Typically the schools in the nation are grouped into categories or strata, homogeneous by type, size, socio-economic level, or location, or by combina-

tions of these characteristics; and entire schools are chosen at random from these strata. Sometimes multistage cluster sampling techniques are employed, involving several steps: random sampling of communities, random sampling of schools within those communities, random sampling of classes within those schools, and occasionally random sampling of students from those classes. When possible, the methods of stratified sampling and cluster sampling are combined to yield norms samples that are not only economical as to size, but also possess the desired levels of reliability and representativeness.

When any particular student is to be evaluated, the best comparison group is a group of students with whom he is in competition or with whom he aspires to compete (or a group as similar to one of these as possible). Thus, if a test is to be used for educational guidance, an appropriate norms group consists of those students with whom the student will be in competition if he undertakes a particular course of study. If the test is to be used for selection at a given college, the appropriate norms group is the group of candidates with whom the student is competing for a place. If a test is to be used for evaluation of achievement in a specific school course, then the ideal group is the rest of the class.

Increasingly the major test publishers are coming around to the point of view that the most valuable norms group may be one that is locally assembled by the test user himself. This does not relieve the publisher of the responsibility of providing more general norms; however, his norms may be considered only supplementary to the data collected on the local group.

OTHER TEST CHARACTERISTICS

Finally, the producer of a standardized test will make available to the test user for his information in selecting and using the instrument a set of data describing the various characteristics of the test: the use to which it is intended or for which it is recommended; an outline of the test content; the item difficulties and discrimination indices; data on the speededness of the test; its reliability and standard error of measurement; its predictive validity for various pertinent criteria; the pattern of growth if the test is designed for use at more than one level; relationships with other tests or forms; and, finally, an evaluation of the strengths and weaknesses of the test for various purposes to which it might be put. The makers of standardized tests are committed to the methods of scientific inquiry; they must also assume the obligations of science—making the results of their inquiry available to the public.

The procedures involved in the process of standardizing tests as they are discussed here are not by any means intended to constitute a set of minimum criteria for a test to be considered "standardized." Some highly useful tests follow the procedures of standardization in somewhat different ways from those that are outlined here. However, aside from the details of procedure, it is certainly reasonable to say that taken together the characteristic features of a standardized test are what make it a scientific measuring instrument, capable of precision and predictive of future achievement. For both human and practical reasons the standardized test is a necessary outcome of the philosophy of a modern democratic society in which large masses of individuals competing for educational awards, or simply seeking better self-understanding, assemble for an objective, unbiased evaluation of their abilities. No other method that we know of today can provide measurement for the tremendous number of individuals who demand objective consideration of their talents. Certainly no other method that we know of today can accomplish this measurement as equitably as can the standardized test.

33. ON THE MEANING OF INTELLIGENCE *

GEORGE D. STODDARD

In measuring intelligence, we perceive an accumulative phenomenon in which learning not only affects the mental age and I.Q. at the time but also, through memory, mental skill, and cognitive structure, progressively affects the scores obtained. If we add to this overlap a measure of environmental constancy, let us say through the impact of speech habits, a planned curriculum, and television, we can expect I.Q. constancy to a mild degree. Until recent years, tens of millions of potentially bright children in Asia, Africa, and Latin America remained illiterate and therefore consistently test-dull. At the same time we may postulate that in advanced countries millions of potentially dull children, under favorable conditions, went up the mental ladder faster and farther thus altering our concept of the norm.

Intelligence is as intelligence does; it is no secret pocket hidden away in the brain like a pituitary gland. Intelligence is indeed based on the brain—on the brain as reconstituted by experience. Childhood education is in part a name for organized experience that is designed to develop intelligence, along with other desirable attributes in personality and behavior, to an optimum degree. At the root of all experience and all education is *the mind as consequence.*

What it has come down to, ever since the first Binet-Simon tryouts, is the identification of behavior deemed intelligent with rather simple cognitive matters—with geared-in information, speech, and problem solving. I have long felt that in the total pattern we need to

* Stoddard, George D., "On the Meaning of Intelligence." From *Proceedings of the 1965 Invitational Conference on Testing Problems.* Copyright © 1966 by Educational Testing Service. All rights reserved. Reproduced by permission of Educational Testing Service and the Author.

insert two additional factors, namely 1) creativity and 2) resistance to emotional or other forces that distort the process of reasoning. The memorizer, the computer, the plodder simply should not be given the highest rank in the field of *general intelligence*. The tested and scored operations exhaust his talent; his assorted mental skills can be measured and totalized. Beyond the standardized test lies open-ended testing not *of* but *for* the emergence of original ideas. Case histories help but do not suffice. Likewise, a merger of mental testing with personality testing will give us clues as to why individual "A" remains intelligent under social, political, or religious pressure while "B," his mental-test equal, becomes confused, misled, or ridiculous.

Of course, creativity cannot be guaranteed. Creativity is no sure outcome of the mastery of even the far reaches of what is known or surmised. Thus in science a solid jumping-off place is needed; intuition does not serve there unless it is intellectually allied to previous knowledge or theory. Jerome B. Wiesner postulates a condition for creativity in the sciences:

> The term "creativity" is principally used to mean activity resulting in contributions that have novelty and value in the intellectual sphere of human experience, including the sciences, as well as literature, music, and the visual arts. In all such contexts, "creativity" universally implies a departure from, and advance beyond, what is conventionally attainable. However, there is an important characteristic of creative contributions in science that is not significantly present in many other fields, namely, quantitatively definable logical relationships to pre-existing scientific knowledge.

Along with studies of what's what in the environment, I should place reliable measures of creativity and intellectual integrity at the top of the heap for new research.

Perhaps two or three additional suggestions are worth considering.

The young girl, further along physiologically and presumably mentally, learns to read sooner and better than the boy. For a time, she holds her own in mathematical and other abstractions, but the boy catches up. He keeps growing for a longer time. It may be that the so-called genius rating—a precarious label—is achieved by a child who starts fast like a girl and perseveres like a boy. In any case, sex-related differences should be reexamined in relation to cognitive theory and test standardization. As long as scores are computed with chronological age as a denominator, we need separate male and female norms.

Doubtless, intelligence tests for the adolescent and the mature adult should break up into branches that reach out from the main stem of general intelligence. In these later stages, intelligent behavior needs to be differentiated in terms of the ability to solve abstract problems that involve acquired formulas and methods, together with certain cognitive tools such as may be found in logic, science, or music. Concrete tools like the telescope, the microscope, the camera, hearing devices, and other detectors may be regarded as extensions of the sensory organs whose contribution to cortical power is indirect. The skills involved in their use are akin to those that the race developed long ago—to cutting and pounding devices and agricultural implements. They help the technician, but they are not necessarily a part of his intellectual structure. Hence, for our purposes we need not measure the motor skills they call for, but only the way in which their sensory revelations transform thinking.

General intelligence becomes a base for special development that may be measured more meaningfully than that afforded by adding discrete items that are validated on the percent passing in a given sampling. It is a profound error in mental measurement to derive the abilities of the "superior adult" from an aggregation of simple tasks. With new test items of the kind Jerome S. Bruner and his colleagues are working on we could carry the concept of general intelligence to more advanced levels before reaching the rational outcome in the branching I have referred to.

For adults it is scarcely a matter of predicting a future mental state. What counts is the ability to perform immediate mental tasks that embody the essence of whole families of tasks. There is a change-over point from interest in the child's present and future levels of accomplishment to what the adult does or is able to do *now*. How shall we test this? After all, for adults, we do not predict anything except a decline—not so much a decline in the basic skills but in mental power that may be applied to real situations. By this time, through heredity and long experience, the intellectual structure is characterized by observable potentials, limits, and stable achievements. While the general trend is downward, as with a river, the immediate capabilities may hold steady or at times surge upward. There can be a late-blooming intelligence as long as the nervous system has not suffered damage or deterioration. Of course, no new brain cells are involved in this phenomenon—there aren't any—only a better coordination of those that remain functional.

Whether intelligence be viewed in terms of current behaviorism or of cognitive psychology, there is postulated a sufficient chemical, physical, and neurological base. Neurological studies are of interest to the psychologist just as cellular studies are to the nutritionist or the physiologist. Nevertheless, psychology is essentially a social science. Men think in man-made symbols or they do not think at all. Intelligence, as an ability that grows through the interaction of nervous structures and mediated social events, may be regarded as our most purely psychological phenomenon. In studying early education that may be designated effective or good, we turn to the significance of images, concepts, formulations, and experiences rather than to actual changes in nervous tissue or in physiological function. Actually, when we find a gain in measured intelligence that is correlated with age or experience, we postulate either a temporary or long-range improvement in the nervous system. Let the biochemist, the physiologist, the neurologist, and the nutritionist discover what they can. It may or may not have discernible psychological outcomes, but it makes sense to improve our knowledge of the substrata of behavior. In fact, therapeutic principles of great importance to an individual or to a whole population may emerge. Consider, for example, the operational difference between brain X_1 that is optimally supplied with oxygen and twin-brain X_2 whose oxygen supply is deficient or in excess.

The brain is not a dead tool or chest of tools. It is not a machine. Its stores of remembered items are not lined up on a shelf or imbedded in an automatic circuit. They are chosen in the first place and once chosen, their quality depends upon their availability on demand for abstract thinking, problem solving, and creativity. That, in turn, depends upon a prior process of coding and integrating. Without the early intervention of speech this whole series of events would be encumbered. In the words of Neal E. Miller:

> We no longer view the brain as merely an enormously complicated telephone switchboard which is passive unless excited from without. The brain is a device for sorting, processing, and analyzing information. The brain contains sense organs which respond to states of internal environment, such as osmotic pressure, temperature and many others. The brain is a gland which secretes chemical messengers, and it also responds to such messengers, as well as to various types of feedback, both central and peripheral.

So much for the inside. In regard to the outside we have, as one example, the flat statement of Harold G. Wolff, a neurologist at the Cornell University School of Medicine: "I am prepared now to say, after four years of inquiry, that the brain may be damaged in the process of attempting to make adaptations to situations that the individual cannot meet."

Language is the great stimulator and the basis of most logical thought. Illiteracy imposes a massive mental defect. A neurosis is a partial mental defect; if our tests do not discover it and negatively incorporate it into the total score of mental ability, so much the worse for the tests. Similarly a psychotic involvement carries a corresponding mental defect, for it rains down intellectual corruption upon the trivial discrete responses which are superficially intact. To decimate activity deemed intelligent is one way of reducing mental ability, although the condition is different from the overall defectiveness of a congenital imbecile. If the psychosis develops relatively late in life, the harmful social effects are compounded. By that time the person may be able to wield power over others.

Granted that each of us is a unique bundle of cellular units, we *learn* to be intelligent, or not to be, and some persons learn faster than others. In fact, for some children such learning is so hard to come by, even under conditions of expert instruction, that we are justified in applying a low I.Q. rating, and in retaining it if the learning difficulties persist, but not otherwise. At times, neurological conditions permit us to predict a permanent mental defect. Lacking such physical evidence, we should be cautious about applying restrictive labels. A functional defect not traceable to brain deficiency or damage may or may not endure; we have to find out by repeated measurements based on differentiated educational stimuli. These, in turn, may call into play novel forms of stimulation, motivation, and achievement. At the other end of the stick, we have to be cautious about predicting an abiding mental superiority. Brains deemed neurologically intact may become addled. In your own community look about you!

J. McV. Hunt has pinpointed a semantic error that runs through much mental testing:

The application of such terms as *dimension* and *scale* may at once tend to carry their meaning in the physical world over to the world of organismic behavior and to imply that the constancy of dimensions is being generalized from static objects to non-static persons and their behavior . . . Fixed intelligence is a conception like the pre-formationistic notion that the bodily structure of a species is to be found within the egg or the sperm . . . Calling intelligence a *dimension* and speaking of tests as *scales* may be unfortunate.

Hunt develops in some detail "the notion of intelligence as central processes developing as a function of the child's interactions with the environment." Here the key word is *interactions,* and its significance for education is emphasized by Hunt: "Inasmuch as development rates are most rapid, in absolute terms, during the early months and first couple of years, this is probably the period of most importance for maximizing intellectual potential."

Since the reliability of infant tests may reach r=.90, their failure to predict later or final mental standing is another way of saying that we do not know what the subsequent environmental encounters will consist of; in fact, we have poor measures of such influences at any stage of development. The studies of

S. A. Kirk and others, comparing I.Q. changes in retarded children, indicate the fruitfulness of such an attack even when the precise forces at work are, to say the least, homogenized. Whatever the events, learnings, and situations may be, it appears that the essence of a fruitful interaction is to get beyond repetitions or aggregations to a spiraling integration. This means a putting away of childish things in the later portions of any mental test. Even to test the hereditary component as a *potential,* we need to give full play to hierarchical experiences and to relate them in time sequences to the intellectual demands of a particular growing child.

So, let us stop worrying about how much of intelligence is due to heredity and how much to environment. It never was a good question. There can be a hereditary or congenital defect so severe as to make an environmental influence negligible. I have myself seen an adult inmate of an institution whose I.Q. might be placed at 1; she could smile, period. On the other hand, potential geniuses who "waste their sweetness on the desert air," for all we know, may be rather numerous. Illiteracy in a society reaching toward literacy not only stamps out genius; it obscures all objective measurement of what is or might have been.

We observe three action worlds: 1) the pre-conception world of eugenics; 2) the prenatal world of nutrition and protection; and 3) the postnatal world of education. The prenatal condition is really a special case: by informing the mother, you safeguard the fetus. Thus Ashley Montagu has shown that the heavy smoking of cigarettes by pregnant women may damage the unborn child. By maximizing beneficent environment, early and late, but especially early, we are in a sound position. With or without formal schooling, the first six years are the most important—logically because all of life follows, and psychologically because this is a period of rapid mental growth. Far in advance of scientific knowledge, we have done rather well, by law, to keep children away from tobacco, alcohol, and narcotics, but we are just beginning to give economic and educational aid on behalf of children below the age of five.

Consider this educational dilemma:

Allowing 182 out of 365 days to formal

schooling and noting that one-half of the waking time of each child during this formal schooling period is spent out of school, we come abruptly upon a sobering thought: in the preschool years, the family and neighborhood carry 100 percent of the educational load; during school years they still carry 75 percent of the load, as they say on Madison Avenue, "timewise." Hence the need for a sound education of the child at home by parents who are soundly educated is urgent. And this is not all. If Benjamin Bloom is right in his hypotheses, this preschool period accounts for as much variance in tested intelligence as all the remaining years of childhood and adolescence. While the kind of testing advocated in this brief paper will search out new cognitive structures and will give scope to emerging factors less appropriate to early childhood, the principle remains: to neglect the young child is to invite a progressive slowdown in intellectual attainment.

To turn a phrase, we can discern the three forces of intellect, namely, home education, school education, and self-education. Technically self-education is all. No one of these simply works *upon,* none directly *impinges* on the child's inherited nervous system—rather, all unite in a vastly complicated interaction between what the child was born with (and has grown into) and the determiners, overt or obscure, in the environment.

The national educational program carried on last summer on behalf of over 500,000 underprivileged preschool children is indeed a *Head Start.* (The new crop of underprivileged children, by the way, will be those who do not get such attention before the age of five.) If the movement spreads, I predict a lifting of the fog that has settled over so many discussions of inferiority due to race, nationality, or parental status. Children differ from one another in their inherited structures, but this cannot be determined by extrapolation from external categories.

We learn in order to make better decisions now and in the future—in order to safeguard and enrich our lives. The aim of education is life fulfillment through learning. It is true that a small amount of learning may produce a vast amount of thinking, but such "thinking" tends to become repetitive and self-defeating.

In our culture pattern, the Dark Ages furnish the supreme example; the people were terribly short of knowledge, or of the scientific method. Who knows but today, with all our vast array of science and technology, we may be judged as being terribly short of *thinking,* that is, of problem solving directed toward viable and humane political structures.

Has not the worldwide drift up to now been on the side of the dysgenic? We have the well-documented population "explosion." We have the prospect of wars which, in the future, will disproportionately kill city people and wipe out their cultural achievements. Still, if education from nursery school to college becomes endemic, social competition will operate as an effective eugenic moderator. We can then forget about large families versus small. Also, except for extremes which rarely run in families, we can forget about "good stock" and "poor stock." Man's ancestry is so unlike the incestuous breeding lines that produce good dogs and horses as to make such comparisons hilarious. In a world of love-at-first-sight, or perhaps on-second-thought, the crossing gene lines are as invisible as the genes themselves.

All animals evolve by natural selection and a responsiveness to the environment. A family group, a tradition, a language, a space ship is as much a part of the environment as a seashore or a tree. Our ancestors climbed down out of trees, made use of sticks and stones, and gradually were changed. Now we climb up into the sky. Since *change* is the universal condition of life, and of sublife for that matter, who can say what human forms will evolve? While a centrifuged, irradiated, weightless person may not expect to see any special effects in his offspring, if we put enough of the breeding segment of the human race in space contraptions, generation after generation, mutations might appear. Perhaps in a hundred thousand years the computer men who never get off the ground will develop so differently from astronauts that a demand for desegregation will arise!

Clearly, the stage is set for interchange, interaction, interdependence. The brain responds to internal and external events. In responding, it changes. Of course it would change anyway through the mechanics of growth and decline, but we like to think we can prevent or postpone deleterious happenings and accentuate what is organismically and behaviorally sound. Therein lies the foundation of the good life for the individual. It is, I suppose, an article of faith that a reliance on actions and experiences deemed favorable *for this child today,* if they are constantly modified by new insights, will also be of long-range value to the human race. The fearful alternative is to lose sight of *this child,* or of *all children,* by poisoning the materials or events that interact with cortical functioning. A sustained indifference to the inroads of disease, injury, ignorance, frustration, or superstition will lower the intelligence level of a given generation and lend a gloomy outlook to the future of man.

34. THE EFFECT OF VARIATIONS IN ENVIRONMENT ON INTELLIGENCE *

BENJAMIN S. BLOOM

We may assume that an individual is born with a nervous system and physiological makeup which are the bases on which general intelligence is developed. Individuals may vary considerably in these characteristics at birth, and this variation is undoubtedly a significant

* From Bloom, Benjamin S., "The Effect of Variations in Environment on Intelligence," in *Stability and Change in Human Characteristics,* New York, John Wiley and Sons, 1964, pp. 68-76.

factor in determining the potential of the individual for the development of general intelligence.

Perhaps our clearest evidence for the inheritance of general intelligence comes from the various studies of twins reared together and reared apart. In Table 1 we have summarized the various studies on the intelligence measurements of twins as well as siblings. Here it will be noted that the identical twins, when

TABLE 1 Correlational studies of the intelligence of twins and siblings reared together and reared apart.

	Group Tests of Intelligence			Individual Tests of Intelligence	
	Burt (1958)	Newman, Freeman, Holzinger (1937)	Husén (1959)	Burt (1958)	Newman, Freeman, Holzinger (1937)
Identical Twins					
Reared together	.94	.92	.90	.92	.91
Reared apart	.77	.73		.84	.67
Nonidentical Twins					
Reared together	.54	.62	.70	.53	.64
Siblings					
Reared together	.52			.49	
Reared apart	.44			.46	
Unrelated Children					
Reared together	.28			.25	

reared apart, correlate +.67 to +.84 as compared with +.90 to +.94 for identical twins reared together. Similarly, the siblings reared together correlate slightly higher than do the siblings reared apart. Here then, we do have evidence that similar hereditary makeup when accompanied by similar environments (at least home environments) does result in very similar levels of general intelligence, whereas similar hereditary makeup accompanied by dissimilar environments results in somewhat different levels of general intelligence.

This point is further clarified by Anastasi (1958, p. 299) in a table showing the differences in I.Q.'s of identical twins reared apart as related to environmental differences (See Table 2). It is especially noteworthy that the differences in I.Q. for identical twins separated during the first three years are highly related to the differences in educational advantage (+.79) but have only moderate relationships with the difference in social and physical advantages in the environments of the separated twins (+.51, +.30).[1] Thus, if the identical twins are separated but placed in very similar environments, it is likely that they will have very similar intelligence test scores, whereas if placed in very different environments, their intelligence test scores will be quite different.[2]

Various workers have attempted to determine the proportions of the variance attributable to heredity and environment. Woodworth (1941) estimates 60% attributable to heredity, Newman, Freeman, and Holzinger (1937) estimate 65% to 80% attributable to heredity, Burks (1928) estimates 66% to heredity,

[1] Reported by Newman, Freeman, Holzinger (1937, p. 340).
[2] We have divided the separated twins into two groups. For one group of 11 pairs, each pair of separate twins had very similar educational environments. The rank correlation for their I.Q. scores was +.91, whereas for the eight pairs that had the least similar educational environments, the rank correlation for their I.Q. scores was only +.24.

TABLE 2 Environmental differences and I.Q. differences for identical twins reared apart (Anastasi, 1958).

| Case No. | Sex | Age at Separation | Age at Testing | Environmental Differences | | | | I.Q. Differences† |
				1. Years of Schooling	2. Educational Advantages	3. Social Advantages	4. Physical Advantages	
11	F	18 mo.	14	37	37	25	22	24
18	M	1 yr.	27	4	28	31	11	19
4	F	5 mo.	29	4	22	15	23	17
8	F	3 mo.	15	1	14	32	13	15
2	F	18 mo.	27	10	32	14	9	12
1	F	18 mo.	19	1	15	27	19	12
17	M	2 yr.	14	0	15	15	15	10
12	F	18 mo.	29	5	19	13	36	7
6	F	3 yr.	59	0	7	10	22	8
9	M	1 mo.	19	0	7	14	10	6
10	F	1 yr.	12	1	10	15	16	5
5	F	14 mo.	38	1	11	26	23	4
16	F	2 yr.	11	0	8	12	14	2
13	M	1 mo.	19	0	11	13	9	1
15	M	1 yr.	26	2	9	7	8	1
7	M	1 mo.	13	0	9	27	9	−1
14	F	6 mo.	39	0	12	15	9	−1
3	M	2 mo.	23	1	12	15	12	−2
20	F	1 mo.	19	0	2	?	?	−3
19	F	6 yr.	41	0	9	14	22	−9

† Difference in favor of the individual with the educational advantage is shown as positive.

Leahy (1935) estimates 78%, whereas Burt (1958) estimates 77% to 88% attributable to heredity. We do not propose to attempt to settle this controversy other than to recognize that although the estimates vary, all are apparently agreed that some portion of the variance must be attributed to the effect of the environment in which the children are reared.

We shall consider the evidence as to what constitutes a favorable or abundant environment for the development of intelligence and shall do the same for an unfavorable or deprived environment. We take the view that intelligence is a developmental characteristic in that the mental age or I.Q. compares the general learning of an individual with the progress in the learning of selected samples of behavior made by representative samples of individuals at different ages. It would seem that with such an operational concept of intelligence, the environment could clearly block and retard certain developments in an individual, whereas it is likely (but less clear) that the environment could facilitate and accelerate these developments (Hunt, 1961). If general intelligence is a developmental characteristic and is related to the time it takes the individual to learn various concepts, skills, etc., it would seem reasonable that lack of such learning in one time period may be difficult or impossible to make up fully in another period, whereas unusually excellent learning in one time period is not likely to be lost in a subsequent period.

What then is likely to happen if the individual lives in a deprived or abundant environment (as it affects intelligence) for varying periods of time in his development? Let us assume that the long-term effect of

extreme environments may affect the I.Q. to the extent of 1.25 standard deviations on the I.Q. norms, that is, about 20 I.Q. points. This seems a reasonable amount since the three pairs of identical twins reared under the most different environments (see Table 2) had an average difference of 20 I.Q. points, while Sontag (1958) found the individuals in his study changing as much as 20 I.Q. points under what he considered to be favorable and unfavorable environments. This is about the figure cited by Burks (1928) as the effect of extreme environments. We are not firmly convinced of the magnitude of the differences produced by abundant and deprived environments, but do regard 20 I.Q. points as a fair estimate of this amount. With this figure as a first approximation, and with our estimates of the extent of development of intelligence at various ages as determined by the Overlap Hypothesis related to the work of Thorndike (1927) on an absolute scale of intelligence, we are in a position to set up a hypothetical table of the possible effects of various environments on the development of intelligence.

In Table 3 we have hypothesized the possible effects on the individual's intelligence of living under different environments. It will be noted that we are here concerned only with the first 17 years of life. Furthermore, we have assumed that the loss of development in one period cannot be fully recovered in another period. We shall discuss this point later. What we have hypothesized is that extreme environments can have far greater effects in the early years of development than they can in later years. That is, deprivation in the first four years can have far greater consequences than deprivation in the ten years from age 8

TABLE 3 Hypothetical effects of different environments on the development of intelligence in three selected age periods.

Age Period	Percent of Mature Intelligence	Variation from Normal Growth in I.Q. Units			
		Deprived	Normal	Abundant	Abundant-Deprived
Birth–4	50	−5	0	+5	10
4–8	30	−3	0	+3	6
8–17	20	−2	0	+2	4
Total	100	−10	0	+10	20

through age 17. Put in other terms, extreme environments each year in the first four may affect the development of intelligence by about an average of 2.5 I.Q. points per year, whereas extreme environments during the period of age 8 to 17 may have an average effect of only 0.4 I.Q. points per year.

Is there any evidence in support of the values hypothesized in Table 3? We will first consider a number of the studies on the effects of deprivation in relation to our hypothesized values, then the studies of the effects of abundance, and finally the studies of individuals who have moved from one type of environment to another. In each study, we cannot be certain of how extreme the environment was, but we will attempt to characterize briefly the environment and show the reported effect in contrast with our hypothesized values. For convenience, we have put the research findings and the hypothesized values in Table 4.

In all but one of the studies reported in Table 4 the observed difference is greater than our hypothesized changes. The one study in which the observed and hypothesized values are most similar is Newman, Freeman, Holzinger (1937) in which the identical twins with the most radically different educational environments are compared. In this study most of the children had been separated in the first year of life and they were tested at maturity; thus the entire period of growth was considered. In the other studies we have seriously underestimated the amount of change. However, it is of interest to note that the rank order correlation between the observed and hypothesized change is +.95, suggesting that the basic difficulty is not in the general conception of decreasing change with increasing age, but it is in the fixing of the amount of change likely to take place at each age period. It is our hope that future research will establish more accurate estimates of the amount of change which can take place under various environmental conditions at different age periods.

The two studies which we believe to be most crucial in establishing the pattern of change in relation to the environment are those by Kirk (1958) and Lee (1951). In each of these studies, children in contrasting environments were repeatedly tested. In the Kirk study, mentally retarded children in an institution were given a one year preschool experience intended to stimulate their learning. The children were tested prior to the preschool experience at about age 4½. They were retested at the end of the preschool experience, and then again several years later. Another group of children in the institution was used for purposes of contrast. The pre- and posttest scores are shown in Chart 1 for the experimental and contrast groups. It will be seen that with only two exceptions, individuals in the experimental group gained in a rather consistent pattern. The two children in the experimental group who showed decreases in I.Q. consisted of a child with brain damage and a child who appeared to be emotionally disturbed. The children in the contrast group generally decreased in measured intelligence with only two children gaining.[3]

The Lee (1951) study followed several groups of Negro children with repeated tests until grade 9. In Chart 2, it will be seen that the children who were born in Philadelphia maintained about the same mean scores from grades 1 to 9. The children who were born in the South and moved to Philadelphia by age 6 gained an average of 6½ I.Q. points from grades 1 to 9. The children who were born in the South and moved to Philadelphia by grade 4 gained about 3 I.Q. points from grades 4 to 9, whereas the children who were born in the South and moved to Philadelphia by grade 6 gained only 2 I.Q. points during the period grades 6 to 9.[4]

The point of the Lee study is the decreasing effect of an improved environment with increasing age. It is also of interest to note that the greatest changes take place in the first few years in the new environment. Although there are strong indications that the environ-

[3] Six of the 15 children in the experimental group showed enough improvement to be released from the institution. None of the children in the contrast group was released.

[4] Lee used grade placement of the students in the Philadelphia schools rather than age at entrance. It is likely that if age samples were used (and these were typical of Southern rural communities), the group would show decreasing levels of intelligence with increase in length of time spent in the South.

TABLE 4 Effects of Deprivation and Abundance on I.Q. in Contrast with Hypothesized Effects.

Author and Date	Environment	Test	Ages	I.Q. at Initiat and Retest	Observed Differences	Hypothesized Change
Deprivation						
Dennis and Najarian (1957)	Orphanage with minimum of adult-child contact	Goodenough, Draw a Man	4–6	93–89	−4	−2.5
Newman, Freeman, Holzinger (1937)	Identical twins reared apart; 4 pairs with most extreme environments	Stanford-Binet	Tested at maturity		18	20
Kirk (1958)	Retarded children in institutions	Stanford-Binet	4.8–7.3	57–51	−6	−2
Wheeler (1932)	Isolated mountain children (1930)		6 versus 16	94.7–73.5	−21.2	−3.3
Wheeler (1942)	Less isolated mountain children		6 versus 16	102.6–81.3	−21.3	−3.3
Sontag et al. (1958)	Children with low need achievement	Stanford-Binet	3–12	128–115	−13	−5.1
Abundance						
Sontag et al. (1958)	Children with high need achievement	Stanford-Binet	3–12	118–138	+30	+5.1
Deprivation to Improved Environment						
Kirk (1958)	Retarded children in institution presented with preschool stimulation	Stanford-Binet	4.4–7.3	61–71.2	−10.2	+2.25
Lee (1951)	Negro children born in South and moved to Philadelphia at various ages		Deprived 1–6 Improved 7–15	86.5–92.8	+6.3	+2.3
			Deprived 1–9 Improved 10–15	86.3–89.4	+3.1	+1.1
			Deprived 1–11 Improved 12–15	88.2–90.2	+2.0	+0.4

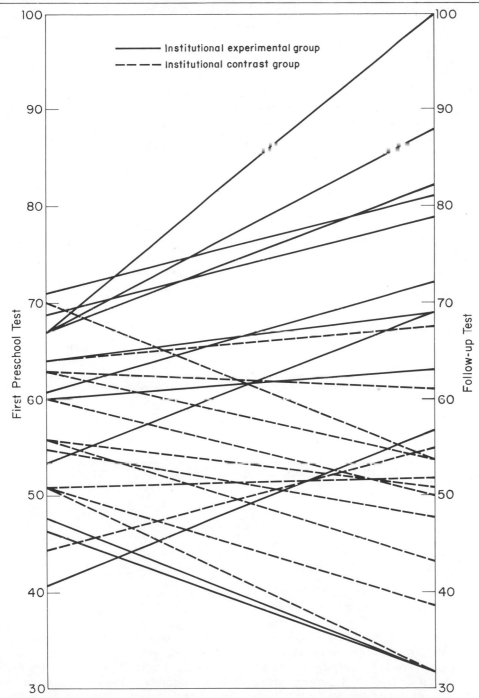

CHART 1 Changes in intelligence for two groups of children in an institution.

ment from which the children came in the South could be characterized as a deprived environment for the development of intelligence, we do not believe that the Philadelphia environment should be regarded as an abundant or stimulating one, even though it did represent an improvement over the earlier environment for these children.

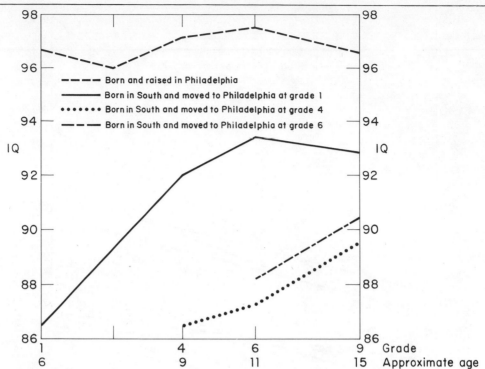

CHART 2 Changes in intelligence for Negro students born in Philadelphia and Negro students born in the South and moving to Philadelphia at various grades (adapted from Lee, 1951).

35. MISCONCEPTIONS ABOUT INTELLIGENCE TESTING *

WARREN R. GOOD

There seems to be a lot of confusion nowadays about intelligence tests and the meaning of intelligence quotients. For example, many teachers now in service have been taught that 60 percent of the children have IQ's 90-109, 14 percent 110-119 and again 80-89, 6 percent 120-129 and 70-79, 1 percent above 130, and 1 percent below 70; and that those with IQ's below 70 are feebleminded. None of this is "true" today. Many teachers have

* From Good, Warren R., "Misconceptions about Intelligence Testing," *University of Michigan School of Education Bulletin*, May 1964.

been easily converted to an ill-founded confidence in verbal and nonverbal IQ's, primary abilities, and culture-free tests. Whatever the merits of these "newer" developments may be, teachers should choose and interpret on the basis of understanding rather than acceptance of propaganda. These and other blunders apparently result from poor knowledge of fundamental intelligence-test theory.

When we try to measure intelligence we seek an indication of *capacity* for learning and adaptation. This indication must be obtained by inference, because the potentiality for development is constantly in the process of being realized. Hence we must resort to the assumption that mental ability—what the individual knows and can do on intellectual tasks—will vary with capacity if opportunities for development and motivation have been equal. And we infer "intelligence" from mental ability. But we cannot measure ability directly, either; what we measure is performance. And so, it goes like this: we measure performance, from which we infer ability, from which we infer capacity.

The basic conditions for validity of our inferences—equality of opportunity and motivation—demand what might reasonably be called "normal" environment, comparable, so far as test effects are concerned, with that of the children on whom the test was standardized. And opportunities to have learned the kinds of things involved in the specific test items must be equalized. Our chances of getting such equalization are certainly best at zero (no opportunity at all) and infinity, or to be practical, at *plenty*—far more opportunity than would be needed to learn the thing if the individual were mature enough. For example, children have abundant opportunities to learn what arms, legs, nose, ears, and hair are, and to learn the names and uses of familiar household objects. Intelligence tests are often at fault because a good many items relate to special interests or opportunities, but even the best tests will be unsatisfactory for some children in almost any group, because of differences in background.

Once this principle of equal opportunity is understood, teachers can judge for themselves whether test items are suitable for measuring intelligence, and will soon learn to choose good tests for the purpose. In the last analysis the validity of intelligence test items always depends on judgment.

The pathetic arguments favoring "nonverbal IQ's" for duller children are at best questionable. In general, language is a highly sensitive indicator of intelligence and, barring specific handicap, there is no evidence that those who cannot understand or use their native language with facility are likely to be endowed with some special kind of "general mental ability" that cannot be adequately measured by verbal tests. The issue here, as always in intelligence testing, is equality of opportunity to have learned the kind of thing demanded. One technique for evening out the accidental differences in opportunity is to sample broadly from the many types of items and activities that are judged to show "relative facility in learning." But, to avoid language in an intelligence test is to reject the most versatile and most important means of communicating thought. In case of specific handicap—defect of speech or hearing, or difference of languages—we resort to nonlanguage tests through necessity, not because they are "just as good." Even for young children, our best intelligence tests make considerable use of language, although that does not necessarily mean having the pupil read—which is not a suitable means of setting the task unless he can read well enough for the purpose.

I have just been examining the test booklets filled out by 133 high school students on a test which purports to yield a verbal and a nonverbal IQ. The correlation between the two is only .36 for this group, and the helter-skelter differences are highly questionable in consideration of (1) the very unsatisfactory statistical characteristics of the subtests, (2) the dubious validity of many specific items, and (3) internal evidence on the quality of responses.

As for verbal and nonverbal IQ's, there has never been any justification for such terminology. What we have is verbal and nonverbal test items or tests, all designed to measure general intelligence; and if IQ's obtained with verbal and nonverbal tests differ greatly there is reason for grave doubt of the validity of either or both.

The broad sampling needed for good intelligence tests may have to be restricted for special purposes, such as obtaining comparable measurements where languages differ or cultural patterns are conspicuously dissimilar. Such an attempt was illustrated by the "culture-free" tests which have been so severely criticized. Here too, the major criterion is equality of opportunity to have learned the kind of thing demanded, and American schools do not require the exclusion of the common culture to achieve cultural fairness in intelligence tests. To exclude it is to throw out our most useful indicators of mental ability.

The search for "primary mental abilities" is concerned with finding the major components of the groups of abilities which may be judged to reflect intelligence. But so far, competent analysts are not agreed on the identification of such abilities or on the validity of tests which purport to measure them as separate abilities.

A common characteristic of intelligence tests is that they yield IQ's. The original Binet tests measured directly in mental age credits, but nearly all tests nowadays are point scales, the IQ's being determined statistically from the distribution of point scores. If these determinations were valid in relation to the definition of an IQ, the distributions of IQ's obtained from the various tests on the market would be alike—they would have the same standard deviation—and the IQ's would be comparable, in this respect, at least. But these standard deviations vary from about 10 to about 26; so a very bright youngster might have, taking extremes, an IQ of 130 on one test and an IQ of 178 on another. Or, a child might have an IQ of 80 on one test and be judged a bit subnormal, and have an IQ of 48 on another and be classified as an imbecile.

The standard deviation of IQ's on the first Stanford-Binet scale was about 13. The distribution of IQ's given in the first paragraph of this article was based on the scale, which has been obsolete since 1937, when it was superseded by the present revision. The newer standard deviation is reported as 16.4, and makers of many other intelligence tests now try to get about the same dispersion—with considerably varying degrees of success.

An IQ, then, is likely to be a pretty shifty measure of mental ability unless it is interpreted in terms of how commonly such an IQ occurs in the general population; that is, in terms of the statistical characteristics of the test used. The IQ's yielded by different tests cannot be assumed to be comparable. At least some teachers in each school, therefore, should know enough about elementary statistics to make the necessary analysis.

Many teachers are disturbed by the increasing numbers of "feeble-minded" children in school, as indicated by IQ's below 70. As Tredgold pointed out many years ago, the sound definition of feeble-mindedness refers to the lowest x percent of the population. Without an agreement on x, we formerly had estimates running all the way from one feeble-minded person in 2500 to one in 16. The American consensus on what x should be was expressed for the old Stanford-Binet as the portion having IQ's below 70. That was 1 percent. On the present Stanford-Binet it's nearly 4 percent. To identify the feeble-minded as the lowest 1 percent nowadays we should take those with IQ's below 60 on the Stanford-Binet and other tests with similar IQ dispersion.

The term IQ has been so grossly abused and it is so inappropriate to the shifting values yielded by various tests the writer thinks that we probably should abandon it altogether. The test scores would be far easier to interpret if the school made its own conversion of the raw point scores into standard scores of some sort (Z-scores, for example, which have a mean of 50 and a standard deviation of 10), and made comparisons with national norms if requisite data were available.

In any case, I should say that we do too much intelligence testing and then misinterpret—or ignore—the results. Once in three or four years should be often enough to measure a student's mental ability, and the tests then used should not attempt the speculative or the impossible. In considering tests for selection, fancy claims and high costs should be automatically suspect, and tests under favorable consideration should be carefully studied (and actually taken by the teachers who made the selection) to make judgments of local validity, ease of administration and scoring, adequacy of manuals, and so on. Finally, the results of the intelligence testing should be interpreted in light of the characteristics of the test used, and especially—until we can do better—of the IQ distribution for that test.

36. ON TELLING PARENTS ABOUT TEST RESULTS *

JAMES H. RICKS

Like any other organization dealing with people, a school has many confidences to keep. School administrators, teachers, and especially guidance workers inevitably come to know items of private information. A gossip who carelessly passes such information around abuses his position and his relationship with his students. It is both right and important that some kinds of information be kept in confidence.

What about test results? Do they belong in the category of secrets, to be seen only by professional eyes and mentioned only in whispers? Or is their proper function best served when they become common knowledge in the school and its community? (In some towns, names and scores have been listed in the local newspaper, much like the results of an athletic contest.)

We think neither extreme is a good rule. Sometimes there is reason to make group data —figures such as the average and the range from high to low generally public. Seldom should individual results be published except for the happy announcement of a prize won, a scholarship awarded, and the like. But short of general publication, school guidance workers face a particularly important question: Should parents be told their children's test results?

Hard questions often are hard because they deal with genuinely complicated problems. Simple "solutions" to such questions are likely to be a trap rather than an aid if their effect is to divert our attention from the difficulties we truly face. Simple rules or principles, on

* From Ricks, James H., "On Telling Parents About Test Results," *Test Service Bulletin No. 54,* The Psychological Corporation, 1959, pp. 1-4.

the other hand, can be of real help as one tackles complex problems and situations. This article will present some rules that we have found useful in facing questions such as— "What should I say when a mother wants to know her son's IQ?" "Should we send aptitude test profiles home with the children?" "We feel that parents in our school ought to know the results of the achievement tests we give, but then it's hard to explain the discrepancies between these and the teachers' grades."

No single procedure, obviously, can be appropriate for every kind of test. Nor for every kind of parent. To Mr. Jones, a well-adjusted and well-educated father, a report of his daughter's test scores may enhance his understanding of her capacities and of what the school has been giving her. To Mr. Green, a somewhat insecure and less knowledgeable man, the identical information may spark an explosion damaging to both child and school. And the counselor or teacher often has no sure way of knowing which kind of parent he will be reporting to.

Two principles and one verbal technique seem to us to provide a sound basis for communicating the information obtained from testing. The two "commandments" are absolutely interdependent—without the second the first is empty, and without the first the second is pointless.

The first: PARENTS HAVE THE RIGHT TO KNOW WHATEVER THE SCHOOL KNOWS ABOUT THE ABILITIES, THE PERFORMANCE, AND THE PROBLEMS OF THEIR CHILDREN.

The second: THE SCHOOL HAS THE OBLIGATION TO SEE THAT IT COMMUNICATES UNDERSTANDABLE AND USABLE KNOWLEDGE. Whether by written report or by individual conference, the school must make sure it is giving real information—not just the illusion of information that bare numbers or canned interpretations often afford. And the information must be in terms that parents can absorb and use.

Few educators will dispute the first principle. It is in parents that the final responsibility for the upbringing and education of the children must lie. This responsibility requires access to all available information bearing on educational and vocational decisions to be made for and by the child. The school is the agent to which parents have delegated part of the educational process—but the responsibility has been delegated, not abdicated. Thoughtful parents do not take these responsibilities and rights lightly.

The parents' right to know, then, we regard as indisputable. But, to know what?

Suppose that as a result of judicious testings the school knows that Sally has mastered social studies and general science better than many in her ninth grade class, but that few do as poorly as she in math. In English usage she stands about in the middle, but her reading level is barely up to the lower border of the students who successfully complete college preparatory work in her high school. The best prediction that can be made of her probable scores on the College Boards three years hence is that they will fall in the range which makes her eligible for the two-year community college, but not for the university. She grasps mechanical concepts better than most boys, far better than most girls. Looking over the test results and her records, her experienced teacher recognizes that good habits and neatness of work have earned Sally grades somewhat better than would be expected from her test scores.

All of these are things Sally's parents should know. Will they know them if they are given the numbers—Sally's IQ score, percentiles for two reading scores, percentiles on another set of norms for several aptitude tests, and grade-placement figures on an achievement battery?

Telling someone something he does not understand does not increase his knowledge (at least not his correct and usable knowledge

—we are reminded of the guide's observation about the tenderfoot, "It ain't so much what he don't know, it's what he knows that ain't so that gits him in trouble."). Transmitting genuine knowledge requires attention to content, language, and audience. We have already referred to some of the characteristics of parents as an audience. Let's look at the other two elements.

Content means that to begin with we must ourselves know what we are trying to get across.

We need to know just what evidence there is to show that these test results deserve any consideration at all. We need equally to know the margins and probabilities of error in predictions based on tests. If we don't know both what the scores mean and how much confidence may properly be placed in them, we are in trouble at the start—neither our own use of the information nor our transmission of it to others will be very good.

Content—what we are going to say—and language—how we are going to put it—are inseparable when we undertake to tell somebody something. In giving information about test results, we need to think about the general content and language we shall use and also about the specific terms we shall use.

To illustrate the general content-and-language planning, a guidance director may decide that he wants first to get across a sense of both the values and the weaknesses of test scores. One excellent device for his purpose would be an expectancy table or chart. Such a chart can make it clear to persons without training in statistics that test results are useful predictors and that the predictions will not always be precise. Local studies in one's school or community are of greatest interest. But the guidance director who lacks local data may still find illustrative tables from other places helpful in preparing parents and students to use test results in a sensible way.

Specific terms used in expressing test results vary considerably in the problems they pose. Consider, for example, the different kinds of numbers in which test results may be reported.

IQ's are regarded as numbers that should rarely if ever be reported as such to students or to their parents. The reason is that an IQ is likely to be seen as a fixed characteristic of the person tested, as somehow something more than the test score it really represents. The effect, too often, is that of a final conclusion about the individual rather than that of a piece of information useful in further thinking and planning. Few things interfere more effectively with real understanding than indiscriminate reporting of IQ scores to parents.

Grade-placement scores or standard scores of various kinds are less likely to cause trouble than IQ scores are. Still, they may substitute an illusion of communication for real communication. Standard scores have no more meaning to most parents than raw scores unless there is opportunity for extensive explanations. Grade placements seem so simple and straightforward that serious misunderstandings may result from their use. As noted in a very helpful pamphlet (Katz, 1958), a sixth-grade pupil with grade-placement scores of 10.0 for reading and 8.5 for arithmetic does not necessarily rank higher in reading than he does in arithmetic when compared to the other sixth-graders. (Both scores may be at the 95th percentile for his class—arithmetic progress much more than reading progress tends to be dependent on what has been taught, and thus to spread over a narrower range at any one grade.)

Percentiles probably are the safest and most informative numbers to use provided their two essential characteristics are made clear: (1) that they refer not to percent of questions answered correctly but to percent of people whose performance the student has equaled or surpassed, and (2) who specifically are the people with whom the student is being compared. The second point—a definite description of the comparison or "norm" group—is especially important in making the meaning of test results clear.

Much more can be said about the kinds of numbers used to convey test score information. But a more fundamental question remains—are any numbers necessary?

We intend nothing so foolish as suggesting a ban on the use of numbers in reporting test results. But we have been struck repeatedly by the fact that some of the very best

counselors and many of the best-written reports present numerical data only incidentally or not at all.

Along with the two "commandments" at the beginning of this article, we mentioned a verbal technique. Generally we dislike formulas for writing or speaking. This one, however, seems to have advantages that outweigh the risks attending its suggestion. It's just a few words: "YOU SCORE LIKE PEOPLE WHO . . ." Or, to a parent, "Your son (or daughter) scores like students who . . ."

The sentence, of course, requires completion. The completion depends on the test or other instrument, the reason for testing, and the person to whom the report is being given. Some sample completions:

YOU SCORE LIKE

". . . people who don't find selling insurance a very satisfactory choice. Three out of four who score as you do and become insurance salesmen leave the job for something else in less than a year."

". . . people who are pretty good at office work, fast and accurate enough to hold a job and do it well."

". . . students who find getting into liberal arts college and getting a B.A. degree something they can attain only with extra hard work. On the other hand, they find a year or two of technical school interesting and they probably do well in the jobs to which that leads."

". . . students who are disappointed later if they don't begin a language in the ninth grade and plan to take some more math and science. It's easier to head toward business later if you still want to than to go from the commercial course into a good college."

". . . students who don't often—only about one out of four—manage to earn a C average their freshman year at State."

". . . students who have more than average difficulty passing in arithmetic—you (or, to a parent, he) may need some extra help on this in the next few years."

Many more samples will come readily to mind. The most important thing to note is that a satisfactory report combines two kinds of information:

1. the test results of the individual person, and
2. something known about the test or battery and its relationship to the subsequent performance of others who have taken it.

Also, a satisfactory completion puts the school or the counselor out on a limb, at least a little. Some variant of "That's not so!" or, more politely, "How do you know?" will be the reaction in some cases, probably less frequently voiced than it is felt.

Well, let's face it. The decision to use a test at all is a step out on a limb. Some limbs are broad and solid and the climber need feel little or no anxiety. Some are so frail that they offer only hazard, with the bait of an improbable reward. We climb out on some limbs of medium safety because there is evidence of a real chance that they will help us, and those whom we test, toward a worthwhile goal.

The words of the formula need not actually be used in each case. Sometimes percentiles, grade placement scores, or a profile may be what the parents should receive. But it is well to try first mentally stating the meaning of the results in the language suggested above. If this proves difficult or discomforting, a warning signal is on—reporting the numbers is likely not to be constructive in the case at hand!

The audience of parents to which our test-based information is to be transmitted includes an enormous range and variety of minds and emotions. Some are ready and able to absorb what we have to say. Reaching others may be as hopeless as reaching TV watchers with an AM radio broadcast. Still others may hear what we say, but clothe the message with their own special needs, ideas, and predilections.

The habit of using the formula and of thinking a bit about what answer to give if the response is a challenging or doubting one puts the interpreter of test scores in the strongest position he can occupy. In the case of achievement tests it requires him to understand why and how the particular test or battery was chosen as appropriate for his school and his purpose. In the case of aptitude (including scholastic aptitude or intelligence) tests it requires him to examine the evidence offered in the test manual and research studies to back up the test's claim to usefulness. And it reminds him always that it is in the end his thinking, his weighing of the evidence, his soundness and helpfulness as an educator or counselor that is exposed for judgment—not the sometimes wistful ideas of the test author or publisher.

The school—or the counselor—is exposed for judgment when telling parents about the abilities and performances of their children. The parents have the right to know. And knowledge in terms they can understand and absorb is what the school must give.

Chapter VII

THE PSYCHOLOGY OF TEACHING
AND THE TEACHER

Because the so-called "simple act" of teaching usually involves some kind of premeditated attempt by an adult to affect some other person, usually a child, it is important to focus on what we might call the psychology of this act. By the psychology we mean all the many factors influencing the adult involved in teaching, his perceptions, his motives, his emotions, and his attitudes—both toward the learning process and toward the pupils. Often we, as people, do not clearly understand our own attitudes and we certainly have difficulty in trying to assess our own motives. These psychological constructs or personality factors are even more complex when viewed from the standpoint of the teacher. It is a generalization that applies to both children and adults, that our attitudes, values, motives (e.g., our psychological dispositions) continuously affect how we act.

In classical psychology it was Sigmund Freud who first popularized the ideas of unconscious motivation, which simply means that much of what we do as human beings, does not occur as the result of careful rational planning. The disparity between what we often *say* and what we actually *do*, denotes the importance of motives and attitudes as causes of how we behave.

As an example, Margaret Mead (1950) has described three types of teachers in *The School in American Culture*. Speaking from the context of anthropology, she notes that in primitive cultures there are three distinctively different patterns of raising children: (1) that of the "grandmother," (2) that of the "parent," and (3) that of the "child nurse." The values, attitudes, and role of each are different. The *grandmother*, with respect and admiration for the past, exemplifies the unchanging nature of the world; she is a conservative "classicist" who clings to the old ways. The *parent* is seen as one who wishes to instill in the child habits of industriousness, of practicality, and of ambition. The *child-nurse*, who is still close to babyhood herself, wants to keep the child close to infancy. Mead suggests that teachers in American schools fall into similar categories. An interesting exercise in testing out Margaret Mead's types might be a review of our own experience in elementary and secondary school to see if some of the teachers we had might reappear in our mind's eye as grandmother, parent, or child-nurse. Regardless of whether or not we can actually find pure "types," the exercise will surely illustrate the variety of attitudes and values that may be guiding and directing the teacher in her approach to both the subject matter and the pupil.

There is obviously much more to teaching than the application of teaching methods. If this were the case the solution to the problem of teaching would be clear—have each teacher learn an array of techniques (e.g., how to give a lecture, conduct class discussions, manage recitations, etc.). This obviously is insufficient since it leaves out the personality, motives, attitudes, perceptions, etc., of the teacher. Recently it has been fashionable to examine such questions in the framework suggested by Marshall McLuhan, a philosopher who has popularized the phrase "The medium is the message." In other words it is not the content that is so important but how the message is transmitted. In teaching, the subtle nuances of attitudes, unwittingly held by the teacher both in regard to the pupils and the subject matter, may be more relevant than the sophistication of a formal lesson plan. How the material is communicated by the teacher or how the teacher feels about certain pupils, either positively or negatively, may strongly facilitate or deter instruction. We have all experienced instruction at the hands of a grudging tutor, someone who told us in so many words "I don't think you'll be able to understand this but listen anyway." Or we've all at one time or another realized deep down inside us that the person we've been talking to hasn't really been listening to what we've been saying but has just been going through the motions. In these instances the medium indeed is the message; and instruction or learning or teaching all suffer. It is surely not surprising that pupils (being people like us) are sensitive in detecting attitudes that others hold toward them. What is often not understood, however, is the great influence that these attitudes have on learning.

There is always the danger that in entering the murky waters of motivation we may be opening a Pandora's box. We may find things that we don't want to discover. We may learn that some of our stereotypes about teachers and teaching are simply that—empty stereotypes. We may find the professed concern of the educator to educate each child to reach his "maximum" and to realize his potential is all to often honored only in the breach. We may realize that the oft-cited "discovery" from psychology, of individual differences and unique potential, remains only a catchy phrase and has not become a basis for instruction. It does seem crucial that all those who are going to work in the education enterprise as teachers, counselors, or principals should fully understand the importance of what we might call the "hidden agenda" or the "implicit curriculum." The hidden agenda of teaching is not made up of lesson plans or curriculum content—it is made up of the expectations, attitudes, and values of the teacher. These determine how the lesson plan is conveyed. The process of communication will determine in a significant way how much the children really learn. The readings in this section have been selected to elaborate on this theme as well as to underscore its importance.

In the late 1920s, a significant study was done by Wickman that illustrated both the importance of the perceptions with which pupils were regarded and the marked difference in these perceptions when held by teachers and psychologists. Teachers, in viewing children in the classroom, were most concerned about aggressive and disruptive behavior by pupils. Psychologists, on the other hand, were much more concerned about the children who appeared very shy and withdrawn. The psychologists assumed that passive, quiet, and shy children—even though they obviously caused no "trouble" in class, would not learn much because of their passivity. Psychologists have generally viewed learning as an aggressive activity, one that demands initiative. On the other hand, the teachers obviously entertained a completely different set of values about learning, They felt that physical activity, noise, and aggressiveness would inhibit learning. This controversy has never really been resolved. Today psychologists generally maintain that teachers are overly concerned about "normal" aggressiveness in pupils; and teachers maintain that psychologists are overly concerned about "normally" quiet pupils. This all serves to illustrate one underlying issue—that the values and perceptions accorded to pupils differ significantly when they are perceived by psychologists and when they are perceived by teachers. Also it is obvious that within a group of teachers, there is considerable variation in their attitudes towards pupils. Someone interested in teaching might do well to examine his own views on these and similar issues. Although we may never fully comprehend our own "hidden agenda" we can at least become more aware of some of the values and attitude dimensions within ourselves.

Thus far we have deliberately focused on but one aspect of the many dimensions involved in classroom learning. We have discussed in a general way the influence of attitudes towards the children as a critical variable in examining the psychology of teaching. We would be remiss, however, if we left the reader with the impression that other attitudes may not be equally important. In a sense the teacher's attitude toward the learning process, or the teacher's perception of knowledge, may be as significant as his or her attitude towards pupils. The question itself is broad, and is based on one's conception of knowledge or assumptions about learning.

For example a teacher might perceive knowledge as largely being "fact gathering." Before the children can form their own opinions, so this teaching view goes, they have to memorize and repeat information in order to master the material. What this meant in practice in the not too distant past was that in geography, for example, the children were required to memorize the dates of admission to the Union of all the states, along with their capital cities and principal commercial products. Or in English, a child might memorize Portia's mercy speech from the *Merchant of Venice,* or "Snowbound" by Whittier, or Mark Antony's oration in *Julius Caesar.* The belief was that through repetition and memorization (really assuming the mind was merely like a muscle) we could keep the "mind" active and learning.

Another view or attitude toward knowledge, sharing equal prominence with fact gathering, was the emphasis on techniques, accuracy, and neatness. Pupils used to be taught to write by being forced to endlessly make circles and lines on page after page of "practice paper." Similarly, teachers would stress neatness, as did the first grade teacher who insisted that all the children carefully color within the lines of a prescribed outline. Careful attention to margins, the form and heading of each work paper, and the deliberate reward for tidiness—all these obviously would convey quickly to the pupils a particular set of attitudes towards learning.

If we look for a moment at the fact-gathering attitude or the neatness disposition, we can readily understand how such attitudes would influence learning. If children learn in school that the teacher knows everything or has all the answers, then the pupils will also learn to follow directions, do what the teacher wants, say what the teacher wants to hear, etc. Such an atmosphere, of course, could lay the groundwork for a very passive attitude toward learning in the pupils. Similarly, if a teacher emphasizes neatness and orderliness, the pupils will quickly understand that this dimension is of major importance as a definition of knowledge with concomitant attitudes.

John Dewey many years ago warned of the sterilized curriculum and an antiseptic view of knowledge—that is, learning as material to be injected into children. This view carried with it by-products that seemed to make learning a painful and uninteresting process. One of Dewey's main considerations in his attack upon the classical curriculum that emphasized memorization (often meaningless) and repetition (often parrot-like) was that the most important outcome of learning may well be the *formation of enduring attitudes* toward knowledge. The teacher's implicit conception of knowledge may be among the most important messages that is communicated to the children.

In this introduction, we have stressed three aspects of attitudes and values in relation to teachers and teaching. As was so clearly seen by Margaret Mead, the teacher's attitude towards himself as both a person and a teacher is significant. By no means less important however, are the other two attitudes, those towards the pupils and those about "knowledge" and the learning process. Thus emerges the three part system of self attitudes, views regarding pupils, and assumptions about learning. These taken together make for a complicated picture of the psychology of teaching. It would be impossible to say which set is most important, nor is the question meaningful. All three parts are in constant interaction. A teacher's view of himself affects his view of students, and both views obviously influence his understanding of the learning process.

AN OVERVIEW OF THE READINGS FOR THIS CHAPTER

The first article (Selection 37) by William James is one of his famous *Talks With Teachers*. James, who has been called the father of American psychology, was among the first of the "new breed" of psychologists in this country, who at the turn of the century focused on the psychology of teaching. In one sense he makes a careful differentiation between teaching as an art and psychology as a science. This distinction needs to be reiterated today as well. Psychology can increase our understanding of child behavior and adult behavior as James notes. However, and this is the crux of his argument, do not expect that psychological knowledge can guarantee good teaching any more than the science of logic can guarantee "a man reason rightly."

Teaching is thus application, but again James warns of the complexity. He presents a striking analogy in comparing the principles of teaching to those of warfare. What appears so simple in theory (e.g., just work your pupil into a corner . . .), fails miserably in practice. The failure of this "simple" teaching is apparent because so often the teacher forgets that the pupil may be working at cross purposes. It is, after all, difficult to discern the motives of pupils. James concludes, however, that teachers should not become psychologists because if they did they would simultaneously become poor teachers.

If it is difficult for teachers to discern motives in their pupils, it does not follow that pupils cannot grasp attitudes and motives of teachers. The second article (Selection 38) by Rosenthal and Jacobson makes this clear. These authors tested out the so-called self-fulfilling prophecy. This is a very interesting phenomenon in human behavior. Our expectations, or what we think "ought" to happen in a particular situation, do indeed occur. The irony is that apparently we actually bring about the result unwittingly. This is not to suggest some kind of magical communication or extrasensory perception; but rather we unintentionally convey these expectations to others and they act in a way that is confirmatory. Rosenthal and Jacobson provide rather dramatic information on this point in their article. They show the effect of certain artificially created expectations on pupil learning and even on measured intelligence. The teachers were led to believe that particular students would experience a "growth spurt" of intellectual development. The results of such expectations were startling. Thus the study itself raises important questions about classroom climates and atmospheres created from within the personality of the teacher.

Howard Becker's article (Selection 39) on the "Social-Class Variations in the Teacher-Pupil Relationship," provides further evidence of differential attitudes within teachers toward pupils. The framework of the study is descriptive and direct. The author interviewed a number of teachers in one school system and then classified their "talk" into three categories: (1) teaching problems, (2) discipline problems, and (3) moral acceptability of children. Sociologists, of course, have long been interested in the influence of one's social class and background upon attitudes, perceptions, and values. Perceptions (that is, what one "sees") are often colored or distorted by what one "wants" to see. Becker shows how middle class teachers "see" pupils from upper class, middle class, and lower class backgrounds. In reading the excerpts, imagine the impact of the implicit attitudes in terms of what the teachers expect from children whose backgrounds are dissimilar to those of the teacher.

The fourth article (Selection 40) in this chapter by Meyer and Thompson presents evidence on the variations in patterns of approval and disapproval by teachers. The research report, "Sex Differences in the Distribution of Teacher Approval and Disapproval Among Sixth Grade Children," raises further questions about the hidden agenda in teaching.

Parts of the article are somewhat technical, particularly in the presentation of statistical tests of significance. In order not to obscure the meaning of the results, we will present an interpretation of Table 1, "Sex Differences in Frequency of Teachers' Disapproval Contacts." In the table, "N" stands for the number of pupils in each classroom. "Mean" indicates the arithmetical average number of disapproval contacts. For example, in classroom "A," the boys received an average of 11.1 negative contacts while the girls received an average of only 2.67. S.D. refers to the "standard deviation," a statistic that describes how much spread or variation exists around the mean in the number of contacts. Since the numbers are 7.62 for the boys as against 2.18 for girls, it is obvious that there is much less variation in the average contacts for the girls. The next notation in the table, "t," refers to a test of significance. It indicates ($t = 3.20$) that the difference between the average for the boys (11.10) and the girls (2.67) could occur by chance only one time in a hundred. This is a convention adopted by statisticians as a way of agreeing whether computed differences are significant or are simply the result of chance. The notation "F" refers to a test of the statistical significance regarding the amount of variation or spread of the number of contacts. Again the convention in this case indicates that this much spread would occur by chance only one time in a hundred implying that chance is *not* the reason for the difference. Of course the authors show more than just that teachers blame boys more than girls, for they also demonstrate that all the pupils are aware of these differences. What effect such an awareness within the pupils might have on their academic performance we will leave to the reader to ponder! However it is interesting to consider their discussion of the teachers' responses to the normal aggressiveness and activity of young male pupils. This discussion is particularly important since it has long been held that normal aggressiveness is a main component of effective learning. When we speak of "hitting the books" or "grabbing an idea," these everyday expressions represent learning as an active, aggressive process rather than a passive acceptance of someone else's view. Squelching the boys' active behavior in general may then inhibit the development of active mastery in learning. The short run advantage of quiet orderliness to the teacher may bring a long run decrement in pupil learning.

The last two articles represent a more general and hence more philosophical view toward teachers and the teaching role. David Reisman's article (Selection 41), "Changes in the Role of Teacher," presents his analysis of the opportunity for significant influence by teachers. Because modern society has removed so many other adults from within the ken of children, the teacher is almost the single remaining parent surrogate. Combined with this change, he discerns a general shift in our society away from self-direction and self-reliance (inner direction) and toward conformity and other direction. This means we have a greater tendency to act in accord with other people's desires than on the basis of our own view. He then indicates how this shift toward "other direction" acts to inhibit intellectual growth. The teacher may become an opinion leader emphasizing adjustment rather than presenting challenging ideas. There is a danger of over-simplifying Reisman's position to the old dichotomy of the "whole child" theory versus academic attainment. Note carefully that he's saying much more than just "bad guys" (e.g., anti-intellectual, adjustment-oriented, soft teachers) versus "good guys" (e.g., hard-nosed, brilliant, inspiring scholars).

The final article (Selection 42) by Thelen, "The Triumph of Achievement over Inquiry in Education," touches yet another aspect of teaching. By now the reader is hopefully aware of the series of issues, the multiple positions, and the wide array of variables that make up what we have called the hidden agenda of teaching. Thelen presents us with a note of closure in raising the fundamental issue of "teaching for what?". He sees too much of our present teaching oriented toward an academic hit-and-run process, emphasizing outcome (e.g., grades), rote memorization, and collecting facts. He brings the selection to a close with his almost eloquent plea for teachers to stress intrinsic interest in learning. Otherwise we may be doomed to become a nation of sheep!

37. PSYCHOLOGY AND THE TEACHING ART *

WILLIAM JAMES

In the general activity and uprising of ideal interests which every one with an eye for fact can discern all about us in American life, there is perhaps no more promising feature than the fermentation which for a dozen years or more has been going on among the teachers. In whatever sphere of education their functions may lie, there is to be seen among them a really inspiring amount of searching of the heart about the highest concerns of their profession. The renovation of nations begins always at the top, among the reflective members of the State, and spreads slowly outward and downward. The teachers of this country, one may say, have its future in their hands. The earnestness which they at present show in striving to enlighten and strengthen themselves is an index of the nation's probabilities of advance in all ideal directions. The outward organization of education which we have in our United States is perhaps, on the whole, the best organization that exists in any country. The State school systems give a diversity and flexibility, an opportunity for experiment and keenness of competition, nowhere else to be found on such an important scale. The independence of so many of the colleges and universities; the give and take of students and instructors between them all; their emulation, and their happy organic relations to the lower schools; the traditions of instruction in them, evolved from the older American recitation-method (and so avoiding on the one hand the pure lecture-system prevalent in Germany and Scotland, which considers too little the individual student, and yet not involving

the sacrifice of the instructor to the individual student, which the English tutorial system would seem too often to entail),—all these things (to say nothing of that coeducation of the sexes in whose benefits so many of us heartily believe), all these things, I say, are most happy features of our scholastic life, and from them the most sanguine auguries may be drawn.

Having so favorable an organization, all we need is to impregnate it with geniuses, to get superior men and women working more and more abundantly in it and for it and at it, and in a generation or two America may well lead the education of the world. I must say that I look forward with no little confidence to the day when that shall be an accomplished fact.

No one has profited more by the fermentation of which I speak, in pedagogical circles, than we psychologists. The desire of the schoolteachers for a completer professional training, and their aspiration toward the 'professional' spirit in their work, have led them more and more to turn to us for light on fundamental principles. And in these few hours which we are to spend together you look to me, I am sure, for information concerning the mind's operations, which may enable you to labor more easily and effectively in the several schoolrooms over which you preside.

Far be it from me to disclaim for psychology all title to such hopes. Psychology ought certainly to give the teacher radical help. And yet I confess that, acquainted as I am with the height of some of your expectations, I feel a little anxious lest, at the end of these simple talks of mine, not a few of you may experience some disappointment at the net results. In

* James, William, "Psychology and the Teaching Art," *Talks with Teachers*, New York: Norton, 1958, pp. 21-27.

other words, I am not sure that you may not be indulging fancies that are just a shade exaggerated. That would not be altogether astonishing, for we have been having something like a 'boom' in psychology in this country. Laboratories and professorships have been founded, and reviews established. The air has been full of rumors. The editors of educational journals and the arrangers of conventions have had to show themselves enterprising and on a level with the novelties of the day. Some of the professors have not been unwilling to co-operate, and I am not sure even that the publishers have been entirely inert. 'The new psychology' has thus become a term to conjure up portentous ideas withal; and you teachers, docile and receptive and aspiring as many of you are, have been plunged in an atmosphere of vague talk about our science, which to a great extent has been more mystifying than enlightening. Altogether it does seem as if there were a certain fatality of mystification laid upon the teachers of our day. The matter of their profession, compact enough in itself, has to be frothed up for them in journals and institutes, till its outlines threaten to be lost in a kind of vast uncertainty. Where the disciples are not independent and critical-minded enough (and I think that, if you teachers in the earlier grades have any defect—the slightest touch of a defect in the world—it is that you are a mite too docile), we are pretty sure to miss accuracy and balance and measure in those who get a license to lay down the law to them from above.

As regards this subject of psychology, now, I wish at the very threshold to do what I can to dispel the mystification. So I say at once that in my humble opinion there *is* no 'new psychology' worthy of the name. There is nothing but the old psychology which began in Locke's time, plus a little physiology of the brain and senses and theory of evolution, and a few refinements of introspective detail, for the most part without adaptation to the teacher's use. It is only the fundamental conceptions of psychology which are of real value to the teacher; and they, apart from the aforesaid theory of evolution, are very far from being new.—I trust that you will see better what I mean by this at the end of all these talks.

I say moreover that you make a great, a very great mistake, if you think that psychology, being the science of the mind's laws, is something from which you can deduce definite programmes and schemes and methods of instruction for immediate schoolroom use. Psychology is a science, and teaching is an art; and sciences never generate arts directly out of themselves. An intermediary inventive mind must make the application, by using its originality.

The science of logic never made a man reason rightly, and the science of ethics (if there be such a thing) never made a man behave rightly. The most such sciences can do is to help us to catch ourselves up and check ourselves, if we start to reason or to behave wrongly; and to criticise ourselves more articulately after we have made mistakes. A science only lays down lines within which the rules of the art must fall, laws which the follower of the art must not transgress; but what particular thing he shall positively do within those lines is left exclusively to his own genius. One genius will do his work well and succeed in one way, while another succeeds as well quite differently; yet neither will transgress the lines.

The art of teaching grew up in the schoolroom, out of inventiveness and sympathetic concrete observation. Even where (as in the case of Herbart) the advancer of the art was also a psychologist, the pedagogics and the psychology ran side by side, and the former was not derived in any sense from the latter. The two were congruent, but neither was subordinate. And so everywhere the teaching must *agree* with the psychology, but need not necessarily be the only kind of teaching that would so agree; for many diverse methods of teaching may equally well agree with psychological laws.

To know psychology, therefore, is absolutely no guarantee that we shall be good teachers. To advance to that result, we must have an additional endowment altogether, a happy tact and ingenuity to tell us what definite things to say and do when the pupil is before us. That ingenuity in meeting and pursuing the pupil, that tact for the concrete situation, though they are the alpha and omega of the teacher's art, are things to which psychology cannot help us in the least.

The science of psychology, and whatever science of general pedagogics may be based on it, are in fact much like the science of war. Nothing is simpler or more definite than the principles of either. In war, all you have to do is to work your enemy into a position from which the natural obstacles prevent him from escaping if he tries to; then to fall on him in numbers superior to his own, at a moment when you have led him to think you far away; and so, with a minimum of exposure of your own troops, to hack his force to pieces, and take the remainder prisoners. Just so, in teaching, you must simply work your pupil into such a state of interest in what you are going to teach him that every other object of attention is banished from his mind; then reveal it to him so impressively that he will remember the occasion to his dying day; and finally fill him with devouring curiosity to know what the next steps in connection with the subject are. The principles being so plain, there would be nothing but victories for the masters of the science, either on the battlefield or in the schoolroom, if they did not both have to make their application to an incalculable quantity in the shape of the mind of their opponent. The mind of your own enemy, the pupil, is working away from you as keenly and eagerly as is the mind of the commander on the other side from the scientific general. Just what the respective enemies want and think, and what they know and do not know, are as hard things for the teacher as for the general to find out. Divination and perception, not psychological pedagogics or theoretic strategy, are the only helpers here.

But, if the use of psychological principles thus be negative rather than positive, it does not follow that it may not be a great use, all the same. It certainly narrows the path for experiments and trials. We know in advance, if we are psychologists, that certain methods will be wrong, so our psychology saves us from mistakes. It makes us, moreover, more clear as to what we are about. We gain confidence in respect to any method which we are using as soon as we believe that it has theory as well as practice at its back. Most of all, it fructifies our independence, and it reanimates our interest, to see our subject at two different angles,—to get a stereoscopic view, so to speak, of the youthful organism who is our enemy, and, while handling him with all our concrete tact and divination, to be able, at the same time, to represent to ourselves the curious inner elements of his mental machine. Such a complete knowledge as this of the pupil, at once intuitive and analytic, is surely the knowledge at which every teacher ought to aim.

Fortunately for you teachers, the elements of the mental machine can be clearly apprehended, and their workings easily grasped. And, as the most general elements and workings are just those parts of psychology which the teacher finds most directly useful, it follows that the amount of this science which is necessary to all teachers need not be very great. Those who find themselves loving the subject may go as far as they please, and become possibly none the worse teachers for the fact, even though in some of them one might apprehend a little loss of balance from the tendency observable in all of us to overemphasize certain special parts of a subject when we are studying it intensely and abstractly. But for the great majority of you a general view is enough, provided it be a true one; and such a general view, one may say, might almost be written on the palm of one's hand.

Least of all need you, merely *as teachers*, deem it part of your duty to become contributors to psychological science or to make psychological observations in a methodical or responsible manner. I fear that some of the enthusiasts for child-study have thrown a certain burden on you in this way. By all means let child-study go on,—it is refreshing all our sense of the child's life. There are teachers who take a spontaneous delight in filling syllabuses, inscribing observations, compiling statistics, and computing the per cent. Child-study will certainly enrich their lives. And, if its results, as treated statistically, would seem on the whole to have but trifling value, yet the anecdotes and observations of which it in part consists do certainly acquaint us more intimately with our pupils. Our eyes and ears grow quickened to discern in the child before us processes similar to those we have read of as noted in the children,—processes of which we might otherwise have remained inobservant. But, for Heaven's sake, let the rank and file of teachers be passive readers if they so prefer, and feel free not to contribute to the accumulation. Let not the prosecution of it be preached as an imperative duty or imposed by regulation on those to whom it proves an exterminating bore, or who in any way whatever miss in themselves the appropriate vocation for it. I cannot too strongly agree with my colleague, Professor Münsterberg, when he says that the teacher's attitude toward the child, being concrete and ethical, is positively opposed to the psychological observer's, which is abstract and analytic. Although some of us may conjoin the attitudes successfully, in most of us they must conflict.

The worst thing that can happen to a good teacher is to get a bad conscience about her profession because she feels herself hopeless as a psychologist. Our teachers are overworked already. Every one who adds a jot or tittle of unnecessary weight to their burden is a foe of education. A bad conscience increases the weight of every other burden; yet I know that child-study, and other pieces of psychology as well, have been productive of bad conscience in many a really innocent pedagogic breast. I should indeed be glad if this passing word from me might tend to dispel such a bad conscience, if any of you have it; for it is certainly one of those fruits of more or less systematic mystification of which I have already complained. The best teacher may be the poorest contributor of child-study material, and the best contributor may be the poorest teacher. No fact is more palpable than this.

So much for what seems the most reasonable general attitude of the teacher toward the subject which is to occupy our attention.

38. TEACHERS' EXPECTATIONS AS SELF-FULFILLING PROPHECIES * [1]

ROBERT ROSENTHAL AND LENORE JACOBSON

There is increasing concern over what can be done to reduce the disparities of education, of intellectual motivation and of intellectual

* Rosenthal, Robert and Jacobson, Lenore, "Teachers' Expectations as Self-Fulfilling Prophecies," Paper presented at APA Div. 13, Washington, D.C., 1967.

[1] This research was supported by the Division of Social Sciences of the National Science Foundation (GS-177, GS-714, and GS-1741). We are grateful to Dr. Paul Nielsen, Superintendent, South San Francisco Unified School District, for making this study possible. We also thank Nate Gage, Jerome Kagan, David Marlowe, Jerome Singer, and especially Bruce Biddle for their valuable advice, and Mae Evans and George Smiltens for their assistance. A much more extended treatment of this and of additional material has been published in 1968 by Holt, Rinehart and Winston as a book entitled *Pygmalion in the Classroom: Teacher expectation and pupils' intellectual development.*

Prepared for presentation at the Cattell Fund Award Papers Session of Division 13 at the

competence that exist between the social classes and the colors of our school children. With this increasing concern, attention has focused more and more on the role of the classroom teacher, and the possible effects of her values, her attitudes, and, especially, her beliefs and expectations. Many educational theorists have expressed the opinion that the teacher's expectation of her pupils' performance may serve as an educational self-fulfilling prophecy. The teacher gets less because she expects less.

The concept of the self-fulfilling prophecy is an old idea which has found application in clinical psychology, social psychology, soci-

meetings of the American Psychological Association, Washington, D.C. September 4, 1967. This paper is a condensation of a fuller report prepared as a chapter for Deutsch, Katz, and Jensen (Eds.) *Social Class, Race, and Psychological Development.* Holt, Rinehart and Winston, 1968.

ology, economics, and in everyday life. Most of the evidence for the operation of self-fulfilling prophecies has been correlational. Interpersonal prophecies have been found to agree with the behavior that was prophesied. From this, however, it cannot be said that the prophecy was the cause of its own fulfillment. The accurate prophecy may have been based on a knowledge of the prior behavior of the person whose behavior was prophesied, so that the prophecy was in a sense "contaminated" by reality. If a physician predicts a patient's improvement, we cannot say whether the doctor is only giving a sophisticated prognosis or whether the patient's improvement is based in part on the optimism engendered by the physician's prediction. If school children who perform poorly are those expected by their teachers to perform poorly, we cannot say whether the teacher's expectation was the "cause" of the pupils' poor performance, or whether the teacher's expectation was simply an accurate prognosis of performance based on her knowledge of past performance. To help answer the question raised, experiments are required in which the expectation is experimentally varied and is uncontaminated by the past behavior of the person whose performance is predicted.

Such experiments have been conducted and they have shown, that in behavioral research, the experimenter's hypothesis may serve as self-fulfilling prophecy (Rosenthal, 1966). Of special relevance to our topic are those experiments involving allegedly bright and allegedly dull animal subjects. Half the experimenters were led to believe that their rat subjects had been specially bred for excellence of learning ability. The remaining experimenters were led to believe that their rat subjects were genetically inferior. Actually, of course, the animals were assigned to their experimenters at random.

Regardless of whether the rat's task was to learn a maze or the appropriate responses in a Skinner box, the results were the same. Rats who were believed by their experimenters to be brighter showed learning which was significantly superior to the learning by rats whose experimenters believed them to be dull. Our best guess, supported by the experimenters' self-reports, is that allegedly well-endowed animals were handled more and handled more gently than the allegedly inferior animals. Such handling differences, along with differences in rapidity of reinforcement in the Skinner box situation, are probably sufficient to account for the differences in learning ability shown by allegedly bright and allegedly dull rats.

If rats showed superior performance when their trainer expected it, then it seemed reasonable to think that children might show superior performance when their teacher expected it. That was the reason for conducting the Oak School Experiment (Rosenthal and Jacobson, 1966).

THE "OAK SCHOOL" EXPERIMENT

To all of the children in the Oak School, on the West Coast, the "Harvard Test of Inflected Acquisition" was administered in the Spring of 1964. This test was purported to predict academic "blooming" or intellectual growth. The reason for administering the test in the particular school was ostensibly to perform a final check on the validity of the test, a validity which was presented as already well-established. Actually, the "Harvard Test of Inflected Acquisition" was a standardized relatively nonverbal test of intelligence, Flanagan's Tests of General Ability.

Within each of the six grades of the elementary school, there were three classrooms, one each for children performing at above-average, average, and below-average levels of scholastic achievement. In each of the 18 classrooms of the school, about 20% of the children were designated as academic "spurters." The names of these children were reported to their new teachers in the Fall of 1964 as those who, during the academic year ahead, would show unusual intellectual gains. The "fact" of their intellectual potential was established from their scores on the test for "intellectual blooming."

Teachers were cautioned not to discuss the test findings with either their pupils or the children's parents. Actually, the names of the 20% of the children assigned to the "blooming" condition had been selected by means of a table of random numbers. The difference, then, between these children, earmarked for intellectual growth, and the undesignated control group children was in the mind of the teacher.

Four months after the teachers had been given the names of the "special" children, all the children once again took the same form of the nonverbal test of intelligence. Four months after this retest the children took the same test once again. This final retest was at the end of the school year, some eight months after the teachers had been given the expectation for intellectual growth of the special children. These retests were not, of course, explained as "retests" to the teachers but rather as further efforts to predict intellectual growth.

The intelligence test employed, while relatively nonverbal in the sense of requiring no speaking, reading, or writing, was not entirely nonverbal. Actually there were two subtests, one requiring a greater comprehension of English—a kind of picture vocabulary test. The other subtest required less ability to understand any spoken language but more ability to reason abstractly. For shorthand purposes we refer to the former as a "verbal" subtest and to the latter as a "reasoning" subtest. The pretest correlation between these subtests was $+.42$.

For the school as a whole, the children of the experimental groups did not show a significantly greater gain in verbal IQ (2 points) than did the control group children. However, in total IQ (4 points) and especially in reasoning IQ (7 points) the experimental group children gained more than did the control group children $(p=.02)$. In 15 of the 17 classrooms in which the reasoning IQ posttest was administered children of the experimental group gained more than did the control group children $(p=.001)$. Even after the four month retest this trend was already in evidence though the effects were smaller $(p<.10)$.

When we examine the results separately for the six grades we find that it was only in the first and second grades that children gained significantly more in IQ when their teacher expected it of them. In the first grade, children who were expected to gain more IQ gained over 15 points more than did the control group children $(p<.002)$. In the second grade, children who were expected to gain more IQ gained nearly 10 points more than

did the control group children $(p<.02)$. In the first and second grades combined, 19% of the control group children gained 20 or more IQ points. Two-and-a-half times that many, or 47%, of the experimental group children gained 20 or more IQ points.

When educational theorists have discussed the possible effects of teachers' expectations, they have usually referred to the children at lower levels of scholastic achievement. It was interesting, therefore, to find that in the present study, children of the highest level of achievement showed as great a benefit as did the children of the lowest level of achievement of having their teachers expect intellectual gains.

At the end of the school year of this study, all teachers were asked to describe the classroom behavior of their pupils. Those children from whom intellectual growth was expected were described as having a significantly better chance of becoming successful in the future, as significantly more interesting, curious, and happy. There was a tendency, too, for these children to be seen as more appealing, adjusted, and affectionate and as lower in the need for social approval. In short, the children from whom intellectual growth was expected became more intellectually alive and autonomous or at least were so perceived by their teachers. These findings were particularly striking among the first grade children; those were the children who had benefited most in IQ gain as a result of their teachers' favorable expectancies.

We have already seen that the children of the experimental group gained more intellectually so that the possibility existed that it was the fact of such gaining that accounted for the more favorable ratings of these children's behavior and aptitude. But a great many of the control group children also gained in IQ during the course of the year. Perhaps those who gained more intellectually among these undesignated children would also be rated more favorably by their teachers. Such was not the case. The more the control group children gained in IQ the more they were regarded as *less* well adjusted $(r=-.13, p<.05)$, as *less* interesting $(r=-.14, p<.05)$ and as *less* affectionate $(r=-.13, p<.05)$. From these results it would seem that when

children who are expected to grow intellectually do so, they are considerably benefited
in other ways as well. When children who are
not especially expected to develop intellectually
do so, they seem either to show accompanying
undesirable behavior or at least are perceived
by their teachers as showing such undesirable
behavior. If a child is to show intellectual
gain it seems to be better for his real or perceived intellectual vitality and for his real
or perceived mental health if his teacher has
been expecting him to grow intellectually. It
appears that there may be hazards to unpredicted intellectual growth.

A closer analysis of these data, broken down
by whether the children were in the high,
medium, or low ability tracks or groups,
showed that these hazards of unpredicted intellectual growth were due primarily to the
children of the low ability group. When these
slow track children were in the control group
so that no intellectual gains were expected of
them, they were rated more unfavorably by
their teachers if they did show gains in IQ.
The greater their IQ gains, the more unfavorably were they rated, both as to mental
health and as to intellectual vitality. Even
when the slow track children were in the
experimental group, so that IQ gains were
expected of them, they were not rated as
favorably relative to their control group peers
as were the children of the high or medium
track, despite the fact that they gained as
much in IQ relative to the control group children as did the experimental group children
of the high group. It may be difficult for a
slow track child, even one whose IQ is rising
to be seen by his teacher as a well-adjusted
child, and as a potentially successful child,
intellectually.

THE QUESTION OF MEDIATION

How did the teachers' expectations come to
serve as determinants of gains in intellectual
performance? The most plausible hypothesis
seemed to be that children for whom unusual
intellectual growth had been predicted would
be more attended to by their teachers. If
teachers were more attentive to the children
earmarked for growth, we might expect that
teachers were robbing Peter to see Paul grow.
With a finite amount of time to spend with

each child, if a teacher gave more time to the
children of the experimental group, she would
have less time to spend with the children of
the control group. If the teacher's spending
more time with a child led to greater gains,
we could test the "robbing Peter" hypothesis
by comparing the gains made by children of
the experimental group with gains made by
children of the control group in each class.
The robbing Peter hypothesis predicts a negative correlation. The greater the gains made
by the children of the experimental group
(with the implication of more time spent
on them) the less should be the gains made
by the children of the control group (with
the implication of less time spent on them).
In fact, however, the correlation was positive,
large and statistically significant (rho = +.57,
$p = .02$, two tail). The greater the gain made
by the children of whom gain was expected,
the greater the gain made in the same classroom by those children from whom no special
gain was expected.

Additional evidence that teachers did not
take time from control group children to spend
with the experimental group children comes
from the teachers' inability to recall which
of the children in her class were designated
as potential bloomers and from her estimates
of time spent with each pupil. These estimates
showed a tendency, which was not significant
statistically, for teachers to spend *less* time
with pupils from whom intellectual gains were
expected.

That the children of the experimental group
were not favored with a greater investment of
time seems less surprising in view of the
pattern of their greater intellectual gains.
If, for example, teachers had talked to them
more, we might have expected greater gains
in verbal IQ but, the greater gains were found
not in verbal but in reasoning IQ. It may be,
course, that the teachers were inaccurate in
their estimates of time spent with each of their
pupils. Possibly direct observation of the
teacher-pupil interactions would have given
different results, but that method was not
possible in the present study. Even direct
observation by judges who could agree with
one another might not have revealed a difference in the amounts of teacher time invested
in each of the two groups of children. It

seems plausible to think that it was not a difference in amount of time spent with the children of the two groups which led to the differences in their rates of intellectual development. It may have been more a matter of the type of interaction which took place between the teachers and their pupils.

By what she said, by how she said it, by her facial expressions, postures, and perhaps, by her touch, the teacher may have communicated to the children of the experimental group that she expected improved intellectual performance. Such communications, together with possible changes in teaching techniques, may have helped the child learn by changing his self-concept, his expectations of his own behavior, his motivation, as well as his cognitive skills. It is self evident that further research is needed to narrow down the range of possible mechanisms whereby a teacher's expectations become translated into a pupil's intellectual growth. It would be valuable, for example, to have sound films of teachers interacting with their pupils. We might then look for differences in the way teachers interact with those children from whom they expect more intellectual growth compared to those from whom they expect less. On the basis of films of psychological experimenters interacting with subjects from whom different responses are expected, we know that even in such highly standardized situations, unintentional communications can be subtle and complex (Rosenthal, 1967). How much more subtle and complex may be the communications between children and their teachers, teachers who are not constrained by the demands of the experimental laboratory.

SOME IMPLICATIONS

The results of the experiment just now described provide further evidence that one person's expectation of another's behavior may serve as a self-fulfilling prophecy. When teachers expected that certain children would show greater intellectual development, those children did show greater intellectual development.

It may be that as teacher training institutions acquaint teachers-to-be with the possibility that their expectations of their pupils' performance may serve as self-fulfilling prophecies, these teacher trainees may be given a new expectancy—that children can learn more than they had believed possible.

The methodological implications of the evidence presented in this paper are best introduced by citing the results of a well-known "total-push" educational program, which, after three years, led to a 10 point IQ gain by 38% of the children and a 20 point IQ gain by 12% of the children. Such gains, while dramatic, were smaller than the gains found among the first and second grade children of our control group and very much smaller than the gains found among the children of our experimental group.

It is not possible to be sure about the matter, but it may be that the large gains shown by the children of our control group were attributable to a Hawthorne effect. The fact that university researchers, supported by federal funds, were interested in the school in which the research was conducted, may have led to a general improvement of morale and teaching technique on the part of all the teachers. In any case, the possibility of a Hawthorne effect cannot be ruled out either in the present experiment or in other studies of educational practices. Any educational practice which is assessed for effectiveness must be able to show some excess of gain over what Hawthorne effects alone would yield.

When the efficacy of an educational practice is investigated, we want to know its efficacy relative to the Hawthorne effect of "something new and important" but the present paper suggests that another baseline must be introduced. We will want to know, too, whether the efficacy of an educational practice is greater than that of the easily and inexpensively manipulatable expectation of the teacher. Most educational practices are more expensive in time and money than giving teachers names of children "who will show unusual intellectual development."

When educational innovations are introduced into ongoing educational systems, it seems very likely that the administrators whose permission is required, and the teachers whose cooperation is required, will expect the innovation to be effective. If they did not, they would be unlikely to give the required permission and cooperation. The experimental innovation, then, will likely be confounded with favorable expectations regarding their efficacy.

When educational innovations are introduced into newly created educational systems with specially selected and specially trained teachers and administrators, the problems are similar. Those teachers, and those administrators, who elect to go, and are selected to go, into newly created educational systems, are likely to have expectations favorable to the efficacy of the new program. In this situation as that in which changes are introduced into pre-existing systems, teachers' and administrators' expectations are likely to be confounded with the educational innovations. All this argues for the systematic employment of expectancy control groups, a type of control described elsewhere in detail (Rosenthal, 1966). Without the use of expectancy control groups, it is impossible to tell whether the results of experiments in educational practices are due to the practices themselves or to the correlated expectations of the teachers who are to try out the educational reforms.

But to come to an end, we shall want a summary. Perhaps the most suitable summary of the hypothesis discussed in this paper and tested by the described experiment has already been written. The writer is George Bernard Shaw, the play is "Pygmalion" and the speaker is Eliza Doolittle:

"You see, really and truly, . . . the difference between a lady and a flower girl is not how she behaves, but how she's treated. I shall always be a flower girl to Professor Higgins, because he . . . treats me as a flower girl, . . . but I know I can be a lady to you, because you always treat me as a lady, and always will."

REFERENCES

ROSENTHAL, R. *Experimenter effects in behavioral research*. New York: Appleton-Century-Crofts, 1966.

ROSENTHAL, R. Covert communication in the psychological experiment. *Psychological Bulletin*, 1967, *67*, 356-367.

ROSENTHAL, R., and JACOBSON, LENORE. Teachers' expectancies: Determinants of pupils' IQ gains. *Psychological Reports*, 1966, *19*, 115-118.

39. SOCIAL-CLASS VARIATION IN THE TEACHER-PUPIL RELATIONSHIP *

HOWARD S. BECKER

The major problems of workers in the service occupations are likely to be a function of their relationship to their clients or customers, those for whom or on whom the occupational service is performed.[1] Members of such occupations typically have some image of the "ideal" client, and it is in terms of this fiction that they fashion their conceptions of how their work ought to be performed, and

* Becker, Howard S., Social-Class Variation in the Teacher-Pupil Relationship, *J. Educ. Sociology*, 1952, pp. 451-465.

[1] See Howard S. Becker, "The Professional Dance Musician and His Audience," *American Journal of Sociology*, LVII (September, 1951), pp. 136-144 for further discussion of this point.

their actual work techniques. To the degree that actual clients approximate this ideal the worker will have no "client problem."

In a highly differentiated urban society, however, clients will vary greatly, and ordinarily only some fraction of the total of potential clients will be "good" ones. Workers tend to classify clients in terms of the way in which they vary from this ideal. The fact of client variation from the occupational ideal emphasizes the intimate relation of the institution in which work is carried on to its environing society. If that society does not prepare people to play their client roles in the manner desired by the occupation's members there will be conflicts, and problems for the workers in the performance of their work. One of the major factors affecting the production of suitable clients is the cultural diversity of various social classes in the society. The cultures of particular social-class groups may operate to produce clients who make the worker's position extremely difficult.

We deal here with this problem as it appears in the experience of the functionaries of a large urban educational institution, the Chicago public school system, discussing the way in which teachers in this system observe, classify and react to class-typed differences in the behavior of the children with whom they work. The material to be presented is thus relevant not only to problems of occupational organization but also to the problem of differences in the educational opportunities available to children of various social-classes. Warner, Havighurst and Loeb[2] and Hollingshead[3] have demonstrated the manner in which the schools tend to favor and select out children of the middle classes. Allison Davis has pointed to those factors in the class cultures involved which make lower-class children less and middle-class children more adaptable to the work and behavioral standards of the school.[4] This paper will contribute to knowledge in this area by analyzing the manner in which the public school teacher reacts to these cultural differences and, in so doing, perpetuates the discrimination of our educational system against the lower-class child.

The analysis is based on sixty interviews with teachers in the Chicago system.[5] The interviews were oriented around the general question of the problems of being a teacher and were not specifically directed toward discovering feelings about social-class differences among students. Since these differences created some of the teachers' most pressing

problems they were continually brought up by the interviewees themselves. They typically distinguished three social-class groups with which they, as teachers, came in contact: (1) a bottom stratum, probably equivalent to the lower-lower and parts of the upper-lower class; (2) an upper stratum, probably equivalent to the upper-middle class; and (3) a middle stratum, probably equivalent to the lower-middle and parts of the upper-lower class. We will adopt the convention of referring to these groups as lower, upper and middle groups, but it should be understood that this terminology refers to the teachers' classification of students and not to the ordinary sociological description.

We will proceed by taking up the three problems that loomed largest in the teachers' discussion of adjustment to their students: (1) the problem of *teaching* itself, (2) the problem of *discipline,* and (3) the problem of the *moral acceptability* of the students. In each case the variation in the form of and adjustment to the problem by the characteristics of the children of the various class groups distinguished by teachers is discussed.

I

A basic problem in any occupation is that of performing one's given task successfully, and where this involves working with human beings their qualities are a major variable affecting the ease with which the work can be done. The teacher considers that she has done her job adequately when she has brought about an observable change in the children's skills and knowledge which she can attribute to her own efforts:

> Well, I would say that a teacher is successful when she is putting the material across to the children, when she is getting some response from them. I'll tell you something. Teaching is a very rewarding line of work, because you can see those children grow under your hands. You can see the difference in them after you've had them for five months. You can see where they've started and where they've got to. And it's all yours. It really is rewarding in that way, you can see results and know that it's your work that brought those results about.

She feels that she has a better chance of success in this area when her pupils are

[2] W. L. Warner, R. J. Havighurst, and W. J. Loeb, *Who Shall Be Educated?* (New York: Harper and Bros., 1944.)

[3] August Hollingshead, *Elmtown's Youth* (New York: John Wiley & Sons, 1949).

[4] Allison Davis, *Social-Class Influences Upon Learning* (Cambridge: Harvard University Press, 1950).

[5] The entire research has been reported in Howard S. Becker, "Role and Career Problems of the Chicago Public School Teacher," (unpublished Ph. D. dissertation, University of Chicago, 1951).

interested in attending and working hard in school, and are trained at home in such a way that they are bright and quick at school work. Her problems arise in teaching those groups who do not meet these specifications, for in these cases her teaching techniques, tailored to the "perfect" student, are inadequate to cope with the reality, and she is left with a feeling of having failed in performing her basic task.

Davis has described the orientations toward education in general, and schoolwork in particular, of the lower and middle classes:

> Thus, our educational system, which next to the family is the most effective agency in teaching good work habits to middle class people, is largely ineffective and unrealistic with underprivileged groups. Education fails to motivate such workers because our schools and our society both lack *real rewards* to offer underprivileged groups. Neither lower class children or adults will work hard in school or on the job just to please the teacher or boss. They are not going to learn to be ambitious, to be conscientious, and to study hard, as if school and work were a fine character-building game, which one plays just for the sake of playing. They can see, indeed, that those who work hard at school usually have families that already have the occupations, homes, and social acceptance that the school holds up as the rewards of education. The underprivileged workers can see also that the chances of their getting enough education to make their attainment of these rewards in the future at all probable is very slight. Since they can win the rewards of prestige and social acceptance in their own slum groups without much education, they do not take very seriously the motivation taught by the school.[6]

As these cultural differences produce variations from the image of the "ideal" student, teachers tend to use class terms in describing the children with whom they work.

Children of the lowest group, from slum areas, are characterized as the most difficult group to teach successfully, lacking in interest

in school, learning ability, and outside training:

> They don't have the right kind of study habits. They can't seem to apply themselves as well. Of course, it's not their fault; they aren't brought up right. After all, the parents in a neighborhood like that really aren't interested. . . . But, as I say, those children don't learn very quickly. A great many of them don't seem to be really interested in getting an education. I don't think they are. It's hard to get anything done with children like that. They simply don't respond.

In definite contrast are the terms used to describe children of the upper group:

> In a neighborhood like this there's something about the children, you just feel like you're accomplishing so much more. You throw an idea out and you can see that it takes hold. The children know what you're talking about and they think about it. Then they come in with projects and pictures and additional information, and it just makes you feel good to see it. They go places and see things, and they know what you're talking about. For instance, you might be teaching social studies or geography. . . . You bring something up and a child says, "Oh, my parents took me to see that in the museum." You can just do more with material like that.

Ambivalent feelings are aroused by children of the middle group. While motivated to work hard in school they lack the proper out-of-school training:

> Well, they're very nice here, very nice. They're not hard to handle. You see, they're taught respect in the home and they're respectful to the teacher. They want to work and do well. . . . Of course, they're not too brilliant. You know what I mean. But they are very nice children and very easy to work with.

In short, the differences between groups make it possible for the teacher to feel successful at her job only with the top group; with the other groups she feels, in greater or lesser measure, that she has failed.

These differences in ability to do school work, as perceived by teachers, have important consequences. They lead, in the first place, to differences in actual teaching tech-

[6] Allison Davis, "The Motivation of the Underprivileged Worker," *Industry and Society*, ed. William F. Whyte (New York: McGraw-Hill Book Co., 1947), p. 99.

niques. A young high school teacher contrasted the techniques used in "slum" schools with those used in "better" schools:

> At S———, there were a lot of guys who were just waiting till they were sixteen so they could get out of school. L———, everybody—well, a very large percentage, I'll say —was going on to secondary school, to college. That certainly made a difference in their classroom work. You had to teach differently at the different schools. For instance, at S———, if you had demonstrations in chemistry they had to be pretty flashy, lots of noise and smoke, before they'd get interested in it. That wasn't necessary at L———. Or at S——— if you were having electricity or something like that you had to get the static electricity machine out and have them all stand around and hold hands so that they'd all get a little jolt.

Further, the teacher feels that where these differences are recognized by her superiors there will be a corresponding variation in the amount of work she is expected to accomplish. She expects that the amount of work and effort required of her will vary inversely with the social status of her pupils. This teacher compared schools from the extremes of the class range:

> So you have to be on your toes and keep up to where you're supposed to be in the course of study. Now, in a school like the D——— [slum school] you're just not expected to complete all that work. It's almost impossible. For instance, in the second grade we're supposed to cover nine spelling words a week. Well, I can do that up here at the K——— ["better" school]. They can take nine new words a week. But the best class I ever had at the D——— was only able to achieve six words a week and they had to work pretty hard to get that. So I never finished the year's work in spelling. I couldn't. And I really wasn't expected to.

One resultant of this situation—in which less is expected of those teachers whose students are more difficult to teach—is that the problem becomes more aggravated in each grade, as the gap between what the children should know and what they actually do know becomes wider and wider. A principal of such a school describes the degeneration there of the teaching problem into a struggle to get a few basic skills across, in a situation where this cumulative effect makes following the normal program of study impossible:

> The children come into our upper grades with very poor reading ability. That means that all the way through our school everybody is concentrating on reading. It's not like at a school like S——— [middle group] where they have science and history and so on. At a school like that they figure that from first to fourth you learn to read and from fifth to eighth you read to learn. You use your reading to learn other material. Well, these children don't reach that second stage while they're with us. We have to plug along getting them to learn to read. Our teachers are pretty well satisfied if the children can read and do simple number work when they leave here. You'll find that they don't think very much of subjects like science, and so on. They haven't got any time for that. They're just trying to get these basic things over. . . . That's why our school is different from one like the S———.

Such consequences of teachers' differential reaction to various class groups obviously operate to further perpetuate those class-cultural characteristics to which they object in the first place.

II

Discipline is the second of the teachers' major problems with her students. Willard Waller pointed to its basis when he wrote that "Teacher and pupil confront each other in the school with an original conflict of desires, and however much that conflict may be reduced in amount, or however much it may be hidden, it still remains."[7] We must recognize that conflict, either actual or potential, is ever present in the teacher-pupil relationship, the teacher attempting to maintain her control against the children's efforts to break it.[8] This conflict is felt even with those children who present least difficulty; a teacher who

[7] Willard Walter, *Sociology of Teaching* (New York: John Wiley and Sons, 1932), p. 197.

[8] Although all service occupations tend to have such problems of control over their clients, the problem is undoubtedly aggravated in situations like the school where those upon whom the service is being performed are not there of their own volition, but rather because of the wishes of some other group (the parents, in this case).

considered her pupils models of good behavior nevertheless said:

> But there's that tension all the time. Between you and the students. It's hard on your nerves. Teaching is fun, if you enjoy your subject, but it's the discipline that keeps your nerves on edge, you know what I mean? There's always that tension. Sometimes people say, "Oh, you teach school. That's an easy job, just sitting around all day long." They don't know what it's really like. It's hard on your nerves.

The teacher is tense because she fears that she will lose control, which she tends to define in terms of some line beyond which she will not allow the children to go. Wherever she may draw this line (and there is considerable variation), the teacher feels that she has a "discipline" problem when the children attempt to push beyond it. The form and intensity of this problem are felt to vary from one social-class group to another, as might be expected from Davis' description of class emphases on aggression:

> In general, middle-class aggression is taught to adolescents in the form of social and economic skills which will enable them to compete effectively at that level. . . . In lower-class families, physical aggression is as much a normal, socially approved and socially inculcated type of behavior as it is in frontier communities.[9]

These differences in child training are matched by variation in the teachers' reactions.

Children in "slum" schools are considered most difficult to control, being given to unrestrained behavior and physical violence. The interviews are filled with descriptions of such difficulties. Miriam Wagenschein, in a parallel study of the beginning school teacher, gave this summary of the experiences of these younger teachers in lower-class schools:

> The reports which these teachers give of what *can* be done by a group of children are nothing short of amazing. A young white teacher walked into her new classroom and was greeted with the comment, "Another damn white one." Another was "rushed" at her desk by the entire class when she tried to be extremely strict with them. Teachers report having been bitten, tripped, and

pushed on the stairs. Another gave an account of a second grader throwing a milk bottle at the teacher and of a first grader having such a temper tantrum that it took the principal and two policemen to get him out of the room. In another school following a fight on the playground, the principal took thirty-two razor blades from children in a first grade room. Some teachers indicated fear that they might be attacked by irate persons in the neighborhoods in which they teach. Other teachers report that their pupils carry long pieces of glass and have been known to threaten other pupils with them, while others jab each other with hypodermic needles. One boy got angry with his teacher and knocked in the fender of her car.[10]

In these schools a major part of the teacher's time must be devoted to discipline; as one said: "It's just a question of keeping them in line." This emphasis on discipline detracts from the school's primary function of teaching, thus discriminating, in terms of available educational opportunity, against the children of these schools.

Children of the middle group are thought of as docile, and with them the teacher has least difficulty with discipline:

> Those children were much quieter, easier to work with. When we'd play our little games there was never any commotion. That was a very nice school to work in. Everything was quite nice about it. The children were easy to work with. . . .

Children of the upper group are felt hard to handle in some respects, and are often termed "spoiled," "overindulged," or "neurotic"; they do not play the role of the child in the submissive manner teachers consider appropriate. One interviewee, speaking of this group, said:

> I think most teachers prefer not to teach in that type of school. The children are more pampered and, as we say, more inclined to run the school for themselves. The parents are very much at fault. The children are not used to taking orders at home and naturally they won't take them at school either.

[9] Allison Davis, *Social-Class Influence Upon Learning*, pp. 34-5.

[10] Miriam Wagenschein, "Reality Shock" (Unpublished M. A. thesis, University of Chicago, 1950), pp. 58-9.

Teachers develop methods of dealing with these discipline problems, and these tend to vary between social-class groups as do the problems themselves. The basic device used by successful disciplinarians is to establish authority clearly on the first meeting with the class:

You can't ever let them get the upper hand on you or you're through. So I start out tough. The first day I get a new class in, I let them know who's boss. . . . You've got to start off tough, then you can ease up as you go along. If you start out easy-going, when you try to get tough they'll just look at you and laugh.

Having once established such a relation, it is considered important that the teacher be consistent in her behavior so that the children will continue to respect and obey her:

I let them know I mean business. That's one thing you must do. Say nothing that you won't follow through on. Some teachers will say anything to keep kids quiet, they'll threaten anything. Then they can't or won't carry out their threats. Naturally, the children won't pay any attention to them after that. You must never say anything that you won't back up.

In the difficult "slum" schools, teachers feel the necessity of using stern measures, up to and including physical violence (nominally outlawed):

Technically you're not supposed to lay a hand on a kid. Well, they don't, technically. But there are a lot of ways of handling a kid so that it doesn't show—and then it's the teacher's word against the kid's, so the kid hasn't got a chance. Like dear Mrs. ———. She gets mad at a kid, she takes him out in the hall. She gets him stood up against the wall. Then she's got a way of chucking the kid under the chin, only hard, so that it knocks his head back against the wall. It doesn't leave a mark on him. But when he comes back in that room he can hardly see straight, he's so knocked out. It's really rough. There's a lot of little tricks like that that you learn about.

Where such devices are not used, there is recourse to violent punishment, "tongue lashings." All teachers, however, are not emotionally equipped for such behavior and must find other means:

The worst thing I can do is lose my temper and start raving. . . . You've got to believe in that kind of thing in order for it to work. . . . If you don't honestly believe it it shows up and the children know you don't mean it and it doesn't do any good anyway. . . . I try a different approach myself. Whenever they get too rowdy I go to the piano and . . .play something and we have rhythms or something until they sort of settle down. . . . That's what we call "soft-soaping" them. It seems to work for me. It's about the only thing I can do.

Some teachers may also resort to calling in the parents, a device whose usefulness is limited by the fact that such summonses are most frequently ignored. The teacher's disciplinary power in such a school is also limited by her fear of retaliation by the students: "Those fellows are pretty big, and I just think it would take a bigger person than me to handle them. I certainly wouldn't like to try."

In the school with children of the middle group no strong sanctions are required, mild reprimands sufficing:

Now the children at Z——— here are quite nice to teach. They're pliable, yes, that's the word, they're pliable. They will go along with you on things and not fight you. You can take them any place and say to them, "I'm counting on you not to disgrace your school. Let's see that Z——— spirit." And they'll behave for you. . . . They can be frightened, they have fear in them. They're pliable, flexible, you can do things with them. They're afraid of their parents and what they'll do to them if they get into trouble at school. And they're afraid of the administration. They're afraid of being sent down to the principal. So that they can be handled.

Children of the upper group often act in a way which may be interpreted as "misbehavior" but which does not represent a conscious attack on the teacher's authority. Many teachers are able to disregard such activity by interpreting it as a natural concomitant of the "brightness" and "intelligence" of such children. Where such an interpretation is not possible the teachers feel hampered by a lack of effective sanctions:

I try different things like keeping them out of a gym period or a recess period. But that doesn't always work. I have this one little boy who just didn't care when I used those punishments. He said he didn't like gym anyway. I don't know what I'm going to do with him.

The teacher's power in such schools is further limited by the fact that the children are able to mobilize their influential parents so as to exert a large degree of control over the actions of school personnel.

It should be noted, finally, that discipline problems tend to become less important as the length of the teacher's stay in a particular school makes it possible for her to build a reputation which coerces the children into behaving without attempting any test of strength:[11]

I have no trouble with the children. Once you establish a reputation and they know what to expect, they respect you and you have no trouble. Of course, that's different for a new teacher, but when you're established that's no problem at all.

III

The third area of problems has been termed that of *moral acceptability,* and arises from the fact that some actions of one's potential clients may be offensive in terms of some deeply felt set of moral standards; these clients are thus morally unacceptable. Teachers find that some of their pupils act in such a way as to make themselves unacceptable in terms of the moral values centered around health and cleanliness, sex and aggression, ambition and work, and the relations of age groups.

Children of the middle group present no problem at this level, being universally described as clean, well dressed, moderate in their behavior, and hard working. Children from the "better" neighborhoods are considered deficient in the important moral traits of politeness and respect for elders:

Where the children come from wealthy homes. That's not so good either. They're not used to doing work at home. They have

[11] This is part of the process of job adjustment described in detail in Howard S. Becker, "The Career of the Chicago Public School Teacher," *American Journal of Sociology,* LVII (March 1952).

maids and servants of all kinds and they're used to having things done for them, instead of doing them themselves. . . . They won't do anything. For instance, if they drop a piece of cloth on the floor, they'll just let it lay, they wouldn't think of bending over to pick it up. That's janitor's work to them. As a matter of fact, one of them said to me once: "If I pick that up there wouldn't be any work for the janitor to do." Well, it's pretty difficult to deal with children like that.

Further, they are regarded as likely to transgress what the teachers define as moral boundaries in the matter of smoking and drinking; it is particularly shocking that such "nice" children should have such vices.

It is, however, the "slum" child who most deeply offends the teacher's moral sensibilities; in almost every area mentioned above these children, by word, action or appearance, manage to give teachers the feeling that they are immoral and not respectable. In terms of physical appearance and condition they disgust and depress the middle-class teacher. Even this young woman, whose emancipation from conventional morality is symbolized in her habitual use of the argot of the jazz musician, was horrified by the absence of the toothbrush from the lives of her lower-class students:

It's just horribly depressing, you know. I mean, it just gets you down. I'll give you an example. A kid compained of a toothache one day. Well, I thought I could take a look and see if I could help him or something so I told him to open his mouth. I almost wigged when I saw his mouth. His teeth were all rotten, every one of them. Just filthy and rotten. Man, I mean, I was really shocked, you know. I said, "Don't you have a toothbrush?" He said no, they were only his baby teeth and Ma said he didn't need a toothbrush for that. So I really got upset and looked in all their mouths. Man, I never saw anything like it. They were all like that, practically. I asked how many had toothbrushes, and about a quarter of them had them. Boy, that's terrible. And I don't dig that crap about baby teeth either, because they start getting molars when they're six, I know that. So I gave them a talking to, but what good does it do? The kid's mouth was just rotten. They never heard of a toothbrush or going to a dentist.

These children, too, are more apt than the other groups to be dishonest in some way that will get them into trouble with law enforcement officials. The early (by middle-class standards) sexual maturity of such children is quite upsetting to the teacher:

> One thing about these girls is, well, some of them are not very nice girls. One girl in my class I've had two years now. She makes her money on the side as a prostitute. She's had several children. . . . This was a disturbing influence on the rest of the class.

Many teachers reported great shock on finding that words which were innocent to them had obscene meanings for their lower-class students:

> I decided to read them a story one day. I started, reading them "Puss in Boots" and they just burst out laughing. I couldn't understand what I had said that had made them burst out like that I went back over the story and tried to find out what it might be. I couldn't see anything that would make them laugh. I couldn't see anything at all in the story. Later one of the other teachers asked me what had happened. She was one of the older teachers. I told her that I didn't know; that I was just reading them a story and they thought it was extremely funny. She asked me what story I read them and I told her "Puss in the Boots." She said, "Oh, I should have warned you not to read that one." It seems that Puss means something else to them. It means something awful—I wouldn't even tell you what. It doesn't mean a thing to us.[12]

Warner, Havighurst and Loeb note that "unless the middle-class values change in America, we must expect the influence of the schools to favor the values of material success, individual striving, thrift, and social mobility."[13] Here again, the "slum" child violates the teacher's moral sense by failing to display these virtues:

> Many of these children don't realize the worth of an education. They have no desire to improve themselves. And they don't care much about school and schoolwork as a result. That makes it very difficult to teach them.
>
> That kind of problem is particularly bad in a school like ———. That's not a very privileged school. It's very under-privileged, as a matter of fact. So we have a pretty tough element there, a bunch of bums, I might as well say it. That kind you can't reach at all. They don't want to be there at all, and so you can't do anything with them. And even many of the others— they're simply indifferent to the advantages of education. So they're indifferent, they don't care about their homework.

This behavior of the lower-class child is all the more repellent to the teacher because she finds it incomprehensible; she cannot conceive that any normal human being would act in such a way. This teacher stresses the anxiety aroused in the inexperienced teacher by her inability to provide herself with a rational explanation for her pupils' behavior:

> We had one of the girls who just came to the school last year and she used to come and talk to me quite a bit. I know that it was just terrible for her. You know, I don't think she'd ever had anything to do with Negroes before she got there and she was just mystified, didn't know what to do. She was bewildered. She came to me one day almost in tears and said, "But they don't want to learn, they don't even want to learn. Why is that?" Well, she had me there.

It is worth noting that the behavior of the "better" children, even when morally unacceptable, is less distressing to the teacher, who feels that, in this case, she can produce a reasonable explanation for the behavior. An example of such an explanation is the following:

> I mean, they're spoiled, you know. A great many of them are only children. Naturally, they're used to having their own way, and they don't like to be told what to do. Well, if a child is in a room that I'm teaching he's going to be told what to do, that's all there is to it. Or if they're not spoiled that way, they're the second child and they never got the affection the first one did, not that their mother didn't love them, but they didn't get as much affection, so they're not so easy to handle either.

---

[12] Interview by Miriam Wagenschein. The lack of common meanings in this situation symbolizes the great cultural and moral distance between teacher and "slum" child.

[13] *Op. cit.*, p. 172.

IV

We have shown that school teachers experience problems in working with their students to the degree that those students fail to exhibit in reality the qualities of the image of the ideal pupil which teachers hold. In a stratified urban society there are many groups whose life-style and culture produce children who do not meet the standards of this image, and who are thus impossible for teachers like these to work with effectively. Programs of action intended to increase the educational opportunities of the under-privileged in our society should take account of the manner in which teachers interpret and react to the cultural traits of this group, and the institutional consequences of their behavior.[14] Such programs might profitably aim at producing teachers who can cope effectively with the problems of teaching this group and not, by their reactions to class differences, perpetuate the existing inequities.

[14] One of the important institutional consequences of these class preferences is a constant movement of teachers away from lower-class schools, which prevents these schools from retaining experienced teachers and from maintaining some continuity in teaching and administration.

A more general statement of the findings is now in order. Professionals depend on their environing society to provide them with clients who meet the standards of their image of the ideal client. Social class cultures, among other factors, may operate to produce many clients who, in one way or another, fail to meet these specifications and therefore aggravate one or another of the basic problems of the worker-client relation (three were considered in this paper).

In attacking this problem we touch on one of the basic elements of the relation between institutions and society for the differences between ideal and reality place in high relief the implicit assumptions which institutions, through their functionaries, make about the society around them. All institutions have embedded in them some set of assumptions about the nature of the society and the individuals with whom they deal, and we must get at these assumptions, and their embodiment in actual social interaction, in order fully to understand these organizations. We can, perhaps, best begin our work on this problem by studying those institutions which, like the school, make assumptions which have high visibility because of their variation from reality.

40. SEX DIFFERENCE IN THE DISTRIBUTION OF TEACHER APPROVAL AND DISAPPROVAL AMONG SIXTH GRADE CHILDREN *

W. J. MEYER AND G. C. THOMPSON

This study was designed to investigate the relative frequency of women teachers' approval and disapproval evaluations of sixth-grade male as contrasted with female pupils. The relevant data for this study were obtained by means of two independent techniques:

* Meyer, W. J. and Thompson, G. C., "Sex Difference in the Distribution of Teacher Approval and Disapproval Among Sixth Grade Children," *Journal of Educational Psychology*, 1959, 47, pp. 385-396.

thirty hours of direct observation of teacher-pupil interactions in each of three classrooms; and, the use of a modification of the "Guess Who?" technique to determine if the children themselves were aware of any sex differences in their teachers' approval and disapproval evaluations.

There is considerable agreement among psychologists that the use of approval by the teacher results in better learning and probably in better over-all adjustment (Hurlock, 1924;

Ojemann and Wilkinson, 1939). Some studies (Olson and Wilkinson, 1938; Snyder, 1947) have shown that personal maladjustments in teachers have deleterious effects on the adjustment level of the children in their classes.

In a series of studies by Anderson and Brewer (1945, 1946) and Anderson, Brewer, and Reed (1946), using a sample of kindergarten-age children, the data indicate that teachers typically use statements of a dominative nature in their interactions with the children in their classes. Anderson further reports that the teachers in his study tended to levy most of their dominative and/or integrative overtures on only a few pupils to the relative neglect of the other children in the classroom. Further evidence of this nature is reported in a study by deGroat and Thompson (1949) using four sixth-grade classrooms. In addition to reporting inequities in teacher approval and disapproval they also found that teachers give more praise to the youngsters who are brighter, better adjusted and higher achievers. The more poorly adjusted and the duller children were observed by these investigators to receive more disapproval from their teachers.

The purpose of the present investigation is to shed more light on the ways in which teachers respond toward the pupils in their classrooms. Extensive research findings have been reported in the literature[1] which consistently show that boys are more aggressive and generally more "unmanageable" than girls. It is our hypothesis that this "masculine" behavior will result in male pupils receiving a larger number of dominative, or punitive, contacts than girls from their teacher, who is usually a woman from the middle socio-economic stratum of our society. That is, we feel that the behavior of boys in the typical classroom is of such a nature as to make it less acceptable to teachers who probably attempt to perpetuate certain middle-class standards of what "good" classroom behavior should be. We believe that girls usually display behavior more in conformity to the standards perceived as "good" by the average elementary school teacher and will therefore receive fewer disapproval contacts

and more approval contacts from their teachers.

Assuming that the above hypotheses are supported by the data we would also predict that children of elementary school age will recognize, and take for granted, that boys receive more disapproval and blame from their teachers than girls.

EXPERIMENTAL PROCEDURE

In order to test the hypothesis that boys receive a larger number of dominative, or disapproval, evaluations from their teachers than do girls, teacher-pupil interaction within three sixth-grade classrooms were recorded for a total sample of thirty hours per classroom. These time samples of classroom behavior were spread over an entire school year. Among other things being studied, interactions between teachers and pupils were classified into two categories: (a) praise contacts (teacher initiated interactions with a child in which she verbally expressed approval of some behavior which the child had displayed), and (b) blame contacts (teacher initiated interactions with a child in which she verbally expressed disapproval for some bit of behavior which the child had displayed). Observer agreement for the praise classification ranged from eighty-four to one hundred per cent with a median of approximately ninety-two per cent. Observer agreement for the blame classification ranged from fifty-seven to one hundred per cent, with a median of approximately ninety-three per cent.

In an attempt to cast some light on children's perceptions of any sex differences in teacher disapproval, a modified "Guess Who?" approach was employed. The "Guess Who?" approach used in this study required each child to nominate fellow class members for a number of situations in which children are receiving approval or disapproval from their teacher for some behavior. (See deGroat and Thompson [1949] for a more complete description of these scales and information about their reliabilities.) The behavior descriptions were selected on the basis of their familiarity to children and contain a fairly representative sample of situations in which children typically receive either approval or disapproval from their teachers. Each child was required

[1] Goodenough (1931); Hayes (1943); Radke (1946); Sears (1951); Tuddenham (1952).

TABLE 1 Sex differences in frequency of teachers' disapproval contacts.

	Classroom A		Classroom B		Classroom C	
	Boys	Girls	Boys	Girls	Boys	Girls
N	10	9	12	14	17	16
Mean	11.10	2.67	10.75	2.79	10.06	1.44
S.D.	7.62	2.18	9.27	2.42	14.42	1.59
t	3.20**		3.11**		2.37*	
F	12.22**		14.67**		130.36**	
t.01†	3.30		3.10		2.92	

   * Significant at the five percent level.
  ** Significant at the one per cent level.
   † See footnote 2.

to list the names of four of his classmates whom he thought fitted each of the behavior descriptions most adequately.

RESULTS

Fisher's test was used to determine the reliability of the obtained sex differences.[2] The difference between disapproval contacts received by boys and by girls from their teachers was statistically significant in each of the three classrooms. As predicted, the boys received the larger number of disapproval contacts. These differences may be

interpreted according to our hypothesis as supporting the notion that teachers are responding with counter-aggression to the greater expression of aggression by boys. The results obtained in analyzing the teachers' praise contacts with boys and girls are presented in Table 2. The only statistically significant differences obtained for this variable was in school B. However the boys received more praise than the girls in each of the classrooms. It may be that the teachers are attempting to reinforce any positive behavior that the boys may display. Or this tendency to praise boys more than girls may reflect compensatory behavior for guilt feelings created in the teacher by her excessive aggressiveness towards boys. Either interpretation, or any one of the several others that could be offered, is highly speculative.

The data presented above are based on the extensive observations of an objective ob-

[2] This test assumes that the samples being compared are homogeneous with respect to their variances. Frequently this assumption had to be rejected in some of the group comparisons. In such cases a more conservative test of significance was used which makes some allowance in the error term for heterogenicity of variance. This technique is presented in detail in Cochran and Cox (1950).

TABLE 2 Sex differences in frequency of teachers' approval contacts.

	Classroom A		Classroom B		Classroom C	
	Boys	Girls	Boys	Girls	Boys	Girls
N	10	9	12	14	17	16
Mean	9.90	9.67	10.50	5.50	3.71	2.69
S.D.	6.10	7.65	5.33	2.53	2.95	1.99
t	0.074		2.50*		1.15	
F	1.57		4.43**		2.19	
t.05†	———		2.19		———	

   * Significant at the five percent level.
  ** Significant at the one per cent level.
   † See footnote 2.

TABLE 3 Sex differences in children's nominations for teacher disapproval.

	Classroom A		Classroom B		Classroom C	
	Boys	Girls	Boys	Girls	Boys	Girls
N	10	9	12	14	17	16
Mean	21.60	5.33	42.33	9.71	33.82	5.18
S.D.	13.33	5.68	43.06	8.13	55.87	8.26
t	3.39**		2.79**		2.03	
F	5.51**		28.07**		19.21**	
$t_{.01}$†	3.26		3.10		——	

** Significant at the one per cent level.
  † See footnote 2.

server who played no functional role in the classrooms. The data presented in the following section reflect the teachers' approval and disapproval contacts as viewed by their pupils.

"GUESS WHO?" DATA

Analysis of the "Guess Who?" data was performed along the same lines as the data obtained by direct observation. A comparison of the pupils' nominations of their peers on the disapproval items revealed statistically significant differences between boys and girls for two of the three schools. This can be interpreted as showing that the boys are viewed by the girls as well as by their peers as being involved in more situations which evoke disapproval from their teachers.

Analysis of the children's responses to the items related to teacher approval produced no significant differences between boys and girls.

A final analysis of the "Guess Who?" data was performed in an attempt to determine how boys as contrasted with girls perceived the teacher's approval and disapproval biases. The choices made by the boys and by the girls for the approval and disapproval items were separately analyzed. It seemed unreasonable to use the t test in this situation because of the unequal numbers of boys and girls in the classroom. Therefore the groups were equated by converting the frequencies of nominations to percentages and working with percentage differences.

The results of the statistical analysis of boys nominations on the disapproval items show that boys respond as if they usually received more blame from teachers than do girls. It would appear that boys are quite sensitive to the disapproval of their teachers. Table 5 shows that the girls also respond as if boys receive more teacher disapproval.

There is little consistency in the nominations made by the boys for the praise items. In schools B and C the boys react as though

TABLE 4 Sex differences in children's nominations for teacher approval.

	Classroom A		Classroom B		Classroom C	
	Boys	Girls	Boys	Girls	Boys	Girls
N	10	9	12	14	17	16
Mean	11.00	34.33	23.58	31.42	23.71	21.60
S.D.	12.93	32.64	18.51	25.08	35.75	25.70
t	2.09		0.856		0.242	
F	6.376**		1.835		19.35**	
$t_{.01}$†	——		——		——	

** Significant at the one per cent level.
  † See footnote 2.

TABLE 5 Choices made by boys and girls on teacher disapproval items.

	Classroom A				Classroom B				Classroom C			
	Boys Choosing		Girls Choosing		Boys Choosing		Girls Choosing		Boys Choosing		Girls Choosing	
	B	G	B	G	B	G	B	G	B	G	B	G
N	8	9	8	9	14	12	14	12	17	16	17	16
%	89.77	23.23	83.09	16.91	88.37	11.63	73.05	26.95	88.70	11.20	82.21	17.79
CR	5.60**		3.64**		6.10**		2.65**		7.03**		4.84**	

** Significant at the one per cent level.

they typically receive more praise than girls, although this difference is not statistically significant. In contrast to the boys' responses, the girls feel that they receive more praise, particularly in school B where the difference is statistically significant. These results might be interpreted as meaning that children fail to recognize any definite dichotomy in the teacher's distribution of praise contacts.

DISCUSSION

The general findings of this study support the hypothesis that the male pupil receives reliably more blame from his teacher than the female pupil. Moreover, the boys recognize that they are the recipients of a higher incidence of teacher disapproval. We feel that these data lend indirect support to the notion that "masculine" behavior is not tolerated by the typical teacher who in turn attempts to inhibit such behavior by means of punishment.

Davis and Havighurst (1947) have discussed at length the divergence of cultural mores between lower-class children and their middle-class teachers. Their work may best be summarized in the assertion that the goals defined by the middle-class teacher do not receive reinforcement from the lower-class child's peer group or from his family. Teacher initiation of punishment for "misbehavior" only serves to reinforce an already existing dislike for school and further leads to peer group reinforcement. A similar (but by no means identical) interpretation appears relevant to the present discussion. Our society's definitions of acceptable male and female behavior are divergent particularly with respect to aggression. For example Radke (1946) in her monograph on the relationship of parental authority to child behavior reports that the fathers in her sample felt that aggressive, assertive behavior on the part of boys was less undesirable than the identical behavior in girls (and in many cases was deemed highly desirable). The mothers felt that aggression was unacceptable behavior in either sex but in general they were in agreement that ag-

TABLE 6 Choices made by boys and by girls on teacher approval items.

	Classroom A				Classroom B				Classroom C			
	Boys Choosing		Girls Choosing		Boys Choosing		Girls Choosing		Boys Choosing		Girls Choosing	
	B	G	B	G	B	G	B	G	B	G	B	G
N	8	9	8	9	17	16	14	12	14	12	17	16
%	36.98	63.01	34.07	65.92	57.56	42.43	24.58	75.42	56.95	43.04	46.22	53.77
CR	1.11		1.38		0.88		3.01**		0.72		0.44	

** Significant at the one per cent level.

gressive behavior is more unacceptable in girls. In another study specifically related to the notion that aggressive behavior is more unacceptable in the female culture is a study by Sears, Pintler, and Sears (1946). These writers predicted that in father-absent homes, wherein the child is brought up by the mother, boys would be less aggressive than in father-present homes in which the boy models his behavior after the father. The results of their study support the "sex-typing" hypothesis as presented above. Bach (1946) reports similar evidence in support of the "sex-typing" hypothesis.[3] Apparently the social mores of the typical female teacher, at least with respect to aggressive, assertive behavior, are in sharp contrast to the behavioral tendencies of the typical male youngsters. The behavioral tendencies of the female child are, however, in close agreement with those of her teachers. We feel that the above generalization accounts to a high degree for the data reported in this study. Our argument becomes somewhat stronger when the work of Wickman (1938) and a follow-up study by Mitchell (1942) are included in the discussion. These investigators found that teachers perceive aggressive nonconforming behavior as more serious than withdrawal behavior. More recently Kaplan (1951-1952) has reported that the aggressive child was deemed annoying to almost three-quarters of the teachers in his sample. The present investigation suggests that perhaps teachers react to the aggressive behavior of children with counter-aggression, a vicious circle for both pupil and teacher.

Consistent with the above interpretation is the larger amount of variation found among the male pupils as contrasted with female pupils. In a culture such as ours in which the father is away from the home during most of the child's waking hours (and in some instances pays only cursory attention to the youngster when at home), it appears obvious that both the male and female child are more directly influenced by the mother. Many boys, however, will be influenced more by their

fathers and peer culture than by the mother because of identification with the masculine role in our culture. Our belief is that these more "masculine" boys are the ones who receive the greater share of teacher disapproval. Such an interpretation appears consistent with the work of Sears, Pintler, and Sears (1946) and Bach (1946).

The foregoing discussion has certain implications for the student of child development and education. If our interpretation of the teacher and male-pupil relationship is accurate, then the fact that boys dislike school more than girls is understandable. The daily punishment received by the boy for behavior he really does not consider "bad" must certainly be anxiety producing. If the anxiety created in the school situation becomes sufficiently intense, it seems reasonable that tension reduction can be achieved by means of avoiding school. It is known that more boys leave school at 'an earlier age than girls (Tanenbaum, 1939-1940).

Perhaps of even more importance is the effect of this teacher-disapproval generated anxiety on the general personality adjustment of male pupils. It is unfortunate that we do not have evidence on the changes in adjustment level of the children in our sample, but studies by Ojemann and Wilkinson (1939) and others indicate that consistent teacher dominance has deleterious effects on the adjustment of children. We can only speculate as to the nature of these adjustment problems but such behavioral manifestations as nervousness, withdrawal and lack of self-confidence are a few of the known symptoms.

We feel that the consistent trends in our findings imply that teachers' negative attitudes towards their male pupils arise from a lack of appreciation for the term "normal" male child. In our culture, aggressive outgoing behavior is as normal in the male as quiescent nonassertive behavior is in the female. The teacher who attempts to thwart this behavior by means of threats and punishment can only meet with frustration since the boy is confronted with a conflicting social code. A more reasonable plan to follow would seem to be one in which the excess energy and tensions of the male child could be discharged on some constructive activity.

[3] Though there is insufficient evidence at this time the present writers feel that the factor of innate sex defferences in aggressive tendencies should not be overlooked. See Beach (1948) for suggestive findings.

Planned physical education classes will do much to dissipate aggressive needs in a socially acceptable manner. Perhaps most important of all, however, is the knowledge that some degree of aggressive behavior is a normal part of development in both boys and girls and should be treated not as a personal threat to the teacher but as sign of "normal" social and personality development.

SUMMARY

The purpose of this study was to investigate sex differences in teacher distribution of approval and disapproval among three sixth-grade classrooms. Data relevant to the children's perceptions of their teachers' attitudes towards boys and girls were also collected. Using the discrepancies in attitude between males and females in our culture toward aggressive behavior as the basic underlying variable, the hypothesis was offered that boys, who are more aggressive and nonconforming than girls, would receive more disapproval contacts from their teachers than girls. Girls being quiescent and more conforming than boys would as a consequence receive more approval from their teachers than boys. We further hypothesized that both boys and girls will be aware of the differences in their teachers' attitudes towards them.

In order to test the foregoing hypothesis three sixth-grade teachers and their pupils were directly observed for a total of thirty hours per classroom. All teacher initiated contacts of an approval or disapproval nature were recorded. The measurement of the children's perceptions of teacher attitude was accomplished by means of a variation of the "Guess Who?" technique. The pupils were asked to list the names of four students who best fitted a series of statements of a teacher approval nature and of disapproval nature. Analysis was made of the number of children of each sex chosen for the approval items and for the disapproval items.

Statistical analysis of the data clearly supports our hypothesis with respect to male pupils. In all three schools the boys received reliably more disapproval from their teachers than the girls. We also found that both the boys and the girls nominated more boys for the disapproval items than girls. This differ-

ence was statistically reliable. With respect to the second hypothesis concerning girls, the data did not yield any clear-cut differences. If any trend was present it was in a direction opposite to that predicted. These results indicated that the teachers in our sample tended to have fewer contacts with girls in their classrooms.

The results of this investigation were interpreted as being consistent with the notion of a sex difference in attitude towards aggressive behavior. The conclusion was drawn that teachers attempt to "socialize" the male child by means of dominative counter-aggressive behavior. The negative consequences of this situation for the child are discussed.

GUESS-WHO? SCALE

Directions:

In this booklet are some word pictures of members of your class. Read each statement and write down the names of the people whom you think the description fits. *Remember—*

1. Several people may fit one picture. You may write down after each description as many names as you think belong there.
2. The same person may be mentioned for more than one word-picture.
3. If you cannot think of anyone to match a particular word-picture go on to the next one.
4. Write the first and last names of the people chosen, not their nicknames or initials.
5. Do not use your own name.

1. Here is someone whose work is often put up on the bulletin board.*
2. Here is someone whose work is often pointed out as being very neat.
3. Here is someone whom the teacher often scolds for whispering.
4. Here is someone who is often praised for good writing on all papers handed in.
5. Here is someone whom the teacher often scolds for disturbing the class in some way (shooting paper wads, chewing gum, etc.)
6. Here is someone who is often scolded by the teacher because he or she pays little attention to what is going on in class.

* Each item has four lines.

41. CHANGES IN THE ROLE OF THE TEACHER *

DAVID RIESMAN, NATHAN GLAZER, AND REUEL DENNY

THE TEACHER'S ROLE IN THE STAGE OF INNER-DIRECTION

One important authority, however, remains: a proxy parent whose power has probably increased as a consequence of the shift to other-direction. This is the schoolteacher, and we turn now to a fuller exploration of the change in her role.

In the period when inner-direction insures middle-class conformity, school starts relatively late—there are few nursery schools. The teacher's task is largely to train the children in decorum and in intellectual matters. The decorum may be the minimum of discipline needed to keep order in the classroom or the maximum of polish needed to decorate girls of the upper social strata. As schools become more plentiful and more readily accessible and "democratic," the obligation to train the child in middle-class speech and manners—that he may be aided in his rise above his parents' rank—falls upon the teacher. But the teacher does not work close to the child's emotional level. And the teacher regards her job as a limited one, sharply demarcated from the equally rigorous task of the home.

The physical arrangements of the school, both in this period and the next, symbolize its psychological impact and play a part in that impact. Seating in the preprogressive era is arranged formally—all face front—and often alphabetically. The walls are decorated with the ruins of Pompeii and the bust of Caesar. For all but the few exceptional children who can transcend the dead forms of their classical education and make the ancient world come alive, these etchings and statues signify the irrelevance of the school to the emotional problems of the child.

The teacher herself has neither understanding of nor time for these emotional problems, and the child's relation to other children enters her purview only in disciplinary cases. Often she has simply no authority: she is a common scold with too large a brood. Or she manages to maintain discipline by strictures and punishments. But these absorb the emotional attention of the children, often uniting them, at least within social class lines, in opposition to authority.

In the recent Swedish movie *Torment* we see this pattern still at work in the near-contemporary scene. Teachers and parents share the task of instilling inner-directed values. The villain is a harsh and overbearing, neurotic prep-school teacher. All the boys hate him; some fear him; no self-respecting boy would dream—despite the teacher's groping efforts—of being his friend. The hero is a boy who rebels, not so much because he wants to as because he is forced to by his teacher. He and his friends suffer, but their parents and teachers do not invade their lives, and they have privacy with each other and with girls, so long as no serious breach of decorum is evident. This rebellion itself—its success is not the issue—is part of the process of developing an inner-directed character.

An equally moving portrait is Antonia White's novel of a girl's convent school, *Frost in May*. Though the nuns at the school go quite far in "molding character" and viciously

* Riesman, David, et al. "Changes in the Role of the Teacher," from *The Lonely Crowd*, Abridged Edition, New Haven, Connecticut: Yale University Press, pp. 55-64, Copyright © 1950, 1953, 1961 by Yale University Press.

cut down signs of spontaneity and open-mindedness in the gifted heroine, they have back of them only the old-fashioned sanctions of penance and salvation. Their charges break or bend or run away or join the church—they do not open up to the nuns as friends. The very existence of uniforms, as in a military school, symbolizes the walls that separate the authorities from the children.

We may sum all this up by saying that the school of this period is concerned largely with impersonal matters. The sexes are segregated from each other. The focus is on an intellectual content that for most children has little emotional bite. Elocution, like female accomplishment, is impersonal, too; the child is not asked to "be himself"—nor does the school aim to be like "real life." Teachers, whether spinsterly or motherly types, do not know enough, even if they had the time and energy, to take an active hand in the socialization of tastes or of peer-group relations. While parents may permit the teachers to enforce certain rules of morality directly related to school, such as modesty of dress and honesty in examinations, and to inculcate certain rules of manners directly related to social ascent, they hardly allow interference with play groups, even in the interests of enforcing ethnic or economic democracy. The teacher is supposed to see that the children learn a curriculum, not that they enjoy it or learn group cooperation. The present practice of progressive grammar schools which decide whether or not to take a child by putting him in his putative group and seeing how he fits in would hardly have been conceivable.

Nevertheless, despite the social distance between teacher and child, the school's unquestioning emphasis on intellectual ability is profoundly important in shaping the inner-directed character. It affirms to the child that what matters is what he can *accomplish,* not how nice is his smile or how cooperative his attitude. And while the objectivity of the criteria for judging these skills and competences is rightfully called into question today—when we can see very clearly, for instance, the class bias in intelligence tests and paper examinations—the inner-directed school is not aware of such biases, and hence its standards can appear unequivocal and unalterable. For

this reason these standards can be internalized both by those who succeed and by those who fail. They are felt as real and given, not as somebody's whim. Thus the school reinforces the home in setting for the child goals that are clear to all and that give direction and meaning to life thereafter.

Whatever the security that children gain from knowing where they stand—a security they no longer have in the other-directed progressive school—we must not forget how harshly this system bears on those who cannot make the grade: they are often broken; there is little mercy for them on psychological grounds. Brains, status, perhaps also docility win the teacher, rather than "personality" or "problems." Some of the failures rebel. But these, too, are hammered into shape by the school—bad shape. Occasionally the frontier and other opportunities for mobility provide an exit for the academically outclassed; and still more occasionally, the rebel returns, like a mythical hero, having lived his troubles down, to alleviate the guilt of other misfits and give them hope for their own future. By and large, however, the very unequivocality of the school's standards that gives the children a certain security also means that the standards will be internalized even by those who fail. They will carry with them the after-effects of emotional shock whose violence lies beyond criticism—sometimes even beyond recall.

THE TEACHER'S ROLE IN THE STAGE OF OTHER-DIRECTION

Progressive education began as a movement to liberate children from the crushing of talent and breaking of will that was the fate of many, even of those whose inner-direction might have seemed to them and to the observer stable and sound enough. Its aim, and to a very considerable degree, its achievement, was to develop the individuality of the child; and its method was to focus the teacher's attention on more facets of the child than his intellectual abilities. Today, however, progressive education is often no longer progressive; as people have become more other-directed, educational methods that were once liberating may even tend to thwart individuality rather than advance and protect it. The story can be quickly told.

Progressive schools have helped lower the age of school entry; the two- to five-year-old groups learn to associate school not with forbidding adults and dreary subjects but with play and understanding adults. The latter are, increasingly, young college graduates who have been taught to be more concerned with the child's social and psychological adjustment than with his academic progress—indeed, to scan the intellectual performance for signs of social maladjustment. These new teachers are more specialized. They don't claim to "understand children" but to have studied under Gesell on the "fives" or the "nines"; and this greater knowledge not only prevents the children from uniting in a wall of distrust or conspiracy against the school but also permits the teacher to take a greater hand in the socialization of spheres—consumption, friendship, fantasy—which the older-type teacher, whatever her personal desires, could not touch. Our wealthier society can afford this amount of individuation and "unnecessary" schooling.

Here also physical arrangements—in seating, age grading, decoration—symbolize the changes in the teacher's function. The sexes are mixed. Seating is arranged "informally." That is, *alphabetic* forms disappear, often to be replaced by *sociometric* forms that bring together compeers. This often means that where to sit becomes problematical—a clue to one's location on the friendship chart. Gesell grading is as severe as intellectual grading was in the earlier era; whatever their intellectual gifts, children stay with their presumed social peers.[1] The desks change their form,

too; they are more apt to be movable tables with open shelves than places where one may hide things. The teacher no longer sits on a dais or struts before a blackboard but joins the family circle.

Above all, the walls change their look. The walls of the modern grade school are decorated with the paintings of the children or their montages from the class in social studies. Thus the competitive and contemporary problems of the children look down on them from walls which, like the teacher herself, are no longer impersonal. This looks progressive, looks like a salute to creativeness and individuality; but again we meet paradox. While the school de-emphasizes grades and report cards, the displays seem almost to ask the children: "Mirror, mirror on the wall, who is fairest of us all?"[2]

What is perhaps most important, while the

[1] Howard C. Becker, a graduate student at the University of Chicago now engaged in a study of schoolteachers under the direction of Everett C. Hughes, has been observing the classroom consequences of the decline of the practice both of skipping grades and of holding children back who must repeat the grade. The teachers, faced with a group of identical age but vastly different capacities and willingness, meet the situation by dividing the class into two or three like-minded groups. Mobility between groups is discouraged, and children are encouraged to imitate their groupmates. The teacher herself, in the public schools, is probably inner-directed, but she is forced by her situation to promote other-direction among her charges.

Though in interview material it is always difficult to distinguish ideology from character, it is possible that the following quotation from one of Mr. Becker's interviews is a poignant example of the unwilling promotion of other-direction, as a result of this teacher's practice of using "telling time" and group shame as pressure on the child to have more interesting week ends: "Every class I have I start out the year by making a survey. I have each child get up and tell what he did over the week end. These last few years I've noticed that more and more children get up and say, 'Saturday I went to the show, Sunday I went to the show' . . . I've been teaching twenty-five years, and it never used to be like that. Children used to do more interesting things, they would go places instead of 'Saturday I went to the show, Sunday I went to the show' . . . What I do is to give a talk on all the interesting things that could be done—like going to museums and things like that. And also things like playing baseball and going on bike rides. By the end of the term a child is ashamed if he has to get up and say, 'Saturday I went to the show, Sunday I went to the show.' All the rest of the children laugh at him. So they really try to do some interesting things."

[2] Still more paradoxically, it often happens that those schools that insist most strongly that the child be original and creative by this very demand make it difficult for him to be so. He dare not imitate an established master nor, in some cases, even imitate his own earlier work. Though the introduction of the arts into the school opens up the whole art world to many children, who would have no time or stimulation outside, other children are forced to socialize performances that would earlier have gone unnoticed to peers and adults.

children's paintings and montages show considerable imaginative gift in the preadolescent period, the school itself is still one of the agencies for the destruction of fantasy, as it was in the preceding era. Imagination withers in most of the children by adolescence. What survives is neither artistic craft nor artistic fantasy but the socialization of taste and interest that can already be seen in process in the stylization of perception in the children's paintings and stories. The stories of the later progressive grades are apt to be characterized by "realism." This realism is subtly influenced by the ideals of the progressive movement. Caesar and Pompeii are replaced by visits to stores and dairies, by maps from *Life,* and by *The Weekly Reader;* and fairy tales are replaced by stories about trains, telephones, and grocery stores, and, later, by material on race relations or the United Nations or "our Latin American neighbors."

These changes in arrangement and topic assist the breakdown of walls between teacher and pupil; and this in turn helps to break down walls between student and student, permitting that rapid circulation of tastes which is a prelude to other-directed socialization. Whereas the inner-directed school child might well have hidden his stories and paintings under his bed—like the adult who, as we saw, often kept a diary—the other-directed child reads his stories to the group and puts his paintings on the wall. Play, which in the earlier epoch is often an extracurricular and private hobby, shared at most with a small group, now becomes part of the school enterprise itself, serving a "realistic" purpose.

The teacher's role in this situation is often that of opinion leader. She is the spreader of the messages concerning taste that come from the progressive urban centers. She conveys to the children that what matters is not their industry or learning as such but their adjustment in the group, their cooperation, their (carefully stylized and limited) initiative and leadership.

Especially important is the fact that the cooperation and leadership that are inculcated in and expected of the children are frequently contentless. In nursery school it is not important whether Johnny plays with a truck or in the sandbox, but it matters very much

whether he involves himself with Bill—via any object at all. To be sure, there are a few, a very few, truly progressive schools where the children operating on the Dalton plan and similar plans exercise genuine choice of their program, move at their own pace, and use the teacher as a friendly reference library; here cooperation is necessary and meaningful in actual work on serious projects. Far more frequently, however, the teacher continues to hold the reins of authority in her hands, hiding her authority, like her compeer, the other-directed parent, under the cloak of "reasoning" and manipulation. She determines the program and its pace—indeed, often holding the children back because she fails to realize that children, left to themselves, are capable of curiosity about highly abstract matters. She may delay them by making arithmetic "realistic" and languages fun—as well as by substituting social studies for history. In extreme forms of this situation there is nothing on which the children have to cooperate in order to get it done. The teacher will do it for them anyway. Hence when she asks that they be cooperative she is really asking simply that they be nice.

However, though the request seems simple, it is not casually made: the teacher is very tense about it. Deprived of older methods of discipline, she is, if anything, even more helpless than the parents who can always fall back on those methods in a pinch, though guiltily and rather ineffectively. The teacher neither dares to nor cares to; she has been taught that bad behavior on the children's part implies poor management on her part. Moreover, she herself is not interested in the intellectual content of what is taught, nor is this content apt to come up in a staff meeting or PTA discussion. These adult groups are often concerned with teaching tolerance, both ethnic and economic; and the emphasis on social studies that results means that intellectual content and skill become still more attenuated. Consequently, the teacher's emotional energies are channeled into the area of group relations. Her social skills develop; she may be sensitive to cliques based on "mere friendship" and seek to break them up lest any be left out. Correspondingly, her love for certain specific children may be trained out of her

All the more, she needs the general cooperation of all the children to assure herself that she is doing her job. Her surface amiability and friendliness, coupled with this underlying anxiety concerning the children's response, must be very confusing to the children who will probably conclude that to be uncooperative is about the worst thing one can be.

Of course the teacher will see to it that the children practice cooperation in small matters: in deciding whether to study the Peruvians or the Colombians, in nominating class officers for early practice in the great contemporary rituals of electioneering and parliamenteering, and in organizing contributions for the Red Cross or a Tag Day. Thus the children are supposed to learn democracy by underplaying the skills of intellect and overplaying the skills of gregariousness and amiability —skill democracy, in fact, based on respect for ability to *do* something, tends to survive only in athletics.

There is, therefore, a curious resemblance between the role of the teacher in the small-class modern school—a role that has spread from the progressive private schools to some of the public schools—and the role of the industrial relations department in a modern factory. The latter is also increasingly concerned with cooperation between men and men and between men and management, as technical skill becomes less and less of a major concern. In a few of the more advanced plants there is even a pattern of democratic decision on moot matters—occasionally important because it affects piecework rates and seniority rules, but usually as trivial as the similar decisions of grammar-school government. Thus the other-directed child is taught at school to take his place in a society where the concern of the group is less with what it produces than with its internal group relations, its morale.

42. THE TRIUMPH OF ACHIEVEMENT OVER INQUIRY IN EDUCATION *

HERBERT A. THELEN

Principals, teachers, parents, professors, or practice teachers who try to improve instruction in the classroom soon find themselves in a trap.

It is a fascinating trap built by people who know better. The fact that they built the trap very much against their will does not make the trap any less a trap. But it does show that one can get swept along by forces at work in the larger society.

In big, broad terms, the trap is the conflict between the Organization Man, who continually seeks to reassure himself of his place in

society, and the Inquiring Man, who seeks to better himself and his society. In narrower terms, the conflict is between the way we try to teach children and the way we measure what they have learned. In middle-sized terms, the conflict is between education and achievement as school goals.

CLOSE-UP OF A TRAP

I should like to begin by describing the trap —by reporting on the conflicts and contradictions that make up the trap. So I shall talk about practices, not sentiments or theories.

My testimony comes mostly from thoughtful teachers who think wistfully about the possibility of improving their own courses. They are tired of just covering the ground, by which

* Reprinted from "The Triumph of Achievement over Inquiry in Education," in *Elementary School Journal, 60,* 1960, by permission of the University of Chicago Press.

they mean exposing the pupil to a prescribed body of already organized ideas. They would like to get some inquiry going. They would like to see pupils study because there is something important to learn, something important to the pupils, that is.

As these teachers see it, the chief obstacle to making this shift is the way achievement is now defined by the public and measured by tests. The teachers perceive that their pupils are realistic enough to know that their job is to pass tests; this is what academic aspirations means; this is what achievement means to pupils and to the public.

Of course, some of these teachers say, "We don't mark exclusively on tests. We take other things into account." But these "other things" are subjective and unconfidently known. At best, they merely blur the harsh outline of test results.

And here we can point to the heart of the conflict. Teachers try to set up learning experiences based on one set of views while they measure achievement based on a different set of views. The disparity can be disconcerting to pupils, parents, and concerned citizens as well as teachers. Let's look at some aspects of the conflict.

Pupils feel that testing puts them in competition with one another. But the teacher wants them to co-operate, not compete.

In class discussion and class projects, the teacher seems to want class members to share ideas. But on tests, pupils see their classmates as rivals who are required to get the better of one another.

There are even conflicting economic connotations here. In testing it is usually assumed that there are not enough A's to go around; in teaching it is assumed that everyone can have an A—if he earns it.

Our tests teach pupils that academic status, not learning, is the goal of education.

If learning were the goal, achievement would be measured as the difference between pre-tests and post-tests on the material of the course. Since pre-tests are seldom used, the teacher has no way of knowing how much the pupil learned. The mark testifies to final status, not to what was learned during the course.

Pupils work for marks rather than in response to the challenge of the subject.

The purpose of learning is to gain status, symbolized in a mark, rather than to master the discipline of the subject. Good marks mean promotion and the regard of adults. Snap subjects and "soft" teachers are the sensible route to good marks. Moreover, acceptance or capitulation by the teacher to the mark-getting routine tends to free him from his professional obligation to make study meaningful in its own right.

Pupils study the teacher rather than the subject.

Often the main object of inquiry in the classroom is the sort of question the teacher is likely to ask, the bases he uses for marking, his biases and enthusiasms. This experience, over the years, has no doubt helped mold the Organization Man, who studies the boss for the same reasons that he once studied the teacher. In good teaching, the demands the pupil faces come from the problem situation, not from the teacher.

Learning becomes a kind of academic hit-and-run. The class hits the test and runs on to a new unit.

Once knowledge is tested, it can be safely forgotten. This notion directly contradicts the idea of education as a "deepening and enriching" experience. The unit plan, originally designed to organize learning into significant wholes, has become a package plan, with each package wrapped up by a unit test.

Pupils learn that specific information is an end in itself rather than the means to broad understanding of universal principles.

The easiest way to make a reliable test is to use a large number of independent, specific, and separate items. This discovery about testing dealt a severe blow to the educational goal of understanding. The educated citizen is the quiz kid, not the wise man. And cramming for examinations, whether in school or on TV shows, is the basic learning process.

Pupils learn from experience with tests that all questions have clear-cut answers certified by authority. Such "thought questions" as the teacher uses are asked just to keep conversation going.

Compared with "getting the facts," the process of reasoning from data to probable conclusions is at best an intriguing parlor game. The teacher, himself conditioned by tests, may strive to be a walking encyclopedia rather than a guide to inquiry. We present to children a world in which all the lovely mottled grays of the adult world are squeezed into black-and-white certainties.

Post-Sputnik pressures, aided by the nationally standardized test, are rapidly turning the school into a processing plant rather than a place for inquiry.

In this processing plant, the teacher's role is that of a technician, not a professional. The professional, like the learner, must be aware of alternatives in a situation, choose among them, and test the consequences of his choice. The technician, like the rote learner, treats all situations alike, using prescribed rules and memorized procedures.

The range of choices that require mature judgment of the teacher is rapidly narrowing, and with this change the climate for inquiry is becoming less favorable. If we no longer trust the teacher, our confidence might be restored if we gave him better preparation, especially in his major subject. Detailed specifications for content, method, and activities were appropriate for war-time crash programs by the armed forces charged with the task of turning out technicians in quantity, but crash programs of this nature will not produce enlightened citizens and creative leaders.

The pupil is being taught to escape from freedom for the sake of material reward and social approval.

Freedom can exist only if self-knowledge is valued. Our procedures for measuring achievement do not help the pupil find out who he is or discover his strengths and weaknesses as a person. Our tests only tell us how well the pupil is conforming to a specified 1960 super-technical model.

But we do have a conscience. Having conditioned the pupil, through awards and other forms of social approval, into submissiveness, we then propose to put him in a liberal arts college to develop his human spirit!

Our 1960 super-technical model is defined by tests that give the pupil feedback about his growing strengths, his self-concept, and his abilities. These are expressed in terms that we prescribe, not necessarily in the areas where growth and development are taking place.

In teaching, we hunt for growth areas because it is through them that the pupil puts forth effort and gives attention. In testing, we have to disregard categories of information of unique importance to particular individuals, partly because we have to test everybody with the same instrument and partly because we simply do not know the ways in which children at various stages of growth relate to ideas and subject disciplines. Thus we teach the pupil that his own life and interests are irrelevant to education.

What do our present practices in measuring achievement contribute to education? Tests can be used to supply extrinsic motivation. This kind of motivation is considered undesirable by those who regard pupils as human beings rather than as manpower for technological enterprises.

Tests can also be used to spot children who need help. Many pupils have received remedial help because an appropriate screening test revealed their need. Most of us would agree that it is desirable to use tests in this way.

Tests can be used to guide teaching. But tests are generally given too late to serve this purpose. By the time the test results are known, the class has already moved on to a new unit. To help guide instruction, the teacher may, of course, devise short questionnaires of his own and use them at frequent intervals.

As diagnostic tools for helping the pupil understand himself and set his life goals, tests have little value for at least two reasons. First, what is past is past. We do not go back. We are satisfied to say how much the pupil learned, but not to help him master presumably important learnings. Second, achievement tests are not constructed to tell much about a pupil's unique strengths. This fact about our tests is an unfortunate one, since the pupil's strengths are all that he and the teacher have to build on.

ALTERNATIVES

Having described school practices in destructive, cynical, or perhaps honest, terms, I now ask: Do we have to be content with this kind of evaluation?

The answer is no, and many test-makers would be the first to agree. Their responsibility for the present state of affairs is no more and no less than the responsibility of atomic physicists for Hiroshima. The bomb was dropped because of a complex alignment of social forces. The triumph of "achievement" over education is a sign of the times rather than the intention of educational evaluators. Moreover, like atomic energy, evaluation is taking an increasingly important place in our lives.

But the proper use of evaluation will not come about through the singlehanded efforts of evaluators, teachers, or any other one group. Evaluation will contribute to education rather than to narrow goals in achievement only after widespread effort by many groups. As far as each school is concerned, the problem involves the attitudes, expectations, and goals of the entire community.

How can we return to the goal of education?

First, we could try to measure the pupil's growth as a whole, unique person, with his own goals, his own way of viewing people and the world. Individuals differ in their way of life. By *way of life* I mean the pattern of attitudes, abilities, and habits by which an individual lives and develops his strengths. If we could determine each child's general pattern, we could follow him as a whole person and help him make choices appropriate to the effective development of his way of life. We could be concerned with how he is organizing subject matter in his subjective world and the relationship between this world and his behavior in all situations.

But such evaluations can be achieved only if we start with children. We will not succeed if we start by asking: What does chemistry teach? What does history teach? We shall have to ask: How is the pupil assimilating the discipline of chemistry? Of history? How well is he mastering the method of the chemist? Of the historian? What do his learnings in chemistry and history mean for

his way of life? This last question is the proper concern of the teacher, and it is a very different concern from the one that now motivates schools and communities.

My second suggestion recognizes that it is the purpose of education not only to develop individual powers but also to prepare effective citizens. Our schools have the responsibility of helping children live as self-realizing people, not in a vacuum or a hermitage, but in a complex society. In short, we recognize that children are going to have to take roles in a real world. They are going to manage others; interpret the world around them; make discoveries; create social, political, and economic alternatives; ferret out facts; and persuade, promote, criticize, analyze, guide, console, and teach.

Education is at least partly an inquiry into the kinds of roles boys and girls may be fitted for. We must not seal off pathways before children's tendencies are thoroughly demonstrated, and we must always allow for unexpected changes in tendencies. But we can ask, as the Strong Vocational Interest Blanks ask in regard to occupations: What kinds of roles are children developing potential for? And we could keep records through the school years of profiles that show the child's aptitudes and readiness for certain roles.

RECOMMENDATIONS

The first thing we must do is to free the schools from the pressures that keep them from their proper job of educating boys and girls. We must reduce the pressures, so fashionable at present, for achievement, for covering ground, for mass production of pseudo-experts.

Let the schools concentrate on doing something for our children. Let the others—college faculties and employers—worry about what they are going to do about our pupils after the schools have done all they can. In other words, let's stick to our proper job of saying what has happened to our pupils and what goals they are moving toward. Let each college decide whether the student is ready to embark on its study program. Let the industrialists decide whether they want to hire him. Let the parents decide whether they are satisfied with him. These are their decisions, not ours.

Many of us in the schools know that our marks have always been monstrous. They try to signify two things that cannot be measured together. They try to measure the pupil's standing, judged against standards we have assumed (often erroneously) the higher school or college desired.

Marks also try to measure what the child has done compared with what he might be capable of doing. The criteria for measuring the pupil's standing must be the same for all pupils. Yet the criteria for measuring capability or growth of powers must differ from one pupil to the next.

The confusion over marks is a symptom of the larger confusion over the mission of the school. Let us commit ourselves to the educational job defined earlier, and let us find appropriate means for describing the results.

My second recommendation has to to with both the means and the measurement of education. Let us confront the pupil with the events, the ideas, the attitudes, and the practices that he must cope with. Let us help him cope with them, and from time to time let us assess his growth in the ability to cope.

In teaching let us use situations that are vital and lifelike, though not necessarily a slice of natural life. The situations we provide should have the validity of significant human activity. They should release the essentially dramatic quality of purposeful human endeavor. In testing, perhaps the simplest way of stating the recommendations is to say that more *complete* situations should be used.

I would like to see us experiment with sound movies. The pupil views a situation on the screen, tells what he would do in the situation, and justifies his response.

I would like to see us make much more use of role-playing. Certainly one of the major goals of the disciplines of history, anthropology, and psychology is to develop the individual's ability to put himself in the place of people who lived at other times and other places. In role-playing, we can watch the pupil as he tries to feel and understand situations from another's point of view. As we watch, we should be as interested in the child's actions and expressions as in his words. I

would like to see these techniques used in our assessment of the pupil's powers as manifested in performance, not in puzzles.

I do not see any reason why we cannot use situations in the community to probe development. We have had a lot of talk about democracy. All right, let the pupil see a club or a board of directors in action. Let him come back and tell us about it. Let's note what he observes, what he responds to, what is important to him. Isn't this the sort of information we need to plan further activities and to assess educational growth?

I would like to get at the ideas to which the pupil is committed. What ideas are important to him? What causes is he nurturing? Is he developing any life goals? Any compelling purposes? Are his intellectual interests expanding?

To discover answers to these questions, we must occasionally give the pupil opportunities for free choice. In planning his work, we can offer him six or eight kinds of activities from which to choose. Which does he select? Why?

I maintain that this is relevant and interpretable information and that it has the feel of life. But let's let him choose among activities, not just among phrases written on a piece of paper.

THE DOCTOR AND THE DETECTIVE

John H. Watson, M.D., wrote what may well be the longest and the most complete case study on record. His subject was Sherlock Holmes, the detective. In *A Study in Scarlet,* Watson attempts, after some weeks of acquaintance, to assess Holmes, and he writes out a report card in the best achievement tradition.

He certifies Holmes' knowledge of literature, philosophy, and astronomy to be nil. Politics —feeble. Botany—strong on poisons but weak on practical gardening. Geology—recognizes mud stains from various parts of London. Chemistry—profound. Sensational literature —knows "every detail of every horror perpetrated in the last century." Anatomy— "accurate, but unsystematic." Good violinist, expert amateur athlete, "good practical knowledge of British law." And Watson, with rare insight into his own evaluative processes, labels the report card "Sherlock Holmes—*his limits*" (italics mine).

But with all this observation, which is quite accurate, Watson misses the essence of Holmes, and Sherlock has to tell him, finally, what his powers and abilities are and what social role organizes these powers and abilities into an effective personality and contributor to society.

What Watson missed, because he had never seen Holmes perform in an appropriate situation, was his intuition for unraveling crimes, his ability to apply special knowledge to problems, his conscious use of rules of deduction, his habit of observation. And the report card could never have led Watson to predict Holmes' role of "consulting detective."

Watson, I am afraid, embodies the achievement point of view in our schools. He represents the traditional, academic, propaedeutic view of education, which asks after achievement in its own categories but fails to comprehend, and therefore to educate, the child.

Sherlock is unique, as human personality is unique; and he represents that part of every man which must be understood within its own frame of reference and commitments. The categories useful for understanding Sherlock are not the categories most useful for understanding Watson.

Watson talks about his own education in language that is typical of certification and achievement. He "took his degree" and proceeded "to go through the course prescribed for surgeons."

Holmes never talks about his education. But he does talk about problems to be solved, inquiries to be conducted, and methods of thought that he values. For the most part, Holmes educated himself. His studies were "very desultory and eccentric, but he . . . amassed a lot of out-of-the-way knowledge which would astonish his professors." And the habit of inquiry—which the university could not stamp out—survived.

Can we say as much for our pupils?

Chapter VIII

CULTURAL DEPRIVATION: NEW PROBLEMS IN TEACHING AND LEARNING

Until recently educational psychology has paid scant attention to social class variables or social class influences on learning. In general, there were always a few academics from other disciplines—particularly sociology or anthropology—who would point with obvious disdain to the middle class or lower-middle class orientation of schools and/or teachers. Such criticism was intended apparently to poke at the legal fictions surrounding middle class America and the few voices raised were pretty much sounds in the wilderness. In the field of educational psychology too, there were occasional psychological studies illustrating, for example, that lower class children perceived rewards somewhat differently from middle class children, or that lower class children did not delay gratification of impulse as much as middle class children, or that teachers themselves had somewhat different attitudes toward pupils according to social class background.

In general, however, education as a form of social intervention or as a means to enhance, nurture, and develop children in accord with society's charge was based on the assumption that schooling in its present form would provide all children with equal opportunity. No special consideration or programs or particular knowledge was necessary. Yes, tinkering adjustments might be called for, but no major shift in the direction of our educational enterprise seemed necessary. Nevertheless, we knew, at least at the margin of awareness, that some schools in some of the more antiquated segments of our cities or rural areas were not as "good" as say some of the "flashy" suburban campus-type schools.

In a review of educational research, it would be hard to find any genuine or systematic interest in the educational problems presented by children of the poor. For one thing, we tended to maintain a somewhat romantic notion of the slums. The Bowery in New York, a skid row section now razed, held a certain fascination and charm that contributed to the myth. Also, there were always a few well publicized examples of individuals who by heroic efforts and good fortune managed to pull themselves out of these settings and achieve success. These few, seen as examples of the

Horatio Alger myth, served to confirm what middle class America really wanted to believe. Success was simply a question of willpower, hard work, and effort. If the poor chose not to work, it was, after all, only their own fault. This "happy" state of affairs allowed us to sermonize and pontificate to and about the poor, much of this sermonizing being in the let-em-eat-cake tradition of the eighteenth century French aristocracy.

The first appeal for a more comprehensive understanding of the urban educational problem was broadcast to an unresponsive nation in 1961 in the second Conant Report on the American high school, *Slums and Suburbs*. In ringing phrases Conant called our attention to the "social dynamite" festering in our slum schools. Yet this call to national action largely went unheeded. The nation slept. Five years later we awoke as the riots began in practically every major city above the Mason-Dixon Line.

Only gradually did we understand what was happening. At first we regarded it as a communist plot, or the work of a few hot heads. Then we took a second look. The cities were in fact decaying. Once proud and prominent urban educational systems were suffering from a complex blight. Racial isolation in the cities was increasing. Great migrations had taken place. Seventy-five percent of our Negro population now lived in cities; whereas just forty years ago eighty percent lived on farms. Because of social, economic, and other more insidious barriers, these groups simply filled up the cities, being able to move no farther. Increasingly city schools became populated exclusively by the poor. In a study in 1967 of fifteen leading metropolitan areas it was reported that the school enrollments averaged eighty percent non-white. While the schools themselves became overcrowded, the financial resources necessary for new programs, new buildings, and new hope diminished each year.

The Conant Report presented the problem in broad, subjective terms. More recently, a second study has been published documenting both the existence and the extent of our newly discovered national educational problems. By congressional action, James Coleman, a sociologist at Johns Hopkins, was given the responsibility of providing data on the question of equality of educational opportunity. Since the tenor of the events at that time led us to anticipate a report that would document the differences between white and Negro educational opportunity (which is great indeed), it came as a genuine surprise that social class background of pupils was the single most important variable in educational attainment. Of course it must be remembered that in this country the non-white population makes up a large portion of the low social and economic class. The problem, however, goes beyond the racial question. The inherent weakness in our educational system seems to be the class-linked nature of most schools. By keeping lower class children in the same schools regardless of the racial composition of the schools, we may well defeat efforts to change. Daniel P. Moynihan, an urbanologist (a new type of social scientist devoted to the study of urban problems), has noted that class background of the children is the determining factor in providing anything like equality of educational opportunity. He suggested by way of analogy that the segregated nature of Catholic parochial education in the nineteenth century retarded the development of equality of opportunity not because the schools were composed of all Catholic children, but mostly because they were all poor children.

It is almost a truism to say that this country in the sixth decade of the twentieth century has just discovered its poor people. Whether we have simply pretended until now that they did not really exist (like the Germans in pre-World War II days who did not "know" about the concentration camps) is beside the point. The first step in developing solutions is the acknowledgement of the problem itself. Certainly long range, comprehensive solutions are needed. Although it is beyond the scope of this volume to deal directly with specific changes, it may not be an overstatement to say that for too long our city school children have been sacrificed to the principle of local control. In the late 1920s we, as a country, confronted a similar situation in the Great Depression. At first it was felt that the problem had to be solved at the local level with local resources, but gradually as the bread and soup lines increased and employment rates decreased, we realized that we faced a national problem. The problem posed by the Depression affected all of us. Similarly, the problem posed by urban education is in fact a national concern, for no corner of this country can for long remain untouched by it. After the Supreme Court decision of 1954, the North tended to feel complacent. The great problems were all safely below the Mason-Dixon Line. Events, however, have upset this complacency.

What we are beginning to understand in rather simple terms is that schooling may be the only genuine way to provide people with the means to achieve their own goals. We now have nothing at all like equality of educational opportunity. There are two separate but complementary dimensions to the problem that deserve recognition. First, poor children start school in the first grade with serious educational handicaps, and second, their academic deficiencies increase during the course of schooling. This means we can smugly point the finger neither just at the home background nor just at the school. Once again, as we have noted in the other parts of this book, such dichotomies are superficial. The interaction of the early environment and the present school environment in the city slums reflects a deadly combination.

It is no accident that with reference to the educational problems of the poor we return to the issues mentioned in Chapter I of this volume. The reader will recall that we stressed that inherited or genetically determined abilities and aptitudes flourish or decay depending on the interaction with the surrounding environment. The early imprint of experience can become indelible. Theorists from many different frames of references (Freud to

Hess) agree on the importance of early learning experiences, even though their interpretations may vary. Rene Spitz (1945) has shown descriptively what happened to unmothered children in an orphanage. Although the physical needs were met, the psychological needs were not, and 34 of 91 children died. Krech, as we noted, has shown in animal experiments that chemical and structural changes occur after the subjects (rats) experience a stimulating and creative environment. The reverse has also been demonstrated. Calhoun subjected animals (again rats) to severe crowding and demoralizing conditions and found later that as these rats matured they would not care for their offspring. Also, there were certain chemical changes that took place as a result of the overcrowding so that the effect of these early experiences included physiological as well as psychological impairment.[1]

We have been slow to recognize that all these studies and all these theories concerning critical periods and initial learning experiences point to poverty itself as a major epidemiological factor in preventing normal growth. We have seen the results in terms of the enormously high rates of emotional problems, birth defects, epilepsy, and mental retardation among the poor, but for a series of reasons we have avoided the inescapable conclusion that such effects have been caused by poverty itself.

Although this chapter particularly emphasizes the educational problems posed by the poor, we are not suggesting that schools in the "green belt" suburbs represent models for emulation and solution. The educational problems in the suburbs are neither so visible nor so dramatic as those in the cities. The signs are more subtle. City schools have dropouts in large numbers; whereas suburban schools have "bright but low achieving" pupils in significant proportions. In the city there may be open hostility, but in the suburbs pupil distrust takes the form of cynicism and sarcasm. In the cities teacher turnover is apparent; in the suburbs it may take the form of a teacher's turning from individual inquiry and insight in learning to rewarding conformity in thought and passivity in action. Recently two well known educators, specializing in problems of poor children, noted that the urban child and his parents have dared to call attention to the essential irrelevancy of the education provided for them. Fantini and Weinstien (1967) go on to note that in so doing the urban child has become "the spokesman for the middle class child as well."[2]

In an earlier chapter in this volume we presented some of the findings and positions of Coleman, Friendenberg, and Holt, among others. These views, largely on so-called "middle class" schools, suggested a somewhat different type of disadvantage for suburban pupils. Conformity, social

---

[1] Calhoun, J. B., "The Social Aspects of Population Dynamics," *J. Mammalogy, 33*, 1957, 139-59.
[2] Fantini, M. D. and Weinstien, G., "Taking Advantage of the Disadvantaged." A Ford Foundation Reprint from *The Teachers College Record, 69*, 1967, #2.

status consciousness, and conventionalism all indicate this disadvantage too. The corporate nature of many large suburban schools, possibly even including a well staffed bureaucracy, may inflict learning deficits just as surely as do the big city schools. If Fantini and Weinstien are correct, the criticism of urban education will induce a general questioning about the quality and relevancy of schools across the board. If such indeed is the outcome of the urban unrest, we shall owe a particular debt to the urban poor. Edgar Friendenberg has suggested that there is no older tradition in our country than to leave the most difficult jobs to such groups of people.

AN OVERVIEW OF THE READINGS FOR THIS CHAPTER

The lead article (Selection 43) by Malone is entitled "Safety First: Comments on the Influence of External Danger in the Lives of Children of Disorganized Families." The author, a psychiatrist, has investigated the effects on cognitive development in children from multi-problem families. Note that he distinguishes between stable working class families and disorganized families. Crucial to our understanding is his description of the functioning of the latter groups of children. From his presentation of the concomitants of delayed or inhibited cognitive growth, an ironic picture emerges. On one hand the children are uninterested in learning and unresponsive to the material in the preschool; on the other they are old beyond their years. They can shop in busy stores, cross dangerous intersections, and take care of their younger brothers and sisters even though they are themselves only three or four years old. This indicates surely that such children have "learned" something. The formative influences on these children can be seen quite dramatically in Malone's presentation of their experiences. The effort they have to expend to survive may concurrently foreclose their ability for school learning. It is difficult for one in danger of annihilation to concentrate on a lesson plan. Malone suggests that it is just such real external danger in combination with neglect that arrests their cognitive growth. Most revealing, of course, is his analysis of what lies behind their "precocious" abilities and the implications for schooling.

The second article (Selection 44) is from the Department of Labor's report *The Negro Family*. The report provides a specific and detailed picture of what it is like to be not only poor but non-white as well. By indicating from an historical account how the nation has for the past two centuries systematically destroyed the basic social unit of any group, the family, we can understand more clearly the extent of the educational problems we face. In the report's words, that the Negro has survived at all is extraordinary. The price of such survival is a more relevant and immediate concern. The disparities in educational attainment, the matrifocal society in some ghettos, the growing cumulative educational deficit, the unemployment problems that follow, all these are factors which lead to alienation and despair. Although the report may be criticized because it does not "mince words" or carefully qualify all its statements, the general picture of a socially induced pathology must be portrayed in such terms to emphasize the urgency of time running out.

The next selection (45) is from a study committee headed by Bloom, Davis, and Hess specifically devoted to the educational implications for children of poverty. We have included two excerpts from their report: one on the elementary school and the second on adolescents in secondary school. Clearly the authors recognize that the school has a special mission with these children, one that up to now it has failed to fulfill. Present school practices overcome neither the initial differences upon entry to school nor the cumulative deficit. The solutions must not be simplistic. By changing the teacher-pupil ratio slightly or by introducing a few new reading books that include bi-racial pictures, we may feel that we are accomplishing something. Such minor changes, as the authors note, are completely inadequate. In fact the reader can detect in this report many of the themes that have run through the entire set of readings: children learn in a series of modes; there should be a number of approaches to learning; we should develop a learning environment by starting within the child's stage of cognitive and emotional development, within the child's "critical stages."

Since initial learning experiences are important, the elementary program is predicated on the establishment of an effective kindergarten and nursery school experience. Without a changed elementary program, however, the nursery school is only a "head start" to nowhere. Such themes probably provide the best new evidence we have that educational psychology may yet make important contributions to education.

The final article (Selection 46) is by Jonathan Kozol. The selection is from his book on ghetto schools, *Death at an Early Age*. The author provides a subjective assessment of one particular dimension in the first of two selections, the "Reading Teacher." Earlier in this book we have indicated the importance of the "hidden agenda," that is, the effects of implicit attitudes and values. We presented the general case; in the Kozol article we view the specific. He develops a composite character, the reading teacher, and then through a series of dialogues with her demonstrates the latent prejudice behind her comments. This is both an effective and dangerous device because a reader can quickly conclude that no one person could really be that prejudiced and still function as a teacher. Rather than attempt to establish absolute credibility, it is perhaps best to view the descriptions as part of an overall picture of ghetto schools.

In the second selection from his book, Kozol describes "how it really is" in the ghetto classroom. He presents us with the individual differences he confronted in his fourth grade class—the wide disparity in achievement level, the missing records, the broken desks, the missing teachers. He talks of the standardized condescension by the adults and its effects. Also, he presents a poignant description of a little Negro girl picking her way to school past abandoned cars, winos, trash, and insults. Walk with her on her trip to school, as you read, and try to put yourself in her shoes to see "how it really is." If you conclude that it will take more than a few Langston Hughes poems to restore human dignity in that setting, you may be right.

The atmosphere of despair is pervasive in the ghettos. As one mother put it recently to one of the authors of this volume, "When you despair, the children know it. You may think you are putting up a brave front, but the children see through it. You can put up with a lot of hardships for yourself, but if you see no chance for your children to ever know anything better than you have known yourself, you despair. . . ."

If this set of readings appears to overemphasize the educational problems of the poor, it is a result of our past neglect. If the scope of the problems seems overwhelming, it also follows that brief "crash" programs will not alleviate the difficulties. If we have indicated that the time to assess blame has long passed, then maybe we can as a nation join the effort to develop schooling for all children. Other programs almost by definition will be too little and too late. Education offers the opportunity to break the vicious cycle of poverty and halt the inheritance of despair by future generations. Prevention in the form of education seems the only viable solution. As a country we need to take education seriously almost as if our survival depended upon it. It does. However, whether the new programs work, whether financial resources are wisely used, and indeed whether the children themselves will be any better off in the future, will depend on one major ingredient. People will ultimately make the difference. Informed, intelligent, and committed adults are needed. The problems are great, but so is the challenge.

43. SAFETY FIRST: COMMENTS ON THE INFLUENCE OF EXTERNAL DANGER IN THE LIVES OF CHILDREN OF DISORGANIZED FAMILIES *

C. A. MALONE

This paper concerns aspects of the findings, impressions and formulations of three years of intensive work with the preschool offspring of a group of multiproblem, hard-to-reach families living in a Skid-Row area. This work constitutes one effort to meet the complex, difficult and costly challenges of unreached families, as an extension of family-centered child guidance practice into the community.

The designation, "multi-problem, hard-to-reach family," does not refer to a type or specific category, but rather to a loose, heterogeneous group. This group can be demarcated grossly from stable, working-class families at the upper end of the lower-class continuum (7) but is less well distinguished from families nearer the more disorganized end of the range. Thus the multiproblem families with whom we worked represent a segment of the lower class which merges with and is related to other strata on the continuum.

PSYCHOLOGICAL CHARACTERISTICS OF THE CHILDREN[1]

By the time the 21 preschool children entered nursery school, as early as age two-and-a-half to three years, distinctive deviation in their development could be observed. Despite divergent individual histories, native endowment and temperament these three- to five-year-olds shared most of the descriptive characteristics, which we will now present, with only small differences in intensity.

The children were quick, agile, well coordinated and often capable of advanced gross motor feats. Yet heedlessness and general disregard for body care caused them to trip and fall or to stumble into things frequently. Most of them demonstrated a driven, on-the-go quality and tended to discharge tension and stress in disorganized motor activity. Their actions were rarely pleasurable, and their explorations of the environment were minimal and mechanically repetitious.

Typically, the children approached adults with a friendly, shallow, nonspecific eagerness. They displayed considerable skill in manipulating the teacher to secure her attention. Along with this need for attention however, they showed distrust and intolerance of closeness. Contact between the children mainly involved facile imitation of each other's activities as part of their rivalry for the teacher's attention. In fact, imitation of expressions, gestures, words and behavior was a dominant feature of all their interaction with others. Conflicts were largely avoided and aggression seldom was expressed openly except in the form of impulsive grabbing of another's possessions. Instead, aggression appeared covertly in provocativeness and much later in dramatically playing the roles of vindictive, demanding, controlling and punishing figures. Related to this identification with the aggressor, low self-esteem and marked self devaluation were characteristic of these children along with derogation of their products. They had little confidence in their ability and

* Malone, C. A., "Safety First: Comments on the Influence of External Danger in the Lives of Children of Disorganized Families," *American Journal of Orthopsychiatry*, Vol. 36, No. 1, January 1966, pp. 3-12. Copyright, the American Orthopsychiatric Association, Inc. Reproduced by permission.

[1] In developing this description of the children, I am indebted to our nursery school teacher, Mrs. Ilse Mattick, for her careful observations.

very little enjoyment from themselves in play, exploration or achievement.

The children's mode of functioning tended to be by passive response to the cues of others rather than by the use of initiative. Their token, joyless performance of directed routines, often in an overly compliant manner and their inability to handle independently undirected activities pointed to a significant deficit in self-determination and age-appropriate assertiveness. The children didn't ask for appropriate help and often could not accept it when it was offered. They showed, however, pseudoautonomy in that they tended to substitute manipulativeness, compliance, controllingness and appearance of being grown up for voluntary control and independence. Expectation of calamity and guarded fearfulness permeated their daily nursery school lives. They demonstrated a "danger orientation," a perceptual apprehensiveness, in which they watched and listened intently and reacted impulsively as though by proper reading of cues they could forestall trouble for themselves. In contrast, they were unresponsive to other stimuli such as attractive displays or verbal explanations.

When the children first came to nursery school they lacked interest in learning the names and properties of objects. Colors, numbers, sizes, shapes, locations, all seemed interchangeable. Nothing in the room seemed to have meaning for a child apart from the fact that another child had approached or handled it or that the teacher's attention was turned toward it. Even brief play depended on the teacher's involvement and support. The children's language development was retarded, and communication frequently was effected by other means, such as pleading looks, appealing smiles and whimpering. Not only was their vocabulary small, but the language they had was limited in its usefulness. Their infantile speech often was used in an imitative, parroting manner or to gain attention and was little used to seek information and explanations or to solve problems. The simple words and sentences at their command were related mostly to satisfying immediate needs. Concomitant with their language impairment, these children showed delayed cognitive development in spite of low average IQs.

There was an excessive concreteness and literalness, with a corresponding dearth of abstract thought and minimal capacity to generalize and form concepts. Animation of the inanimate appeared more often than would be expected for this age group. The absence of a reliable system of causality, and a lack of knowledge about their surroundings, combined with a low frustration tolerance, made thinking through and solving problems extremely difficult for them. Importantly, related to the children's heavy reliance on external cues, we found that once they learned to do something one way, or one meaning for a new word, it was extremely difficult, or sometimes not possible, to teach them to use another way or a second meaning. Thus, the tendency toward literalness and inflexibility, noted in their imitation and emotional response to people, also was apparent in their language and thought processes.

Finally, with all their immaturity and their efforts to *appear* grown up these children did possess certain abilities above age expectancy. They often took on responsibility beyond their years. They could go shopping across dangerous intersections, feed babies at night, make decisions for their parents and accomplish a variety of other advanced activities. Such advanced capacities coupled with the children's immaturities in other areas resulted in the uneven, disparate development which was perhaps the children's most distinguishing characteristic.

INFLUENCE OF THE ENVIRONMENT

Those familiar with studies on the effects of maternal deprivation in institutionalized children (2, 3, 4, 8, 11) will recognize that many of the leading characteristics of the preschool children described here correspond to those reported in such studies. This raises the possibility that characteristics such as shallow, nonspecific relationships; delayed language and cognitive development; low level of initiative; diminished interest in and enjoyment from themselves and others, and quiet, docile and conforming behavior (despite impaired capacity to modulate and control impulses) may be related to the effect of maternal deprivation, which exists for these children as a dynamic process in spite of their being family-reared. For although the children do not grow up in the sterile, orderly, quiet atmosphere of an institution, they nevertheless lack consistent care from the same person. Growing up in a noisy, hectic apartment with a mother whose physical and emotional presence is unreliable and who is frequently overwhelmed by the manifold burdens of the household and the care of many small children, these children frequently are left alone for hours. As babies they may be put off by themselves in a crib and are isolated from stimulation for most of each day. They are fed with propped bottles without being checked regardless of the cause of their cries. If they lose the nipple and are unable to retrieve it or to hold onto the bottle, their needs may go unattended. When the mothers are present, their own needs interfere with their capacity to give to their children. In general there is little holding, comforting and handling involved in the mother's child care. A quiet child is considered a "good" child, and self-activation and motor capacity are welcome if they answer the mother's need and expectation to have her child grow up fast and do not place any demands upon her. Toys are minimal, usually kept out of reach and often inappropriate. But more important, the children are rarely played with, talked to and given explanations. In short, the varied physical, emotional and intellectual stimulations of a mutually enjoyable relationship to the mother are minimal.

The deviant development of these children, however, cannot be completely described or fully understood in terms of deprivation alone. It is not only a matter of delay and deficiency, it is also uneven and anachronistic.

These disparate features of the children's development led us to consider other formative influences in their environmental and relationship experiences in addition to deprivation. In this quest certain qualities of the children not previously reported or emphasized in studies of deprived children caught our attention. These qualities were the children's danger orientation; their high anxiety level and trend toward diffuse motor discharge; their pseudoautonomy and proclamations of an independence they did not possess; their reliance on visual and auditory hyperalertness to orient and protect themselves, and finally the literalness of their imitation, learning and thinking.

These features led, in our thinking, to an emphasis on the influence of real danger, self-preservation and survival in the children's development. Even brief consideration of their environment underscores the kind of danger these children are exposed to early and continuously in their lives.

They must bear the brunt of harsh punishment and parental loss of control. They are yelled at, slapped, and beaten in inconsistent, confusing ways. They are punished for accidents as well as intentional naughtiness, for things they haven't done as well as things they have done; even for things that previously and on other occasions they have been encouraged to do. They are exposed to their mothers' devaluating criticisms. The children's efforts to achieve and produce, their expressions of assertion and selfhood, their products and even their sexual identities are derogated. Publicly their parents will deride them with comments like, "Who is she; she's a nobody." Or, "He *thinks* he's a boy." These children witness parental drunkenness, battles and sexual activities and experience parental neglect and abuse. Alcoholism, violence, promiscuity and prostitution are not abstract concepts, but home and neighborhood life experiences for them. Unpredictably their mothers leave them alone, or in the unreliable care of others. Threatened desertion, homelessness and police action continually hang over their heads.

Gradually, as we reflected on the impact of these ubiquitous dangers to the children, a conceptual framework emerged. This framework differs from past conceptions in the emphasis it places on the role of outer danger in the children's life adjustment. The remainder of this paper will be devoted to presenting in condensed form the major points of this conceptual framework.

To begin with, disorganized families live in (and their children grow up in) a "desert" and a "jungle." By "desert" we mean the barren wasteland of unmet, neglected needs in their family and social lives which constitute *deprivation*. By "jungle" we mean the confusing, untamed family and neighborhood world of impulsivity, excess and asocial patterning which constitutes *real external danger*. To illustrate our concept of "desert" or deprivation, as opposed to "jungle" or external danger, let us describe a few interrelated contrasts in the children's environment. These children are brought up by narcissistic mothers who are frequently physically or emotionally absent. On the other hand, they are confusedly shifted and shunted around in unpredictable ways among too many adults. Many are permitted to have certain kinds of seductive, physical contact with their mothers. The children are reared by mothers who are limited in their capacity to give and frustrate excessively; on the other hand, the children are overindulged and infantilized. They grow up in a world of general apathy, inactivity and "depression" in a derelict, normless society. By contrast, they are exposed to erratic, violent, aggressive outbursts and instinctually overwhelming sights and sounds. In their homes and neighborhoods toys and play are minimal or absent; on the other hand, they become involved in "games" that are not play and "fun" that is forbidden.

The role of external danger is emphasized because it has generally not been given recognition in the literature on multiproblem families, whereas, by contrast, deprivation has received considerable attention as the dominant or sometimes sole etiological factor. We wish to make it clear, however, that we realize that external danger and deprivation are for the most part inseparable. Deprivations such as separation or temporary desertion and insufficient love and protection are also dangers. Dangers such as harsh punishment and exposure to sexual experiences also involve deprivations in regard to what is missing in the children's experiences with their parents. We further recognize that the most profound influence on the children's development comes from the combined effects of these forces. For example, the depriving and punishing mothers become discomforting, frightening and feared persons, and this overwhelming and dominant quality of the mothers probably has the most far-reaching effects on the children. Nevertheless, external danger in the family and neighborhood lives of the children is so marked and influential that it must be taken into account separately as well as in combination with deprivation. Therefore, for heuristic purposes we will discuss it separately.

THE ROLE OF EXTERNAL DANGER

We postulate that external danger in the children's lives mobilizes early and continuous self-preservative interests and emphasizes survival first and foremost. Hence the children develop an early coping orientation to life and show considerable efforts toward compensation. They use what they have developed to make up for their own deficiencies and to cope with their dangerous family and neighborhood environments. They develop early facility to know well what adults like, dislike or fear; to manipulate the environment and to present themselves endearingly if need be (1).

It is particularly in terms of the ego that danger and survival considerations play a role. Four interrelated characteristics observed in the children illustrate this influence.

1. *Danger orientation.* Although these children showed the facile friendliness and appealing manner which is very like other deprived children, we were struck by their distrustfulness, tension and guardedness. Despite their surface contentment, we were aware that their high level of anxiety and furtive looks betrayed their danger orientation. In the nursery school if something happened suddenly or unexpectedly, they reacted as though it were bad or threatening. If the juice spilled, or a block building were bumped into, all of the children reacted as though they were guilty and would be punished. There was no such thing as an accident; the concept seemed as foreign to them as the idea of intention. Even incidental happenings or passing events were reacted to as dangerous, and the children needed to be ever on the lookout for the worst to occur.

2. *The children showed visual and auditory hyperalertness to some stimuli while they were hypoalert to others.* They were alert to the sounds and sights of the street, to the teacher's whereabouts and attention, to whom she was with, and to who was receiving something. They were hyperreactive in this manner to such an extent that they were not alert to, or sometimes even responsive to, the teacher's spoken directions or to a display of colored paper, scissors and paste set out by her to

stir their curiosity and interest. It was as though these stimuli could not compete for the children's attention in view of their preoccupation with the task of avoiding potentially noxious situations. A feature of the children's hyperreactivity was their use of vision to protect themselves in new situations, when a new person entered the room or when they were uncertain. In these circumstances the children showed intense visual scanning of the environment. They attempted to use visual recognition and analysis as a means of orienting themselves and showed particular adeptness in reading external, observable cues. It appeared that the children "navigated" through life situations by triangulation rather than by a built-in guidance system.

In relation to the children's hyperalertness to the teacher and her whereabouts, we noted that while they attempted to prevent the teacher's being too distant, they also did not let her get too close. It was as though they had to protect both against painful distance (loss of the teacher's attention, experiencing her giving to another, being exposed to her leaving) and against painful closeness (intrusion, vulnerability to their dependent longings, unexpected punishment, rejection or devaluation). Either extreme was too dangerous.

3. In contrast to their vigilance concerning their surroundings, *the children availed themselves to many forms of denial such as avoidance, evasion, obliviousness and ignoring (5).* The children avoided particularly noxious outside stimuli by not being aware of them. For example, they handled the major and repeated threat of actual separation from their mothers by being oblivious to its existence. Similarly, although the children kept careful track of the teacher's whereabouts when she was in the room, they ignored her when she left the room. We saw these as examples of a massive, primitive form of denial by not perceiving.

4. Finally, *the children revealed certain areas of "hypertrophied" ego functioning, areas of advanced ability.* We noted that these "precocious" abilities had high survival value for the children. The kind of above-age expectancy functioning that we have in mind in using the term "precocious" is, for example, the children's role reversal with their parents, such as making decisions for them, baby-sit-

ting, protecting and caring for infants and younger siblings. In this role reversal several of the children's coping capacities, stimulated by danger and survival considerations, combine: their need to avoid parental punishment if they displease, their use of observable cues to orient themselves and their facility to imitate and learn by rote. The process is further reinforced by their parents' demand that they function in certain grown-up ways and the high premium placed by the parents on having their own needs met.

The children's advanced abilities play an important part in their efforts, often successful, to compensate for deficiencies in themselves and others, and to cope with their deviant milieu. By virtue of their getting-along orientation, they are able to maintain elements of security in their lives; by virtue of their use of hearing and vision to scan their environment alertly for signals of possible danger and to size up and adjust to a situation, the children provide themselves with some semblance of safety (*10*). By these means they are less vulnerable to the realistic dangers around them. They have sufficient protection so that the frequent traumata of their existence which can, under other circumstances, disrupt and fragment personalities, do not produce in them atypical, psychotic-like end results. In view of the confusion, danger and disorganization which surrounds them, this is no small or insignificant accomplishment.

Clearly, the children's ability to cope and areas of hypertrophied ego functioning are among their strengths. We believe, however, that these "strengths" are also weaknesses and that in the final analysis they contribute to the children's literalness and inflexibility and to the fixation in their development. *Although the children are assisted by their need for self-preservation and stimulated by external danger to adjust to their special kind of life space, they pay a price for this assistance.*

The children of these families are, for example, pressed into service at an early age, and as young as three years are sent to do the family shopping. To accomplish this they must cross busy, heavily travelled streets without benefit of stop lights; they must find their way to and from the store, and hand or tell the storekeeper a short list of desired items, then give him the money or request that he charge it on the family bill. Now clearly for three- or five-year-old children this is an advanced accomplishment involving multiple skills. On the other hand, when our nursery school teacher on several occasions took the children to visit the neighborhood store in order to build upon this natural skill and common experience, she was surprised. She found that, taken by a different route, they did not seem to know their way around the store, nor the names of common items on the shelves. They showed little interest or curiosity, but when asked, "What do you get at the store?" they rapidly rattled off the names of a few everyday items which obviously came from memorized lists. This illustration reveals the weakness involved in one of the children's "precocious" abilities. The children's shopping ability was not an internal adaptive capacity, but rather a premature coping pattern learned by rote. Consequently, it remained inflexibly stereotyped and did not lend itself to elaboration or generalization. Correspondingly, in dramatic play in nursery school, when it developed, the children did not repeat or elaborate in fantasy "playing store" or "going shopping."

Similarly the children's heavy reliance on vision to read cues, to reflect imitatively and to be on the lookout for danger is useful, but they pay a price for this capability in the degree to which they are further bound to external stimuli. We feel that the children's being bound to external stimuli contributes to the rigid literalness of their learning and imitation and to the concreteness of their thinking (6).

In other words, our descriptive data suggest that under the pressures of outer danger and the need to grow up fast, these children grow up too fast and relinquish their childhoods too early. Their early independence and premature coping and defensive ability do not lead to later full independence. It is our impression that the children's premature capacity to adjust leads to early closure of their development whereby genuine mastery and flexible adaptability are forfeited.

Our findings also suggest that it may be that the children's experiences with their discomforting, inappropriately overstimulating,

punitive, and at times frightening mothers have prompted them to turn away from their mothers and to invest in themselves and their own equipment and capacity to avoid pain (9). This experience has promoted distrust of others; keeping a safe distance and manipulative control of the situation interfere with and substitute for close affective relations. Thus the children have turned away from certain passive experiences involving entrusting oneself completely to another, which would have provided a cornerstone for certain critical inner developments.

SUMMARY

In summary, then, we have attempted to emphasize that multiproblem, hard-to-reach, disorganized families exist on the lower end of a continuum of lower-class families. The composition of the previously unserved children of these families with those of less disorganized families along this range will assist in the overall process of developing a clearer perspective on the important, nationwide problems of "deprived" or "disadvantaged" children, which is necessary if we are to plan, carry out and evaluate therapeutic and/or educational programs for these children carefully and effectively. In an effort to contribute to this process of gaining perspective, we have presented descriptive findings on the psychological characteristics and developmental deviation of 21 preschool children seen in a demonstration, therapeutic-educational nursery school program. We have related some of these characteristics to the presence in the children's family and neighborhood lives of maternal deprivation and real external danger. A conceptualization of the influence of external danger on the children's deviant development was offered. The salient features of this viewpoint are:

1. Disorganized, multiproblem families live in, and their children grow up in, an environment that rightly can be designated as a "desert" (deprivation) and a "jungle" (external danger). The children of these families cannot be understood from the viewpoint of deprivation alone. One can only gain a full perspective on how these children differ from other studied groups of deprived children if one also takes into account the influence of

excess and external danger in their environment.

2. We postulate that external danger in the lives of these children mobilizes early and continuous self-preservative interests and emphasizes survival first and foremost. Hence the children develop an early coping, "getting-along" orientation to life and show considerable efforts toward compensation.

3. We consider that the influence of these factors on ego development is seen particularly in the children's danger orientation, perceptual hyperalertness, use of various forms of denial and areas of advanced or anachronistic development.

4. These areas of advanced ability play an important role in the children's efforts to compensate for deficiencies in themselves and others and to cope with their deviant milieu. But these very abilities, which are among the children's strengths, are also their weaknesses; they contribute to the relative literalness and inflexibility of the children, and to the fixation of their development. These weaknesses pose a major handicap in their lives, especially with regard to successful functioning and learning in school.

REFERENCES

1. BLOS, P. 1963. Discussion in symposium on developmental approach to problems of acting out. *Amer. J. of Child Psychiat.*, 2(1), 68-71.

2. BOWLBY, J. 1951. *Maternal Care and Mental Health*, World Health Organization, Geneva. Monograph No. 2.

3. GESELL, A., and C. AMATRUDA, 1947. Developmental diagnosis: Normal and abnormal child development. In *Clinical Methods and Pediatric Applications.* 2nd Ed., Hoeber, New York.

4. GOLDFARB, W. 1945. Effects of psychological deprivation in infancy and subsequent stimulation. *Amer. J. Psychiat.*, *102*, 18-33.

5. FREUD, A. 1936. *The Ego and the Mechanisms of Defense.* International Universities Press, New York. Pp. 190-191.

6. MALONE, C. A. 1963. Some Observations on children of disorganized families and problems of acting out. *Amer. J. Child Psychiat.*, 2(1), 22-41.

7. PAVENSTEDT, E. 1965. A comparison of the child-rearing environment of upper-lower and very low-lower class families. *Amer. J. Orthopsychiat.*, *35*(1), 89-93.

8. PROVENCE, S., and H. C. LIPTON. 1962. *Infants in Institutions.* International Universities Press, New York.

9. RITVO, S., and A. J. SOLNIT. 1958. Influences of early mother-child interaction on identification processes. *Psychoanalytic Study of the Child*, *13*, 64-85. New York: International Universities Press.

10. SANDLER, J. 1960. The Background of Safety. *Internat. J. Psycho-analysis*, *41*, 352.

11. SPITZ, R. A., and A. M. WOLF. 1946. Hospitalism: an inquiry into the genesis of psychiatric conditions in early childhood. *The Psychoanalytic Study of the Child*, *1*, 53-74. International Universities Press, New York.

44. COMPENSATORY EDUCATION FOR CULTURAL DEPRIVATION *

B. S. BLOOM, A. DAVIS, AND R. HESS

During the past three decades there has been a tremendous influx into the large cities of children who do not seem able to take ad-

* From *Compensatory Education for Cultural Deprivation* by Benjamin S. Bloom, Allison Davis, and Robert Hess. Copyright © 1965 by Holt, Rinehart and Winston, Inc. Reprinted by permission of Holt, Rinehart and Winston, Inc.

vantage of the educational opportunities offered by the conventional elementary school. Methods and materials which have served the average child well do not seem to help the culturally disadvantaged child acquire the vital communication and computation skills which are so necessary to achievement of educational goals. Conventional approaches to the acquiring of these skills make learning demands on disadvantaged children which they simply are not able to meet. The gaps between the learning tasks and the "readiness" of the children are a source of frustration to the teachers as well as the children. All too quickly, the teacher and the child are ready to give up the struggle—both with a terrible sense of being defeated.

As was pointed out in the previous section, the culturally deprived child comes to school with deficits in learning sets and the ability to "learn to learn." Since he lacks particular experiences and since he is at a relatively low level of linguistic development, he is usually not ready to begin his learning at the same level and by the same approach as is characteristic of children from favorable cultural environments. Unless the school reshapes its curriculum and methods to begin with the child where he is, learning cannot proceed in a fruitful and meaningful way.

Present school practices do not succeed in overcoming the initial differences between culturally advantaged and culturally disadvantaged children. Instead, what start as small measurable differences in the first grade become larger each year. By the end of the sixth year of school, there is a cumulative deficit in the school achievement of the culturally disadvantaged children which shows up most clearly in the tool subjects of reading and arithmetic. But, even in the measures of general intelligence many of these children appear to decline during the period of grade 1 to grade 6. It is this cumulative deficit which must be reversed as early as possible in the culturally deprived child's school career.

The child from the culturally deprived home comes to school with an interest in the new experiences but without some of the experiences, skills, and values typical of the middle-class child. The culturally advantaged child has been amply rewarded for his previous learning, and he is likely to begin school valuing achievement (and specifically school achievement) as a good in its own right. In contrast, the culturally deprived child has difficulty in learning for its own sake and in learning for the approval of an adult. He values things and activities which are concrete and which have immediate and tangible rewards. He has difficulty in seeing the relevance of much of school learning since he is unable to comprehend fully or accept the deferred and symbolic gratification that the middle-class child has come to accept. As each year of school goes by, the culturally disadvantaged child suffers further frustration and failure. He is rarely rewarded or approved in the school and is penalized and disapproved of more strongly each year. As this increasing failure becomes apparent to the child and to all who are concerned with him (parents, teachers, school administrators), the child becomes alienated from the school program. He recognizes that there is little likelihood that he will get satisfaction from his schoolwork and he seeks satisfying experiences elsewhere. He usually turns to his peers for more satisfying relations than he has with adults. For this as well as for other reasons, the peer group becomes more central in the life of lower-class children far earlier than it does for middle-class children.

The culturally deprived child has some special difficulties because the school learning environment and materials are so very different from the settings which are familiar to him. However, it is in the reduced physical activity of the school and in the demand for long spans of attention that he is at a special disadvantage as compared with children from culturally advantaged homes. It is difficult for him to learn to be quiet and to attend to a flow of words (many of which he does not understand) from the teacher.

The elementary school teacher is expected to use the conventional materials and methods of the elementary school curriculum for all children. As the teacher becomes frustrated because of the relatively poor progress of the culturally disadvantaged children, she is likely to place the blame on the children (or their parents) rather than on the curriculum and methods of instruction. The discouragement of the teacher is communicated to the children. Finally, the teacher faced with restless children learning poorly views her task as primarily one of maintaining discipline and order. Teacher and child alike seek ways of getting out of what has come to be a bad situation for both. While it is possible for the teachers and school administrators to

blame the home and the parents for the difficulties these children have in learning, this
placement of blame does little good for the
child or the teacher who must deal with him.
Furthermore, this placement of blame does
little to attack the central problem which is
the improvement of the learning of the child
as early as possible in his school career.

The first three years of the elementary
school are critical. If learning is not successful and satisfying in these years, the entire
educational career of the child is seriously
jeopardized. The child's interest in school
learning, the problems of the school dropout,
and the educational and vocational career of
the individual are largely determined by what
takes place in the first few years of public
school.

Even more serious than the lack of effective conventional school learning is the effect
of continuous failure on the child's image of
himself and his attitude toward others. It is
a serious blow to one's pride to suffer failure
time and time again. Success gives one courage to attempt more and more complex tasks
—failure does not.

SOME IMPLICATIONS FOR
THE SCHOOLS

Since the present introductory years of the
elementary school do not effectively prepare
the culturally deprived child for the later years
of school, it is the clear responsibility of the
schools to devise a more effective school program for these children.

The development of a more effective school
program for these children can do much to
help them solve the learning tasks of the school
and at the same time acquire a more adequate
self-image. It is in the interest of the school
to halt the cumulative deficits of these children
as early as possible in order to make later
instruction and learning increasingly effective.
Ideally, a solution to the learning problems of
these children in the first few grades of elementary school should mean that the existing
school programs at later grades are likely to
become more effective, and there will be less
need for drastic modification of these school
curricula.

It would be most efficient and effective if
the early learning in the home prepared these
children for the elementary school. Where
the home cannot provide this preparation, it
would be in the interests of the child and the
school if this could be done during the nursery
school-kindergarten period. If circumstances
prevent these solutions or attacks on the problem, then the earlier in the elementary school
that appropriate school programs are made
available to these children, the better for all
concerned.

There is increasing evidence that elementary
school programs have been developed which
reduce the cumulative deficits in learning.
Some of these school programs appear to have
such powerful effects in the improvement of
reading, language (including speech), and
arithmetic that the differences between culturally disadvantaged and culturally advantaged children become very small.

The schools must recognize the complexity
of the educational problem of these children
and must not expect to solve these problems
by some single change such as a new textbook,
a more favorable teacher-pupil ratio, a teaching machine, etc. The basic problem is to
start with the child where he is and to proceed
by a carefully developed and sequential program to bring him up to a level where he
can learn as well as other children and eventually under the same conditions as other
children.

If an effective program of nursery school
and kindergarten education has already been
established, there should be less need for
marked changes in the methods and curriculum
of the elementary school. The following recommendations are made on the assumption that
the majority of culturally deprived children
still begin school at Grade 1 and that this
will be true for some time to come.

RECOMMENDATIONS

1. *Evidence should be obtained on each child
at the beginning of the first grade to determine
the levels he has reached with regard to perceptual development, language development,
ability to attend, and motivation for learning.*

Such evidence may be obtained by the use
of previous records and special tests as well
as by observing the child in actual learning
situations for several weeks. On the basis of
this evidence, an educational prescription

should be written for the child and he should be placed with others in an appropriate section with a teacher who can best provide what he needs.

2. *In each school, there should be a number of approaches to introductory learning, and each child should be placed in the approach which is most appropriate for him.*

Some of these approaches might stress early learning and readiness, others could stress an experience approach to language and reading; and, still others might stress the present regular programs of reading and arithmetic. Ideally, each teacher should become a specialist in a particular approach to learning as well as a specialist in dealing with a particular range of learning problems.

Since these first years are so important, these should be the years in which each teacher has the smallest number of children (preferably less than 20); each teacher should be aided by specialists in speech, reading, and school psychology; and each teacher should be aided by a pool of curriculum materials, games, self-learning devices, and other learning materials. The use of teaching aids and assistants can do much to improve the effectiveness of instruction in these grades.

3. *The emphasis in the first three years of elementary school should be on the development of each child with careful evaluation records of his progress toward clear-cut tasks and goals. In these years, the child should not be failed or expected to repeat a grade or year. The careful sequential development of each child must be one of continual success at small tasks.*

4. *A national commission of teachers and other specialists should be created to co-ordinate and to develop the curricular guidelines, materials, and methods for the first three years of elementary school for culturally deprived children. This commission should develop several alternative approaches to the problem and should evaluate the effectiveness of such curricula.*

Much of the initial work of this commission may be to appraise the effectiveness of some of the promising approaches already being used in some of the schools in large cities.

5. *The teaching staff for the first three years of school should be carefully selected and have many opportunities for in-service education on the curriculum problems of these years. They should be so organized that they can provide continuity and sequential development for each child. They should regard their central task as helping each child master the fundamental skills in language, reading, and arithmetic as well as develop a general skill in learning itself.*

The teachers must be free to try new approaches to these goals and should regard themselves as the key persons in helping each child create the base on which the entire educational (and vocational) future of the individual depends. Salary, status, and training should be commensurate with this great responsibility.

6. *Since the home is so important in the work of the schools—especially in the elementary school period—every effort must be made to strengthen the relation between the home and the school. Parents must be involved in such a way that they can understand the importance of this level of schooling and so that they can provide support and reinforcement for the learning tasks of the school. Both teachers and parents must come to understand the ways in which the learning progress of all children is a dual task involving home and school.*

The schools must find ways of involving parents by imaginative devices such as special tutoring by the more able parents. Most central is the recognition by teachers and parents of the role of the parents in raising the aspirations of children and in the valuing of education and learning as a major means of gaining security and mobility.

It is hoped that the involvement of the home and appropriate changes in school district regulations to reduce pupil transfers will do much to increase the continuity of relationship between each child and his teacher. This continuity is important in insuring sequence of learning and the establishment of the necessary human relationships for effective learning.

7. *For culturally disadvantaged children who have not had the benefits of a revised curriculum in the first years of school there should be an all out effort to halt the cumulative deficits in learning achievement at the*

later grades. While this is likely to be increasingly difficult as the child gets older, every resource should be available to the teachers at these levels. If it is necessary to sacrifice some aspects of the curriculum in order to bring these children to higher levels of achievement, the emphasis should be on the language development of the child, reading, and arithmetic.

A longer school day, summer programs, small group instruction, teacher assistants and tutoring programs, the aid of specialists, the use of diagnostic instruments, and the development of more effective instructional materials for this age group should all contribute to the educational development of these children.

The adolescent period is the period in which the individual attempts to create a new identity for himself and this is a period when he is especially open to new experiences which will help him determine who he is and what he might become. This is the period in which the peer group becomes very important in the life of the individual while the parents and other adults becomes less central than they were. This is also the period in which the individual looks to the future to determine what are the realities ahead for him and what he must do to prepare for these realities as he perceives them.

If the individual regards higher education as appropriate and available for him, his learning at the adolescent level proceeds relatively smoothly. If he does not hope and aspire for higher education and sees no relevance of secondary education for his occupational future, he "marks time" until he is permitted to drop out of school or until he completes secondary education—if pressed hard to do so.

By the beginning of secondary school, the typical culturally disadvantaged student is reading at a level approximately 3½ years below grade level. He is considerably retarded in arithmetic and other school subjects. His problem solving and abstract thinking is at a very low level as compared with others at this grade or age level. For these students there is a disaffection with school such that the student approaches learning tasks in a most apathetic manner.

There is little participation in the extracurricular activities of the school other than athletics. Indeed, it would appear that most of the school activities are attractive primarily for the college-bound student.

Few of the culturally deprived students at the secondary level have clear vocational goals or the motivation to persist in a learning program which may enable them to make vocational choices.

Combined with these deficits in learning and motivation, many of these students have developed a level of hostility and rebellion against school authorities, teachers, and other adults which interferes with learning and which makes their own lives one of continual resentment against individuals and forces around them.

The culturally disadvantaged student has all too frequently given up hope for the future. Frustrated by the school's demands and by its repeated punishment (and lack of rewards), he sees little relevance in present school learning for the realities he perceives ahead. All that is interesting and meaningful at this stage is his membership in a peer society which finds no place for itself in the school.

The peer society provides for many lower-class youth a very exciting and rewarding life. Such a society enables him to become relatively independent of adult control. In such a society he has opportunities for becoming a leader or for participating in significant activities under leaders he admires and with others who share a common set of interests and values. The peer society frequently provides relationships between girls and boys at a level of intensity far beyond that approved by adults or social institutions like the school, church, or community organizations. Put in other terms, the school with its emphasis on learning tasks, deferred gratifications, and adult-controlled social activity has a difficult time in competing with a peer society which offers exciting and meaningful activity with immediate and powerful rewards quite independent of adult controls.

The secondary school system has functioned as a selective system giving its major attention to the youth who are able to complete it successfully and priding itself primarily on the youth who are in college preparatory programs.

The schools have not been able to find ways of reaching in a very vital way approximately one-third of the youth who begin secondary education.

It is the establishment of one's identity which is undoubtedly the central developmental task of adolescence. The individual is beginning to make a balance sheet of the negative and positive aspects of his personality and character. He sees himself as somewhat alienated and different from his parents and is groping for models of persons who best combine the characteristics he admires. He would like to become more like these models and he begins to imitate some of the more superficial characteristics of these models, that is, dress, appearance, and mannerisms. He is also desperately searching for a set of values and attitudes which will give meaning to his life and which will make him a unique individual who has worth in his own eyes, and perhaps in the eyes of others. Finally, he (or she) is seeking to establish his own adequacy as a male or female in our society. This definition of adequacy involves attractiveness to members of the opposite sex as well as adequacy as a male or female in the eyes of members of his (or her) own sex. In our society this sense of adequacy is also related to being able to enter a vocation (or marriage) which will give him sufficient material resources to enable him to lead at least as good a life as his parents. For some, this notion of a vocation includes satisfaction in the work, status, and the opportunity to contribute to others.

As one views the problems of the adolescent, and especially those of the culturally disadvantaged adolescent, against the present organization and curriculum of the schools, it becomes clear that the schools are not meeting the special needs of this group. This occurs partly because the school is only one of the social institutions in the community which has a sense of responsibility for this group, and all too frequently these different social institutions have no way of working together on a common set of problems. In part, also, the schools and the other social institutions are working in traditional ways while the larger society—the city, the economy, and the government—is changing so rapidly that traditional approaches to the problem are no longer adequate. Finally, the core of the over-all problem is that a rapidly changing society raises questions about traditional values, as does the adolescent society, and there are no simple ways for developing a new set of values quickly.

IMPLICATIONS FOR THE SCHOOLS (AND COMMUNITY)

The schools working alone can do a great deal for some culturally disadvantaged adolescents. Working alone, the schools can do somewhat less for a sizeable portion of this group. Only as the schools combine their efforts with the efforts of other community agencies and cooperate with industry and government can the problems facing the majority of these adolescents be effectively solved.

In a society which has need for a constantly increasing portion of its youth to secure higher education, some more concerted effort must be made to enable a larger portion of these youth to secure higher education. In the culturally disadvantaged group there is a sizeable proportion of the youth (perhaps one-third) who can aspire to higher education and who should be enabled to secure this higher education.

RECOMMENDATIONS

1. *A major effort must be made to identify, by the beginning of secondary education, a sizeable group of deprived students who can with appropriate continual effort on the part of the school be enabled to complete secondary education successfully and begin higher education. These students must be offered special instructional programs, tutorial help as needed, increased counseling, and help on the basic skills and tool subjects (for example, Higher Horizons Project).*

It is quite possible that these students could, by a system of tutoring less able students, be able to satisfy their own needs for service to others and at the same time begin to make their own aspirations for higher education more realistic. (Thus, a system of remuneration for tutoring other students including the younger students could be supported by the state and national government so that each year the student from the 9th through the 12th grade could receive some pay while an equal amount was put in a special higher education fund to be made available when he entered a higher educational institution.) The point of all this is that each individual needs to make real his aspirations for the future while at the same time he needs to have a sense of independence as well as a sense of dedication and service to others. Such a system of earning his way by tutoring others could remove the stigma of being a special recipient of philanthropy or charity.

2. *Culturally disadvantaged adolescents who are having great difficulty with the regular school curricula should have a school program which emphasizes the basic skills of language and reading and they should be permitted to specialize in an area in which they are especially interested.*

Such a program would reduce the emphasis on general education courses and would permit the student to go as far as he can go in some area of specialization. Such specialization could begin as early as the 9th year of school.

It is especially important for these students to have a detailed diagnosis of their special weaknesses and strengths in the basic skills and be helped by appropriate remedial measures, tutorial instruction, and more effective curricular materials.

3. *For these youth, there should be work-study plans in which students can learn in relation to the work. This requires very effective co-operation between schools, industry, and public agencies.*

Work on blind-alley positions which involve little opportunity for learning would have little value for the student. It is quite possible that work-study programs could be developed in which the type of work experiences are arranged in an increasing order of complexity from jobs that could be learned in a single week to jobs that require many weeks to master. If then, students could begin with simple jobs, learn them and then move to more complex jobs, they could develop some of the basic abilities of learning to work and learning to adapt to different work situations. Ideally, a student might have four to six work experiences during the age period 16 to 19. A student in these work experiences should be appropriately supervised and helped to learn both on the job and in the school. The student should be moved to as complex a type of work as he can master and increasingly his work experiences should be related to the types of jobs for which there will be greatest need in industry and the community. Students in these work-study plans will need frequent counseling in order to understand the realities of the job market in relation to their own skills and expectations. A specially trained group of counselors will be needed to help these students with their educational-vocational decisions.

4. *For all youth, and especially for the culturally disadvantaged youth, there should be peer societies which have continuity over the age period 14-19 and which provide opportunities for social relations, service to others, and the development of meaningful value patterns. Such peer societies may be organized by appropriate community agencies with the co-operation of the schools.*

This type of peer society requires much more than the present type of extracurricular and social activities of the high school which do not at present have a place for lower-class youth.

In these peer societies there must be a place for key adult personalities in the community. This type of peer society plays a major role in other countries and provides the youth with a meaningful set of relationships and activities. Associated with the peer society should be opportunities for counseling youth, recreational activities, and facilities for group meetings. Ideally, the peer society should enable youth to find support and help from others at a most critical stage in their lives.

45. THE TANGLE OF PATHOLOGY *

U.S. DEPARTMENT OF LABOR

That the Negro American has survived at all is extraordinary—a lesser people might simply have died out, as indeed others have. That the Negro community has not only survived, but in this political generation has entered national affairs as a moderate, humane, and constructive national force is the highest testament to the healing powers of the democratic ideal and the creative vitality of the Negro people.

But it may not be supposed that the Negro American community has not paid a fearful price for the incredible mistreatment to which it has been subjected over the past three centuries.

In essence, the Negro community has been forced into a matriarchal structure which, because it is so out of line with the rest of the American society, seriously retards the progress of the group as a whole, and imposes a crushing burden on the Negro male and, in consequence, on a great many Negro women as well.

There is, presumably, no special reason why a society in which males are dominant in family relationships is to be preferred to a matriarchal arrangement. However, it is clearly a disadvantage for a minority group to be operating on one principle, while the great majority of the population, and the one with the most advantages to begin with, is operating on another. This is the present situation of the Negro. Ours is a society which presumes male leadership in private and public affairs. The arrangements of society facilitate such leadership and reward it. A sub-

* U.S. Dept. of Labor, "The Tangle of Pathology," *The Negro Family: The Case for National Action*, Washington, D.C., March 1965, pp. 29-37 and 43-45.

culture, such as that of the Negro American, in which this is not the pattern, is placed at a distinct disadvantage.

Here an earlier word of caution should be repeated. There is much evidence that a considerable number of Negro families have managed to break out of the tangle of pathology and to establish themselves as stable, effective units, living according to patterns of American society in general. E. Franklin Frazier has suggested that the middle-class Negro American family is, if anything, more patriarchal and protective of its children than the general run of such families. Given equal opportunities, the children of these families will perform as well or better than their white peers. They need no help from anyone, and ask none.

While this phenomenon is not easily measured, one index is that middle-class Negroes have even fewer children than middle-class whites, indicating a desire to conserve the advances they have made and to insure that their children do as well or better. Negro women who marry early to uneducated laborers have more children than white women in the same situation; Negro women who marry at the common age for the middle class to educated men doing technical or professional work have only four-fifths as many children as their white counterparts.

It might be estimated that as much as half of the Negro community falls into the middle class. However, the remaining half is in desperate and deteriorating circumstances. Moreover, because of housing segregation it is immensely difficult for the stable half to escape from the cultural influences of the unstable one. The children of middle-class Negroes often as not must grow up in, or next to the slums, an experience almost unknown to white middle-class children. They are therefore constantly exposed to the pathology of the disturbed group and constantly in danger of being drawn into it. It is for this reason that the propositions put forth in this study may be thought of as having a more or less general application.

In a word, most Negro youth are in *danger* of being caught up in the tangle of pathology that affects their world, and probably a majority are so entrapped. Many of those who escape do so for one generation only: as things now are, their children may have to run the gauntlet all over again. That is not the least vicious aspect of the world that white America has made for the Negro.

Obviously, not every instance of social pathology afflicting the Negro community can be traced to the weakness of family structure. If, for example, organized crime in the Negro community were not largely controlled by whites, there would be more capital accumulation among Negroes, and therefore probably more Negro business enterprises. If it were not for the hostility and fear many whites exhibit towards Negroes, they in turn would

be less afflicted by hostility and fear and so on. There is no one Negro community. There is no one Negro problem. There is no one solution. Nonetheless, at the center of the tangle of pathology is the weakness of the family structure. Once or twice removed, it will be found to be the principal source of most of the aberrant, inadequate, or anti-social behavior that did not establish, but now serves to perpetuate the cycle of poverty and deprivation.

It was by destroying the Negro family under slavery that white America broke the will of the Negro people. Although that will has reasserted itself in our time, it is a resurgence doomed to frustration unless the viability of the Negro family is restored.

MATRIARCHY

A fundamental fact of Negro American family life is the often reversed roles of husband and wife.

Robert O. Blood, Jr. and Donald M. Wolfe, in a study of Detroit families, note that "Negro husbands have unusually low power," and while this is characteristic of all low income families, the pattern pervades the Negro social structure: "the cumulative result of discrimination in jobs. . ., the segregated housing, and the poor schooling of Negro men." In 44 percent of the Negro families studied, the wife was dominant, as against 20 percent of white wives. "Whereas the majority of white families are equalitarian, the largest percentage of Negro families are dominated by the wife."

The matriarchal pattern of so many Negro families reinforces itself over the generations. This process begins with education. Although the gap appears to be closing at the moment, for a long while, Negro females were better educated than Negro males, and this remains true today for the Negro population as a whole.

The difference in educational attainment between nonwhite men and women in the labor force is even greater; men lag 1.1 years behind women.

The disparity in educational attainment of male and female youth age 16 to 21 who were out of school in February 1963, is striking. Among the nonwhite males, 66.3 percent

TABLE 1 Children born per woman age 35 to 44: Wives of uneducated laborers who married young, compared with wives of educated professional workers who married after age 21, white and nonwhite, 1960.[1]

	Children per Woman	
	White	Nonwhite
Wives married at age 14 to 21 to husbands who are laborers and did not go to high school	3.8	4.7
Wives married at age 22 or over to husbands who are professional or technical workers and have completed 1 year or more of college	2.4	1.9

[1] Wives married only once, with husbands present.
Source: 1960 Census, *Women by Number of Children ever Born*, PC(2)3A, table 39 and 40, pp. 199–238.

TABLE 2 Educational attainment of the civilian noninstitutional population 18 years of age and over, March 1964

Color and sex	Median school years completed
White:	
Male	12.1
Female	12.1
Nonwhite:	
Male	9.2
Female	10.0

Source: Bureau of Labor Statistics, unpublished data.

TABLE 3 Percent of nonwhite youth enrolled in school who are 1 or more grades below mode for age, by sex, 1960.

Age	Male	Female
7 to 9 years old	7.8	5.8
10 to 13 years old	25.0	17.1
14 and 15 years old	35.5	24.8
16 and 17 years old	39.4	27.2
18 and 19 years old	57.3	46.0

Source: 1960 Census, *School Enrollment*, PC(2) 5A, table 3, p. 24.

were not high school graduates, compared with 55.0 percent of the females. A similar difference existed at the college level, with 4.5 percent of the males having completed 1 to 3 years of college compared with 7.3 percent of the females.

The poorer performance of the male in school exists from the very beginning, and the magnitude of the difference was documented by the 1960 Census in statistics on the number of children who have fallen one or more grades below the typical grade for children of the same age. The boys have more frequently fallen behind at every age level. (White boys also lag behind white girls, but at a differential of 1 to 6 percentage points.)

In 1960, 39 percent of all white persons 25 years of age and over who had completed 4 or more years of college were women. Fifty-three percent of the nonwhites who had attained this level were women.

However, the gap is closing. By October 1963, there were slightly more Negro men in college than women. Among whites there were almost twice as many men as women enrolled.

There is much evidence that Negro females are better students than their male counterparts.

Daniel Thompson of Dillard University, in a private communication on January 9, 1965, writes:

As low as is the aspirational level among lower class Negro girls, it is considerably higher than among the boys. For example, I have examined the honor rolls in Negro high schools for about 10 years. As a rule, from 75 to 90 percent of all Negro honor students are girls.

Dr. Thompson reports that 70 percent of all applications for the National Achievement Scholarship Program financed by the Ford Foundation for outstanding Negro high school

TABLE 4 Fall enrollment of civilian noninstitutional population in college, by color and sex—October 1963 (in thousands).

Color and Sex	Population, age 14–34, Oct. 1, 1963	Number enrolled	Percent of youth, age 14–34
Nonwhite			
Male	2,884	149	5.2
Female	3,372	137	4.1
White			
Male	21,700	2,599	12.0
Female	20,613	1,451	7.0

Source: U.S. Bureau of the Census, *Current Population Reports*, Series P-20, No. 129 July 24, 1964, tables 1, 5.

graduates are girls, despite special efforts by high school principals to submit the names of boys.

The finalists for this new program for outstanding Negro students were recently announced. Based on an inspection of the names, only about 43 percent of all the 639 finalists were male. (However, in the regular National Merit Scholarship program, males received 67 percent of the 1964 scholarship awards.)

Inevitably, these disparities have carried over to the area of employment and income.

In 1 out of 4 Negro families where the husband is present, as an earner, and someone else in the family works, the husband is not the principal earner. The comparable figure for whites is 18 percent.

More important, it is clear that Negro females have established a strong position for themselves in white collar and professional employment, precisely the areas of the economy which are growing most rapidly, and to which the highest prestige is accorded.

The President's Committee on Equal Employment Opportunity, making a preliminary report on employment in 1964 of over 16,000 companies with nearly 5 million employees, revealed this pattern with dramatic emphasis.

In this work force, Negro males outnumber Negro females by a ratio of 4 to 1. Yet Negro males represent only 1.2 percent of all males in white collar occupations, while Negro females represent 3.1 percent of the total female white collar work force. Negro males represent 1.1 percent of all male professionals, whereas Negro females represent roughly 6 percent of all female professionals. Again, in technician occupations, Negro males represent 2.1 percent of all male technicians while Negro females represent roughly 10 percent of all female technicians. It would appear therefore that there are proportionately 4 times as many Negro females in significant white collar jobs than Negro males.

Although it is evident that office and clerical jobs account for approximately 50 percent of all Negro female white collar workers, it is significant that 6 out of every 100 Negro females are in professional jobs. This is substantially similar to the rate of all females in such jobs. Approximately 7 out of every 100 Negro females are in technician jobs. This exceeds the proportion of all females in technician jobs—approximately 5 out of every 100.

Negro females in skilled jobs are almost the same as that of all females in such jobs. Nine out of every 100 Negro males

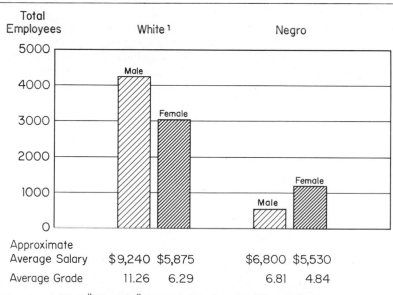

Total Employees	White [1]		Negro	
Approximate Average Salary	$9,240	$5,875	$6,800	$5,530
Average Grade	11.26	6.29	6.81	4.84

1 This is "Non-Negro" and may include some nonwhites other than Negro.

FIGURE 1 Department of Labor employment as of December 31, 1964.

are in skilled occupations while 21 out of 100 of all males are in such jobs.

This pattern is to be seen in the Federal government, where special efforts have been made recently to insure equal employment opportunity for Negroes. These efforts have been notably successful in Departments such as Labor, where some 19 percent of employees are now Negro. (A not disproportionate percentage, given the composition of the work force in the areas where the main Department offices are located.) However, it may well be that these efforts have redounded mostly to the benefit of Negro women, and may even have accentuated the comparative disadvantage of Negro men. Seventy percent of the Negro employees of the Department of Labor are women, as contrasted with only 42 percent of the white employees.

Among nonprofessional Labor Department employees—where the most employment opportunities exist for all groups—Negro women outnumber Negro men 4 to 1, and average almost one grade higher in classification.

The testimony to the effects of these patterns in Negro family structure is widespread, and hardly to be doubted.

WHITNEY YOUNG:

Historically, in the matriarchal Negro society, mothers made sure th..t if one of their children had a chance for higher education the daughter was the one to pursue it.

The effect on family functioning and role performance of this historical experience [economic deprivation] is what you might predict. Both as a husband and as a father the Negro male is made to feel inadequate, not because he is unlovable or unaffectionate, lacks intelligence or even a gray flannel suit. But in a society that measures a man by the size of his pay check, he doesn't stand very tall in a comparison with his white counterpart. To this situation he may react with withdrawal, bitterness toward society, aggression both within the family and racial group, self-hatred, or crime. Or he may escape through a number of avenues that help him to lose himself in fantasy or to compensate for his low status through a variety of exploits.

THOMAS PETTIGREW:

The Negro wife in this situation can easily become disgusted with her financially dependent husband, and her rejection of him further alienates the male from family life. Embittered by their experiences with men, many Negro mothers often act to perpetuate the mother-centered pattern by taking a greater interest in their daughters than their sons.

DETON BROOKS:

In a matriarchal structure, the women are transmitting the culture.

DOROTHY HEIGHT:

If the Negro woman has a major underlying concern, it is the status of the Negro man and his position in the community and his need for feeling himself an important person, free and able to make his contribution in the whole society in order that he may strengthen his home.

DUNCAN M. MACINTYRE:

The Negro illegitimacy rate always has been high—about eight times the white rate in 1940 and somewhat higher today even though the white illegitimacy rate also is climbing. The Negro statistics are symptomatic of some old socioeconomic problems, not the least of which are underemployment among Negro men and compensating higher labor force propensity among Negro women. Both operate to enlarge the mother's role, undercutting the status of the male and making many Negro families essentially matriarchal. The Negro man's uncertain employment prospects, matriarchy, and the high cost of divorces combine to encourage desertion (the poor man's divorce), increases the number of couples not married, and thereby also increases the Negro illegitimacy rate. In the meantime, higher Negro birth rates are increasing the nonwhite population, while migration into cities like Detroit, New York, Philadelphia, and Washington, D.C. is making the public assistance rolls in such cities heavily, even predominantly, Negro.

Robin M. Williams, Jr. in a study of Elmira, New York:

Only 57 percent of Negro adults reported themselves as married—spouse present, as compared with 78 percent of native white American gentiles, 91 percent of Italian-American, and 96 percent of Jewish informants. Of the 93 unmarried Negro youths interviewed, 22 percent did not have their mother living in the home with them, and 42 percent reported that their father was not living in their home. One-third of the youths did not know their father's present occupation, and two-thirds of a sample of 150 Negro adults did not know what the occupation of their father's father had been. Forty percent of the youths said that they had brothers and sisters living in other communities: another 40 percent reported relatives living in their home who were not parents, siblings, or grandparent.

THE FAILURE OF YOUTH

Williams' account of Negro youth growing up with little knowledge of their fathers, less of their fathers' occupations, still less of family occupational traditions, is in sharp contrast to the experience of the white child. The white family, despite many variants, remains a powerful agency not only for transmitting property from one generation to the next, but also for transmitting no less valuable contracts with the world of education and work. In an earlier age, the Carpenters, Wainwrights, Weavers, Mercers, Farmers, Smiths acquired their names as well as their trades from their fathers and grandfathers. Children today still learn the patterns of work

from their fathers even though they may no longer go into the same jobs.

White children without fathers at least perceive all about them the pattern of men working.

Negro children without fathers flounder— and fail.

Not always, to be sure. The Negro community produces its share, very possibly more than its share, of young people who have the something extra that carries them over the worst obstacles. But such persons are always a minority. The common run of young people in a group facing serious obstacles to success do not succeed.

A prime index of the disadvantage of Negro youth in the United States is their consistently poor performance on the mental tests that are a standard means of measuring ability and performance in the present generation.

There is absolutely no question of any genetic differential: Intelligence potential is distributed among Negro infants in the same proportion and pattern as among Icelanders or Chinese or any other group. American society, however, impairs the Negro potential. The statement of the HARYOU report that "there is no basic disagreement over the fact that central Harlem students are performing poorly in school"

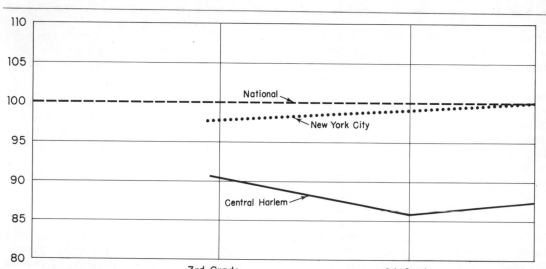

FIGURE 2 By the 8th grade, Central Harlem pupils' average IQ was 87.7 compared to the national norm of 100.

may be taken as true of Negro slum children throughout the United States.

Eighth grade children in central Harlem have a median IQ of 87.7, which means that perhaps a third of the children are scoring at levels perilously near to those of retardation. IQ *declines* in the first decade of life, rising only slightly thereafter.

The effect of broken families on the performance of Negro youth has not been extensively measured, but studies that have been made show an unmistakable influence.

Martin Deutch and Bert Brown, investigating intelligence test differences between Negro and white 1st and 5th graders of different social classes, found that there is a direct relationship between social class and IQ. As the one rises so does the other: but more for whites than Negroes. This is surely a result of housing segregation, referred to earlier, which makes it difficult for middle-class Negro families to escape the slums.

The authors explain that "it is much more difficult for the Negro to attain identical middle- or upper-middle-class status with whites, and the social class gradations are less marked for Negroes because Negro life in a caste society is considerably more homogeneous than is life for the majority group."

Therefore, the authors look for background variables other than social class which might explain the difference: "One of the most striking differences between the Negro and white groups is the consistently higher frequency of broken homes and resulting family disorganization in the Negro group."

Further, they found that children from homes where fathers are present have significantly higher scores than children in homes without fathers.

TABLE 6 Mean intelligence scores of Negro children by school, grade, social class, and by presence of father

Social Class and School Grade	Father present	Father absent
Lowest social class level:		
Grade 1	95.2	87.8
Grade 5	92.7	85.7
Middle social class level:		
Grade 1	98.7	92.8
Grade 5	92.9	92.0

(Adapted from author's table).

	Mean Intelligence Scores
Father Present	97.83
Father Absent	90.79

The influence of the father's presence was then tested *within* the social classes and school grades for Negroes alone. They found that "a consistent trend within both grades at the lower SES [social class] level appears, and in no case is there a reversal of this trend: for males, females, and the combined group, the IQ's of children with fathers in the home are always higher than those who have no father in the home."

The authors say that broken homes "may also account for some of the differences between Negro and white intelligence scores."

The scores of fifth graders with fathers absent were lower than the scores of first

TABLE 5 Father absent from the home.

Lowest social class level		Middle social class level		Highest social class level	
Percent of White	Negro	Percent of White	Negro	Percent of White	Negro
15.4	43.9	10.3	27.9	0.0	13.7

(Adapted from authors' table).

TABLE 7 Percent of nonwhite males enrolled in school, by age and presence of parents, 1960.

Age	Both parents present	One parent present	Neither parent present
5 years	41.7	44.2	34.3
6 years	79.3	78.7	73.8
7 to 9 years	96.1	95.3	93.9
10 to 13 years	96.2	95.5	93.0
14 and 15 years	91.8	89.9	85.0
16 and 17 years	78.0	72.7	63.2
18 and 19 years	46.5	40.0	32.3

Source: 1960 Census, *School Enrollment,* PC(2) 5A, table 3, p. 24.

graders with fathers absent, and while the authors point out that it is cross sectional data and does not reveal the duration of the fathers' absence, "What we might be tapping is the cumulative effect of fatherless years."

This difference in ability to perform has its counterpart in statistics on actual school performance. Nonwhite boys from families with both parents present are more likely to be going to school than boys with only one parent present, and enrollment rates are even lower when neither parent is present.

When the boys from broken homes are in school, they do not do as well as the boys from whole families. Grade retardation is higher when only one parent is present, and highest when neither parent is present.

The loneliness of the Negro youth in making fundamental decisions about education is shown in a 1959 study of Negro and white dropouts in Connecticut high schools. Only 29 percent of the Negro male dropouts discussed their decision to drop out of school with their fathers, compared with 65 percent of the white males (38 percent of the Negro males were from broken homes). In fact, 26 percent of the Negro males did not discuss this major decision in their lives with anyone at all, compared with only 8 percent of white males.

A study of Negro apprenticeship by the New York State Commission Against Discrimination in 1960 concluded:

> Negro youth are seldom exposed to influences which can lead to apprenticeship. Negroes are not apt to have relatives, friends, or neighbors in skilled occupations. Nor are they likely to be in secondary schools where they receive encouragement and direction from alternate role models. Within the minority community, skilled Negro 'models' after whom the Negro youth might pattern himself are rare, while substitute sources which could provide the direction, encouragement, resources, and information needed to achieve skilled craft standing are nonexistent.

* * *

ALIENATION

The term alienation may by now have been used in too many ways to retain a clear meaning, but it will serve to sum up the equally numerous ways in which large numbers of Negro youth appear to be withdrawing from American society.

One startling way in which this occurs is that the men are just not there when the Census enumerator comes around.

According to Bureau of Census population estimates for 1963, there are only 87 nonwhite males for every 100 females in the 30-to-34-year age group. The ratio does not exceed 90 to 100 throughout the 25-to-44-year age bracket. In the urban Northeast, there are only 76 males per 100 females 20-to-24-years of age, and males as a percent of females are below 90 percent throughout all ages after 14.

There are not really fewer men than women in the 20-to-40 age bracket. What obviously is involved is an error in counting: the surveyors simply do not find the Negro man. Donald J. Bogue and his associates, who have studied the Federal count of the Negro man, place the error as high as 19.8 percent at age 28; a typical error of around 15 percent is estimated from age 19 through 43. Preliminary research in the Bureau of the Census on the 1960 enumeration has resulted in similar conclusions, although not necessarily the same estimates of the extent of the error. The Negro male *can* be found at age 17 and 18. On the basis of birth records and mortality records, the conclusion

TABLE 8 Ratio of males per 100 females in the population, by color, July 1, 1963.

	Males per 100 Females	
Age	White	Nonwhite
Under 5	104.4	100.4
5–9 years	103.9	100.0
10–14 years	104.0	100.0
15–19 years	103.2	99.5
20–24 years	101.2	95.1
25–29 years	100.1	89.1
30–34 years	99.2	86.6
35–39 years	97.5	86.8
40–44 years	96.2	89.9
45–49 years	96.5	90.6

Source: *Current Population Reports*, Series P-25, No. 276, table 1, (Total Population Including Armed Forces Abroad).

must be that he is there at age 19 as well.

When the enumerators do find him, his answers to the standard questions asked in the monthly unemployment survey often result in counting him as "not in the labor force." In other words, Negro male unemployment may in truth be somewhat greater than reported.

The labor force participation rates of nonwhite men have been falling since the beginning of the century and for the past decade have been lower than the rates for white men. In 1964, the participation rates were 78.0 percent for white men and 75.8 percent for nonwhite men. Almost one percentage point of this difference was due to a higher proportion of nonwhite men unable to work because of long-term physical or mental illness; it seems reasonable to assume that the rest of the difference is due to discouragement about finding a job.

If nonwhite male labor force participation rates were as high as the white rates, there would have been 140,000 more nonwhite males in the labor force in 1964. If we further assume that the 140,000 would have been unemployed, the unemployment rate for nonwhite men would have been 11.5 percent instead of the recorded rate of 9 percent, and the ratio between the nonwhite rate and the white rate would have jumped from 2:1 to 2.4:1.

Understated or not, the official unemployment rates for Negroes are almost unbelievable.

The unemployment statistics for Negro teenagers—29 percent in January 1965—reflect lack of training and opportunity in the greatest measure, but it may not be doubted that they also reflect a certain failure of nerve.

"Are you looking for a job?" Secretary of Labor Wirtz asked a young man on a Harlem street corner. "Why?" was the reply.

Richard A. Cloward and Robert Ontell have commented on this withdrawal in a discussion of the Mobilization for Youth project on the lower East Side of New York.

What contemporary slum and minority youth probably lack that similar children in earlier periods possessed is not motivation but some minimal sense of competence.

We are plagued, in work with these youth, by what appears to be a low tolerance for frustration. They are not able to absorb setbacks. Minor irritants and rebuffs are magnified out of all proportion to reality. Perhaps they react as they do because they are not equal to the world that confronts them, and they know it. And it is the knowing that is devastating. Had the occupational structure remained intact, or had the education provided to them kept pace with occupational changes, the situation would be a different one. But it is not, and that is what we and they have to contend with.

Narcotic addiction is a characteristic form of withdrawal. In 1963, Negroes made up 54 percent of the addict population of the United States. Although the Federal Bureau of Narcotics reports a decline in the Negro proportion of new addicts, HARYOU reports the addiction rate in central Harlem rose from 22.1 per 10,000 in 1955 to 40.4 in 1961.

There is a larger fact about the alienation of Negro youth than the tangle of pathology described by these statistics. It is a fact particularly difficult to grasp by white persons who have in recent years shown increasing awareness of Negro problems.

The present generation of Negro youth growing up in the urban ghettos has probably less personal contact with the white world than any generation in the history of the Negro American.

Until World War II it could be said that in general the Negro and white worlds lived, if not together, at least side by side. Certainly they did, and do, in the South.

Since World War II, however, the two worlds have drawn physically apart. The symbol of this development was the construction in the 1940's and 1950's of the vast white, middle- and lower-middle class suburbs around all of the Nation's cities. Increasingly the inner cities have been left to Negroes—who now share almost no community life with whites.

In turn, because of this new housing pattern—most of which has been financially assisted by the Federal government—it is probable that the American school system has become *more,* rather than less segregated in the past two decades.

School integration has not occurred in the South, where a decade after *Brown v. Board of Education* only 1 Negro in 9 is attending school with white children.

And in the North, despite strenuous official efforts, neighborhoods and therefore schools are becoming more and more of one class and one color.

In New York City, in the school year 1957-58 there were 64 schools that were 90 percent of more Negro or Puerto Rican. Six years later there were 134 such schools.

Along with the diminution of white middle-class contacts for a large percentage of Negroes, observers report that the Negro churches have all but lost contact with men in the Northern cities as well. This may be a normal condition of urban life, but it is probably a changed condition for the Negro American and cannot be a socially desirable development.

The only religious movement that appears to have enlisted a considerable number of lower class Negro males in Northern cities of late is that of the Black Muslims: a movement based on total rejection of white society, even though it emulates whites more.

In a word: the tangle of pathology is tightening.

RATE – Cases Per 10,000 Population

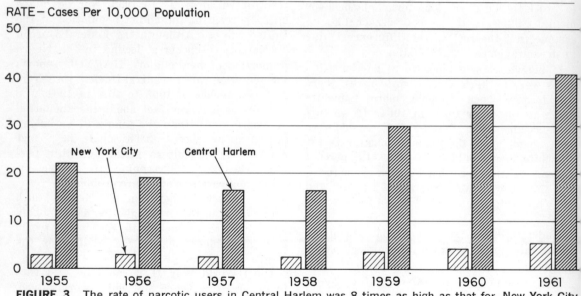

FIGURE 3 The rate of narcotic users in Central Harlem was 8 times as high as that for New York City in 1961.

46. IN NEGRO SCHOOLS *

J. KOZOL

I have described already a few of the people who were teaching in my school, but I have not yet really spoken about the teacher who was, in many ways, the most interesting person of all. She was the Reading Teacher. This lady was interesting to me, first of all, because she was one of the most serious and self-consciously moralistic people whom I have ever known. She was also, by all odds, the most effective and most high-powered of the old-fashioned public school teachers who were still around. She was—finally—an extraordinarily, if at times, quite subtly, bigoted woman. At the same time, however, and like many others in America, she considered herself a politically liberal and enlightened person, was shocked by any imputation of prejudiced behavior and even spoke at great length, and sometimes without much mercy, of certain of the dishonesties and secret bigotries of others. She was, I used to feel, not only one of the most complex people in the school, but also the most tragic. Unlike much of the school faculty, this lady was seldom consciously malevolent to anybody. She worked hard, gave many signs of warmth and fondness to various children, and spoke incessantly of her deep feelings for them. She was precisely the sort of person whom an outside observer would instantly describe as "a dedicated teacher," if for no other reason than because she would tell him so. I think it was this last trait—her capacity for overwhelming self-congratulation — which heightened so greatly the sense of irony that surrounded much of her behavior.

I remember a day when she had come up

into my classroom during lunchtime. She was in one of her moods of exposing the bigotry of other teachers while at the same time rather pridefully extolling her own virtues. "Others may be prejudiced," she was saying to me. "So and so downstairs uses the word 'nigger.' I know, I've heard him say it with my own ears. It makes me sick every time I hear him say that. If a person feels that way I don't know what he's doing teaching at this school. You wouldn't imagine the kinds of things I used to hear . . . Last year there was a teacher in this school who used to call them 'black stuff.' Can you imagine somebody even thinking up a phrase like that? If people are prejudiced, they should not be teaching here."

Another time, she spoke of the same matter in these words: "Others may be prejudiced. I know that I am not. There are hundreds like me. Thank God for that. Some teachers are prejudiced. The majority are not. We are living in a time when everything is changing. Things are going along but they must not change too fast."

I remember that I felt astonished at her certainty. I told her, for my own part, that I would feel very uneasy making that kind of statement. I said that on many occasions I had become convinced that my thinking was prejudiced, sometimes in obvious ways and sometimes in ways that lay deeper and would not have been so easy for other people to observe. Furthermore, I said, I also was convinced that I was prejudiced at a level of depth, and in a manner hardened over so many years, that some of that prejudice undoubtedly would always be within me.

"Well I'm not," she replied to me with much emotion.

* From *Death at an Early Age* by J. Kozol, (Chaps. 3 and 18). Copyright © 1967 Houghton, Mifflin Co., Boston.

I did not try to turn any accusation toward her. Everything I said was directed at "people in general," at "white society," and mainly at myself. I said to the Reading Teacher that, so far as my own feelings were concerned, I had no doubt of what I was saying. I had learned, in some of the work I'd done in Roxbury—certainly in much of the work I'd done for CORE—that more than once I must have hurt somebody's feelings badly by an undercurrent or an unconscious innuendo in my talk or else the people I was talking to just would not have winced the way they had. I said I was certain, from any number of similar moments that there was plenty of regular old-time prejudice in me, just as in almost every other white man I ever saw.

To this, however, the Reading Teacher snapped back at me again, and now with an absolute self-confidence: "In me there is none."

We stood together in the doorway. The children sat in their chairs. It was almost the end of lunchtime. Each child was having his milk except the ones who couldn't afford it. Sometimes white and Negro children chattered with each other, and it was normal and natural and pleasant to watch that, but there were not sufficient white children for it really to happen freely enough. There were not enough children who were not black. The Reading Teacher looked out at the children and she said to me, from where we were standing: "Roger over there, I think, is the most unhappy child in this class." Roger was one of only three white boys in my class. He was sitting behind Stephen. She did not see Stephen sitting in front of him. She said to me: "When I look at them I do not see white or black." I listened to her and looked at her and thought about what she was saying. She said, "I do not see white or black." But I felt really that she saw white much more clearly than she saw black. She saw the quiet and unhappy little white boy. She did not see Stephen before him, his hands all welted and his face all scarred with scabs. "I see no color difference," she told me. "I see children in front of me, not children who are black. It has never made a difference to me. White skin or black skin, they all are made by God."

One day when we talked about it, she told me about a trip she had made to Europe the summer before. She told me that a man on the boat, during the evening, had come across the floor to dance with her. But the man's skin was black. "I knew it was wrong but I honestly could not make myself say yes to that man. It was because he was a Negro. I just could not see myself dancing with that man."

I didn't know if anyone could be condemned for being honest. "What if I fell in love with a Negro girl?" I asked her.

She told me the truth: "I would be shocked."

I said I didn't see why she couldn't dance with a Negro passenger.

"I could not do it."

She also said, "If you married a Negro girl I have to admit that I would feel terribly sad."

I did not have that in my mind, but about what she had been saying I found I was still puzzled. "Would you have Negroes come and visit you or come and have dinner with you in the evening?"

And to that the answer was clear and elucidating and exact: "They could come and visit if I invited them to come but not as you could come to see me. They could not feel free to just drop in on me. I would have to draw the line at that."

Hearing that, I asked myself what this kind of feeling meant in terms of one teacher and one child. This woman had drawn the line "at that" just as the city had drawn the line of the ghetto. A Negro was acceptable, even lovable, if he came out only when invited and at other times stayed back. What did it do to a Negro student when he recognized that his teacher felt that she had to "draw the line at that"? Did it make him feel grateful for the few scraps that he got or did it make him feel bewildered instead that there ought to be any line at all? The Reading Teacher apparently was confident that the line did not descend, in her feelings, to the level of the children—or that, if it did, it would not be detected by them. I gained the impression, on the contrary, that that line was very much in evidence in the classroom and that many of the children were aware of it.

There were two ways in which I thought the Reading Teacher would unknowingly but consistently reveal the existence of that line. One of them, certainly the less important, was in the occasional favors that she showed and in the kinds of arrangements that she would make for various children. To one of my pupils I remember that she brought in and gave as a present a really fine and expensive children's book. I recall that she brought it in and handed it to the child in full view of the class and spoke of how much the little girl deserved it and of how warmly she admired her. For another child, she did something different. He was a poor boy from a large family and so she tried to arrange a stay for him at summer camp. In the case of a third child, she made a friendly contact with his parents, invited them on a couple of occasions to come over and visit in her home, and in general took a warm and decent interest in his up-bringing. The point of this is that all three of these children were white and, while all may well have deserved her help or fondness (and it is hard to imagine what child would not), nonetheless it is striking that the white children in our school were in a very definite and dwindling minority and, during the course of the entire year in which I was teaching, I did not once observe her having offered to do anything of that sort for any child who was Negro, unless it was prompted by a stark emergency. I could not help noticing as well that when I took it on my own initiative to do something similar for a couple of the Negro children in my class, she heard about it immediately and came up to advise me that it was not at all a good idea.

In November I began giving Frederick a lift home after class, for he lived only about three blocks from the school. In December I also started to make occasional visits to see Stephen on the weekends and finally one day I took him over to Harvard to visit at the Peabody Museum. On Christmas Eve I brought him some crayons and some art paper and visited for a while in his home. From all of these trivial actions, but especially from the last, I was seriously discouraged. It was not good practice, it was not in accord

with teaching standards, it could not help but ruin discipline if a teacher got to know a pupil outside class. Yet the person who offered me this criticism had just done many things of a similar nature for a number of white children. It seemed evident to me, as it must by now be evident also to her, that the rule or the standard or the policy or the pattern that dictates a separation between a teacher and his pupil was being understood at our school, and was being explicitly interpreted, in precisely such a way as to maintain a line of color. The rule was there. It was relaxed for white children. It was enforced rigorously for Negroes. In this way the color line grew firm and strong.

There was another way in which the Reading Teacher showed her preference. It was in the matter of expectations: of what you could even hope to look for "in these kinds of children," meaning children who were Negro. Directly hooked onto this, often expressed in the same sentence, was a long and hard-dying panegyric for the past. The last, the panegyric, was one of the most common themes and undercurrents in our conversations all year long. Even at moments when she knew it to be inappropriate almost to the point of cruelty, still it was an emotion that she could not contain. Many of the other teachers in the school expressed the same idea frequently, but the most vivid conversations that I remember from the first part of the year were those with the Reading Teacher.

In the early part of winter, I had to ask the Reading Teacher for permission to take my Fourth Grade pupils on a trip to the Museum. I spoke to her of the fact that we would soon be studying Egypt and the desert, and that I thought a morning's visit to the Boston Museum of Fine Arts to see the Egyptian collection and also to wander around and look at some of the paintings would be a good idea. The Reading Teacher's manner of reacting to this request anticipated the way in which she and certain of the other teachers would respond to many other requests that I was to make later in the year. Her first reaction was to turn me down flat. Then, however, she paused for a moment— and, finally, feeling suddenly the need to justify her refusal, added these words:

"With another sort of child, perhaps. The kind of children that we used to have . . ." The moment of panegyric: "Oh we used to do beautiful work here. Wonderful projects! So many wonderful ideas . . ." The present tense again: "Not with these children. You'd take a chance with *him?* or *her?* You'd take a group like them to the museum?"

In a similar vein, I made a suggestion for another child—not for Stephen, because I knew in advance that it would have been doomed to her refusal, but for a little girl. "I thought about next summer. She's one of the best in drawing. I wanted to try to get her into an art class somewhere starting in June."

The Reading Teacher grilled me about it skeptically. "Where?"

I told her I had two places in mind. One was the school that was attached to the Museum. A summer art class for young children was conducted there. Another class that sounded more adventurous was located in Cambridge. The Cambridge program, in a loft-building near Harvard, was being spoken about with much excitement by many of the people interested in art education and it had already won a certain lively reputation for its atmosphere of openness and freedom. The children of some friends of mine were taking classes there.

"How would she get there?"

I answered that I knew someone who would drive her.

"Who'd pay for it?"

I said the same person had offered to pay for the lessons.

The very idea of this little Negro girl bridging the gap between two worlds seemed inconceivable or mechanically unfeasible to the Reading Teacher. To hear her voice you might well have thought it was an arrogant proposal. It was as if a major defiance of chance and nature and of all proper relations and proportions were being suggested. A moment's pause for thinking and then this answer, finally, from the Reading Teacher:

"I wouldn't do anything for Angelina because I just don't like her. But if you're going to do anything, the Museum School's plenty good enough for a child like her."

Because she respected herself as highly as she did, I wonder if the Reading Teacher would have been astonished if somebody had told her that she sounded rather ungentle? Perhaps she would not have been astonished—because she probably would not have believed it. She was one of the most positive persons I have ever known, and she had the most stupendous capacity to convince herself of the justice of her position on almost any issue at all. At any moment when she was reminded, by herself or someone else, that she was being less Christian or less than charitable to kids who already did not have very much in life, her reaction was apt to be to question whether there was really so much suffering here as people liked so say or whether things were really all that bad. With Stephen, for example, there were only rare moments when she would come face to face with his desperate position. Characteristic of her response to him was the attitude expressed that time when she pointed to the white boy in the seat in back of him and called him the most unhappy child in the class. I remember that when I said to her, "What about Stephen? He doesn't even have parents," the Reading Teacher became instantly defensive and irritated with me and replied: "He has a mother. What are you talking about? He has a foster mother and she is paid by the State to look after his care." But I said maybe it wasn't like having a real mother. And also, I said, the State didn't seem to have time to notice that he was being beaten up by his foster mother while being thoroughly pulverized and obliterated in one way or another almost every day at school. "He has plenty," was her answer. "There are many children who are a great deal worse off. Plenty of white people have had a much harder time than that." Harder than he had? How many? I didn't believe it. Besides, when it got to that point, did it very much matter who, out of many suffering people, was suffering a little bit less or a little bit more? But the Reading Teacher became impatient with the direction of my questioning and she ended it at this point by telling me with finality: "He's getting a whole lot more than he deserves."

It was this, her assumption that people don't deserve a great deal in life, and that a little—even a very, very little for a Negro child—is probably a great deal more than he has earned, which seemed the most disturbing thing about her. And yet at the same time she enjoyed delineating to me the bigotry of others, attacking the Art and Math teachers ruthlessly, when she was not chatting with them, and making hash out of the School Principal when she was not making hash out of someone else. I came into that school as a provisional teacher in October. It was four months, almost the end of February, before I had the courage to begin to speak to her with honesty.

*   *   *

Perhaps a reader would like to know what it is like to go into a new classroom in the same way that I did and to see before you suddenly, and in terms you cannot avoid recognizing, the dreadful consequences of a year's wastage of real lives.

You walk into a narrow and old wood-smelling classroom and you see before you thirty-five curious, cautious and untrusting children, aged eight to thirteen, of whom about two-thirds are Negro. Three of the children are designated to you as special students. Thirty per cent of the class is reading at the Second Grade level in a year and in a month in which they should be reading at the height of Fourth Grade performance or at the beginning of the Fifth. Seven children out of the class are up to par. Ten substitutes or teacher changes. Or twelve changes. Or eight. Or eleven. Nobody seems to know how many teachers they have had. Seven of their lifetime records are missing: symptomatic and emblematic at once of the chaos that has been with them all year long. Many more lives than just seven have already been wasted but the seven missing records become an embittering symbol of the lives behind them which, equally, have been lost or mislaid. (You have to spend the first three nights staying up until dawn trying to reconstruct these records out of notes and scraps.) On the first math test you give, the class average comes out to 36. The children tell you with embarrassment that it has been like that since fall.

You check around the classroom. Of forty desks, five have tops with no hinges. You lift a desk-top to fetch a paper and you find that the top has fallen off. There are three windows. One cannot be opened. A sign on it written in the messy scribble of a hurried teacher or some custodial person warns you: DO NOT UNLOCK THIS WINDOW IT IS BROKEN. The general look of the room is as of a bleak-light photograph of a mental hospital. Above the one poor blackboard, gray rather than really black, and hard to write on, hangs from one tack, lopsided, a motto attributed to Benjamin Franklin: *"Well begun is half done."* Everything, or almost everything like that, seems a mockery of itself.

Into this grim scenario, drawing on your own pleasures and memories, you do what you can to bring some kind of life. You bring in some cheerful and colorful paintings by Joan Miro and Paul Klee. While the paintings by Miro do not arouse much interest, the ones by Klee become an instantaneous success. One picture in particular, a watercolor titled "Bird Garden," catches the fascination of the entire class. You slip it out of the book and tack it up on the wall beside the doorway and it creates a traffic jam every time the children have to file in or file out. You discuss with your students some of the reasons why Klee may have painted the way he did and you talk about the things that can be accomplished in a painting which could not be accomplished in a photograph. None of this seems to be above the children's heads. Despite this, you are advised flatly by the Art Teacher that your naïveté has gotten the best of you and that the children cannot possibly appreciate this. Klee is too difficult. Children will not enjoy it. You are unable to escape the idea that the Art Teacher means herself instead.

For poetry, in place of the recommended memory gems, going back again into your own college days, you make up your mind to introduce a poem of William Butler Yeats. It is about a lake isle called Innisfree, about birds that have the funny name of "linnets" and about a "bee-loud glade." The children do not all go crazy about it but a number of them seem to like it as much as you do and you tell them how once, three years before, you were living in England and you helped a man in the country to make his home from wattles and clay. The children become intrigued. They pay good attention and many of them grow more curious about the poem than they appeared at first. Here again, however, you are advised by older teachers that you are making a mistake: Yeats is too difficult for children. They can't enjoy it, won't appreciate it, wouldn't like it. You are aiming way above their heads . . . Another idea comes to mind and you decide to try out an easy and rather well-known and not very complicated poem of Robert Frost. The poem is called "Stopping By Woods on a Snowy Evening." This time, your supervisor happens to drop in from the School Department. He looks over the mimeograph, agrees with you that it's a nice poem, then points out to you—tolerantly, but strictly—that you have made another mistake. "Stopping By Woods" is scheduled for Sixth Grade. It is not a "Fourth Grade poem," and it is not to be read or looked at during the Fourth Grade. Bewildered as you are by what appears to be a kind of idiocy, you still feel reproved and criticized and muted and set back and you feel that you have been caught in the commission of a serious mistake.

On a series of other occasions, the situation is repeated. The children are offered something new and something lively. They respond to it energetically and they are attentive and their attention does not waver. For the first time in a long while perhaps there is actually some real excitement and some growing and some thinking going on within that one small room. In each case, however, you are advised sooner or later that you are making a mistake. Your mistake, in fact, is to have impinged upon the standardized condescension on which the entire administration of the school is based. To hand Paul Klee's pictures to the children of this classroom, and particularly in a twenty-dollar volume, constitutes a threat to this school system. It is not different from sending a little girl from the Negro ghetto into an art class near Harvard Yard. Transcending the field of familiarity of the administration, you are endangering its authority and casting a blow at its self-confidence. The way the threat is handled is by a continual and standardized underrating of the children: They can't do it, couldn't do it, wouldn't like it, don't deserve it . . . In such a manner, many children are tragically and unjustifiably held back from a great many of the good things that they might come to like or admire and are pinned down instead to books the teacher knows and to easy tastes that she can handle. This includes, above all, of course, the kind of material that is contained in the Course of Study.

Try to imagine, for a child, how great the gap between the outside world and the world conveyed within this kind of school must seem: A little girl, maybe Negro, comes in from a street that is lined with car-carcasses. Old purple Hudsons and one-wheel-missing Cadillacs represent her horizon and mark the edges of her dreams. In the kitchen of her house roaches creep and large rats crawl. On the way to school a wino totters. Some teenage white boys slow down their car to insult her, and speed on. At school, she stands frozen for fifteen minutes in a yard of cracked cement that overlooks a hillside on which trash has been unloaded and at the bottom of which the New York, New Haven and Hartford Railroad rumbles past. In the basement, she sits upon broken or splintery seats in filthy toilets and she is yelled at in the halls. Upstairs, when something has been stolen she is told that she is the one who stole it and is called a liar and forced abjectly to apologize before a teacher who has not the slightest idea in the world of who the culprit truly was. The same teacher, behind the child's back, ponders audibly with imagined compassion: "What can you do with this kind of material? How can you begin to teach this kind of child?"

Gradually going crazy, the child is sent after two years of misery to a pupil adjustment counselor who arranges for her to have some tests and considers the entire situation and discusses it with the teacher and finally files a long report. She is, some months later, put onto a waiting-list some place for once-a-week therapy but another year passes before she has gotten anywhere near to the front of a long line. By now she is fourteen, has lost whatever innocence she had in the back seat of the old Cadillac and, within two additional years, she will be ready and eager for dropping out of school.

Once at school, when she was eight or nine, she drew a picture of a rich-looking lady in an evening gown with a handsome man bowing before her but she was told by an insensate and wild-eyed teacher that what she had done was junk and garbage and the picture was torn up and thrown away before her eyes. The rock and roll music that she hears on the Negro station is considered "primitive" by her teachers but she prefers its insistent rhythms to the dreary monotony of school. Once, in Fourth Grade, she got excited at school about some writing she had never heard about before. A handsome green book, brand new, was held up before her and then put into her hands. Out of this book her teacher read a poem. The poem was about a Negro—a woman who was a maid in the house of a white person—and she liked it. It remained in her memory. Somehow without meaning to, she found that she had done the impossible for her: she had memorized that poem. Perhaps, horribly, in the heart of her already she was aware that it was telling about her future: fifty dollars a week to scrub floors and bathe little white babies in the suburbs after an hour's street-car ride. The poem made her want to cry. The white lady, the lady for whom the maid was working, told the maid she loved her. But the maid in the poem wasn't going to tell any lies in return. She knew she didn't feel any love for the white lady and she told the lady so. The poem was shocking to her, but it seemed bitter, strong and true. Another poem in the same green book was about a little boy on a merry-go-round. She laughed with the class at the question he asked about a Jim Crow section on a merry-go-round, but she also was old enough to know that it was not a funny poem really and it made her, valuably, sad. She wanted to know how she could get hold of that poem, and maybe that whole book. The poems were moving to her . . .

This was a child in my class. Details are changed somewhat but it is essentially one child. The girl was one of the three unplaced special students in that Fourth Grade room. She was not an easy girl to teach and it was hard even to keep her at her seat on many mornings, but I do not remember that there was any difficulty at all in gaining and holding onto her attention on the day that I brought in that green book of Langston Hughes.

Of all of the poems of Langston Hughes that I read to my Fourth Graders, the one that the children liked the most was a poem that has the title "Ballad of the Landlord."

. . . This poem may not satisfy the taste of every critic, and I am not making any claims to immortality for a poem just because I happen to like it a great deal. But the reason this poem did have so much value and meaning for me and, I believe, for many of my students, is that it not only seems moving in an obvious and immediate human way but that it *finds* its emotion in something ordinary. It is a poem which really does allow both heroism and pathos to poor people, sees strength in awkwardness and attributes to a poor person standing on the stoop of his slum house every bit as much significance as William Wordsworth saw in daffodils, waterfalls and clouds. At the request of the children later on I mimeographed that poem and, although nobody in the classroom was asked to do this, several of the children took it home and memorized it on their own. I did not assign it for memory, because I do not think that memorizing a poem has any special value. Some of the children just came in and asked if they could recite it. Before long, almost every child in the room had asked to have a turn.

All of the poems that you read to Negro children obviously are not going to be by or about Negro people. Nor would anyone expect that all poems which are read to a class of poor children ought to be grim or gloomy or heart-breaking or sad. But when, among the works of many different authors, you do have the will to read children a poem by a man so highly renowned as Langston Hughes, then I think it is important not to try to pick a poem that is innocuous, being like any other poet's kind of poem, but I think you ought to choose a poem that is genuinely representative and then try to make it real to the children in front of you in the way that I tried. I also think it ought to be taken seriously by a teacher when a group of young children come in to him one morning and announce that they have liked something so much that they have memorized it voluntarily. It surprised me and impressed me when that happened. It was all I needed to know to confirm for me the value of reading that poem and the value of reading many other poems to children which will build upon, and not attempt to break down, the most important observations and very deepest foundations of their lives.

7050